LEGAL WRITING, ANALYSIS, AND ORAL ARGUMENT

By

LARRY L. TEPLY
Professor of Law
Creighton University

American Casebook Series
St. Paul, Minn.
WEST PUBLISHING CO.
1990

By

WEST PUBLISHING CO.

50 West Kellogg Boulevard

P.O. Box 64526

St. Paul, Minnesota 55164-0526

ISBN 0-314-70250-4

PREFACE

This book focuses on legal analysis, written work in law practice, and appellate oral argument. It is a result of several years of experimentation with various approaches to these subjects.

This book is primarily a self-teaching text. It provides numerous illustrations and highlights important points to facilitate learning. The problems in the text allow readers (1) to "test" their understanding and ability to analyze and (2) to practice applying what they have learned. Readers receive immediate feedback on how well they have done by consulting a detailed discussion in Appendix A.

Chapter 1 of the text presents seven fundamental principles of legal writing. These principles form the underlying basis for the subsequent discussion in the remaining chapters. Chapter 1 also provides a detailed introduction to legal writing style and professional responsibility issues arising in the context of legal writing.

The remaining chapters in this text follow the basic pattern of legal research and analysis in practice. Chapter 2 focuses on analyzing the facts, identifying legal problems, defining a writing project, developing a research plan, and taking research notes. Chapter 3 deals with reading, analyzing, and briefing cases for research purposes. Chapter 4 shows how cases fit into the basic pattern of authority and legal reasoning.

Chapter 5 covers statutory interpretation and analysis, including the use of legislative history in legal arguments. It also introduces students to some elements of legal drafting. Chapter 6 discusses and illustrates how legal research is reported. Chapter 7 reviews editing and proofreading skills used in preparing and revising a first draft of a memorandum reporting legal research (or other written work). Chapter 8 focuses on formulating arguments and using persuasive writing techniques. Chapter 9 discusses appellate brief writing. Chapter 10 presents materials dealing with oral argument of appellate cases.

The author welcomes suggestions for improvement for this book.

L.L.T.

Omaha, Nebraska
October, 1989

ACKNOWLEDGMENTS

I am indebted to Assistant Dean Barbara Gaskins for her review of the various drafts of this text during the past several years. Her suggestions and comments have been invaluable.

I am also indebted to several other colleagues at Creighton Law School for their encouragement and suggestions, including Professors G. Michael Fenner, David A. Larson, R. Colin Mangrum, Kent J. Neumeister, Eric Pearson, Ronald R. Volkmer, and Ralph U. Whitten. I want to thank Creighton Dean Larry Raful, former Creighton Dean Rodney Shkolnick, Creighton Law Library Director Robert Q. Kelly, Doug Murdock (Catalog Librarian), and Paul Hill (Reference Librarian) for their general support of this project.

I want to acknowledge the excellent suggestions, editing, and proofreading by my current research assistants Beth Hansen (Class of 1991) and Lisa Henkel (Class of 1990). I also want to thank my former research assistants Angie Ballentine (Class of 1988) and Beth Heine (Class of 1989) for their work on earlier versions of the manuscript.

I appreciate the efforts of Eileen Schwery, Lori Langholdt, Vicki Simants, and Juli Enright for their accurate and cheerful secretarial assistance.

I wish to acknowledge Frances Nimocks of Hattiesburg, Mississippi, as the source of the stories used in Illustration 1.7 and Illustration B.24. I also wish to acknowledge Mittie Nimocks of Platteville, Wisconsin, as the source of Illustration 7.48. I appreciate these contributions to this text.

I want to thank the following publishers or individuals who have granted me permission to quote or reproduce copyrighted materials in this book:

Figures 2-A and 2-B Reprinted with permission of Macmillan Publishing Company from W. Burton, *Legal Thesaurus* (1980), Copyright 1980 by William C. Burton.

Figures 2-E through 2-N W. Keeton, D. Dobbs, R. Keeton & D. Owen, *Prosser & Keeton on the Law of Torts* (5th ed. 1984), Copyright 1984 by West Publishing Co.

Figure 2-O *North Western Reporter Second*, Copyright 1970 by West Publishing Co.

Figure 2-P *South Eastern Digest Second*, Copyright 1981 by West Publishing Co.

Figures 2-Q through 2-S *American Law Reports Annotated 3d*, Copyright 1973 by The Lawyers Co-operative Publishing Co. and Bancroft-Whitney Co.

North Western Reporter Second, Copyright 1963 by West Publishing Co. (*Theisen* case in Chapter 3).

Ballentine's Law Dictionary (3d ed. 1969), Copyright 1969 by The Lawyers Co-operative Publishing Co. (dictionary entries in Chapter 3).

Black's Law Dictionary (5th ed. 1979), Copyright 1979 by West Publishing Co. (dictionary entries in Chapter 3).

Figures 4-A and 4-B *Shepard's South Western Reporter Citations*, Copyright 1985 by McGraw-Hill, Inc. Reprinted with permission by Shepard's/McGraw-Hill, Inc. Any further reproduction is strictly prohibited.

Figures 4-C thorough 4-E *South Western Reporter Second*, Copyright 1962, 1965, 1966, 1967 by West Publishing Co.

Figure 4-F *North Western Reporter*, Copyright 1883 by West Publishing Co.

Figure 4-G *North Western Reporter*, Copyright 1935 by West Publishing Co.

Gopen, *Let the Buyer in the Ordinary Course of Business Beware: Suggestions for Revising the Prose of the Uniform Commercial Code*, 54 U. Chi. L. Rev. 1178, 1184-93 (1987), Copyright 1987 by the University of Chicago.

Nunez, *The Nature of Legislative Intent and the Use of Legislative Documents as Extrinsic Aids to Statutory Interpretation: A Reexamination*, 9 Cal. W.L. Rev. 128, 129, 131-35 (1972). Copyright 1972 by The United States International University, California Western Law School.

I also appreciate the valuable base of knowledge on which this book rests. This base of knowledge has been developed by many others in this field. Their excellent contributions have been recognized in citations to their works in the footnotes in the text.

Finally, I appreciate the continuing support and encouragement of my family--my wife Frances Gayle and my two children Robert and Benjamin--during the preparation of this book.

L.L.T.

Omaha, Nebraska
October, 1989

SUMMARY OF CONTENTS

TABLE OF CONTENTS

Chapter 1

INTRODUCTION TO LEGAL WRITING

WHAT YOU WILL LEARN IN THIS CHAPTER

* The nature and importance of legal writing in law practice
* The seven fundamental principles of legal writing
* The ethical duties and limitations with which legal writing should comply
* The basic elements of legal writing style
* The importance of attitude and diligence in perfecting legal writing skills

Section 1A. Written Work in Law Practice

1. POPULAR CONCEPTIONS OF LAW PRACTICE

Television programs typically show lawyers interviewing and advising clients, deposing witnesses, negotiating on behalf of their clients, representing clients at hearings, examining or cross-examining witnesses, making closing arguments to juries, and presenting oral arguments in appellate courts.

Although these often dramatic oral skills are in the forefront of the public's mind, persons knowledgeable with the practice of law realize that these *oral* skills are intimately bound up with important research and writing skills.

ILLUSTRATION 1.1

(1) Oral presentations at trial are preceded by: (a) formal written statements by the parties to a lawsuit setting forth their

respective claims and defenses *(pleadings)*; (b) formal applications made to a court to obtain orders or rulings *(motions)*; (c) internal reports memorializing research or outlining litigation strategy *(law office memoranda)*; (d) sworn written statements in support of proposed action to be taken by the court *(affidavits)*; (e) documents discussing the law supporting or opposing requested court action *(trial briefs or memoranda of law for courts)*; (f) formal requests to the opposing party for information *(interrogatories)*; and (g) personal notes that organize a lawyer's preparation for trial for the lawyer's own use *(trial notebooks)*.

(2) Settlement discussions are often preceded by: (a) letters demanding payment of a claim *(demand letters)*; and (b) written settlement proposals *(settlement brochures or proposals)*.

(3) Successful oral negotiations are formalized by: (a) written documents embodying the principal agreement reached by the parties *(contracts)*; (b) written documents collateral to a principal agreement *(such as side drafts, mortgages, notes, or personal guarantees)*; and (c) formal documents in which a claim or right is abandoned *(releases)*.

(4) Oral advice to clients is supplemented by written documents stating the law, analyzing the client's rights and obligations, or advising the client on the legality of proposed action *(opinion letters and memoranda for clients)*.

(5) Appellate oral arguments are preceded by extensive written statements discussing the legal issues on appeal and the legal authorities relied upon by the parties in support of their respective positions *(appellate briefs)*.

2. BASIC CATEGORIES OF WRITTEN WORK IN LAW PRACTICE

The written work in law practice can be divided into the following basic categories:

(1) ***planning and advisory documents*** (e.g., memoranda for clients and opinion letters);

(2) ***agreements and private transactions*** (e.g., sales contracts, wills, franchises, partnerships, mortgages, deeds, and employment contracts);

(3) ***legislative documents*** (e.g., statutes, regulations, and ordinances); and

(4) ***litigation-related documents*** (e.g., complaints, discovery requests, motions, memoranda of law, appellate briefs, and settlement agreements).

3. NATURE AND IMPORTANCE OF LEGAL DRAFTING AND WRITING

LEGAL WRITING IN LAW PRACTICE IS VOLUMINOUS.

Most of the business and legal transactions with which lawyers deal are written. The weighty size of the typical court file or the documentation of any significant business deal underscores this point.

LEGAL WRITING IN LAW PRACTICE IS DEMANDING.

Being an *effective* legal writer is not easy. Legal writing requires concentration, patience, judgment, and skill. Writing requires planning because one fact of legal life is that legal writers face deadlines.

LEGAL WRITING IN LAW PRACTICE IS CRITICAL.

Poor legal writing harms people. Large sums of money are gained and lost as a result of carelessly drafted wills or trusts. Unnecessary disputes and wasteful litigation are caused by poor drafting of statutes, pleadings, contracts, discovery requests, agreements, deeds, insurance clauses, and other legal documents typically prepared by lawyers. Furthermore, there are more subtle reasons for good legal writing.

ILLUSTRATION 1.2

Poor drafting of a memorandum of law or an appellate brief diminishes its persuasive impact on the court and may cause the judges to question the *substantive* quality of the writing as well. Inferior quality written communications also may harm client relations and reduce a lawyer's effectiveness in dealing with others.

On the other hand, the *process* of producing quality written documents develops clear thinking and a good working knowledge of the contents of the documents.

Section 1B. Fundamental Principles of Legal Writing

Focus your attention on what is involved in producing good legal writing. Experience has shown that the essentials can be distilled into seven fundamental principles. These principles (introduced in the following subsections) require your constant attention and provide you with an overall checklist for reviewing the quality of written legal work.

1. ACCURACY IN LEGAL RESEARCH

GOOD LEGAL WRITING REQUIRES ACCURACY IN LEGAL RESEARCH.

Thorough and accurate legal research provides the material and framework for good legal writing. Without it, an otherwise well-written and well-organized document may be disastrous.

ILLUSTRATION 1.3

In *Cicio v. City of New York*,[1] a 51-year-old Staten Island sanitation worker sued the City of New York for three million dollars. The worker claimed that he had been injured when his partner negligently drove the garbage truck over his foot. On appeal to the Appellate Division of the New York Supreme Court, the attorneys for New York City filed an appellate brief urging that the worker's case should have been dismissed because formal notice of the claim had been filed one day after the ninety-day statutory time limit for such claims had run.

In their appellate brief, the attorneys for the city did not discuss, or even cite, several controlling judicial decisions adverse to the city's position. In affirming the lower court's granting of an application for leave to serve a late notice of the claim against the city, the Appellate Division of the New York Supreme Court cited and relied upon several cases that supported the worker's position, including two cases directly on point in which the city itself had been a party. Somewhat miffed at counsels' failure to research the question properly and to present the issue fairly, the court stated:

> [The attorneys' failure to cite these cases] is most disturbing and clearly inexcusable. . . . Had even a modicum of thought and research been given to this case, it would have been self-evident to the city that its position was untenable and this court and the taxpayers would have been spared the costs of a frivolous appeal.[2]

---

[1] 98 A.D.2d 38, 469 N.Y.S.2d 467 (1983).

[2] Id. at 40, 469 N.Y.S.2d at 469. This kind of notoriety is undesirable and is not personally or professionally satisfying.

2. ACCURACY IN LEGAL ANALYSIS

GOOD LEGAL WRITING REQUIRES ACCURACY IN LEGAL ANALYSIS AND REASONING.

For most legal research and writing projects, you will attempt to find relevant statutes, regulations, cases, constitutional provisions, ordinances, and legislative history applicable to the legal problem.

During the research and writing process, you must analyze and summarize these sources accurately. You must be able to draw analogies between the facts of reported cases and the facts with which you are working. You must be able to distinguish cases. You must be able to engage in the often difficult task of case synthesis and rule formulation. You also must be able to apply statutes, regulations, and constitutional provisions.

During this entire process, you must avoid logical fallacies, and you must be adept in the techniques of argumentation commonly used in legal writing.

3. AWARENESS OF THE PURPOSE AND AUDIENCE

GOOD LEGAL WRITING REQUIRES AWARENESS OF THE PURPOSE AND AUDIENCE.

(a) Identify the Purpose of the Document

Documents prepared by lawyers serve a wide variety of purposes. Some, such as contracts, are designed to memorialize understandings and create binding obligations. Others, such as wills and trusts, are designed to express and effectuate clients' wishes. Some, such as memoranda in support of motions and trial or appellate briefs, are concerned mainly with convincing judges or other decision makers of the correctness of clients' positions. Some, such as interrogatories or Freedom of Information Act requests, are designed to secure information.

Other documents, such as law office memoranda, case briefs, and memoranda prepared by judicial clerks, are used for internal communication or preparation of other documents. Some, such as demand letters, settlement brochures, collection letters, and pleadings, are aimed at inducing either voluntary or involuntary action. Still others, opinion letters to clients for example, are designed to convey information or advice.

YOU MUST BE SENSITIVE TO THE WIDE-RANGING PURPOSES OF LEGAL DOCUMENTS BECAUSE EACH REQUIRES AN ADJUSTMENT IN YOUR WRITING STYLE.

ILLUSTRATION 1.4

Law office memoranda for internal use, memoranda for judges prepared by their clerks, and opinion letters for clients traditionally are more objective in the statement of facts and the interpretation of the law than are appellate briefs or memoranda in support of motions.

Pleadings often are drafted with an eye to those pleadings that have been upheld in prior litigation, occasionally sacrificing what appears to be simpler and more direct language to avoid risking a controversy.

In contrast, absolute clarity of expression is a prime concern in the drafting of statutes, contracts, wills, and trusts. Absolute clarity of expression is of less concern in routine correspondence.

(b) Be Aware of the Audience

The audience to whom a legal document is directed should also affect your legal writing style.

ILLUSTRATION 1.5

Will the pleadings be read to the jury or will they be placed only in a court file? Is the document directed to a judge, an opposing counsel, or an unsophisticated layperson?

WHAT MAY BE GOOD LEGAL WRITING STYLE FOR ONE AUDIENCE MAY BE INEFFECTIVE FOR ANOTHER.

ILLUSTRATION 1.6

A legal rule lawyers and judges readily understand often must be restated in simplified language for jurors and other laypersons in jury instructions.

BE ESPECIALLY CAREFUL ABOUT ASSUMING THE AUDIENCE'S FAMILIARITY WITH THE LAW OR THE FACTS OF A CASE.

ILLUSTRATION 1.7

A woman watched a local television newscaster every evening. One day she met the newscaster on the street and greeted him in a very friendly manner. Because he had never seen her before, the newscaster said "hello" politely and continued on his way. Later that day, she complained to one of her friends: "You would think that he would have been more friendly. After all, I see him every night."

The point of this story is simple, but it illustrates a pitfall of many legal writers: Never overestimate the reader's familiarity with the substantive law or the facts in legal writing.

4. COMMAND OF THE ENGLISH LANGUAGE

GOOD LEGAL WRITING REQUIRES A COMMAND OF THE ENGLISH LANGUAGE.

To realize that the particular purpose of a document and its audience should affect the written work product is one thing. To know *how* to make the needed adjustments in tone, emphasis, and content is quite another.

TO MAKE APPROPRIATE ADJUSTMENTS TO REFLECT THE PARTICULAR PURPOSE OF A DOCUMENT AND ITS AUDIENCE, YOU MUST FIRST HAVE A COMMAND OF THE ENGLISH LANGUAGE.

You must avoid rudimentary technical errors. You must be able to move from passive to active voice and vice versa, to shift emphasis within a sentence, and to write with clarity, precision, and brevity. You must be sensitive to shifts in tense, mood, and voice. You must be able to use parallel construction, tabulation, structural guides, coherent paragraphing, and transition sentences effectively.

You must be able to identify, articulate, and order concepts in your writing. You must be able to select words carrying appropriate connotations. You must be willing to work to achieve an appropriate eloquence of expression.

Appendix B contains a self-review of basic English language technical skills. Section D of this chapter introduces the basic elements of legal writing style. Several other sections of the text discuss stylistic skills in the context of writing particular kinds of legal documents.

5. PROPER FORMAT AND LEGAL CITATION

(a) Using the Proper Format

GOOD LEGAL WRITING REQUIRES THE USE OF THE PROPER FORMAT.

The format of a document will often be officially prescribed. You should use that format.

BE SURE TO DETERMINE ANY OFFICIAL CONSTRAINTS ON THE FORMAT OF A DOCUMENT. BE ESPECIALLY CAREFUL TO FOLLOW ANY APPLICABLE PROCEDURAL RULES OR LOCAL COURT RULES.

ILLUSTRATION 1.8

Rule 28 of the Federal Rules of Appellate Procedure dictates the headings and organization of briefs filed in United States courts of appeals and limits the length of the appellate briefs.[3] Rule 32 governs the physical form of appellate briefs, including page size, kind of paper, type size, and color of the cover.[4] Individual circuit court rules further supplement these rules. Similar restrictions frequently are imposed on documents filed in the trial courts.[5]

When official constraints on the format are not prescribed, you must be sensitive to any internal office requirements, local customs, and practices of the bar. In any event, the format of the document should be geared to its eventual use and should aid in accomplishing the purpose of the document.

---

[3] Fed. R. App. P. 28(a), (b), (g). Cf. S. Ct. R. 33.3 and 34 (prescribing the contents, order of presentation, and page limits for briefs filed in the United States Supreme Court). See generally R. Stern, Appellate Practice in the United States 225-310 (2d ed. 1989) (discussing parts of briefs and timing in state and federal appellate practice).

[4] Fed. R. App. P. 32(a). In United States courts of appeals, the cover of the appellant's brief "should be blue; that of the appellee, red; that of an intervenor or amicus curiae, green; that of any reply brief, gray;" the cover of a separate appendix should be white. Id.

[5] See, e.g., Fed. R. Civ. P. 10(a), (b) (captions, paragraphing, and separate statements required in federal district court pleadings); 4 F. Poore & E. Koeber, Cyclopedia of Federal Procedure § 14.29 (rev. 3d ed. 1986) (discussing local district court rules on the size, weight, and color of paper, color of ink, line numbering, spacing of lines, fastening, flat or unfolded filing, and the number of copies to be filed).

(b) Citing Sources in Legal Writing

GOOD LEGAL WRITING REQUIRES EFFECTIVE USE OF LEGAL CITATION.

Much of a lawyer's written work is focused on identifying, predicting, or asserting what the law is or should be. The citation of cases, statutes, and the wide variety of other primary and secondary sources is an integral part of that persuasive process. By citing such authority, lawyers demonstrate the support for a particular position. Good legal writing requires that these authorities be used and cited effectively.

One widely accepted system of citation is *A Uniform System of Citation (USOC)*, known as the "Blue Book" or the "*USOC*."[6] A more flexible system of citation is prescribed in *The University of Chicago Manual of Legal Citation (Chicago Manual)*, known as the "Maroon Book."[7]

Legal citation rules assure the cited sources can be found based on the information provided. Furthermore, many members of the bar and judiciary regard "proper" citation as one indication of quality legal work.

6. PROCEDURAL CONTEXT AND REMEDY SOUGHT

GOOD LEGAL WRITING REQUIRES SENSITIVITY TO THE PROCEDURAL CONTEXT AND TO THE REMEDY SOUGHT.

In litigation-oriented legal writing, sensitivity to the procedural context of the problem is important for several reasons.

THE PROCEDURAL CONTEXT IS IMPORTANT BECAUSE IT USUALLY PROVIDES A PROCEDURAL STANDARD THAT MUST BE MET.

---

[6] The Harvard Law Review Ass'n, Yale Law Journal, Columbia Law Review, and University of Pennsylvania Law Review, A Uniform System of Citation (14th ed. 1986) [hereinafter USOC and USOC Rule].

[7] University of Chicago, The University of Chicago Manual of Legal Citation (1989) [hereinafter Chicago Manual and Chicago Rule].

ILLUSTRATION 1.9

Assume that a complaint has been filed and you have been asked to prepare a motion for a more definite statement (and a memorandum in support of the motion) in response. Under Rule 12(e) of the Federal Rules of Civil Procedure, the procedural standard to be met is whether the pleading "is so vague or ambiguous that a party cannot reasonably be required to frame a responsive pleading . . . ."[8]

Standards such as these provide the point of attack or the focus of memoranda supporting or opposing past or proposed action.

THE PROCEDURAL CONTEXT IS IMPORTANT BECAUSE IT PROVIDES RULES OF CONSTRUCTION AND INTERPRETATION THAT AFFECT YOUR APPROACH IN WRITING A MEMORANDUM OR APPELLATE BRIEF.

ILLUSTRATION 1.10

Assume that you have been asked to prepare a motion (and a memorandum in support of that motion) to dismiss a complaint on the ground that the complaint fails to state a claim upon which relief may be granted. Under the Federal Rules of Civil Procedure, the factual allegations in the complaint are assumed to be true for purposes of the motion.[9]

You also must be sensitive to the remedy sought. In other words, what does your client want: a declaratory judgment, constructive trust, temporary restraining order, reformation, equitable lien, replevin, damages, rescission, garnishment, or some other legal remedy?

EACH REMEDY HAS PECULIAR REQUIREMENTS THAT ROUTINELY MUST BE TAKEN INTO ACCOUNT IN LEGAL WRITING.

Sometimes, legal controversies center not so much on the parties' substantive rights but on the *appropriateness* of particular remedies or questions of their *measurement*.

---

[8] Fed. R. Civ. P. 12(e).

[9] See id. 12(b)(6) (motion to dismiss for failure to state a claim upon which relief may be granted).

ILLUSTRATION 1.11

Is a preliminary injunction proper under the circumstances? Are the damages in a given case to be measured by the plaintiff's loss or the defendant's gain?

7. PROFESSIONAL ETHICAL STANDARDS

GOOD LEGAL WRITING REQUIRES COMPLIANCE WITH PROFESSIONAL ETHICAL STANDARDS.

The following professional ethical rules are relevant to written work in law practice:

(1) the *Model Code of Professional Responsibility*[10] (the minimum standards that attorneys must meet in many jurisdictions); and

(2) the *Model Rules of Professional Conduct*[11] (the current ethical standards adopted by the American Bar Association, which have been adopted as the minimum standards attorneys must meet in a growing number of jurisdictions).

Applicable provisions of the *Model Code* and *Model Rules* are quoted or cited in the next section.

Section 1C. Ethical Duties and Limitations

1. COMPETENT, PREPARED, AND TIMELY REPRESENTATION

Lawyer incompetence and neglect are rarely attributable to deficiencies in basic mental capabilities. Instead, personal problems, overcommitment, sloth, or indifference are the typical sources of the problems. In a legal writing context, these factors manifest themselves in the form of inadequate research, drafting, and revision.

Legal writers should carefully assess how much time a particular matter will take and plan accordingly. When lawyers lack sufficient time to complete a matter competently, they should

---

[10] American Bar Ass'n, Model Code of Professional Responsibility (1980) [hereinafter Model Code].

[11] American Bar Ass'n, Model Rules of Professional Conduct (1983) [hereinafter Model Rules].

get help, refer the matter to a knowledgeable lawyer who has time to handle it, or not accept the new matter.[12]

2. ZEALOUS REPRESENTATION OF THE CLIENT

As part of the adversary system, lawyers should represent their clients zealously within the bounds of the law. Disciplinary Rule 7-101(A)(1) states this duty in negative terms: "A lawyer shall not intentionally . . . [f]ail to seek the lawful objectives of [the] client through reasonably available means permitted by law and the Disciplinary Rules."[13]

Subpart (B) of this rule, however, provides that lawyers may, when "permissible, exercise [their] professional judgment to waive or fail to assert a right or position of [their] client[s]" and may "[r]efuse to aid or participate in conduct that [lawyers believe] to be unlawful, even though there is some support for an argument that the conduct is legal."[14]

Professors Aronson and Weckstein explain the importance of zealous representation in the adversary system in this way:

> The elements of justice--approximation of the truth, respect for human dignity, satisfaction of potential litigants, and party participation in the process of decision-making--can be effectuated only if each litigant is able to call upon a loyal and knowledgeable legal representative to zealously discover the facts, research the law, convincingly present the case to an impartial decision-maker, stand ready to rebut the presentation of adversaries, and safeguard the constitutional and other legal rights of the client. . . . [T]he lawyer is expected to make positive contributions to a reasoned decision in accordance with valid general principles and good public policy through accurate and complete research and effective advocacy.[15]

3. MANDATORY DISCLOSURE OF CONTROLLING LAW

When lawyers present a matter to a tribunal, the rules of professional ethics require them to make certain disclosures to the

---

[12] See Model Code, supra note 10, DR 6-101(A).

[13] Id. DR 7-101(A)(1).

[14] Id. DR 7-101(B)(2).

[15] R. Aronson & D. Weckstein, Professional Responsibility in a Nutshell 271 (1980).

tribunal. Disciplinary Rule 7-106(B)(1) imposes on attorneys a mandatory duty to reveal any legal authority in the "controlling jurisdiction" that they know to be "directly adverse" to their client's position and that opposing counsel has not disclosed.[16]

This rule dovetails with common sense in advocacy. Good advocacy would dictate disclosure of adverse authorities--along with arguments distinguishing or criticizing them. In this way, candor "takes the wind from an opponent's sails and instills judicial trust in the quality and completeness of [the] presentation."[17]

4. MANDATORY DISCLOSURE OF FACTS IN EX PARTE PROCEEDINGS

Lawyers are held to a significantly higher standard of factual candor in ex parte proceedings than in proceedings in which the opposing party is represented. In ex parte proceedings, lawyers are required to inform the court "of all material facts [the lawyer knows to] enable the [court] to make an informed decision, whether or not the facts are adverse."[18]

Failure to disclose all material facts can have serious consequences.

ILLUSTRATION 1.12

In *Weichert v. New York State Bar Association*,[19] a New York attorney was disbarred for filing a knowingly misleading affidavit to secure an ex parte order involving lien priorities.

---

[16] Model Code, supra note 10, DR 7-106(B)(1). Accord Model Rules, supra note 11, Rule 3.3(a)(3). Cf. Uviller, Zeal and Frivolity: The Ethical Duty of the Appellate Advocate to Tell the Truth about the Law, 6 Hofstra L. Rev. 729, 734-38 (1978) ("[T]he Code of Professional Responsibility is too tolerant of legal artifice. Whatever [the lawyer's] cause, a lawyer discussing law implicitly offers a professional opinion. [A lawyer's] ethical obligation to the court . . . is at least as strong as the duty [owed to the lawyer's] client in consultation: to give fair and detached rendition of the law as [the lawyer] understands it").

[17] C. Wolfram, Modern Legal Ethics § 12.8, at 682 (1986). Cf. A. Hornstein, Appellate Advocacy in a Nutshell § 6-3, at 156 (1984) ("[Failing to deal with adverse precedent] will make it appear to the court that the advocate cannot deal with the precedent case successfully. [That] precedent may then become even more damaging for lack of a response to it. . . . [It] is likely to cast doubt either upon the advocate's forthrightness or competence or both. And that sort of doubt may taint the rest of what the advocate has to say").

[18] Model Rules, supra note 11, Rule 3.3(d).

[19] 40 A.D.2d 261, 262-63, 339 N.Y.S.2d 750, 751 (1973).

5. FALSE STATEMENTS OF LAW OR FACTS

Disciplinary Rule 7-102(A)(5) prohibits lawyers in representing their clients from making knowingly false statements of law. This same provision prohibits making knowingly false statements of facts.[20]

ILLUSTRATION 1.13

In an Indiana criminal case, the defendant was tried for first-degree murder after he had drawn a gun, had shot the victim several times, and had continued to shoot the victim after he had fallen to the ground. On appeal to the Indiana Supreme Court, the defendant's attorney referred in his appellate brief to several instances of "uncontroverted evidence" in the record. In its opinion in the case, the Indiana Supreme Court stated:

> We realize that a lawyer should zealously plead his client's case. But surely no one who has read the transcript of the evidence in this case can, in good faith, say the evidence is "uncontroverted" that the appellant fired [the gun] in self-defense. . . . The [c]ourt is entitled to a fair statement of the facts from attorneys on both sides, not an exaggerated, self-serving version of the facts or an omission of crucial facts. When the [c]ourt finds that it can not rely upon the statement of a lawyer, the lawyer has lost his effectiveness . . . and has therefore, in fact, injured his client.[21]

6. ASSERTIONS OF FALSE OR FRIVOLOUS CLAIMS OR DEFENSES

The disciplinary rules prohibit the assertion of patently false claims or defenses. Disciplinary Rule 7-102(A)(2) states that attorneys may not "[k]nowingly advance a claim or defense that is unwarranted under existing law, [unless] it can be supported by [a] good faith argument for an extension, modification, or reversal of

---

[20] Model Code, supra note 10, DR 7-102(A)(5). See also Model Rules, supra note 11, Rule 3.3(a)(1), (2), (4); Uviller, supra note 16, at 731-34 (providing examples of "direct" and "indirect" statements of the law in a discussion of what is meant by a "false statement of law").

[21] Cooper v. State, 261 Ind. 659, 662, 309 N.E.2d 807, 808 (1974). See also Frausto v. Legal Aid Soc'y, 563 F.2d 1324, 1327 n.8 (9th Cir. 1977) ("It is appellate counsel's professional duty to be scrupulously accurate in referring to the record and the authorities upon which he relies in his presentation to the court in his brief or oral argument").

existing law."[22] The consequences for violating this standard can be unpleasant.

ILLUSTRATION 1.14

In the case of *In re Bithoney*,[23] an attorney was fined and suspended from practice for filing petitions for review in immigration cases based on frivolous grounds to secure automatic stays of deportation.

In addition to the requirements of the *Model Code* and *Model Rules*, Rule 11 of the Federal Rules of Civil Procedure imposes an affirmative duty to investigate the facts and the law before taking action:

> The signature of an attorney or party constitutes a certificate by the signer that the signer has read the pleading, motion, or other paper; that to the best of the signer's knowledge, information, and belief formed after reasonable inquiry it is well grounded in fact and is warranted by existing law or a good faith argument for the extension, modification, or reversal of existing law, and that it is not interposed for any improper purpose, such as to harass or to cause unnecessary delay or needless increase in the cost of litigation.[24]

Rule 11 authorizes the following sanctions for asserting improper claims or defenses:

> If a pleading, motion, or other paper is not signed, it shall be stricken unless it is signed promptly after the omission is called to the attention of the pleader or movant. If a pleading, motion, or other paper is signed in violation of this rule, the court, upon motion or upon its own initiative, shall impose upon the person who signed it, a represented party, or both, an appropriate sanction, which may include an order to pay to the other party or parties the amount of the reasonable expenses incurred because of the filing of the [document], including a reasonable attorney's fee.[25]

---

[22] Model Code, supra note 10, DR 7-102(A)(2). See also Model Rules, supra note 11, Rule 3.1.

[23] 486 F.2d 319, 325 (1st Cir. 1973).

[24] Fed. R. Civ. P. 11.

[25] Id.

7. DILATORY TACTICS, HARASSMENT, AND MALICIOUS INFLICTION OF HARM

Sometimes, clients will want lawyers to write letters, file actions, or use dilatory tactics to harass someone. Disciplinary Rule 7-102(A)(1) prohibits lawyers from filing a suit, asserting a position, conducting a defense, delaying a trial, or taking other action on behalf of their clients when they know or "when it is obvious that such action would serve merely to harass or maliciously injure another."[26]

Aronson and Weckstein assert that when "the law is not an obstacle but the client's case is weak on the facts, the lawyer may still pursue it unless the purpose is merely to harass or maliciously injure another person. If that is the client's motivation, the attorney may not file a suit, assert a position, conduct a defense, or delay a trial to effect such a purpose."[27]

In addition to the provisions of Rule 11 quoted above, Federal Rule 26 focuses on the abuse of discovery:

> The signature of the attorney or party constitutes a certification that the signer has read the [discovery] request, response, or objection, and that to the best of the signer's knowledge, information, and belief formed after a reasonable inquiry it is:
>
> (1) consistent with these rules and warranted by existing law or a good faith argument for the extension, modification, or reversal of existing law;
>
> (2) not interposed for any improper purpose, such as to harass or to cause unnecessary delay or needless increase in the cost of litigation; and
>
> (3) not unreasonable or unduly burdensome or expensive, given the needs of the case, the discovery already had in the case, the amount in controversy, and the importance of the issues at stake in the litigation.[28]

8. THREATS OF CRIMINAL PROSECUTION

Lawyers may not threaten criminal charges solely to gain an advantage in a civil matter.[29]

---

[26]Model Code, supra note 10, DR 7-102(A)(1).

[27]R. Aronson & D. Weckstein, supra note 15, at 282.

[28]Fed. R. Civ. P. 26(g).

[29]Model Code, supra note 10, DR 7-105(A). See generally Annotation, Initiating, or Threatening to Initiate, Criminal Prosecution as Ground for Disciplining Counsel, 42 A.L.R.4th 1000 (1985).

ILLUSTRATION 1.15

A lawyer was disciplined for making the following threat in a letter:

> I am giving you an opportunity of making an amicable settlement on behalf of my client . . . for the injuries she has suffered. Unless you show some substantial evidence of your willingness to compensate [her] for her injuries, I shall have no other alternative but to immediately criminally prosecute you for assault against my client. In addition to that, I shall institute civil action for the amount of damages which [my client] has suffered.[30]

9. DIRECT COMMUNICATION WITH REPRESENTED PARTIES

Unless prior consent of the adverse party's lawyer has been obtained or communication is otherwise authorized by law, lawyers may not communicate directly with a party known to be represented by counsel concerning the "subject of the representation."[31]

10. CLIENT CONFIDENCES AND SECRETS

Except in limited circumstances, lawyers may not knowingly reveal information protected by attorney-client privilege. Furthermore, lawyers are obliged not to reveal information outside the attorney-client privilege that (1) the client has requested be kept confidential, (2) would be embarrassing to the client, or (3) would likely be harmful to the client.[32]

Model Rule 1.6 enlarges the Model Code by applying confidentiality restrictions to all information about a client, even though the information is not embarrassing or the client has not requested confidentiality and even if the information is acquired before or after the attorney-client relationship existed.

The Model Code and Model Rules both provide various exceptions. For example, Model Rule 1.6(b) states that a lawyer may reveal confidential information "to the extent the lawyer

---

[30] In re Hyman, 226 A.D. 468, 469, 235 N.Y.S. 622, 623 (1929). Accord In re Cohn, 46 N.J. 202, 203-08, 216 A.2d 1, 2-4 (1966) (bigamy charges used to gain an advantage in civil suit).

[31] Model Code, supra note 10, DR 7-104(A)(1); Model Rules, supra note 11, Rule 4.2. See also Annotation, Attorney's Dealing Directly with Client of Another Attorney as Ground for Disciplinary Proceeding, 1 A.L.R.3d 1113 (1965).

[32] See Model Code, supra note 10, DR 4-101(A), (B)(1).

reasonably believes necessary . . . to prevent the client from committing a criminal act that the lawyer believes is likely to result in imminent death or substantial bodily harm."[33]

11. EX PARTE COMMUNICATION WITH JUDGES

The disciplinary rules prohibit ex parte communications with judges. Specifically, Disciplinary Rule 7-110(B) provides that in an adversary proceeding, a lawyer shall not communicate about the merits of the cause with a judge before whom the proceeding is pending, except

> (1) [i]n the course of official proceedings; (2) [i]n writing if [the lawyer] promptly delivers a copy of the writing to opposing counsel or to the adverse party if [that party] is not represented by a lawyer; (3) [o]rally upon adequate notice to opposing counsel or to the adverse party if [that party] is not represented by a lawyer; or (4) as otherwise authorized by law.[34]

ILLUSTRATION 1.16

A Florida attorney was suspended from the practice of law for one year because of his ex parte communications with justices of the Florida Supreme Court about the merits of a pending case in which his client had an interest. In this instance, the attorney's communications included discussing the case during a golf game with the justice who had been assigned to write the opinion. The attorney later submitted an informal memorandum of law to that justice without notifying counsel of record or having copies served on counsel of record.[35]

12. APPEALS TO RACIAL, RELIGIOUS, NATIONAL, OR REGIONAL PREJUDICES

In legal writing and in appearances before judges and juries, you are required to avoid appeals to prejudices unrelated to the

---

[33] Model Rules, supra note 11, Rule 1.6(b)(1).

[34] Model Code, supra note 10, DR 7-110(B)(1)-(4). See also Model Rules, supra note 11, Rule 3.5. See generally Annotation, Disciplinary Action Against Attorney Based on Communications to Judge Respecting Merits of Cause, 22 A.L.R.4th 917 (1983).

[35] Florida Bar v. Mason, 334 So. 2d 1, 2-3 (Fla. 1976). Accord Heavey v. State Bar, 17 Cal. 3d 553, 559, 551 P.2d 1238, 1241-42, 131 Cal. Rptr. 406, 409-10 (1976) (a California attorney was disciplined for writing to a judge about the merits of a pending case without furnishing a copy of the letters to opposing counsel).

legal and factual merits of cases.[36] In a trial setting, such conduct can lead to a mistrial, new trial, or reversal.[37] "Thus, appeals to racial, religious, national, or regional prejudice have been held to be reversible error (at least when substantially prejudicial and not remedied by trial court instructions) and [to be] unethical conduct."[38]

13. SIMULATION OF LEGAL PROCESS

A lawyer may not simulate legal process for private purposes.[39]

ILLUSTRATION 1.17

In *State v. Ziegler*,[40] a lawyer was suspended indefinitely from the practice of law for sending the following letter simulating a garnishment notice:

WRITTEN NOTICE OF GARNISHMENT

Dr. Sippy

vs

Charles Loughlin [sp]
RR # 1 Box 208 A
Stilwell, Kansas

Since you have refused to pay this debt voluntarily or to keep your arrangements for payment:

Court action is now required.

---

[36] See Model Rules, supra note 11, Rule 3.5 (improper to influence judges, jurors, and others using appeals to prejudices unrelated to the merits of the case).

[37] See Annotation, Counsel's Appeal in Criminal Case to Racial, National, or Religious Prejudice as Ground for Mistrial, New Trial, or Reversal, 45 A.L.R.2d 303 (1956); Annotation, Statement by Counsel Relating to Race, Nationality, or Religion in Civil Action as Prejudicial, 99 A.L.R.2d 1249 (1965).

[38] R. Aronson & D. Weckstein, supra note 15, at 300. Cf. In re Richter, 187 Wis. 490, 499-505, 204 N.W. 492, 494-96 (1925) (attorney disbarred for advancing facts prejudicial to the female plaintiff's "honor and reputation" but never attempting to prove the allegations).

[39] See Model Code, supra note 10, DR 1-102(A)(4) (engaging in conduct involving dishonesty, fraud, deceit, or misrepresentation).

[40] 217 Kan. 748, 755, 538 P.2d 643, 648-49 (1975).

> Therefore be advised, your wages will be garnished. Twenty-five percent (25%) thereof will be taken for the payment of this bill unless the entire balance of $143.00 is paid immediately to Wayne L. Ziegler.[41]

14. CONDUCT ADVERSELY REFLECTING ON A LAWYER'S FITNESS TO PRACTICE LAW

Disciplinary Rule 1-102 provides that lawyers may not "[e]ngage in any . . . conduct that adversely reflects on [their] fitness to practice law."[42]

ILLUSTRATION 1.18

The attorney who sent the above simulated garnishment notice also was found to have violated Disciplinary Rule 1-102(A)(6) by sending the following collection letter:

> OH! THE JOY OF BEING SUED!!
>
> How do you explain to the neighbors and the kids when the Sheriff's car pulls up front and an officer hands you the summons?
>
> OR, how do you explain a garnishment to the boss, and the other fellows at work???
>
> I don't know, but I guess you do; at least you didn't bother to answer my letter. You do not need to send me your check immediately to pay your account, because I am not going to bother you any more . . . but the Sheriff will. Oh yes, I will see you in court.
>
> You owe ______________ $ ____________________
>
> PAY ME NOW!!![43]

15. IMPROPER CRITICISM OF JUDGES OR COURTS

Lawyers must be careful when they openly criticize the actions taken by a court or the competence or integrity of a judge. Model Rule 8.2 provides that "[a] lawyer shall not make

---

[41] Id. at 751, 538 P.2d at 646. Accord In re Dows, 168 Minn. 6, 7-10, 209 N.W. 627, 627-30 (1926) ("Advance and Final Notice Before Suit for Garnishment, Levy, and Sale" simulating legal process improper).

[42] Model Code, supra note 10, DR 1-102(A)(6).

[43] State v. Ziegler, 217 Kan. at 748-49, 538 P.2d at 644.

a statement that the lawyer knows to be false or with reckless disregard as to its truth or falsity concerning the qualifications or integrity of a judge."[44]

ILLUSTRATION 1.19

A lawyer improperly asserted in a brief filed in the Ninth Circuit Court of Appeals that the justices of the California Third District Court of Appeals (1) had acted "unlawfully" and "illegally" in reversing a trial court judgment in his client's favor and (2) had thus become "parties to the theft" of his client's property.

The lawyer also improperly implied in a petition for certiorari filed in the United States Supreme Court that the justices had falsified the record and suggested that the justices' "unblemished" records were undeserved. As a result, the attorney was suspended from law practice.[45]

16. PROBLEMS ON LEGAL ETHICS IN LEGAL WRITING

The following problems deal with professional ethics and legal writing. Be sure to choose an answer before consulting the discussion of the problem in Appendix A at the end of this text.

Unless otherwise stated, the problems are based on the following facts:

Assume that you represent well-known sportscaster, trainer, and avid boxing fan Doc Louis. Your client was recently involved in an automobile accident with six other cars. The drivers of the other cars--Von Kaiser, Piston Honda, Soda Popinski, King Hippo, and Bald Bull--ironically all are professional boxers. Each of these boxers has sued your client for damage to his car resulting from the accident and for personal injuries resulting from an altercation that occurred immediately after the accident. Assume that these actions are properly before a federal district court and that the applicable law provides that no oral provocation is sufficient to justify a battery.

In your initial interview with your client, Louis told you that after the crash he started an argument with the drivers. Apparently, the argument was something about "who was the

---

[44]Model Rules, supra note 11, Rule 8.2(a). See Annotation, Attorney's Criticism of Judicial Acts as Ground of Disciplinary Action, 12 A.L.R.3d 1408 (1967).

[45]Ramirez v. State Bar, 28 Cal. 3d 402, 404-05, 619 P.2d 399, 400, 169 Cal. Rptr. 206, 207 (1980). Accord Wilburn v. Reitman, 54 Ariz. 31, 35-36, 91 P.2d 865, 866-67 (1939) (attorney reprimanded for suggesting in a brief that the trial judge had not only been dominated but actually hypnotized by opposing counsel).

greatest." No one witnessed the accident or the altercation other than the parties to the lawsuits. The facts are clear to you from the interview with your client that Louis started the argument, provoked the fight, and struck the first blows. During the interview, Louis stated that he should have been more careful and that "he caused the accident."

Under the Federal Rules of Civil Procedure, Louis must file a document called an "Answer" (1) admitting or denying each of the plaintiffs' allegations, (2) raising any "affirmative defenses" that he may have, and (3) asserting any "counterclaim" that Louis wants to pursue. Such a counterclaim is "compulsory" if it arises out of the transaction or occurrence that is the subject of the plaintiff's claims. A compulsory counterclaim is lost if the defendant fails to plead it.

PROBLEM 1.1

Assume Louis wants you to deny the allegations that Louis provoked the fight and threw the first punch because Louis thinks that a jury will not believe the plaintiffs. Assume Louis is probably right and that a jury is not likely to believe the plaintiffs. Based on the various rules discussed in this section, a denial would be

(a) proper because you never know for sure whether your client is telling the truth. The professionally prudent course of action in such circumstances is to make the plaintiffs prove the allegation.

(b) proper because the plaintiffs have the burden of proof on all factual issues essential to their claim. In this instance, they must establish that Louis was the aggressor to hold Louis liable for their injuries.

(c) proper because Rule 11 of the Federal Rules of Civil Procedure allows an attorney to form an opinion as to whether a pleading is well grounded in fact after a reasonable inquiry. In this instance, since you have not conducted an inquiry, the rule does not apply. The professionally prudent course of action is to protect your client.

(d) improper because Rule 11 of the Federal Rules of Civil Procedure requires you to plead in good faith to the best of your knowledge, information, and belief. If you denied the allegations, you would be making a false statement of fact (the denial would be directly contrary to information your client gave you in the interview). Therefore, you must admit the allegation.

Stop here, and choose an answer before consulting the discussion of this problem in Appendix A.

PROBLEM 1.2

Assume that Louis also wants you to file a counterclaim asserting that the plaintiffs negligently caused the crash. Recall that during the interview, Louis stated that he should have been more careful and that "he caused the accident." Based on the various rules discussed in this section, the *best* argument that it is *ethical* to file this counterclaim would be

(a) an attorney never knows for sure when the client is telling the truth.

(b) an attorney does not have to rely on a client's interpretation of complex factors involved in a negligence case, particularly the issue of causation. If the attorney's view of the facts, however remote, would support plaintiff liability, the professionally prudent course of action is to preserve your client's claim.

(c) an attorney must zealously represent a client without regard to the facts. The system is an adversary one. Furthermore, because the adverse information was received from the client, the information is protected from disclosure by the attorney-client privilege.

(d) an attorney may make a good faith argument for the extension, modification, or reversal of existing law.

Stop here, and choose an answer before consulting the discussion of this problem in Appendix A.

PROBLEM 1.3

The *best* argument that it is *unethical* to file the counterclaim described in Problem 1.2 would be

(a) filing the counterclaim is intended to delay trial.

(b) filing the counterclaim constitutes a knowingly false statement of fact. The counterclaim is simply a "nuisance claim" in which the attorney could not have a good faith belief in its merits.

(c) filing the counterclaim would be considered a frivolous claim. In doubtful situations, an attorney does not have the right to "protect" a client by filing a counterclaim.

(d) filing the counterclaim would be contrary to the facts apparently known by the attorney at the time. An attorney has an obligation to make a reasonable inquiry before filing the counterclaim and cannot simply follow the client's strategy unless the counterclaim "to the best of his knowledge, information, and belief . . . is well grounded in fact."

Stop here, and choose an answer before consulting the discussion of this problem in Appendix A.

PROBLEM 1.4

Assume further that Louis had specifically told you the only reason he wants you to file the counterclaim is that he believes that "the best defense is a good offense" and that he is sure the cost of litigating the counterclaim will induce a settlement in the case. Assume further that (1) you now believe your client has such a weak case that no possibility exists that a jury could plausibly find in Louis' favor and (2) if the jury would find in favor of Louis, that finding would be reversed on appeal under the applicable rules of appellate review.

Filing the counterclaim would be

(a) proper because everyone is entitled to his or her day in court regardless of the merits of an individual's claim.

(b) proper because an attorney is ethically obligated to represent a client zealously. A client's motivation is irrelevant.

(c) improper because the attorney should know the counterclaim is intended to harass or maliciously injure the opposing parties.

(d) improper because a weak case is always treated the same as a frivolous case.

Stop here, and choose an answer before consulting the discussion of this problem in Appendix A.

PROBLEM 1.5

Assume instead that (1) Louis lies to you and claims the plaintiffs started the altercation; (2) Louis wants you to file a counterclaim against the plaintiffs asserting that they provoked and initiated the altercation; (3) Louis wants you to threaten to seek to have the proper authorities file a criminal complaint asserting that the plaintiffs provoked and initiated the altercation; (4) a jury might award substantial damages on the counterclaim in the civil action; and (5) a jury could plausibly convict the defendants based on Louis' testimony in a criminal proceeding.

Assume also that Louis explains that the prospect of the criminal charges would induce a substantial settlement in the case (of which you would receive a third) because a conviction may lead to barring the boxers from participating in future boxing matches. Your preliminary investigation establishes that no one except the parties witnessed the events and either your client or the other parties are lying.

In light of these new assumptions, which one of the following statements is correct?

(a) Filing the counterclaim and criminal complaint would be proper because everyone is entitled to have his or her rights protected based on what the client has told an attorney.

√(b) In absence of some direct or indirect indication that your client is lying, filing the counterclaim would be proper because an attorney is ethically obligated to represent a client zealously. Filing the criminal complaint, however, would be improper because an attorney may not threaten criminal charges solely to gain advantage in a civil matter.

(c) Filing the counterclaim would be improper because the attorney should know the claim is intended to harass or maliciously injure the opposing parties. Filing the criminal complaint would be improper for the reason stated in (b) above.

(d) Filing the counterclaim would be improper because the attorney lacks a reasonable basis to support the counterclaim. Filing the criminal complaint would be proper because you can use the threat of a legitimate criminal action even if the indirect consequence of threatened action is to gain advantage in a civil action.

Stop here, and choose an answer before consulting the discussion of this problem in Appendix A.

PROBLEM 1.6

Assume that Soda Popinski's attorney refuses to discuss settlement or to convey your settlement offer of $50,000 to Popinski. Louis wants you to send the offer directly to Popinski to get the matter settled. Louis is sure that Popinski will accept the offer. The proposed course of action would be

(a) unethical because the settlement offer is an ex parte communication related to a pending cause.

√(b) unethical because an attorney is prohibited from communicating directly with a party known to be represented by counsel.

(c) ethical because Popinski's attorney has no right to withhold this information from the client.

(d) ethical because offers of settlement are not part of "the subject of the representation."

Stop here, and choose an answer before consulting the discussion of this problem in Appendix A.

PROBLEM 1.7

Assume that you decide not to contact Soda Popinski directly. Which of the following courses of action on the facts of the preceding problems would be the *clearest* violation of professional ethics?

(a) Talking to the judge privately about the merits of the case and the refusal of Popinski's counsel to communicate the offer to Popinski.

(b) Holding a press conference and announcing the proposed settlement offer (assuming the case is legitimately newsworthy).

(c) Allowing your client to communicate the offer directly to Popinski.

(d) Threatening to report the opposing counsel's refusal to the disciplinary committee of the state bar association unless the offer is promptly conveyed to the client.

Stop here, and choose an answer before consulting the discussion of this problem in Appendix A.

PROBLEM 1.8

Assume that a legal issue has arisen in the lawsuit concerning whether professional boxers have a special duty to avoid participating in fist fights outside the professional ring. Assume that in the course of your research you have found that the courts in the jurisdiction where the litigation is taking place have not considered the issue. Other jurisdictions have considered the issue and are split on the question of whether a special duty exists.

Assume further that you have told your client about these decisions. The court has requested each side to prepare a memorandum of law for the court on this issue. Louis wants you to cite only the favorable cases in support of your position. Your client strongly feels that you should not be doing the other side's work for them. This course of action would

(a) violate the disciplinary rules because an attorney must disclose every adverse precedent to the court.

(b) violate the disciplinary rules because the failure to disclose the adverse precedents is tantamount to making a false statement of law.

(c) not violate the disciplinary rules because mandatory disclosure of adverse cases from other jurisdictions is not required.

(d) not violate the disciplinary rules because mandatory disclosure of adverse cases is required only in ex parte proceedings.

Stop here, and choose an answer before consulting the discussion of this problem in Appendix A.

PROBLEM 1.9

Assume that during your research you have found a favorable case (*Sandman v. Tiger*) from a neighboring jurisdiction that directly supports your legal position. Upon further research, you have discovered the *Sandman* case has been substantially undermined by another recent decision (*Flamenco v. Machoman*) in that jurisdiction.

Assume further that you have told your client about these two cases and Louis thinks that you should cite only the *Sandman* case. Louis maintains you do not have to make the other side's case for them by explaining how a recent case has affected an earlier one. The *best* argument that this proposed course of action would be *unethical* is

(a) the disciplinary rules prohibit citing a case or a statute when an attorney knows the case has been overruled or the statute has been repealed. Citing a case which an attorney knows has been substantially undermined is different only in degree, not kind, from citing an overruled case and, therefore, should be considered a knowingly false statement of law.

(b) an attorney must disclose every adverse precedent to the court. Because the *Flamenco v. Machoman* case undermines the cited case, the *Flamenco* case is adverse and must be disclosed.

(c) the failure to disclose the existence and effect of the subsequent case is a prohibited dilatory tactic designed to needlessly increase the cost of litigation. If this information was disclosed, the opposing party would not need to conduct the research to find this information and thus the litigation process would be speeded up.

(d) an attorney must disclose directly adverse precedents in the controlling jurisdiction, assuming that opposing counsel has not previously revealed the relationship of the cases to the court.

Stop here, and choose an answer before consulting the discussion of this problem in Appendix A.

Section 1D. Basic Elements of Legal Writing Style

This section presents the basic elements of legal writing style used in written work for judges, lawyers, or other legal audiences.

1. CAPITALIZATION

(a) Descriptive Names of the Litigants

DO NOT CAPITALIZE PLAINTIFF, DEFENDANT, APPELLANT, OR OTHER DESCRIPTIVE NAMES FOR THE LITIGANTS IN LEGAL WRITING TEXT.

Descriptive names for the litigants in legal writing text should not be capitalized.

ILLUSTRATION 1.20

The respondent failed to appear at the deposition.
The court held defendant Smith in contempt.

(b) References Derived From Names of Specific Laws, Constitutions, and Titles of Governmental Officers

CAPITALIZE REFERENCES DERIVED FROM PROPER NAMES OF SPECIFIC LAWS.

In addition to capitalizing the proper names of specific laws, references derived from those names should be capitalized in legal writing. Note, however, that many secretaries have been trained not to capitalize common-noun references to laws (e.g., the code).

ILLUSTRATION 1.21

the Act (referring to the Federal Trade Commission Act)
the Code (referring to the Uniform Commercial Code)
code pleading (referring, for example, to the reform of common-law pleading by the various state codes)

CAPITALIZE "CONSTITUTION," STANDING ALONE, ONLY WHEN IT REFERS TO THE U.S. CONSTITUTION.

Capitalize "Constitution," standing alone, only when it refers to the United States Constitution.[46]

ILLUSTRATION 1.22

the constitution (referring to the New Mexico Constitution)
the Constitution (referring to the U.S. Constitution)

CAPITALIZE NAMES OF PARTS OF CONSTITUTIONS, STATUTES, OR OTHER GOVERNMENTAL ACTS ONLY WHEN THEY ARE CONSIDERED TO BE A DISCRETE BODY OF LAW.

Parts of constitutions, statutes, and other governmental acts are not capitalized, especially in law review writing.[47]

ILLUSTRATION 1.23

article I, section 8, clause 2 of the Constitution
the twenty-first amendment
section 201 of the Civil Rights Act of 1964

On the other hand, when they are "generally considered to be discrete from the remainder of the governmental act," common-noun substitutes referring to parts of constitutions, statutes, or other federal, state, and international governmental acts are capitalized.[48]

ILLUSTRATION 1.24

The "Bill of Rights" is considered to be a discrete body of law.[49]

REFERENCES TO AMENDMENTS TO CONSTITUTIONS MAY BE CAPITALIZED IN PERSUASIVE WRITING.

---

[46]USOC, supra note 6, at 32 (Rule 8). Accord Chicago Manual, supra note 7, at 30 (Appendix 1).

[47]See USOC, supra note 6, at 32 (Rule 8). Cf. Chicago Manual, supra note 7, at 30 ("Names of parts of a constitution or statute may be capitalized when used in an English sentence as proper nouns . . . .").

[48]Texas Law Review, Manual of Style 3 (4th ed. 1979) (hereinafter Texas Style Manual) (Rule 1:9). Cf. USOC, supra, note 6, at 32 ("Bill of Rights"); Chicago Manual, supra note 7, at 30 (parts may be capitalized).

[49]See USOC, supra note 6, at 32 (Rule 8).

In persuasive legal writing, you may capitalize amendments to the Constitution (for example, the "Seventh Amendment" or "First Amendment") to emphasize their importance when it is to your advantage.

CAPITALIZE REFERENCES DERIVED FROM TITLES OF GOVERNMENTAL OFFICERS.

ILLUSTRATION 1.25

the Commissioner (referring to the Commissioner of Internal Revenue)

(c) Governmental Entities and Subdivisions

CAPITALIZE REFERENCES DERIVED FROM PROPER NAMES OF GOVERNMENTAL AGENCIES.

ILLUSTRATION 1.26

the Board (referring to the National Labor Relations Board)
the Commission (referring to the Federal Trade Commission)

IN LEGAL WRITING, DO NOT CAPITALIZE "FEDERAL GOVERNMENT."

In legal writing, "federal government" should not be capitalized even though it is used to refer to the United States Government.

CAPITALIZE WORDS DESIGNATING POLITICAL SUBDIVISIONS WHEN THEY ARE ESSENTIAL ELEMENTS OF SPECIFIC NAMES; IN LAW REVIEW WRITING, DO NOT CAPITALIZE THEM WHEN THEY STAND ALONE OR PRECEDE A PROPER NAME.

Words designating national, regional, or local political subdivisions ordinarily are capitalized when they are essential elements of specific names.

ILLUSTRATION 1.27

Washington State
Douglas County

The general rule is that words designating national, regional, or local political subdivisions are not capitalized when they precede a proper name or stand alone, especially in law review writing.[50]

ILLUSTRATION 1.28

county of Douglas
county governments
the state of Washington

IN PERSUASIVE LEGAL WRITING, CAPITALIZE "STATE" WHEN IT REFERS TO A SPECIFIC STATE OR TO THE STATE AS A LITIGANT (BUT NOT WHEN IT REFERS TO THE STATE GENERALLY OR AN INTERNATIONAL ENTITY) TO EMPHASIZE RESPECT FOR THE STATE.

Many legal writers apply a special rule for "state" in persuasive legal writing. To emphasize the sovereignty of a state, these writers capitalize "state" whenever it refers to a specific state or to the state as a litigant but not when it refers to the state generally or to an international entity.

ILLUSTRATION 1.29

State of Washington
State (referring to the State of Washington as a litigant)
the state courts (referring to the state generally)
the state's witness (referring to the state generally)
Upper Volta is a state (referring to the state as an international entity)

(d) "Court," "Supreme Court," "Justice," "Term," and Other References to Specific Courts

---

CAPITALIZE THE FULL NAMES OF SPECIFIC COURTS. CAPITALIZE REFERENCES DERIVED FROM THOSE NAMES, EXCEPT WHEN "COURT" OR "SUPREME COURT" IS USED ALONE.

In addition to capitalizing the *full* names of *specific* courts, references derived from those names should be capitalized, except when "court" and "supreme court" are used alone.

ILLUSTRATION 1.30

---

[50] See id. at 33 (Rule 8).

ILLUSTRATION 1.30

Supreme Court of Iowa (full name of a specific court)
Iowa Supreme Court (full name of a specific court)
United States District Court for the District of New Jersey (full name of a specific court)
First Circuit (referring to the United States Court of Appeals for the First Circuit)

A general reference, however, should not be capitalized.

ILLUSTRATION 1.31

the court of appeals (general reference)
a federal district court (general reference)
the circuit courts (general reference)
a county court (general reference)

CAPITALIZE "COURT," "SUPREME COURT," "JUSTICE," AND "TERM," STANDING ALONE, ONLY WHEN THEY REFER TO THE U.S. SUPREME COURT OR ONE OF ITS TERMS. IN PERSUASIVE WRITING, THEY MAY BE CAPITALIZED.

When standing alone, "court" and "supreme court" should be capitalized only when they refer to the U.S. Supreme Court.[51]

ILLUSTRATION 1.32

The Court [referring to the United States Supreme Court] granted the stay of execution.

The court [referring, for example, to the United States Court of Appeals for the Ninth Circuit] reversed the judgment of the trial court.

The Supreme Court [referring to the United States Supreme Court] noted probable jurisdiction.

The supreme court [referring to the Wisconsin Supreme Court] dismissed the appeal because it was moot.

An exception to the above rule may be made when it is to your advantage to emphasize respect for the court.

ILLUSTRATION 1.33

If you were litigating in the state courts of Minnesota, it may be to your advantage as an advocate to capitalize "supreme

---

[51] Id. at 32 (Rule 8). Accord Chicago Manual, supra note 7, at 30. Cf. Texas Style Manual, supra note 48, at 6 (Rule 1:15) (capitalized only if "court" refers to the United States Supreme Court or to an international court).

court," standing alone, when you refer to the Minnesota Supreme Court.

Capitalize "term" and "justice," standing alone, only when they respectively refer to a Term of the United States Supreme Court or to one of its Justices.

ILLUSTRATION 1.34

Two Justices [referring to U.S. Supreme Court Justices] recused themselves.

During this term [referring to a term of the Florida Supreme Court], the justices heard forty-five criminal appeals.

In persuasive legal writing, you may want to capitalize "justice" when you are referring to a state supreme court justice, particularly when the written product is directed to that court.

(e) Trademarks and Service Marks

CAPITALIZE TRADEMARKS AND SERVICE MARKS.

Capitalize trademarks and services, especially when they belong to your clients. Failure to capitalize words claimed as trademarks or service marks can contribute to the "generic deterioration" of such words. The lack of capitalization may be used as evidence to prove the mark has become a generic word (which may result in the loss of the right to exclusive use of the mark).[52]

(f) Headings and Titles

IN HEADINGS AND TITLES APPEARING IN LEGAL WRITING, CAPITALIZE THE INITIAL WORD, THE WORD IMMEDIATELY FOLLOWING A COLON, AND ALL OTHER WORDS EXCEPT ARTICLES, CONJUNCTIONS, AND PREPOSITIONS OF FOUR OR FEWER LETTERS. USE THIS SAME RULE WHEN YOU CITE NAMES OR TITLES.

Unless otherwise directed, follow the *USOC* rule that requires capitalization of the initial word, the word immediately

---

[52] See, e.g., Haughton Elevator Co. v. Seeberger, 85 U.S.P.Q. (BNA) 80, 81 (Comm'r Pat. 1950) ("escalator" generic) (misused in patent applications, correspondence, and advertising).

following a colon, and all other words except articles, conjunctions, and prepositions of four or fewer letters in (1) headings, (2) titles, (3) cited names, and (4) cited titles.[53] According to the *USOC*, this rule should be followed even when it causes a departure from the capitalization used in the cited source.[54]

ILLUSTRATION 1.35

Assume that the title of the annotation you are going to cite is given in the *A.L.R.* volume as follows:

Religious activities as doing or transaction of business under "long-arm" statutes or rules of court

Pursuant to the *USOC* rule, this title would be capitalized as:

Annotation, <u>Religious Activities as Doing or Transaction of Business Under "Long-Arm" Statutes or Rules of Court</u>, 26 A.L.R.4th 1176 (1983). (Both words in hyphenated compounds ("Long-Arm" Statutes) should be capitalized.)

(g) Words Following Colons

IN LEGAL WRITING TEXT, CAPITALIZE THE INITIAL LETTER OF THE WORD FOLLOWING A COLON ONLY WHEN IT IS USEFUL TO EMPHASIZE THAT WORD.

Capitalize the initial letter of the word following a colon in the text only when it is useful to emphasize that word.

ILLUSTRATION 1.36

The court should identify three categories of consumers: those for whom the mark is solely source-significant and not the generic name of the product; those for whom the mark lacks any source significance and is the generic name of the product; and those for whom it performs both functions. (Emphasizing "those" would not serve a useful purpose.)

Of all the procedural rules that must be learned, remember this one: Never omit a compulsory counterclaim. (Emphasizing "never" is accomplished by capitalizing it.)

---

[53] <u>USOC</u>, <u>supra</u> note 6, at 31 (Rule 8).

[54] <u>Id</u>. at v.

PROBLEM 1.10

For each of the sentences below, indicate the letters that should be capitalized by triple underlining beneath the letter. Indicate letters that should be typed in lower case by making a slash mark through the letter and by writing "lc" above the letter. Assume these sentences appear in an office memorandum of law and are related to each other.

(a) The eighth circuit affirmed the refusal to grant the injunction.

(b) The U.S. Department of Justice then sought review in the United States Supreme Court.

(c) The U.S. Attorney General argued on behalf of the Federal Government that (1) the federal district courts did have the power to hear the case even though the state of Minnesota was a party to the action and (2) the U.S. District Court for the District of Minnesota could enjoin the Minnesota supreme court from hearing the case.

(d) On the other hand, the Respondents argued that the Eleventh Amendment to the U.S. Constitution and the Anti-Injunction Act, 28 U.S.C. § 2283, applied to this case.

(e) Under that act, writs of injunction to stay proceedings in any court of a state have been prohibited since 1793. See Durfee & Sloss, Federal Injunctions against Proceedings in State Courts: the Life History of a Statute, 30 Mich. L. Rev. 1145 (1932).

(f) In an opinion accompanying the court's refusal to hear the case this term, the justices refused to speculate on whether the constitution or that act applied to a state court appeal because the issue was moot.

Stop here, and edit the capitalization in the above sentences before consulting the discussion of this problem in Appendix A.

2. QUOTATIONS

PUNCTUATE QUOTED MATERIAL FOLLOWING THE TRADITIONAL RULES: (1) PLACE COMMAS AND PERIODS WITHIN THE QUOTATION MARKS; (2) PLACE SEMICOLONS AND COLONS OUTSIDE THE QUOTATION MARKS; AND (3) PLACE QUESTION MARKS WITHIN THE QUOTATION MARKS WHEN THEY APPLY TO THE QUOTED MATTER ONLY; OTHERWISE, PLACE THEM OUTSIDE THE MARKS.

Place commas and periods within the quotation marks.

ILLUSTRATION 1.37

The Court essentially agreed, stating that "an unexpressed purpose to nullify a state's control over its officers and agents is not lightly to be attributed to Congress." (The period is within the quotation marks.)

Place semicolons and colons outside the quotation marks.

ILLUSTRATION 1.38

This concept is known by the term, "free ride"; if one person, for example, erects a lighthouse, many will "free ride" on its benefits. (The semicolon is outside the quotation marks.)

Place question marks within the quotation marks when they apply to the quoted matter only; place them outside the marks when they refer to the whole sentence.

ILLUSTRATION 1.39

In some instances the seller will probably encounter the consumer response, "I agree that it looks like plexiglass, but if your substitute brand of cast acrylic sheet is really 'Plexiglass,' then why isn't it called that?" (The question mark refers to only the quotation and, therefore, is within the quotation marks. Quotes within quotes are indicated by single quotation marks.)

Does "Wilson Art" brand decorative laminated plastics really possess the durability that consumers associate with "Formica"? (The question mark refers to the entire sentence and, therefore, is outside the quotation marks.)

DO NOT USE QUOTATION MARKS WHEN FIFTY WORDS OR MORE ARE QUOTED; INSTEAD, INDENT THEM FROM BOTH THE LEFT AND RIGHT MARGINS.

ILLUSTRATION 1.40

Assume that the following appears in a memorandum. Because the material quoted from the case is more than fifty words,[55] the quotation is indented from both the left and right margins.

---

[55] See USOC, supra note 6, at 25 (Rule 5) (stating the above 50-word rule). Cf. Chicago Manual, supra note 7, at 29 (stating that quotations running more than six lines of text should be in block form).

In Theisen v. Milwaukee Automobile Mutual Insurance Co., 18 Wis. 2d 91, 118 N.W.2d 140 (1962), the Wisconsin Supreme Court held that falling asleep at the wheel of an automobile is negligence as a matter of law. The court explained:

> Normally no harm will be done if one falls asleep reading the newspaper after dinner or this opinion. In the horse and buggy days, one might have fallen asleep while driving and the horse quite likely would have had enough horse sense to stop or even to take the driver home through habit and instinct quite safely. But falling asleep behind a wheel of an auto propelled by 200 or 300 mechanical horses having no horse sense is entirely a different matter in terms of your duty to others. . . . When one is under a duty to use care not to injure another, he cannot fulfill the duty by falling asleep.
>
> We must approach a sleeping driver case on the premise the driver has the duty to stay awake while he drives and it is within his control either to stay awake, to cease driving, or not to drive at all when sleepy. . . .
>
> . . . .
>
> We exclude from this holding those exceptional cases of loss of consciousness resulting from injury inflicted by an outside force or fainting or heart attack, epileptic seizure, or other illness which suddenly incapacitates the driver of an automobile and when the occurrence of such disability is not attended with sufficient warning or should not have been reasonably foreseen.

18 Wis. 2d at 97-99, 118 N.W.2d at 143-44.

The citation ("18 Wis. 2d at 97-99, 118 N.W.2d at 143-44.") is not included with the indented material. As shown above, it is given on the line immediately following the block quotation at the left-hand margin.[56] In double-spaced legal writing, block quotations are traditionally single-spaced.

When a block quotation is used, the paragraph structure of the quoted material should be shown by further indenting the first line of each paragraph. The first quoted paragraph should be indented, however, only when the first quoted word is in fact the first word of the original paragraph.[57]

---

[56]USOC, supra note 6, at 25 (Rule 5.1). Accord Chicago Manual, supra note 7, at 29.

[57]USOC, supra note 6, at 28 (Rule 5.4) ("Normally" at the beginning of the quotation in the above example was the first word in the paragraph in the original).

ENCLOSE ALTERATIONS OF QUOTATIONS IN BRACKETS.

Brackets should be used to indicate alterations in quoted material or to add clarification.[58]

ILLUSTRATION 1.41

The court specifically pointed out that "[n]o warranty nor representation was made by the insured." ("N" in "no" was capitalized in the opinion quoted.)

"When a restraint upon trade is the result of valid governmental action, no violation of the [Sherman] Act can be made out." ("Sherman" was added for clarification.)

USE BRACKETS TO ENCLOSE "SIC" TO INDICATE SIGNIFICANT MISTAKES IN QUOTED MATERIAL.

"Sic" means "intentionally so written" and is used immediately after a quoted word or words to indicate that the original has been exactly reproduced. Errors in the original should be retained; significant ones should be followed immediately by "[sic]."[59]

ILLUSTRATION 1.42

The contract stated, "the insurer [sic] shall notify the insurer of any loss." ("Sic" is used to indicate the error in the original. "Insurer" should have been "insured" in the original.)

USE ELLIPSES TO INDICATE OMISSIONS IN QUOTED MATERIAL.

Ellipses are punctuation marks indicating an omission. Some publishers use asterisks (* * *) or other marks to indicate omissions, but in most legal writing three periods are used, set off by a space before the first, after the last, and in between each period.[60]

---

[58] Id. at 26 (Rule 5.2). Accord Chicago Manual, supra note 7, at 29.

[59] See USOC, supra note 6, at 26 (Rule 5.2). Accord Chicago Manual, supra note 7, at 29.

[60] See id. at 26 (Rule 5.3).

ILLUSTRATION 1.43

Consider the following portion of the *Theisen* opinion:

> Normally no harm will be done if one falls asleep reading the newspaper after dinner or this opinion. In the horse and buggy days, one might have fallen asleep while driving and the horse quite likely would have had enough horse sense to stop or even to take the driver home through habit and instinct quite safely. But falling asleep behind a wheel of an auto propelled by 200 or 300 mechanical horses having no horse sense is entirely a different matter in terms of your duty to others. We recently pointed out the increase in the frequency and in the seriousness of the consequences of automobile accidents today resulting from modern, high-powered vehicles. The increase in risks and hazards of driving an automobile on public highways demands greater skill and attention than 40 years ago. When one is under a duty to use care not to injure another, he cannot fulfill the duty by falling asleep.
>
> We must approach a sleeping driver case on the premise the driver has the duty to stay awake while he drives and it is within his control either to stay awake, to cease driving, or not to drive at all when sleepy. Up to now no decision has gone beyond the limits of the well established rule that the fact the driver of an automobile goes to sleep while driving is a proper basis for an inference of negligence sufficient to make a prima facie case and support a verdict for recovery if no circumstances tending to excuse or justify such conduct are proven. This problem is the subject of an extensive annotation, Automobile--Illness or Drowsiness, 28 A.L.R.2d 12.[61]

Note how ellipses would be used to indicate the following omissions in a quotation of the above opinion:[62]

[1] In the horse and buggy days, one might have fallen asleep while driving and the horse quite likely would have had enough horse sense to stop or even to take the driver home through habit and instinct quite safely.	[1] Omission at the beginning of the quotation (no ellipses used)

---

[61] Theisen v. Milwaukee Auto. Mut. Ins. Co., 18 Wis. 2d 91, 97, 118 N.W.2d 140, 143 (1962) (footnote omitted).

[62] See USOC, supra note 6, at 27-28 (Rule 5.3).

But falling asleep behind a wheel of an auto . . . is [2] entirely a different matter in terms of your duty to others. . . . When [3] one is under a duty to use care not to injure another, [a driver] [4] cannot fulfill the duty by falling asleep.

We must approach a sleeping driver case on the premise the driver has the duty to stay awake . . . .[5] Up to now no decision has gone beyond the limits of the well established rule that the fact the driver of an automobile goes to sleep while driving is a prima facie case and support a verdict for recovery if no circumstances tending to excuse or justify such conduct are proven. [6]

[2] Omission of material ("propelled by 200 or 300 mechanical horses having no horse sense") in the middle of the quoted sentence shown by ellipses.
[3] Omission of material after the end of a quoted sentence, by the insertion of three periods after the final punctuation mark of the sentence. Note the *USOC* leaves only one space after the final period before beginning the next sentence.
[4] Brackets indicate the change in quoted material ("he" changed to "a driver").
[5] Omission of material at the end of a quoted sentence, shown by ellipses inserted between the last quoted word and the final punctuation mark. Note the difference in the spacing of ellipses with that in [3].
[6] Omission of material after the last quoted sentence (no ellipses).

In the above Illustration, the quoted language stood by itself as full sentences. When the material quoted appears as a clause or phrase in one of your sentences, ellipses are not used to indicate language omitted before or after the quoted material.

ILLUSTRATION 1.44

Assume that the following is your sentence:

In <u>Theisen v. Milwaukee Automobile Mutual Insurance Co.</u>, 18 Wis. 2d 91, 118 N.W.2d 140 (1962), the Wisconsin Supreme Court specifically pointed out that "no decision ha[d] gone beyond the limits of the well established rule that the fact the driver of an automobile goes to sleep while driving is a proper basis for an inference of negligence sufficient to make a prima facie case." <u>Id</u>. at 97, 118 N.W.2d at 143. (No ellipses are used).

When you omit material from within the quoted language used in one of your sentences as a phrase or clause, ellipses should be used.

ILLUSTRATION 1.45

In Theisen v. Milwaukee Automobile Mutual Insurance Co., 18 Wis. 2d 91, 118 N.W.2d 140 (1962), the Wisconsin Supreme Court specifically pointed out that "no decision ha[d] gone beyond the limits of the well established rule that the fact the driver of an automobile goes to sleep while driving is . . . sufficient to . . . support a verdict for recovery if no circumstances tending to excuse or justify such conduct are proven." Id. at 97, 118 N.W.2d at 143.

When one or more entire paragraphs have been omitted from material included in a block quotation, four periods should be inserted and indented on a new line between the first part of the quoted material and remaining part.[63] Refer to the block quotation in Illustration 1.40 above for an example of the omission of an entire paragraph from a block quotation.

USE QUOTATION MARKS TO ENCLOSE MATTER THAT FOLLOWS CERTAIN INTRODUCTORY EXPRESSIONS, SUCH AS "ENTITLED," "SIGNED," "ENDORSED," "MARKED," "THE TERM," OR "THE WORD."

Items introduced by "entitled," "signed," "endorsed," "marked," "the term," "the word," and similar expressions should be enclosed in quotation marks.

On the other hand, quotation marks ordinarily are not used with "known as," "called," or "so-called."

ILLUSTRATION 1.46

The check had been endorsed, "[i]n entire settlement of all claims, Sharon Theisen." (Quotation marks are used with "endorsed.")

The so-called diversity jurisdiction of the federal courts requires complete diversity of citizenship between adverse parties to the suit. (Quotation marks are not used with "so-called.")

3. CLARITY OF EXPRESSION

BREAK UP LONG NOUN STRINGS.

[63] Id. at 28 (Rule 5.4).

When several nouns are strung together, readers often find it difficult to comprehend the exact relationship between those nouns. To break up noun chains, Wydick suggests that nonessential descriptive words be omitted and that some prepositions be inserted.[64]

ILLUSTRATION 1.47

Wydick gives the following example of a long noun chain:[65]

Pretrial Document Identification Request Responses (long noun chain)

Responses to Plaintiff's Request for Pretrial Identification of Documents (noun chain broken up)

AVOID ELEGANT VARIATION IN LEGAL WRITING.

Elegant variation is the use of different names for the same referent. Fowler points out that "[i]t is the second-rate writers, those intent rather on expressing themselves prettily than on conveying their meaning clearly, and still more those whose notions of style are based on a few misleading rules of thumb, that are chiefly open to the allurements of elegant variation."[66]

In legal writing, the best approach is to use the same term for the same referent throughout a document or statutory provision. Otherwise, elegant variation in the references may confuse the reader and create legal ambiguities.[67]

ILLUSTRATION 1.48

Consider the following example of the ambiguities created by elegant variation: "The use fee shall be 1% of Franchisee's gross revenue. Franchise payment shall be made on or before the 15th day of each month." (Are "franchise payments" something

---

[64] R. Wydick, Plain English for Lawyers 61 (2d ed. 1985).

[65] Id.

[66] H. Fowler, A Dictionary of Modern English Usage 148 (2d ed. 1965).

[67] See Dickerson, How to Draft a Statute, 31 Notre Dame L. Rev. 14, 24 (1955) ("The cardinal rule of all drafting, sometimes called 'the draftsman's golden rule,' can be stated in four words: Use your terms consistently. For one thing, don't vary your terminology when referring to the same thing. For example, don't refer to an automobile as an 'automobile' in one place and as a 'motor car' in another").

different from the "use fee"? If so, what are they, and when must the use fee be paid?)[68]

AVOID USING THE SAME WORD IN DIFFERENT SENSES IN THE SAME SENTENCE (OR PARAGRAPH).

Avoid using a word twice in the same sentence (or paragraph) in different senses because the reader tends to assume that the word retains its same meaning.[69]

ILLUSTRATION 1.49

Block provides the following example of this type of writing fault: "My client has a *cause* of action against the defendant because the *cause* of my client's injuries was defendant's conduct." ("My client can maintain an action against the defendant because the defendant's conduct caused my client's injuries.")[70]

PLACE CLAUSES AND PHRASES NEAR THE WORDS THAT THEY MODIFY.

Ordinarily, a relative pronoun ("that," "which," "who") should be placed immediately after its antecedent in the sentence.[71] On occasion, an ambiguity may still arise.

ILLUSTRATION 1.50

Wydick gives the following example: "Claims for expenses, which must not exceed $100, must be made within 30 days."[72] This sentence should be rewritten to make clear whether the claims or the expenses must not exceed $100:

---

[68] R. Wydick, supra note 64, at 60 (stating the example used in the above illustration) ("Don't be afraid to repeat a word if it is the right word, and if repeating it will avoid confusion"). See also G. Block, Effective Legal Writing 61-62 (3d ed. 1986) ("Rule: Choose clarity over elegance").

[69] See H. Fowler, supra note 66, at 328-29 (calling the practice "legerdemain with two senses"). Cf. Dickerson, supra note 67, at 24 ("Don't use the same term to refer to different things. For example, don't use the term 'military' to mean just the land forces in one section [of a statute] and then use the same term to include the naval forces in another section. Consistency is a sine qua non of all effective communication").

[70] G. Block, supra note 68, at 62-63 (also noting some linguists call this type of fault "ultraquistic subterfuge").

[71] See W. Strunk & E. White, The Elements of Style 29 (3d ed. 1979).

[72] R. Wydick, supra note 64, at 46.

Expenses must not exceed $100. Claims for expenses must be made within 30 days.

Claims for expenses must not exceed $100 and must be made within 30 days.[73]

The same rule (placing the modifier immediately after its antecedent) applies to prepositional phrases used as adjectives. By proofreading carefully, you usually will be able to identify instances in which you have separated related parts of a sentence.

ILLUSTRATION 1.51

Wydick illustrates the improper positioning of a prepositional phrase in a legal context with this example: "My client has discussed your proposal to fill the drainage ditch with his partners."[74]

DO NOT CREATE AN AMBIGUITY BY USING A PRONOUN WHEN ITS REFERENCE IS TOO FAR REMOVED.

Avoid placing a pronoun in a position that is too far removed from its antecedent.

ILLUSTRATION 1.52

Consider the ambiguity created by the use of "he" in the following example:

In these situations, the master is absolved from liability only when the injured party is aware of the servant's negligence and then disregards it. It is not enough that he *(who?)* has a notion that there is a remote possibility that he *(who?)* might be injured.

DO NOT USE "THIS" BY ITSELF TO REFER TO PRECEDING MATERIAL, CONCEPTS, OR ARGUMENTS; INSTEAD, ADD A SPECIFIC REFERENCE.

Confusion can often be caused by vague uses of "this." Rombauer asserts that indefinite use of "this" is responsible "for

---

[73] Id.

[74] Id. at 44. This type of error also occurs frequently in a nonlegal context. See, e.g., Slips of the TV Tongue, Omaha World-Herald Magazine of the Midlands, Oct. 30, 1983, at 12, col. 1 ("Dr. Barney Clark spent his 62nd day with an artificial heart glued to the TV set").

more fuzzy writing by law students than any other word."[75] Indeed, "this" is used to refer indefinitely to entire paragraphs, prior ideas, reasoning, arguments, or even things not previously mentioned.[76]

ILLUSTRATION 1.53

Consider what "this" refers to in the following example:

Smith's sudden mental illness caused her to lose control of her automobile. This satisfies the test established by the court in Breunig.

Does the loss of control satisfy the test? Is the suddenness of the mental illness the critical element? Is the causal connection between the sudden mental illness and the inability to control the automobile crucial? Or is more than one of these elements necessary to satisfy the test?

Ambiguous references can be avoided by adding the desired reference after "this." Rombauer maintains that the best practice is simply "never to use 'this' without a following word that identifies what is referred to" by the author.[77] Thus, after the word "this" add the proper reference (conclusion, view, idea, rule, theory, holding, etc.).

AVOID THE USE OF MULTIPLE NEGATIVES.

"No," "not," "never," "nobody," and similar words have negative meanings. Many other words, such as "except," "unless," "save," "excluding," "until," "deny," "failure," and "absent," also have negative meanings or connotations.

Multiple negatives in a sentence often make it difficult to understand. To the extent possible, use the positive instead (unless you intend to emphasize the negative).

AVOID UNCLEAR SHIFTS IN YOUR POINT OF VIEW.

---

[75] M. Rombauer, Legal Problem Solving: Analysis, Research and Writing 306 (4th ed. 1983).

[76] Id.

[77] Id.

Block points out that "[w]henever you write, you make an implicit promise to your readers not to shift your point of view unless you let them know about it."[78]

ILLUSTRATION 1.54

Block provides the following example of the confusion that unclear shifts in the point of view can cause.

> Although zoning ordinances should furnish owners of historic properties some relief from the financial burden of maintaining their property for public benefit, decline in market value [of what?] and diminished expectations [whose? about what?] are not sufficient injuries [who received? who caused?] to constitute a taking of property [who took?] without just compensation [to whom?].[79]

Block suggests the following revisions to make clear the subjects and objects of the clauses:

> Zoning ordinances should furnish owners of historic properties some relief from the financial burden of maintaining their property for public benefit. However, the injury to the landowners of a decline in the market value of their property or their diminished expectation of income from the property is not sufficient for the court to find that the state has taken private property without compensation to the property owners.[80]

PROBLEM 1.11

Assume that you are reviewing a proposed elevator maintenance contract. Your client wants you to be sure that the contract provides protection against the various possible equipment failures that might occur. What do you think of the following provision?

This company will repair or replace worm and gear bearings and housings.

Would you find this provision acceptable? Why or why not?

---

[78] G. Block, <u>supra</u> note 68, at 51.

[79] <u>Id.</u>

[80] <u>Id.</u>

Stop here and consider these questions before consulting the discussion of this problem in Appendix A.

PROBLEM 1.12

Correct the misplaced clauses and phrases in the following sentences. This problem is based on examples collected by James J. Kilpatrick in his "The Writer's Art" newspaper column.[81]

(a) The French government is preparing television commercials encouraging the use of condoms that are blunt enough to shock even liberal Americans.

(b) Establishments such as the Bright Star in Bessemer, for instance, will have lines of people waiting for seats extending outside their own premises.

(c) On Monday, March 30, at 7:30 p.m., there will be an Interfaith Support Group meeting for parents who have lost a child [through] death at the First Presbyterian Church.

(d) One pharmacist told us of a trying moment recently when he had to explain to a young woman how to administer a douche in front of a small audience of onlookers.

Stop here, and edit the above sentences before consulting the discussion of this problem in Appendix A.

PROBLEM 1.13

Correct remote, ambiguous, or improper references in the following related sentences. Write in changes using a caret symbol to indicate insertions. Cross out or circle words or phrases in a manner showing to where they should be moved or indicating that they should be deleted.

(a) Holding social hosts liable for injuries to third parties caused by their drunken driving would cause practical problems.

(b) In this instance, for example, it was impossible for a host to keep his "eye" on each guest and for him to monitor his drinking habits.

(c) When they left, the host and hostess went with the guests to the door, wished them good night, and reminded everyone who was driving to use caution.

---

[81] James J. Kilpatrick has published an entertaining and educational selection of articles from his newspaper column in his book The Writer's Art (1985).

(d) Clearly, this indicated that the social hostess exercised the same degree of care that a reasonable person would have exercised toward social guests under these circumstances.

Stop here, and correct the remote or ambiguous references before consulting the discussion of this problem in Appendix A.

4. TONE AND WORD CHOICE

(a) Archaic Terminology, Inflated Language, and Legal Jargon

AVOID ARCHAIC TERMINOLOGY, INFLATED LANGUAGE, AND LEGAL JARGON

The language of the Anglo-American law reflects the influence of Latin, French, and old and middle English. As the language of the law evolved over several hundred years, legal writers and the courts have tended to use archaic terminology, inflated language, and legal jargon in judicial opinions and legal documents. Good legal writing today should avoid this kind of "legalese."[82]

ILLUSTRATION 1.55

will (*not* "last will and testament"--coupled synonyms)
give (*not* "give, devise, and bequeath"--coupled synonyms)
the premises (*not* "said" or "aforesaid premises"--old and middle English)
beneficiary of the trust (*not* "cestui que trust"--French)

(b) Legal Terms of Art

USE ACCEPTED LEGAL TERMS OF ART RATHER THAN OTHER TERMS IN FORMAL LEGAL WRITING. WHEN THE READERS WILL BE UNFAMILIAR WITH LEGAL TERMINOLOGY, YOU SHOULD EXPLAIN, DEFINE, OR ILLUSTRATE THE TERMS.

---

[82] See G. Block, supra note 68, at 44-46 ("Don't Use Jargon"); D. Mellinkoff, Legal Writing: Sense and Nonsense 126-27, 187-96 (1982) (providing numerous examples of "Ordinary Old and Middle English," "Coupled Synonyms," "Old Formalisms," "Law Latin," and "Law French"); D. Pratt, Legal Writing: A Systematic Approach 178-80 (1989) (short summary of the "Origins of Legalese").

Knowledge of the legal terms of art comes from careful observation of how terms are used in legal sources and the study of law generally. In formal legal writing (such as in legal memoranda and appellate briefs), accepted legal terms of art, not ordinary terms, should be used.

ILLUSTRATION 1.56

A suddenly incapacitated driver *loses culpability* (should be "is not liable") when control of the vehicle is taken away without any fault on the driver's part. ("Liable" is the accepted legal term of art in this context.)

The court *differentiated* (should be "distinguished") the two cases. ("Distinguished" is the accepted legal term of art here.)

The trial court *abused its discretion* (should be "erred") when the court granted a motion striking sudden mental illness as a defense on the ground that this defense was insufficient as a matter of law. ("Abuse of discretion" is properly used only when the court is ruling on a motion that allows a judge to exercise some degree of latitude in deciding whether or not a motion should be granted. A defense is either recognized or not, and thus no discretion is involved.)

The defense of sudden mental illness was incorrectly *barred* (should be some other term, such as "disallowed") by the trial court. ("Bar" is a legal term of art used in describing the res judicata effect of a prior judgment. It would be better to avoid using bar in its ordinary sense--prevented or forbidden.)

In some situations, such as deeds or contracts, careful legal writers must use legal or technical terms for substantive purposes. To help persons who are unfamiliar with those terms understand the document, you should consider defining, explaining, or illustrating the terms immediately after the terms are first used or in an accompanying cover letter.

ILLUSTRATION 1.57

The accompanying deed grants you an *easement* (the right to pass over another person's land).

The defendant asserted that your claim could not be maintained because of *laches* (an unreasonable delay or neglect in pursuing your claim or right).

AVOID USING CONTRACTIONS IN FORMAL LEGAL WRITING.

Legal writing tends to follow certain traditional formalities, particularly in appellate briefs, memoranda, contracts, and legislation. One of those formalities is avoiding the use of contractions.

ILLUSTRATION 1.58

The contractions should be separated in the following sentences:

The protagonist *hasn't* (should be "has not") been charged with a crime. Therefore, he *isn't* (should be "is not") protected by the sixth amendment.

AVOID USING COLLOQUIAL LANGUAGE IN FORMAL LEGAL WRITING.

Colloquial language is that used in familiar and informal conversation. This type of language and this type of writing style are considered inappropriate for formal legal writing.

ILLUSTRATION 1.59

The following sentences should be rephrased using more formal terminology:

The opinion *went on to say* that . . . . (too colloquial)
The defendant *was hot to trot* . . . . (too colloquial)

Informal references to the position of the court should be avoided in legal writing.[83]

ILLUSTRATION 1.60

The court *believed* (argued, felt, etc.) that the reason for the delay was untenable. (too informal)

The court *wrestled with* the question . . . . (too informal)

The Supreme Court *came up with* a three-part test . . . . (too informal)

Instead, it would be more appropriate to state:

The court decided (recognized, held, suggested, etc.) that the reason for the delay was untenable.

The court considered . . . .

The Supreme Court adopted a three-part test . . . .

---

[83] See M. Rombauer, supra note 75, at 306-07.

In legal writing, judges and justices should be referred to in a formal manner. Do not refer to them by their last name alone.[84]

ILLUSTRATION 1.61

Chief Justice Smith
Judge Wilson

AVOID USING A CASE NAME OR CASE CITATION AS THE SUBJECT OF THE SENTENCE.

In formal legal writing (such as legal memoranda and appellate briefs), using a case name or case citation as the subject of a sentence should be avoided.

ILLUSTRATION 1.62

In Erie Railroad Co. v. Tompkins, 304 U.S. 64 (1938), the Court overruled the Swift case. (*not* "Erie Railroad Co. v. Tompkins, 304 U.S. 64 (1938) overruled the Swift case.")

AVOID A PERSONALIZED WRITING STYLE IN FORMAL LEGAL WRITING.

In formal legal writing, a personalized writing style should be avoided.

ILLUSTRATION 1.63

Consider the following three illustrations of a personalized writing style:

We assert that the court below erred. (too personalized)
I plan to discuss three critical issues. (too personalized)
For purposes of this memorandum, *I* am assuming that the illness was sudden and unexpected. (too personalized)

A better approach would be to delete the personal references:

The appellant asserts that the court below erred.
Three critical issues will be discussed.
For purposes of this memorandum, the illness is assumed to have been sudden and unexpected.

---

[84] See USOC, supra note 6, at 33 (Rule 9).

PROBLEM 1.14

Assume that the following sentences appear in an office memorandum of law. Revise these sentences to reflect a proper legal writing style.

(a) In this memorandum, I'll discuss the law concerning incontestability clauses in insurance contracts.

(b) The court refused to tackle certain kinds of violations, such as the failure to pay parking tickets.

(c) The rule is simple: Never fail to file the complaint on time.

(d) Smith distinguished the Jones case.

Stop, and revise these sentences before consulting the discussion of this problem in Appendix A.

Section 1E. Legal Writing in Perspective

This section considers several perspectives on legal writing and provides some advice about learning legal writing skills.

1. LEGAL WRITING IN RELATION TO OTHER LEGAL SKILLS

In practice, lawyers soon discover clients often seek their services not in times of joy but in times of sorrow, stress, and conflict. At these times, the ability of lawyers to listen to clients and empathize with them is probably the most important service that lawyers have to offer.

But in terms of accomplishing client objectives (for example, obtaining compensation for personal injuries, defending a malpractice suit, creating a corporation, establishing a binding agreement, or effecting an estate plan), legal writing and related research and analytical skills play a critical role.

2. PERSUASION IN LEGAL WRITING

The most fundamental aspect of legal writing is communication--the exchange of information between individuals through a common system of symbols and signs. The purpose of most legal writing is more than simple communication. For instance, lawyers often must focus on precision and exactness of the language to avoid latent ambiguities or disputes about meaning. At other times, lawyers must persuade and influence in their legal writing. Accomplishing this goal requires skillful use of legal reasoning and rhetoric.

PERSUASION AND LEGAL REASONING DEPEND ON A LEGAL WRITER'S ABILITY TO CONCEPTUALIZE AND CHARACTERIZE.

Never forget the "same thing" can be said in many different ways.

ILLUSTRATION 1.64

"brutal murder" vs. "unfortunate incident"

Remember, the way you choose to say something should be the most effective one in light of your particular purpose or purposes.

PROBLEM 1.15

Read the following "Statement of Facts" and "Summary of Argument" in the Petitioner's Opening Brief in *California v. Krivda*, 409 U.S. 33 (1972). After reading the presentation, answer the following four questions:

1. How does the petitioner characterize the case?
2. What parts of the presentation are not strictly necessary (and thus perhaps designed to influence and persuade)?
3. Does the argument seem convincing?
4. How would you respond? In other words, what seem to be the weak points on these facts and in the legal arguments?

In the *Krivda* case, the Superior Court of Los Angeles had dismissed a prosecution for the possession of marijuana after a motion to suppress evidence had been granted. The evidence suppressed had been obtained in a warrantless police search of the defendant's trash. The California Supreme Court affirmed the dismissal. The State of California sought review in the United States Supreme Court. The references to "App." are to the Appendix to the Appellant's Brief.

Statement of Facts

> On July 1, 1968, Officer Stephen C. Gates of the Los Angeles Police Department received a telephone call from an anonymous female informant who told him that "Rodger" and "Judy" were engaging in narcotic activities, i.e., smoking marijuana and injecting methedrine. (App. pp. 12-13) The informant indicated that there were many sex parties

at their 1901 Nolden residence in Los Angeles and that a Lesbian named "Frankie" was living there. The informant also indicated that both Rodger and Judy were injecting the two children who resided at that location with methedrine. The informant said that she had heard this from Judy, who said she enjoyed the effects of methedrine and that she also wanted her children to experience the feeling of being under the influence of methedrine. (App. pp. 12-13)

After receiving this information, Officer Gates and his partner, Officer William Marsden, located the address and observed two young female children in front of the premises. Officer Gates then ran a utility check which indicated that Judy Krivda was paying for the utilities at 1901 Nolden. (App. 13, 48) Officer Gates also checked criminal records with the Los Angeles Police Department and determined that three individuals with the last name of Krivda had been arrested in Los Angeles. Upon further investigation Officer Gates discovered that one of these individuals, Edward Joseph Krivda, had a wife named Judy. (App. p. 13) The records also indicated that Edward Joseph Krivda had been arrested [1] for possession of dangerous drugs for sale and [2] also for sale of dangerous drugs. (App. p. 14)

At about 11 a.m. on July 9, 1968, Officer Gates and his partner returned to the vicinity of 1901 Nolden. The residence at that address was a single family dwelling. (App. p. 14) From their vantage point, the officers observed several trash barrels directly in front of the house at 1901 Nolden. (App. pp. 14-15, 17) The trash barrels were in the parkway adjacent to the sidewalk, thirty to forty yards from the house. (App. pp. 17, 28) The home adjacent to 1901 Nolden was approximately twenty feet down the hill. (App. p. 15)

The officers observed refuse collectors approximately a block away from the house at 1901 Nolden. (App. p. 14) Officer Gates stopped the collectors approximately half a block west of the premises. (App. pp. 14, 18) After identifying himself as a police officer, Officer Gates told the trash collectors that he was interested in looking at the contents of the trash barrels in front of 1901 Nolden. (App. pp. 14-18) He asked them to empty the well of their truck, to pick up the trash in front of the house at 1901 Nolden, and to meet Officer Gates and his partner approximately one block north of the location. (App. pp. 14, 18, 70)

Officer Gates observed the refuse collectors drive their truck to the front of the premises at 1901 Nolden. He observed them go to the back of the truck, take the trash barrels in the well, and then drive north to where he and Officer Marsden were waiting. Officer Gates had examined the well of the trash truck prior to the emptying of these specific garbage cans into the well. There had been no refuse at all in the well prior to the emptying of the garbage cans at 1901 Nolden. Officer Gates did not observe the collectors empty any other garbage cans into the well of the truck between the time they placed the trash from those cans into the well and the time the truck arrived at his location. (App. pp. 18-19)

When Officer Gates examined the contents of the well of the trash truck, he observed approximately five brown paper sacks among the refuse. Upon examining the sacks, he found that they contained what appeared to be marijuana debris and marijuana seeds. (App. p. 19) In one of the bags, Officer Gates found approximately four to six partially burned marijuana cigarettes. (App. pp. 20, 57) Also among the contents in the well of the trash truck, Officer Gates found an envelope with the name Edward Krivda and the address 1901 Nolden, a handwritten letter with the name Frankie mentioned in it, and a three-by-five card with the names Rodger and Judy on it. (App. pp. 20-21)

After Officer Gates had examined the contents of the well of the trash truck, he went back to his former vantage point. There he observed respondent Rodger Minor come from the premises at 1901 Nolden and picked up the trash barrels which had contained the marijuana debris. Respondent Minor, wearing only a towel around his waist, took the trash barrels to the front porch of the house. (App. pp. 21-22, 81)

At this point Officer Gates and his partner requested the assistance of a uniformed sergeant. The uniformed officer and Officer Gates approached the front of the premises while Officer Marsden positioned himself at the rear. When respondent Minor met Officer Gates at the front door, Officer Gates placed him under arrest for possession of marijuana. (App. pp. 22, 40, 43) The officers then effected entry, discovered respondent Krivda in the residence, and recovered additional marijuana and paraphernalia. (App. pp. 23-25, 46)

Summary of Argument

When the police examined the respondents' trash in the well of the trash truck parked a block away from the respondents' home, the trash was abandoned property. The respondents' acts of (1) discarding the trash into their trash barrels and (2) then placing the trash barrels on the parkway for collection unambiguously demonstrated the requisite intent to abandon. It is well established that "[t]here can be nothing unlawful in the [g]overnment's appropriation of abandoned property." *Abel v. United States*, 362 U.S. 217, 241 (1960).

Furthermore, the respondents had no "reasonable expectation of privacy" either as to the location of the search or as to the items seized from the trash. The well of a trash truck parked a block away from respondents' home is not within those areas immediately adjacent to the home which are protected by the Fourth Amendment. After the barrels were placed on the parkway, their contents were subject to numerous risks of public exposure. Respondents had also given the trash collector such complete and unrestricted control over their trash that they may be said to have accepted the risk that he might permit the police to examine the contents of their trash barrels. The Fourth Amendment does not protect "[a] wrongdoer's misplaced belief that a person to whom he confides his wrongdoing will not reveal it." *Hoffa v. United States*, 385 U.S. 293, 302 (1966). There is no indication that society generally expects garbage to remain private after it has come to rest in the well of a trash truck. To extend Fourth Amendment protection to the trash abandoned by respondents would elevate the trash barrel to the status of a constitutional sanctuary for the concealment and disposal of evidence of crime.

Apart from the question of whether the Fourth Amendment protects a right of privacy in one's trash, this case raises the issue of whether the exclusionary rule should have any application to the type of police conduct involved here. The law at the time of the search clearly permitted the appropriation of abandoned property. The exclusionary rule should not be used to discipline police officers who have attempted to act within the constitutional limits of the Fourth Amendment. The entire deterrent rationale of the exclusionary rule is open to serious question which may require its abandonment. Short of a complete reconsideration of the wisdom of retaining the exclusionary rule, petitioner proposes that the rule be limited to flagrant violations of the Fourth Amendment where the conduct of the police is truly lawless.[85]

Stop here, and answer the questions posed at the beginning of this problem before consulting the discussion of this problem in Appendix A.

The true test for persuasive legal writing is how well it performs the task at hand. In other words, what is the ultimate outcome? In most situations, legal writers will be concerned with exploiting the strengths of the case and minimizing its weaknesses. This outcome orientation is limited by professional ethics.

3. ADVISORY LEGAL WRITING

In addition to advocacy, legal writing often involves making critical judgments and insightful recommendations. In making such decisions, you must keep in mind the practical realities of litigation, not merely whether the "law" is on a client's side.

IN ADVICE TO CLIENTS, LEGAL WRITERS SHOULD NOT IGNORE THE HUMAN AND PRACTICAL SIDE OF LEGAL SITUATIONS OR THEY MAY FIND THAT THEY HAVE WASTED A CLIENT'S TIME AND MONEY IN FRUITLESS LITIGATION.

ILLUSTRATION 1.65

Consider the realities of the following story about a trial in Clay County, Alabama:

> It seems that a sharecropper was charged with the crime of stealing the mule of the landlord. The latter was rich and domineering, without many friends among the common people. The evidence against the defendant was overwhelming, so much so that he did not take the stand. The judge charged the jury, laying down the law meticulously. In five minutes the jury returned.
>
> "Have you reached a verdict, Mr. Foreman?" asked the judge.
>
> "We have, Your Honor."
>
> "Then hand it to the clerk."
>
> The clerk put on his glasses, took the paper, unfolded it, cleared his throat, and said, "We the jury

---

[85] Petitioner's Opening Brief at 5-9, California v. Krivda, 409 U.S. 33 (1972).

find the defendant not guilty, provided he returns the mule."

The judge brought his gavel down sharply, saying, "There is no such verdict in the law. The defendant is either guilty or not guilty." After giving the charge all over again, judge told the jury to retire and come back with a lawful verdict.

The jury returned in five minutes and the judge asked the foreman, "Have you reached a verdict?"

"We have, Your Honor."

"Then hand it to the clerk."

The clerk put on his glasses, unfolded the paper, cleared his throat, and read: "We the jury find the defendant not guilty. He can keep the mule."[86]

4. PERFECTING LEGAL WRITING SKILLS

PRODUCING QUALITY LEGAL WRITING IS HARD WORK. UNLESS A LEGAL WRITER IS A RARE INDIVIDUAL OR FACES AN EMERGENCY SITUATION, A FIRST DRAFT OF A MEMORANDUM OR BRIEF SHOULD NEVER BE THE FINAL PRODUCT.

From the outset, legal writers need to develop the habit of allowing enough time for revision and proofreading. Indeed, procrastination is the bane of law students, lawyers, and others preparing legal documents. Failure to allow time for revision and proofreading probably accounts for more of the wretched writing submitted in law offices, law schools, and courts than any other cause.

Remember a legal writer is responsible for quality control; the secretary's errors are regarded as the errors of the legal writer; and it is hard to separate yourself from your written work.

IN SUM, YOUR WRITTEN WORK REFLECTS YOUR WORTH; IT DEMONSTRATES YOUR THINKING; AND IT REFLECTS YOUR ABILITIES.

---

[86] W. Douglas, Go East, Young Man 451 (1974) (relating this story, which was told by Justice Black).

Chapter 2

ANALYZING THE FACTS, IDENTIFYING LEGAL PROBLEMS, DEFINING THE WRITING PROJECT, DEVELOPING A RESEARCH PLAN, AND TAKING RESEARCH NOTES

WHAT YOU WILL LEARN IN THIS CHAPTER

* How to identify and analyze legal research problems
* How to develop a research and writing plan
* How to use law dictionaries and other sources to gain perspective on unfamiliar terminology
* How to use indexes in texts, treatises, and similar sources
* How to record the results of your research in notes
* How to develop your research efficiently by using West's topics and key numbers, *A.L.R.* annotations, and other methods (basic approaches)
* How to update your research (basic approaches)

Section 2A. Factual Investigation, Analysis, and Preliminary Identification of Legal Issues

Facts play a critical role in legal research and writing. For a lawyer with a client, facts provide the legal problem, generate specific legal issues, and guide a lawyer's research. The principal sources of facts for legal research and writing purposes are (1) client interviews, (2) witness statements, and (3) documents. For certain writing projects, the facts may be disputed or only partially known. For other writing projects, the facts may be established by the procedural context, such as the trial court's findings of fact on appeal.

ILLUSTRATION 2.1

MEMORANDUM

To: Law Firm
From: William Klink, No-Pay Adjuster
Re: Irma Marie Delira (Our Policy No. 89-199)
Date: January 10, 19xx

We have received a summons and complaint from S.W. Lash naming No-Pay as a co-defendant in a negligence action. Lash is suing for damages based on an automobile accident that occurred between Lash and our insured (Irma Marie Delira) on November 1, 19xx in the newly admitted State of Utopia, U.S.A. We were not notified by our insured apparently because she has been in a mental institution since the accident.

The plaintiff's complaint, which I am forwarding with this memorandum, provides some of the details about the accident. I am also attaching a copy of the police report and a transcript of my brief interview with our insured. Please prepare an answer and advise us of your preliminary evaluation of this situation.

****

UNITED STATES DISTRICT COURT FOR
THE DISTRICT OF UTOPIA

Civil Action, File Number XXX

SNIDELY W. LASH, Plaintiff, v. NO-PAY CASUALTY CO. and IRMA M. DELIRA, Defendants.	COMPLAINT

PLAINTIFF Snidely Whip Lash, by his attorneys, alleges:

1. Plaintiff is a citizen of the State of Collapse, U.S.A., and the defendant I.M. Delira is a citizen of the State of Utopia, U.S.A. Defendant No-Pay Casualty Company is a corporation incorporated under the laws of the State of Depression and having its principal place of business in a state other than the State of Utopia. The amount in controversy exceeds, exclusive of interest and costs, the sum of $50,000.

2. The defendant No-Pay Casualty Company is licensed to do business in the State of Utopia and issues, among other things, automobile liability policies. Prior to November 1, 19xx, defendant No-Pay Casualty Company issued and delivered for a valuable consideration its policy of liability insurance to defendant I.M. Delira. In this policy, defendant No-Pay Casualty Company agreed to pay any liability incurred on account of damages sustained by others by reason of the negligent operation of a motor vehicle owned and operated by I.M. Delira. This policy of insurance was in full force and effect on November 1, 19xx. By reason of this policy and the laws of the State of Utopia, defendant No-Pay Casualty Company is a proper defendant in this action and is liable to the plaintiff for the damages and injuries resulting from the accident described in paragraph 3 of this complaint.

3. On November 1, 19xx, on Highway 8 in Lincoln County, Utopia, defendant I.M. Delira negligently crossed the center line of the highway and negligently drove her vehicle against the plaintiff's vehicle. The defendant I.M. Delira was negligent at the time and place of the accident in the following particulars:

(a) In negligently and carelessly failing to operate her automobile to the right of the center line of the highway;

(b) In negligently and carelessly operating her automobile at an excessive rate of speed;

(c) In negligently and carelessly failing to maintain a proper lookout;

(d) In negligently and carelessly failing to properly manage and control her automobile; and

(e) In negligently and carelessly failing to stay awake at the wheel of her automobile.

4. The accident and resulting injuries and damages sustained by the plaintiff were proximately caused by the negligence of the defendant I.M. Delira and were not caused or contributed to in any manner by any negligence on the part of the plaintiff.

5. As a result of the accident, plaintiff has sustained injuries described generally as a whiplash, a herniated disk, and multiple other contusions, lacerations, and abrasions over his entire body.

6. As the result of these injuries, plaintiff was confined to the hospital under the care of doctors and has sustained great pain and suffering, medical expense, and loss of income. Plaintiff is informed and believes that his injuries are permanent and that he will sustain additional pain and suffering in the future leading to

additional loss of income and medical expense, all to his damage in the sum of $750,000.

Wherefore, plaintiff demands judgment against the defendants in the sum of $750,000, together with his costs and disbursements.

Signed: /s/

FOGG & HORN
Attorneys for the Plaintiff
100 Hospital Drive
City of Lincoln, Utopia 00001

****

TRANSCRIPT OF INTERVIEW WITH IRMA MARIE DELIRA AT FREUD MEMORIAL MENTAL HOSPITAL
(Our Policy No. 89-199)
William Klink, No-Pay Adjuster
January 8, 19xx

[The beginning portion of the interview has been omitted.]

Klink: Do you know where you are now?

Delira: In a hospital.

Klink: Do you know why you are here?

Delira: I was hurt in an accident.

Klink: Do you understand that I work for your automobile insurance company?

Delira: Yes.

Klink: Would you mind answering some questions about your accident?

Delira: I would be glad to help you.

Klink: Do you remember anything about the accident?

Delira: The accident happened shortly after midnight, but it wasn't my fault. I couldn't control the car.

Klink: What do you mean?

Delira: My car was controlled by an alien creature. I was totally powerless to do anything.

Klink: Could you see this alien creature?

Delira: No. I could only feel its presence. The creature must have wanted to keep me from delivering the beer.

Klink: The police report stated that there were three cases of beer on the front seat of your car. What were you doing with all that beer?

Delira: I was taking it to the dead people.

Klink: What dead people?

Delira: The ones that communicated to me while I was watching television. They came out of the grave yard and were calling for "Miller Lite." They chased me into a house, but I was able to get rid of them by handing them bottles of beer. I promised to get them some more if they would leave me alone.

Klink: Are you talking about the "Miller Lite" beer commercial that was shown around Halloween?

Delira: Did you see the message too?

Klink: . . . . Had you been drinking before the accident?

Delira: No. I never drink when I am on a mission.

Klink: Where did you get the beer?

Delira: After I saw the message on T.V., I went to the liquor store on the corner near my apartment. I was lucky because they were about to close for the night.

Klink: Where do you live?

Delira: 155 South Main Street here in Lincoln.

Klink: Do you live with anyone else?

Delira: No. I live alone. I was just discharged from the U.S. Army.

Klink: Exactly where were you taking the beer?

Delira: To the graveyard outside of town, of course. That's when I was attacked by the alien creature. . . .

Klink: Why didn't you notify us about the accident?

Delira: They wouldn't let me. Besides, it wasn't my fault like I told you. Say, I really need to get out of here. Do you think you could help me?

[The remainder of the interview has been omitted.]

STATE OF UTOPIA STANDARD POLICE TRAFFIC COLLISION REPORT

Sheet 1 of 2

DATE OF ACCIDENT	TIME	ACCIDENT INVOLVED
11-1-19xx	1:20 a.m.	Two motor vehicles

LOCATION (Name of street\highway)	CITY OR COUNTY
Highway 8 at Milepost 12	Lincoln County

VEHICLE NO. 1	VEHICLE MAKE	MODEL	YEAR
	Jeep	Cherokee	1989

LICENSE NO.	STATE	ODOMETER	IDENTIFICATION NO.
U-110467	Utopia	8,124	3K199VG106F402

OPERATOR NO. 1	FULL NAME	SEX
	Irma Marie Delira	F

ADDRESS		DATE OF BIRTH
	155 S. Main St., Apt. 3 City of Lincoln, Utopia	4-16-64

DRIVER'S LICENSE NO. 150GP444 STATE Utopia

VEHICLE NO. 2	VEHICLE MAKE	MODEL	YEAR
	BMW	525e	1988

LICENSE NO.	STATE	ODOMETER	IDENTIFICATION NO.
CC-193434	Collapse	12,998	5C344XG559B506

OPERATOR NO. 2	FULL NAME	SEX
	Snidely W. Lash	M

ADDRESS		DATE OF BIRTH
	2400 Lakeshore Drive Crater Lake, Collapse	10-31-47

DRIVER'S LICENSE NO. GL125564 STATE Collapse

FIRST AID BY: Bystander, Police, and Ambulance Attendant
INJURED REMOVED TO: Lincoln County General Hospital
REMOVED BY: Ambulance
VEHICLE NO. 1 TOWED TO: Police Lot
VEHICLE NO. 2 TOWED TO: Al's Garage in Lincoln
POLICE NOTIFIED: 1:30 a.m.
POLICE ARRIVED: 1:38 a.m.
REPORTING OFFICER: Matthew Dillon
UNIT: 22 BADGE NO. 406 DATE: 11-3-19xx

WITNESSES: Mike D. Banner, 1444 Military Rd., Fort Utopia, U.S.A.	Sheet 2 of 2

ACCIDENT DIAGRAM

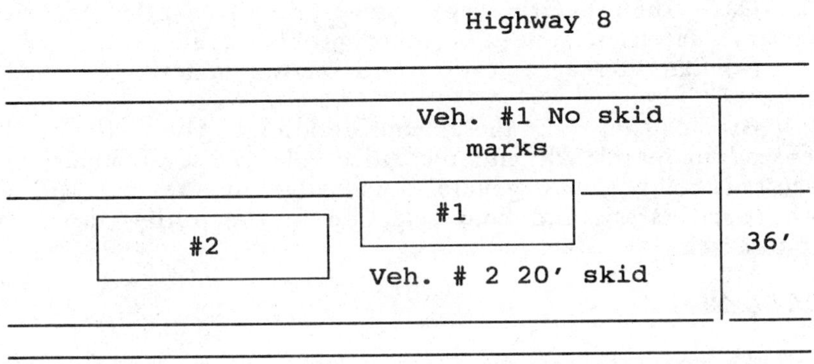

ACCIDENT DESCRIPTION
Vehicle #1 crossed the center line and struck Vehicle #2 on the driver's side head-on. The driver of Vehicle #2 stated that he put on his brakes when he realized that Vehicle #1 had suddenly crossed into his lane. The driver of Vehicle #1 stated that she was a real "Wonder Woman." She claimed that she was from Paradise Island, which was "hidden deep within the Bermuda Triangle." Upon further inquiry, she claimed to be an "Amazing Amazon" and that she was unable to control her vehicle because an alien creature had attacked her. She stated, "I was totally powerless to do anything." I recommended that the driver of Vehicle #1 be taken to Lincoln General Hospital for a psychiatric exam.

ROAD CONDITIONS Blacktop payment, soft shoulders
Road surface dry, weather clear

ALCOHOL INDICATED Vehicle #1 had three cases of beer on the front seat, but the driver of Vehicle #1 did not appear intoxicated. No tests given.

CITATIONS Negligent driving citation issued to the driver of Vehicle #1

VEHICLE DAMAGE SEVERITY Both vehicles suffered severe damage.

Before beginning research on a client's problem, you first should analyze the facts that you have developed or that have been provided. This analysis involves four basic considerations:

(1) the legal subjects involved;
(2) the specific terms used to describe the parties, places, and things involved;
(3) the specific legal issues involved--the theories of recovery, defenses, relief, or other problems; and
(4) any research leads based on the material received.

By focusing on these considerations, you will be better prepared to search for and recognize relevant legal materials. As discussed below, your general knowledge of the law will affect both your analysis and your selection of the initial starting point for research.

PROBLEM 2.1

Assume that you work for a law firm representing No-Pay Casualty Company and that you have been given the documents reproduced in Illustration 2.1 to review. Prepare a preliminary analysis of this information by answering the following questions in the space provided below.

(a) What legal subject(s) are involved in this research problem?

(b) What words could be used to describe the parties, places, and things involved in this research problem?

(c) What words could be used to describe the legal issues (theories, defenses, relief, and others) involved in this research problem?

(d) What research leads are there?

Stop here, and prepare your analysis before consulting the discussion of this problem in Appendix A.

Section 2B. Defining the Writing Project and Developing a Research Plan

The memorandum from No-Pay Casualty Co. in Illustration 2.1 in the preceding section requests that the law firm assess liability under the circumstances described and answer the complaint. In this instance, you will have several writing projects, which may include the following:

1. Answer (or motion in response to the complaint);
2. Memorandum of law (reporting your research on the legal issues);
3. Cover letter to No-Pay and Delira (accompanying the answer); and
4. Letter to No-Pay summarizing your assessment of the case.

You probably will have to research the legal issues before you can begin any of these writing projects. The preliminary analysis in Problem 2.1 should have suggested some possible topics or directions for research. Prior to beginning your research, you should formulate a tentative research plan.

The most important legal issue appears to be whether Delira's insanity provides a defense to a negligence action. Because in this instance there are no research leads to specific primary sources for the No-Pay research project (such as a relevant case or statute), the best initial source will be a secondary source.

You may be readily aware of a relevant secondary source covering tort or negligence law, and you could directly consult these topics in a legal encyclopedia. You could identify other treatises and secondary sources by consulting the subject card catalog.

If you are unfamiliar with the area of law involved in your research problem, consulting a dictionary is a useful preparatory step. Consulting a dictionary will help your general understanding of the research problem and may generate several new terms. Developing working definitions and learning the relevant terminology also will aid you later when you use the subject card catalog, tables of contents, and indexes as part of your research.

PROBLEM 2.2

Your analysis of Problem 2.1 should have provided you several words and phrases that might be usefully consulted in a legal dictionary or thesaurus, including: insanity, insane or mental delusion, negligence, and direct action.

Examine the entries for "insane," "insanely deluded," "insaneness," "*insania*," "insanity," and "*insanus*" in the Index shown in Figure 2-A below and the main entry for "insanity" in Burton's *Legal Thesaurus* shown in Figure 2-B on the following page. What is a synonym for "insanely deluded"?

inrush inflow
insagacious inept *(inappropriate)*
insalubrious adverse *(negative)*, blameful, blameworthy, deleterious, detrimental, disadvantageous, harmful, inadvisable, malignant, noxious, peccant *(unhealthy)*, pernicious, pestilent
insalubriousness disadvantage
insalubris insalubrious, peccant *(unhealthy)*
insalubrity disease
insane deranged, lunatic, non compos mentis
insanely deluded non compos mentis
insaneness lunacy
insania insanity
insanity lunacy, paranoia
insanus deranged, frenetic
insatiabilis insatiable
insatiability greed
insatiable gluttonous, rapacious
insatiableness greed
insatiate rapacious
insciens unintentional, unwitting
inscientia ignorance
inscitia ignorance, incapacity
inscitus incompetent
inscius unacquainted, unaware, unwitting
inscribe book, brand *(mark)*, dedicate, enroll, enter *(record)*, file *(place*

FIGURE 2-A
W. BURTON, LEGAL THESAURUS

INQUISITIVE, ***adjective***
audiendi, cupidus, curiosus, curious, eager for knowledge, fond of investigation, given to research, inquiring, interested, interrogative, investigative, questioning, quizzical, scrutinizing, searching, seeking, speculative

INSALUBRIOUS, ***adjective***
baleful, baneful, calamitous, damaging, dangerous, deleterious, destructive, detrimental, disadvantageous, disastrous, fraught with danger, *gravis,* harmful, hazardous, hurtful, injurious, *insalubris,* lethal, lethiferous, malefic, maleficent, menacing, mephitic, miasmal, miasmatic, miasmatical, miasmic, morbific, morbifical, mortiferous, noisome, noxious, ominous, pathogenic, perilous, pernicious, pestiferous, *pestilens,* pestilent, pestilential, poisonous, risky, ruinous, threatening, toxic, unclean, unfavorable to health, unhealthful, unhealthy, unhygienic, unsafe, unsanitary, unwholesome, venomous, virulent

INSANITY, ***noun***
aberration, aberration of mind, abnormality, alienation, alienation of mind, amentia, brain damage, craziness, daftness, delirium, delusion, dementedness, *dementia,* deranged intellect, derangement, diseased mind, disordered intellect, disordered mind, disordered reason, disorientation, frenzy, hallucination, *insania,* loss of reason, lunacy, madness, mental abnormality, mental alienation, mental decay, mental deficiency, mental derangement, mental disease, mental incapacity, mental infirmities, mental instability, mental sickness, mental unsoundness, paranoia, raving, unbalanced mind, unsound mind, unsoundness of mind, *vecordia,* want of comprehension, want of reason
ASSOCIATED CONCEPTS: adjudication of insanity, diminished capacity, habitual insanity, incompetency, insane delusion, insane impulse to act, insanity defense, insanity plea, irresistible impulse
FOREIGN PHRASES: ***Furiosus nullum negotium contrahere potest.*** An insane person can make no contract. ***Furiosus stipulare non potest nec aliquid negotium agere, qui non intelligit quid agit.*** An insane person who knows not what he is doing, cannot contract nor transact any business. ***Furiosi nulla voluntas est.*** A madman has no will. ***Furiosus solo furore punitur.*** A madman is punished by his madness alone. ***Furor contrahi matrimonium non sinit, quia consensu opus est.*** Insanity prevents a marriage from being contracted, because consent is required. ***Ira furor brevis est.*** Anger is short insanity. ***Furiosus absentis loco est.*** A madman is considered as a person who is absent. ***Insanus est qui, abjecta ratione, omnia cum impetu et furore facit.*** A person is insane who, deprived of reason, does everything with violence and rage.

FIGURE 2-B
W. BURTON, LEGAL THESAURUS

Stop here, and find a synonym before consulting the discussion of this problem in Appendix A.

Assume that you decide to find treatises on tort law in the card catalog. Shown in the Figures 2-C and 2-D are some cards from the subject heading "TORTS-UNITED STATES":

```
KF
1250      Morris, Clarence, 1903-
.M67        Morris on torts / Clarence Morris, C.
1980      Robert Morris. -- 2d ed. -- Mineola,
          N.Y. : Foundation Press, 1980.
            443 p. ; 27 cm.
            Includes index.


            1.>Torts--United States.  I. Morris,
          C. Robert, 1928-       joint author.
          II. Title

        18 APR 80     5946417  CLLAsc        80-170
```

```
KF
1250      Prosser and Keeton on the law of torts
.P73        / W. Page Keeton, general editor ; W.
1984        Page Keeton ... [et al.]. — 5th ed.
            -- St. Paul : West, 1984.
            xxxi, 1286 p. ; 26 cm.
            Rev. ed. of: Handbook of the law of
          torts / William L. Prosser. 4th ed.
          1971.
            Includes bibliographical references
          and index.
            ISBN 0-314-74880-6

            1.>Torts--United States.  I. Keeton,
          Page.  II. Prosser, William Lloyd,
          1898-      Handbook of the law of torts.
          III. Title: Law of torts 5th ed.

        19 SEP 84     9971374  CLLAsc      83-19830
```

FIGURE 2-C
SUBJECT CARDS FROM THE CARD CATALOG

```
KF
1250      Harper, Fowler Vincent, 1897-1965.
.H37        The Law of torts / Fowler V. Harper,
1986x     Fleming James, Jr., Oscar S. Gray. --
          2nd ed. -- Boston ; Toronto : Little,
          Brown, 1986.
            6 v. ; 24 cm.
            Kept up to date with pocket
          supplements.
            Includes bibliography and index.
            ISBN 0-316-32587-2


            1.>Torts--United States.  I. James,
          Fleming, 1904-      II. Gray, Oscar S.
          1926-       III. Title


       06 JUN 86    13611469   CLLAsc
```

```
KF
1250      Kionka, Edward J., 1939-
.Z9         Torts in a nutshell : injuries to
K53       persons and property / by Edward J.
          Kionka. St. Paul, Minn. : West Pub.
          co., 1977.
            xxviii, 434 p. ; 19 cm. (West
          nutshell series)
            Includes index.


            1.>Torts--United States.   I. Title


       21 FEB 79    3239734    CLLAsc      77-78248
```

FIGURE 2-D
SUBJECT CARDS FROM THE CARD CATALOG

Assume that you have decided to begin your research with Prosser and Keeton's leading hornbook on tort law which you identified by consulting the subject card catalog. Assume that the book is in front of you and that you are going to consult the index in that book.

PROBLEM 2.3

Based on the preliminary analysis of the No-Pay research problem discussed earlier, which index entry or entries would you try to consult *first*?

Stop here, and decide under which index entry or entries you would look at before consulting the discussion of this problem in Appendix A.

PROBLEM 2.4

Assume that you have decided initially to consult the entries for "Negligence" and "Insanity" (the relevant parts of which are shown in Figure 2-E below and Figure 2-F on the following page). Underline the entries that you feel might direct you to a relevant discussion of law relating to the No-Pay research problem.

FIGURE 2-E
PROSSER AND KEETON ON THE LAW OF TORTS

FIGURE 2-F
PROSSER AND KEETON ON THE LAW OF TORTS

Stop here, and underline the relevant entries before consulting the discussion of this problem in Appendix A.

Section 2C. Note Taking in Legal Research

One question that arises during the course of legal research is how and to what extent should notes be taken? The answer depends directly on the nature and purpose of the legal research.

Generally speaking, if the research involves simply finding a specific case, statute, or some other source, little, if any, note taking will be needed. In these situations, making a photocopy ordinarily will be the most useful approach. On the other hand, extensive, orderly, and accurate note taking will prove to be essential for a major research project that will form the basis for a memorandum, appellate brief, or article.

The best conceived system of note taking in a legal context is presented in Vom Bauer's article "How to Look Up Law and Write Legal Memoranda--Revisited," published in the *Practical Lawyer*.[1] In taking notes, Vom Bauer recommends that three basic concepts be utilized.

FIRST, EACH NEW PRINCIPLE, CASE, STATUTE, OR OTHER SOURCE THAT APPEARS TO BE APPLICABLE TO THE RESEARCH PROBLEM SHOULD BE RECORDED IMMEDIATELY AS IT IS IDENTIFIED.

As Vom Bauer points out, "Don't wait. Don't slur over any one of them, thinking that you'll think it over and maybe come back later. It may slip your mind or you may have great difficulty finding again the book or page that contained the idea or case."[2] All information needed to cite each source, to the extent that it is available, should be recorded when the source is first examined.

SECOND, EACH IDEA OR LEGAL PRINCIPLE SHOULD BE RECORDED ON A SEPARATE SHEET OF PAPER.

---

[1] Vom Bauer, How to Look Up Law and Write Legal Memoranda--Revisited, 11 Prac. Law., May 1965, at 23.

[2] Id. at 28.

This approach allows you to compile authorities (and notes thereon) supporting a single idea or legal principle without interference or confusion with other ideas. It also allows you to arrange and rearrange those ideas or principles conveniently without rewriting.[3]

THIRD, FULL NOTE TAKING INCLUDES RECORDING THE SIGNIFICANCE OF PARTICULAR SOURCES AND THE STEPS THAT HAVE BEEN TAKEN.

Specifically, you should develop a personal system to indicate when:

(1) you have read a particular source (for example, by means of a check mark in front of the reference to the source);

(2) the source is not pertinent (for example, by means of an "X" in front of the reference to the source);

(3) the source is especially relevant or is a leading case (for example, by means of an asterisk (*) in front of the reference to the source); and

(4) other steps in the research process, such as updating, have been completed.[4]

PROBLEM 2.5

Assume that in your research using Prosser and Keeton on Torts you decide to start with the references to pages 1072 through 1075 because they appear to be the most relevant. Turning to page 1072, you would see that section 135 on "Insanity" begins on that page. Read this page and the ones that follow shown in Figures 2-G, 2-H, 2-I, and 2-J. As you read, mark in the margin the portions of the discussion that appear to relate to the research question.

---

[3] Id.

[4] See id. at 29-33. To record Shepard's Citations updating, for example, Vom Bauer suggests that you mark a line across the check in front of the reference to a source after each Shepard's volume and pamphlet covering a source has been consulted. Vom Bauer recommends that all Shepard's volumes and pamphlets be searched one at a time. You should read cited cases and record notes on each cited case before you move to another phase of your research. You should always start with the most recent Shepard's pamphlet and work backwards. Vom Bauer points out that this approach "a great timesaver. The most recent cases may not only change or vary the legal principles announced by an older decision; they may also articulate and explain them in expanded terms. . . . [T]his system . . . will provide an ironbound system for enabling you to complete the 'Shepardizing' process thoroughly, despite a number of interruptions." Id. at 30-31.

1072 IMMUNITIES Ch. 25

had contracted for a safe ride,[9] but courts once held that there was only a contract duty in such cases and that it could be avoided by disaffirmance.[10] Similarly, agency is created by contract and courts have usually held that an infant cannot be vicariously liable because of this contractual element.[11] Or again, a minor may escape liability for trivial or negligent misuse of bailed property on the ground that his duties were created by contract,[12] but where the misuse is a serious one courts regarded it as a violation of duties imposed by law for which he is liable in tort.[13]

Another problem in applying the independent obligation test occurs when the infant fraudulently induces another to enter a contract, usually by representing that he is an adult and can make a binding contract. A few cases hold that the minor is not liable even for such a fraud, because the fraud is inseparably connected with contract.[14] Most, however, impose liability in tort for fraudulent misrepresentations,[15] unless the representation is construed to be a mere warranty that can be disaffirmed.[16] A few courts go further and hold that the infant's fraud works an estoppel so that he is liable on the contract itself and not merely in tort.[17]

Probably the independent obligation test is workable only if it is applied with an understanding that the contract immunity is intended to provide a shield against bad bargains, not a sword for the commission of torts.

WESTLAW REFERENCES

211k59

§ 135. Insanity

Mentally disabled persons usually have been classed with infants, and held liable for their torts.[1] The rule seems to have originated in a dictum in a case[2] decided in 1616, at a time when the action of trespass still rested upon the older basis of strict liability without regard to the fault of the individual. When the modern law developed to the point of holding the defendant liable only for wrongful intent or negligence, the dictum was still repeated, and there have been numerous decisions in accord with it. Thus an insane person has been held liable in a tort action for assault and battery,[3] false imprisonment,[4] trespass on land,[5] destruction

9. See Pokriefka v. Mazur, 1967, 379 Mich. 348, 151 N.W.2d 806; Friedhoff v. Engberg, 1967, 82 S.D. 522, 149 N.W.2d 759.

10. See Brown v. Wood, 1940, 293 Mich. 148, 291 N.W. 255, 127 A.L.R. 1436, overruled in Pokriefka v. Mazur, 1967, 379 Mich. 348, 151 N.W.2d 806.

11. Government Employees Insurance Co. v. Edelman, Tex.Civ.App.1975, 524 S.W.2d 546, refused n.r.e. (joint venture). But see State Farm Mutual Automobile Insurance Co. v. Fields, D.Mo.1970, 325 F.Supp. 1135 (liability insurance procured by father as agent for minor is valid), affirmed 8th Cir. 1971, 441 F.2d 659; 1972, 37 Mo.L.Rev. 150; G.(A.) v. G.(T.), [1970] 2 Q.B. 643, [1970] 3 All.Eng.Rep. 546.

12. Eaton v. Hill, 1870, 50 N.H. 235. Young v. Muhling, 1900, 48 App.Div. 617, 63 N.Y.S. 181.

13. Smith v. Moschetti, 1948, 213 Ark. 968, 214 S.W.2d 73; Vermont Acceptance Corp. v. Wiltshire, 1931, 103 Vt. 219, 153 A. 199.

14. Raymond v. General Motorcycle Co., 1918, 230 Mass. 54, 119 N.E. 359; Greensboro Morris Plan Co. v. Palmer, 1923, 185 N.C. 109, 116 S.E. 261.

15. Doenges-Long Motors, Inc. v. Gillen, 1958, 138 Colo. 31, 328 P.2d 1077; Royal Finance Co. v. Schaefer, Mo.App., 1959, 330 S.W.2d 129.

16. Collins v. Gifford, 1911, 203 N.Y. 465, 96 N.E. 721.

17. Nichols v. English, 1967, 223 Ga. 227, 154 S.E.2d 239, 29 A.L.R.3d 1265 (estopped to repudiate conveyance).

§ 135

1. Second Restatement of Torts, § 283B.

2. Weaver v. Ward, 1616, Hob. 134, 80 Eng.Rep. 284.

3. Mullen v. Bruce, 1959, 168 Cal.App.2d 494, 335 P.2d 945; Kaczer v. Marrero, Fla.App. 1976, 324 So.2d 717; McGuire v. Almy, 1937, 297 Mass. 323, 8 N.E.2d 760; Barylski v. Paul, 1972, 38 Mich.App. 614, 196 N.W.2d 868.

Cf. Vosnos v. Perry, 1976, 43 Ill.App.3d 834, 2 Ill. Dec. 447, 357 N.E.2d 614 (shooting resulting in death).

4. Krom v. Schoonmaker, N.Y.1848, 3 Barb. 647.

5. Cathcart v. Matthews, 1916, 105 S.C. 329, 89 S.E. 1021; Amick v. O'Hara, Ind.1843, 6 Blackf. 258.

FIGURE 2-G
PROSSER AND KEETON ON THE LAW OF TORTS

§ 135 INSANITY 1073

of property,[6] conversion,[7] wrongfully suing out an injunction,[8] alienation of affections,[9] infringement of a patent,[10] and injuries caused by the defective condition of his property.[11]

A number of different explanations have been given for the liability of the mentally disabled, none of which has gone unchallenged.[12] It has been said that "where one of two innocent persons must suffer a loss, it should be borne by the one who occasioned it." [13] So far as this is anything more than an historical survival, it represents a conclusion that it is better that the estate of the lunatic should be taken to give compensation for the damage he has done than that it should remain to be administered by guardians for his own incompetent benefit.[14] It has been said also that if he is held liable, his custodians and those interested in his estate will be stimulated to keep him in order; [15] and that since insanity is easily feigned, there would be too much temptation to pretend it.[16] Coupled with this is perhaps an unexpressed fear of introducing into the law of torts the confusion and unsatisfactory tests attending proof of insanity in criminal cases.[17]

Against the liability of mentally disabled it has been said that the rule of liability is a product of an era when confinement of the mentally limited was the accepted social goal, as it no longer is,[18] that it is unjust to impose responsibility without fault upon the disabled when fault is the standard of liability for others,[19] and that at the very least the incompetent should be relieved of any duty of reasonable care toward those who know of his disability and can protect themselves from it.[20]

6. Morse v. Crawford, 1893, 17 Vt. 499 (killing an ox); Cross v. Kent, 1870, 32 Md. 581; Mutual Fire Insurance Co. v. Showalter, 1897, 3 Pa.Super. 452; In re Guardianship of Meyer, 1935, 218 Wis. 381, 261 N.W. 211.

7. Morse v. Crawford, 1893, 17 Vt. 499.

8. Behrens v. McKenzie, 1867, 23 Iowa 333.

9. Shedrick v. Lathrop, 1934, 106 Vt. 311, 172 A. 630; Sweeney v. Carter, 1939, 24 Tenn.App. 6, 137 S.W.2d 892.

10. Avery v. Wilson, W.D.N.C.1884, 20 F. 856.

11. Filip v. Gagne, 1962, 104 N.H. 14, 177 A.2d 509; Morain v. Devlin, 1882, 132 Mass. 87; Campbell v. Bradbury, 1918, 179 Cal. 364, 176 P. 685. Contra, Ward v. Rogers, 1906, 51 Misc. 299, 100 N.Y.S. 1058.

12. See Ellis, Tort Responsibility of Mentally Disabled Persons, 1981 A.B.Found.Res.J. 1081; Seidelson, Reasonable Expectations and Subjective Standards in Negligence Law, 1981, 50 G.W.L.Rev. 17; Curran, Tort Liability of the Mentally Ill and Mentally Deficient, 1960, 21 Ohio St.L.J. 52; Sadoff, 1967, Tortious Liability of the Insane, 39 Pa.Bar.Q. 73; Ague, The Liability of Insane Persons in Tort Actions, 1956, 60 Dick.L.Rev. 211; Bohlen, Liability in Tort of Infants and Insane Persons, 1924, 23 Mich.L.Rev. 9; Hornblower, Insanity and the Law of Negligence, 1905, 5 Colum.L.Rev. 278; Comment, The Tort Liability of Insane Persons for Negligence, 1972, 39 Tenn.L.Rev. 705.

13. See Kaczer v. Marrero, Fla.App.1976, 324 So.2d 717; Seals v. Snow, 1927, 123 Kan. 88, 90, 254 P. 348, 349; Williams v. Hays, 1894, 143 N.Y. 442, 447, 38 N.E. 449, 450; Karow v. Continental Insurance Co., 1883, 57 Wis. 56, 64, 15 N.W. 27, 30.

14. See McGuire v. Almy, 1937, 297 Mass. 323, 8 N.E.2d 760; Bohlen, Liability in Tort of Infants and Insane Persons, 1924, 23 Mich.L.Rev. 9, 17–18.

15. See McGuire v. Almy, 1937, 297 Mass. 323, 8 N.E.2d 760; McIntyre v. Sholty, 1887, 121 Ill. 660, 13 N.E. 239; Seals v. Snow, 1927, 123 Kan. 88, 254 P. 348; Williams v. Hays, 1894, 143 N.Y. 442, 38 N.E. 449.

16. See Young v. Young, 1910, 141 Ky. 76, 132 S.W. 155, and cases cited in the preceding footnote.

17. See Bohlen, Liability in Tort of Infants and Insane Persons, 1924, 23 Mich.L.Rev. 9; Note, 1938, 22 Minn.L.Rev. 853, 862.

18. Ellis, Tort Responsibility of Mentally Disabled Persons, 1981 A.B.Found.Res.J. 1079.

19. Seidelson, Reasonable Expectations and Subjective Standards in Negligence Law: The Minor, the Mentally Impaired, and the Mentally Incompetent, 1981, 50 G.W.L.Rev. 17.

20. Seidelson, Reasonable Expectations and Subjective Standards in Negligence Law: The Minor, the Mentally Impaired, and the Mentally Incompetent, 1981, 50 G.W.L.Rev. 17. Quite apart from insane persons, it would seem that the duty owed toward a person of limited capacity depends on whether the actor knew or should have known of that capacity. See Bexiga v. Havir Manufacturing Corp., 1972, 60 N.J. 402, 290 A.2d 281; Rue v. State Department of Highways, La.1979, 372 So.2d 1197, on remand 376 So.2d 525; Warner v. Kiowa County Hospital Authority, Okl.App. 1976, 551 P.2d 1179. Similarly if an injured person knows he is dealing with a person of limited capacity, the duty of the mentally disabled person may be reduced accordingly. This may be accomplished through the doctrine of contributory negligence, but only fortuitously, because of the difference in burden of proof on "no duty" and contributory negligence and because of

FIGURE 2-H
PROSSER AND KEETON ON THE LAW OF TORTS

1074 IMMUNITIES Ch. 25

The traditional view, however, has emphasized the fact that a mentally limited person may be capable of having an intent to bring about a specific result, even though the intent is induced by a delusion; and in that respect his acts are to be distinguished from those of an epileptic or a person seized with temporary unconsciousness, which are regarded as involuntary and accidental.[21] If tort liability without fault is to be imposed upon sane persons who make reasonable mistakes,[22] an incompetent who acts under a perpetual mistake, unreasonable in the eyes of the community, may very well be held liable for his intentional torts. It has been recognized, however, that his insanity may be such that he is incapable of entertaining the specific intent necessary for a particular tort, such as deceit,[23] malicious prosecution,[24] defamation,[25] or even battery,[26] and so he should not be liable simply because he has not committed the tort. This, however, has not always been carried through very effectively. As to defamation, there has been almost a complete failure to distinguish between the "legal malice" implied as a fiction from the intent to publish the defamatory words, and the "malice in fact" which will defeat a qualified privilege.[27] It would appear that the insane person may properly be charged with the former, but not the latter.[28] It seems well settled that insanity may be shown to disprove evil intent and mitigate actual damages,[29] and that where the insanity is notorious, it may disprove special damage because no one believes what is said.[30] Since the lunatic is regarded as incapable of the necessary guilty mind, and admonition to him is obviously futile, punitive damages are not recoverable against him,[31] at least unless it can be shown that in spite of his mental incapacity he entertained a mental outlook that makes punitive damages appropriate.[32]

So far as negligence is concerned, the common law cases have usually said that an insane person is liable for failure to conform to the standard of conduct of the reasonable person,[33] with the civil law in Louisiana going the other way.[34] But there has been judicial[35] as well as scholarly criticism of the common law rule, and Wisconsin has taken the view,[36] supported by a Canadian deci-

the widespread adoption of comparative negligence, which would have no effect on a limited duty rationale.

21. See supra, § 29.

22. See supra, § 17.

23. Becker v. Becker, 1954, 207 Misc. 17, 138 N.Y.S.2d 397.

24. Beaubeauf v. Reid, 1926, 4 La.App. 344. But cf. Behrens v. McKenzie, 1867, 23 Iowa 333.

25. Irvine v. Gibson, 1904, 117 Ky. 306, 77 S.W. 1106; Bryant v. Jackson, 1845, 25 Tenn. (6 Humph.) 199; Horner v. Marshall's Administratrix, 1817, 19 Va. (5 Munf.) 466.

26. See Mullen v. Bruce, 1959, 168 Cal.App.2d 494, 335 P.2d 945; also Morriss v. Marsden, [1952] 1 All Eng.Rep. 925, followed in Beal v. Hayward, [1960] N.Z.L.Rep. 131, and Phillips v. Soloway, [1956] 6 Dom. L.Rep.2d 570.

27. See Notes, 1938, 22 Minn.L.Rev. 853, 859–860; 1934, 34 Col.L.Rev. 185.

28. See Gatley, Libel and Slander, 2d ed. 1929, 430, 437; Ullrich v. New York Press Co., 1898, 23 Misc. 168, 50 N.Y.S. 788.

29. See Yeates v. Reed, Ind.1838, 4 Blackf. 463; Gates v. Meredith, 1856, 7 Ind. 440; Dickinson v. Barber, 1812, 9 Mass. 225. Cf. Warner v. Lockerby, 1884, 31 Minn. 421, 18 N.W. 145, rehearing denied 31 Minn. 421, 18 N.W.2d 821 (heat of passion); Alderson v. Kahle, 1914, 73 W.Va. 690, 80 S.E. 1109.

30. Wilson v. Walt, 1933, 138 Kan. 205, 25 P.2d 343; see Dickinson v. Barber, 1812, 9 Mass. 225.

31. Jewell v. Colby, 1890, 66 N.H. 399, 24 A. 902; see Moore v. Horne, 1910, 153 N.C. 413, 69 S.E. 409.

32. Schumann v. Crofoot, 1979, 43 Or.App. 53, 602 P.2d 298.

33. Williams v. Hays, 1894, 143 N.Y. 442, 38 N.E. 449, qualified in 1899, 157 N.Y. 541, 52 N.E. 589; Sforza v. Green Bus Lines, 1934, 150 Misc. 180, 268 N.Y.S. 446; Shapiro v. Tchernowitz, 1956, 3 Misc.2d 617, 155 N.Y.S.2d 1011; Johnson v. Lambotte, 1961, 147 Colo. 203, 363 P.2d 165; Ellis v. Fixico, 1935, 174 Okl. 116, 50 P.2d 162 (statute); Kuhn v. Zabotsky, 1967, 9 Ohio St. 2d 129, 224 N.E.2d 137, 38 O.O.2d 302; Turner v. Caldwell, 1980, 36 Conn.Sup. 350, 421 A.2d 876; Annot., 49 A.L.R.3d 189.

34. See Turner v. Bucher, La.1975, 308 So.2d 270, 273–74 (nondiscerning persons not morally guilty and not liable but their curators are liable).

35. Fitzgerald v. Lawhorn, 1972, 29 Conn.Sup. 511, 294 A.2d 338.

36. Breunig v. American Family Insurance Co., 1970, 45 Wis.2d 536, 173 N.W.2d 619, 49 A.L.R.3d 179.

FIGURE 2-I
PROSSER AND KEETON ON THE LAW OF TORTS

§ 135 INSANITY 1075

sion,[37] that where insanity occurs suddenly and without warning, it is to be treated like a heart attack, so that the insane defendant is not held to the reasonable man standard under those circumstances. Judicial doubts about the rule are also expressed in the contributory negligence cases, where the mentally disturbed or defective person is usually held only to the standards he can personally meet.[38]

In the light of these cases, the permanent direction of the law may be in doubt even now. Proposals have been made to compensate the injured through payments by the state and at the same time to relieve the insane defendant.[39] This would avoid the harshness of liability for the insane and at the same time protect the injured. Since similar proposals have received some support elsewhere in tort law, this may represent the course of future development.[40]

WESTLAW REFERENCES

liab! /s insan! sane sanity "mental** ill!" /s negligen** intent!
257Ak411
257Ak412

37. Buckley & Toronto Transp. Comm'n v. Smith Transport, Ltd., [1946] Ont.L.Rep. 798, [1946] 4 Dom.L. Rep. 721.

See Picher, The Tortious Liability of the Insane in Canada, 1975, 13 Osgoode Hall L.J. 193.

38. E.g., Mochen v. State, 1974, 43 A.D.2d 484, 352 N.Y.S.2d 290; Comment, 1972, 39 Tenn.L.Rev. 705. The Second Restatement of Torts, § 464 expressly refused to take a position on this.

39. Sadoff, 1967, Tortious Liability of the Insane, 39 Pa.Bar.Q. 73.

40. Crime Victims' Compensation Acts operate on a similar principle. See, e.g., Rothstein, How the Uniform Crime Victims Reparations Act Works, 1974, 60 A.B.A.J. 1531. A number of states reach a similar result where state officials are sued by indemnifying them. See supra, § 132.

FIGURE 2-J
PROSSER AND KEETON ON THE LAW OF TORTS

Stop here, and mark the relevant portions of the discussion in the above section before consulting the discussion of this problem in Appendix A.

Assume that you are now ready to begin taking notes on this material. What should you write down?

As discussed earlier in this section, Vom Bauer suggests that you begin taking notes immediately in a way that usefully summarizes what you have found "rather than expecting somehow to summarize everything all of a sudden at the end."[5] Recall that each new legal principle or idea should be recorded on a separate sheet of paper.

After you have stated the principle or idea, you should then make *complete* listing of citations to authorities of every description supporting the principle or idea.[6] Using this system

---

[5] Id. at 28.

[6] Id. at 28-30.

of note taking, you would start several sheets based on your reading of the above section.

ILLUSTRATION 2.2

The first legal principle or idea recorded could be based on the discussion accompanying footnotes 36 and 37 in Figures I and J above. You could state this legal principle or idea in several ways. One of those ways is shown below:

> When it occurs suddenly and without warning, insanity should be treated like a heart attack; in such circumstances, insane defendants are not held to the standard of conduct of the reasonable person which is ordinarily used in negligence actions.

Following the system of note taking suggested in this chapter, you should identify the source of this principle or idea:

> ✓ W. Prosser & W. Keeton, The Law of Torts § 135, at 1074-75 (5th ed. 1984) (pointing out this line of authority).

To indicate that you have personally read the material in the source, you should place a *check mark* in front of it. Also under this system, you would write all of the citations given by the source as supporting this principle or, at least those applicable to your jurisdiction (depending on the time available and the scope of your research).[7] In this instance, a Wisconsin case (footnote 36) and a Canadian case and a law review article (footnote 37) are cited in support of the proposition.

These authorities should be listed under the citation to Prosser and Keeton:

> * Breunig v. American Family Insurance Co., 45 Wis. 2d 536, 173 N.W.2d 619 (1970) (annotated at 49 A.L.R.3d 179).

> * Buckley & Toronto Transportation Commission v. Smith Transport, Ltd., [1946] Ont. L. Rep. 798, [1946] 4 Dom. L. Rep. 721.

> Picher, The Tortious Liability of the Insane in Canada, 13 Osgoode Hall L.J. 193 (1975).

These two cases appear to be leading cases directly on point. To indicate their significance, you should place a *star* in front of each of them.

---

[7] Id. at 29-30.

You should remember that clients and others requesting research do not always supply the right information. One of the important functions of research is to identify shortcomings in the available information so that additional facts can be sought from the client or other sources. When researchers discover that relevant facts are missing, they often must proceed on alternative assumptions to complete the research.

Furthermore, sometimes during the course of the research, you will discover that the assigned research issue was not formulated accurately or that the opposing party has erred in stating the issue. Or more often, the initial formulation of the legal issue will need to be focused more specifically to reflect the true crux of the matter.

ILLUSTRATION 2.3

In this instance, the facts that you were given referred to Delira's apparently sudden insanity, but note that the above principle requires that the insanity also must be "without warning." Did Delira have a previous history of mental illness? Were there any prior signs of mental problems?

At this point, you probably should proceed on alternative assumptions: (1) the mental illness in fact was sudden and without warning; and (2) the current attack--although perhaps sudden--was, in fact, part of a prior pattern of mental illness and in that way could have been "expected." This approach seems especially warranted because Prosser and Keeton indicate that the sudden mental illness rule is an *exception* to the generally accepted rule that insane persons are liable for their failure to conform to the standard of conduct of reasonable persons.

Pursuing these alternative assumptions, the second principle (see the text at footnote 33) could be stated at the top of a separate sheet:

> Under the common law, in negligence actions insane persons are liable for their failure to conform to the standard of conduct of reasonable persons.

Under this principle, you would refer again to Prosser and Keeton's text. A full citation to it, however, is unnecessary because this information has been recorded fully already:

✓ W. Prosser & W. Keeton, § 135, at 1074.

Footnote 33 contains the support for this principle, and the sources cited therein should be recorded under the citation to Prosser and Keeton:

> Williams v. Hays, 143 N.Y. 442, 38 N.E. 449 (1894), qualified in 157 N.Y. 541, 52 N.E. 589 (1899).

Sforza v. Green Bus Lines, 150 Misc. 180, 268 N.Y.S. 446 (_______ 1934).

Shapiro v. Tchernowitz, 3 Misc. 2d 617, 155 N.Y.S.2d 1011 (_______ 1956).

Johnson v. Lambotte, 147 Colo. 203, 363 P.2d 165 (1961).

Ellis v. Fixico, 174 Okla. 116, 50 P.2d 162 (1935) (statute).

Kuhn v. Zabotsky, 9 Ohio St. 2d 129, 224 N.E.2d 137 (1967).

Turner v. Caldwell, 36 Conn. Supp. 350, 421 A.2d 876 (_______ 1980).

Annotation,________________________________
________________, 49 A.L.R.3d 189 (______).

The citations should be recorded in proper form so that they can be easily used later in legal writing. Furthermore, leave blanks for information not given (for example, the title and date of the *A.L.R.3d* annotation is missing), so you will be alerted to fill in the missing information when that source is consulted.

YOU SHOULD AVOID THE TEMPTATION TO SKIP LISTING ANY OF THE CITED SOURCES (UNLESS THEY CLEARLY ARE IRRELEVANT OR UNNECESSARY IN LIGHT OF THE SCOPE OF THE RESEARCH PROJECT), EVEN IF IT RESULTS IN A LENGTHY LIST AS ABOVE.

Vom Bauer points out that you may have difficulty finding the book or the page that cites these sources again and that in the long run you may end up wasting time if you fail to summarize and record fully as you proceed.[8]

In reading the excerpt, you should have noted several other points. Prosser and Keeton indicate that the common-law rule requiring insane persons to conform to the standard of reasonable persons has not been followed in Louisiana (based on the civil law derived from the law of France) and that the common-law rule has been criticized (see the text at footnote 34). Although the unique law of Louisiana will not apply to the presumably common-law state of Utopia, you might want to note this idea

---

[8] Id. at 28 ("[D]on't half-do it the first time, half-do it the second time, half-do it a third time, and then expect it to be suddenly right at the end").

and the case cited in support of it in footnote 34 for the purpose of possibly criticizing the common-law rule.

More importantly, you would want to record that the common-law rule has been criticized. If it turns out to be justified, this criticism may provide you with a second defense. Even if Delira fails to meet the requirements of the sudden insanity defense, it still may be appropriate to assert that the State of Utopia should reject the common-law rule applied to insane persons generally. For this reason, you would write at the top of another sheet of paper:

> The common-law rule requiring insane persons to conform to the standard of conduct of reasonable persons has been criticized.
>
> ✓ W. Prosser & W. Keeton, § 135, at 1074.
>
> Fitzgerald v. Lawhorn, 29 Conn. Supp. 511, 294 A.2d 338 (______ 1972).

The origin, development, justifications, and criticism of the common-law approach holding insane persons liable for their torts is discussed earlier in the section. Each relevant principle or idea on this topic should be recorded before leaving this section. The text initially points out that mentally disabled persons are usually held liable for their torts (see the text accompanying footnote 1). This entry is important because the *Restatement (Second) of Torts* is cited in support of that view. This point (and the relevant supporting authorities) should be recorded on another sheet of paper.

The origin of the rule (see the text accompanying and following footnote 2) is important because it seems to have originated as dictum in a case when strict liability was applied rather than fault (on which the modern law of negligence is based). This idea should be recorded on a separate sheet too.

One way of understanding and evaluating any rule is to examine the reasons or justification given in support of it. The text discusses the reasons or justifications for the common-law rule (see the text accompanying footnotes 12 through 17), and each should be recorded on a separate sheet. Each of the arguments against the rule should be recorded on separate sheets (see the text accompanying footnotes 18 through 20).

You also might record that judicial doubts about the rule have been expressed in contributory negligence cases (see the text accompanying footnote 38), and have led Prosser and Keeton to conclude that "the permanent direction of the law may be in doubt even now" (see the text following footnote 38). Finally, you might note that proposals have been made to develop a compensation system that ultimately might represent a better way of handling this problem (see the text accompanying footnotes 39 and 40).

At this point, you have extracted everything useful from this section of Prosser and Keeton. Vom Bauer warns that you should avoid the impulse to rush from one source to another without making full notes.[9] In this instance, recall that the index to Prosser and Keeton also indicated possibly relevant material on page 176 under the heading "Negligence"/"Mental capacity." This material should be checked before consulting another source. After all, you could have chosen to start there.

PROBLEM 2.6

Read Prosser and Keeton's discussion of "Mental Capacity" that begins on page 176 in Figures 2-K, 2-L, and 2-M. As you read, mark in the margin the portions of the discussion that appear to relate to the research question.

---

[9] Id. at 31 ("Extract the full juice from each [source] before going on").

or deaf,[17] or lame, or is otherwise physically disabled,[18] is entitled to live in the world and to have allowance made by others for his disability,[19] and the person cannot be required to do the impossible by conforming to physical standards which he cannot meet. Similar allowance has been made for the weaknesses of old age.[20] At the same time, the conduct of the handicapped individual must be reasonable in the light of the person's knowledge of his infirmity, which is treated merely as one of the circumstances under which the person acts. A blind man may be negligent in going into a place of known danger, just as one who knows that he is subject to epileptic fits, or is about to fall asleep, may be negligent in driving a car.[21] It is sometimes said that a blind man must use a greater degree of care than one who can see; [22] but it is now generally agreed that the more accurate way to state the rule is that he must take the precautions, be they more or less, which the ordinary reasonable person would take if he were blind.[23] Under the latter formulation, the standard remains essentially the same, but has added flexibility for taking the actor's physical deficiencies into account.

Mental Capacity

As to mental peculiarities of the actor, the standard remains of necessity an external one. "The law," says Mr. Justice Holmes in a much quoted passage, "takes no account of the infinite varieties of temperament, intellect, and education which make the internal character of a given act so different in different men. It does not attempt to see men as God sees them, for more than one sufficient reason." [24] The fact that the indi-

667, affirmed 404 So.2d 1221 (walking without cane not negligent in circumstances).

Compare, as to impaired vision, Masters v. Alexander, 1967, 424 Pa. 65, 225 A.2d 905; Bernard v. Russell, 1960, 103 N.H. 76, 164 A.2d 577; Pennington v. Southern Pacific Co., 1956, 146 Cal.App.2d 605, 304 P.2d 22; Shepherd v. Gardner Wholesale, Inc., 1972, 288 Ala. 43, 256 So.2d 877 (cataracts).

17. McCann v. Sadowski, 1926, 287 Pa. 294, 135 A. 207; Jakubiec v. Hasty, 1953, 337 Mich. 205, 59 N.W.2d 385; Rhimer v. Davis, 1923, 126 Wash. 470, 218 P. 193; Kerr v. Connecticut Co., 1928, 107 Conn. 304, 140 A. 751; Otterbeck v. Lamb, 1969, 85 Nev. 456, 456 P.2d 855.

18. Texas & New Orleans Railroad Co. v. Bean, 1909, 55 Tex.Civ.App. 341, 119 S.W. 328, error refused (club foot); Borus v. Yellow Cab Co., 1977, 52 Ill.App. 3d 194, 9 Ill.Dec. 843, 367 N.E.2d 277 (recovering from prior injuries); Memorial Hospital v. Scott, 1973, 261 Ind. 27, 300 N.E.2d 50 (multiple sclerosis); Stephens v. Dulaney, 1967, 78 N.M. 53, 428 P.2d 27 (no sense of smell; gas fumes exploded by cigarette). Cf. Sterling v. New England Fish Co., W.D.Wash.1976, 410 F.Supp. 164 (short leg). Accord, as to short stature, Mahan v. State of New York, to Use of Carr, 1937, 172 Md. 373, 191 A. 575; Singletary v. Atlantic Coast Line Railroad Co., 1950, 217 S.C. 212, 60 S.E.2d 305.

19. Thus a city must govern its excavations on sidewalks by the expectation that the blind will use them. Fletcher v. City of Aberdeen, 1959, 54 Wn.2d 174, 388 P.2d 743. See also Garbutt v. Schechter, 1959, 167 Cal. App.2d 396, 334 P.2d 225 (200 pound woman): Robinson v. Pioche, Bayerque & Co., 1885, 5 Cal. 460, 461 (drunk): "A drunken man is as much entitled to a safe street, as a sober one, and much more in need of it." Cf. Sterling v. New England Fish Co., W.D.Wash.1976, 410 F.Supp. 164 (safety of place of employment).

20. Brunner v. John, 1954, 45 Wn.2d 341, 274 P.2d 581; Kitsap County Transportation Co. v. Harvey, 9th Cir. 1927, 15 F.2d 166; Garner v. Crawford, La.App. 1973, 288 So.2d 886; Borus v. Yellow Cab Co., 1977, 52 Ill.App.3d 194, 9 Ill.Dec. 843, 367 N.E.2d 277 (dictum). But the actor's advanced age alone should not be considered unless it is shown to have impaired his abilities. See O'Connor & Raque Co. v. Bill, Ky.1971, 474 S.W.2d 344.

21. See supra, § 29. Cf. Felton v. Horner, 1896, 97 Tenn. 579, 37 S.W. 696 (aged and infirm person risking jolt of train); King v. Investment Equities, Inc., La. App.1972, 264 So.2d 297 (spastic paraplegic failed to observe large hole); Sterling v. New England Fish Co., W.D.Wash.1976, 410 F.Supp. 164 (short legged seaman should have gripped railing on steep and slippery ramp).

22. Winn v. City of Lowell, 1861, 83 Mass. (1 Allen) 177; Karl v. Juniata County, 1903, 206 Pa. 633, 56 A. 78; King v. Investment Equities, Inc., La.App.1972, 264 So.2d 297 (spastic paraplegic). See also Armstrong v. Warner Brothers Theatres, 1947, 161 Pa.Super. 385, 54 A.2d 831 (age).

23. See Second Restatement of Torts, § 283C ("a reasonable man under like disability"); Hill v. City of Glenwood, 1904, 124 Iowa 479, 100 N.W. 522; Borus v. Yellow Cab Co., 1977, 52 Ill.App.3d 194, 9 Ill.Dec. 843, 367 N.E.2d 277 (disabled); Memorial Hospital v. Scott, 1973, 261 Ind. 27, 300 N.E.2d 50 (disabled); Shepherd v. Gardner Wholesale, Inc., 1972, 288 Ala. 43, 256 So.2d 877 (impaired vision); Otterbeck v. Lamb, 1969, 85 Nev. 456, 456 P.2d 855 (deaf mute); Stephens v. Dulaney, 1967, 78 N.M. 53, 428 P.2d 27 (no sense of smell); Roberts v. State, La.App.1981, 396 So.2d 566, writ granted 400 So.2d 667, affirmed 404 So.2d 1221 (blind).

24. Holmes, The Common Law, 1881, 108. See Jolley v. Powell, Fla.App.1974, 299 So.2d 647.

FIGURE 2-K
PROSSER AND KEETON ON THE LAW OF TORTS

vidual is a congenital fool, cursed with inbuilt bad judgment,[25] or that in the particular instance the person "did not stop to think," [26] or that the person is merely a stupid ox, or of an excitable temperament which causes him to lose his head and get "rattled," obviously cannot be allowed to protect him from liability.[27] Apart from the very obvious difficulties of proof as to what went on in the person's head, it may be no bad policy to hold a fool according to his folly. The harm to his neighbors is quite as great, and may be greater, than if the person exhibited a modicum of brains; [28] and if the person is to live in the community, he must learn to conform to its standards or pay for what he breaks. As to all such mental deficiency of a minor nature, no allowance is made; [29] the standard of reasonable conduct is applied, and "it is not enough that the defendant did the best he knew how." [30]

As for more severe mental disabilities, including total insanity, where the actor entirely lacks the capacity to comprehend a risk or avoid an accident, one might expect a relaxation of the standard similar to the physical disability rule. Yet, for a variety of reasons, the law [31] has developed the other way, holding the mentally deranged or insane defendant accountable for his negligence as if the person were a normal, prudent person.[32] Against the apparent injustice of making persons responsible according to a standard they cannot meet,[33] several rationales have been offered to support the decision to hold mentally deranged defendants accountable for their negligence and certain other torts,[34] including the difficulty of distinguishing true incapacity from mere bad judgment, the belief that the custodians of incompetents will be encouraged by the rule to watch them more closely and keep them under control, and the perceived sense of fairness, even in the absence of moral blame, of a rule requiring mental defectives who live among the rest of society to conform to the general standards of con-

25. Fritscher v. Billiot, La.App.1959, 112 So.2d 755; Vaughan v. Menlove, 1837, 3 Bing.N.C. 467, 132 Eng. Rep. 490.

26. Cronin v. Columbian Manufacturing Co., 1909, 75 N.H. 319, 74 A. 180; Masters v. Public Service Co. of New Hampshire, 1942, 92 N.H. 85, 25 A.2d 499.

27. Cf. Crosslin v. Alsup, Tenn.1980, 594 S.W.2d 379 (plaintiff agitated and preoccupied).

28. "If, for instance, a man is born hasty and awkward, is always hurting himself or his neighbors, no doubt his congenital defects will be allowed for in the courts of Heaven, but his slips are no less troublesome to his neighbors than if they sprang from guilty neglect. His neighbors accordingly require him, at his peril, to come up to their standard, and the courts which they establish decline to take his personal equation into account." Holmes, The Common Law, 1881, 108.

29. Feldman v. Howard, 1966, 5 Ohio App.2d 65, 214 N.E.2d 235, reversed on other grounds 10 Ohio St. 2d 189, 226 N.E.2d 564; Johnson v. Texas & Pacific Railway Co., 1931, 16 La.App. 464, 133 So. 517, rehearing denied 16 La.App. 464, 135 So. 114; Riesbeck Drug Co. v. Wray, 1942, 111 Ind.App. 467, 39 N.E.2d 776.

30. Vaughan v. Menlove, 1837, 3 Bing.N.C. 468, 471, 132 Eng.Rep. 490.

31. Statutory in California, Montana, North Dakota, Oklahoma and South Dakota. "A minor, or person of unsound mind, of whatever degree, is civilly liable for a wrong done by him, but is not liable in exemplary damages unless at the time of the act he was capable of knowing that it was wrongful." West's Ann.Cal.Civ. Code § 41.

32. Kuhn v. Zabotsky, 1967, 9 Ohio St.2d 129, 224 N.E.2d 137; Johnson v. Lambotte, 1961, 147 Colo. 203, 363 P.2d 165; Jolley v. Powell, Fla.App.1974, 299 So.2d 647 (defendant shot plaintiff's intestate; acquitted in earlier homicide prosecution by reason of insanity); Schumann v. Crofoot, 1979, 43 Or.App. 53, 602 P.2d 298 (lawyer malpractice); Vosnos v. Perry, 1976, 43 Ill. App.3d 834, 2 Ill.Dec. 447, 357 N.E.2d 614 (defendant shot plaintiff's intestate). But see Fitzgerald v. Lawhorn, 1972, 29 Conn.Sup. 511, 294 A.2d 338 (defendant shot plaintiff; insanity good defense to assault claim). See generally Annot., 1973, 49 A.L.R.3d 189.

33. See generally Ague, The Liability of Insane Persons in Torts Actions, 1956, 60 Dick.L.Rev. 211; Curran, Tort Liability of the Mentally Ill and Mentally Deficient, 1960, 21 Ohio St.L.J. 52; Alexander & Szasz, Mental Illness as an Excuse for Civil Wrongs, 1967, 43 Notre Dame L.Rev. 24; Seidelson, Reasonable Expectations and Subjective Standards in Negligence Law: The Minor, the Mentally Impaired, and the Mentally Incompetent, 1981, 50 Geo.Wash.L.Rev. 17; Ellis, Tort Responsibility of Mentally Disabled Persons, 1981 Am. Bar Found.Res.J. 1079; Note, 1972, 39 Tenn.L.Rev. 705.

34. As to the tort liability of insane persons generally, see infra, § 135.

FIGURE 2-L
PROSSER AND KEETON ON THE LAW OF TORTS

178 NEGLIGENCE: STANDARD OF CONDUCT Ch. 5

duct or pay their innocent victims for the damage they cause.[35]

Similar to the cases involving sudden illness or unconsciousness,[36] there is some sentiment for treating a sudden delerium or loss of mental faculties as a "circumstance" depriving the actor of control over his conduct, thus shielding him from liability, provided that the lapse was unforeseeable.[37]

In the case of mentally defective or insane plaintiffs, where the issue involves the contributory or comparative fault of such persons, the policy arguments outlined above lose much of their force.[38] In particular, the question shifts from which of two innocents should bear the loss to whether a negligent defendant should pay for the loss he has partially caused to a mentally incapacitated person incapable of properly looking after himself. Because of the obviously different equities in this situation, the great majority of courts in the contributory negligence context apply a lower standard of care and consider the plaintiff's incapacity as only one of the "circumstances" to be considered in judging the quality of his conduct.[39]

Whether intoxication is to be regarded as a physical or a mental disability depends on how the accident occurs. On either basis, it is common enough; and it is uniformly held that voluntary[40] or negligent intoxication cannot serve as an excuse for acts done in that condition which would otherwise be negligent. One who so becomes intoxicated is held thereafter to the same standard as if he were a sober person.[41] One good reason is that an excuse based on such intoxication would be far too common and too easy to assert; another is that drunkenness is so antisocial that one who indulges in it ought to be held to the consequences.[42] Yet intoxication is not negligence in itself, and it must be shown to have caused the actor's behavior to have deviated from that of a reasonable per-

35. See, e.g., Jolley v. Powell, Fla.App.1974, 299 So. 2d 647; Schumann v. Crofoot, 1979, 43 Or.App. 53, 602 P.2d 298; Second Restatement of Torts, § 283B, Comment *b*. The rationales are critiqued in Note, 1972, 39 Tenn.L.Rev. 705.

36. See supra, § 29.

37. See Breunig v. American Family Insurance Co., 1970, 45 Wis.2d 536, 173 N.W.2d 619; Buckley & Toronto Transp. Comm'n v. Smith Transport, Ltd., [1946] Ont.L.Rep. 798, [1946] 4 Dom.L.Rep. 721. Cf. Restatement of Torts, § 283C, com. *b*. But see Kuhn v. Zabotsky, 1967, 9 Ohio St.2d 129, 224 N.E.2d 137.

38. See Second Restatement of Torts, § 464, Comment *g*.

39. Emory University v. Lee, 1958, 97 Ga.App. 680, 104 S.E.2d 234; De Martini v. Alexander Sanitarium, 1961, 192 Cal.App.2d 442, 13 Cal.Rptr. 564; Johnson v. Texas & Pacific Railway Co., 1931, 16 La.App. 464, 133 So. 517; Lynch v. Rosenthal, Mo.App.1965, 396 S.W.2d 272; Feldman v. Howard, 1966, 5 Ohio App.2d 65, 214 N.E.2d 235, reversed on other grounds, 1967, 10 Ohio St.2d 189, 226 N.E.2d 564.

Some earlier opinions held the plaintiff who was not totally insane to the same standard of safety for his own protection as a normal person. E.g., Wright v. Tate, 1967, 208 Va. 291, 156 S.E.2d 562, criticized in Note, 1968, 9 W. & M.L.Rev. 897. Recent decisions have rejected such distinctions and permit the trier of fact to determine if the plaintiff's mental condition deprived him of the ability to perceive or avoid the harm. Young v. State, 1978, 92 Misc.2d 795, 401 N.Y.S.2d 955; Miller v. Trinity Medical Center, N.D.1977, 260 N.W.2d 4; Snider v. Callahan, W.D.Mo.1966, 250 F.Supp. 1022.

40. Involuntary, non-negligent intoxication, as where the old lady who never has tasted whiskey is given a cup of "tea," is held to be treated like illness or physical disability. Cf. Davies v. Butler, 1979, 95 Nev. 763, 602 P.2d 605 (death by alcohol poisoning from forced consumption as initiation into college drinking club); Greenberg v. McCabe, E.D.Pa.1978, 453 F.Supp. 765, affirmed without opinion, 3d Cir. 1979, 594 F.2d 854 (improperly administered drugs; psychiatric malpractice action). As to the problem of the chronic alcoholic, who escapes criminal liability, see Driver v. Hinnant, 4th Cir. 1966, 356 F.2d 761; Easter v. District of Columbia, 4th Cir. 1966, 361 F.2d 50; Note, 1967, 52 Corn.L.Q. 470.

41. Hamilton v. Kinsey, Ala.1976, 337 So.2d 344; Shuman v. Mashburn, 1976, 137 Ga.App. 231, 223 S.E.2d 268; Harlow v. Connelly, Ky.App.1977, 548 S.W.2d 143; Folda v. City of Bozeman, 1978, 177 Mont. 537, 582 P.2d 767. For drug cases, see Haber v. County of Nassau, 2d Cir. 1977, 557 F.2d 322; Mikula v. Balogh, 1965, 9 Ohio App.2d 250, 224 N.E.2d 148. See generally McCoid, Intoxication and Its Effect Upon Civil Responsibility, 1956, 42 Iowa L.Rev. 38; Dooley & Mosher, Alcohol and Legal Negligence, 1978, 7 Contemp.Drug Prob. 145; Annot., 1973, 49 A.L.R.3d 189.

42. The consequences may include punitive damages. See Taylor v. Superior Ct., 1979, 2 Cal.3d 890, 157 Cal.Rptr. 693, 598 P.2d 854 (drunk driving).

FIGURE 2-M
PROSSER AND KEETON ON THE LAW OF TORTS

Stop here, and mark the relevant portions of the discussion in the above section before consulting the discussion of this problem in Appendix A.

In footnote 36, a cross-reference is given to section 29 of the text. Before moving to another source, you should check this section to see if it is relevant.

PROBLEM 2.7

The beginning page of section 29 from Prosser and Keeton's hornbook is shown on the following page. Read the following page and determine how the section is relevant to the research problem, if at all.

162 NEGLIGENCE: STANDARD OF CONDUCT Ch. 5

§ 29. Unavoidable Accident

An unavoidable accident[1] is an occurrence which was not intended and which, under all the circumstances, could not have been foreseen or prevented by the exercise of reasonable precautions. That is, an accident is considered unavoidable or inevitable at law if it was not proximately caused by the negligence of any party to the action, or to the accident.[2] No accident, of course, is entirely inevitable, so long as it results from a voluntary human act. If the defendant rides a horse, which runs away with him and injures the plaintiff, the accident is not strictly inevitable, since the defendant intentionally rode the horse, and might have prevented all harm by keeping him in the barn. But the runaway is called "unavoidable" if it did not result from any lack of foresight or proper care in the management of the horse, because both wrongful intent and negligence are lacking. There is no liability in such a case.[3] Upon the same basis, the driver of an automobile who suddenly loses control of the car because the driver is seized with a heart attack, a stroke, a fainting spell, or an epileptic fit is not liable, unless the driver knew that he might become ill, in which case he may have been negligent in driving the car at all.[4] The same conclusions are reached when a driver strikes a child[5] or an animal[6] which darts in front of the car or when his attention is diverted by an unusual event.[7] Such rules are adopted because the

§ 29

1. Other terms include "inevitable accident," "mere accident," "pure accident," and "accident." The unavoidable accident doctrine logically subsumes the narrower doctrines of Act of God and sudden emergency. Cf. Bass v. Aetna Insurance Co., La.1979, 370 So.2d 511 (Act of God defense inapplicable to case where worshiper, "trotting under the Spirit of the Lord," collided with another worshiper praying in the aisle). See generally Rees, Unavoidable Accident—A Misunderstood Concept, 1964, 5 Ariz.L.Rev. 225; Kirchner, Sudden Illness as a Defense in Auto Accidents, 1967, 16 Clev.-Marsh.L.Rev. 523; Berry, The Unavoidable Accident Instruction, 1968, 17 Defense L.J. 259; Notes, 1976, 25 Drake L.Rev. 754 (Act of God defense); 1973, 52 Neb.L.Rev. 559; 1966, 19 Okla.L.Rev. 308; Annots., 1959, 65 A.L.R.2d 12 (auto cases); 1979, 93 A.L.R.3d 326 (auto accident from blackout or sudden unconsciousness).

2. Definitions vary from state to state, reflecting the nature and scope of the doctrine as applied in the jurisdiction. E.g., Hyatt Creek Builders-Engineers Co. v. Board of Regents, Tex.Civ.App.1980, 607 S.W.2d 258, 266, error dismissed ("an event * * * which was not proximately caused by the negligence of any party to the event"); Howard v. Howard, Ky.App.1980, 607 S.W.2d 119, 120 ("unforeseen and unexpected, occurring externally to all persons affected by it"); Zayre of Georgia, Inc. v. Haynes, 1975, 134 Ga.App. 15, 213 S.E.2d 163, 165 ("It may be an 'act of God' * * * or a pure casualty which exists without fault or carelessness on the part of either party * * * [or] an accident to the parties where * * * any negligence involved was attributable to one not a party to the suit or one too young to be legally chargeable therewith."). See also Anderton v. Montgomery, Utah 1980, 607 P.2d 828, 834 ("Unavoidable accident, rather than being a separate legal doctrine, is simply a recognition of the fact that an incident causing injury to the plaintiff does not necessarily give rise to liability in the defendant.").

3. Gibbons v. Pepper, 1695, 1 Ld.Raym. 38, 91 Eng. Rep. 922; Steudle v. Rentchler, 1872, 64 Ill. 161.

4. *Compare* Moore v. Presnell, 1977, 38 Md.App. 243, 379 A.2d 1246 (blackout unforeseeable despite hypertension medication); Cox v. Vernieuw, Wyo.1980, 604 P.2d 1353 (no reason to anticipate blackout from heart condition; yet Act of God rule inapplicable to a defendant's physical affliction); and Frechette v. Welch, 1st Cir. 1980, 621 F.2d 11 (unforeseeable blackout); *with* Reliance Insurance Co. v. Dickens, La.App. 1973, 279 So.2d 234 (epileptic attack foreseeable to driver with 8-year history of seizures). See generally Kraig, Heart Attack as a Defense in Negligence Actions, 1963, 12 Clev.-Marsh.L.Rev. 59; Kirchner, Sudden Illness as a Defense in Auto Accidents, 1967, 16 Clev.-Marsh.L.Rev. 523; Annot., 1979, 93 A.L.R.3d 326.

Although falling asleep at the wheel is often deemed negligent as a matter of law, see Annot., 1953, 28 A.L.R.2d 12, some courts permit a jury to find for the defendant in such a case if there was no prior warning of drowsiness. See Smith v. McIntyre, 1964, 20 A.D.2d 711, 247 N.Y.S.2d 361. Cf. Price v. Glosson Motor Lines, Inc., 4th Cir. 1975, 509 F.2d 1033. See generally Kaufman & Kantrowitz, The Case of the Sleeping Motorist, 1950, 25 N.Y.U.L.Q.Rev. 362; Notes, [1950] Wis. L.Rev. 334; 1944, 18 St.Johns.L.Rev. 95.

5. Compare Yarborough v. Berner, Tex.1971, 467 S.W.2d 188 (defendant entitled to unavoidable accident instruction if evidence at retrial showed 4-year-old child darted in front of car), with Alley v. Siepman, 1974, 87 S.D. 670, 214 N.W.2d 7 (defendant not entitled to instruction where accident occurred at time and place where pedestrian crossing road could well have been anticipated).

6. Rush v. State Farm Mutual Automobile Insurance Co., La.App.1973, 274 So.2d 461 (darting cow: unavoidable).

7. See Seals v. Morris, La.App.1980, 387 So.2d 1220, writ granted 393 So.2d 745 (green snake crawling on driver's shoulder: accident unavoidable), reversed 410

FIGURE 2-N
PROSSER AND KEETON ON THE LAW OF TORTS

Stop here, and consider how this section is relevant to the research problem, if at all, before consulting the discussion of this problem in Appendix A.

At this point, you have now extracted all the useful material relevant to this research problem from Prosser and Keeton's hornbook. By selecting a good secondary-search source and by resisting the temptation to go to some other source before you have used it fully, you now have a fair working knowledge of the contours of the research problem. If you were forced to do so in an emergency situation or if you could not justify spending more research time on this project at this point, you could report a tentative answer based on this research.

Section 2D. Basic Methods for Developing Your Research

The preceding section illustrated how notes should be taken on secondary-search sources, such as treatises, legal encyclopedias, or law review articles. The preceding section also illustrated how you may be able to formulate a tentative answer to a research question based on such sources. The next chapter will illustrate how you should take notes on cases for research purposes.

Under normal circumstances, you would plan to develop your research by consulting the cited primary sources or other secondary sources, such as a legal encyclopedia, an *A.L.R.* annotation, or a law review article. Cross-references within materials published by the same company often facilitate this process. This section introduces three basic methods for developing your research.

1. USING TOPICS AND KEY NUMBERS

During this stage of research, one particularly useful technique involves the use of West's topics and key numbers. West Publishing Company prepares headnotes that abstract the legal rules and points of law involved in every judicial opinion it publishes. West assigns to each headnote a topic and key number in its comprehensive system. These headnotes are collected and arranged by topic and key numbers in numerous digests covering cases from an individual state, a region, a particular court, or all courts nationwide.

Once the relevant topic and key number have been identified in a case from *any* jurisdiction or from some other source, all relevant cases on that point from every other jurisdiction (or just the one that is relevant) can be found by consulting that topic and key number in the appropriate digest.[10]

PROBLEM 2.8

Assume that you are specifically interested in determining whether a "sudden mental illness" is a defense to a negligence action in West Virginia (instead of the State of Utopia as previously assumed). Assume that you want to check West's digests covering West Virginia (the South Eastern Digest or Virginia & West Virginia Digest). How could you determine the relevant topic and key number under which you should look to find West Virginia cases on point (if any exist)?

Stop here, and consider this question before consulting the discussion of this problem in Appendix A.

PROBLEM 2.9

Assume that you decide to consult the *Breunig* opinion to determine the relevant topic(s) and key number(s). The page containing the relevant headnotes from the *Breunig* opinion is reproduced on the following page. Examine these headnotes, and place a check by the headnotes that appear to contain relevant points of law. Remember that the headnotes summarize points of law discussed in the opinion.

---

[10] See L. Teply, Legal Research and Citation 70, 293-300 (3d ed. 1989).

620 Wis. 173 NORTH WESTERN REPORTER, 2d SERIES

The Circuit Court for Dane County, Norris Maloney, J., entered judgment for the truck driver after he accepted reduction in damages and filed remittitur. The insurance company appealed. The Supreme Court, Hallows, C. J., held that whether motorist had knowledge of her schizophrenic, paranoid condition and of likelihood of hallucination while driving automobile was question for jury.

Affirmed.

1. Negligence ⚷105

Although some forms of insanity are defense to and preclude liability for negligence, not all types of insanity vitiate responsibility for a negligent tort and question of liability in every case must depend upon kind and nature of the insanity.

2. Automobiles ⚷157

Effect of mental illness or mental hallucinations or disorder must be such as to affect the person's ability to understand and appreciate duty which rests upon him to drive his automobile with ordinary care, or if insanity does not affect such understanding in operation, it must affect his ability to control his automobile in ordinarily prudent manner and there must be absence of notice or forewarning to the person that he may be suddenly subject to such a type of insanity or mental illness before insanity is defense to liability for negligence.

3. Automobiles ⚷157

Sudden mental incapacity equivalent in its effect to such physical causes as sudden heart attack, epileptic seizure, stroke or fainting by motorist is defense to liability for negligence in automobile collision case.

4. Evidence ⚷571(1)

Psychiatrist's opinion that there was no forewarning which would reasonably lead motorist to believe that her hallucinations would occur and be such as to affect her driving an automobile was expert's opinion and was not conclusive on jury in personal injury action.

5. Evidence ⚷570

It is for the jury to decide whether facts underpinning an expert opinion are true.

6. Automobiles ⚷245(35)

Whether motorist had knowledge of her schizophrenic, paranoid condition and of likelihood of hallucination while driving automobile was question for jury in personal injury action arising out of collision.

7. Negligence ⚷134

The evidence to sustain verdict of jury in personal injury action need not constitute the great weight and clear preponderance.

8. Trial ⚷337

For verdict to be perverse, there must be something to warrant finding that considerations which were ulterior to reasonably fair application of judgment of the jury to the evidence under trial court's instructions controlled or materially influenced the jury.

9. Trial ⚷337

That jury knows effect of its answer does not make its verdict perverse, but verdict is perverse when trial court instructs or tells jury the effect of its answer.

10. Trial ⚷29(4)

Trial judge is not mere moderator or referee; conversely, his duty is not to try the case but to hear it.

11. Trial ⚷29(4)

Trial judge must control conduct of trial but he is not responsible for the proof.

12. Trial ⚷29(4)

While litigants are entitled to fair trial, trial judge does not have to enjoy giving it.

13. Trial ⚷29(1, 4)

Responsibility for atmosphere of impartiality during course of trial rests upon

FIGURE 2-O
NORTH WESTERN REPORTER SECOND

Stop here, and mark the relevant headnote(s) before consulting the discussion of this problem in Appendix A.

PROBLEM 2.10

Assume that you have found the relevant page from West's *South Eastern Digest* showing Automobiles 157. That page is reproduced in the figure on the following page. Examine that entry, and determine whether a West Virginia case has dealt with this point of law.

5 S E D 2d—621

AUTOMOBILES ⇨158

For references to other topics, see Descriptive-Word Index

Va. 1953. A truck is not an "inherently dangerous instrumentality" when operated by a normal licensed driver, but it is a dangerous instrumentality when under control of an inexperienced person or an immature boy.

Meek v. Graybeal, 78 S.E.2d 593, 195 Va. 381.

Va. 1952. A mere failure to skillfully operate an automobile under all conditions, or to be alert and observant and to act intelligently and operate an automobile at a low rate of speed, may or may not be a failure to do what an ordinarily prudent person would have done under the circumstances and thus amount to lack of ordinary care; but such lack of attention and diligence, or mere inadvertence, does not amount to wanton or reckless conduct, or constitute culpable negligence for which automobile driver will be responsible to an invited guest.

Carr v. Patram, 70 S.E.2d 308, 193 Va. 604.

Va. 1937. The driver of an automobile cannot go to sleep without being chargeable with negligence.

Lee v. Moore, 191 S.E. 589, 168 Va. 278.

W.Va. 1955. Where driver of vehicle suddenly becomes physically or mentally incapacitated without warning, he is not liable for injury resulting from operation of vehicle while so incapacitated, but where a prima facie case of negligence has been established by plaintiff, burden is on defendant to show sudden illness or attack and that illness or attack was unanticipatable and unforeseen.

Keller v. Wonn, 87 S.E.2d 453, 140 W.Va. 860.

⇨158. Willful, wanton, or reckless acts or conduct.

Library references

C.J.S. Motor Vehicles § 258.

Ga. 1962. Motorist's reckless and wanton disregard of consequences, evincing willingness to inflict injury or produce death, may amount to wilfulness, though there is no direct proof of actual intention to inflict injury or produce death.

Carr v. John J. Woodside Storage Co., 123 S.E.2d 261, 217 Ga. 438, conformed to 123 S.E.2d 267, 104 Ga.App. 862.

Ga.App. 1971. That automobile was proceeding at about 60 or 65 miles per hour before collision was not wilful and wanton conduct.

Adams v. U. S. Fidelity & Guaranty Co., 186 S.E.2d 784, 125 Ga.App. 232.

Ga.App. 1963. Where conditions which would give police officers special statutory privileges in operation of automobile did not exist, court, in determining whether officers were guilty of wanton misconduct, must apply same standards as it would apply to any private individual. Code, § 68–1604.

Poole v. City of Louisville, 130 S.E.2d 157, 107 Ga.App. 305.

Police officers, who were pursuing motorist on highway under conditions which did not give officers right to exercise statutory privileges, owed motorist duty not to recklessly disregard his safety nor wantonly injure him. Code, § 68–1604.

Poole v. City of Louisville, 130 S.E.2d 157, 107 Ga.App. 305.

Whether police officers were guilty of wanton misconduct in pursuing motorist at night in unmarked police automobile without giving any sign to show that they were police depended upon whether reasonably prudent person would have foreseen strong probability of injury or danger to pursued motorist and guarded against it.

Poole v. City of Louisville, 130 S.E.2d 157, 107 Ga.App. 305.

Ga.App. 1943. Motorist is not guilty of "gross negligence" where alleged momentary inattentiveness to road is induced by promptings of a natural and humane instinct.

Edwards v. Ford, 26 S.E.2d 306, 69 Ga. App. 578.

Ga.App. 1936. Convalescent woman who suffered from convulsions resulting from fright when truck driven by defendant's employee left street, crashed through fence, and came to rest near porch where woman was sitting, held not entitled to maintain action on grounds of trespass on her property, criminal negligence, and assault on her person or will-ful, wanton, and intentional injury.

Elrod v. Brown Transfer & Storage Co., 187 S.E. 705, 54 Ga.App. 286.

N.C. 1967. Violation of statute prohibiting reckless driving is negligence per se and gives rise to both civil and criminal liability. G.S. § 20–140.

Ingle v. Roy Stone Transfer Corp., 156 S.E.2d 265, 271 N.C. 276.

Violation of reckless driving statute constitutes culpable negligence. G.S. § 20–140.

Ingle v. Roy Stone Transfer Corp., 156 S.E.2d 265, 271 N.C. 276.

Mere failure of motorist to keep reasonable lookout does not constitute reckless driving in absence of dangerous speed or perilous operation. G.S. § 20–140.

Ingle v. Roy Stone Transfer Corp., 156 S.E.2d 265, 271 N.C. 276.

Neither the intentional nor the unintentional violation of traffic law without more constitutes reckless driving.

Ingle v. Roy Stone Transfer Corp., 156 S.E.2d 265, 271 N.C. 276.

FIGURE 2-P
WEST'S SOUTH EASTERN DIGEST SECOND

Stop here, and determine whether a West Virginia case has dealt with this point of law before consulting the discussion of this problem in Appendix A.

If you are not focusing on the law of a particular jurisdiction, it is strongly recommended that you not become engaged in reading primary sources too quickly. Thus, instead of consulting the *Breunig* case after finishing your note taking on Prosser and Keeton's hornbook, you should consult additional secondary sources, such as a legal encyclopedia or one or more of the law review articles cited in Prosser and Keeton. In this way, you will get a broader view of the subject.

When your focus is not on a particular jurisdiction, you will usually find secondary sources more useful. Primary sources will serve more as examples or illustrations. You could continue to examine the sources, take notes, and prepare additional sheets. When you encounter material that is not relevant, Vom Bauer suggests that you should mark an "X" next to it in the margin.[11]

AT ALL TIMES, YOU SHOULD MODIFY THE SYSTEM OF NOTE TAKING DESCRIBED IN THIS CHAPTER AS NECESSARY TO RECORD YOUR RESEARCH IN AN EFFICIENT MANNER, PROVIDED IT IS CONSISTENT WITH THE GENERAL PRINCIPLES OF GOOD NOTE TAKING.

2. USING A.L.R. ANNOTATIONS

Another method for developing your research and focusing on the law of a particular jurisdiction is to identify an *A.L.R.* annotation on point.[12]

PROBLEM 2.11

In the notes taken from Prosser and Keeton's hornbook, an annotation (49 A.L.R.3d 189) was recorded. Such an annotation will generally discuss all cases within the scope of the topic. Examine the annotation scheme and index of 49 A.L.R.3d 189 in the following two figures. Which section discusses sudden insanity?

---

[11] Vom Bauer, supra note 1, at 30.

[12] See L. Teply, supra note 10, at 87, 287-93.

189

ANNOTATION

LIABILITY OF INSANE PERSON FOR HIS OWN NEGLIGENCE

by

J. A. Bryant, Jr., J.D., LL.M.

INDEX

TOTAL CLIENT-SERVICE LIBRARY® REFERENCES

41 Am Jur 2d, Incompetent Persons §§ 104, 108, 110; 57 Am Jur 2d, Negligence § 82

8 Am Jur Proof of Facts 1, Mental Disorder and Incapacity

ALR Digests, Incompetent Persons

ALR Quick Index, Incompetent or Insane Persons; Negligence

Consult POCKET PART in this volume for later case service

FIGURE 2-Q
AMERICAN LAW REPORTS ANNOTATED

190 TORTS—INSANITY AS DEFENSE 49 ALR3d

§ 1[a] 49 ALR3d 189

TABLE OF JURISDICTIONS REPRESENTED

Consult POCKET PART in this volume for later case service

Ala	§§ 4, 7
Colo	§ 4
Md	§§ 4, 7
Mass	§§ 2, 4
Minn	§ 4
NY	§§ 4, 5[a], 6
Ohio	§§ 4, 5[b]
Okla	§§ 1[a], 2, 4
W Va	§§ 3, 5[b]
Wis	§§ 2, 3, 5[b]
Eng	§ 2

§ 1. Introduction

[a] Scope

This annotation[1] collects the cases which consider the liability of an insane or incompetent person[2] for his own[3] negligence.[4] Liability of such persons for intentional torts is treated at 51 ALR 833, and 89 ALR 476, and the civil liability of insane or other mentally disordered persons for the specific torts of assault or battery is considered at 77 ALR2d 625. For a treatment of contributory negligence, see the comment note entitled "Contributory negligence of mentally incompetent or mentally or emotionally disturbed person," at 91 ALR2d 392.

A number of cases may be found which, without making any distinction between those torts which would ordinarily be classed as intentional and those which would be classed as negligent, state in broad terms that an insane person is liable for his torts. No attempt has been made to collect those cases unless the particular factual situation involved was one indicating that the court was considering a negligent tort.

State statutes often make provision as to the liability of insane persons,[5] and since this annotation treats statutes only insofar as they are involved in the cases herein and only as necessary to a discussion thereof, the attorney is advised

1. The annotations at 51 ALR 833 and 89 ALR 476 no longer need be consulted as to the subject matter of this annotation.

2. The annotation is concerned with mental illness, including temporary aberrations and temporary insanity. It is not concerned with physical illnesses such as epilepsy, nor with mere stupidity or excitability.

3. For cases considering the liability of an incompetent person for torts of others, see 41 Am Jur 2d, Incompetent Persons § 111, and also the annotation entitled "Liability of incompetent's estate for torts committed by guardian, committee, or trustee in managing estate," at 40 ALR2d 1103.

4. As to the liability of the guardian of an incompetent person for torts committed by the incompetent person, see 39 Am Jur 2d, Guardian and Ward § 188.

5. Such a statute was involved in Ellis v Fixico (1935) 174 Okla 116, 50 P2d 162, infra § 4.

FIGURE 2-R
AMERICAN LAW REPORTS ANNOTATED

Stop here, and determine which section is the most relevant one before consulting the discussion of this problem in Appendix A.

PROBLEM 2.12

Examine the "Table of Jurisdictions Represented" shown on the preceding page. In which sections of the annotation could you find New York cases?

Stop here, and determine which sections are most relevant before consulting the discussion of this problem in Appendix A.

PROBLEM 2.13

Examine section 1[a] dealing with the scope of the annotation shown on the preceding page. Where can a discussion of contributory negligence of the mentally ill be found?

Stop here, and determine which source is the most relevant one before consulting the discussion of this problem in Appendix A.

PROBLEM 2.14

Examine the first page of section 5(b) in the following figure.

(a) Does the annotation conclude that it is foreseeable that sudden and unforeseeable mental illness might be recognized as a defense to a negligence claim?

(b) What argument does the annotation make (in footnote 13) about § 283C of the *Restatement (Second) of Torts?*

49 ALR3d TORTS—INSANITY AS DEFENSE 199
49 ALR3d 189 § 5[b]

and prudent man would ordinarily give to his own vessel, the court noted, and what prudent man could do more than to care for his vessel until overcome by physical and mental exhaustion? Familiar legal maxims include those that the law intends what is agreeable to reason and does not suffer an absurdity, and that impossibility is an excuse in law and there is no obligation to perform impossible things. Applying those maxims to the case here, the court said, the fallacy of the reasoning by the trial court becomes apparent, and it should not be sustained.[9]

It appears that although there is much discussion of the law relative to the liability of insane persons for their own negligence in the Williams Cases, supra, the cases seem merely to involve an application of the reasonable man standard to a situation in which, without fault attributable to him, the events connected with the actor's line of duty were such as might render a reasonable man insane.[10]

[b] **Sudden insanity**

Sudden physical illness is generally recognized as a defense in tort cases,[11] particularly those involving automobiles.[12] It is foreseeable, therefore, that sudden and unforeseeable mental illness might likewise be recognized as a defense to a negligence charge.[13] The following cases have specifically considered the point.[14]

Thus, in Keller v Wonn (1955) 140 **W Va** 860, 87 SE2d 453, involving an accident which occurred when a driver lost control of his car upon suffering a massive cerebral hemorrhage, the court held that where the driver of a motor vehicle suddenly becomes physically or mentally incapacitated without warning, he cannot be held liable for any injury resulting from the operation of his vehicle while he is so incapacitated, but where a prima facie case of negligence has been established by the plaintiff, the burden is upon the defendant to show the sudden illness or attack, and to further show that the illness or attack was unanticipatable and unforeseen.

Recognizing that there were authorities which generally held that insanity is not a defense in tort cases except for intentional torts, the court in Breunig v American Family Ins. Co. (1970) 45 **Wis** 2d 536, 173 NW2d 619, 49 ALR3d 179, nonetheless concluded that the statement that insanity is no defense is too broad when applied to a negligence case where a driver is suddenly over-

9. This case is discussed at length in most of the law review articles cited in § 1[b], supra, and portions of the trial transcript are quoted in the discussion of the case in Hornblower, Insanity and the Law of Negligence (1905) 5 Columbia L Rev 278.

10. It should be noted that some commentators do not interpret Williams v Hays in this manner, but content themselves with criticizing the lucidity of reasoning of the court. The conclusion reached above was also reached in Harper and James, The Law of Torts § 16.8 note 19 (noting that the opinion was obscure).

11. American Law Institute Restatement of Torts 2d § 283C.

12. See, for example, Keller v Wonn (1955) 140 **W Va** 860, 87 SE2d 453, infra. And see generally 8 Am Jur 2d, Automobiles and Highway Traffic § 693.

13. Comment b to § 283C of the Restatement of Torts 2d contains indications in this direction. It is there stated that a transitory delirium falls under the rule of § 283C, concerning physical disability, and not under § 283B, involving mental deficiency and insanity, and therefore is to be regarded in the same way as is a heart attack, or as is temporary dizziness due to fever or nausea. Thus, a transitory delirium is to be treated as a circumstance to be taken into account in determining what the reasonable man would do in the same situation.

14. Cases which in fact involved sudden insanity, but in which no significance was attached by the court to the fact of its suddenness, are not included in this section.

FIGURE 2-S
AMERICAN LAW REPORTS ANNOTATED

Stop here, and answer the questions posed based on the page of the A.L.R. annotation reproduced on the preceding page before consulting the discussion of this problem in Appendix A.

3. SHEPARD'S CITATIONS

Another technique that is particularly useful at this stage involves the use of *Shepard's Citations*. One feature of *Shepard's Citations* is that it allows a researcher who has found a citation to a case that deals with the problem being researched to readily find cases in other jurisdictions that have cited that case.[13] This method of search will be discussed in a later chapter.

4. USING LEGAL PERIODICALS

Legal periodicals are another important means of developing your research. In the above research problem, several articles were cited. They could be consulted to find additional citations and analysis.

In addition, legal periodical indexes could be consulted under the subject headings of "Negligence," "Mental Illness," and "Insanity" to find other articles. The two principal indexes of legal periodical literature are (1) the *Index to Legal Periodicals* (which was established in 1908 and closely resembles the *Reader's Guide to Periodical Literature*) and (2) the *Current Law Index* (which was established in 1980).[14]

Section 2E. Updating and Concluding Your Research

Change is an inherent aspect in our legal system. Before research projects are completed, researchers must bring the research up to date. The failure to realize that a statute has been repealed or amended or that an important case has been overruled, qualified, or otherwise limited in a significant way may lead to embarrassment and faulty conclusions and liability for malpractice. Similarly, a recent decision or recently enacted statute may clarify an unsettled question of law and may dramatically change the conclusions and recommendations resulting from the prior research.

The updating process involves the use of *Shepard's Citations* (to determine, *inter alia*, whether a case has been overruled or a

---

[13] See id. at 300-08.

[14] See id. 162-67, 320-21.

statute repealed or amended), supplements, pocket parts, "advance sheets" (to find recent decisions), legislative services, and slip laws (to update statutory research).

Eventually, you will start to find the same cases and citations over and over again. This repetition should mark the end of your research, unless a prior time deadline has forced you to rely on your preliminary findings. You should be certain that you personally have read all the cases which you may cite in a subsequent product (such as a memorandum or appellate brief) and that the relevant sources have been "shepardized" or otherwise updated. Likewise, you should check to see that you have briefed those cases which you are likely to discuss in a subsequent written report of the research. As Vom Bauer points out, under this system you will develop confidence in your research and a firm conviction about the law.[15]

Toward the end of a major research project, you should consider adding special refinements in light of your particular purposes.

ILLUSTRATION 2.4

If the research is for an appellate brief, you may want to find quotations or illustrations for the brief. References to nonlegal literature may be helpful in supporting policy arguments or providing a broader perspective. You may also want to compile photocopies of the critical materials for an appendix.

---

[15]Vom Bauer, supra note 1, at 33.

Chapter 3

READING, ANALYZING, AND BRIEFING CASES FOR LEGAL RESEARCH AND WRITING PURPOSES

WHAT YOU WILL LEARN IN THIS CHAPTER

* The ten basic characteristics of judicial opinions
* How to master the facts, transactions, or occurrences giving rise to the litigation on which judicial opinions are based
* How to understand the procedural aspects of judicial opinions
* How to analyze the substance of judicial opinions
* A suggested approach for briefing judicial opinions for legal research and writing purposes

Section 3A. Basic Characteristics of Judicial Opinions

Good builders know the basic characteristics of their materials and how to work with them effectively. In legal research and writing, judicial opinions are one of the key building blocks. This chapter focuses on how to read, understand, and brief them effectively for research purposes.

Perhaps you can remember a time when you began to work with something and you quickly became enmeshed in all the details without ever seeing the "big picture." Or perhaps you can remember a time when you worked with something so much that you tended to forget about its basic nature and general characteristics. Either of these situations can happen to those who work with judicial opinions.

Because of this risk, it is useful to step back at times and consider the nature of judicial opinions from a broader perspective. The following are basic characteristics of judicial opinions that should be recognized and remembered.

JUDICIAL OPINIONS REFLECT THE PRINCIPAL ACTIVITIES OF COURTS IN THE LEGAL SYSTEM.

Courts review the validity of legislative enactments, interpret their meaning, and determine their application. They perform a similar function with respect to administrative and executive actions. Courts also develop and enforce the unwritten common law through their decisions and maintain the procedural and administrative integrity of the judicial system through their orders, rules, and decisions. It is one or more of these matters with which judicial opinions will be concerned.

UNLIKE LEGISLATURES, COURTS MUST WAIT FOR LITIGANTS TO PRESENT DISPUTES TO THEM FOR DECISION, AND THESE DISPUTES MUST BE REAL ONES.

Judicial opinions are based on *actual* controversies, not hypothetical situations that may or may not arise. Furthermore, the courts must wait for the litigants to present these controversies for decision.

EXCEPT IN LIMITED CIRCUMSTANCES, COURTS MUST DECIDE CASES WITHIN THE SCOPE OF THEIR SUBJECT-MATTER JURISDICTION.

Subject-matter jurisdiction (a court's authority to hear certain types of cases) is determined by constitutional and statutory provisions. Judges cannot avoid deciding cases within their jurisdiction because the issues are too controversial or difficult. Occasionally, however, judges will devote a judicial opinion to explaining why they are refusing to decide a matter. The most common reasons include mootness, ripeness, and political questions.

THE ANGLO-AMERICAN SYSTEM OF LITIGATION IS AN ADVERSARY ONE, AND JUDICIAL OPINIONS NECESSARILY REFLECT THE PARTIES' POSITIONS AND ARGUMENTS.

Courts frequently refer to the parties' contentions in the text of opinions, and sometimes reporters will summarize the parties' arguments. The parties' briefs often are available separately. Clearly, knowing what each party argued enhances one's understanding of the opinion. However, failure to distinguish between what a party has asserted and what the court has decided frequently confuses the reader of judicial opinions.

COURTS STATE THE REASONS FOR THEIR DECISIONS IN THEIR OPINIONS.

In their opinions courts usually state the reasons for their decisions. This practice forces a court to carefully consider its decision and to inform the parties why it decided the case the way it did. This practice also assists others in predicting how the court may rule in similar situations in the future. Thus, in reading judicial opinions, significant emphasis should be placed on the reasoning articulated by the court.

JUDGES STATE THE FACTS OF THE CASE IN THEIR OPINIONS.

Judicial opinions ordinarily state in detail the facts of the case. Such statements ordinarily go beyond those facts that might be viewed as strictly relevant to the stated bases for the decision. These detailed factual statements play an important role in the process of growth and change in the law.

WHEN LEGISLATION DOES NOT GOVERN A DISPUTE, COURTS WILL USE THE COMMON LAW TO RESOLVE THE MATTER.

The early English courts developed the common law by applying principles of justice, reason, and common sense to the particular situations presented for decision. The early English court reports, certain English statutes, and the texts of certain great English writers, such as Blackstone, Coke, and Bracton, were the sources of the American common law. Over time, American courts developed and modified this body of law received from England to meet American conditions and circumstances.

In judicial opinions applying the common law, the legal rule and the reasons given in support of that rule often are intertwined in such a way that it may be difficult to distinguish clearly between the rule and its justifications. This characteristic plays an important role in the subsequent interpretation of an opinion.

IN THEIR OPINIONS, COURTS ARTICULATE GENERAL RULES THAT COVER A CLASS OF DISPUTES OR SITUATIONS.

The courts usually articulate general rules that cover a *class* of disputes or situations in their opinions. In this way, judicial opinions are important sources of legal rules which order society and regulate human behavior. But remember that over time courts may find that they have stated a rule too broadly or too narrowly or that exceptions should displace the rule.

JUDICIAL DECISIONS NEED NOT BE UNANIMOUS.

Judges do not always agree. In deciding a case, the opinion of the majority of the court determines the outcome. Concurring and dissenting opinions may be filed. These opinions often are useful for understanding the rationale of the majority of the court.

JUDICIAL OPINIONS VARY IN STYLE, COMPLETENESS, ACCURACY, AND CLARITY.

Reading judicial opinions is like mining. Sometimes, the valuable ore or gems are lying right on the surface and can be picked up easily. Other times, they are buried in tons of slag, and it takes a long time before the miner sees the light at the end of the tunnel. Remember too that miners who carelessly speed ahead in their work and fail to do a good job sometimes get crushed in the resulting cave-in or get blown away in an unexpected explosion. In your research, take the time to find the gems.

Section 3B. Mastering the Facts, Transactions, and Occurrences Reported in Judicial Opinions

The task that law students and lawyers face in reading judicial opinions can be divided into three separate elements: (1) mastering the facts, transactions, or occurrences giving rise to the litigation; (2) understanding the procedural aspects of the decision; and (3) analyzing the substance of the case (the parties' contentions and the court's holding and reasoning). This section and the two that follow consider these elements.

In many instances, such as criminal cases (other than some white-collar crimes), tort and insurance litigation, and domestic-relations disputes, the facts, transactions, or occurrences involved in the lawsuit will be apparent. In other situations, however, you may be confused about the events or circumstances of the litigation. What should you do to master the facts, transactions, or occurrences involved in the case? The first step in mastering the facts and transactions is to organize your thinking.

MASTERING THE FACTS, TRANSACTIONS, AND OCCURRENCES REPORTED IN JUDICIAL OPINIONS

1. Who were the parties involved in the lawsuit? Who commenced the action? Against whom was it brought?
2. What was the basic legal nature of the action? (e.g., trespass to land)
3. What were the basic facts? (e.g., the tenant refused to vacate the premises when the lease expired)
4. What relief or remedy was sought? (e.g., to enjoin repeated trespasses)

If the facts, transactions, or occurrences are still unclear after trying to answer these questions, the next step is to determine the *source* of the problem. Does the problem lie with the opinion or with you?

As previously mentioned, judicial opinions vary in their completeness, accuracy, and style. Thus, ***the opinion may be written in an unclear or incomplete manner.*** If that is the problem, one approach is to consult the statements of facts in the parties' briefs, the editor's case synopsis, or the official syllabus. Another approach is to examine the trial court's opinion, which will often contain a more detailed statement of the facts or events.

If these approaches do not solve the problem, you may be forced (1) to make assumptions or (2) to recognize simply that an ambiguity exists. In either case, this uncertainty may diminish the usefulness of the opinion for legal writing purposes. Another source of the problem may be that ***you, as the reader, may be so unfamiliar with the subject of the dispute, the underlying business transaction, or the purpose of the litigation that it is hard for you***

to comprehend the events or circumstances involved--even though those things might be quite clear to those who are familiar with such matters.

When you are unfamiliar with the type of dispute or underlying business transaction, the best approach is to consult background references. A legal dictionary is probably the single most valuable tool for this purpose. Other useful sources include articles in law reviews, general legal encyclopedias, specialized encyclopedias, looseleaf services, and trial practice materials.

ILLUSTRATION 3.1

For example, you might consult a general legal encyclopedia, such as *Corpus Juris Secundum*, a specialized encyclopedia, such as *Lawyer's Medical Cyclopedia of Personal Injuries and Allied Specialties*, or trial practice materials, such as *American Jurisprudence Trials*. If the case involved business or corporate law, you might consult a straightforward text discussing sole busniess organizations[1] or other aspects of corporate finance.[2]

IN SUM, IT IS IMPORTANT TO MASTER THE FACTS, TRANSACTIONS, OR OCCURRENCES INVOLVED IN AN OPINION. OFTEN SUCH A MASTERY CAN BE ACHIEVED THROUGH CAREFUL READING OF THE OPINION. SOMETIMES, HOWEVER, YOU WILL HAVE TO GO OUTSIDE THE OPINION. WHERE YOU LOOK DEPENDS ON THE SOURCE OF THE PROBLEM--THE AMBIGUITY OR INCOMPLETENESS OF THE OPINION ITSELF OR YOUR OWN LACK OF BACKGROUND KNOWLEDGE.

Read the following excerpts from a 1962 Wisconsin judicial opinion. Then answer the questions concerning the facts and occurrences involved. Notes and dictionary references to *Black's Law Dictionary*[3] and *Ballentine's Law Dictionary*[4] have been added to assist you in your reading.

---

[1]See, e.g., W. Kline, Business Organization and Finance (1980) (proprietorships, partnerships, corporations, basic corporate investment devices, valuation, and financial strategy).

[2]See, e.g., B. Manning, A Concise Textbook on Legal Capital (2d ed. 1981) (corporate capital accounts, par and no par stock, stated capital, distributions to shareholders, asset write-downs or write-ups, and promoters' liability).

[3]Black's Law Dictionary (5th ed. 1979) (hereinafter Black's).

[4]Ballentine's Law Dictionary (3d ed. 1969) (hereinafter Ballentine's).

NORTHWESTERN REPORTER SECOND
WEST PUBLISHING COMPANY
COPYRIGHT 1963

WEST KEY NUMBER SYSTEM

18 Wis.2d 91

Sharon THEISEN, an infant, by Fred Theisen, her guardian, et al., Plaintiffs-Respondents,

v.

MILWAUKEE AUTOMOBILE MUTUAL INSURANCE COMPANY, a corporation, Defendant-Appellant.

Supreme Court of Wisconsin.

Nov. 27, 1962.

Rehearing Denied Feb. 5, 1963.

BALLENTINE'S:

infant. In ordinary usage, a child of a tender and helpless age. In law, a person who has not reached the age of majority, usually 21 years, at which the law recognizes a general contractual capacity. 27 Am Jlst Inf § 2.

In some states females become of age at the end of the eighteenth year and the statutes of some states make all persons adults upon their marriage. See 27 Am Jlst Inf § 5.

See **emancipation of minor; legal capacity; majority; natural infancy.**

BLACK'S:

Guardian. A person lawfully invested with the power, and charged with the duty, of taking care of the person and managing the property and rights of another person, who, for defect of age, understanding, or self-control, is considered incapable of administering his own affairs. One who legally has the care and management of the person, or the estate, or both, of a child during its minority.

When you are reading a case, you should first note its "style" (the heading by which it is identified). The style of this case is *Theisen v. Milwaukee Automobile Mutual Insurance Co.*

This case has been reprinted from the *Northwestern Reporter Second*, published by the West Publishing Company. Its citation (not shown) is 118 N.W.2d 140. Above the designation of the parties is the official citation of the case, "18 Wis. 2d 91." This official citation is referred to as the "parallel citation" because the opinion is published in both the *North Western Reporter Second* and *Wisconsin Reports Second*. This case would be cited: *Theisen v. Milwaukee Automobile Mutual Insurance Co.*, 18 Wis. 2d 91, 118 N.W.2d 140 (1962). Note that the official citation (when there is one) is always listed first.

Just below the designation of the parties is the date of the decision and the name of the court. Also noted is that a request for a rehearing (a reconsideration of the issues by the same court) was denied on February 5, 1963.

Sometimes, a rehearing will be granted when the party requesting it points out that some matter was overlooked or an important ambiguity in the opinion of the court should be corrected. More often, rehearings are granted when the case has been heard by only a part or division (usually three judges) of an entire court (usually seven or nine judges). Such a rehearing is called a rehearing en banc. In federal courts of appeals, such rehearings "will not be ordered except (1) when consideration by the full court is necessary to secure or maintain uniformity of its decisions, or (2) when the proceeding involves a question of exceptional importance."[5]

In West's reporters, a brief synopsis of the case prepared by West's editors follows the date.

> Guest-host action. The Circuit Court for Buffalo County, Robert G. Varnum, Circuit Judge, rendered judgment for plaintiffs, and defendant appealed. The Supreme Court, Hallows, J., held that falling asleep at wheel of automobile is negligence as a matter of law, and no facts can exist which will excuse such negligence.
>
> Judgment reversed and new trial granted on questions of negligence only.

---

[5] Fed. R. App. P. 35(a).

BLACK'S:

Guest. A person receiving lodging for pay at inn, motel, or hotel on general undertaking of keeper thereof. A traveler who lodges with the consent of the keeper or owner.

Guest is a person who is received and entertained at one's home, club, etc., and who is not a regular member. Stadelmann v. Glen Falls Ins. Co. of Glen Falls, 5 Mich.App. 536, 147 N.W.2d 460, 463.

A "guest" in an automobile is one who takes ride in automobile driven by another person, merely for his own pleasure or on his own business, and without making any return or conferring any benefit on automobile driver. Guest is used to denote one whom owner or possessor of vehicle invites or permits to ride with him as gratuity, without any financial return except such slight benefits as are customarily extended as part of ordinary courtesies of road. Rothwell v. Transmeier, 206 Kan. 199, 477 P.2d 960, 963, 966. See **Guest statute.**

Business guest. See **Business.**

One advantage of reading cases in reporters rather than casebooks is that the reader has the benefit of editorial features. One important feature is West's numbered headnotes, classified by West's topics and key numbers. These headnotes summarize the points of law discussed in the text of the opinion. Below, all but the first have been omitted.

1. Automobiles 🔑157

Falling asleep at wheel of automobile is negligence as a matter of law, and no facts can exist which will excuse such negligence; overruling earlier cases.

BALLENTINE'S:

negligence as a matter of law. An undisputed fact or facts, so conclusive of negligence in conduct or omission in violation of a standard of care which is clear in its requirements and in its application to the case, that there is no question to be submitted to the jury and the court must declare that negligence is established. 38 Am J1st Negl § 344.

See **negligence per se.**

After the headnotes, West prints the syllabus that appears in the official reporter (if any). The official syllabus often provides greater factual detail than West's synopsis. Sometimes, it will recount the court's holdings on the issues.

> This guest-host action was brought by 17-year-old Sharon Theisen and her father Fred Theisen to recover damages for personal injuries sustained while Sharon Theisen was a guest in an automobile driven by Louis Shepherd who was insured by the defendant Milwaukee Automobile Mutual Insurance Company. The accident occurred sometime after 3:00 a. m. on November 17th, 1960, when the automobile left Highway 95 approximately three miles west of Arcadia, Wisconsin, and collided with a large tree stump located 10 feet north of the edge of the blacktop pavement. The plaintiff received injuries including a broken jaw and leg; Shepherd was killed.
>
> The jury found Shepherd causally negligent in respect to management and control and apportioned 95% of the negligence to him. Sharon Theisen was found negligent in entering and riding in the car driven by Shepherd but such negligence was not causal. The jury also found Sharon Theisen causally negligent as to lookout and apportioned 5% of the total negligence to her. Damages were assessed for both plaintiffs and judgment entered on the verdict. The defendant appeals.

BLACK'S: **(APPORTIONMENT)**

> *Liability.* Legal responsibility of parties to a transaction or tort may be distributed or apportioned among them by statute or by agreement. See **Comparative negligence; Contribution.**

***BLACK'S* (CROSS-REFERENCE FROM APPORTIONMENT/Liability):**

> **Comparative negligence.** Under comparative negligence statutes or doctrines, negligence is measured in terms of percentage, and any damages allowed shall be diminished in proportion to amount of negligence attributable to the person for whose injury, damage or death recovery is sought. Many states have replaced contributory negligence acts or doctrines with comparative negligence. Where negligence by both parties is concurrent and contributes to injury, recovery is not barred under such doctrine, but plaintiff's damages are diminished proportionately, provided his fault is less than defendant's, and that, by exercise of ordinary care, he could not have avoided consequences of defendant's negligence after it was or should have been apparent.

BALLENTINE'S:

> **comparative negligence.** The negligence of the defendant in an action to recover damages for negligence as compared with that of the plaintiff, the comparison being made for the purpose of applying the rule of admiralty, which has been adopted by statute for negligence cases generally in some jurisdictions, that the more gross the negligence of the defendant appears, the less degree of care is required of the plaintiff to permit a recovery by him; that the negligence of the plaintiff operates, not to relieve the defendant entirely from liability, but merely to diminish the damages recoverable. 38 Am J1st Negl §§ 231-233.

Immediately following the syllabus from the official report are the names of the attorneys who appeared in the action on both sides of the lawsuit (shown on the following page).

The text of the opinion begins immediately after the author of the opinion (Justice Hallows) is identified. Justice Hallows' opinion begins with a statement of the facts.

Hale, Skemp, Hanson, Schnurrer & Skemp, La Crosse, for appellant.

Fugina, Kostner & Ward, Arcadia, for respondent.

HALLOWS, Justice.

This is a case of a sleeping driver. On the evening of November 16th, 1960, the plaintiff and Shepherd participated in the Arcadia high school senior class play in which Shepherd had the leading role. The play was over about 10:15. The members of the cast and those associated with the production, numbering in all about 30, were invited to a party at the home of Alfred Service, father of one of the members of the cast. Service lived about seven miles west of Arcadia on Highway 95. After the play, the young folks went to a cafe in Arcadia, then to a dancehall and danced, and about midnight started for the Service home. Upon arriving there, the girls prepared a lunch. The party then went on a hayride for about an hour, and upon returning to the house, played the piano, danced and talked. Shepherd brought a fifth of liquor to the house. At the party, beer or sloe gin, or both, were consumed, but there is no evidence anyone became intoxicated. Some of the girls testified the liquor could not be felt or not very much, or made them tired or sleepy or drowsy. The only evidence concerning Shepherd's drinking is by one of the girls who said she saw him with a drink in his hand.

About 3:00 a. m. the party broke up and five girls, including the plaintiff, got into Shepherd's car for the ride home. The plaintiff sat in the rear left seat. These girls testified they were tired and one stated the car was warm which just naturally made them drowsy. About four miles from the Service home the Shepherd car, as it was traveling east toward Ar-

> cadia on a straight level stretch of Highway 95, gradually veered from its right lane to the left lane and onto the shoulder of the road. At this time, at least all the girls were asleep or dozing. When the car left the pavement, one of the girls in the front seat woke up and shouted, "Louis, lookout" but there was no reaction; she thought Louis was asleep. Another girl hollered "Louie" but Shepherd did not move. The car proceeded on its course 270 feet until it hit a large tree stump on the north side of the road about 10 feet from the edge of the blacktop.

To test your comprehension of the facts, transactions, and occurrences involved in the above opinion, answer the following questions (based on the portion of the opinion that you have read so far).

PROBLEM 3.1

Who of the following were parties to the lawsuit?

(a) Sharon Theisen (Plaintiff)

(b) Estate of Louis Shepard (Defendant)

(c) Fred Theisen (Plaintiff)

(d) Milwaukee Automobile Mutual Insurance Co. (Defendant)

Stop here, and choose your answer or answers before consulting the discussion of this problem in Appendix A.

PROBLEM 3.2

Which *one* of the following descriptions of the basic legal nature of the action is the *most* accurate?

(a) Comparative negligence action

(b) Guest-host action for breach of contract to carry a passenger safely

(c) Negligent homicide action

(d) The case of the sleeping driver

Stop here, and choose your answer before consulting the discussion of this problem in Appendix A.

PROBLEM 3.3

Which *one* of the following descriptions *most* accurately states the basic facts involved in the action?

(a) Louis Shepard brought a fifth of liquor to a cast party after the senior class play. He consumed part of it, and beer was also served at the party. Apparently influenced by the consumption of this alcohol, Shepard fell asleep at the wheel of the car he was driving on the way home from the party. Sharon Theisen, a minor who was a guest passenger sleeping in the rear seat of the car, was injured when the car struck a large tree stump. Shepard, who was insured by the defendant Milwaukee Automobile Mutual Insurance Company, was killed.

(b) Louis Shepherd, a participant in the senior class play, attended a party at the home of one of the members of the cast. Some liquor was served at the party, but there was no evidence that anyone became intoxicated. About 3:00 a.m. the party broke up and five girls, including the plaintiff Sharon Theisen, got into Shepherd's car for the ride home. About four miles from the party, Shepherd fell asleep at the wheel. The car left the road and hit a tree. Sharon Theisen, who at the time of the accident was sleeping in the rear seat of the car, was injured. Shepard, who was insured by the defendant Milwaukee Automobile Mutual Insurance Company, was killed.

Stop here, and choose your answer before consulting the discussion of this problem in Appendix A.

PROBLEM 3.4

Which of the following answers indicates the relief sought by the plaintiff in this action?

(a) Sequestration of the insurance company's assets to compensate the plaintiff for her injuries

(b) Damages

(c) Punitive damages

(d) Death penalty for Shepard

Stop here, and choose your answer or answers before consulting the discussion of this problem in Appendix A.

Section 3C. Understanding the Procedural Aspects of Appellate Decisions

Another important aspect of effective reading of judicial opinions is understanding the procedural aspects of appellate decisions. Reading judicial opinions without a basic understanding of trial and appellate procedure is like setting off on a journey without knowing the rules of the road and what the road signs mean. Without this knowledge, a traveler may eventually end up at the proper destination but only after making wrong turns, wasting time, and feeling lost.

With regard to the procedural aspects of judicial opinions, you should get your thinking organized by trying to answer the following questions:

UNDERSTANDING THE PROCEDURAL ASPECTS OF APPELLATE DECISIONS

1. In what lower court or courts did the proceedings take place?
2. In what court was review sought?
3. Who won in the trial court?
4. What was the appellate court's disposition of the action?

Ordinarily, the answers to these questions will be readily apparent when you read an opinion. Review of two areas of knowledge necessary for the efficient reading of judicial opinions at this point will be useful: (1) the methods of obtaining appellate review and (2) the orders or other actions resulting from appellate review.

1. METHODS OF OBTAINING REVIEW

A fundamental principle underlying appellate review is that one (or more) of the parties ordinarily must initiate appellate review of a trial court decision.

ILLUSTRATION 3.2

Under Rule 3 of the Federal Rules of Appellate Procedure, an appeal from a federal district court decision is initiated by one of the parties filing a notice of appeal with the clerk of the district court.

A record on appeal then will be prepared. The record consists of the original papers and exhibits filed in the district court, the transcript of proceedings, if any, and a certified copy of the docket entries. Ordinarily, the parties will then file briefs and the appellate court will hear the attorneys' oral arguments of the case. Special rules apply for the review of interlocutory (non-final) decisions, such as preliminary injunctions.

Procedures for initiating review vary in state courts, but they generally follow the same basic steps as appellate review in the federal courts. One variation, however, is that in some states the parties first must file with the trial court a "bill of exceptions" in which their objections to a trial judge's rulings or jury instructions are stated for the record.

The specific methods of obtaining appellate review can be divided into four basic categories: (a) appeals as a matter of right; (b) discretionary review; (c) certification; and (d) extraordinary writs.

(a) Appeals as a Matter of Right

Some appeals are as a matter of right. The dividing line between appeals as a matter of right and those within a court's discretion generally is set by statute. The first level of appeal ordinarily will be of right.

ILLUSTRATION 3.3

Appeal from the final decision of a federal district court to a federal court of appeals is a matter of right.

(b) Discretionary Review

Review of some decisions is at the discretion of the appellate court. In such instances, a party first must ordinarily file a petition, usually called a petition for a writ of certiorari. In this petition, the party seeking review must convince the court that it should hear the appeal. After a petition has been filed, the other party will ordinarily file a brief in opposition.

Today, almost all of the cases heard by the United States Supreme Court are a result of discretionary review. Detailed requirements for timing and contents of a petition filed in the Supreme Court are contained in Supreme Court Rules. Several states that have intermediate appellate courts also use a system of discretionary review as a means of determining which cases will reach the highest courts of those states. These systems generally follow the same pattern as that described for the United States Supreme Court.

(c) Certification

Another method of review is certification of a question *before* decision.

ILLUSTRATION 3.4

A federal court of appeals may certify to the United States Supreme Court "any question of law in any civil or criminal case as to which instructions are desired."[6] Certification is one exception to the earlier statement that appellate review is initiated by the litigants. In this instance, a federal court of appeals (that is in doubt and desires instructions) may certify a question to the Supreme Court. The Supreme Court has discretion to answer. The use of this procedure is rare. A few states also provide for certification prior to a decision by an intermediate appellate court.

More common is the certification of an interlocutory appeal by a federal district court judge under § 1292(b) of Title 28. This section permits such appeals when the trial judge certifies that the matter "involves a controlling question of law as to which there is a substantial ground for difference of opinion and that an immediate appeal from the order may materially advance the ultimate termination of the litigation."[7]

The federal court of appeals has discretion to review the question. Although they deviate in some ways, a number of states have similar methods of certification for review of interlocutory orders not otherwise appealable.

Certification of questions by courts of *other* jurisdictions to state supreme courts is also available when a state has authorized this type of review. About half of the states permit certification from a federal court to their respective state supreme courts. A few permit appellate courts of other states to do so also. This method of determining state law is particularly useful for the federal courts as a means of fulfilling their obligation under the Rules of Decision Act to apply state substantive law in diversity cases.

(d) Extraordinary Writs

A petition for an extraordinary writ technically commences an original action in the appellate court. Such a petition, however, often involves objections arising out of lower court proceedings.

---

[6] 28 U.S.C.A. § 1254(3) (West Supp. 1989).

[7] 28 U.S.C.A. § 1292(b) (West Supp. 1989).

ILLUSTRATION 3.5

One of the principal extraordinary writs is ***mandamus***, which traditionally has been issued in response to abuses of judicial power. When judges refuse to take some action that they are required to take or they take some action that they are not empowered to take, a writ of mandamus may be proper.

Another extraordinary writ that may be used to obtain "review" of judicial proceedings is ***prohibition***, which traditionally has been issued by a superior court to prevent an inferior court from usurping matters not within its jurisdiction. It is directed to the judge and the parties involved in the action in the inferior court.

Still another extraordinary writ is ***habeas corpus***, which primarily is used to test the legality of a prisoner's detention. Mandamus, habeas corpus, and other extraordinary writs such as ***quo warranto*** (traditionally used to determine who has title to a public office) may be directed to public officers other than judges, and original jurisdiction over these actions may be vested in a trial court.[8]

The power of federal courts to issue these extraordinary writs is based upon their inherent power and the "all writs" authority established by § 1651 of Title 28. Section 1651 provides that "[t]he Supreme Court and all lower courts established by Congress may issue all writs necessary or appropriate in aid of their respective jurisdictions and agreeable to the usages and principles of law."[9] These writs generally are available only in extraordinary circumstances, principally when all other judicial remedies have failed or are considered to be inadequate.

2. ORDERS AND OTHER ACTIONS RESULTING FROM APPELLATE REVIEW

The goal of the party who is bringing an appeal is ordinarily ***reversal*** (which is one method for the appellate court to annul the inferior court's judgment). A reversal, however, may not end the controversy, and further proceedings in a lower tribunal often may be necessary. Thus, a case may be ***remanded*** with a general instruction for "further proceedings consistent with this opinion" or with specific instructions. Sometimes the appellate court may use the term "vacated" or "set aside" instead of "reversed."

---

[8] See, e.g., 28 U.S.C.A. § 1361 (West 1982) (jurisdiction vested in federal district court for actions in the nature of mandamus to compel an officer or federal employee to perform a duty owed to the plaintiff).

[9] 28 U.S.C.A. § 1651 (West 1966).

The prevailing party below ordinarily argues for an ***affirmance*** of the lower court decision by the appellate court.[10] If the judgment, decree, or order is affirmed, it is declared valid and correct. In some instances, however, the goal of the prevailing party will be a ***denial***.

ILLUSTRATION 3.6

The prevailing party may ask the appellate court to enter an order denying a petition for a writ of certiorari.

Rather than affirming or reversing a judgment, the appellate court may ***modify*** a judgment in order to limit, clarify, or otherwise change it. Likewise, injunctions or other orders may be modified on appeal. Other actions that may result from appellate court decisions include reinstatement of pleadings or proceedings, imposition of sanctions, dismissal of an appeal for untimeliness or mootness, and quashing of a frivolous, vexatious, or dilatory appeal.

To test your comprehension of the procedural aspects of the *Theisen* case reproduced in the preceding section, answer the following questions. Refer to the opinion to refresh your memory as necessary.

PROBLEM 3.5

In what lower court or courts did the proceedings take place?

(a) Wisconsin Circuit Court

(b) Supreme Court of Wisconsin

(c) Wisconsin County Court

(d) Wisconsin Compensation Court

Stop here, and choose the correct answer or answers before consulting the discussion of this problem in Appendix A.

PROBLEM 3.6

In what court was review sought?

(a) Wisconsin Court of Appeals

(b) Supreme Court of Wisconsin

---

[10] Prevailing parties also may appeal or cross-appeal from the judgment below if they are dissatisfied with the judgment in some way.

(c) United States Supreme Court

(d) Wisconsin Appellate Court of Compensation

Stop here, and choose the correct answer or answers before consulting the discussion of this problem in Appendix A.

PROBLEM 3.7

Who won in the trial court?

(a) Sharon Theisen/Fred Theisen

(b) Louis Shepard

(c) Estate of Louis Shepard

(d) Milwaukee Automobile Mutual Insurance Co.

Stop here, and choose the correct answer or answers before consulting the discussion of this problem in Appendix A.

PROBLEM 3.8

The defendant sought review by what means?

(a) Certiorari

(b) Appeal

(c) Certification

(d) Extraordinary writ

Stop here, and choose the correct answer or answers before consulting the discussion of this problem in Appendix A.

PROBLEM 3.9

What was the appellate court's disposition of the action?

(a) Affirmed

(b) Reversed and judgment entered for the defendant

(c) Reversed and new trial granted on questions of negligence only

(d) Reversed and new trial granted to determine the amount of the plaintiff's damages

Stop here, and choose the correct answer or answers before consulting the discussion of this problem in Appendix A.

Section 3D. Reading Judicial Opinions for Substance

Ordinarily, the principal purpose of reading a judicial opinion is for "substance." In other words, you usually will be extracting a "proposition" from the opinion.

ILLUSTRATION 3.7

You may want to cite the opinion as a precedent for a proposition of law:

> Falling asleep at the wheel of an automobile is negligence as a matter of law. Theisen v. Milwaukee Auto. Mut. Ins. Co., 18 Wis. 2d 91, 98-99, 118 N.W.2d 140, 144 (1962).

Or you may to want to cite the opinion as "authority" for a broader proposition of law:

> In Theisen, the court recognized that if (1) a person should have reasonably anticipated a physical disability or loss of consciousness and (2) that person is physically able to avoid a dangerous situation that requires due care but fails to do so, then such action is negligence as a matter of law. Theisen v. Milwaukee Auto. Mut. Ins. Co., 18 Wis. 2d 91, 99, 118 N.W.2d 140, 144 (1962).

To organize your thinking about extracting matters of substance such as these from an opinion, you should focus on the following questions when you read an opinion:

READING JUDICIAL OPINIONS FOR SUBSTANCE

1. What specific rulings or actions were claimed to be erroneous?
2. What were the parties' contentions about these alleged errors?
3. What standard of review did the appellate court use?
4. What did the court decide about each of the parties' contentions?
5. What reasons did the court give?
6. What general rules or legal principles did the court announce or apply?

The first question (concerning allegedly erroneous rulings or actions) and the third question (concerning the standards of review) require some background. The first two subparts of this section discuss these two topics. Then you will be asked to read the *Theisen* opinion for substance.

1. TYPES OF ERRORS REVIEWED

A fundamental principle underlying appellate review is that the appellate court will be focusing on errors committed below, ordinarily rulings by the court.

ILLUSTRATION 3.8

If the judge granted a motion for a directed verdict, the party against whom it was granted will be claiming on appeal that the judge erred in granting the motion.

(a) Errors in Granting or Denying Motions

During litigation the principal means of requesting the court to rule on a matter is by *motion* (which is simply an application to the court for an order).

ILLUSTRATION 3.9

Such motions may request a dismissal of the action by attacking the sufficiency of the pleadings or the court's jurisdiction over the subject matter or over the person (personal jurisdiction). They may request entry of judgment in a party's favor (judgment on the pleadings, summary judgment, or judgment notwithstanding the verdict). They may request that a new trial be granted or a default be set aside. They may request that a subpoena be quashed or that discovery be ordered.

Allegedly erroneous rulings on such motions are a frequent basis for appeals.

(b) Errors in Evidentiary Rulings

During the course of a trial a party may object to evidence offered by the opposing party.

ILLUSTRATION 3.10

Under the Federal Rules of Evidence, a party may object that the evidence is irrelevant (Rule 402), the person is incompetent to be a witness (Rule 601), the answer to a question is hearsay (Rule 802), or an expert is not properly qualified to state an opinion (Rule 702). In each instance, the trial judge's ruling on the evidentiary objection may give rise to error.

(c) Errors in Instructing the Jury

Before the jury retires to deliberate, the judge will instruct the jury. These instructions summarize the applicable law and provide information on weighing the evidence and viewing the credibility of the witnesses. Attorneys on either side of the lawsuit may submit proposed instructions, but it is the ultimate responsibility of the judge to prepare proper jury instructions. In federal district courts, if they want to assign the giving or the failure to give an instruction as an error, the parties must object before the jury retires.

(d) Errors in Review by Inferior Appellate Courts

In addition to reviewing errors committed by trial courts, appellate courts also consider errors committed by inferior appellate courts. Generally, these errors will relate to (1) the use of the wrong standard of review or (2) the erroneous statement or application of substantive law by the inferior appellate court.

2. STANDARDS OF REVIEW

Another important aspect of understanding appellate court opinions is the recognition of the standard of review used by the reviewing court.

(a) De Novo Review

Sometimes, a trial de novo (anew) is held before the appellate court, and the evidence is presented again as if the suit originally had been filed in the appellate court. Appeals from courts of limited jurisdiction (e.g., justices of the peace) frequently are handled in this manner. Another kind of de novo review is based upon the appellate court's examination of the entire record made below and then forming its own opinion about the facts.

Generally speaking, appellate courts in these situations give no attention to the trial court's findings and judgment except to the extent they may be helpful in reasoning.

(b) Abuse of Discretion

Throughout a lawsuit the trial judge has varying degrees of discretion in ruling on particular motions, offers of evidence, and other matters.

ILLUSTRATION 3.11

The trial court has a certain degree of discretion concerning the scope of discovery, the order of presentation of evidence at trial, the propriety of severing or consolidating cases for trial, and a host of other matters.

In reviewing a trial judge's rulings, the appellate court will give the trial court considerable leeway. Thus, although it may disagree with the trial judge's exercise of discretion, the appellate court will not intervene unless it finds that the judge's ruling(s) or action(s) were clearly improper.

(c) Review of Factual Determinations

Appellate court review of a jury's determinations of fact is limited. If the jury might have reasonably found as it did, its factual determinations will not be set aside. This standard of review is, in effect, the same test as that for a directed verdict, but with the further limitation that some insight will be accorded to the trial court judge's conclusion as to whether the jury verdict should stand. Thus, in most instances, the appellate court will be forced to accept the jury's factual determinations.

Although the exact statement of the standard varies from jurisdiction to jurisdiction, review of factual findings made by a judge sitting without a jury likewise will be limited. In civil litigation in the federal system, Rule 52 of the Federal Rules of Civil Procedure provides that "[f]indings of fact shall not be set aside unless clearly erroneous, and due regard shall be given to the opportunity of the trial court to judge the credibility of the witnesses."[11]

(d) Conclusions of Law

Trial judges ordinarily make formal conclusions of law in two situations. First, under the Federal Rules of Civil Procedure, they must do so when they try a civil action without a jury. Rule 52 requires the court to find the facts specially and to state separately its conclusions of law thereon. Second, judges must make formal conclusions of law when they grant or refuse interlocutory injunctions.

The "clearly erroneous" standard of review, discussed in the preceding subsection, does not apply to the federal district court's conclusions of law. The appellate court is free to form its own view of the law and is not precluded in any degree by the trial court's view. You should be aware that the dividing line between

---

[11] Fed. R. Civ. P. 52(a).

fact and law is not always clear. In cases of a mixed question of law and fact, the outcome may depend on the predominance of one over the other.[12]

(e) Jury Instructions

When an appellate court reviews jury instructions given by a trial court, the function of the appellate court is to satisfy itself that the instructions show no tendency to confuse or mislead the jury with respect to the applicable principles of law. The jury instructions will be considered as a whole in determining whether a prejudicial error has been committed.

(f) Harmless Error

Not all errors committed by the trial court will be considered prejudicial. In considering various errors on appeal, a federal appellate court is bound by section 2111 of Title 28: "On the hearing of any appeal or writ of certiorari in any case, the court shall give judgment after an examination of the record without regard to errors or defects which do not affect the substantial rights of the parties."[13] This concept of distinguishing between harmful and harmless errors applies at the trial level as well.[14]

3. READING THE *THEISEN* OPINION FOR SUBSTANCE

The *Theisen* opinion discusses several fundamental concepts that are useful in reading any judicial opinion: causes of action, a prima facie case, inferences, burden of proof, prima facie evidence, direct and circumstantial evidence, offers of proof, presumptions, and erroneous jury instructions.

The opinion also provides an opportunity to examine several basic substantive concepts in tort law: negligence, negligence as a matter of law, contributory negligence, assumption of risk, implied assumption of risk, causation, comparative negligence, and direct actions.

These concepts are among the most difficult that you will encounter in reading judicial opinions.

---

[12] See, e.g., Backar v. Western States Producing Co., 547 F.2d 876, 884 (5th Cir. 1977) (clearly erroneous standard applied because factual questions and credibility choices in the finding predominated over the legal aspects).

[13] 28 U.S.C.A. § 2111 (West 1982).

[14] See Fed. R. Civ. P. 61; Fed. R. Crim. P. 52; Fed. R. Evid. 103.

THIS SECTION DEMONSTRATES THAT BY READING AND BY CONSULTING APPROPRIATE SOURCES (SUCH AS LEGAL DICTIONARIES, ENCYCLOPEDIAS, AND TREATISES), EVEN THE MOST DIFFICULT LEGAL CONCEPTS CAN BE MASTERED.

Continue reading the *Theisen* opinion. Answer the problems based on the text of the opinion and the accompanying excerpts.

PROBLEM 3.10

> [1] The defendant contends Shepherd's going to sleep was an unknown physical impairment which caused him to lose control of the car and, consequently, could not constitute negligence. The gist of the argument is Shepherd went to sleep unknowingly from physical exhaustion and the case should be governed by the principles applicable to sudden unforeseen physical disability over which a driver has no control, such as being the victim of a heart attack, epileptic seizure, or other loss of consciousness which is sudden and unforeseen. Arguendo, it may be stated acts done while one is asleep are not voluntary and in and of themselves do not constitute negligence. Bushnell v. Bushnell (1925), 103 Conn. 583, 131 A. 432, 44 A.L.R. 785. See also Steele v. Lackey (1935), 107 Vt. 192, 177 A. 309; Kaplan v. Kaplan (1931), 213 Iowa 646, 239 N.W. 682 [recklessness]. The basis, however, for liability of the sleeping driver is his negligence in falling asleep.

BLACK'S:

> **Arguendo** /àrgyuwéndow/. In arguing; in the course of the argument. A statement or observation made by a judge as a matter of argument or hypothetical illustration, is said to be made *arguendo*, or in the abbreviated form, *arg*.

BLACK'S:

Negligence. The omission to do something which a reasonable man, guided by those ordinary considerations which ordinarily regulate human affairs, would do, or the doing of something which a reasonable and prudent man would not do.

Negligence is the failure to use such care as a reasonably prudent and careful person would use under similar circumstances; it is the doing of some act which a person of ordinary prudence would not have done under similar circumstances or failure to do what a person of ordinary prudence would have done under similar circumstances. Amoco Chemical Corp. v. Hill, Del.Super., 318 A.2d 614, 617. Conduct which falls below the standard established by law for the protection of others against unreasonable risk of harm; it is a departure from the conduct expectable of a reasonably prudent person under like circumstances. Pence v. Ketchum, La., 326 So.2d 831, 836.

The term refers only to that legal delinquency which results whenever a man fails to exhibit the care which he ought to exhibit, whether it be slight, ordinary, or great. It is characterized chiefly by inadvertence, thoughtlessness, inattention, and the like, while "wantonness" or "recklessness" is characterized by willfulness. The law of negligence is founded on reasonable conduct or reasonable care under all circumstances of particular case. Doctrine of negligence rests on duty of every person to exercise due care in his conduct toward others from which injury may result.

See also Actionable negligence; Active negligence; Cause; Comparative negligence; Concurrent negligence; Fault; Imputed negligence; Invitation; Joint negligence; Laches; Legal negligence; Palsgraph doctrine; Parental liability; Product liability; Reasonable man doctrine; Reckless; Simple negligence; Standard of care; Strict liability; Supervening negligence.

Which of the following statements *best* explains the defendant's argument addressed by the court in the preceding paragraph of the opinion?

(a) Acts done while a person is asleep cannot constitute negligence. Because Shepard hit the tree while he was asleep, he could not have been negligent (and thus was not liable).

(b) Negligence is based on fault, and a person who suffers from a physical impairment, such as a heart attack, epileptic seizure, or other loss of consciousness, is always an innocent victim of that impairment. Such a person cannot be said to be "at fault."

(c) The direct cause of the accident was the car hitting the tree, not Shepard's falling asleep. Thus, Shepard was not at fault and cannot be liable.

(d) This case should be governed by the general rule that a driver is not liable for an accident caused by a sudden and unforeseen disability (such as a heart attack). Shepard unknowingly fell asleep from physical exhaustion without warning. Under such circumstances, it would be unfair to hold him responsible because the subsequent acts were involuntary.

Stop here, and choose the correct answer or answers before consulting the discussion of this problem (Problem 3.10) in Appendix A.

PROBLEM 3.11

> Normally no harm will be done if one falls asleep reading the newspaper after dinner or this opinion. In the horse and buggy days, one might have fallen asleep while driving and the horse quite likely would have had enough horse sense to stop or even to take the driver home through habit and instinct quite safely. But falling asleep behind a wheel of an auto propelled by 200 or 300 mechanical horses having no horse sense is entirely a different matter in terms of your duty to others. We recently pointed out [1] the increase in the frequency and in the seriousness of the consequences of automobile accidents today resulting from modern, high-powered vehicles. The increase in risks and hazards of driving an automobile on public highways demands greater skill and attention than 40 years ago. When one is under a duty to use care not to injure another, he cannot fulfill the duty by falling asleep.
>
> We must approach a sleeping driver case on the premise the driver has the duty to stay awake while he drives and it is within his control either to stay awake, to cease driving, or not to drive at all when sleepy.
>
> 1. McConville v. State Farm Mut. Auto. Ins. Co. (1962), 15 Wis.2d 374, 113 N.W.2d 14.

BLACK'S:

Duty. A human action which is exactly conformable to the laws which require us to obey them. Legal or moral obligation. Obligatory conduct or service. Mandatory obligation to perform. Huey v. King, 220 Tenn. 189, 415 S.W.2d 136. See also **Obligation.**

A thing due; that which is due from a person; that which a person owes to another. An obligation to do a thing. A word of more extensive signification than "debt," although both are expressed by the same Latin word *"debitum."* Sometimes, however, the term is used synonymously with debt.

Those obligations of performance, care, or observance which rest upon a person in an official or fiduciary capacity; as the *duty* of an executor, trustee, manager, etc.

In negligence cases term may be defined as obligation, to which law will give recognition and effect, to conform to particular standard of conduct toward another. Rasmussen v. Prudential Ins. Co., 277 Minn. 266, 152 N.W.2d 359, 362. The word "duty" is used throughout the Restatement of Torts to denote the fact that the actor is required to conduct himself in a particular manner at the risk that if he does not do so he becomes subject to liability to another to whom the duty is owed for any injury sustained by such other, of which that actor's conduct is a legal cause. Restatement, Second, Torts § 4. See **Care; Due care.**

In its use in jurisprudence, this word is the correlative of *right.* Thus, wherever there exists a right in any person, there also rests a corresponding duty upon some other person or upon all persons generally.

It also denotes a tax or impost due to the government upon the importation or exportation of goods. See also **Customs; Tariff; Toll; Tonnage duty.**

See also **Legal duty; Obligation.**

Based on the above discussion by the court, which of the following *best* identifies the court's basic approach?

(a) Greater skill and attention are needed in driving an automobile now than were needed forty years ago. This change justifies liability without fault if one falls asleep while driving.

(b) To recover in a negligence action, the defendant must have breached a duty of care owed to others. Because of the risks involved, drivers have a duty to stay awake while they are driving, and it is within their control either to stay awake, to cease driving, or not to drive at all when they are sleepy.

(c) Modern, high-powered automobiles have become inherently dangerous. Because of this increased danger, a special duty arises to cease driving if one becomes sleepy.

(d) Physical impairments are no longer a valid excuse because of the increase in the frequency and in the seriousness of the consequences of accidents involving modern automobiles.

Stop here, and choose the correct answer before consulting the discussion of this problem (Problem 3.11) in Appendix A.

PROBLEM 3.12

The preceding paragraph of the opinion continues:

> Up to now no decision has gone beyond the limits of the well established rule that the fact the driver of an automobile goes to sleep while driving is a proper basis for an inference of negligence sufficient to make a prima facie case and support a verdict for recovery if no circumstances tending to excuse or justify such conduct are proven. This problem is the subject of an extensive annotation, Automobile—Illness or Drowsiness, 28 A.L.R.2d 12. In Krantz v. Krantz (1933), 211 Wis. 249, 248 N.W. 155, this court recognized that rule and relied on the leading case of Bushnell v. Bushnell, supra, which sets forth a medical basis for the rule. The inference of negligence which arises from "sleeping at the wheel" is based on the judicial recognition that sleep ordinarily does not occur without some notice and to fall asleep while driving is the usual result of negligence in failing to heed the warning. See for medical and psychological theories of the nature of sleep, Kaplan v. Kaplan, supra; Paulson v. Hanson (1939), 226 Iowa 858, 285 N.W. 189 and Rice-Stix Dry Goods Co. v. Self (1935), 20 Tenn.App. 498, 101 S.W.2d 132.

BLACK'S:

> **Prima facie** /práymə féyshiy(iy)/. Lat. At first sight; on the first appearance; on the face of it; so far as can be judged from the first disclosure; presumably; a fact presumed to be true unless disproved by some evidence to the contrary. State ex rel. Herbert v. Whims, 68 Ohio App. 39, 38 N.E.2d 596, 599, 22 O.O. 110.

BLACK'S:

Prima facie case. Such as will prevail until contradicted and overcome by other evidence. Pacific Telephone & Telegraph Co. v. Wallace, 158 Or. 210, 75 P.2d 942, 947. A case which has proceeded upon sufficient proof to that stage where it will support finding if evidence to contrary is disregarded. In re Hoagland's Estate, 126 Neb. 377, 253 N.W. 416.

A prima facie case consists of sufficient evidence in the type of case to get plaintiff past a motion for directed verdict in a jury case or motion to dismiss in a nonjury case; it is the evidence necessary to require defendant to proceed with his case. White v. Abrams, C.A.Cal., 495 F.2d 724, 729. Courts use concept of "prima facie" case in two senses: (1) in sense of plaintiff producing evidence sufficient to render reasonable a conclusion in favor of allegation he asserts; this means plaintiff's evidence is sufficient to allow his case to go to jury, and (2) courts used "prima facie" to mean not only that plaintiff's evidence would reasonably allow conclusion plaintiff seeks, but also that plaintiff's evidence compels such a conclusion if the defendant produces no evidence to rebut it. Husbands v. Com. of Pa., D.C.Pa., 395 F.Supp. 1107, 1139.

Inference. In the law of evidence, a truth or proposition drawn from another which is supposed or admitted to be true. A process of reasoning by which a fact or proposition sought to be established is deduced as a logical consequence from other facts, or a state of facts, already proved or admitted. Com. v. Whitman, 199 Pa.Super. 631, 186 A.2d 632, 633. Inferences are deductions or conclusions which with reason and common sense lead the jury to draw from facts which have been established by the evidence in the case.

An inference is a deduction of fact that may logically and reasonably be drawn from another fact or group of facts found or otherwise established in the action. Calif.Evid.Code.

See also **Reasonable inference rule.** *Compare* **Presumption.**

Why is proof of falling asleep enough to establish an inference of negligence for purposes of a prima facie case and, under prior cases, what was the effect of that proof?

(a) Sleep does not ordinarily occur without some notice and to fall asleep while driving is the usual result of negligence in failing to heed the warnings. The case goes to the jury and a verdict for the plaintiff will be upheld if no circumstances tending to excuse or justify such conduct are proven.

(b) No circumstances can be proven that would justify any conclusion other than that the driver had been negligent by falling asleep while driving. The plaintiff wins and is entitled to a directed verdict.

(c) The inference of negligence is based on the well-established medical principle that sleep is always accompanied by premonitory warnings. A jury verdict may be based on falling asleep after receiving those warnings and will be upheld on appeal because no circumstances can be proven to excuse or justify that conduct.

(d) Sleeping is inherently negligent. Thus, proof of sleep at the wheel allows the case to go to the jury and will support a jury verdict in favor of the plaintiff if the court is satisfied that it was the proximate cause of the accident.

Stop here, and choose the correct answer before consulting the discussion of this problem (Problem 3.12) in Appendix A.

PROBLEM 3.13

> Whatever the medical and scientific basis may be for the inference, we find no justification in the common experience of mankind for one's falling asleep with his foot on the accelerator, his hands on the wheel and his auto transformed into an instrument of destruction. The process of falling asleep—normal and healthy sleep—is a matter of common experience and usually attended by premonitory warnings or is to be expected. Such warnings or reasonable expectations of sleep are especially accentuated when one is conscious of his duty to stay awake while driving and the failure to heed such warnings and permitting oneself to fall asleep while driving an automobile must be deemed negligence as a matter of law. If while driving a car one is in such a state of exhaustion that he falls asleep without any premonitory warning, he is chargeable with the knowledge of any ordinarily prudent man that such exhaustion is reasonably likely to cause sleep while driving. Wis. Natural Gas Co. v. Employers Mut. Liability Ins. Co. (1953), 263 Wis. 633, 58 N.W.2d 424. Although it has been argued the liability of a sleeping driver should be absolute on the grounds of an extra haz-

ardous activity,[2] we do not base our decision on that ground but hold that falling asleep at the wheel is negligence as a matter of law because no facts can exist which will justify, excuse or exculpate such negligence. The language in earlier Wisconsin cases that falling asleep while driving may be excusable is overruled.

2. The Case of the Sleeping Motorist, 25 N.Y.University Law Rev. 362.

BLACK'S:

Chargeable. This word, in its ordinary acceptation, as applicable to the imposition of a duty or burden, signifies capable of being charged, subject to be charged, liable to be charged, or proper to be charged.

Prudence. Carefulness, precaution, attentiveness, and good judgment, as applied to action or conduct. That degree of care required by the exigencies or circumstances under which it is to be exercised. This term, in the language of the law, is commonly associated with "care" and "diligence" and contrasted with "negligence." See those titles.

Prudent. Sagacious in adapting means to end; circumspect in action, or in determining any line of conduct. Practically wise, judicious, careful, discreet, circumspect, sensible. Tureen v. Peoples Motorbus Co. of St. Louis, Mo.App., 97 S.W.2d 847, 848. In defining negligence, practically synonymous with cautious.

Absolute liability. Responsibility without fault or negligence. Rylands v. Fletcher, 3 H.L. 330; Clark-Aiken Co. v. Cromwell-Wright Co., Inc. (Mass.), 323 N.E.2d 876. See **Strict liability**.

Excusable. Admitting of excuse or palliation. As used in the law, this word implies that the act or omission spoken of is on its face unlawful, wrong, or liable to entail loss or disadvantage on the person chargeable, but that the circumstances attending it were such as to constitute a legal "excuse" for it, that is, a legal reason for withholding or foregoing the punishment, liability, or disadvantage which otherwise would follow. See **Justification; Legal excuse.**

> **Legal excuse.** Doctrine by which one seeks to avoid the consequences of his own conduct by showing justification for acts which would otherwise be considered negligent or criminal; *e.g.* killing of another in self defense. Gibbs v. Wilmeth, 261 Iowa 1015, 157 N.W.2d 93, 96. See also **Excusable; Justification; Legal impossibility.**

The court declared that a person's falling asleep while driving an automobile is negligence as a matter of law. The effect of this declaration on future cases is that

(a) the court will determine whether any excuse is sufficient to be submitted to the jury.

(b) negligence will no longer be a question of fact to be submitted to the jury when the plaintiff alleges that the defendant driver fell asleep at the wheel.

(c) defendants will be held strictly liable because no facts can exist which will justify, excuse, or exculpate falling asleep at the wheel.

(d) all the plaintiff needs to prove is the fact of falling asleep. If the plaintiff proves this fact, the plaintiff is entitled to recover, assuming the other elements of his cause of action are sufficiently shown.

Stop here, and choose the correct answer before consulting the discussion of this problem (Problem 3.13) in Appendix A.

PROBLEM 3.14

In the above excerpt, the court also states, "If while driving a car one is in such a state of exhaustion that he falls asleep without any premonitory warning, [the defendant] is *chargeable* with the knowledge of any ordinary prudent man that such exhaustion is reasonably likely to cause sleep while driving" (emphasis added). This statement means that

(a) even if credible evidence could be offered that, because of inexperience, the driver *in fact* did not know that a result of exhaustion is falling asleep, the defendant would not be allowed to offer that evidence under the rule established by the court.

(b) on retrial, the plaintiff must show that Shepard was an ordinary prudent person.

(c) on retrial, the plaintiff must show that Shepard was in a state of exhaustion; otherwise, the burden shifts to the defendant to show that ordinary prudent persons, faced with the same circumstances as those facing the defendant, would have attempted to drive.

(d) on retrial, the defendant will have to show through medical and scientific proof that in some instances sleep resulting from exhaustion can *in fact* occur without premonitory warning in order to win.

Stop here, and choose the correct answer before consulting the discussion of this problem (Problem 3.14) in Appendix A.

PROBLEM 3.15

> We exclude from this holding those exceptional cases of loss of consciousness resulting from injury inflicted by an outside force or fainting or heart attack, epileptic seizure, or other illness which suddenly incapacitates the driver of an automobile and when the occurrence of such disability is not attended with sufficient warning or should not have been reasonably foreseen. When, however, such occurrence should have been reasonably foreseen, we have held the driver of a motor vehicle negligent as a matter of law, as in the sleep cases. Eleason v. Western Casualty & Surety Co. (1948), 254 Wis. 134, 35 N.W.2d 301 (epilepsy); Wis. Natural Gas Co. v. Employers Mut. Liability Ins. Co., supra. Likewise, in Krueger v. Krueger (1929), 197 Wis. 588, 222 N.W. 784, decided before implied assumption of risk was abolished, we held a guest assumed the risk as a matter of law of the driver falling asleep when the guest had knowledge of the driver's condition and sleep was reasonably to be expected.

BLACK'S:

> **Implied.** This word is used in law in contrast to "express"; *i.e.*, where the intention in regard to the subject-matter is not manifested by explicit and direct words, but is gathered by implication or necessary deduction from the circumstances, the general language, or the conduct of the parties. Term differs from "inferred" to the extent that the hearer or reader "infers" while the writer or speaker "implies".

> **Assumption of risk.** The doctrine of assumption of risk, also known as volenti non fit injuria, means legally that a plaintiff may not recover for an injury to which he assents, *i.e.*, that a person may not recover for an injury received when he voluntarily exposes himself to a known and appreciated danger. The requirements for the defense of volenti non fit injuria are that: (1) the plaintiff has knowledge of facts constituting a dangerous condition, (2) he knows the condition is dangerous, (3) he appreciates the nature or extent of the danger, and (4) he voluntarily exposes himself to the danger. An exception may be applicable even though the above factors have entered into a plaintiff's conduct if his actions come within the rescue or humanitarian doctrine. Clarke v. Brockway Motor Trucks, D.C.Pa., 372 F.Supp. 1342, 1347.
>
> A defense to action of negligence which consists of showing that the plaintiff, knowing the dangers and risk involved, chose to act as he did. An affirmative defense which the defendant in a negligence action must plead and prove. Fed.R.Civil P. 8(c). It is not a defense under state workers' compensation laws or in FELA actions. Many states have abolished the defense of assumption of risk in automobile cases with the enactment of no-fault insurance acts or comparative negligence acts.

Assume that on retrial the defendant could offer *credible* medical evidence from Shepard's autopsy that Shepard's falling asleep was caused by his first (and last) attack of narcolepsy (a condition characterized by brief attacks of deep sleep). Based on the court's opinion, which of the following is the *best* argument in favor of allowing the defendant to introduce this evidence?

(a) The plaintiff assumed the risk as a matter of law that the defendant might be struck with an attack of narcolepsy.

(b) Narcolepsy is different from ordinary sleep because it involves deep sleep. Thus, this case does not fall within the court's rule excluding justifications or excuses for ordinary sleep.

(c) Narcolepsy is an illness which occurred without warning and resulted in a sudden incapacitation of the driver.

(d) Narcolepsy does not involve "permitting oneself to fall asleep." Driving under such circumstances should not be *deemed* to be negligence as a matter of law.

Stop here, and choose the correct answer before consulting the discussion of this problem (Problem 3.15) in Appendix A.

PROBLEM 3.16

[2] The party claiming the driver fell asleep while driving has the burden of proving the driver in fact, fell asleep. If the evidence, whether direct or by permissible inference, tends to establish the fact, such evidence casts a burden upon the party seeking to excuse the driver's loss of consciousness—the burden of showing the greater probability that the loss of consciousness is excusable on some nonactionable basis.

BLACK'S:

Burden of proof. (Lat. *onus probandi.*) In the law of evidence, the necessity or duty of affirmatively proving a fact or facts in dispute on an issue raised between the parties in a cause. The obligation of a party to establish by evidence a requisite degree of belief concerning a fact in the mind of the trier of fact or the court.

Burden of proof is a term which describes two different concepts; first, the "burden of persuasion", which under traditional view never shifts from one party to the other at any stage of the proceeding, and second, the "burden of going forward with the evidence", which may shift back and forth between the parties as the trial progresses. Ambrose v. Wheatley, D.C.Del., 321 F.Supp. 1220, 1222.

The burden of proof may require a party to raise a reasonable doubt concerning the existence or nonexistence of a fact or that he establish the existence or nonexistence of a fact by a preponderance of the evidence, by clear and convincing proof, or by proof beyond a reasonable doubt. Except as otherwise provided by law, the burden of proof requires proof by a preponderance of the evidence. Calif.Evid.Code, § 115.

In a criminal case, all the elements of the crime must be proved by the government beyond a reasonable doubt. In re Winship, 397 U.S. 358, 90 S.Ct. 1068, 25 L.Ed.2d 368.

Term has been used to mean either the necessity of establishing a fact, that is, the burden of persuasion, or the necessity of making a prima facie showing, that is, the burden of going forward. State Farm Life Ins. Co. v. Smith, 29 Ill.App.3d 942, 331 N.E.2d 275, 278.

Based on the above paragraph of the opinion, which of the following statements about the "burden of proof" in cases involving allegedly sleeping drivers is correct?

(a) The party claiming that the driver fell asleep has the initial burden of going forward with the evidence tending to show that the driver fell asleep.

(b) If the party claiming that the driver fell asleep presents evidence tending to establish that fact, the burden of going forward with the evidence shifts to the other side to show that the driver did not fall asleep. For example, that the driver suffered a heart attack.

(c) If the burden shifts as described in answer (b), the driver will be held negligent as a matter of law unless the driver can show that a greater probability exists that the loss of consciousness is excusable on some nonactionable basis, such as a heart attack.

(d) The court does not appear to be addressing the ultimate burden of proof (persuasion), which remains on the plaintiff throughout the proceeding.

Stop here, and choose the correct answer before consulting the discussion of this problem (Problem 3.16) in Appendix A.

PROBLEM 3.17

> [3] The trial court excluded an offer of proof made by the defendant which would have shown Shepherd was not an habitual user of alcoholic beverages and was physically exhausted from the loss of considerable sleep for some six weeks prior to the accident practicing for the play, getting to bed later than his normal bedtime and continuing his usual farm chores. It was not error of the trial court to reject this evidence offered to prove a justification for going to sleep. On the contrary, such proof would have tended to show Shepherd should have known, as a reasonable prudent man, he was likely to have fallen asleep. Such offer of proof, of course, is immaterial under our holding that falling asleep while driving is negligence as a matter of law.

BLACK'S:

> **Offer of proof.** At a trial or hearing, when an objection to a question has been sustained, the party aggrieved by the ruling may indicate for the record (out of the presence of the jury) the answer which would have been given if the question had not been excluded. The appellate court is then in a position to determine from the record the correctness of the ruling and the prejudice in its exclusion, if any. See Fed.Evid.Rule 103(a)(2).

BALLENTINE'S:

> **immaterial.** Not material; not pertinent; of no consequence.

> **immaterial evidence.** Evidence which is offered to prove or disprove a fact or proposition which is not at issue. 29 Am J2d Ev § 252.
> See **material evidence.**

BLACK'S:

> **Holding.** The legal principle to be drawn from the opinion (decision) of the court. Opposite of dictum (*q.v.*). Also, general term for property, securities, etc. owned by person or corporation. See also **Dicta.**
> In English law, a piece of land held under a lease or similar tenancy for agricultural, pastoral, or similar purposes.

The trial court's exclusion of the defendant's offer of proof concerning Shepard's physical exhaustion was not error because the evidence

(a) was offered for the purpose of proving a proposition which was not properly at issue.

(b) lacked any tendency to make the existence of any fact more probable or less probable than it would have been without the evidence.

(c) was based on a preconceived view of the facts which would have confused the determination of liability.

(d) tended to prove a proposition favorable to the *plaintiff*, not the defendant (who offered the evidence). Only evidence favorable to one's side may be offered by that side.

Stop here, and choose the correct answer before consulting the discussion of this problem (Problem 3.17) in Appendix A.

PROBLEM 3.18

The opinion continues with a discussion of another of the alleged errors committed by the trial court.

> [4–6] The defendant contends Shepherd was entitled to an instruction on the presumption of due care accorded a deceased party, relying on Seligman v. Hammond (1931), 205 Wis. 199, 236 N.W. 115. Later cases have not followed the strong language of that case which characterized the presumption as very substantial and, although not constituting affirmative evidence that due care was exercised, as requiring proof to the contrary in order to remove its persuasive force. This presumption is a limited one, is not evidence and is sufficient only to place upon the other party the risk incidental to a failure to come forward with such testimony as may be in his control. It involves no rule as to the weight of the evidence necessary to meet it. Fiedler v. Kapsa (1949), 255 Wis. 559, 39 N.W. 2d 682. This court is committed to the doctrine that when evidence is introduced which would support a jury finding contrary to the presumption, the presumption is eliminated and drops out of the case entirely and no instruction to the jury should be given upon the subject. Atkinson v. Huber (1955), 268 Wis. 615, 68 N.W. 2d 447. See also Evjen v. Packer City Transit Line, Inc. (1960), 9 Wis.2d 153, 100 N.W.2d 580; and Weber v. Mayer (1954), 266 Wis. 241, 63 N.W.2d 318.

BLACK'S:

Presumption. A presumption is a rule of law, statutory or judicial, by which finding of a basic fact gives rise to existence of presumed fact, until presumption is rebutted. Van Wart v. Cook, Okl.App., 557 P.2d 1161, 1163.

In all civil actions and proceedings not otherwise provided for by Act of Congress or by these rules, a presumption imposes on the party against whom it is directed the burden of going forward with evidence to rebut or meet the presumption, but does not shift to such party the burden of proof in the sense of the risk of nonpersuasion, which remains throughout the trial upon the party on whom it was originally cast. Federal Evidence Rule 301.

A presumption is an assumption of fact resulting from a rule of law which requires such fact to be assumed from another fact or group of facts found or otherwise established in the action. Uniform Evidence Rule 13.

A presumption is a rebuttable assumption of fact resulting from a rule of law which requires such fact to be assumed from another fact or group of facts found or otherwise established in the action. N.J. Evidence Rule 13.

A presumption is an assumption of fact that the law requires to be made from another fact or group of facts found or otherwise established in the action. A presumption is not evidence. A presumption is either conclusive or rebuttable. Every rebuttable presumption is either (a) a presumption affecting the burden of producing evidence or (b) a presumption affecting the burden of proof. Calif.Evid.Code.

See also **Disputable presumption; Inference; Juris et de jure; Raise a presumption.**

Due care. Just, proper, and sufficient care, so far as the circumstances demand it; the absence of negligence. That care which an ordinarily prudent person would have exercised under the same or similar circumstances. Strickland v. Hughes, 2 N.C.App. 395, 163 S.E.2d 24, 26. "Due care" is care proportioned to any given situation, its surroundings, peculiarities, and hazards. It may and often does require extraordinary care. "Due care," "reasonable care," and "ordinary care" are often used as convertible terms.

This term, as usually understood in cases where the gist of the action is the defendant's negligence, implies not only that a party has not been negligent or careless, but that he has been guilty of no violation of law in relation to the subject-matter or transaction which constitutes the cause of action.

Although in the defendant's brief an argument is made the cause of Shepherd's conduct in operating the car rested on speculation, this case was tried and argued on the basis Shepherd fell asleep from physical exhaustion. The only reasonable inference from the evidence is that Shepherd did fall asleep. There is no evidence of any other cause. The other occupants who had participated in the events of the night and early morning preceding the accident fell asleep. We have no sudden turning of the car to the wrong side of the highway or of a mechanical defect which might have explained the presence of the car on the wrong side of the road and traveling off the highway. The distance from the position of Shepherd's automobile in its right lane on the highway when it began to veer to the left to the point of impact with the tree stump was approximately 500 feet. There is no testimony of a fainting spell, or an epileptic seizure or any other unanticipated mental or physical condition of Shepherd which would cause him to lose consciousness other than falling asleep.

BLACK'S:

Speculation. Buying or selling with expectation of profiting by a rise or fall in price. Also, engaging in hazardous business transactions, or investing in risky securities or commodities, with the hope of an unusually large profit.

Speculation, upon which neither court in nonjury case nor jurors in jury case may base verdict, is the art of theorizing about a matter as to which evidence is not sufficient for certain knowledge. Jaramillo v. U. S., D.C.N.Y., 357 F.Supp. 172, 175.

The defendant also contends the operation of the car on the wrong side of the highway is not sufficient to rebut the presumption of due care accorded the deceased or to overcome it. Traveling on the wrong side of the road and onto the shoulder in a straight line for almost a distance of 500 feet with no explanation other than the driver was asleep raises an inference of fact sufficient to sustain a verdict of negligence on the part of the deceased driver and sufficient to overcome the presumption of due care. It has been said the mere operation of an automobile on the wrong side of the highway is sufficient if unexplained. In Hamilton v. Reinemann (1940), 233 Wis. 572, 290 N.W. 194, we discussed the Seligman case and Booth v. Frankenstein (1932), 209 Wis. 362, 245 N.W. 191, and stated the mere operation of a car upon the wrong side of the highway makes at least a prima facie case of negligence and is enough in the absence of an explanation which the jury is bound to accept to warrant an inference of negligence on the part of its operator. We find no error in the court's refusal to instruct the jury upon the presumption of due care; the presumption dropped out of this case entirely.

BLACK'S:

Rebut. In pleading and evidence, to defeat, refute, or take away the effect of something. When a plaintiff in an action produces evidence which raises a presumption of the defendant's liability, and the defendant adduces evidence which shows that the presumption is ill-founded, he is said to "rebut it." See **Rebuttable presumption; Rebuttal evidence.**

BLACK'S:

Rebuttable presumption. In the law of evidence, a presumption which may be rebutted by evidence. Otherwise called a "disputable" presumption. A species of legal presumption which holds good until evidence contrary to it is introduced. Beck v. Kansas City Public Service Co., Mo.App., 48 S.W.2d 213, 215. It shifts burden of proof. Heiner v. Donnan, 285 U.S. 312, 52 S.Ct. 358, 362, 76 L.Ed. 772. And which standing alone will support a finding against contradictory evidence. Lieber v. Rigby, 34 Cal.App.2d 582, 94 P.2d 49, 50. See also **Presumption.**

Rebuttal evidence. Evidence given to explain, repel, counteract, or disprove facts given in evidence by the acverse party. That which tends to explain or contradict or disprove evidence offered by the adverse party. Layton v. State, 261 Ind. 251, 301 N.E.2d 633, 636. Evidence which is offered by a party after he has rested his case and after the opponent has rested in order to contradict the opponent's evidence.

Also evidence given in opposition to a presumption of fact or a *prima facie* case; in this sense, it may be not only counteracting evidence, but evidence sufficient to counteract, that is, conclusive. See **Rebuttable presumption.**

The defendant contended that an instruction should have been given on the presumption of due care accorded a deceased party. Why did the defendant want this instruction given?

(a) Had the instruction been given, the driver would have been conclusively presumed to have operated the vehicle with due care.

(b) Had the instruction been given, the verdict would have been improper because it rested on speculation.

(c) Because there was no direct evidence of the cause of the driver's loss of consciousness, the defendant wanted the jury to be told that the driver should be presumed to have acted with due care. This instruction would have been favorable to the defendant, who could have tried to convince the jury that the plaintiff was only speculating as to the cause of the loss of consciousness and thus had not met the required burden of rebutting the presumption.

(d) Because no direct evidence of the cause of the driver's loss of consciousness was offered by the plaintiff, the defendant would have been entitled to a directed verdict had the instruction been given.

Stop here, and choose the correct answer before consulting the discussion of this problem (Problem 3.18) in Appendix A.

Next, the court addressed the defendant's assertion that an instruction on implied "assumption of risk" should have been given and alleged errors in the jury instructions. Although the court rejected the defendant's assertion about use of the assumption-of-risk doctrine, the court did find that the trial court erred in instructing the jury in the questions about the plaintiff's negligence in riding with Shepard under the circumstances and the causal connection of the negligence.

The court then devoted the remaining portion of the opinion to giving further guidance to the courts below and the lawyers. At that point, since those matters were not currently before the court for decision, the court was stating dicta. The final disposition of the action is stated at the end of the opinion.

> Several other interesting questions have been raised by the defendant, but as this case must be reversed and a new trial granted it would serve no useful purpose to discuss them and further discussion might be soporific. Neither the defendant nor plaintiff raises any question that the amount of damages was sustained by the evidence or resulted from the accident and there is no reason for including this issue in the new trial.
>
> Judgment reversed, and a new trial granted on the questions of negligence only.

Section 3E. Briefing Judicial Opinions for Legal Research and Writing Purposes

During the course of your legal research, you will want to record what you find in the form of notes. With regard to judicial opinions, such notes are called "case briefs."

CASE BRIEFS PREPARED FOR RESEARCH AND WRITING PURPOSES SHOULD BE TAILORED TO THE QUESTION BEING RESEARCHED AND THE PURPOSE FOR WHICH IT IS LIKELY TO BE USED.

You will need to record in such briefs all the information necessary for you to use the opinion in writing, for example, a memorandum of law or an appellate brief. This section provides suggestions on how you can effectively and efficiently record the necessary information.

A BRIEF PREPARED FOR RESEARCH AND WRITING PURPOSES TYPICALLY DOES NOT EMPHASIZE A FORMAL STRUCTURE.

Experienced researchers generally do not list headings in briefs (which is a frequent suggestion made for classroom briefs). They also frequently intermix the court's holding and reasoning in the form of *statements* rather than separately recording the "issue," "decision," and "reasoning."

When cases are briefed for research purposes, you often will have examined the opinion in reference to a particular legal proposition.

ILLUSTRATION 3.12

The case may have been cited in a secondary source (such as a legal encyclopedia or treatise) in support of a stated legal proposition or the opinion itself may have stated the proposition.

Furthermore, when you encounter a case in the course of legal research, you frequently will also reach some tentative conclusion on how you will use that case.

ILLUSTRATION 3.13

You may be particularly interested in the facts of the opinion or in other aspects of the decision for purposes of distinguishing that case from a current situation that you are confronting.

> In *Theisen*, the court held that falling asleep at the wheel of an automobile is negligence as a matter of law. In that case, the guest proved that the car was driven on the wrong side of the road, the other occupants who had participated in the events of the night had fallen asleep, and every other circumstance indicated that the driver had fallen asleep. In the present case, however, the driver's loss of consciousness is totally unexplained. The accident occurred in the afternoon rather than at three o'clock in the morning. Unlike in *Theisen*, the car did not cross the center line, and no passengers other than the injured guest were in the car. The cause of the driver's loss of conscious is truly speculative. For instance, it could have been caused by a sudden and unexpected fainting spell. In these circumstances,

insufficient evidence exists to eliminate the presumption that the deceased driver exercised due care, and the jury should have been so instructed.

Thus, if a case seems contrary to your position and you are interested in distinguishing it (as illustrated above), you should pay close attention to the facts, the exact statement of the rule, the procedural context, and the court's reasoning. While you are preparing your case brief, any ideas that occur to you on how the case might be distinguished should be added at the end of your case brief.

WHEN YOU PREPARE A RESEARCH BRIEF, YOU SHOULD BRIEF ONLY THOSE ISSUES THAT ARE RELEVANT TO THE PROBLEM YOU ARE RESEARCHING. FURTHERMORE, YOU SHOULD TAILOR THE CONTENT OF THE BRIEF TO THE PURPOSE FOR WHICH YOU ARE LIKELY TO USE IT.

An experienced researcher's brief of the *Theisen* opinion might read as follows. Assume that the issue relevant for research purposes was the exclusion of evidence attempting to justify falling asleep and that it is likely that this case will be cited in support of the proposition that such evidence should be excluded.

ILLUSTRATION 3.14

Falling asleep at the wheel of an automobile is negligence as a matter of law, and no facts can exist that will excuse that negligence.

> Theisen v. Milwaukee Auto. Mut. Ins. Co., 18 Wis. 2d 91, 118 N.W.2d 140 (1962).
>
> The plaintiff, a passenger in a car, commenced a negligence action for damages in a Wisconsin circuit court after she was injured when the driver fell asleep late at night and the car hit a tree. At trial, the defendant, the deceased driver's insurer, attempted to offer, as a justification for the driver's falling asleep, evidence that the driver was not a habitual user of alcoholic beverages and that he was physically exhausted from his activities prior to the time of the accident. Id. at ___, 118 N.W.2d at 144. This evidence was excluded. The jury found for the plaintiff, and judgment in the plaintiff's favor was entered on the verdict.
>
> The Wisconsin Supreme Court upheld the trial court's exclusion of this offer on the ground that

falling asleep is negligence as a matter of law and that no facts can exist which will justify, excuse, or exculpate such negligence. The court reasoned that (a) because it is within a driver's control to stay awake, to cease driving, or not to drive at all when sleepy and (b) because falling asleep does not occur without warning, falling asleep at the wheel of an automobile is so opposed to the dictates of common prudence that no careful person would permit it to occur. Id. at ___, 118 N.W.2d at 143-44.

The judgment for the plaintiff, however, was reversed on other grounds, and the case was remanded for a new trial on the negligence issues.

For purposes of comparison, Appendix C contains a "classroom" brief of the portion of the Theisen opinion reproduced in the preceding section. It follows a formal structure and includes all the issues.

BEGIN A RESEARCH BRIEF WITH A STATEMENT OF THE LEGAL PRINCIPLE OR IDEA INVOLVED. IF THE CASE CONTAINS MORE THAN ONE PRINCIPLE OR IDEA THAT YOU WANT TO RECORD, PREPARE SEPARATE BRIEFS FOR EACH PRINCIPLE OR IDEA.

As discussed in Chapter 2, a good system for coordinating legal research, analysis, and note taking relies, in part, on recording each idea or legal principle on a *separate* sheet of paper.[15] ***This approach allows you to compile authorities (and notes thereon) without interference or confusion with other ideas and to arrange--and rearrange--these principles or ideas without rewriting.*** It is for this reason that it is suggested that you begin the case brief with the legal principle or idea involved.

CITE THE CASE ACCURATELY AND IN PROPER FORM.

Because you often will want to cite the judicial opinion in a written product based on your research, ***you should develop the habit of citing a case accurately and in proper form.*** The citation should follow immediately after the statement of the legal principle or idea to allow quick identification of the case brief. Leave blanks for missing information (e.g., missing parallel citations).

---

[15] See Vom Bauer, How to Look Up Law and Write Legal Memoranda--Revisited, 11 Prac. Law., May 1965, at 23.

ILLUSTRATION 3.15

Theisen v. Milwaukee Auto. Mut. Ins. Co., ___ Wis. 2d ___, 118 N.W.2d 140 (1962).

AT A MINIMUM, STATE THE ESSENTIAL FACTS OF THE CASE IN A RESEARCH BRIEF. IF THE FACTS ARE INTEGRALLY RELATED TO THE ULTIMATE USE OF THE BRIEF OR THE PURPOSE FOR WHICH IT IS BEING PREPARED, STATE THE FACTS IN DETAIL.

Generally speaking, in a classroom brief, the content of the section stating the facts is limited to those facts that were essential to the outcome. The focus is on the gist of the controversy. Compare the following two descriptions of the facts of *Theisen*:

> (1) P, a passenger in a car, was injured in an accident late at night when the driver, insured by D, fell asleep and the car hit a tree.
>
> (2) Louis Shepherd, having participated in the senior class play, attended a party at the home of one of the members of the cast. Some liquor was served at the party, but there was no evidence that anyone became intoxicated. About 3:00 a.m., the party broke up and five girls, including P, got into Shepherd's car for the ride home. About four miles from the party, Shepherd, insured by D, fell asleep at the wheel. The car left the road and hit a tree. Shepherd was killed and P was injured.

The first description is typical of the brief summary of the facts included in a classroom brief. It also represents the *minimum* that should be included in a research brief. The second description might be used in a research brief when the facts are important (for example, because the facts of the case are similar to your "research facts").

WHEN THE FACTS ARE COMPLICATED OR NUMEROUS PARTIES ARE INVOLVED, USE A DIAGRAM IN THE "FACTS" SECTION.

Diagrams are helpful when the relationships and other facts are complicated, particularly in descent and distribution litigation or in other complex or multi-party litigation.

USE DESCRIPTIVE TERMS TO IDENTIFY THE PARTIES.

In addition to identifying the parties involved as the plaintiff, defendant, and the like, it is ordinarily helpful to use factual or legal descriptions in a case brief.

ILLUSTRATION 3.16

P, a passenger in a car,
P, the vendor,
D, a taxpayer,
D, the employer's agent,
P, a mistaken improver, etc.

INCLUDE THE PROCEDURAL CONTEXT OF THE CASE IN YOUR RESEARCH BRIEF. AT A MINIMUM, INCLUDE A CONCISE STATEMENT OF THE NATURE OF THE ACTION.

A research brief should include a statement of the procedural context. At a minimum, that statement should include a brief description of the nature of the action.

ILLUSTRATION 3.17

Suit to enjoin repeated trespasses
Criminal prosecution for manslaughter
Damage action for breach of contract
Suit for ejectment and mesne profits

Note how this type of description was integrated into the sample research brief of the *Theisen* opinion shown earlier:

ILLUSTRATION 3.18

> The plaintiff, a passenger in a car, commenced a negligence action for damages in a Wisconsin circuit court after she was injured late at night when the driver fell asleep and the car hit a tree.

FOCUS ON THE CRITICAL ACTIONS TAKEN BY THE COURT THAT ARE RELEVANT TO THE PRINCIPLE OR IDEA COVERED IN THE BRIEF.

As noted earlier in this chapter, appellate courts focus on errors committed below, generally rulings by the court. The purported erroneous actions or rulings of the court below should be identified in the case brief. For example, the court may have excluded evidence, refused to instruct the jury in a certain manner, directed a verdict, ordered a new trial, dismissed the complaint, etc. By focusing on the purported erroneous actions or ruling below, you will find it much easier to formulate the issues.

ILLUSTRATION 3.19

The information on the purported erroneous actions was included in the sample research brief of the *Theisen* case in the following way:

> At trial, the defendant, the deceased driver's insurer, attempted to offer, as a justification for the driver's falling asleep, evidence that the driver was not a habitual user of alcoholic beverages and that he was physically exhausted from his prior activities at the time of the accident. Id. at ___, 118 N.W.2d at 144. This evidence was excluded.

BE SURE TO STATE THE RESULT IN THE LOWER COURT AND ON APPEAL. BE SURE TO STATE THOSE RESULTS CLEARLY AND ACCURATELY.

A research brief should include a statement of the result below and on appeal (if the opinion is an appellate one). If the opinion briefed is that of a trial court, then the result in that court should be given.

ILLUSTRATION 3.20

Note how this information was integrated into the sample research brief:

> The jury found for the plaintiff, and judgment was entered on the verdict. . . .
>
> The Wisconsin Supreme Court upheld the trial court's exclusion of this offer on the ground that falling asleep is negligence as a matter of law and that no facts can exist which will justify, excuse, or exculpate such negligence. . . .
>
> The judgment for the plaintiff, however, was reversed on other grounds, and the case was remanded for a new trial on the negligence issues.

Be sure to use the correct terminology in your case brief.

ILLUSTRATION 3.21

Do not use "verdict" when the case was tried without a jury because verdicts are rendered only by juries.

Also, be sure to indicate the orders or other actions resulting from the appellate review.

ILLUSTRATION 3.22

The judgment for the plaintiff was affirmed.

The judgment for the plaintiff was reversed, and the case was remanded for a new trial.

IF MORE THAN ONE COURT HEARD THE CASE PRIOR TO THE PRESENT APPEAL, BE SURE TO INDICATE THE RESULTS IN EACH LOWER COURT.

If there is more than one court below (e.g., a trial court and an intermediate appellate court), the result in each court should be indicated.

ARTICULATE THE COURT'S REASONING--WHY IT DECIDED AS IT DID.

The reasoning of the court should be stated. Tie the facts and the procedural context of the case together with the justifications and reasons for the rule.

ILLUSTRATION 3.23

Consider the following example from the sample research brief:

> The court reasoned that (a) because it is within the driver's control to stay awake, to cease driving, or not to drive at all when sleepy and (b) because falling asleep does not occur without warning, falling asleep at the wheel of an automobile is so opposed to the dictates of common prudence that no careful person would permit it to occur. Id. at ___, 118 N.W.2d at 143-44.

When it is necessary, greater detail should be given, particularly if the proposition is controversial.

In sum, remember that case briefs prepared for research and writing purposes differ from those prepared for classroom purposes. You should strive to prepare case briefs that are accurate, functional, and sufficiently detailed in light of the research purposes for which they will be used. Above all, quality briefs depend on your ability to master the facts, to understand the procedural aspects of the case, and to distill the substance of an opinion.

Chapter 4

AUTHORITY OF JUDICIAL DECISIONS, BASIC LEGAL REASONING, AND CASE SYNTHESIS

Section

WHAT YOU WILL LEARN IN THIS CHAPTER

* The differences between a variety of important and sometimes confusing doctrines and concepts relating to the "authority" of judicial opinions
* The various factors that affect the persuasive value of judicial opinions
* The use of basic deductive reasoning to form legal arguments
* The technique of reasoning by analogy in legal analysis and writing
* The synthesis of judicial opinions

Section 4A. The Doctrine of Stare Decisis

Judicial decisions define and dispose of the dispute before the court. They also may serve as authority for deciding future cases: a question of law or statutory interpretation ordinarily will be decided in the same way it was in the prior decision ("precedent"). In other words, the courts will "stand by [their] decisions and [will] not disturb settled points."[1] The Latin phrase for this doctrine is stare decisis. This doctrine was part of the English common-law tradition accepted in the United States.

Several justifications exist for using stare decisis in our system of jurisprudence. (1) Stare decisis encourages even-handed treatment of those who come before the courts. (2) Stare decisis saves time and energy because the courts do not have to hear the same arguments on a point over and over again. (3) By contributing to the predictability of the law, stare decisis facilitates planning by private parties and encourages settlement of disputes. (4) Stare decisis provides a certain degree of protection from capricious or arbitrary judicial rulings. (5) Stare decisis helps maintain public faith in the judiciary.[2]

THE DOCTRINE OF STARE DECISIS CALLS FOR SETTLEMENT OF PRINCIPLE AND CONSISTENCY OF RULING WHEN A COURT HAS GIVEN "DUE CONSIDERATION" TO A POINT.

Nevertheless, the courts, particularly those in the United States, recognize that stare decisis does not require that clear error be continued.[3] A court may overrule a prior decision which is clearly wrong.

A word of caution should be added, however, about the likelihood of a court overruling a decision interpreting the application or meaning of a statute.

DECISIONS INVOLVING LONG-STANDING INTERPRETATIONS OF STATUTES ARE NOT LIKELY TO BE OVERRULED EVEN IF THEY APPEAR TO HAVE BEEN ERRONEOUS OR APPEAR TO BE INCONSISTENT WITH SUBSEQUENT DEVELOPMENTS.

ILLUSTRATION 4.1

In 1922, in *Federal Baseball Club v. National League of Professional Baseball Clubs*,[4] the Supreme Court held that

---

[1] See Black's Law Dictionary 1261 (5th ed. 1979).

[2] See Morgane v. United States Marine Lines, 398 U.S. 375, 403-05 (1970).

[3] See R. Cross, Precedent in English Law 17-19 (3d ed. 1977) (stare decisis never followed in the United States as rigidly as it once was in England).

[4] 259 U.S. 200 (1922).

professional baseball was merely a "sport" and not interstate "commerce" and, therefore, it was not subject to the federal antitrust laws.[5] In 1953, the Court reaffirmed this holding in *Toolson v. New York Yankees*.[6] Even though all other professional sports subsequently had been held to involve interstate commerce and subjected to the federal antitrust laws, the Court again in 1972 refused to overrule its prior decisions. In *Flood v. Kuhn*,[7] the Court explained:

> [W]e adhere once again to *Federal Baseball* and *Toolson*. . . . If there is any inconsistency or illogic in all this, it is an inconsistency and illogic of long standing *that is to be remedied by the Congress and not by this Court*. If we were to act otherwise, we would be withdrawing from the conclusion as to congressional intent made in *Toolson* and from the concerns of retrospectivity therein expressed. Under these circumstances, there is merit in consistency even though some might claim that beneath that consistency is a layer of inconsistency.[8]

Section 4B. The Difference Between "Mandatory" and "Persuasive" Precedents

One important aspect of the doctrine of stare decisis is that all judicial decisions do not have the same weight of authority. Some judicial decisions are "binding" or "mandatory." All others are, at most, "persuasive."

RECOGNIZING THE DIFFERENCE BETWEEN MANDATORY PRECEDENTS (THOSE THAT MUST BE FOLLOWED BY LOWER TRIBUNALS) AND PERSUASIVE PRECEDENTS (THOSE THAT MAY BE INFLUENTIAL BUT ARE NOT BINDING) IS CRITICAL TO LEGAL WRITING.

---

[5] Id. at 208-09.

[6] 346 U.S. 356 (1953).

[7] 407 U.S. 258 (1972).

[8] Id. at 284 (emphasis added). But cf. Erie R.R. v. Tompkins, 304 U.S. 64, 77-78 (1938), overruling Swift v. Tyson, 41 U.S. (16 Pet.) 1 (1842) ("If only a question of statutory construction [of the Rules of Decision Act of 1789] were involved, we should not be prepared to abandon a doctrine so widely applied throughout nearly a century. But the unconstitutionality of the course pursued has now been made clear, and compels us to do so") (footnote omitted) (emphasis added).

TRIAL COURTS DO NOT MAKE BINDING PRECEDENTS.

In a court system with inferior tribunals, the trial (lowest-level) courts do not make binding precedents.[9]

DECISIONS OF INFERIOR APPELLATE TRIBUNALS DO NOT BIND OTHER CO-EQUAL (OR HIGHER) TRIBUNALS WITHIN THE SAME SYSTEM.

Under the doctrine of stare decisis, decisions of inferior appellate tribunals are not binding on other *co-equal* (or higher) tribunals within the same system. Nonetheless, the decisions of inferior appellate tribunals may be accorded significant weight as persuasive precedents.

ILLUSTRATION 4.2

The United States Court of Appeals for the Eighth Circuit need not follow a decision of the United States Court of Appeals for the First Circuit. The views of the First Circuit may be *persuasive*, but they are not binding. Nevertheless, the Eighth Circuit may give the First Circuit's opinion great weight:

> [Three other] circuit courts [have] carefully analyzed the constitutional questions; in our judgment their reasoning is impervious to further attack and needs no further amplification. Although we are not bound by another circuit's decision, we adhere to the policy that a sister circuit's reasoned decision deserves great weight and precedential value. As an appellate court, we strive to maintain uniformity in the law among the circuits, wherever reasoned analysis will allow, thus avoiding unnecessary burdens on the Supreme Court docket. Unless [the] courts of appeals are thus willing to promote a cohesive network of national law, needless division and confusion will encourage further splintering and the formation of otherwise unnecessary additional tiers in the framework of our national court system.[10]

---

[9] See Fenske v. Public Employees' Retirement Sys. Bd., 103 Cal. App. 3d 590, 596, 163 Cal. Rptr. 182, 185-86 (1980).

[10] Aldens, Inc. v. Miller, 610 F.2d 538, 541 (8th Cir. 1979), cert. denied, 446 U.S. 919 (1980).

UNDER THE STARE DECISIS DOCTRINE, ALL INFERIOR TRIBUNALS MUST ADHERE TO DECISIONS OF THEIR RESPECTIVE HIGHER TRIBUNALS UNTIL THOSE DECISIONS HAVE BEEN OVERRULED OR ALTERED BY LEGISLATION.

Inferior tribunals have a duty to adhere to the decisions of their respective higher courts until those decisions have been overruled or altered by legislation.

ILLUSTRATION 4.3

All federal district courts in the First Circuit must follow a rule announced by the First Circuit Court of Appeals even though some of the district courts in that circuit may prefer a rule announced by some other circuit. Similarly, when the court of last resort (in this illustration, the United States Supreme Court) has decided a question, its decision becomes a mandatory precedent binding on all inferior courts until it has been overruled or altered by legislation.

A United States Supreme Court decision on a question of *federal* law binds not only the federal courts of appeals and all other federal courts but also all state courts. This binding effect on state courts results from our constitutional scheme, which vests the Supreme Court (and Congress) with the final authority to determine federal law.[11]

In contrast, the final authority to decide the law of a particular state rests with the court of last resort in that state.

ILLUSTRATION 4.4

The California Supreme Court (along with the California legislature) exclusively determines California law authoritatively. Thus, a Florida Supreme Court decision applying California law would not be a mandatory precedent for the California courts--although the decision may have some persuasive value if the California courts have not yet considered the question.

IF A JURISDICTION HAS PATTERNED ITS LEGISLATION AFTER LEGISLATION IN ANOTHER JURISDICTION, THE JUDICIAL DECISIONS OF THAT OTHER JURISDICTION WILL ORDINARILY BE HIGHLY PERSUASIVE IN THE COURTS OF THE ADOPTING JURISDICTION.

---

[11] See U.S. Const. art. VI, § 2 (supremacy clause).

Sometimes a jurisdiction will pattern its legislation after legislation of a neighboring jurisdiction. Although they will not be binding, the judicial decisions of the neighboring jurisdiction ordinarily will be highly persuasive in the courts of the jurisdiction adopting the law.

ILLUSTRATION 4.5

In *State v. Mackey*,[12] the Arizona Court of Appeals stated "[t]he [Arizona] statutes in question were adopted from California and we therefore look with great interest to [decisions in] that jurisdiction").[13] A similar pattern exists when a state has substantially adopted federal rules or legislation.[14]

IN DIVERSITY ACTIONS IN FEDERAL COURT (DIVERSITY OF CITIZENSHIP AND MORE THAN $50,000 IN CONTROVERSY), THE FEDERAL COURTS MUST APPLY STATE SUBSTANTIVE LAW.

Mandatory precedents also play a role in the diversity jurisdiction of federal courts--actions in which a diversity of citizenship exists between the opposing parties and the matter in controversy exceeds $50,000, exclusive of interest and costs.[15] Under the current interpretation of the Rules of Decision Act,[16] the federal courts must apply *state* substantive law in such cases.[17]

Thus, when the court of last resort of a state has authoritatively determined state substantive law, its decision becomes a mandatory precedent for federal courts, irrespective of what the federal courts think the law ought to be. If the state court decision is out of the line of modern authority, however, a federal court may disregard the decision if there is some

---

[12] 15 Ariz. App. 417, 489 P.2d 80 (1971).

[13] Id. at 419, 489 P.2d at 82.

[14] See, e.g., Gous v. Daray Motor Co., 373 So. 2d 571, 577-78 (La. Ct. App. 1979) (federal interpretations of the substantive provisions of the Federal Trade Commission Act "are proper sources for guidance" when the state statute closely tracks the federal act); Ex parte Dorsey Trailers, 397 So. 2d 98, 103 (Ala. 1981) ("cases construing the Federal Rules of Civil Procedure are authority for construction of the Alabama Rules of Civil Procedure").

[15] See 28 U.S.C.A. § 1332(a) (West Supp. 1989) (diversity jurisdiction of federal district courts).

[16] 28 U.S.C.A. § 1652 (West 1966).

[17] See Erie R.R. v. Tompkins, 304 U.S. 64 (1938) ("Erie" doctrine).

indication that state law would be different today.[18] Furthermore, although decisions of lower state courts are technically only persuasive, the Supreme Court has held that under the Rules of Decision Act they should be disregarded only when other persuasive data convinces a federal court that the highest court of the state would decide otherwise.[19]

Section 4C. Operation of Stare Decisis Rules

1. DICTA IN JUDICIAL OPINIONS

THE DOCTRINE OF STARE DECISIS DOES NOT APPLY TO DICTA IN JUDICIAL OPINIONS.

An important aspect of the doctrine of stare decisis is that the doctrine does not apply to judicial statements or observations that are unnecessary to the ascertainment of the right or title in question between the parties. Such statements or observations are called "dicta" or less frequently "obiter dicta" ("a remark by the way").[20]

ILLUSTRATION 4.6

In considering the construction of a state statute concerning the devise of property in *Carroll v. Lessee of Carroll*,[21] the United States Supreme Court stated:

> [If a judicial statement] was not a matter in judgment, if it might have been decided either way without affecting any right brought into question, then, according to the principles of the common law, an opinion on such a question is not a decision. To make it so, there must have been an application of the judicial mind to the precise question necessary to be determined to fix the rights of the parties and decide to whom the property in contestation belongs.[22]

---

[18] See Bernhardt v. Polygraphic Co. of Am., 350 U.S. 198, 204, 209-12 (1956).

[19] See, e.g., West v. American Tel. & Tel. Co., 311 U.S. 223, 237 (1940).

[20] See Black's Law Dictionary 409 (5th ed. 1979).

[21] 57 U.S. (16 How.) 275 (1854).

[22] Id. at 286-87.

In the same opinion, the Court noted the principal reason why dictum is treated in this way:

> It is a maxim not to be disregarded that general expressions in every opinion are to be taken in connection with the case in which those expressions are used. If they go beyond the case, they may be respected, but ought not to control the judgment in a subsequent suit, when the very point is presented. The reason of this maxim is obvious. The question actually before the court is investigated with care, and considered in its full extent; other principles which may serve to illustrate it are considered in their relation to the case decided, but their possible bearing on all other cases is seldom completely investigated.[23]

ALTHOUGH IT IS NOT BINDING, DICTA MAY BE INFLUENTIAL AND SHOULD NOT BE IGNORED.

Even though lower courts are not bound by dicta for the reasons just stated, dicta in judicial opinions still may be persuasive.

ILLUSTRATION 4.7

A California Court of Appeal, for example, explained:

> It is apparent from the context of the [California] Supreme Court's comments that the issue of compensation was discussed by counsel and was a consideration entering into the majority's decision, probably in anticipation of the issue arising upon further proceedings in the trial court. Because the issue was not necessary to the decision in a narrow sense, real parties in interest argue that what the Supreme Court said was dicta and need not be followed. We do not agree. Dicta are not to be ignored. Dicta may be highly persuasive, particularly where made by the Supreme Court after that court has considered the issue and deliberately made pronouncements thereon intended for guidance of the lower court upon further proceedings.[24]

---

[23] Id. at 287 (quoting Chief Justice Marshall's explanation in Cohens v. Virginia, 19 U.S. (6 Wheat.) 264, 399 (1821), in which the Court refused to follow certain statements made in Marbury v. Madison).

[24] County of Fresno v. Superior Court, 82 Cal. App. 3d 191, 194, 146 Cal. Rptr. 880, 881-82 (1978).

2. DECISIONS BY LESS THAN A MAJORITY OF ALL MEMBERS OF AN APPELLATE COURT

Appellate courts ordinarily consist of several judges, often seven or nine. For example, the United States Supreme Court consists of a Chief Justice and eight Associate Justices, any six of whom constitute a quorum. It is thus possible for an appellate court to have a quorum (e.g., seven of nine) and to decide cases (e.g., on a vote of four to three) with less than a majority of the entire court concurring in the decision.

PROBLEM 4.1

In *Fuentes v. Shevin*,[25] the United States Supreme Court held that a state statute providing for replevin without notice and a meaningful opportunity to be heard prior to the actual seizure of the property violated the due process clause of the fourteenth amendment of the U.S. Constitution. In *Fuentes*, the Court was divided four-to-three, with two Justices not participating. Based on the preceding discussion of stare decisis, do you think the binding nature of the decision is affected because a majority (five Justices) did not concur in the result?

Stop here, and consider this question before consulting the discussion of this problem in Appendix A.

3. DECISIONS BY AN EQUALLY DIVIDED COURT

AFFIRMANCES RESULTING FROM AN EQUALLY DIVIDED COURT DO NOT HAVE A STARE DECISIS EFFECT.

When an appellate court is equally divided, the judgment of the lower court is affirmed. In light of the preceding discussion, it should be apparent that affirmances resulting from an equally divided court do not have a stare decisis effect. In *Hertz v. Woodman*,[26] the United States Supreme Court explained:

> [A]n affirmance by an equally divided court is, as between the parties, a conclusive determination and adjudication of the matter adjudged, but the principles of law involved not having been agreed upon by a majority of the court sitting prevents the case from

---

[25] 407 U.S. 67 (1972).

[26] 218 U.S. 205 (1910).

> becoming an authority for the determination of other cases, either in this or in inferior courts.[27]

The same rule prevails in state court systems.[28]

4. SUMMARY AFFIRMANCE OR DISMISSAL

Although the United States Supreme Court no longer must hear appeals as a matter of right,[29] the United States Supreme Court was required for many years to hear such appeals. Because of its heavy case load, the Supreme Court frequently used memorandum decisions to affirm judgments of lower federal courts and to dismiss appeals from state court decisions "for want of a substantial federal question."

A memorandum decision summarily states the court's ruling. A memorandum decision does not set forth the reasons for the decision. Sometimes, such a decision is called a "per curiam" decision.[30]

In a series of decisions, the United States Supreme Court attempted to clarify the considerable debate that has taken place concerning the precedential value of memorandum decisions. In *Hicks v. Miranda*,[31] the Court found that a federal district court had erred in holding that it was not bound by a prior United States Supreme Court memorandum decision that summarily dismissed, for want of a substantial federal question, an appeal from a state appellate court decision sustaining the constitutionality of a state obscenity statute. The Court observed that votes to affirm summarily or to dismiss for want of a substantial federal question are votes on the merits of a case. The Court noted, however, that its summary action (memorandum decision) is decisive only to the extent that the issues in the two cases are sufficiently the same.[32]

---

[27] Id. at 213-14.

[28] See, e.g., Frank v. City of Cody, 572 P.2d 1106, 1109-10 n.5 (Wyo. 1977) (affirmance by equally divided court not given weight because it should not be considered as settling any principle).

[29] See Act of June 27, 1988, Pub. L. No. 100-352, 102 Stat. 662 (eliminating appeals as a matter of right).

[30] See Black's Law Dictionary 1023 (5th ed. 1979) ("per curiam" also is used to refer to an opinion, often short in length, of the whole court).

[31] 422 U.S. 332 (1975).

[32] Id. at 343-44.

In *Illinois State Board of Elections v. Socialist Workers Party*,[33] the Court further explained the extent of the binding effect of a summary disposition (memorandum decision). According to the Court, a summary disposition (memorandum decision) can extend no farther than the precise issues presented and necessarily decided. It affirms only the judgment below, and "no more may be read into our action than was essential to sustain that judgment."[34] Questions that merely "lurk in the record" are not resolved by the disposition, and "no resolution of them may be inferred."[35]

In contrast to the binding effect of United States Supreme Court summary dispositions, several federal courts of appeals do not regard their own summary dispositions as precedents. This approach is related to the limited publication of their opinions, discussed below.

SUMMARY AFFIRMANCES AND DISMISSALS MUST BE CAREFULLY EVALUATED TO DETERMINE THE EXTENT TO WHICH THEY HAVE PRECEDENTIAL VALUE.

5. CASES IN WHICH NO SINGLE THEORY COMMANDS A MAJORITY OF THE APPELLATE COURT

In certain cases, a majority may agree on the disposition of the appeal, but no single theory commands a majority of the court.

ILLUSTRATION 4.8

In *Robins v. California*,[36] a majority (6-3) of the Court agreed that the decision below should be reversed. Justices Brennan, White, and Marshall joined in Justice Stewart's opinion. Justice Powell filed a separate opinion concurring in the judgment, and the Chief Justice concurred in the judgment without joining in either opinion. Justices Blackmun, Rehnquist, and Stevens filed separate dissenting opinions.

---

[33] 440 U.S. 173 (1979).

[34] Id. at 182-83.

[35] Id. at 183. Accord Mandel v. Bradley, 432 U.S. 173, 176 (1977). See Annotation, Precedential Weight of Supreme Court's Memorandum Decisions Summarily Affirming Lower Federal Court Judgment on Appeal or Summarily Dismissing Appeal from State Court--Federal Cases, 45 L. Ed. 2d 791 (1975).

[36] 453 U.S. 420 (1981).

A decision in which a majority agrees on the disposition of the action, but no single theory commands a majority of the court is regarded as having only limited precedential value. Such a decision should be treated like a decision without an opinion (summary affirmances and dismissals) discussed in the preceding subsection.

IN GENERAL, A DECISION IN WHICH A MAJORITY AGREES ON THE DISPOSITION OF THE ACTION, BUT NO SINGLE THEORY COMMANDS A MAJORITY OF THE COURT, GOVERNS FUTURE CASES IN INFERIOR COURTS IN WHICH THE SAME ISSUES ARE PRESENTED ON INDISTINGUISHABLE FACTS. IT DOES NOT GOVERN CASES IN WHICH THE FACTS PRESENT SOME ISSUES WITHOUT OTHERS.

A student note in the *Columbia Law Review*, however, asserts that the "lower courts have the responsibility to look beneath the surface of the various opinions in order to determine which lines of reasoning, if any, reflect the view of a majority."[37] This student note further asserts that "any line of reasoning that has the support of a clear majority of the Court should be regarded as authoritative, even if that reasoning does not seem convincing to a lower court."[38]

6. DENIAL OF PETITION FOR A WRIT OF CERTIORARI

When an appellate court is given the discretion to decide whether it will review a lower court decision, a party must first request the appellate court to review the decision below. In the United States Supreme Court and many other appellate courts, the party would petition the court to issue a writ of certiorari ordering the lower court to certify the record and send the record to the appellate court for review.

What is the precedential effect of the denial of the petition? Does it give added weight to the decision below? The short answer, according to the United States Supreme Court, is that a denial of discretionary review "carries with it no implication whatever regarding the Court's views on the merits of a case it has declined to review."[39]

---

[37] Note, The Precedential Value of Supreme Court Plurality Decisions, 80 Colum. L. Rev. 756, 780 (1980).

[38] Id. at 779. See also Note, Plurality Decisions and Judicial Decisionmaking, 94 Harv. L. Rev. 1127 (1981).

[39] Maryland v. Baltimore Radio Show, 338 U.S. 912, 919 (1950).

THE DENIAL OF A WRIT OF CERTIORARI DOES NOT GIVE ADDED WEIGHT TO THE DECISION BELOW.

7. DENIAL OR REFUSAL OF A PETITION OR APPLICATION FOR A WRIT OF ERROR

Another type of review available in some states is review pursuant to a writ of error. This type of writ is used to review errors of law apparent on the record. If a petition or application for the writ of error is granted, the court will issue the writ calling for the record of the action for review. Again, what is the precedential effect of a denial of a petition for a writ of error? Does it give added weight to the decision below?

In general, a denial of a writ of error means that the court that denied review approved the result reached by the lower court but not necessarily the lower court's opinion. In addition, such a refusal may not even mean approval of the result below when the error was not preserved and presented to the reviewing court.

IN SEVERAL STATES, A DENIAL OF A WRIT OF ERROR MEANS THAT THE APPELLATE COURT APPROVED THE RESULT BELOW BUT NOT NECESSARILY THE LOWER COURT'S OPINION. WHEN THE ERROR WAS NOT PRESERVED AND PRESENTED TO THE REVIEWING COURT, THE REFUSAL MAY NOT EVEN MEAN APPROVAL OF THE RESULT BELOW.

In this regard, a peculiar practice of the Texas Supreme Court should be considered. The Texas Supreme Court notes the significance of its refusal of an application for a writ of error, as shown in the table on the next page.[40]

[40] See Simpson, Notations on Applications for Writs of Error, 12 Tex. B.J. 547, 574-75 (1949).

TEXAS WRIT HISTORY

WRIT REFUSED (writ ref'd)

9/1/1892 to 6/14/1927--The Texas Supreme Court approved the result reached by the civil court of appeals but did not necessarily approve of the opinion. Refusal might not even mean approval of the result reached when the error was not preserved and presented to the Texas Supreme Court.

6/14/1927 to PRESENT--The judgment of the civil court of appeals was correct and principles of law declared in the opinion were correctly determined.

WRIT REFUSED FOR WANT OF MERIT (writ ref'd w.o.m.)

9/1/1941 to 2/1/1946--The judgment of the civil court of appeals was correct but the Texas Supreme Court was not satisfied that the opinion in all respects had declared the law correctly.

WRIT REFUSED, NO REVERSIBLE ERROR (writ ref'd n.r.e.)

2/1/1946 to PRESENT--The Texas Supreme Court was not satisfied that the opinion of the civil court of appeals in all respects had declared the law correctly but was of the opinion that the application presented no error which required reversal.

WRIT DISMISSED FOR WANT OF JURISDICTION (writ dism'd w.o.j.)

9/1/1892 to 7/1/1917--The Texas Supreme Court lacked jurisdiction to consider the application.

7/1/1917 to 6/14/1927--Same as above, except extended to include cases otherwise within the Texas Supreme Court's jurisdiction when the error committed, if any, was not of such importance to the jurisprudence of the state, in the opinion of the Texas Supreme Court, that a correction was required.

6/14/1927 to 3/1/1939--(1) The Texas Supreme Court lacked jurisdiction to consider the application; (2) in cases within the Texas Supreme Court's jurisdiction, the judgment of the civil court of appeals was correct but the Texas Supreme Court was not satisfied that the opinion of the civil court of appeals in all respects had declared the law correctly.

3/1/1939 to PRESENT--The Texas Supreme Court lacked jurisdiction to consider the application.

WRIT DISMISSED FOR WANT OF JURISDICTION--CORRECT JUDGMENT (writ dism'd judgmt cor.)

3/1/1939 to 9/1/1941--In cases within the jurisdiction of the Texas Supreme Court, the judgment below was correct but the Texas Supreme Court was not satisfied that the opinion of the civil court of appeals in all respects had declared the law correctly.

EVEN IF YOU ARE NOT PRACTICING IN TEXAS, KNOWLEDGE OF THE TEXAS SUPREME COURT'S PRACTICE OF NOTING THE PARTICULAR SIGNIFICANCE OF ITS DENIAL OF WRITS OF ERROR IS NECESSARY TO EVALUATE THE STRENGTH OF TEXAS COURT OF APPEALS CASES CITED AS PERSUASIVE PRECEDENTS.

The most readily available source of the writ history of Texas cases is *Shepard's Citations*. The following pages from *Shepard's South Western Reporter Citations* illustrate how the Texas writ history is indicated in *Shepard's* for cases appearing in volume 306 of the *South Western Reporter Second* and thereafter. Prior to that volume, an asterisk was used to alert the researcher to writ history without stating the specific nature or disposition of the writ.

PROBLEM 4.2

Assume that you have found the following case during the course of your research: *Plata v. Gohman*, 359 S.W.2d 163 (Tex. Civ. App. 1962). Examine the page reproduced from *Shepard's South Western Reporter Citations* covering the entry for this case in Figure 4-A. The page numbers on which specific cases begin in Volume 429 of the reporter are shown in bold type in the columns. Figure 4-B shows *Shepard's* table of abbreviations for Texas writ history. Based on these figures, determine the writ history of *Plata v. Gohman*.

SOUTHWESTERN REPORTER, 2d SERIES **Vol. 359**

441SW[3]687
442SW[3]169
517SW[4]719
588SW[2]480
93Æ2 1211n

– 852 –
s347SW242
d595SW[3]45
d595SW[5]45
d595SW[6]45
659SW[3]232
f669SW[3]565
f669SW[4]565

– 859 –
cc295SW62
363SW[16]642
369SW[7]588
373SW[12]34
395SW[6]739
395SW[7]739
453SW[16]677
481SW[1]600
d551SW[1]862
d551SW[2]862
d551SW[3]862
d551SW[4]863
d551SW[8]863
d580SW[3]315
585SW[15]556
673SW[16]468
Ky
406SW[3]396
Minn
145NW876
NJ
266A2d293
48Æ2 104s
85Æ3 820n

– 867 –
380SW[4]436
389SW[4]217
389SW[5]217
394SW[7]342
e403SW[4]609
e403SW[5]610
411SW[5]94
418SW55
431SW[6]185
431SW[7]186
437SW[4]165
475SW[3]102
503SW[7]68
538SW771
646SW[5]374
363F2d[2]156

– 874• –
R
387SW[5]709
d393SW[5]331
398SW[2]320
401SW[2]642
410SW[5]636
471SW[4]451
526SW[4]219
532SW[5]108
540SW[2]690
558SW954
581SW[2]673
581SW[3]675
604SW[2]216
631SW798
673SW336

– 878 –
402SW[2]934
502SW[2]843

– 880 –
381SW[1]219
470SW[1]282

– 883• –
RNRE
384SW[5]400
411SW[5]950
571SW[5]549
577SW[5]531

– 889• –
RNRE
396SW[5]916
459SW[6]872
461SW[6]447
542SW735
545SW[5]207
614SW886

– 898• –
RNRE
360SW[3]568
458SW[3]510

– 902• –
RNRE
f380SW839
d391SW52
408SW[4]299
419SW[9]710
d420SW[6]430
447SW[9]733
468SW[4]611
f474SW[10]333
475SW[10]371
501SW939
518SW[3]621
518SW[4]621
523SW[9]453
554SW[3]710
572SW[9]76
612SW[3]957
643SW[9]487
662SW[9]419
TCLM§10.18

– 907• –
RNRE
h512SW[2]349
524SW[2]267
524SW[3]276
544SW[2]178
Ariz
409P2d723

– 920 –
388SW[2]23
462SW[2]619
685SW[11]686
322F2d[2]39
18Æ2 443s
50Æ2 458s
93Æ2 1052n

– 934• –
RNRE
458SW[2]184
477SW[3]384
560SW[1]485

– 936• –
RNRE
469SW[1]220
469SW[4]221
94Æ3 1139n

– 941 –
403SW[2]212

– 943 –
443SW[5]381
526SW[1]629
553SW[1]428
553SW[2]428
660SW641
686SW[2]608
11BRW641
Ark
398SW[1]62
NM
414P2d228
55Æ2 1044s
17Æ3 1383n

– 947 –
384SW[2]205
410SW[3]854
446SW[2]926

– 950 –
381SW[2]364
454SW[1]278
470SW[3]775
520SW[1]926
520SW[2]926
576SW[1]893
576SW[2]894
630SW[1]468

– 952 –
16Æ2 3s
37Æ2 391s
11Æ3 266n
2COA167§9

– 955 –
519SW[2]229
582SW[1]504
599SW[2]841
633SW[1]324

– 956• –
G
r366SW922
s369SW53
e364SW[2]842

Vol. 359

– 1 –
(49TnA662)
427SW[6]33
h491SW[3]850
f518SW[7]233
600SW[7]731
379F2d[4]623
d395F2d[6]329
440F2d[3]653
W Va
151SE686
40Æ2 168s
63Æ3 748n
ICD§5.12

– 23 –
362SW[3]751
374SW[8]410
375SW[1]585
479SW[3]187
479SW[4]187
481SW[1]642
484SW[3]668
584SW[3]105

– 29 –
457SW[2]755
f661SW[5]661

– 33 –
364SW[4]348
631SW[2]953
d659SW[2]535

– 38 –
379SW[1]892
8Æ3 1288n
8Æ3 1309n

– 40 –
d366SW[5]73
d379SW568
d410SW[5]113
410SW[3]114
410SW[2]116
d420SW[5]278
454SW[2]626
454SW[4]626
526SW[1]843
d536SW[2]745
d536SW[3]745
d536SW[4]745
542SW[3]70
565SW[2]680
637SW[5]733
Ill
344NE515
465NE520
69Æ2 9s

– 48 –
(163Tex545)
s351SW932
362SW[1]382
369SW[5]642
370SW[5]23
372SW[8]551
383SW[9]650
384SW[10]403
387SW[4]443
387SW[8]443
387SW[9]443
390SW[7]392
392SW[3]891
398SW[3]389
400SW[9]14
403SW[3]337
403SW[8]337
403SW[9]338
j403SW[9]339
d426SW[5]846
443SW[9]603
446SW[9]356
447SW[9]744
451SW[9]958
d452SW[9]710
469SW[9]928
480SW[5]425
480SW[6]426
483SW[1]312
f490SW[7]217
496SW[1]542
508SW[2]664
512SW[8]764
513SW[9]208
518SW[5]597
533SW[7]369
f533SW[6]372
535SW[1]944
535SW[2]944
535SW[9]947
535SW[10]947
541SW[7]875
j543SW[10]735
564SW486
575SW[9]633
592SW[9]33
595SW[9]179
595SW[8]180
606SW[9]4
624SW[9]663
641SW[10]216
664SW[1]108
331F2d[6]352
406F2d[5]338
Ind
315NE723
333NE86
Iowa
148NW473
218NW579
49Æ2 521s

– 52 –
(172TxCr470)

– 54• –
G
r363SW431
482SW[2]668
55Æ2 673s

– 56• –
G
r371SW548

– 62• –
G
a367SW322
e399SW[2]870
456SW[3]444
496SW[3]676
573SW[3]295
j583SW933

– 68• –
RNRE
378SW[7]120
403SW[11]173
509SW[11]417
367F2d[12]497

– 77 –
366SW[2]635
604SW[2]535

– 86• –
G
r367SW312

– 91 –
419SW[3]677
572SW[3]15
590SW[3]741
592SW[3]64

– 95• –
RNRE
s362SW298
f363SW[1]901
387SW[2]757
393SW[1]431
400SW[2]302
410SW[1]841
426SW[1]320
497SW[3]804
516SW[2]476
516SW[1]478
538SW[1]683
616SW[2]374
j631F2d511
Ariz
650P2d500
33Æ3 157n
46Æ3 777n
46Æ3 784n
46Æ3 789n

– 97 –
46Æ3 1254n

– 99 –
381SW[2]725
f407SW[1]31
495SW[4]35

– 101 –
412SW[1]387
465SW[1]223
509SW[1]876

– 103• –
G
r364SW177
q377SW[4]857

– 106 –
472SW[2]577
89Æ3 808n

– 108• –
RNRE
s337SW376
s349SW715
Mo
480SW[3]895

– 112• –
RNRE
447SW[1]450

– 114 –
374SW[6]452
407SW[4]880
427SW[6]331
429SW[6]165
432SW[6]554
462SW[6]544
557SW[5]585
601SW[2]546
635SW[4]875
NM
671P2d1139
70Æ2 1250s

– 116• –
RNRE
361SW[1]435
366SW[1]658
370SW[1]10
378SW[1]155
384SW[1]916
387SW[1]949
395SW[1]662
400SW[5]10
j406SW[1]196
j406SW[4]197
435SW[1]190
439SW[1]396
d441SW[6]912
453SW[1]358
454SW[1]267
457SW[1]153
466SW[1]20
472SW[1]825
507SW[1]309
507SW[2]309
29Æ2 5s
39Æ2 15s

– 120• –
G
r359SW882
cc381SW945
d369SW639

– 122 –
414SW[5]61
605SW[1]718
DC
383A2d14

– 126• –
D
604SW[2]392
346F2d[4]205

– 128• –
R
384SW[4]418
386SW[4]194
d396SW[2]109
d572SW[4]581
42Æ3 57n

– 131• –
G
a365SW628
403SW[2]882
453SW[6]201
12Æ4 833n

– 134 –
j404SW[2]146
445SW[1]807

– 136• –
RNRE

– 146 –
417SW[5]424
548F2d[2]1221
656F2d[2]204
317FS[2]1181

– 152• –
RNRE
d393SW395
486SW[4]159

– 156• –
RNRE
cc382SW354
387SW[3]716
433SW[2]730
433SW[3]730
433SW[5]730
517SW[5]347
577SW[5]512
76Æ2 1172s

– 163• –
RNRE
d390SW[4]383
404SW[4]926
408SW[2]952
408SW[4]952
408SW[1]953
413SW[5]771
419SW[2]438
431SW[6]778
445SW[6]818
d505SW[3]950
570SW[2]485

– 168 –
s319SW820
s330SW690
s337SW107
s373SW100
398SW[1]785
427SW[1]126
509SW[1]876

– 171 –
s365SW700
465SW[2]397
507SW[2]343
507SW[3]343
d517SW[3]372
523SW[2]17
647SW[3]90
40BRW[2]611

– 177• –
RNRE
433SW[7]734
442SW[1]439
442SW[2]439
442SW[4]439
477SW[12]329
e485SW[12]778
517SW[12]349
561SW[2]220
561SW[4]220
561SW[11]222
18Æ2 725s
56Æ3 24n
56Æ3 48n
56Æ3 111n

– 184• –
D
D362SW646
f369SW[1]437
458SW[1]653
Fla
215So2d779
10Æ2 1035s

– 190• –
RNRE
401SW[1]720
414SW[1]749
417SW[1]356
491FS[1]1149
491FS[2]1149

– 200 –
389SW169
399SW[4]184
404SW[4]919
463SW[4]231
Continued

*Texas cases involving writs. See page xii

1021

FIGURE 4-A
SHEPARD'S SOUTH WESTERN REPORTER CITATIONS

ABBREVIATIONS

Disposition of Texas Writs

CD–Application for certiorari denied.
D–Application for writ of error dismissed for want of jurisdiction.
DAP–Application for writ of error dismissed by agreement of parties.
DJC–Application for writ of error dismissed, judgment correct.
DMA–Dismissed on motion of applicant.
DWB–Dismissed for want of bond.
DWP–Dismissed for want of prosecution.
G–Application for writ of error granted.
MA–Mandamus awarded.
MD–Application for writ of mandamus dismissed for want of jurisdiction.
MDen–Application for writ of mandamus denied.
MG–Motion for mandamus granted.
MGP–Application for mandamus granted in part.
MI–Writ of mandamus will issue.
MO–Motion for mandamus overruled.
MR–Application for writ of mandamus refused.
MRP–Application for writ of mandamus refused in part.
R–Application for writ of error refused.
RNRE–Application for writ of error refused, no reversible error.
RWM–Application for writ of error refused for want of merit.

FIGURE 4-B
SHEPARD'S SOUTH WESTERN REPORTER CITATIONS

Stop here, and determine the writ history of Plata v. Gohman, 359 S.W.2d 163 (Tex. Civ. App. 1962) before consulting the discussion of this problem in Appendix A.

PROBLEM 4.3

The refusal of the application for the writ of error in the *Plata* case (above) means that

(a) the authority of the decision below is strengthened.

(b) the principles declared in the opinion of the Texas Court of Civil Appeals were decided correctly.

(c) the authority of the decision below must be analyzed carefully because the Texas Supreme Court was not convinced that the opinion of the Texas Court of Civil Appeals correctly stated the law in all respects.

(d) the Texas Supreme Court lacked jurisdiction to hear the case, and thus it refused the application for the writ of error. A refusal of the writ indicates that "no reversible error" existed.

Stop here, and choose one or more answers before consulting the discussion of this problem in Appendix A.

Shepard's South Western Reporter Citations begins listing the specific writ history with volume 306 of the *South Western Reporter Second*. How would you find the writ history of cases reported prior to volume 306?

Shepard's state edition (*Shepard's Texas Citations*) indicates the specific disposition of the writ begins with volume 256 of the *South Western Reporter Second*. The writ history of all Texas cases also can be checked by using West's *Texas Writ of Error Table* (not available in many law libraries outside of Texas). This table is updated by consulting the most recent advance sheets of the *South Western Reporter* and, if available, the most recent *Texas Supreme Court Journal*.[41]

Section 4D. Res Judicata and Related Doctrines

This section considers the following four related, but distinct doctrines: (1) res judicata (claim preclusion), (2) collateral estoppel (issue preclusion), (3) law of the case, and (4) full faith and credit. These four doctrines should be carefully distinguished from stare decisis.

1. RES JUDICATA (CLAIM PRECLUSION)

In subsequent litigation between the parties and their privies involving the same claim, the doctrine of res judicata (also referred to as "claim preclusion") makes a final *judgment* by a court of competent jurisdiction conclusive.

ILLUSTRATION 4.9

Assume Caesar sued Brutus to recover for personal injuries, but the jury found for Brutus. In such a case, the court would enter a judgment that the "plaintiff take nothing." If Caesar sued Brutus again because he was dissatisfied with the result in the first action, Brutus could raise the defense of res judicata ("a thing decided"). In other words, the judgment in the first suit would be a "bar" to the second action.

The purpose of res judicata in the above situation is to establish a finality to litigation. In that sense, res judicata is like stare decisis. The same points, once they are settled, will not be

---

[41] See Texas Law Review, Texas Rules of Form 11-12 (5th ed. 1983).

considered again. Stare decisis, however, relates to the binding effect of the legal principles decided or the rule involved, not to the particular judgment that results from them. Res judicata binds the parties and privies to the judgment. Stare decisis governs the decisions of the same questions of law in other actions between strangers to the prior action. Another important difference is that stare decisis applies to the legal principles and rules which have been "duly considered." In contrast, res judicata may preclude aspects of a claim that could have been raised but were not.

ILLUSTRATION 4.10

Assume that Caesar had won his suit against Brutus and that a judgment for $10,000 had been entered in his favor. Assume that in the suit Caesar presented evidence of the extent of his personal injuries and his pain and suffering but failed to ask for lost wages or to present evidence concerning them. Res judicata would be a defense to a second suit by Caesar to recover for his lost wages. The judgment in the plaintiff's favor extinguished the entire claim that was the subject of the first suit. The claim, it is said, "merged" into the judgment. Thus, Caesar no longer could sue on the original claim or any part of it even if something was omitted unintentionally from his original claim.

2. COLLATERAL ESTOPPEL (ISSUE PRECLUSION)

Stare decisis also should be distinguished from the doctrine of collateral estoppel ("issue preclusion").

ILLUSTRATION 4.11

Assume that Caesar signed a contract to sell Brutus a dagger (Contract #l) and that Brutus also entered into a separate, identically worded contract to acquire another dagger from Antony (Contract #2). Assume that Caesar decided that it would not be a good idea to fulfill his contract with Brutus. Brutus then sued Caesar for specific performance of the contract.

Assume that in the course of the litigation a dispute arose concerning the legal effect of certain language in the contract and that the dispute was decided against Brutus. Even though he had lost his suit against Caesar, Brutus was not worried because he still had the contract with Antony to acquire another dagger. Antony, however, also refused to fulfill his contract, and Brutus sued Antony for specific performance of the contract.

Assume that the same issue concerning the legal effect of the contract language then was raised. Under the modern law of collateral estoppel, the decision against Brutus in the prior proceeding (*Brutus v. Caesar*) ordinarily would preclude relitigation of the same issue by a party to the prior proceeding (here Brutus) in a subsequent action (*Brutus v. Antony*) on a different claim (the breach of contract #1 and #2 are different claims).

This preclusion occurs assuming that the party against whom collateral estoppel is going to be applied (Brutus) had a full and fair opportunity to litigate the issue in the prior action. The legal principle or rule concerning the legal consequences of the contract language announced in *Brutus v. Caesar* may have an effect on actions between entire strangers to the *Brutus v. Caesar* action.

ILLUSTRATION 4.12

Suppose that Cleopatra subsequently entered into a contract to buy an asp in a basket of figs from a rustic person and that she used the same contract language that Brutus and Caesar had used. If an action on that contract is brought before the same court, the issue is likely to be decided in the same way.

The reason would be stare decisis, not res judicata (because these are different claims and different parties) nor collateral estoppel (neither Cleopatra nor the rustic person could be bound because neither had been a party to the prior action).

3. LAW OF THE CASE

Stare decisis likewise should be distinguished from the closely related doctrine of the "law of the case." Like stare decisis, the law of the case applies to determinations of questions of law. Unlike stare decisis, which is used in *other* subsequent cases involving the same legal issue, the doctrine of the law of the case applies to all subsequent stages of the *same* case. Once a question of law in the case has been determined, that determination will be treated as correct throughout the case (until the question is reviewed by a higher court).

ILLUSTRATION 4.13

A trial court will treat its own earlier rulings as conclusive in subsequent proceedings. Likewise, when an appellate court has decided a legal issue on an interlocutory appeal (one occurring during litigation that does not determine the entire merits of the controversy), the decision on the legal issue ordinarily will not be reconsidered by the same appellate court if the case later is heard on appeal from the final judgment.

4. FULL FAITH AND CREDIT

As noted previously in section B above, only the federal courts (and Congress) have the final authority to determine federal law, just as each state has the final authority to determine state law. Nevertheless, under some circumstances a court may not reject determinations of its law by other courts even though the court views such determinations as clearly incorrect.

ILLUSTRATION 4.14

Assume that Ponce de Leon, a Florida resident, sued Big Foot, another Florida resident, for fraud in a Florida state court. In the course of the litigation, the Florida court decided to apply California law to certain legal issues because the misrepresentation that was the basis of the action had been made in California. Assume that the Florida court erroneously determined California law and entered judgment for the plaintiff. Because the defendant lacked sufficient assets in Florida to satisfy the judgment, Ponce de Leon then sued in a California state court to enforce the Florida judgment against the defendant's property in California.

Under these circumstances, assuming that the Florida court properly had jurisdiction over the defendant and the proceedings were otherwise valid, the California court would be "bound" to enforce a valid Florida judgment even though the California court realized that the judgment was based upon on an erroneous determination of California law. This result is not one of stare decisis but rather one of "full faith and credit." The statute implementing the full faith and credit clause of the Constitution[42] provides, "[The] judicial proceedings [of every state] shall have the same full faith and credit in every court in the United States . . . as they have by law or usage in the courts of [the state] from which they are taken."[43] A separate provision governs full faith and credit for child custody determinations.[44]

The following problems review the basic concepts relating to the authority of judicial opinions discussed in this and preceding sections. Unless otherwise stated, these problems are based on the following facts:

Ms. Hood was walking through the woods one day on the way to her grandmother's house. Wolf, a door-to-door salesman, had sold Grandmother Hood a complete line of pots and pans. Upon hearing that Hood was coming to the house, Wolf tied Grandmother Hood up and put her in the closet. When Ms. Hood arrived, Wolf pretended to be Hood's grandmother. Not being fooled, Ms. Hood gave him three swift Karate kicks, and Wolf surrendered. Assume that Ms. Hood and her grandmother

---

[42]U.S. Const. art. IV, § 1.

[43]28 U.S.C.A. § 1738 (West 1966).

[44]<u>See</u> 28 U.S.C. § 1738A (West Supp. 1989).

commenced separate actions in a California state trial court (California Superior Court) against Wolf to recover damages.

PROBLEM 4.4

Grandmother Hood's attorneys sought to take the oral deposition (pretrial testimony taken under oath) of Peter Hood, Ms. Hood's younger brother. Wolf objected that Peter was too young to testify. After the parties took the appropriate procedural steps to present the issue to the trial court for decision, the trial judge ruled that Peter was competent and allowed his deposition to be taken. At trial, Wolf again objected that Peter was incompetent to testify. Which of the following doctrines would be the proper basis for denying Wolf's objection?

(a) stare decisis

(b) res judicata

(c) full faith and credit

(d) law of the case

Stop here, and choose an answer before consulting the discussion of this problem in Appendix A.

PROBLEM 4.5

Assume that Grandmother Hood won her action against Wolf and that Ms. Hood's action was then brought to trial. Ms. Hood called her little brother (Peter) to testify, and Wolf objected on the ground that Peter was too young to testify reliably. Which of the following doctrines would support the trial judge's denial of Wolf's motion?

(a) stare decisis

(b) collateral estoppel

(c) full faith and credit

(d) law of the case

Stop here, and choose one or more answers before consulting the discussion of this problem in Appendix A.

PROBLEM 4.6

At trial, Wolf claimed that "he didn't touch Ms. Hood" and that she had attacked him without provocation. Assume that the jury believed Wolf's testimony and that the trial court entered a judgment in favor of Wolf based on the jury's verdict. Dissatisfied with that result, Hood sued again on the same claim in a different California Superior Court. That second action would be barred by

(a) the doctrine of stare decisis.

(b) the doctrine of res judicata.

(c) the doctrine of full faith and credit.

(d) the doctrine of law of the case.

Stop here, and choose an answer before consulting the discussion of this problem in Appendix A.

PROBLEM 4.7

Assume that instead of filing a new action, Hood appealed the judgment entered on the jury's verdict to a California Court of Appeal. On appeal, Ms. Hood asserted that the trial court erred when it allowed certain testimony that Hood considered to be inadmissible hearsay evidence. Assume that the California Supreme Court had decided a prior case involving the same point of evidence law and similar facts. The California Court of Appeal would be bound by that earlier decision based on

(a) the doctrine of stare decisis.

(b) the doctrine of collateral estoppel.

(c) the doctrine of full faith and credit.

(d) the doctrine of law of the case.

Stop here, and choose an answer before consulting the discussion of this problem in Appendix A.

Section 4E. Other Factors Affecting the Authority of Judicial Opinions

This section considers other factors affecting the "authority" of judicial opinions.

1. DECISIONS BY A WELL-KNOWN AND RESPECTED JUDGE

In terms of persuasive value, a decision written by a well-known and well-respected judge, such as Benjamin Cardozo, Learned Hand, Roger Traynor, Henry J. Friendly, or Oliver Wendell Holmes, may be more influential than others.

ILLUSTRATION 4.15

For instance, Learned Hand's influence on the law of unfair business practices, trademarks, copyright, and commercial law is evidenced by the number of times other courts have favorably cited his opinions as well as the number of times casebooks on these subjects have included or referred to his opinions.

2. DISSENTING OPINIONS

What is the precedential value of a dissenting opinion written by a judge who disagrees with the action taken by the majority of the court? Referring to a recently decided Colorado case that had addressed the point in dispute, the Wyoming Supreme Court gave the following answer:

> The appellant-plaintiff here cites as his authority the dissent in that case. We must remind [counsel] that a dissent has no precedential value nor does the fact that an appellate court is split take anything away from the weight of the majority. A dissent lends comfort to the losing party but adds nothing to the jurisprudence of the [s]tate until perhaps in the indefinite future it is adopted as controlling.[45]

Karl Llewellyn provides a different perspective on dissenting opinions in his book *The Bramble Bush*:

> [W]hile it is very hard to generalize about the effect of a dissenting opinion in the future, certain things seem probable. First, that in the court which decides the case a dissenting opinion proves that a fight has been had and is settled, and that the majority will almost certainly stay put, at least so long as the same personnel is on the bench. The great exceptions to this rule (and they are rare) are cases in which the dissent in the words of Cardozo "was the voice of a new day," too unfamiliar to have found as yet the acceptance that awaited it. Outside of the court which announced the decision the effect of a dissenting opinion is ambiguous. Always it somewhat weakens the authority of the case. Partly because it is by a divided court, partly because side by side with the reasoning of the majority and weakening its psychological effect appears another line of reasoning. Yet the argument is often met with, and seems sometimes to have weight, that the very fact of a dissent proves peculiarly careful consideration, and

[45] Woodward v. Haney, 564 P.2d 844, 846 (Wyo. 1977).

should therefore strengthen rather than weaken the case as an authority.[46]

DISSENTING OPINIONS ARE NOT MANDATORY AUTHORITY. BE CAREFUL IN RELYING ON DISSENTING OPINIONS AS PERSUASIVE PRECEDENTS. SOMETIMES, HOWEVER, COURTS OUTSIDE THE JURISDICTION WILL REGARD ARGUMENTS MADE BY DISSENTING JUDGES AS MORE PERSUASIVE THAN THOSE MADE IN THE MAJORITY OPINION.

3. CONTENT OF AN OFFICIAL SYLLABUS

A syllabus is ordinarily an introductory summary of the points of law discussed in the opinion and sometimes the facts of the case. It is not part of the opinion and ordinarily is not an authoritative statement even when it is prepared by the court.[47] In a few states, however, a syllabus prepared by the court does have authoritative value, and the content of the syllabus can make statements of law in the text of the opinion (that otherwise appear relevant to the decision) not binding for purposes of stare decisis.

ILLUSTRATION 4.16

Consider, for example, the Ohio Supreme Court's view:

> The law in Ohio since 1858 has been that it is the syllabus of the [Ohio] Supreme Court decisions which states the law, i.e., the points of law decided in a case are to be found in the syllabus. Therefore, [when] the justice assigned to write the opinion discusses matters or expresses his opinion on questions not in the syllabus, the language is merely the personal opinion of the writer. Consequently, the language in [the case] relied upon by the appellant is merely obiter dicta.[48]

---

[46] K. Llewellyn, The Bramble Bush 64 (1930).

[47] See, e.g., Burbank v. Ernst, 232 U.S. 162, 165 (1914) ("Reliance is also placed upon the headnote of the decision [that] inaccurately represents the reasoning of the judgment. . . . [W]e look to the opinion for the original and authentic statement of the grounds of decision").

[48] State v. Wilson, 58 Ohio St. 52, 60, 388 N.E.2d 745, 751 (1979) (footnote and emphasis deleted).

IN MOST JURISDICTIONS, A SYLLABUS DOES NOT CONSTITUTE PART OF AN OPINION, AND IT DOES NOT HAVE PRECEDENTIAL VALUE. IN A FEW STATES, HOWEVER, A SYLLABUS IS AUTHORITATIVE AND CONTROLS THE POINTS OF LAW DECIDED.

4. EN BANC VERSUS PANEL DECISIONS

En banc decisions are those in which the entire membership of the court participates. In many state appellate courts and in the federal courts of appeals, cases usually are heard and decided by panels of judges. Rule 35(a) of the Federal Rules of Appellate Procedure provides that an en banc hearing "is not favored and ordinarily will not be ordered except (1) when consideration by the full court is necessary to secure or maintain uniformity of its decisions, or (2) when the proceeding involves a question of exceptional importance."[49]

In terms of precedent, courts in other jurisdictions will consider a panel decision to be less persuasive than an en banc decision on the same point. Furthermore, courts have consistently held that a panel cannot modify a prior en banc decision and that a prior panel decision does not bind the entire court.[50]

A PANEL DECISION IS CONSIDERED TO BE LESS PERSUASIVE THAN AN EN BANC DECISION ON THE SAME POINT. BE AWARE THAT DIFFERENT PANELS, DIVISIONS, OR DEPARTMENTS OF A COURT MAY FOLLOW INCONSISTENT APPROACHES OR STANDARDS UNTIL THE ISSUE IS FINALLY RESOLVED BY THE ENTIRE COURT.

5. UNPUBLISHED AND UNOFFICIALLY REPORTED OPINIONS

Opinions written in a number of cases are not officially or unofficially published. For example, only a small portion of

---

[49] Fed. R. App. P. 35(a).

[50] See, e.g., Ewing v. Williams, 596 F.2d 391, 397 (9th Cir. 1979); Spann v. State, 126 Ga. App. 370, 374, 190 S.E.2d 924, 927 (1972). Until the entire court resolves a matter, different panels, divisions, or departments of a court may follow inconsistent standards or approaches. See M. Rombauer, Legal Problem Solving: Analysis, Research and Writing 51 (4th ed. 1983) (noting that this possibility must be taken into account in evaluating the authoritative value of an opinion).

opinions written by the federal district courts are published in the *Federal Supplement*. Nevertheless, unpublished opinions are available to attorneys and the general public as part of the public record of the case. Do these unpublished opinions have precedential value?

In absence of a court restriction prohibiting their use, unpublished opinions appear to have persuasive value, but apparently they are not considered binding in a stare decisis sense.

ILLUSTRATION 4.17

Consider the following discussion of this issue by the Tennessee Supreme Court:

> The [plaintiff-in-error's] able brief . . . relies upon the common[-]law rule that such an act does not constitute the crime of sodomy [in this state]. . . .
>
> . . . .
>
> This [c]ourt in an unpublished opinion of *Lester Brewer v. State*, Knox Criminal, November 1943, supports and upholds the position taken by the State in the instant case, that is, that the [Tennessee] [s]tatute covers the crime. This [c]ourt in that opinion relied upon what it there called the leading case of *State v. Cyr* [an Oregon Supreme Court decision rejecting the common-law view].
>
> Of course counsel for the plaintiff[-]in[-]error did not have access to this unpublished opinion. We do not like to nor do we ordinarily refer to unpublished opinions. Normally the opinions are not published because . . . authority on the matter [has] already [been] published in the State. When there is no authority for it and the opinion is not published the opinion is *not* to be taken as general authority. . . . We think though that the reasoning of the [c]ourt is *very persuasive* and we must adopt such a reasoning in this case and hold that under the indictment herein it is an offense against the [s]tatute--a crime against nature.[51]

When opinions have not been designated for official publication, but they have been published in an unofficial

---

[51] Fisher v. State, 197 Tenn. 594, 595-96, 277 S.W.2d 340, 340-41 (1955) (emphasis added).

reporter, special subject reporter, legal newspaper, or some other source, some courts have considered such opinions to be binding.[52]

ILLUSTRATION 4.18

In *Estate of Little*,[53] an intermediate appellate court quoted extensively from a 1909 California Supreme Court opinion that had not been reported officially. The opinion, however, did appear in *California Unreported Cases*, a seven-volume series published in 1913 that covered unreported cases from 1855-1910. The California appellate court stated, "This case has never been overruled and is therefore binding upon this court. The fact that this case was not ordered reported in the official report of the [California] Supreme Court does not detract from its binding force."[54]

In an attempt to reduce the number of opinions published, some courts have authorized only selective, official publication of their opinions.

ILLUSTRATION 4.19

Pursuant to Rule 976, the California Supreme Court has reduced substantially the publication of opinions of the California courts of appeals and the California appellate departments of superior courts.[55] To discourage private publication of reported opinions not designated for official publication, Rule 977, as amended in 1985, provides:

> (a) [Unpublished opinions] An opinion that is not ordered published shall not be cited or relied on by a court or a party in any other action or proceeding except as provided in subdivision (b).
> (b) [Exceptions] Such an opinion may be cited or relied on:
> (1) when the opinion is relevant under the doctrines of law of the case, res judicata, or collateral estoppel; or

---

[52]See Vestal, Reported Opinions of the Federal District Courts: Analysis and Suggestions, 52 Iowa L. Rev. 379, 396, n.63 (1966) (citing unofficial sources of early unreported opinions in California, Louisiana, Michigan, Mississippi, Nebraska, New York, Ohio, Tennessee, Texas, and Virginia). West Publishing Company also has included in its reporters a number of opinions that are not officially published. Id. (citing as examples Iowa Supreme Court opinions in the Northwestern Reporter designated as "Not to be officially reported" and California opinions in the California Reporter superseded by the granting of a hearing, rehearing, or other judicial action).

[53]23 Cal. App. 2d 40, 72 P.2d 213 (1937).

[54]Id. at 43, 72 P.2d at 215.

[55]See Cal. Sup. Ct. R. 976.

(2) when the opinion is relevant to a criminal or disciplinary action or proceeding because it states reasons for a decision affecting the same defendant or respondent in another such action or proceeding.

(c) [Citation procedure] A copy of any opinion citable under subdivision (b) shall be furnished to the court and all parties by attaching it to the document in which it is cited, or, if the citation is to be made orally, within a reasonable time in advance of citation.

(d) [Opinions ordered published by Supreme Court] An opinion of the Court of Appeals ordered published by the Supreme Court pursuant to rule 976 is citable.[56]

Through court rule, many of the federal courts of appeals also have prohibited the citation of unreported decisions in briefs or oral arguments presented in unrelated cases.

BE AWARE THAT COURT RULES MAY PROHIBIT CITATION OF UNREPORTED DECISIONS OR DISPOSITIONS DESIGNATED NOT FOR PUBLICATION. IN ABSENCE OF A RESTRICTION, UNPUBLISHED OPINIONS APPEAR TO HAVE PERSUASIVE VALUE, BUT APPARENTLY THEY ARE NOT CONSIDERED BINDING IN A STARE DECISIS SENSE.

6. ADVISORY OPINIONS

An advisory opinion (rendered at the request of the government or an interested party) indicates how the court would rule on a matter should adversary litigation develop. The federal government and most states do not permit their courts to render advisory opinions. A few states, however, require their appellate courts to render advisory opinions.

ILLUSTRATION 4.20

The Maine Constitution provides that "[t]he Justices of the Supreme Judicial Court shall be obliged to give their opinion upon important questions of law, and upon solemn occasions, when required by the Governor, Senate or House of Representatives."[57]

---

[56] Cal. Sup. Ct. R. 977. See Chavin, A Survey of the Writing and Publication of Opinions in Federal and State Appellate Courts, 67 L. Lib. J. 362 (1974).

[57] Me. Const. art. VI, § 3.

Advisory opinions should be considered to have about the same persuasive value as an attorney general's opinion. Advisory opinions may contain persuasive arguments, but they are certainly not binding.

ILLUSTRATION 4.21

As the Maine Supreme Judicial Court has stated, advisory opinions have "no precedential value and no conclusive effect as a judgment upon any party" and are "not binding upon even the individual [j]ustice rendering it in any subsequent litigated matter" heard by the court.[58]

BECAUSE THEIR JURISDICTION HAS BEEN RESTRICTED TO CASES OR CONTROVERSIES, MOST COURTS WILL NOT RENDER ADVISORY OPINIONS. A FEW STATES, HOWEVER, PERMIT ADVISORY OPINIONS. SUCH OPINIONS MAY CONTAIN PERSUASIVE REASONING BUT ARE NOT BINDING.

---

7. DATE OF THE DECISION

Rombauer points out that "[t]he older the decision, the less authority it may have, particularly if the trend of recent decisions in the problem area has been away from an established view or if related social attitudes have been changing."[59] Generally speaking, this statement is correct, but it is subject to one important exception: if the decision was one of statutory interpretation, its value as a precedent ordinarily is *increased* by age of the decision, as discussed in section A (example of baseball and the federal antitrust laws).

IN THE MODERN JUDICIAL CLIMATE, BE ESPECIALLY CAREFUL IN RELYING ON OUTDATED PRECEDENTS. ON THE OTHER HAND, A DECISION INVOLVING STATUTORY INTERPRETATION ORDINARILY INCREASES IN PRECEDENTIAL VALUE WITH AGE.

---

[58] Opinion of the Justices, 396 A.2d 219, 223 (Me. 1979).

[59] M. Rombauer, supra note 50, at 50.

8. CHANGE IN JUDGES ON THE COURT

An underlying tenant of stare decisis is that changes in personalities and philosophies of judges on a court ought not to affect the value of a decision as a precedent.

ILLUSTRATION 4.22

The New York Court of Appeals followed a "troublesome" precedent despite its completely asymmetrical conformance to prior law

> because it would have been scandalous for a court to shift within less than two years because of the replacement of one of the majority in the old court by one who now intellectually would have preferred to have voted with the old minority [to make a] new [majority].
>
> The ultimate principle is that a court is an institution and not merely a collection of individuals; just as a higher court commands superiority over a lower not because it is wiser or better but because it is institutionally higher. This is what is meant, in part, as the rule of law and not of men.[60]

Nonetheless, significant changes in court personnel, particularly on the United States Supreme Court, apparently may undercut the value of a precedent.

ILLUSTRATION 4.23

Consider Justice Stewart's dissent in *Mitchell v. W.T. Grant Co.*:[61]

> A substantial departure from precedent can only be justified, I had thought, in the light of experience with the application of the rule to be abandoned or in the light of an altered historic environment. Yet the Court today has unmistakably overruled a considered decision of this Court that is barely two years old, without pointing to any change in either societal perceptions or basic constitutional understandings that might justify this total disregard of stare decisis.

---

[60] People v. Hobson, 39 N.Y.2d 479, 491, 348 N.E.2d 894, 903, 384 N.Y.S.2d 419, 427 (1976).

[61] 416 U.S. 600 (1974).

> . . . The only perceivable change that has occurred . . . is in the makeup of this Court [Justice Powell and Rehnquist were appointed].
>
> A basic change in the law upon a ground no firmer than a change in our membership invites the popular misconception that this institution is little different from the two political branches of the [g]overnment. No misconception could do more lasting injury to this Court and to the system of law which it is our abiding mission to serve.[62]

9. SUBSEQUENT TREATMENT OF THE DECISION

One aspect of the weight accorded a precedent already has been discussed. A prior decision may be overruled and thus it may no longer be of value as a precedent. Furthermore, the court that decided a case subsequently may limit or otherwise criticize, harmonize, question, or distinguish the decision. This subsequent treatment may affect significantly the weight accorded to a decision. Similarly, courts in other jurisdictions may follow or criticize the decision and their treatment may influence how other jurisdictions view the case.[63]

How do you determine the subsequent treatment of a case by the deciding court or other courts? The principal means is *Shepard's Citations*. A full discussion of *Shepard's Citations* will be left to materials on legal research, but one example will illustrate the basic method used by *Shepard's*. Assume that you have found the following case during the course of your research: *Plata v. Gohman*, 359 S.W.2d 163 (Tex. Civ. App. 1962).

To find this case in *Shepard's Citations*, you would check the *Shepard's* volumes covering the *South Western Reporter Second* and look for the volume number of the reporter in the top corner of the page (Vol. 359) and the page number (**-163-**) on which the opinion begins (in bold type in the columns). After the page entry (**-163-**), various information is given, including citations to other cases that have cited the *Plata* case.

Shepard's uses symbols to indicate specific subsequent treatment of the case (e.g., o = overruled, d = distinguished, no letter = cited). *Shepard's* indicates the point of law cited or treated by noting the headnote number of the point of law immediately after the reporter abbreviation.

---

[62] Id. at 634-36.

[63] See M. Rombauer, supra note 50, at 53.

PROBLEM 4.8

Find the entry for *Plata v. Gohman*, 359 S.W.2d 163 (Tex. Civ. App. 1962) on the page of Shepard's Citations reproduced in Figure 4-A in section 4C of this chapter. Assume that you are particularly interested in the subsequent treatment of the point of law summarized in headnote 4 of the opinion.

> **4. Automobiles ⚿206**
>
> Even one who has the right-of-way is not excused from exercising ordinary care for his own safety, and even though one is not required to anticipate negligent conduct on part of motorist, he is not entitled to close his eyes to that which is plainly visible and which would have been observed by person of ordinary prudence similarly situated.

FIGURE 4-C
SOUTH WESTERN REPORTER SECOND

What subsequent treatment of headnote 4 is indicated on the page reproduced from *Shepard's*?

Stop here, and determine what treatment, if any, is indicated in Shepard's before consulting the discussion of this problem in Appendix A.

USING SHEPARD'S CITATIONS TO UPDATE A CASE TO DETERMINE ITS CURRENT STATUS IS AN INTEGRAL PART OF LEGAL RESEARCH. THE SUBSEQUENT TREATMENT OF A CASE MUST BE TAKEN INTO ACCOUNT IN EVALUATING ITS PRECEDENTIAL OR PERSUASIVE VALUE.

10. QUALITY OF THE ARGUMENTS PRESENTED

Finally, the persuasive value of a precedent may be undermined significantly when it can be shown "that a particular line of precedents or reasoning was not presented to the court in counsels' briefs [nor later raised in oral argument], and hence it cannot be presumed that it was considered by the court."[64]

---

[64] Id.

Section 4F. Deductive Reasoning

As previously discussed, judicial decisions serve as authority or precedent for deciding future cases.

PROBLEM 4.9

Assume, for example, that a trial judge in Wisconsin is asked to decide whether a defendant should be permitted to offer evidence to prove certain unusual circumstances in an attempt to excuse the defendant's apparent negligence in the operation of his automobile. Assume further that the request to rule on the admissibility of the evidence occurred after the decision of *Theisen v. Milwaukee Automobile Mutual Insurance Co.*, 18 Wis. 2d 91, 118 N.W.2d 140 (1962), discussed in Chapter 3. How would you, as the plaintiff's attorney, attempt to convince the court that the evidence should be excluded?

Stop here, and decide how you would present your argument before consulting the discussion of this problem in Appendix A.

LAWYERS TYPICALLY USE DEDUCTIVE REASONING IN ANALYZING LEGAL PROBLEMS AND PRESENTING ARGUMENTS TO COURTS. THE DEDUCTIVE PROCESS INVOLVES ESTABLISHING A MAJOR PREMISE AND A MINOR PREMISE AND THEN DERIVING A CONCLUSION THAT FOLLOWS NECESSARILY FROM THE PREMISES.

Section 4G. Reasoning by Analogy

In the preceding problem, only one legal rule (major premise) was considered. Sometimes *another* legal rule will be urged to apply to the situation that would, by deduction, lead to the opposite result.

WHEN ARGUMENTS ARE BASED ON DEDUCTIVE REASONING, THE FOCUS OF DISAGREEMENT USUALLY IS ON ONE OR BOTH OF THE PREMISES. IN DECIDING BETWEEN COMPETING LEGAL PREMISES, THE COURTS RELY ON ANALOGY TO DETERMINE WHICH OF THE PREMISES BEST FITS THE SITUATION. THE STRENGTH OF THE ANALOGIES ARE TESTED, IN PART, BY EXAMINING THE PURPOSES OF EACH COMPETING RULE AND THE REASONS SUPPORTING THE RULES.

ILLUSTRATION 4.24

In the *Theisen* case, the defendant urged the following major premise: if a driver of an automobile becomes mentally or physically incapacitated by reason of a sudden and unforeseen attack, the driver is not liable for any injuries resulting from the operation of the vehicle. The minor premise was that the driver fell asleep unknowingly and unexpectedly from physical exhaustion.

The defendant's argument in Illustration 4.24 was drawn from a series of decisions involving heart attacks, convulsions, epileptic seizures, cerebral hemorrhages, and fainting spells. The defendant maintained that falling asleep from exhaustion was *like* one of these incapacitating events. All of these events (including falling asleep from exhaustion) are based upon physical causes. Likewise, all of these events involve an inability to function and a loss of consciousness, sensory perception, or physical control after the event occurs. Presumably, the defendant argued that falling asleep from physical exhaustion likewise could occur unexpectedly and unknowingly.

The defendant thus could point out a number of *similarities*. The problem the defendant faced, however, was whether falling asleep from physical exhaustion was *sufficiently like* the other situations to which the rule had been applied to justify the application of the rule to this situation. The issue is not the number of the resemblances but rather the *strength* of the resemblances. How can the strength of the resemblances be judged? One method is to examine the *purposes* of the rule and the *reasons* supporting it.

ILLUSTRATION 4.25

For instance, what is the basis for relieving a person from liability for negligence when a loss of consciousness results from fainting, heart attack, epileptic seizure, or other illnesses that occur suddenly and unexpectedly? The law of negligence provides a legal ground for demanding compensation for injuries caused by the *fault* of another person. When an accident could not have been foreseen or prevented by the exercise of reasonable precautions, the accident is considered to be "unavoidable," and no liability will be imposed. Thus, to be unavoidable, the loss of consciousness must be without sufficient warning and could not have been reasonably foreseen.

The defendant's argument in *Theisen* was not successful. The Wisconsin Supreme Court viewed the analogy between sudden illness and falling asleep as insufficient because, according to the court, a person always is given conscious warnings of drowsiness. If a person fails to heed those warnings, continues to drive, and causes injury to another, the driver is at fault (negligent) under such conditions.

Section 4H. Synthesizing Opinions

When there has been a series of related decisions, sometimes a cohesive general rule of law tying them together will not be clear. Perhaps such a rule will not have emerged because the opinions used different (but perhaps related) concepts or terminology to discuss and resolve the matter. For example, one decision may relieve the driver from liability because the driver's heart attack was an "act of God." Another may relieve a driver from liability in similar circumstances because the accident could not have been prevented by the exercise of reasonable precautions and thus the accident was "unavoidable." Another may emphasize that the acts done after loss of consciousness could not be a basis of negligence because the driver was no longer capable of sensory perceptions or judgment.

A further barrier to the emergence of a cohesive, general rule may be the diversity of factual contexts of the cases. One may involve a driver who suffers a heart attack; one may involve someone who becomes insane while driving; one may involve someone who faints, etc. The problem is like not seeing the forest for the trees. A general rule encompassing all the cases will become apparent only after a number of cases have been decided and synthesized.

Be aware that later decisions may emphasize or de-emphasize specific factual aspects of prior decisions in formulating the rule of law inherent in the prior decisions, even though these factual aspects may or may not have been articulated as previously important. For example, the first "heart attack" decision may have stated the rule of law to be that "a driver is not liable for damages in a negligence action if a heart attack incapacitated the driver." A second, later case may involve a driver who had been warned not to drive because a severe heart attack in the near future was likely.

In an action brought on these latter facts, the court may see similarities as well as significant differences between the two cases. If in the first case the attack occurred without warning (even though that was not emphasized or articulated in the legal rule actually stated by the court), the court in the second case may *restate* the general rule or ratio decidendi of the *first* case to be that "a driver is not liable for damages in a negligence action if a heart attack incapacitated the driver *without warning*." This rule then is applied to the second case. In this example, recovery would be denied.

This process of case synthesis has been summarized as follows:

> The basic pattern of legal reasoning is . . . a three-step process . . . in which a proposition

> descriptive of the first case is made into a rule of law and then applied to a next similar situation. The steps are these: similarit[ies] [and differences are] seen between cases; . . . the rule inherent in the first case is announced; then the rule is made applicable to the second case.[65]

The rule also may be "expanded" or "contracted" over time by stating it at *varying levels of generality*. For example, assume that after the first two "heart attack" cases, the court is presented with a third case involving a fainting spell that occurred without warning. Assume that the rule stated by the court in the second "heart attack" case was that "a driver is not liable for damages in a negligence action if a *heart attack* incapacitated the driver without warning." In light of the facts in the third case, the lawyer for the defendant would urge that the rule inherent in the first two cases is that a driver is not liable for damages in a negligence action if a *sudden illness* incapacitated the driver without warning.

Thus, depending on the facts in later cases, other *classifications* could be substituted or other *qualifications* could be added. In other words, "[T]he legal process is one in which the classification changes as the classification is made [and] [t]he rules change as the rules are applied."[66]

PROBLEM 4.10

Assume again the basic facts presented in Chapter 2 involving Irma Marie Delira. Recall that she was a defendant in a lawsuit arising out of an automobile accident. Apparently, Delira had suffered a sudden mental aberration that caused her to lose conscious control of the automobile she was driving. Assume that all the details are still not known at this time because Delira currently is institutionalized. You can assume, however, that she caused the accident by not controlling her vehicle in a prudent manner. Assume that (1) you have found three Wisconsin opinions during your research that appear to be related to this problem and (2) you are going to analyze and apply the principles in those cases to the facts of the Delira problem.

The first case is *Karow v. Continental Insurance Co.*, 57 Wis. 56, 15 N.W. 27 (1883). Note the basic facts of the *Karow* case and decide what its holding is. Mark in the margin the parts of the opinion that are relevant to the research problem.

FIGURE 4-F NORTHWESTERN REPORTER, COPYRIGHT 1883 BY WEST PUBLISHING CO.

---

[65] E. Levi, An Introduction to Legal Reasoning 1-2 (1948).

[66] Id. at 3-4.

(57 Wis. 56)

KAROW and others *v.* CONTINENTAL INS. CO. OF NEW YORK.

Filed February 20, 1883.

Where the only evidence tending to prove insanity is the commission of a given crime, such *act of itself* is not sufficient to establish the insanity, and the mere fact that a man commits suicide does not even raise a presumption of insanity at the time. It is, however, a fact which, in connection with other evidence, becomes very pertinent to the issue, especially where the suicide is immediately preceded by the murder, or attempted murder, of members of the suicide's family, and the destruction of his property without any apparent motive or even provocation.

Where there is nothing in the policy to the contrary, a fire-insurance company is not relieved from liability because the property was burned by the assured while in a state of insanity, nor unless the burning was caused by the *voluntary act*, assent, procurement, or design of the assured.

In the absence of fraud or design, a fire-insurance company is not relieved from liability on its policy by reason of loss by fire through the negligence of the assured or his servants.

Appeal from circuit court of Winnebago county.

The plaintiffs are the daughters, only heirs at law, and legal representatives of John Wiskow, who is claimed to have died January 12, 1881. This action is upon two fire-insurance policies issued by the defendant to him in his life time, upon the buildings constituting his homestead, for the sum of $1,150 It is claimed, and for the purposes of this case we must regard the facts as established, that at about half-past 6 o'clock in the evening of January 12, 1881, the assured, John Wiskow, struck and severely injured one of the plaintiffs, then killed his wife, and then set fire to the buildings above mentioned, and then either killed himself or allowed himself to perish in the flames of one of the burning buildings. At the close of the trial, under the charge of the court, the jury returned a special verdict to the effect that John Wiskow was dead; that he set fire to the buildings, and was not insane when he did it. The plaintiffs moved for judgment on the ground that the defendant had waived the defense of the buildings being burned by Wiskow, but the motion was denied and the plaintiffs excepted. Judgment was thereupon entered upon the special verdict in favor of the defendant, from which this appeal is brought.

G. W. Burnell, for appellants, Wilhelmina Karow and others. *C. W. Felker* for respondent, Continental Ins. Co. of New York.

CASSODAY, J. Assuming that the defendant called for proofs of loss, yet we do not think such call was made with such knowledge of the facts as to waive the defense alleged that the assured burned his own buildings. In submitting the question of insanity, the court, in effect, charged the jury that they must look outside of the commission of the act of which the assured was charged, and could only find him insane from other and independent testimony in no way connected or associated with the crime. Assuming that the plaintiffs had the right to have the question of insanity submitted to the jury, then the mental condition of Wiskow at the time of the burning was the material subject of inquiry. Certainly his acts, being of the character indicated, tended to show what his mental condition was at that time. It is undoubtedly the law that where the only evidence tending to prove insanity is the commission of a given crime, such act of itself is not sufficient to establish insanity. The mere fact that a man commits suicide does not even raise a presumption of insanity at the time. It is, however, a fact which, in connection with other evidence, becomes very pertinent to the issue. Especially is this so where the suicide is immediately preceded by the murder or attempted murder of members of the suicide's family, and the destruction of his property without any apparent motive or even provocation. The rule is elementary, and must exist from the very nature of the question to be determined.

The learned counsel for the defendant virtually concedes the rule. For this manifiest error in the charge, therefore, the case must be reversed, unless the determination of the question of insanity was immaterial, as urged by counsel for the defendant. He claims that the burning of the building by the assured relieved the company from all liability, regardless of the question whether he was at the time sane or insane, and such seems to have been the opinion of the court during a portion of the trial. The question is important, and the principal one discussed upon the argument. Counsel on both sides concede their inability to find any adjudicated case directly in point. Upon the part of the plaintiffs it is urged that the case is the same in principle as the liability of a life insurance company, where the assured has committed suicide; and he cites several cases which hold, in effect, that if the assured was insane at the time of the suicide, then the company is liable, otherwise not. On the other hand, it is claimed upon the part of the defense that those cases have no application to fire insurance; that the two classes of contracts are essentially different; that a policy of fire insurance is a contract of indemnity,—a contract for compensation for damages actually sustained; whereas, a policy of life-insurance is a contract to pay a certain sum of money upon the death of a person named, which is sure to happen, and that such payment is to be made, regardless of the value or worthlessness of the life insured.

Having thus distinguished the two classes of cases, the learned counsel contends that, while an insane person cannot be guilty of a crime, nor liable for a tort wherein the *intent* is a necessary ingredient, yet that a lunatic has always been held liable for other torts resulting in damage. In support of this, counsel cite several cases, and argues from them that if a lunatic burns the buildings of A., he is liable to A. for the amount of the actual damages sustained; and that, since this is so, it must follow that a lunatic cannot burn his own buildings upon which he has previously obtained an insurance, and then turn around and recover of the insurer the damages he has sustained by reason of his own act.

The argument is plausible, and deserves very careful consideration, especially in the absence of any direct authority upon the question involved. In order to appreciate its force, it may be well to consider the precise ground upon which such liability is predicated. *Krom* v. *Schoonmaker*, 3 Barb. 657, was an action for false imprisonment on void process issued by the defendant when a lunatic, and Judge HARRIS stated the rule thus: "He (a lunatic) is not a free agent, capable of intelligent, voluntary actions, and therefore is incapable of a guilty intent, which is the very essence of crime; but a civil action, to recover damages for an injury, may be maintained against him, *because the intent with which the act is done is not material.* * * * Ordinarily, in an action for a personal injury, the amount of damages is, at least to a considerable extent, governed by the motive which influenced the party in committing the act. * * * But in respect to the lunatic, *as he has properly no will*, it follows that the only proper measure of damages in an action against him for a wrong, is the mere compensation of the party injured."

In *Morse* v. *Crawford*, 17 Vt. 499, the defendant, while insane, killed the plaintiff's ox, and in an action against him therefor the court said: "It is a common principle that a lunatic is liable for any tort which he may commit, though he is not punishable criminally. When one receives an injury from the act of another, this is a trespass, though done by mistake or *without design*. Consequently, no reason can be assigned why a lunatic should not be held liable." To the same effect, *Behrens* v. *McKenzie*, 23 Iowa, 333. In *Beals* v. *See*, 10 Pa. St. 61, Chief Justice GIBSON said: "As an insane man is civilly liable for his torts, he is liable to bear the consequences of his infirmity, as he is liable to bear his misfortunes, on the principle that where a loss must be borne by one of two innocent persons, it shall be borne by him who occasioned it." This was quoted approvingly in *Lancaster* v. *Moore*, 78 Pa. St.

433, and is substantially the ground of liability, as stated in Cooley, Torts 99, 103. Thus the liability is made in no way dependent upon intent or design to commit the act complained of, but is based upon the theory that the lunatic has no will, hence can form no design nor have any intent. It is solely upon the ground that where a loss must fall upon one of two persons equally innocent, it must be borne by the one who caused it. To relieve the defendant from liability upon the strength of the above authorities, therefore, we must go to the extent of holding that there can be no recovery in such case if the destruction of the property was in consequence of any act of the assured, unmoved and unprompted by any intent or design, and when such assured was, in legal contemplation, without any will of his own, and hence incapable of forming any design or having any intent to destroy. Is such the law of fire insurance? It is conceded that there is no express stipulation in the policy relieving the company from liability in such case. But it is a maxim of the insurance law of all commercial nations that the assured cannot recover for loss produced by his own wrongful act. *Thompson* v. *Hopper*, 6 El. & Bl. 191.

This brings us to the question, whether he can recover if he happens to set fire to the building without any intent or design to injure any one. In the absence of fraud or design, there can be no question but that a fire insurance company is not relieved from liability on its policy by reason of loss by fire through the negligence of the assured or his servants. *Dobson* v. *Sotheby*, 1 Moody & M. 90; *Busk* v. *The Royal Exchange*, 2 Barn. & Ald. 73; *Walker* v. *Maitland*, 5 Barn. & Ald. 171; *Shaw* v. *Robberds*, 6 Adol. & E. 75; *Catlin* v. *The Springfield*, 1 Sumn. 434; *Columbian* v. *Lawrence*, 10 Pet. 507; *Waters* v. *The Merchants*, 11 Pet. 213; *St. Louis* v. *Glasgow*, 8 Mo. 713; *Nelson* v. *Suffolk*, 8 Cush. 477; *Gates* v. *The Madison*, 5 N. Y. 469; *Matthews* v. *The Howard*, 11 N. Y. 14; *Huckins* v. *The People's*, 11 Foster, 247; *Johnson* v. *Berkshire*, 4 Allen, 388; *Mickey* v. *Ins. Co.* 35 Iowa, 174; *Cumberland* v. *Douglass*, 58 Pa. St. 423; *National* v. *Webster*, 83 Ill. 470; *Gove* v. *The Farmer's*, 48 N. H. 41.

In *Dobson* v. *Sotheby*, *supra*, Lord TENTERDEN, C. J., said that "one of the great objects of insuring is security against the negligence of servants and workmen." In *Shaw* v. *Robberds*, *supra*, Lord DENMAN, C. J., reiterated the same doctrine, and added: "But it is argued that there is a distinction between the negligence of servants or strangers and that of the assured himself. We do not see any ground for such distinction, and are of opinion that, in the absence of all fraud, the proximate cause of the loss only is to be looked to." Page 84.

In *Gates* v. *The Madison*, *supra*, the court states that "there can be no doubt that one of the objects of insurance against fire is to protect the insured from loss, as well against his own negligence as that of his servants and others, and therefore the simple fact of negligence in either, however great in degree, has never been held to be a defense in such policy." Page 478.

In *Mickey* v. *Ins. Co.*, *supra*, the stove-pipe passed from below through the floor of the second story. The pipe in the second story was removed and a bed placed over the hole by the assured's wife, with the intention of removing the stove below, but which was not done. Subsequently, the weather becoming colder, she made a fire in the stove, without thinking of the removed pipe and the bed above. The result was that the house was consumed, and the company was held liable.

In *Cumberland* v. *Douglass*, *supra*, Mr. Justice STORY said: "A fire policy is a protection against fire caused by the assured's own negligence, unless the negligence amounts to fraud."

In *Breasted* v. *The Farmer's*, 8 N. Y. 306, it was, as here, urged, in an action on a life insurance policy, "that because a person *non compos mentis* is liable *civiliter* for torts committed while in a state of insanity, therefore insanity has no effect to qualify this exception (if he shall die by his own hand) in the policy. That conclusion is not a legitimate deduction from the premises. * * * A death by accident and a death by the party's own hand, when deprived of reason, stand on principle in the same category. In both cases the act is done without a controlling mind."

Of course, negligence involves a want of care in one who ought to bestow care. It is an omission of duty. But the law imposes no duty—no obligation of care—upon one who has no control over his mental faculties, and hence no control over his physical action. Being under no obligation of care, and under no restraint of duty, and incapable of exercising either, it would be inapt, if not inaccurate, to say that, by his omission, an insane person was guilty of negligence. Since burning through the negligence of an insured who is sane does not relieve the company from liability, for a much stronger reason the same act by one who is incapable of care would not. But while the negligent burning by the assured of his own property does not relieve the company from liability, yet the negligent burning of another person's property would subject him to damages on the ground of negligence. So, while the burning of his own property by an assured under no restraint of duty and incapable of care, and without any intent or design, does not relieve the company from liability, yet the same act of burning another's property might subject such person to damages therefor, not on the ground of negligence, as that word is usually understood, but in the language of Chief Justice GIBSON, *supra*, "on the principle that where a loss must be borne by one of two *innocent* persons, it should be borne by him who occasioned it."

For the reasons given, it follows as a logical sequence that the non-liability of a fire-insurance company cannot be predicated upon the fact that the act of burning by the assured, if done to the property of another instead of his own, would have made him liable in damages. The authorities holding a lunatic liable for the actual damage occasioned by his torts, therefore, furnish no ground for relieving the defendant from liability in the case before us. The act of burning the property of another necessarily destroys the property burned, and injures the owner to the extent of its value. But the act of burning one's own property does not necessarily injure an insurance company. Whether it does or not depends upon whether the company has, for the time being, assumed the risk of such burning. It is because the company, for a consideration paid, has, for the time being, assumed the risk of burning and hence relieved the owner from such risk, that the liability continues, even where the burning is by the assured's own negligence, or that of his agents or servants. Such policy covers all risks from loss by fire not excepted therefrom, nor affected by the intent, design, or procurement of the assured. Such being the risk which the defendant here by its contract expressly assumed, it cannot be relieved therefrom merely because the assured burned the property, if it is made to appear that at the time of such burning the assured was incapable of forming a design or intention to injure.

Counsel for the defendant concedes, that if the assured was insane at the time, then he could not be guilty of a crime, nor liable for a tort wherein the intent is a necessary ingredient. The authorities cited by him fully support this concession, and hold that a lunatic "is not a free agent, capable of intelligent, voluntary actions, and therefore is incapable of a guilty intent." The same authorities substantially hold that a lunatic has, properly, no will, but acts without design, and is influenced by no motive. Can the act of such a person, even in the burning of his own property, relieve an insurance company from a risk which he has paid it for insuring?

In *Gove* v. *The Farmer's, supra*, the wife of the assured, while insane and alone in the house, burned his buildings, and it was there held that "the defendants will be liable for the loss, unless they can show actual design or such a degree of negligence and carelessness on the part of the husband as will evince a corrupt design or a fraudulent purpose on his part." After citing authorities indirectly bearing upon the question, the learned judge, giving the opinion of the court in that case, said: "It appears to us it would be a misnomer of terms that she, being admitted to be in this state, [insane,] could so far control her reasoning powers as to be able to plan or design the act done by her beforehand, in such a manner as to render herself responsible as a moral agent. The word 'insane' implies unsoundness or derangement of mind or intellect, not a mere temporary or slight delirium which might be occasioned by fever or accident, and we cannot attach moral accountability to a wrongful act admitted to be done by an insane person."

The court then considered the question whether the company was relieved by the husband's negligence in leaving his wife alone in the house while in the condition stated, and concluded that it was not. Applying to that case, the rule in respect to negligence sanctioned by Lord DENMAN, *supra*, that there is no distinction between the act of the assured and his servants, and assuming that a wife left by her husband alone and in charge of his house is, as to its care and custody, the servant if not the agent of the husband, and it follows that if such burning by her while insane will not relieve the company, then neither would such burning by him while insane relieve the company. Of course, such act of burning by such insane wife was not, under the authorities cited, a criminal act, but at most a tort committed without any design or intent to injure, and by one incapable of controlling her reasoning powers, and hence incapable of planning or designing such act in advance, or comprehending its consequences, especially to the insurance company. Such burning by such insane wife, being a mere tort of the character indicated, was, therefore, imputable to the husband, for it is well-settled that the husband is liable for the torts of his wife, (*Head* v. *Brisco*, 5 Car. & P. 484; *Heckle* v. *Luvey*, 101 Mass. 344; *Fowler* v. *Chichester*, 26 Ohio St. 9; *Ball* v. *Bennett*, 21 Ind. 427; *Brazil* v. *Moran*, 8 Minn. 236; *Hildreth* v. *Camp*, 41 N. J. Law, 306; and he may be arrested therefor, (*Solomon* v. *Wass*, 2 Hilton, 179; *Schram* v. *Putscher*, 25 How. Pr. 463.)

Such being the law, it is evident that had such insane wife burned the house of a neighbor instead of the house of her husband, the husband would, on the principle of the authorities cited, have been liable for the tort; but having burned her husband's house, and such risk of burning having, for value received, been expressly assured by the insurance company for the very purpose of relieving the assured therefrom, it would seem that the case was rightly decided. Whether the criminal act of intentional burning by a sane wife, without the knowledge, privity, or consent of the husband, would relieve the company from liability to him, need not be here considered.

In the recent case of the *Midland Ins. Co.* v. *Smith*, L. R. 6 Q. B. Div. 561; S. C. 29 English, (Moak's,) 710, the company sought to cancel the policy held by the husband for such act of criminal burning by the wife, but a demurrer to the bill was sustained. It was there observed that "the loss or damage caused by the wrongful act of the wife either is or is not a loss which the company have agreed to indemnify the husband against. Now, if it is such a loss, an attempt by the company to enforce against the husband a return, indemnity, or reimbursement, is at variance with the very substance of their undertaking to indemnify him. If, on the other hand, the loss, by reason of its having arisen from the act of the wife, is not within the risks and losses covered by the policy, then this action is as wholly misconceived, unnecessary, and unfounded as if the loss had been caused by any other risk not covered by the policy." The court continued, and gave opinion upon the "real and substantial contention on the part of the insurance company," although conceding that it did not and could not arise in the case, as follows: "I have no hesitation in saying that it appears to me to be upon principle perfectly clear and free from doubt that such a loss would be covered by an ordinary policy against loss caused by fire. Under such a policy the company would be liable for every loss caused by fire, unless the fire itself was caused and procured by the willful act of the assured himself, or some one acting with his privity and consent. In order to escape from responsibility for such a loss as the present, the company ought to introduce into their policy an express exception."

The substance of the decisions seem to be that a fire policy covers all risks of loss or damage by fire, save only such as are excepted by the terms of the policy and such as are caused by the voluntary act, assent, procurement, or design of the assured himself. In this respect the law of fire insurance seems to be in harmony with the law of life insurance.

In *Horn* v. *The Anglo Australian*, 7 Jurist, (N.S.) 673, Vice-Chancellor WOOD said: "It appears to me clear that where there is no express provision in the policy that in the event of the assured dying by his own hand the policy shall become void, that policy is not vacated by the circumstance of his having died by his own hand while in a state of temporary insanity." This seems to be the acknowledged law of life insurance. May, § 323. Such being the law of life insurance, a clause is usually inserted in the policy to the effect that the insurer will not be liable in case the insured should "die by suicide, felonious or otherwise, sane or insane." But even then these words are only held to include cases of intentional self-destruction, and not unintentional or accidental death, though brought about by acts of the deceased, involving negligence or carelessness. *Pierce* v. *The Traveler's*, 34 Wis. 389.

In *The Knickerbocker* v. *Peters*, 42 Md. 414, it was held that suicide by the insured while "in a fit of insanity which overpowered his consciousness, reason, and will," did not come within the clause exempting the company in case the assured should "die by his own hand or act." See, also, *Penfold* v. *The Universal*, 85 N. Y. 317, and cased cited by counsel for the plaintiff. But, as already suggested in the policy before us, there is no exemption from liability in case the assured should burn the property feloniously or otherwise, sane or insane, nor anything of that nature.

For the reasons given we must hold that where, as here, there is nothing in the policy to the contrary, the insurance company is not relieved from liability because the property was burned by the assured while in a state of insanity, nor unless the burning was caused by the voluntary act, assent, procurement, or design of the assured. What has already been said in regard to the charge of the court to the jury renders it unnecessary to apply the principle there suggested to the alleged error in excluding the expert testimony, as the same ruling is not likely to be repeated.

The judgment of the circuit court is reversed, and the cause is remanded for a new trial.

Stop here, and decide (1) what the basic facts and holding of the Karow case were and (2) how this case might (or might not) support a defense on the assumed facts before consulting the discussion of this problem in Appendix A.

PROBLEM 4.11

Read the second Wisconsin case, *In re Meyer's Guardianship*, 218 Wis. 381, 261 N.W. 211 (1935), reproduced below. Mark in the margin the parts of the case that are relevant to the research issue. When you have finished reading this case, consider how it could be related to the research problem and the *Karow* case.

FIGURE 4-G
NORTHWESTERN REPORTER, COPYRIGHT 1935 BY WEST PUBLISHING COMPANY

IN RE MEYER'S GUARDIANSHIP Wis. 211
261 N.W.

causation. If the ratio of negligence was 10 to 90 as found, the respective acts of negligence necessarily contributed according to that ratio to produce the collision if they contributed at all.

[4] (3) It was held in McGeehan v. Gaar, Scott & Co., 122 Wis. 630, 100 N. W. 1072, that a question of a verdict answered by the jury where they were instructed to answer it in case they had answered a previous question "Yes" and they had answered that question "No," should be disregarded as surplusage. But we did not so regard the answer in the Hayes Case, supra, upon what we there considered good reason, and the same reason applies here. There is no conflict between the rulings in the McGeehan Case and the Hayes and the instant cases. In the former the answer to the question which the jury were not required to answer in view of their former answer was immaterial. The verdict was sufficient to support a judgment without it.

We are of opinion that in the instant case the verdict should have been corrected by changing the answer of the question as to causation of plaintiff's negligence from "No" to "Yes," and that as so corrected it establishes the respective proportions of the contributing negligence of the parties, and requires a judgment for the plaintiff for 90 per cent. of his damages as assessed by the jury instead of the whole amount.

The judgment of the circuit court is reversed and the record remanded with direction for correction of the verdict and entry of judgment in accordance with this opinion.

In re MEYER'S GUARDIANSHIP.

GERMAN MUT. FIRE INS. SOC. OF LIBERTY, GRANT COUNTY, WIS., v. MEYER.

Supreme Court of Wisconsin.
June 4, 1935.

1. Insane persons ⚷80

Insurer who paid fire losses, and who was assigned causes of action which insureds had against persons who set fire to building, *held* entitled to recover sum paid in settlement of fire losses from person who set fire to building, notwithstanding insanity of such person.

2. Appeal and error ⚷1176(1)

In action in which defendant's liability was clearly established on trial and in which plaintiff was entitled to judgment notwithstanding verdict, order granting new trial would be reversed with directions to enter judgment in favor of plaintiff under statute permitting discretionary reversal (St. 1933, § 251.09).

Appeal from an order of the Circuit Court for Grant County; S. E. Smalley, Circuit Judge.

In the matter of the guardianship of Gustav Meyer, insane. Action by the German Mutual Fire Insurance Society of Liberty, Grant County, against Gustav Meyer, by guardian. From an order setting aside a special verdict and granting a new trial, defendant appeals.—[By Editorial Staff.]

Order reversed, with directions.

This is an appeal from an order of the circuit court for Grant county, setting aside a special verdict and granting a new trial of the action for what the trial court regarded as error in the submission of the first question of said special verdict. Order granted October 29, 1934.

The material facts will be stated in the opinion.

George F. Frantz, of Fennimore, and Kopp & Brunckhorst, of Platteville, for appellant.

Carthew & Meyer, of Lancaster, for respondent.

MARTIN, Justice.

The appellant, hereinafter called defendant, while employed as a farm hand on the farm of one Louisa P. Napp in the town of Fennimore, Grant county, being operated by her son Clyde E. Napp, on September 29, 1932, caused the destruction by fire of a barn and contents located on said farm, resulting in a loss to said Louisa P. Napp in the sum of $2,550 and to the said Clyde E. Napp in the sum of $1,100. Defendant was charged with the crime of arson, in which proceedings he was examined as to his sanity and found to be insane and thereupon was committed to the Central State Hospital for the Criminal Insane at

⚷For other cases see same topic and KEY NUMBER in all Key Number Digests and Indexes

Waupun, and the trial of said defendant for the crime of arson was postponed indefinitely under the provisions of section 357.13, Stats.

On December 12, 1932, the respondent, German Mutual Fire Insurance Society, settled and adjusted the fire loss sustained by the said Louisa P. Napp for the sum of $2,500 and settled the fire loss sustained by Clyde E. Napp for the sum of $935, whereupon said Louisa P. Napp and Clyde E. Napp by instruments in writing sold, assigned, and transferred to said German Mutual Fire Insurance Society their respective claims, demands, rights, or causes of action which they had against the defendant Gustav Meyer. Thereafter on December 29, 1932, in proceedings had in the county court of Grant county, Pauline Meyer was by said court appointed general guardian of the said Gustav Meyer, insane; that an order was entered by the court fixing and limiting the time within which claims might be filed against the estate of said defendant. The respondent filed its claim in said guardianship proceedings, to which objections were filed by Pauline Meyer as such general guardian; whereupon pleadings were made and filed in the county court and defendant gave notice of his demand for a jury trial under section 324.17, Stats. Thereupon the county court entered an order transferring the matter to the circuit court for Grant county as provided for by said section 324.-17. The two cases, the one involving the claim of Louisa P. Napp and the one involving the claim of Clyde E. Napp, were consolidated and tried together.

The trial court submitted the following special verdict, to which the jury made answers as indicated:

"1. Did the defendant, Gustav Meyer, intentionally set the fire which destroyed the Napp property on the 29th of September, 1932? Answer: No.

"2. At the time the fire occurred on September 29, 1932, was the defendant, Gustav Meyer, insane? Answer: Yes.

"3. What was the fair value of the Napp barn just prior to its destruction on September 29, 1932? Answer: $2,100.00.

"4. What was the fair value of the machine shed just prior to its destruction by fire on September 29, 1932? Answer: $350.00.

"5. What sum of money would be required to repair the damage to the silo on said farm as a result of the fire. Answer: $100.00.

"6. What was the fair value:

"(a) of the hay and straw destroyed by said fire? Answer: $350.00.

"(b) of the grain destroyed by said fire? Answer: $400.00.

"(c) of the farm machinery destroyed by said fire? Answer: $250.00.

"(d) of the mule destroyed by said fire? Answer: $100.00."

Defendant moved for judgment upon the special verdict and the files and proceedings had. The respondent filed alternative motions, among others for judgment upon the pleadings and undisputed evidence, for judgment upon the special verdict, for judgment notwithstanding the special verdict, and if the foregoing motions be denied, for an order changing the answer to the first question from "No" to "Yes" and for judgment upon the special verdict when so amended and upon the uncontradicted evidence, and finally if all foregoing motions be denied to set aside the verdict and for a new trial because of alleged errors in the admission and rejection of evidence; because of error in the form of the first question of the special verdict and in submitting the first question to the jury; because there is no evidence to sustain the finding of the jury to the first question and that the answer is perverse and contrary to the overwhelming weight of the evidence; and because justice has not been done.

[1] The trial court denied all motions except the respondent's motion for a new trial. As to that, the order provides: "It is further ordered, on motion of the plaintiff, and in the exercise of the court's discretion, that the special verdict herein is hereby set aside and a new trial ordered because the court is satisfied justice has not been done, for the reason that the issue as to whether the defendant set the fire was not properly submitted to the jury." From this order defendant appealed. Plaintiff made no motion for a directed verdict at the conclusion of the evidence and made no motion for review after defendant took his appeal to this court. Had plaintiff moved for a directed verdict in the court below on the undisputed evidence in the record, judgment should have been directed in favor of the plaintiff and against the defendant for the sum it paid in settlement of the fire losses. That defend-

ant set the fire was proven beyond question of doubt. The only defense made was that on and prior to September 29, 1932, and at all times since said date, said defendant was insane, and as will be observed by the authorities hereinafter referred to, insanity was no defense.

In 14 Ruling Case Law, § 51, p. 596, the rule is stated thus: "It is the well settled rule that a person non compos mentis is liable in damages to one injured by reason of a tort committed by him unless evil intent or express malice constitutes an essential element in the plaintiff's recovery. This rule is usually considered to be based on the principle that where a loss must be borne by one of two innocent persons, it shall be borne by him who occasioned it, and it has also been held that public policy requires the enforcement of the liability in order that those interested in the estate of the insane person, as relatives or otherwise, may be under inducement to restrain him and that tortfeasors may not simulate or pretend insanity to defend their wrongful acts causing damage to others. * * *".

The question of the civil liability of an insane person for his torts has seldom been presented to this court for its consideration. In Huchting v. Engel, by his Guardian, 17 Wis. 230, at page 231, 84 Am. Dec. 741, which was an action involving the civil liability of an infant, in an action for compensatory damages for a trespass, we find the following quotation in the opinion by Chief Justice Dixon: "'Where the minor has committed a tort with force, he is liable at any age; for in case of civil injuries with force, the intention is not regarded; *for in such a case a lunatic is as liable to compensate in damages as a man in his right mind.*'"

In Karow v. New York Continental Ins. Co., 57 Wis. 56, 15 N. W. 27, 46 Am. Rep. 17, which was an action on an insurance policy by the heirs of their father who had set fire to his homestead and then either killed himself or allowed himself to perish in the flames, the issue of the father's insanity was involved. The court said, 57 Wis. 56, at page 60, 15 N. W. 27, 28, 46 Am. Rep. 17:

"* * * the learned counsel contends that, while an insane person cannot be guilty of a crime, nor liable for a tort wherein the intent is a necessary ingredient, yet that a lunatic has always been held liable for other torts resulting in damage. In support of this, counsel cites several cases, and argues from them that if a lunatic burns the buildings of A., he is liable to A. for the amount of the actual damages sustained; and that, since this is so, it must follow that a lunatic cannot burn his own buildings upon which he has previously obtained an insurance, and then turn around and recover of the insurer the damages he has sustained by reason of his own act.

"The argument is plausible, and deserves very careful consideration, especially in the absence of any direct authority upon the question involved. In order to appreciate its force, it may be well to consider the precise ground upon which such liability is predicated. Krom v. Schoonmaker, 3 Barb. [(N. Y.) 647] 650, was an action for false imprisonment on void process issued by the defendant when a lunatic, and Judge Harris stated the rule thus: 'He (a lunatic) is not a free agent, capable of intelligent, voluntary actions, and therefore is incapable of a guilty intent, which is the very essence of crime; but a civil action, to recover damages for *an injury, may be maintained against him, because the intent with which the act is done is not material.* * * * Ordinarily, in an action for a personal injury, the amount of damages is, at least to a considerable extent, governed by the motive which influenced the party in committing the act. * * * But in respect to the lunatic, *as he has properly no will*, it follows that the only proper measure of damages in an action against him for a wrong, is the mere compensation of the party injured.'"

And in 57 Wis. 56, at page 64, 15 N. W. 27, 30, 46 Am. Rep. 17, the court said: "But while the negligent burning by the assured of his own property does not relieve the company from liability, yet the negligent burning of another person's property would subject him to damages on the ground of negligence. So, while the burning of his own property by an assured under no restraint of duty and incapable of care, and without any intent or design, does not relieve the company from liability, yet the same act of burning another's property might subject such person to damages therefor, not on the ground of negligence, as that word is usually understood, but in the language of Chief Justice Gibson, supra [Beals v. See, 10 Pa. 56, 61, 49 Am. Dec. 573] 'on the principle that where a loss must be borne by one of two innocent persons, it should be borne by him who occasioned it.'"

In Williams v. Hays, 143 N. Y. 442, at page 446, 38 N. E. 449, 450, 26 L. R. A. 153, 42 Am. St. Rep. 743, discussing the question of civil liability of an insane person, the court said: "The general rule is that an insane person is just as responsible for his torts as a sane person, and the rule applies to all torts, except, perhaps, those in which malice, and therefore intention, actual or imputed, is a necessary ingredient, like libel, slander, and malicious prosecution. In all other torts, intention is not an ingredient, and the actor is responsible, although he acted with a good and even laudable purpose, without any malice. The law looks to the person damaged by another, and seeks to make him whole, without reference to the purpose or the condition, mental or physical, of the person causing the damage. The liability of a lunatic for his torts, in the opinions of judges, has been placed upon several grounds. The rule has been invoked that, where one of two innocent persons must bear a loss, he must bear it whose act caused it. * * * The lunatic must bear the loss occasioned by his torts, as he bears his other misfortunes, and the burden of such loss may not be put upon others."

In Cross v. Kent, 32 Md. 581, an action of trespass against defendant for setting fire to and burning plaintiff's barn, proof was offered on the part of the defendant that at the time of the trespass, he was, and for many years before and from his infancy had been, an idiot and insane person. Upon the issues joined, the court found the defendant did commit the wrong complained of and gave judgment in favor of the plaintiff. At the trial the defendant contended that the idiocy of the defendant, if found by the court, is a bar to the action; that such idiocy or insanity is evidence in mitigation of damages; and that if the court found the burning was the result of accident and not the intentional or deliberate act of the defendant, such accidental burning, if not a bar to the action, is, nevertheless, a mitigation of the damages claimed by the plaintiff. The court said, 32 Md. 581, at page 583: "The distinction between the liability of a lunatic or insane person in civil actions for torts committed by him, and in criminal prosecutions, is well defined, and it has always been held, and upon sound reason, that though not punishable criminally, he is liable to a civil action for any tort he may commit."

In Brown, Adm'r, v. Howe, 9 Gray (Mass.) 84, 69 Am. Dec. 276, an insane person carelessly set fire to the dwelling house of his guardian, and while it was held that the guardian could not be allowed the amount of his damages above the amount received from the insurance in his probate account, it was held that his only course was to sue the administrator of the lunatic who had died, in a court of law, and have a judgment fixing his damages and collect it from the assets, if the estate was solvent; if not, to share with the other creditors.

In McIntyre, Adm'r, v. Sholty, Adm'r, 121 Ill. 660, 13 N. E. 239, 240, 2 Am. St. Rep. 140, an action for damages for the killing of plaintiff's intestate by a lunatic, the court said: "There is, to be sure, an appearance of hardship in compelling one to respond for that which he is unable to avoid, for want of the control of reason. But the question of liability in these cases is one of public policy. If an insane person is not held liable for his torts, those interested in his estate, as relatives, or otherwise, might not have a sufficient motive to so take care of him as to deprive him of opportunities for inflicting injuries upon others. There is more injustice in denying to the injured party the recovery of damages for the wrong suffered by him than there is in calling upon the relatives or friends of the lunatic to pay the expense of his confinement, if he has an estate ample enough for that purpose. The liability of lunatics for their torts tends to secure a more efficient custody and guardianship of their persons."

In Seals v. Snow, Adm'r, 123 Kan. 88, 254 P. 348, 349, 51 A. L. R. 829, in an action brought by plaintiff against defendant for the shooting and killing of her husband, the jury returned a verdict in favor of the plaintiff. With the verdict were special findings among which was one that Snow was insane when he shot plaintiff's husband. Notwithstanding, plaintiff was given judgment on the verdict, which was affirmed on appeal. The court said: "* * * It is conceded that the great weight of authority is that an insane person is civilly liable for his torts. This liability has been based on a number of grounds, one that where one of two innocent persons must suffer a loss, it should be borne by the one who occasioned it.

Another, that public policy requires the enforcement of such liability in order that relatives of the insane person shall be led to restrain him and that tort-feasors shall not simulate or pretend insanity to defend their wrongful acts causing damage to others, and that if he was not liable there would be no redress for injuries, and we might have the anomaly of an insane person having abundant wealth depriving another of his rights without compensation. * * * 'Therefore, the law, in giving redress, has in view the case of the party injured, and the extent of his injury, and makes what he suffers the measure of compensation. * * *'" See Annotation "Liability of Insane Person for Tort," 51 A. L. R. 833.

[2] The defendant's civil liability having been clearly established on the trial, respondent being entitled to judgment notwithstanding the verdict, we deem it our duty under section 251.09, Stats., to reverse the order granting a new trial herein with directions to enter judgment in favor of the plaintiff against the defendant in the sum of $3,435, with interest from the date of the verdict with costs.

Order granting new trial reversed, with directions for judgment in favor of plaintiff and against defendant in the sum of $3,435 with interest from date of verdict, with costs.

Stop here, and decide (1) what the basic facts and holding of the Meyers' Guardianship case were, (2) how this case might (or might not) support a defense on the assumed facts stated earlier, and (3) how this case relates to the Karow case before consulting the discussion of this problem in Appendix A.

PROBLEM 4.12

Assume that the third Wisconsin case that you have found is *Theisen v. Milwaukee Automobile Mutual Insurance Co.*, 18 Wis. 2d 91, 118 N.W.2d 140 (1962), reproduced in Chapter 3. Examine that case again.

Stop here, examine the Theisen opinion, and decide how that case might support a possible defense. Consider also how the Theisen case relates to the Karow case and Meyers' Guardianship case before consulting the discussion of this problem in Appendix A.

Based on the above cases, a synthesis could be prepared in which cohesive rules of law are formulated and related to the assumed facts. Consider the following suggestions about how to draft such a synthesis:

UNLESS OTHERWISE INSTRUCTED, USE A MEMORANDUM FORMAT TO PRESENT YOUR ANALYSIS.

Presented in Appendix D is a draft of the synthesis of the *Karow*, *Meyer's*, and *Theisen* cases. Refer to that draft as an example of an acceptable memorandum format for presenting a case synthesis.

STATE THE RELEVANT FACTS OF THE PROBLEM (IF ASSUMED FACTS WERE GIVEN TO YOU OR THE FACTS ARE OTHERWISE KNOWN).

The draft of the synthesis in Appendix D contains a summary of the assumed facts in a separate section.

ORGANIZE YOUR PRESENTATION IN A LOGICAL MANNER.

In general, you have three basic choices in organizing your synthesis. First, if a series of opinions appear to support a clear rule, then the best approach is to state the rule and to cite all (or a representative sample) of the cases. Then you could discuss only one of the cases fully to illustrate the common factual pattern and the court's handling of it.[67] Second, if a series of opinions appear to support a rule but have significant variations in the facts or legal analysis, then a good approach is to organize the discussion based on the variables.[68]

Third, if the rule of law is emerging or unclear in the opinions to be synthesized, a chronological approach may be a good one. Remember that rules often develop over time and that

---

[67] See M. Rombauer, supra note 50, at 57 ("Nothing more is needed if factual or other differences among the cases are not significant and if the court or courts have used substantially similar reasoning").

[68] Id. ("For example, if the result is the same for all the cases, but the reasoning differs, the rule applied can be stated, the cases cited, and the illustrative case statement made; the cases can then be regrouped on the basis of the reasoning used (state one reasoning approach, cite supporting opinions; state second approach, cite supporting opinions")).

a chronological order may help the reader follow that development. Furthermore, the opinions themselves frequently refer to (and sometimes distinguish or limit) earlier opinions and can be more readily presented if the prior cases have already been discussed.

IN GENERAL, TEXTUALLY DISCUSS A CASE IN THE FOLLOWING MANNER: (1) STATE THE NATURE OF THE ACTION; (2) GIVE THE FACTS AND CONTENTIONS IN THE CASE; (3) STATE THE HOLDING OF THE CASE; AND (4) DISCUSS THE RELEVANT ASPECTS OF THE OPINION.

The draft of the synthesis in Appendix D illustrates a good way of discussing the relevant cases in a synthesis. First, the nature of the action is stated. Second, the facts and contentions are given. Third, the holding of the case is stated. Fourth, the relevant aspects of the opinion are discussed in detail.

RELATE THE CASES AND THE LEGAL RULES TO THE KNOWN OR ASSUMED FACTS OR CIRCUMSTANCES.

Be sure to relate the cases and the legal rules to the known or assumed facts. Usually, the best approach is to compare the facts and to point out possible significant differences (if any). With respect to the various legal rules, the best approach ordinarily is simply to demonstrate how they would apply to the known or assumed facts.

BE SURE TO REACH A CONCLUSION.

Even though it may be difficult to do, be sure to reach a conclusion. When you cannot give a definite conclusion, you should provide your best estimate of the possible legal rules and the most likely result.

Examine the first draft of the synthesis of the Karow, Meyer's, and Theisen cases in Appendix D.

Chapter 5

STATUTORY INTERPRETATION AND ANALYSIS

WHAT YOU WILL LEARN IN THIS CHAPTER

* The role and importance of legislation as a source of law
* The basic steps of the legislative process and the documents (legislative history) that this process generates
* The nature and scope of judicial review of legislation
* The basic steps in analyzing and applying statutes
* The intrinsic and extrinsic aids to determining legislative intent
* The framing of issues and organization of memoranda involving statutory issues

Section 5A. Legislation as a Source of Law

The Anglo-American legal system relies on two principal sources of law. One of these sources is the unwritten common law developed and enforced through judicial decisions. The other principal source is *legislation*.

Legislation takes several forms. On the local level, legislation takes the form of municipal ordinances. Between states, legislation is embodied in interstate compacts. Between nations, legislation takes the form of treaties and other international agreements. Legislation also includes constitutional provisions adopted by the people and statutes enacted by legislative bodies. Statutory law is often supplemented by administrative regulations promulgated pursuant to legislative authority. Court rules (established pursuant to enabling acts) also have the force of law.

LEGISLATION TODAY IS THE DOMINANT SOURCE OF LAW.

The volume and scope of legislation in the United States have dramatically increased during this century. Statutory schemes, rules, and regulations now permeate both the workplace and the marketplace in one form or another. Statutory schemes, in large measure, have removed broad areas from common-law development.

ILLUSTRATION 5.1

Workers' compensation, securities regulation, labor law, environmental legislation, landlord-tenant law, and evidence are examples of broad areas that have been removed from common-law development.

In other areas, the common law has been codified or significantly changed.

ILLUSTRATION 5.2

Much of commercial law is now governed by the Uniform Commercial Code. Modern insurance contracts are, for the most part, statutorily prescribed. Legislation has abrogated specific common-law doctrines, such as assumption of risk and contributory negligence. Furthermore, statutes such as the medical malpractice acts have imposed limits on liability.

LEGISLATIVE CREATION OF LEGAL RIGHTS AND RELATIONS HAS SEVERAL ADVANTAGES OVER COMMON-LAW DEVELOPMENT OF LEGAL RULES.

As a source of law, legislation has several advantages over common-law creation and evolution of legal rules. First, legislation and administrative regulations may address an entire field of law rather than just the specific issues presented for decision in court cases.

Second, legislation and administrative regulations may deal with a problem in its incipiency rather than waiting for parties to commence litigation. As Fuller points out,

> [t]he predicament of the common[-]law judge, who cannot make rules in advance, but must wait for the cases to come to him, suggests the analogy of a builder attempting to construct a house with no control over the arrival of his materials, so that the shingles come before the foundation stones and the

chimney bricks arrive on the site before the flooring.[1]

Third, most court decisions operate retrospectively. In contrast, ex post facto legislation is not permitted.[2]

Fourth, legislation and administrative regulations are well suited to problem solving. In contrast, courts are generally ill-equipped to plan and supervise complex solutions.

Fifth, legislation, by amendment or repeal, can be more easily adapted to deal with rapidly changing conditions than can judicially created rules.[3]

A PRINCIPAL DIFFICULTY ARISING FROM INCREASED LEGISLATIVE ACTIVITY IS INTERPRETING THE EFFECT OF LEGISLATION ON THE PRIOR COMMON LAW.

This outpouring of legislation, despite its advantages, is responsible for several difficulties. As Justice Traynor aptly pointed out:

> A judge's responsibility is the greater now that legislatures fabricate laws in such volume. The endless cases before [judges] increasingly involve the meaning or applicability of a statute, or on occasion its constitutionality. Such statutes, reflecting their sponsors or draftsmen or author-legislators, are of infinite variety in purpose, range, and quality. . . . [A statute] may cast a heavy shadow on the common law or a light one, or it may idly plane until some incident sends it careening into action. The hydra-headed problem is how to synchronize the unguided missiles launched by legislatures with a going system of common law.[4]

FROM A RESEARCH AND WRITING PERSPECTIVE, THE FOCUS WILL BE ON APPLICATION OF LEGISLATION TO A PARTICULAR SITUATION AND ITS EFFECTS.

---

[1] L. Fuller, Anatomy of the Law 95 (1968).

[2] See id. at 97-103.

[3] See id. at 108-10.

[4] Traynor, Statutes Revolving in Common-Law Orbits, 17 Cath. U. L. Rev. 401, 401-02 (1968).

As a legal researcher, you will have two principal concerns about legislation. First, you will often want to know whether legislation of any kind applies to a client's situation or problem. Second, if a statute is applicable, you will want to determine what its particular effect or impact will be--in other words, what specific conduct is required, prohibited, or regulated.[5]

Section 5B. The Legislative Process

Understanding the legislative process is important because, *inter alia*, the legislative process identifies some of the possible sources of "legislative" history useful in interpreting statutes and regulations. The legislative process also explains why statutes and regulations, on occasion, may be less than perfect models of draftsmanship. Consider the following observation:

> Ambiguities and inconsistencies may appear because of careless drafting or because, just as with [judicial] opinions, a statute may have multiple authors. For example, different portions of an [a]ct may have been drafted by different persons; amendments suggested by the controlling legislative committee or by legislators on the floor may have been adopted. Similarly, the pressure for agreement may lead to intentional use of broad or vague language.[6]

This section briefly considers the following aspects of the legislative process: (1) the enactment of statutes; (2) the promulgation of administrative regulations; (3) the enactment of ordinances; (4) the adoption of court rules; (5) the consent and proclamation of treaties; and (6) the approval of interstate compacts.

1. ENACTMENT OF STATUTES

The basic constitutional principle of separation of powers places the responsibility for creating statutory laws on the legislative branch of government. On the federal level, to become law, a bill must be passed in the same form by a majority of the House of Representatives and a majority of the Senate. The bill can be vetoed by the President. That veto can be overridden by

---

[5] See J. Dernback & R. Singleton, A Practical Guide to Legal Writing and Legal Method 58 (1981).

[6] M. Rombauer, Legal Problem Solving: Analysis, Research and Writing 78 (4th ed. 1983).

a two-thirds vote in favor of enactment in both the House and Senate.[7] A similar process is generally followed in most states.

The route to enactment of a statute may be a long and tortuous one. Numerous bills of varying content as well as Presidential messages or reports by executive agencies may precede an enacted bill. Likewise, the bill may be the subject of numerous congressional hearings. During this process, legislators may make various compromises or amendments.

THE PROCESS OF CONSIDERING PROPOSED LEGISLATION GENERATES THE PRINCIPAL DOCUMENTS COMPRISING THE LEGISLATIVE HISTORY OF A LAW.

During the process of considering proposed legislation, a variety of documents are created, including: (1) Presidential messages, (2) bills, (3) published hearings, (4) debates printed in the *Congressional Record*, (5) committee reports, (6) conference reports, and (7) records of constitutional conventions. Materials on legal research examine the nature of these documents in detail. As discussed later in this chapter, your primary concern with them here will be when and how they can be used to "interpret" a statute.

2. PROMULGATION OF REGULATIONS

Statutes passed by legislatures may create administrative agencies and often empower those agencies to issue rules or regulations. Valid administrative rules or regulations have the same binding force as statutes. They are ordinarily promulgated pursuant to a specific statutory delegation of authority.[8]

TO CREATE VALID RULES AND REGULATIONS, THE ADMINISTRATIVE BODY MUST FOLLOW PROSCRIBED STEPS.

Traditional administrative rulemaking procedures provide for notice of the proposed rulemaking. On the federal level, notice is given by means of publication in the *Federal Register*. That

---

[7] U.S. Const. art. I, § 7.

[8] See, e.g., Federal Trade Commission Improvement Act, 15 U.S.C.A. § 57a (West Supp. 1989) (Federal Trade Commission authorized to promulgate "rules which define with specificity acts or practices which are unfair or deceptive acts or practices in or affecting commerce").

notice is followed by a comment period during which interested persons may present their views in writing or at hearings. The final version of the proposed rules is then published.[9] On the federal level, the rules are codified in the *Code of Federal Regulations*. A similar process is generally followed on the state level.

OFFICIAL PUBLICATION OF ADMINISTRATIVE RULES AND REGULATIONS PROVIDES CONSTRUCTIVE NOTICE OF THEIR CONTENT AND APPLICABILITY.

Publication in the *Federal Register* of properly adopted regulations is constructive notice of their contents and their applicability.[10]

3. ENACTING ORDINANCES

Subordinate political subdivisions such as city councils and county boards enact ordinances governing local matters. Constitutional provisions and related legislation generally set the extent of the authority of a subordinate political subdivision to enact ordinances.

Unlike legislation at the state and national levels, legislative history of ordinances is ordinarily extremely limited. To the extent that it exists, legislative history of ordinances will not be widely available.

4. COURT RULES

Sometimes legislatures establish by statute various rules governing court practice and procedure. Sometimes that power is delegated to the courts.[11] Often, advisory committees assist courts in preparing those rules. The legislative history of the delegating act and the advisory committee notes are the principal research sources concerning intent and application of those rules.

---

[9] See 5 U.S.C.A. § 552(a)(1) (West 1977) (publication in the Federal Register of all "substantive rules of general applicability" is required to "adversely affect" a person who otherwise has not had actual and timely notice of the rules).

[10] See, e.g., Diamond Ring Ranch, Inc. v. Morton, 531 F.2d 1397 (10th Cir. 1976) (publication of regulations requiring a permit for the spraying of government land constituted constructive notice of the requirement to the owners of the ranch).

[11] See, e.g., Rules Enabling Act, 28 U.S.C.A. § 2072 (West Supp. 1989) (authorizing the United States Supreme Court to establish rules of civil procedure for the federal courts).

5. THE MAKING OF TREATIES

In the United States, the President, with the advice and consent of the Senate, has the power to negotiate and make treaties with foreign nations, provided two-thirds of the Senators present for the vote concur.[12] The Senate is not required to adopt or reject a proposed treaty as a whole. Instead, the Senate may modify the proposal.[13]

SELF-EXECUTING TREATIES HAVE THE SAME FORCE OF LAW AS A FEDERAL STATUTE.

If a properly adopted treaty is "self-executing" (in other words, the treaty does not require legislation to put its provisions into effect), it becomes the supreme law of the land.[14] As such, the treaty is equivalent to an act of Congress.[15]

6. APPROVAL OF INTERSTATE COMPACTS

Interstate compacts are agreements between states. Typical subjects of interstate compacts include water rights, boundaries, development of ports, exchange of tax data, adjustment of land grants, and construction and maintenance of bridges.[16]

INTERSTATE COMPACTS MUST BE APPROVED BY CONGRESS.

The Constitution prohibits a state of the United States from entering into any agreement or compact with another state or a foreign power without the consent of Congress.[17] Thus, when states have agreed on a compact, the compact must be submitted to Congress for approval. After Congress has enacted authorizing

---

[12]U.S. Const. art. II, § 2.

[13]See Haver v. Yaker, 76 U.S. (9 Wall.) 32, 35 (1870) (recognizing the Senate's right to amend a treaty prior to ratification). Cf. New York Indians v. United States, 170 U.S. 1, 21-24 (1898) (conditional ratification ineffective because the proviso apparently did not receive the sanction or approval of the President).

[14]See U.S. Const. art. VI, § 2 (supremacy clause).

[15]Foster v. Neilson, 27 U.S. (2 Pet.) 253, 314 (1829).

[16]See generally 72 Am. Jur. 2d States, Territories, & Dependencies § 5, at 411 (1974).

[17]U.S. Const. art. I, § 10, cl. 3.

legislation or otherwise manifested its consent, the compact becomes binding on the states which are parties to the compact and on their citizens.[18]

Section 5C. Judicial Review of the Validity of Legislative and Executive Actions

Under the system of government in the United States, one of the functions of the courts is to review the validity of legislative and executive actions.

WITH REGARD TO THE VALIDITY OF LEGISLATIVE AND EXECUTIVE ACTIONS, THE PRINCIPAL FOCUS OF JUDICIAL REVIEW IS TO DETERMINE COMPLIANCE WITH CONSTITUTIONAL REQUIREMENTS. WITH REGARD TO THE VALIDITY OF ADMINISTRATIVE ORDERS AND RULES, THE PRINCIPAL FOCUS OF JUDICIAL REVIEW IS TO DETERMINE IF THE ACTION IS WITHIN THE SCOPE OF DELEGATED AUTHORITY.

Legislative and executive actions, in the first instance, must conform to constitutional standards.[19] Furthermore, administrative orders and rules, as well as enactments of local governmental bodies, must be within the scope of authority delegated to those bodies.

1. CONSTITUTIONAL REVIEW

Courts consider several different types of constitutional questions in reviewing the validity of legislative and executive actions. First, courts will consider whether a federal statute is within the enumerated powers of Congress, as set forth by the Constitution.[20] Second, courts will consider whether a state or federal statute or executive action invades an individual's

---

[18] See Hinderlider v. La Plata River & Cherry Creek Ditch Co., 304 U.S. 92, 106-08 (1938).

[19] See Marbury v. Madison, 5 U.S. (1 Cranch) 137, 176-79 (1803).

[20] See, e.g., Trade-Mark Cases, 100 U.S. 82, 96-99 (1879) (first federal trademark law unconstitutional because Congress failed to limit that law to interstate or foreign commerce).

constitutional rights.[21] Third, courts will consider whether one branch of government has improperly invaded the sphere of authority of another branch.[22] Fourth, courts will consider whether a state statute invades powers exclusively reserved to Congress by the Constitution or whether the state statute otherwise conflicts with federal law.[23] Fifth, courts will consider whether the legislature has complied with the constitutional provisions governing the manner of enacting statutes.[24]

2. DELEGATED AUTHORITY

Another aspect of judicial review of legislation relates to the validity of local ordinances and administrative orders and rules.

ILLUSTRATION 5.3

Courts will consider claims that an administrative agency lacked authority to issue various rules, orders, or licenses.[25] Likewise, courts will decide whether a local governmental body went beyond the scope of its *delegated authority*.[26]

---

[21] See, e.g., Virginia State Bd. of Pharmacy v. Virginia Citizens Consumer Council, 425 U.S. 748, 771-73 (1976) (state statute banning prescription drug price advertising unconstitutional because the statute violated the consumers' first amendment right to receive information).

[22] See, e.g., INS v. Chadha, 462 U.S. 919, 957-59 (1983) (one-House legislative "vetoes" of administrative action unconstitutional).

[23] See, e.g., Sears, Roebuck & Co. v. Stiffel Co., 376 U.S. 225, 231-33 (1964) (state unfair competition law protecting unpatentable item unconstitutional because the state law conflicted with the exclusive power of the federal government to grant patents).

[24] See, e.g., State ex rel. Heck's Discount Centers v. Winters, 147 W. Va. 861, 876-78, 132 S.E.2d 374, 383-84 (1963) (statute invalid because it was passed beyond the time provided by the state constitution for the expiration of the legislative session, even though the time as shown on the clock in the legislative chamber was seasonable).

[25] See, e.g., Lynch v. Tilden Produce Co., 265 U.S. 315, 320-22 (1924) (administrative regulation defining adulterated butter invalid because the regulation was inconsistent with the federal statute authorizing the regulations and thus beyond the delegated authority of the agency).

[26] See, e.g., City of Miami v. Kichinko, 156 Fla. 128, 134-35, 22 So. 2d 627, 629 (1945) (municipal ordinance invalid because the state legislature intended to prohibit the exercise of all municipal powers except those specifically enumerated in the state beverage law on intoxicating liquors).

Section 5D. Reading and Analyzing Statutes

This section examines methods for reading and analyzing legislation.

YOU CANNOT IGNORE ANY PORTION OF A STATUTE.

Unlike portions of judicial opinions which may be treated as dictum, all language in legislation should be regarded as significant. Thus, ideally, "an interpretation should give meaning to all the language without inconsistencies."[27]

USE MECHANICAL OR LOGICAL METHODS TO UNTANGLE STATUTES.

The best approach to reading and understanding legislation (and to identify possible ambiguities) is to analyze structurally the text of legislation. These methods of reading and analysis include: (1) simple underlining; (2) key-element listing; (3) simple structured rewriting; (4) "capsule" versions; (5) "reader expectation" principles; (6) flow charts; and (7) logic trees.

1. UNDERLINING SIMPLE STATUTES

Rombauer suggests underlining the basic structure (subjects, verbs, objects) of simple legislation to highlight its content.[28]

ILLUSTRATION 5.4

For the purpose of this section, the tax situs of each motor vehicle shall be in the county, precinct, township, city, village, and school district where the motor vehicle is principally stored or kept.

2. KEY-ELEMENT LISTING

Another suggested approach to reading and analyzing legislation is to identify and list the "key elements" of the provision to determine the requirements or application of a statute.

---

[27] M. Rombauer, supra note 6, at 78.

[28] Id. at 79.

The elements of a statute, for example, may be narrower than the sections or subdivisions of a statute.[29]

PROBLEM 5.1

In the space provided below, identify and list what you regard to be the key elements of the following Wisconsin statute:

> No cardholder shall use a credit card issued to him or allow another person to use a credit card issued to him with intent to defraud the issuer, a person or organization providing money, goods, services or anything else of value or any other person.[30]

1.

2.

3.

4.

5.

6.

7.

8.

Stop here, and list up to eight key elements that could be separately analyzed before consulting the discussion of this problem in Appendix A. You may properly decide to list fewer than eight elements.

By breaking down the statute quoted in Problem 5.1 into its key elements, its meaning and the possible ambiguities can more easily be identified.

ILLUSTRATION 5.5

Is a check-cashing identification card a "credit card"? Does the word "use" in the statute encompass merely showing the card for identification purposes but making no charges on it? Does a person's name have to be printed on the face of the card to be "issued to him"?

---

[29] See W. Statsky, Legislative Analysis: How to Use Statutes and Regulations 50-53 (1975).

[30] Wis. Stat. Ann. § 943.41(5)(b) (West 1982).

3. SIMPLE STRUCTURED REWRITING

For more complicated statutes, such as those containing qualifications or exceptions, Rombauer suggests a "structured rewriting." Such a rewriting places in CAPITAL LETTERS the main elements of the statute. Qualifications are placed in roman type under each of the main elements but with critical conjunctions capitalized.[31] Thus, by reading the capitalized parts, you can recognize the principal thrust of the statute. By reading the parts in roman letters, you can focus on the limitations.

ILLUSTRATION 5.6

Assume that you have encountered the following Wisconsin statute concerning bribery of public officers:

> Whoever, with intent to influence the conduct of any public officer or public [employee] in relation to any matter which by law is pending or might come before him in his capacity as such officer or [employee] or with intent to induce him to do or omit to do any act in violation of his lawful duty transfers or promises to him or on his behalf any property or any personal advantage which he is not authorized to receive [is guilty of a Class D felony].[32]

Using Rombauer's approach, this Wisconsin statute could be structurally rewritten as follows:

WHOEVER

> with intent to influence the conduct of any public officer or public [employee] in relation to any matter which by law is pending or might come before him in his capacity as such officer or [employee]
>
> OR with intent to induce him to do or omit to do any act in violation of his lawful duty

TRANSFERS OR PROMISES TO HIM [PUBLIC OFFICER OR EMPLOYEE] OR ON HIS BEHALF ANY PERSONAL PROPERTY OR ANY PERSONAL ADVANTAGE

> which he is not authorized to receive
>
> **IS GUILTY OF A CLASS D FELONY.**

---

[31] M. Rombauer, <u>supra</u> note 6, at 78.

[32] Wis. Stat. Ann. § 946.10(1) (West 1982).

4. CAPSULE VERSIONS OF STATUTES

Sometimes, statutes contain extensive listings of included items. Consider the following illustration.

ILLUSTRATION 5.7

Subdivision (1) of section 132.16 of the *Wisconsin Statutes* provides as follows:

> (1) Any association, lodge, order, fraternal society, beneficial association, or fraternal and beneficial society or association, historical, military, or veterans' organization, labor union, foundation, federation, or any other society, organization or association, degree, branch, subordinate lodge, or auxiliary thereof, whether incorporated or unincorporated, the principles and activities of which are not repugnant to the constitution and law of the United States or of this state, may register, in the office of the secretary of state, a facsimile, duplicate, or description of its name, badge, motto, button, decoration, charm, emblem, rosette or other insignia, and may, by reregistration, alter or cancel the same.[33]

By devising and substituting a conceptual label for each related listing in the statute, you will be able to more easily work with (or revise) the statute.

ILLUSTRATION 5.8

Consider how much easier the statute would read if the following two concepts were identified and substituted in the statute:

Association/Organization = Association, lodge, order, fraternal society, beneficial association, or fraternal and beneficial society or association, historical, military, or veterans' organization, labor union, foundation, federation, or any other society, organization or association, degree, branch, subordinate lodge, or auxiliary thereof, whether incorporated or unincorporated, the principles and activities of which are not repugnant to the constitution and law of the United States or of this state.

Motto/Insignia = Badge, motto, button, decoration, charm, emblem, rosette or other insignia.

> (1) Any association/organization may register, in the office of the secretary of state, a facsimile,

[33] Wis. Stat. Ann. § 132.16(1) (West 1989).

> duplicate, or description of its name, motto/insignia, and may, by reregistration, alter or cancel the same.[34]

5. USING READER EXPECTATION PRINCIPLES TO UNTANGLE STATUTES

As indicated in Section 5B above, legislation is often multi-authored, contains spur-of-the-moment changes or compromises, and deals with a sometimes complex judicial or historical background. As a result, the wording of statutes often violates basic "reader's expectations." When these expectations are not met, the chances of reader misunderstanding greatly increase.[35]

Reader expectations generally focus on sentence structure. First, readers tend to expect that the point the writer (in this instance, the legislature) intended to emphasize will appear in the "stress position"--the end of the sentence. Gopen points out that the stress position can change in size from sentence to sentence and that a sentence can have internal stress positions:

> Sometimes [the stress position] is a single word; sometimes it can be several lines long. The definitive factor: a reader is in the stress position when the reader knows there is nothing but the present material left in the sentence. A whole list, numbered and indented, can be the stress position of a sentence *if* it has been clearly announced that the list is all that remains in that sentence. Each member of that list, in turn, may have its own internal stress position since stress positions are created by syntactic closure (a semi-colon, a colon, a period, or the end of a numbered and indented example). That concluding punctuation mark tells a reader to release the "reader energy" that has been

---

[34]Subsection (7) provides that

> [a]ny person who shall wilfully wear, exhibit, display, print, or use, for any purpose, the [motto/insignia] of [the association/ organization], herein mentioned, duly registered, unless he or she shall be entitled to use and wear the same under the constitution and by-laws, rules, and regulations of [the association/organization], shall be guilty of misdemeanor, and, upon conviction, shall be punished by a fine not exceeding one hundred dollars, and, in default of payment, committed to jail for a period of not to exceed sixty days.

Id. § 132.16(7).

[35]See Gopen, Let the Buyer in the Ordinary Course of Business Beware: Suggestions for Revising the Prose of the Uniform Commercial Code, 54 U. Chi. L. Rev. 1178, 1186 (1987).

> used for the perception of the local ongoing syntax.[36]

Second, readers tend to expect the focus of the discourse to be announced at the beginning of the discourse unit.[37] This position can be referred to as the "topic position."[38] Gopen explains this principle as follows:

> Readers expect a unit of discourse to be *about* whoever shows up first. "John loves Mary" and "Mary is loved by John" are two different sentences about the same facts. The first tells us something about John, the second about Mary. Despite the passivity of the second, both are good sentences. "John loves Mary" is actually an inferior sentence to "Mary is loved by John" *if* the former sentence appears in a paragraph that is telling us all about Mary. We need, therefore, to put at the beginning of each unit of discourse the people (or things) whose "story" that unit intends to recount.[39]

Third, readers tend to expect the action of a sentence to be located in the verb or in verb phrases. Gopen explains this principle as follows:

> When [the action of the sentence is located in the verb or verb phrases], the reader can "hear" that the verb phrase is indeed the clause's action. When the verb phrase does not articulate the action, . . . the reader must search for it elsewhere in the sentence, with no structural clue as to which of the several other words it might be.[40]

Fourth, readers tend to expect a grammatical subject will be immediately followed by the verb, which then will be followed immediately by the complement of the sentence. Gopen explains this principle as follows:

> Anything of length that intervenes between subject and verb or between verb and complement is read as an interruption, as something of lesser importance. . . . The longer an interruption continues, the more

---

[36] Id. at 1187 (placing emphatic material in the stress positions).

[37] Id. at 1118.

[38] Id. at 1192.

[39] Id. at 1188 ("announcing 'whose story' it is at the beginning of the discourse units" in the "topic position").

[40] Id. ("articulating action in the verb phrases").

> baggage the reader has to carry about while searching for the verb. If the interrupting material extends far enough, the reader eventually uses all of his or her available reader energy for perceiving structure; this in turn dissipates the energy that could have been used for perceiving substance and thereby necessitates a re-reading of the sentence.[41]

Fifth, readers tend to expect changes in the occupant of the topic position to indicate that the focus has shifted away from the previous occupant of the topic position.

> Since any given topic position announces whose story this particular unit is, a number of consecutive topic positions being filled by the same occupant suggests to the reader that the story of that occupant is being told continuously. Conversely, when a topic position presents an occupant different from the previous one, the reader should be able to infer safely that the story's focus has shifted away from the previous occupant to the present occupant.[42]

These reader expectation principles can be combined with other basic stylistic techniques to improve the clarity of statutory provisions. These other basic stylistic techniques include: (1) avoiding double negatives; (2) providing the reader semantic "flags" signaling what is being presented next, such as using the word "either" to begin a new series of alternatives; (3) making a clear use of "and" and "or"; and (4) avoiding the inclusion of exceptions in the statements of the general rule.[43]

In addition to improving the clarity of statutory provisions, this process of revision can also reveal (but not substantively resolve) the ambiguities in statutory provisions.[44]

PROBLEM 5.2

In his article, Gopen applies the above principles to several provisions of the Uniform Commercial Code, including the following subsection. Decide "whose story" this provision is primarily attempting to tell.

---

[41] Id. at 1190 ("subject-verb-complement separation").

[42] Id. at 1192 (consistent use of the "topic position").

[43] See id. at 1196-98. These and other basic grammar and style techniques are discussed elsewhere in this text.

[44] See id. at 1189, n.15, 1191, 1212, n.20, 1213-14.

§ 1-102(3) . . . *Variation by Agreement* (original)

> The effect of provisions of this Act may be varied by agreement, except as otherwise provided in this Act and except that the obligations of good faith, diligence, and reasonableness and care prescribed by this Act may not be disclaimed by agreement but the parties may by agreement determine the standards by which the performance of such obligations is to be measured if such standards are not manifestly unreasonable.

Stop here, and decide "whose story" this provision is attempting to tell before consulting the discussion of this problem in Appendix A.

PROBLEM 5.3

Focus on the two exceptions in the provision ("except as otherwise provided in this Act and except that the obligations of good faith, diligence, and reasonableness and care prescribed by this Act").

Stop here, and decide "whose story" the exceptions are attempting to tell before consulting the discussion of this problem in Appendix A.

PROBLEM 5.4

Recall that the provision begins, "The effect of provisions of this Act may be varied by agreement, except as otherwise provided . . . ." Assume now that the provision is going to begin with the word "Parties."

What verb or verb phrase could you use to locate the action of the sentence (what the parties are allowed to do) in that verb or verb phrase?

Stop here, and decide what verb or verb phrase you could use before consulting the discussion of this problem in Appendix A.

PROBLEM 5.5

Reconsider the original provision (above) again. How many stress positions does the original version have?

Stop here, re-examine the original provision, and decide how many stress positions it has before consulting the discussion of this problem in Appendix A.

PROBLEM 5.6

Section 1-102(3) has several points to make, but only one place in it to indicate emphasis to the reader. What is needed are additional stress positions. Consider Gopen's revision of this subsection:

> § 1-102(3) . . . *Variation by Agreement* (revision)
>
> Parties are free to agree to vary the effects of the provisions of this Act except
>
> (a) when this Act explicitly provides otherwise, and
> (b) when this Act prescribes obligations of good faith, diligence, reasonableness and care.
>
> When the obligations listed in Section 1-102(3)(b) are involved, parties may agree to determine the standards by which the performance of the obligations is to be measured, as long as those standards are not manifestly unreasonable.[45]

How many stress positions are there in this revised version?

Stop here, and answer this question before consulting the discussion of this problem in Appendix A.

PROBLEM 5.7

Gopen also illustrates the use of reader expectation principles by revising the following U.C.C. provision:

> § 2-202 *Final Written Expression: Parol or Extrinsic Evidence* (original)
>
> Terms with respect to which the confirmatory memoranda of the parties agree or which are otherwise set forth in a writing intended by the parties as a final expression of their agreement with respect to such terms as are included therein may not be contradicted by evidence of any prior agreement or of a contemporaneous oral agreement but may be explained or supplemented
>
> (a) by course of dealing or usage of trade (Section 1-205) or by course of performance (Section 2-208); and
> (b) by evidence of consistent additional terms unless the court finds the writing to have been

---

[45]Id.

> intended also as a complete and exclusive statement of the terms of the agreement.

Identify the principal subject-verb separation in the above provision.

Stop here, re-examine the provision, and identify the separation before consulting the discussion of this problem in Appendix A.

6. FLOW CHARTS

Another means of understanding a statute with many conditions is to use a flow chart.[46]

A flow chart is simply a linear portrayal of the paths provided by the statute to the "successful" end result. A flow chart is especially useful when some of the conditions are in the *conjunctive* (each condition must be satisfied to achieve legal "success") and some are *disjunctive* (any one of the conditions, if satisfied, will lead to legal "success"). In a flow chart, a linear series along the pathway can be used to portray conjunctives. Forks in the pathway can be used to portray disjunctives.

ILLUSTRATION 5.9

Shown on the following page is a flow chart for the Wisconsin bribery statute discussed in Illustration 5.6:

> Whoever, with intent to influence the conduct of any public officer or public [employee] in relation to any matter which by law is pending or might come before him in his capacity as such officer or [employee] or with intent to induce him to do or omit to do any act in violation of his lawful duty transfers or promises to him or on his behalf any property or any personal advantage which he is not authorized to receive [is guilty of a Class D felony].[47]

In the flow chart that follows, C = condition and R = result.

---

[46] See Allen & Engholm, Normalized Legal Drafting and the Query Method, 29 J. Legal Educ. 380, 384-96 (1978) (discussing and illustrating "language normalization" and the use of flow charts).

[47] Wis. Stat. Ann. § 946.10(1) (West 1982).

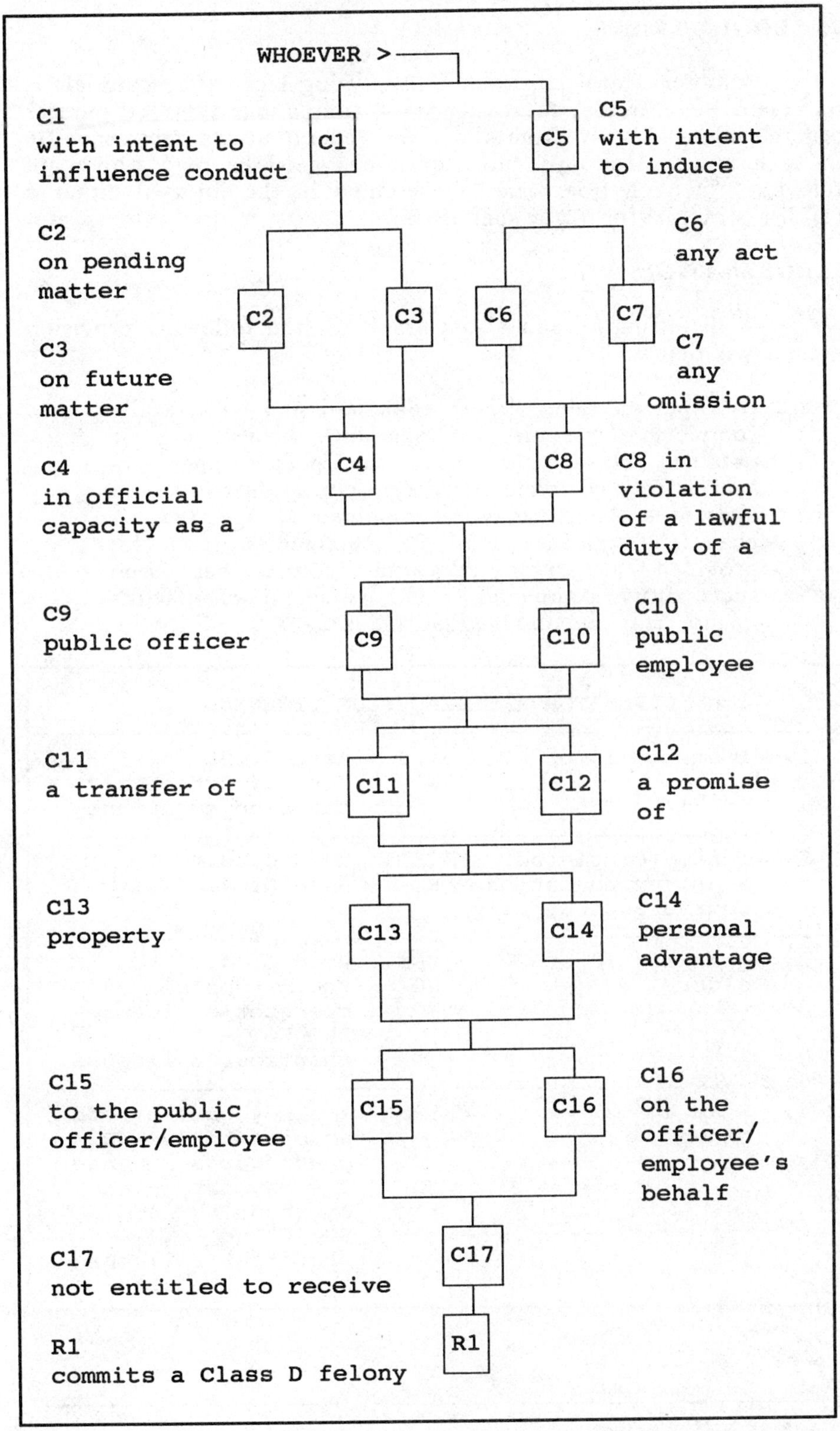
WHOEVER >
C1
with intent to
influence conduct
C1
C5
C5
with intent
to induce
C2
on pending
matter
C2
C3
C6
C7
C6
any act
C3
on future
matter
C7
any
omission
C4
in official
capacity as a
C4
C8
C8 in
violation
of a lawful
duty of a
C9
public officer
C9
C10
C10
public
employee
C11
a transfer of
C11
C12
C12
a promise
of
C13
property
C13
C14
C14
personal
advantage
C15
to the public
officer/employee
C15
C16
C16
on the
officer/
employee's
behalf
C17
not entitled to receive
C17
R1
commits a Class D felony
R1

7. LOGIC TREES

Another useful approach in analyzing legislative materials is to create logic trees: "a sequence of simple questions or phrases ordered hierarchically from the most general to the most specific in such a way that only those questions need be read which are relevant."[48] Such trees can be presented in the form of either a (1) list structure or (2) visual graph.

ILLUSTRATION 5.10

A list structure and visual graph for the following provision are shown below:

> If a person takes driver education and successfully completes the course, an operator's license may be obtained at age 16. If the person does not successfully complete the driver education course, an operator's license may be obtained at age 18. A chauffeur's license may be obtained at age 18, provided a driver education course has been successfully completed. Otherwise, a chauffeur's license may be obtained at age 21.

OPERATOR AND CHAUFFEUR LICENSES

1.	I am age 16 or older	YES NO	Read Q. 2. You may not obtain any kind of license
2.	I have completed a driver education course successfully	YES NO	Read Q. 3. Read Q. 4.
3.	I am age 18 or older	YES NO	Read Q. 4. You may obtain an operator's license BUT NOT a chauffeur's license
4.	I am age 21 or older	YES NO	You may obtain both an operator's AND a chauffeur's license You may obtain an operator's license BUT NOT a chauffeur's license

[48]Wason, The Drafting Rules, 118 New L.J. 548, 548 (1968).

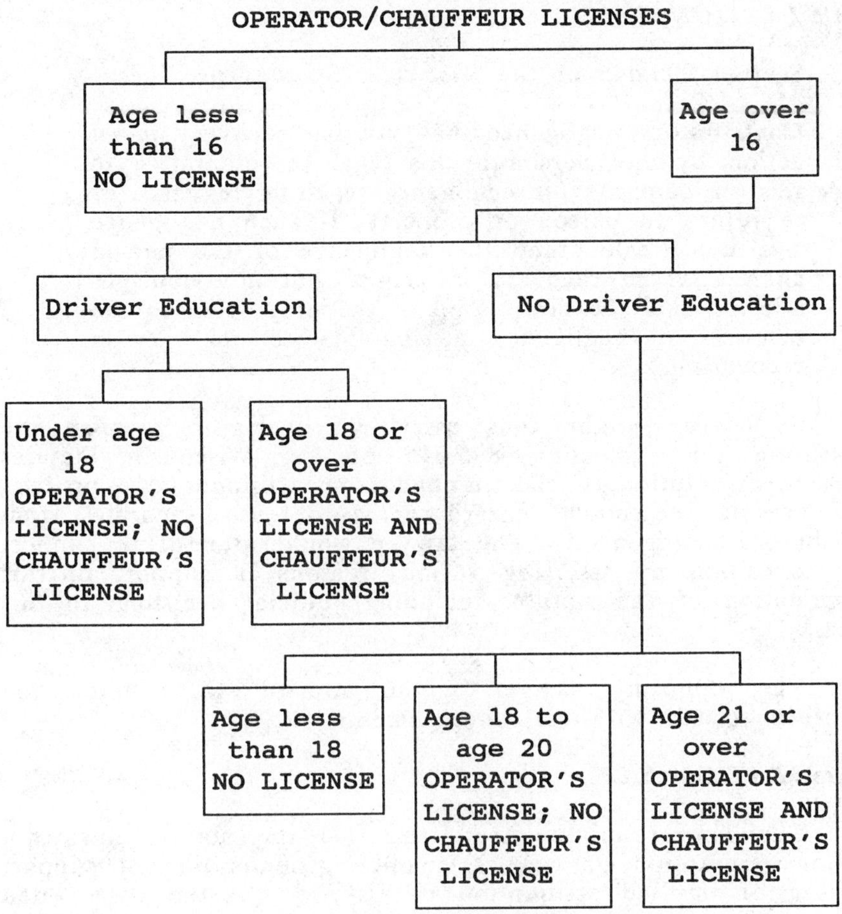

Section 5E. Applying Legislation

This section describes the basic reasoning process that lawyers and courts use in applying legislation.

1. DERIVING A PROPOSITION FROM A STATUTE

ORDINARILY, STATUTES AND OTHER LEGISLATION ARE APPLIED BY DEDUCTIVE REASONING.

Chapter 4 demonstrated that the "ratio decidendi" of a judicial decision can be used as the major premise of a syllogism. A proposition derived from a statute or other legislation can be used in the same way.

ILLUSTRATION 5.11

Section 895.045 of the *Wisconsin Statutes* provides:

> Contributory negligence shall not bar recovery in an action by any person or his legal representative to recover damages for negligence resulting in death or in injury to person or property, if such negligence was not greater than the negligence of the person against whom recovery is sought, but any damages allowed shall be diminished in the proportion to the amount of negligence attributable to the person recovering.[49]

A lawyer might thus assert as a major premise the proposition that "[s]ection 895.045 of the Wisconsin Statutes abolished assumption of risk implied from willingness to proceed in favor of a known hazard as a defense separate from contributory negligence." The lawyer would attempt to support this proposition by asserting various reasons in support of this interpretation of the statute, including judicial decisions to this effect.[50]

The opposing lawyer might attempt to counter the proposition stated with various arguments.

ILLUSTRATION 5.12

The lawyer might assert that (1) the statute does not mention assumption of risk, (2) policy grounds do not support abolition of implied assumption of risk, or (3) the cases cited were wrongly decided. The lawyer might even attack the validity of the statute. For example, the lawyer may attempt to show that the legislature violated a provision in the state constitution when it enacted the law.

2. CLASSIFICATION AND DEDUCTIVE REASONING

The lawyer seeking to apply the statute would then assert a minor premise and a conclusion.

ILLUSTRATION 5.10

"The proposed jury instruction ('Did the plaintiff willingly expose himself to the risk of injury . . . ?') is based on an implied assumption of the risk." The lawyer would again support

---

[49] Wis. Stat. Ann. § 895.045 (West 1983).

[50] See, e.g., McConville v. State Farm Mut. Auto. Ins. Co., 15 Wis. 2d 374, 113 N.W.2d 14 (1962); Baird v. Cornelius, 12 Wis. 2d 284, 107 N.W.2d 278 (1961).

this premise by prior decisions and contrasting the wording of an instruction based upon contributory negligence. The lawyer would then assert the conclusion: "The proposed jury instruction is invalid and should not be given."

The opposing lawyer again might attempt to avoid this conclusion by making various arguments.

ILLUSTRATION 5.14

The opposing lawyer might assert that the jury instruction is directed to an *express* assumption of risk, not an implied one. Thus, the lawyer would be seeking (most likely unsuccessfully) to *classify* the instruction in a way to put the instruction outside the scope of the asserted minor premise.

This process of classification is not always easy. To illustrate this point, consider the following problem.

PROBLEM 5.8

In 1938, Congress enacted the Fair Labor Standards Act,[51] which made the minimum wage and overtime provisions applicable to employees engaged in the production of goods for commerce, or in occupations or processes "necessary" to such production.[52]

Assume that you are trying to decide whether minimum wages must be paid to the following persons performing various services at a factory producing goods for commerce. In other words, are they engaged in occupations *"necessary"* to production?[53]

(a) janitors who clean the floors of the factory

(b) persons who wash the windows of the factory

(c) persons who sell sandwiches to the factory workers

(d) employees who exterminate cockroaches in the factory buildings

Stop here, and decide whether these persons must be paid minimum wages before consulting the discussion of this problem in Appendix A.

---

[51] Fair Labor Standards Act of 1938, ch. 676, 52 Stat. 1060.

[52] See id. §§ 2(a), 3(j), 52 Stat. 1060-61.

[53] See F. Cooper, Writing in Law Practice 306-07 (1963) (presenting the legislative history of this provision).

PROBLEM 5.9

Various courts and the administrative agency enforcing the Act in the preceding problem have found that all of the above types of employees were covered by the Act.[54] Were the courts and the administrative agency correct? What information would be helpful to you in evaluating their decisions about the application of the provision cited in the preceding problem?

Stop here, and decide what information would be helpful to you before consulting the discussion of this problem in Appendix A.

Section 5F. Determining Legislative Intent

In the Illustrations based on Section 895.04 of the *Wisconsin Statutes* given in the preceding section, the lawyers might raise the question of whether the Wisconsin Legislature *intended* to abolish the implied assumption of risk defense by enacting that statute. The issue of the legislature's intent could also be raised regarding the minimum wage provisions of the Fair Labor Standards Act of 1938 examined in Problems 5.8 and 5.9 above.

PROPER METHODS OF STATUTORY INTERPRETATION CENTER ON LEGISLATIVE INTENT.

Questions concerning legislative intent arise in a multitude of situations. Indeed, courts view the intent of the legislature as the controlling factor in interpreting legislation.[55] Consider what is meant by "legislative intent." Nunez suggests that there are really three major categories of legislative intent (ranked from the most general to the most specific):

> (1) Legislative intent concerning solution of a general social problem. For example, a statute enacted in response to the pollution problem is not

---

[54] See, e.g., Martino v. Michigan Window Cleaning Co., 327 U.S. 173, 177 (1946) (window-cleaning was an occupation necessary to production). See also F. Cooper, supra, note 53, at 306-09 (using this provision to illustrate the difficulty in drafting language capable of equitable application to unforeseen contingencies).

[55] See, e.g., United States v. Stone & Downer Co., 274 U.S. 225, 239 (1927) ("In this case, as in every other involving the interpretation of a statute, the intention of Congress is an all-important factor"); Carr v. New York State Bd. of Elections, 40 N.Y.2d 556, 559, 356 N.E.2d 713, 715, 388 N.Y.S.2d 87, 89 (1976) ("In statutory interpretation, legislative intent is the great and controlling principle").

> intended to be used with respect to other social problems in which pollution plays an insignificant role. Mr. Justice Cardozo, speaking of the importance of the larger social problem, stated that "the meaning of a statute is to be looked for, not in any single section, but in all the parts together and *in their relation to the end in view*."
>
> (2) Legislative intent concerning the general purposes of a specific statute. For example, a Selective Service statute intended to recruit men for military service is not intended to be employed to suppress political dissent. "[T]he *general purpose* is a more important aid to the meaning than any rule which grammar or formal logic may lay down."
>
> (3) Legislative intent concerning the meaning of a specific statutory word or phrase. It is this category that is usually thought of when the words "legislative intent" are debated. There is often a need to know whether the statute covers the particular case in mind, or whether the administrator possesses the specific power he wishes to exercise. Because most of the debate in the profession is focused upon the single category of legislative intent, the debaters are pressed to prove the existence or nonexistence of this single category of intent. If, in the debate, the concept of intent in this category is rejected, then all legislative intent is apparently rejected, and the legislative process appears as a mindless operation.
>
> At the beginning of each debate on the existence or nonexistence of legislative intent, we should start with these questions: Which intent? At what level of generality? Are we interested in the larger social policy, the general purpose of the statute, or the meaning of specific words?[56]

Furthermore, in considering the methods of determining legislative intent set forth below, you should be aware that sometimes the court's treatment of legislative intent involves a legal fiction:

> It is possible for a legislature to have a clear and discernible intent concerning the social policy and the general purpose of the statute, and yet not have devoted a single moment of thought to the specific meaning of a word or phrase. Among the

---

[56] Nunez, The Nature of Legislative Intent and the Use of Legislative Documents as Extrinsic Aids to Statutory Interpretation: A Reexamination, 9 Cal. W.L. Rev. 128, 129 (1972) (footnotes omitted).

> documents there may be evidence of specific intent; most often there is none. If the specific legislative intent does not exist and yet we act as though it does, we are acting upon a legal fiction. And even when legislative intent exists on a higher level of generality, it is still likely to be a legal fiction when applied to a word or phrase.[57]

Despite criticism and inherent weaknesses involved in using legislative intent to interpret statutes, the courts have traditionally used several methods of determining legislative intent as a means of properly interpreting and applying legislation: (1) "plain meaning" rule; (2) intrinsic aids; and (3) extrinsic aids. The following sections discuss these methods.

1. "PLAIN MEANING" RULE

One common method of interpreting legislative intent is simply to rely on the "plain meaning" of the words of the statute. A classic statement and application of the this rule is given in *Caminetti v. United States.*[58] In this case, Drew Caminetti was charged with the transportation of "a certain woman from Sacramento, California, to Reno, Nevada, in interstate commerce, for the purpose of debauchery, and for an immoral purpose, to wit, that [she] should be and become his mistress and concubine" in violation of the White Slave Traffic Act of 1910.[59] Appealing a fine and sentence of eighteen months imprisonment, Caminetti argued that Congress did not intend to cover private, non-commercial vice in this Act.[60]

The United States Supreme Court stated that "the meaning of the statute must, in the first instance, be sought in the language in which the act is framed, and if that is plain, . . . the *sole function* of the courts is to enforce it according to its terms."[61] The Court then examined the provisions of the Act, which prohibited, *inter alia*, the taking of "any woman or girl"

---

[57]Id. at 130. See also Radin, Statutory Interpretation, 43 Harv. L. Rev. 863, 869-70 (1930) (arguing that a legislative body, in fact, had no common intent and could have none; alternatively, if a search revealed an actual "legislative intent," that intent should not govern the application of the statute).

[58]242 U.S. 470 (1917).

[59]Id. at 482-83.

[60]Id. at 484-85.

[61]Id. at 485 (emphasis added).

across state lines "for the purpose of prostitution or debauchery, or for any other immoral purpose."[62]

Although there seemed to be ample evidence supporting the defendant's position in the House Report and statements by the sponsor of the bill, the Court refused to consider that evidence and found "no ambiguity" in the terms of the statute. The Court explained:

> [W]hen words are free from doubt they must be taken as the final expression of the legislative intent, are not to be added to or subtracted from by consideration drawn from titles or designating names or reports accompanying their introduction, or from any extraneous source. In other words, the language being plain, and not lending to absurd or wholly impracticable consequences, it is the sole evidence of the ultimate legislative intent.[63]

This approach may be a method of justifying the application of a statute to a specific situation that the legislating body had never contemplated, but is reasonably covered by the language of the statute. The plain meaning rule is also a method of ignoring or cutting short reference to other materials in the legislative history. Several commentators have suggested that the plain meaning rule is often merely "table thumping" to reinforce confidence in an interpretation that has been arrived at on other grounds.[64]

BE CAREFUL NOT TO RELY BLINDLY ON THE PLAIN MEANING RULE.

Although lawyers might urge that the meaning of the language is plain and, therefore, the court's sole function is to enforce the provision according to its terms, careful lawyers realize that they would be taking a risk if they were to expect a court to blindly apply the plain meaning rule. In *United States v.*

---

[62] See 18 U.S.C.A. § 2421 (West Supp. 1989) (similar provision in force today).

[63] 242 U.S. at 490.

[64] See, e.g., 2A C. Sands, Sutherland's Statutory Construction § 46.01, at 49 (4th ed. 1973). See also R. Dickerson, The Interpretation and Application of Statutes 233 (1975) (suggesting "that much of the judicial talk about 'plain meaning' [may be] a device for assigning the burden of persuasion as between the parties contending over the meaning of a statute"); Metz, The Meaninglessness of the Plain Meaning Rule, 4 Dayton L. Rev. 31, 37-38 (1979).

American Trucking Associations,[65] the United States Supreme Court has recognized the problems of a mechanical application of the "plain meaning" rule and its use to exclude other relevant sources concerning the purpose of the legislation:

> There is, of course, no more persuasive evidence of the purpose of a statute than the words by which the legislature undertook to give expression to its wishes. Often these words are sufficient in and of themselves to determine the purpose of the legislation. In such cases we have followed their plain meaning. When that meaning has led to absurd or futile results, however, this Court has looked beyond the words to the purpose of the act. Frequently, however, even when the plain meaning did not produce absurd results but merely an unreasonable one "plainly at variance with the policy of the legislation as a whole" this Court has followed that purpose, rather than the literal words. When aid to construction of the meaning of words, as used in the statute, is available, there certainly can be no "rule of law" which forbids its use, however clear the words may appear on "superficial examination."[66]

Generally speaking, the party asserting an interpretation that varies upon the apparent "plain meaning" usually bears the burden of showing why the apparent meaning should not be applied. The usual reasons for not applying the apparent plain meaning are as follows: (1) the plain meaning interpretation would be contrary to some other part of the statute; (2) it would be contrary to the statute as a whole; (3) it would be contrary to some other statute; (4) it would lead to an absurd result or injustice; or (5) the legislature used language that had a special or technical meaning different from their meaning in an ordinary sense.

2. INTRINSIC AIDS

The first two of the reasons suggested above for not applying the plain meaning rule (plain meaning contrary to (1) some other part of the statute or (2) the statute as a whole) reflect intrinsic aids to statutory interpretation. This subsection examines those aids originating within the statute itself.

---

[65] 310 U.S. 534 (1940).

[66] Id. at 543-44 (footnotes omitted).

(a) Preambles and Statutory Statements of Legislative Findings

CHECK FOR PREAMBLES OR LEGISLATIVE FINDINGS (USUALLY AT THE BEGINNING OF THE STATUTE) TO DETERMINE LEGISLATIVE INTENT.

Sometimes, statutes contain preambles or legislative findings that recite the reasons for the legislation. Preambles and legislative findings are particularly useful for determining the purpose of the legislation. Preambles may also direct the court to adopt a certain method of construction in considering the provision or the statute.

ILLUSTRATION 5.15

Consider, for instance, the preamble to the Nebraska Seller-Assisted Marketing Plan Act:

> (1) The Legislature finds and declares that the widespread sale of seller-assisted marketing plans, often connected with the sale of vending machines, vending racks, or work-at-home paraphernalia, has created numerous problems in Nebraska for purchasers which are inimical to good business practice. Often purchasers of seller-assisted marketing plans are individuals inexperienced in business matters who use their life savings to purchase the seller-assisted marketing plan in the hope that they will earn enough money in addition to retirement income or salary to become or remain self-sufficient. Many purchasers are the elderly who are seeking a way to supplement their fixed incomes. The initial payment is usually in the form of a purchase of overpriced equipment or products. Nebraska purchasers have suffered substantial losses when they have failed to receive full and complete information regarding the seller-assisted marketing plan, the amount of money they can reasonably expect to earn, and the previous experience of the seller-assisted marketing plan seller. Seller-assisted marketing plan sellers have a significant impact upon the economy and well-being of this state and its local communities. The provisions of sections 59-1701 to 59-1761 relating to seller-assisted marketing plans are necessary for the public welfare.
>
> (2) It is the intent of sections 59-1701 to 59-1761 to provide each prospective seller-assisted marketing plan purchaser with the information necessary to make an intelligent decision regarding

> seller-assisted marketing plans being offered, to safeguard the public against deceit and financial hardship, to insure, foster, and encourage competition and fair dealing in the sale of seller-assisted marketing plans by requiring adequate disclosure, to prohibit representations that tend to mislead, and to prohibit or restrict unfair contract terms. Sections 59-1701 to 59-1761 shall be construed liberally in order to achieve such purposes.[67]

This preamble provides researchers (and courts) with important information about the purposes of this Act.

(b) *Statutory Definitions*

Statutes often contain definitions of various terms used in the statute.

ILLUSTRATION 5.16

Consider the following definition of "seller" in the Nebraska Seller-Assisted Marketing Plan Act:

> Seller shall mean a person who sells or leases or offers to sell or lease a seller-assisted marketing plan and:
>
> (1) Has sold, leased, represents, or implies that the seller has sold or leased, whether in Nebraska or elsewhere, at least five seller-assisted marketing plans within twenty-four months prior to a solicitation; or
>
> (2) Intends, represents, or implies that the seller intends to sell or lease, whether in Nebraska or elsewhere, at least five seller-assisted marketing plans within twelve months following a solicitation.[68]

Definitions such as these provide another means of establishing the meaning of other parts of the statute in which the defined terms are used.

(c) *Titles*

In early English practice, the title was not part of the act; instead, the title was supplied by a clerk of one of the houses of

---

[67] Neb. Rev. Stat. § 59-1701 (1988).

[68] Id. § 59-1705.

Parliament. English courts thus ruled that the title could not be used to interpret the meaning of the act. This view influenced a number of American courts to take a similar position.[69]

Nevertheless, courts today regard the title as one means of resolving ambiguities or for correcting obvious errors. According to the courts, however, the title cannot override the plain words of the enactment.[70] The same approach is generally taken for section headings and marginal notes.[71]

(d) Punctuation

Some early American decisions stated that punctuation of an enactment is not part of the act, and courts disregarded the punctuation or even repunctuated a statute. Like the treatment of titles, this rule had its origin in early English practice.[72] The modern view is that punctuation can be used as an aid to indicate the intention of the legislature:

> [I]t is more satisfactory to treat the rules of punctuation on a parity with other rules of interpretation. When punctuation discloses a proper legislative intent or conveys a clear meaning, the courts should give weight to it as evidence. When the act as punctuated is inconsistent with what is otherwise established to be the clear intent or meaning, the punctuation should be disregarded.[73]

(e) Ejusdem Generis

Another intrinsic aid is the doctrine of ejusdem generis (meaning "of the same kind"). This doctrine originated in the *Archbishop of Canterbury's Case*.[74] Ejusdem generis is widely applied to statutes using specific words followed by general words. Dickerson explains this rule:

> [I]f a series of more than two items ends with a catch-all term that is broader than the category into

---

[69] See 2A C. Sands, supra note 64, § 47.03, at 72.

[70] Id.

[71] See id. § 47.14.

[72] Id. § 47.15. See Marcin, Punctuation and the Interpretation of Statutes, 9 Conn. L. Rev. 227, 233-41 (1977).

[73] 2A C. Sands, supra note 64, § 47.15, at 98.

[74] 76 Eng. Rep. 519 (K.B. 1596).

which the preceding items fall but which those items do not exhaust, the catch-all term is presumably intended to be no broader than that category. Thus, in the phrase "oaks, elms, and other vegetation," the term "vegetation" presumably means trees.[75]

BECAUSE DRAFTERS ARE OR SHOULD BE AWARE OF THE EJUSDEM GENERIS DOCTRINE, COURTS WILL INFER THAT THE LEGISLATURE (AND OTHERS) INTENDED TO LIMIT THE CLASS OF MATTERS TO THOSE SIMILAR TO THE ONES SPECIFICALLY ENUMERATED.

PROBLEM 5.10

Based on the principle of ejusdem generis, which of the following should *not* be included within "other vegetation" in the phrase, "oaks, elms, and other vegetation"?

(a) grass

(b) clover

(c) honey locust trees

(d) palm trees

Stop here, and decide which of the above kinds of vegetation should not be included within "other vegetation" before consulting the discussion of this problem in Appendix A.

How do you determine whether a particular situation is within the enumerated class? How do you recognize the possibilities? Statsky recommends the following four steps in analyzing whether a statute containing a list with an ending "catch-all" phrase applies to an unenumerated situation:

First: Separate the relevant *specific language* from the general language in the legislation.

Second: Identify the possible common characteristics of the specific language.

Third: Connect the common characteristics to the general language.

---

[75] R. Dickerson, The Interpretation and Application of Statutes 234 (1975).

Fourth: Assess whether the common characteristics of the specific language could apply to the key facts of your problem.[76]

PROBLEM 5.11

(a) Apply Statsky's first and second steps to the phrase, "oaks, elms, and other vegetation."

Specific Language: General Language:

(b) List the possible common characteristics of the specific language. The possibility mentioned above (trees) is listed for you.

1. Oaks and elms are *trees*.

2.

3.

4.

Stop here, and finish the above analysis before consulting the discussion of this problem in Appendix A.

REMEMBER THAT THE EJUSDEM GENERIS RULE ITSELF DOES NOT IDENTIFY WHICH COMMON CHARACTERISTICS ARE THE CRITICAL ONES.

The third and fourth steps simply involve the formulation of a proposition and its application. In the third step, you would articulate the possibilities: "Other vegetation was probably meant to include only trees or deciduous trees." In the fourth step, you would apply that proposition.

ILLUSTRATION 5.17

For instance, in Problem 5.11, grass would still clearly be excluded. A close question would be created concerning the honey locust and palm trees. Honey locust trees would be included in any event because they are deciduous trees. Palm trees would be included if the class of "other vegetation" consisted

[76] W. Statsky, supra note 29, 100-01.

of all trees. Clover might be included if "other vegetation" meant all plant life in the same plant family (locust trees and clover, for example, belong to the same plant family).

(f) Maxims

The ejusdem generis doctrine is derived from the general maxim, *noscitus a sociis*, which provides that the meaning of a word may be determined from the accompanying words. Over the years, courts have developed a variety of other general maxims to interpret the text of the statutes.

ILLUSTRATION 5.18

Some of the more common maxims include: *reddendo singula singulis* (referring each phrase to its appropriate object); *expressio unius est exclusio alterius* (the expression of one thing is the exclusion of another); *ut res magis valeat quam pereat* (that the thing may have effect rather than be destroyed); and *generalia specialibus non derogant* (general words do not derogate from the special).[77]

BE ESPECIALLY CAREFUL IN RELYING ON MAXIMS.

The authors of the texts on statutory interpretation are unanimous in their view that maxims should be used with caution. It seems that they are often applied to cure poor drafting or to describe results reached by other means.[78]

Furthermore, many of the maxims are inconsistent with other maxims.

ILLUSTRATION 5.19

Karl Llewellyn has collected several of these inconsistent maxims under the categories "Thrust and Parry." On the following page are a few examples from Llewellyn's list:[79]

---

[77] See Black's Law Dictionary 521, 616, 1148, 1386 (5th ed. 1979).

[78] See R. Dickerson, supra note 75, at 234-35.

[79] K. Llewellyn, The Common Law Tradition: Deciding Appeals 525-26 (1960) (Appendix C) (also listing a set of "Thrusts" and "Counterthrusts").

THRUST	PARRY
Every word and clause must be given effect.	If inadvertently inserted or repugnant to the rest of the statute, they may be rejected as surplusage.
The same language used repeatedly in the same connection is presumed to bear the same meaning throughout the statute.	This presumption will be disregarded [when] it is necessary to assign different meanings to make the statute consistent.
Words are to be interpreted according to their proper grammatical effect of arrangement within the statute.	Rules of grammar will be disregarded [when] strict adherence would defeat their purpose.

3. EXTRINSIC AIDS

Sources outside the text of a statute are extrinsic aids to determining legislative intent. One category of such aids is legislative material, such as transcripts of hearings, committee reports, and debates. Another category of such aids is non-legislative material, such as journal articles, bar committee proposals and reports, restatements of the law, and acquiescence in known administrative interpretations.[80]

The Uniform Law Commissioners recommend that courts consider, *inter alia*, the following extrinsic aids to determine legislative intent when a statute is ambiguous:

(1) the object sought to be attained;
(2) the circumstances under which the statute is enacted;
(3) the legislative history;
(4) the common law or former statutory provisions, including laws upon the same or similar subjects;
(5) the consequences of a particular construction;
(6) the administrative construction of the statute; and

---

[80] See Nunez, supra note 56, at 130-31.

(7) the preamble.[81]

The nature of the legislative process creates a significant potential for abuse of legislative history. Nunez explains:

> The most common form of extrinsic evidence used to establish legislative intent is legislative documents. Now more than ever, caution must be exercised in the use of legislative documents to "discover" legislative intent. The legislative process is more open and accessible than ever before in our history. For that reason, more "evidence" of legislative intent is available and consequently more skepticism of each document is necessary. Until recent years, in major constitutional cases scholars and judges looked to "the intent of the framers" found in the *The Federalist Papers* and a few personal diaries. The field of documents was small and well worked over. Today, great improvements in legislative procedures--particularly in state legislatures, with published debates, committee hearings and reports made readily available through inexpensive means of copying--have produced a mountain of documents on every major piece of legislation. It is now possible to pick and choose one's "evidence" from that mountain; in effect, to pick and choose any reasonable legislative intent.[82]

Nunez also points out that

> [a]nyone who has observed or participated in the legislative process is aware of the numerous diverse motives and understandings that produce a final statute. Only on the broadest level of generalizations (such as "this bill permits abortions in this State," or "The State will license television repairmen under this bill") can we honestly assume that there existed a consensus among the legislators as to the intent of the statute. Below the level of broad general purpose, the discovery of meaning through intent is clearly *nunc pro tunc* reasoning. For major pieces of legislation, it has become an increasingly common practice for state legislatures to add a preface or preamble which attempts to explain in narrative language the social problem existing, as well as the general purpose of the ensuing statute. While helpful in placing the legislation in its proper perspective, preambles rarely settle disputes on specific statutory language.

---

[81]Model Statutory Construction Act § 15.

[82]Nunez, supra note 56, at 131-32 (footnote omitted).

Assuming we are able to recognize a statement of legislative intent when we see one, we still must determine where in the legislative process to look for it. The common places for the search are among the transcripts of floor debates, minutes of committee meetings or public hearings, and special documents. Undoubtedly, these sources are valuable and tend to shed some light upon a statute. Again, however, caution is needed. To quote a single legislator or document is to misunderstand the nature of the legislative process itself, which is an open, decision-making process where the "thinking" as well as the final decision are available for inspection. In this open process, a legislator and other participating individuals, such as the governor, commissioners and private citizens, are, within bounds of decorum, permitted to offer any argument they wish in opposition to or support of proposed legislation. It is the thinking process of the legislature, replete with persuasive arguments, that is captured in the transcripts and minutes, not clear statements of legislative intent.

Another barrier to finding legislative intent is often created by lobbyists and legislators opposed to a bill. Knowing the openness of the process and the common use of legislative documents in the search for legislative intent, they often attempt to have inserted into the records their own statements of legislative intent in the hope that, if the legislation is enacted, such statements will be argued by future searchers as actually being the legislature's intent. In such case, the researcher will be quoting the legislative intent as expressed by the opponents of the bill, rather than by supporters who presumably speak for the consensus of the legislature, but who failed to discuss particular wording in the bill. In addition, there is an irony to be found in the search through legislative documents: it is not the sections of the statute that were fully discussed, but the sections that were not, which usually create problems as to legislative intent. Consequently, there is less likely to be evidence on the doubtful points of a statute, and this paucity of evidence increases the likelihood of misinterpretation and dependence upon fictions.

The reliability of a particular legislative document is also related to the time sequence of the legislative process involved. The greater the time lapse between the date of the document and the date of the final enactment, the more the document should be doubted as evidence of legislative intent. Before a proposed bill emerges as a statute, it must pass through numerous and well-known stages--committees, public hearings, floor debates, joint legislative committees and so forth. At these stages the bill may be redrafted, amended, or given a new interpretation, so that the final statute may bear scant resemblance to any earlier proposal. A memorandum or report submitted by the sponsors to explain the purpose of the original proposal may be useless in understanding the final statute as enacted. Similarly, initial debates and documents may fully state the legislative intent of a provision that is subsequently removed or so radically amended that the earlier legislative document may well lead to misinterpretation of the final law. Over the "life" of a proposed bill, the legislature's intent itself may also change several times before the proposal becomes a statute.

When searching for the meaning of a word or phrase, one must also keep in mind the nature of the legislative process that produced the troublesome language within the statute. The essential nature of the legislative process is compromise, bargain and consensus. Legislatures often resort to vagueness in language in order to obtain agreement among the widest number of legislators, or to avoid thorny issues that would be exposed were exactness demanded. In the legislature, vagueness keeps the process moving. Justice Frankfurter colorfully described this situation: "The Court no doubt must listen to the voice of Congress. But often Congress cannot be heard clearly because its speech is muffled." Thus, a subsequent attempt to read into a statute an exact meaning when exactness was purposefully avoided can only be described as a legal fiction. The aim of this warning is to point out that legislative documents have no inherent value as evidence of legislative intent.[83]

IN SUM, BE CAREFUL NOT TO RELY TOO HEAVILY ON GENERAL STATEMENTS OF MEANING OR INTENT IN THE LEGISLATIVE HISTORY OF A STATUTE.

[83] Id. at 133-35 (footnotes omitted). See also R. Dickerson, supra note 75, at 137-97 ("Uses and Abuses of Legislative History").

Chapter 6

REPORTING LEGAL RESEARCH

WHAT YOU WILL LEARN IN THIS CHAPTER

* The purpose of law office memoranda
* The traditional parts of a law office memorandum
* The common pitfalls in reporting legal research and ways those pitfalls can be avoided
* The way to coordinate the use of an outline and research notes in preparing the first draft of the memorandum

Section 6A. Purpose and Form of "Office" Memoranda

1. PURPOSE OF AN "OFFICE" MEMORANDUM

After research on a particular issue or problem has been completed, you will often report the results of that research in an "office" memorandum of law (sometimes simply called a memorandum of law). The purpose of such a memorandum may be (1) to assist someone else, such as a senior partner, in making a decision or preparing an opinion letter, tax return, motion, pleading, appellate brief, or some other legal document; or (2) to memorialize the research for future use. Writing a memorandum also helps organize the research and encourages accurate analysis.

2. FORMAT

Ordinarily, an office memorandum begins with a heading ("Memorandum" or "Memorandum of Law"). This heading is followed by the name of the person to whom the memorandum is addressed or by whom it was requested ("To" or "Requested By").

If the memorandum is written merely to memorialize research, it often is addressed to the "File."

Next, the name of the writer ("From") and the date the memorandum was written are given. Other identifying information ("Title," "Subject," or "Re"), such as the relevant case title, office file number, court docket number, or topic, may be noted.

ILLUSTRATION 6.1

A typical office memorandum might begin as follows:

MEMORANDUM

TO: Senior Partner
FROM: John Q. Clerk
DATE: February 29, 19xx
RE: Sudden Mental Illness as a Defense to a Negligence Action

Following this introductory material are four substantive sections, variously labeled and arranged:

(1) "Question(s)" or "Question(s) Presented"
(2) "Answer," "Brief Answer," or "Conclusion"
(3) "Facts" or "Statement of Facts"
(4) "Discussion," "Analysis," or "Law"

WHEN IT WOULD BE USEFUL TO THE READER, QUOTE THE STATUTE OR CONTRACT PROVISION INVOLVED AT THE BEGINNING OF THE MEMORANDUM. IF YOU DECIDE NOT TO QUOTE THE STATUTE, CITE IT.

Some writers also include a section citing or quoting the "Statute Involved" or the "Contract Provision Involved" if such a section is relevant. This section usually is placed before the "Question."[1]

If a memorandum is lengthy and covers several issues, a "Conclusion" is usually added at the end. In long memoranda, you can also have a "Table of Contents" derived from the headings and subheadings used in the "Discussion" section.

Likewise, you may want to provide a "Table of Citations" listing (in alphabetical order) all cases, statutes, regulations, secondary material, and other sources cited in the memorandum. Both tables should indicate the page numbers in the memorandum

---

[1] See M. Rombauer, Legal Problem Solving: Analysis, Research and Writing 298 (4th ed. 1983) (discussing the "Applicable Statutes" section of memoranda).

where the section or subsection begins and where each cited authority is discussed.

Section 6B. Formulating and Writing the Questions

The first substantive part of an office memorandum traditionally is the question or questions presented section. As a guide to formulating questions in office memoranda, consider the following suggestions.

1. MANNER OF FRAMING THE QUESTIONS

STATE THE QUESTIONS CLEARLY AND CONCISELY.

In office memoranda, you should state the questions clearly and concisely. Vague questions will confuse the reader. Incomplete questions will fail to orient the reader. Misdescriptive questions will mislead the reader.

PROBLEM 6.1

Consider the ways in which the following research question (involving the viability of sudden mental illness as a defense to a negligence action) have been stated. How can each of these questions be specifically criticized?

(a) Does the defendant have a valid defense to the plaintiff's cause of action?

(b) Whether a sudden mental illness, which a motorist asserts after a negligence claim by another motorist, is a defense to such an action?

(c) Is a sudden and unforeseeable mental illness equivalent in effect to a sudden and unforeseeable physical illness, and therefore, should a sudden and unforseeable mental illness be recognized as a defense?

Stop here, and consider how these questions can be criticized before consulting the discussion of this problem in Appendix A.

WHEN THE RESEARCH REPORTED IS BASED ON A GIVEN SET OF FACTS, DO NOT FORMULATE THE QUESTIONS IN TERMS OF ABSTRACT LEGAL QUESTIONS OR CONCLUSIONS.

How the questions are framed depends primarily on the task involved or the focus of the research request. If you are simply reporting on the law generally without reference to particular facts, you will ordinarily have to frame the questions abstractly.

ILLUSTRATION 6.2

Is full-line forcing a violation of section 1 of the Sherman Act?

Is there civil liability for defaming a dead person?

When specific facts have been given, you should include the significant ones in the questions. The inclusion of the significant facts will give the questions added meaning.

ILLUSTRATION 6.3

Is section 1 of the Sherman Act (which prohibits unreasonable "contracts, combinations, or conspiracies" in restraint of trade) violated by a provision in a franchise agreement requiring a dealer to carry the manufacturer's entire line of computer software ("full-line forcing")?

If the significant facts cannot be interwoven effectively into the questions, the statement of facts section should precede the questions so that the questions can be understood.[2]

FRAME ISSUES OF STATUTORY CONSTRUCTION OR APPLICATION NARROWLY AND SPECIFICALLY; INCLUDE THE RELEVANT KEY FACTS AND BRIEFLY QUOTE THE AMBIGUOUS PORTION OF THE STATUTE.

Statsky points out that legal issues of statutory construction are simply statements of questions "arising from the ambiguities in

---

[2] See H. Weihofen, Legal Writing Style 228 (2d ed. 1980). Accord M. Rombauer, supra note 1, at 297. See also J. Dernbach & R. Singleton, A Practical Guide to Legal Writing and Legal Method 116 (1981) (suggesting that this problem may be handled by summarizing or condensing a group of closely related facts for purposes of framing the questions).

the legislation when applied to the facts."[3] Thus, be sure to include the relevant key facts and the ambiguous portion of the statute in your questions.

ILLUSTRATION 6.4

Consider the following three examples of poor drafting of issues or questions involving statutory research:

> Does section 504 apply?
>
> [The] issue is the meaning of "reasonable care."
>
> Does the plaintiff have the burden of proof under the statutes governing the motion?[4]

Statsky explains why these statements of the issues or questions are defective:

> Legal disputes do not arise in the abstract. . . . One cannot comprehend the issue until one knows the facts that gave birth to that issue. This does not mean that the statement of the issue must contain a statement of all the facts; only the *key* facts . . . need be stated. . . . [T]he three statements of issues above are incomplete because they do not quote from the *key* language in the legislation that is in dispute (i.e., that is ambiguous) when applied to the key facts.[5]

INCLUDE ONLY SIGNIFICANT FACTS IN THE QUESTIONS; PUT FACTUAL DETAIL IN THE STATEMENT OF FACTS.

Excessive factual detail makes questions cumbersome and ineffective. Thus, in the question section, limit the facts to significant ones.

ILLUSTRATION 6.5

Compare the following question containing too much factual detail to its counterpart in Illustration 6.3 above:

---

[3] W. Statsky, Legislative Analysis: How to Use Statutes and Regulations 41 (1975).

[4] Id.

[5] Id.

Does paragraph 16(a) of the Smith-Jones "Computer World" franchise agreement, which requires Jones, the franchisee, to carry Smith's entire line of computer software, currently consisting of six hundred fifty-two programs ("full-line forcing"), violate section 1 of the Sherman Act which provides that "[e]very contract, combination, or conspiracy, in restraint of trade or commerce among the several States, or with foreign nations, is hereby declared to be illegal."

TRY TO STATE THE LAW BEFORE THE FACTS AND TO MOVE FROM THE GENERAL TO THE SPECIFIC WHEN SEVERAL FACTS ARE INCLUDED IN A SINGLE QUESTION.

When specific facts and the law are included in a single question, the law should be stated before the facts. Squires and Rombauer suggest that "[i]f the subject matter permits, the facts should be arranged from the more general to the most particular" when several facts are included in the question. Thus, "[t]he question itself should . . . move from the general area of law, at the beginning, to the most particular fact, at the end."[6]

ILLUSTRATION 6.6

Compare again the two questions involving full-line forcing stated in Illustration 6.3 and 6.5 above. The question in Illustration 6.3 refers to the law before facts. The facts move from the general (the franchise agreement) to the specific (the relevant provision in the agreement).

STATE THE QUESTIONS SO THAT EACH IS MEANINGFUL STANDING ALONE.

Each question in the memorandum should be written to be meaningful if it stood alone.[7]

PROBLEM 6.2

Consider the following two questions. How can each of these question be specifically criticized?

(a) Is the franchisor liable for treble damages for violating the Sherman Act?

---

[6] L. Squires & M. Rombauer, Legal Writing § 6.3, at 152 (1982).

[7] Id. § 6.3, at 151.

(b) Is it necessary to evaluate the necessity and proportionality of the foreign sovereign's action to determine the illegality of the foreign sovereign's acts?

Stop here, and consider how each of these questions can be criticized before consulting the discussion of this problem in Appendix A.

2. ORGANIZATION OF THE QUESTIONS

AVOID USING TOO MANY QUESTIONS OR SUBQUESTIONS.

The use of a large number of questions deflects the reader's focus and often fails to convey the issues effectively.

PROBLEM 6.3

Consider the following series of questions based on the sudden mental illness research problem mentioned in Problem 6.1. How could they be revised to avoid the specific problem of having too many questions? Note that in addition to their excessive number, the questions suffer from other defects as well.

1. Is mental illness a general defense to negligence?

2. Is sudden physical illness a defense to negligence?

3. Is sudden mental illness a defense to negligence?

4. Is sudden mental illness likely to be recognized as a defense to negligence in Utopia?

Stop here, and consider how these questions could be appropriately revised before consulting the discussion of this problem in Appendix A.

WHEN THE FACTS ARE COMPLICATED, USE SUBQUESTIONS TO PRESENT THE PRECISE LEGAL ISSUES.

If the matter is so complicated that several questions must be used, the best approach is to use principal questions with a series of subquestions. One benefit of this approach is that the number of facts that must be placed in the principal questions can be reduced.[8]

PROBLEM 6.4

Consider the following problem based on an example in Rombauer's *Legal Problem Solving: Analysis, Research and Writing* text. Does the question below appear to state the legal issue clearly? Would subquestions be helpful to more fully present the significant facts or the precise legal issue or issues?

> Can a broker, licensed in Montana but not in Washington, recover a promised commission for procuring a purchaser for hotel furnishings and a lease on the hotel property, located in Washington, whe[n]:
>
> 1. the oral promise to pay a commission was made in Montana,
>
> 2. the broker found the purchaser in Montana, and
>
> 3. the seller accepted the purchaser's offer, sent from Montana, by telegram sent from Seattle?[9]

Stop here, and consider whether the legal issue appears to be stated clearly and whether subquestions might be helpful in presenting the significant facts and precise legal questions before consulting the discussion of this problem in Appendix A.

INCORPORATE IN EACH SUBQUESTION ONLY THE FACTS THAT ARE PECULIARLY SIGNIFICANT TO THAT SUBQUESTION.

When subquestions are used in office memoranda, each subquestion should incorporate only the facts that are peculiarly significant to it.[10] Refer again to the suggested revision of the question in the discussion of Problem 6.4 for an illustration of this suggested approach.

DO NOT USE ONLY ONE SUBQUESTION (OR OTHER SUBDIVISION).

---

[8] See id. § 6.3, at 152-53.

[9] M. Rombauer, supra note 1, at 296.

[10] Id.

To use only one subquestion is inappropriate. The requirement of at least two subquestions is derived "from the logic of division," namely, "if something is divided into parts, there must be at least two parts."[11]

PROBLEM 6.5

Consider the following example of the improper use of only one subquestion. How would you solve this problem?

1. Should a driver be excused from liability for negligence when he is suddenly overcome, without warning, by a mental disability that prevents him from conforming his conduct to the standard of a reasonable person under like circumstances?

a. Should the question of liability in every case depend on the nature and extent of the driver's insanity?

Stop here, and consider how you would revise the improper use of only one subquestion before consulting the discussion of this problem in Appendix A.

PLACE THE QUESTIONS IN A LOGICAL ORDER.

Placing the questions in a logical order assists the reader in following the problems that the memorandum addresses. Ask whether one of the questions naturally precedes the others. One of the most obvious examples is when one question is dependent on the answer to a preceding question. In this regard, reexamine the subquestions in the second question in the discussion of Problem 6.4 in Appendix A (using "assuming" in the second subquestion).

Section 6C. Stating the Facts

The "Brief Answer" follows the "Questions." Because the answers are normally written after the "Discussion" section has been prepared, a discussion of how to write the answers will be presented after the section in this chapter covering the "Discussion." The "Statement of Facts" usually follows the brief answer. It presents a detailed summary of the relevant facts and assumptions on which the research is based.

---

[11] L. Squires & M. Rombauer, supra note 6, § 6.3, at 153-54.

1. MANNER OF STATING THE FACTS

STATE THE FACTS CLEARLY AND CONCISELY.

Two important aspects of good legal writing are clarity and conciseness. To write the statement of facts clearly and concisely when the facts are provided to you in a written request for research is relatively easy. On the other hand, when the relevant facts are based on depositions, transcripts, client interviews, answers to interrogatories, and stipulations, a researcher must take extra care to present the facts clearly and concisely.

PROBLEM 6.6

Consider the following two statements of facts given by Grey in his article in *Case and Comment*.[12] How would you edit or rewrite them to state the facts more clearly and concisely?

> [1] The defendant, ABC, an Ohio Corporation for profit, is engaged in the subsidized housing business and incident thereto is the owner of six dwelling units containing 46 apartment units housing 100 people. To provide for the culinary and sanitary needs of the occupants the defendant purchases from LeAx approximately 5300 gallons (22 tons) of water per day, and since opening for business in July 1975 has purchased 11,308,000 gallons of water which is all collected following use, placed in a sewage plant, treated, and discharged into a drainage ditch, which in turn discharges onto the plaintiff's property.
>
> [2] This case involves an incident which occurred on November 16, 1978. The plaintiff, Oilcorp, was the owner of a drilling rig which was located in a rural section of Athens County for the purpose of drilling for petroleum. Prior to November 16, 1978, it had been determined that the drilling was completed and it was necessary to move the rig to another location. The defendant was notified of this need and was requested to bring equipment to the drill site for the purpose of moving the drilling rig and associated apparatus from that location to a new location.[13]

---

[12] Grey, Writing a Good Appellate Brief, 88 Case & Comm., Nov.-Dec. 1983, at 44.

[13] Id. at 49.

Stop here, and decide how you would edit or rewrite these statements to state the facts more clearly before consulting the discussion of this problem in Appendix A.

INDICATE ANY ASSUMPTIONS OF FACT THAT HAVE BEEN MADE AND ANY FACTUAL INQUIRIES THAT NEED TO BE UNDERTAKEN.

One problem a researcher may face is that the facts provided may be incomplete once the substantive law on a matter has been determined. In such a situation, the researcher has two choices: (1) to seek additional information before writing the memorandum or (2) to make alternative assumptions. If facts are assumed, the assumptions should be identified in the statement of facts. Furthermore, the memorandum should point out the specific factual inquiries that should be undertaken.[14]

A related problem is lack of clear communication between the person requesting the research and the researcher. Vom Bauer suggests that the best way to avoid misunderstanding is for the person requesting the research to state the facts or questions in writing. If the assignment is made orally, the researcher may want to write a statement that can be reviewed prior to beginning the research. Another way to avoid misunderstandings is to have a conference after the researcher has undertaken some preliminary research.[15]

DO NOT OMIT SIGNIFICANT FACTS. WHEN YOU ARE IN DOUBT, ERROR ON THE SIDE OF INCLUSION.

Including all significant facts is important.[16] The omission of a significant fact can mislead the recipient of the memorandum and can cause serious errors of judgment. If a researcher is in doubt about the relevance of certain facts, Weihofen appropriately suggests that the doubt should be resolved in favor of inclusion.[17]

---

[14] See M. Cohen, How to Find the Law 489 (7th ed. 1976).

[15] Vom Bauer, How to Look Up Law and Write Legal Memoranda--Revisited, 11 Prac. Law., May 1965, at 23, 25. See also H. Weihofen, supra note 2, at 226-27 (recommending conferences); W. Statsky & R. Wernet, Case Analysis and Fundamentals of Legal Writing 411-20 (1977) ("The Art of Receiving Instructions for an Office Memorandum of Law").

[16] See M. Rombauer, supra note 1, at 298; J. Dernbach & R. Singleton, supra note 2, at 109-11 (identify both the legally significant facts and key background facts to put the legally significant facts in context).

[17] See H. Weihofen, supra note 2, at 229 ("Let your superior decide whether [a fact] can be disregarded").

STATE THE FACTS IN THE PAST TENSE.

The facts should be stated in the past tense. Recognize, however, that the past perfect tense may be necessary to express the proper relationship of prior events.

DISTINGUISH BETWEEN ALLEGED AND ESTABLISHED FACTS; NOTE SIGNIFICANT FACTUAL ISSUES BY REFERRING TO INCONSISTENT INFORMATION OR ALLEGATIONS.

Legal research does not always involve established facts. Lawyers often must work with facts that they hope the trier of fact will find to be true. Only foolhardy lawyers forget the old adage that there are two sides to every story or dispute.

A good statement of facts (and any other part of the memorandum as well) carefully distinguishes between alleged and established facts. Squires and Rombauer thus appropriately recommend the use of verbs such as "alleged," "testified," and "found by the court" to alert the reader to the differences.[18]

2. ORGANIZATION OF THE FACTS

ORDINARILY, STATE THE FACTS IN CHRONOLOGICAL ORDER. IF THE FACTS ARE COMPLICATED OR MULTIPLE PARTIES ARE INVOLVED, CONSIDER USING A TOPICAL ORGANIZATION WITH TOPIC HEADINGS.

As a general rule, the best way to state the facts is chronologically.[19] Squires and Rombauer suggest that the key facts of the transaction or occurrence should be stated in the first sentence or two, followed by a chronological narration. To assist

---

[18] L. Squires & M. Rombauer, supra note 6, § 6.3, at 155.

[19] H. Weihofen, supra note 2, at 229. Accord J. Dernbach & R. Singleton, supra note 2, at 111 ("the most sensible and convenient method of organization is to relate the facts in chronological order"); H. Shapo, M. Walter, & E. Fajans, Writing and Analysis in the Law 70 (1989) ("For many of the assignments you receive, the best and easiest way to develop the events is chronologically, that is, in the order in which the events occurred").

the reader in understanding the chronology, each paragraph could be opened with relevant dates (if appropriate).[20]

Special circumstances might justify some other order. "For example, if a problem stems from separate transactions, it may be more effective to state the facts separately for each transaction; if one or two facts are crucial, it may be well to give emphasis to them by stating them first."[21] A similar approach can be used when multiple parties are involved. Squires and Rombauer, however, caution that a researcher should "[b]e careful to introduce and conclude a [topical] fact summary and to provide explicit transitions and headings."[22]

Section 6D. Writing the Discussion Section

In the discussion section of a legal memorandum, the various issues and facts are discussed in conjunction with the relevant authorities. The discussion should be designed to inform the reader without forcing the reader to independently consult those sources.

1. ORGANIZATION OF THE DISCUSSION

DIVIDE THE DISCUSSION INTO HEADINGS AND SUBHEADINGS TO ORGANIZE THE MEMORANDUM AND ASSIST THE READER.

Before drafting the discussion section, carefully review the questions (as they have been initially formulated) and prepare an outline of the discussion.[23] This outline may serve as a means of generating the headings and subheadings of the discussion section. These headings and subheadings will assist the reader in following

---

[20] L. Squires & M. Rombauer, supra note 6, § 6.3, at 155.

[21] M. Rombauer, supra note 1, at 298.

[22] L. Squires & M. Rombauer, supra note 6, § 6.3, at 156.

[23] See Vom Bauer, supra note 15, at 35.

the discussion. In this way, they form an integral part of the discussion section.[24]

In making organizational decisions, the watchwords are "flexibility," "judgment," and "common sense." When there is some doubt about which direction or approach to take, consider the "audience" of the memorandum and ask yourself which direction or approach will best meet the needs of the readers. In this regard, recall the discussion in Chapter 1 of the principle, "Good legal writing requires awareness of the purpose and audience."

Pratt points out that there are two steps in organizing the material for a memorandum of law: (1) deciding on a "gross" organization (the order of issues and sub-issues) and (2) deciding on the "fine" organization (the order within each issue or sub-issue).[25] In terms of gross organization, for example, you might discuss the issues in order of importance[26] or in logical order.[27] Pratt suggests that when substantive and procedural issues being discussed, "it normally makes sense to put the substantive issues before the procedure issues"--unless some other organizational scheme would be better.[28]

One good way to start the discussion of an issue is to give the reader background information about the general area of law. This information may be followed by a statement of the controlling statute(s) or case(s). Then discuss how the statutes or rules apply to the situation that is the subject of the memorandum.[29]

---

[24] See H. Weihofen, supra note 2, at 232 (recommending liberal use of headings and subheadings); H. Cohen, supra note 14, at 485 (recommending use of "mechanical aids" as a guide to the reader in the discussion section). See also V. Charrow & M. Erhardt, Clear and Effective Legal Writing 178-91 (1986) (applying graphic design elements--structure, type, white space, special treatments, and paper--to legal writing).

[25] D. Pratt, Legal Writing: A Systematic Approach 107 (1989).

[26] Id. at 107-08 ("In order to take advantage of the reader's attention [at the beginning of the memorandum], begin with the most important issue and arrange the others in order of decreasing importance").

[27] Id. at 108 ("Sometimes the issues have a logical order . . . . If, for example, the case is a personal injury case and the issues are liability, damages, and attorney fees, the logical order suggests beginning with the liability issue. If there is no liability, the reader does not want to waste . . . time reading about damages and attorney fees").

[28] Id. Pratt also lists the "most complete relief" as another example of gross organization: "If . . . federal and state causes of action are available to the client, but one has the greater possibilities for relief, this is the place to begin." Id. (recognizing that this organization may also be the most logical and the order of greatest importance).

[29] See H. Weihofen, supra note 2, at 231.

A GOOD APPROACH TO ORGANIZING THE DISCUSSION SECTION INVOLVING A STATUTE IS TO DISCUSS SEPARATELY EACH "ELEMENT" OF THE STATUTE, SUBDIVIDING THAT DISCUSSION INTO THE ARGUMENTS FOR EACH POSSIBLE INTERPRETATION AND THEN TO REACH A CONCLUSION ABOUT WHICH ARGUMENT SHOULD PREVAIL ON THAT ELEMENT.

As noted in Chapter 5, one of the common methods of analyzing and applying legislation is to break the legislation down into its "elements" and discuss each one separately. Legal issues concerning the interpretation and application of those elements will generate various "pro" and "con" arguments.

A good way to organize the discussion section involving statutory interpretation is to discuss each of those elements separately, subdividing the discussion into the arguments for each possible interpretation. At the end of the discussion, you can reach a conclusion about which argument should prevail for each element in dispute.[30]

2. MANNER OF PRESENTING THE DISCUSSION

BE OBJECTIVE IN PRESENTING AND DISCUSSING THE AUTHORITIES ON ALL SIDES OF THE RELEVANT QUESTIONS.

One of the most frequent suggestions made concerning the discussion section of an office memorandum is to be "objective."[31] Thus, the authorities on all sides of the relevant questions should be presented and analyzed. Rombauer properly emphasizes this point as follows:

> The purpose of a memorandum is to explore the strength of your opponent's case as well as the strength of your client's case. You should therefore discuss fully any authorities contrary to your client's position as well as those favoring his or her position. You should, of course, attempt to distinguish, limit, or

---

[30] See W. Statsky, supra note 3, at 53-62 (recommending this approach).

[31] See, e.g., L. Squires & M. Rombauer, supra note 6, § 6.3, at 157; H. Weihofen, supra note 2, at 230; M. Cohen, supra note 14, at 480 ("The exposition of the law upon which legal advice is to be predicated must necessarily be more objective and expose more pitfalls than a legal exposition designed to sway a court"); W. Statsky, Legal Research and Writing: Some Starting Points 214-15 (3d ed. 1986) ("The primary feature of an internal memorandum is its objectivity").

criticize contrary authorities and to present the best possible arguments that can be made for your client's position, but do not lay a trap for your reader by failing to point out the weakness of the arguments you suggest.[32]

LET THE READER KNOW THE CONCLUSIONS AT AN EARLY POINT IN THE DISCUSSION.

The tendency of some researchers, particularly in the first draft, is to reveal their conclusions only at the end of the discussion section (which reflects the normal analytical process). Rombauer describes this approach as a "mystery style of development" and criticizes it because the mystery style fails to orient the reader early in the memorandum.[33]

STATE THE PURPOSES OF LEGAL RULES AND THE REASONS SUPPORTING THEM, ESPECIALLY WHEN THEY ARE NOT READILY APPARENT.

In discussing the authorities, state the purposes and reasons for legal rules, especially when they are not apparent on the face of the rule. In this regard, recall the discussion of reasoning by analogy in Chapter 4. One method of judging the strength of the similarities between cases is to examine the purposes of legal rules and the reasons supporting them.

RELATE THE CASES AND OTHER AUTHORITIES CITED TO THE FACTS OR CIRCUMSTANCES OF THE RESEARCH PROBLEM.

The cases and other materials cited or quoted should be related to the facts or circumstances of the research problem. One method is by use of specific comparisons.

ILLUSTRATION 6.7

In Theisen v. Milwaukee Automobile Mutual Insurance Co., 18 Wis. 2d 91, 118 N.W.2d 140 (1962), a passenger in a car

---

[32] Rombauer, supra note 1, at 301. Accord H. Weihofen, supra note 2, at 230 (suggesting that you should be as much concerned with the weaknesses of the case as with the favorable aspects).

[33] Id. at 300. Accord J. Dernbach & R. Singleton, supra note 2, at 93 ("Tell Your Reader Where You Are Going").

commenced a comparative negligence action against the deceased driver's insurer in a Wisconsin circuit court. The passenger was injured when the car hit a tree at three o'clock in the morning. At trial, the passenger proved that the car was driven on the wrong side of the road, the other passengers in the car had fallen asleep, and every other circumstance indicated that the driver also had fallen asleep. Unlike the instant case, in which the loss of consciousness is totally unexplained, the insurer apparently did not dispute that the driver had fallen asleep.

Instead, as justifications for the driver's apparently sudden falling asleep, the insurer attempted to prove that the driver was not a habitual user of alcoholic beverages and that he was physically exhausted at the time of the accident. The trial court rejected the defendant's offer of proof, and judgment was entered for the plaintiff upon a jury verdict. The Wisconsin Supreme Court upheld the trial court's exclusion of this offer and held that falling asleep at the wheel of an automobile is negligence as a matter of law. The case, however, had to be remanded for a new trial because of errors in the jury instructions relating to issues of contributory negligence and causation.

This decision is distinguishable on its facts. Unlike Theisen, in the instant case the accident occurred in the afternoon rather than early in the morning. Furthermore, the car did not cross the center line, and there were no passengers in the car other than the injured guest.

Another method of relating the cases and authorities cited is through citation signals and parentheticals.

ILLUSTRATION 6.8

Official entries in an appellate court docket book should be admissible without proof of compliance with the Business Records Act. Cf. State v. Jones, 579 S.W.2d 670, 670 (Mo. Ct. App. 1979) (entries in permanent record book of trial court admissible without compliance); State v. Edmonds, 347 S.W.2d 158, 163-64 (Mo. 1961) (certified penitentiary records admissible without compliance).

INCLUDE THE FACTS, PROCEDURAL CONTEXT, AND FINAL DISPOSITION IN THE DISCUSSION OF A CASE.

When a case is discussed, its facts and procedural context should be mentioned. In this way, the reader can better judge its relevance and significance. The facts and procedural context lend perspective to the court's holding and final disposition. In this regard, reconsider the example discussing the *Theisen* case in Illustration 6.7 above.

IN DISCUSSING JUDICIAL OPINIONS, STATE THE FACTS OF THE CASE AND THE COURT'S RULINGS IN THE PAST TENSE; HOWEVER, STATE LEGAL RULES IN THE PRESENT TENSE.

The facts of relevant cases and the court's rulings in them should be stated in the past tense. On the other hand, legal rules should be stated in the present tense.[34] The past perfect tense may be necessary to show the proper temporal relationship of the events discussed.

3. CITATIONS IN THE DISCUSSION SECTION

DO NOT USE A LONG SERIES OF CASE CITATIONS (EXCEPT IN UNUSUAL CIRCUMSTANCES).

A string citation is a long series of case citations as authority for a point. The commentators on legal writing generally agree that string citations should be avoided.[35] One exception might be when the point is not generally accepted. Even then, however, it ordinarily is more effective to discuss the cases individually rather than merely to include them in a string citation.

4. QUOTATIONS IN THE DISCUSSION SECTION

AVOID EXCESSIVE RELIANCE ON QUOTATIONS IN PRESENTING THE DISCUSSION.

To move from quotation to quotation in the discussion is inappropriate. Excessive quotation is likely to irritate the reader. Furthermore, excessive quotation diminishes the impact of the quotations that should remain in the text.

---

[34] See H. Weihofen, supra note 2, at 229; M. Rombauer, supra note 1, at 307.

[35] See, e.g., M. Rombauer, supra note 1, at 301 ("String citations are rarely necessary or effective"). Cf. Younger, Citing Cases For Maximum Impact, A.B.A. J., Oct., 1986, at 110, 110 (in persuasive writing, string citations are "hideous on the page and useless to the judge").

USE QUOTATIONS FROM AUTHORITIES TO SUPPORT CONCLUSIONS THAT MIGHT BE DISPUTED, TO IDENTIFY CRITICAL LANGUAGE, AND TO EMPHASIZE CRITICAL POINTS IN THE DISCUSSION.

The commentators on legal writing are not in complete agreement on the use of quotations in the discussion section. Vom Bauer suggests that a researcher should:

> quote where relevant, and don't be afraid to quote generously, for quotations are most helpful in persuading the reader. The reader will be more apt to take the court's word on a legal proposition than yours. Also, when the memorandum has been typed in final form, you may find some unexpected nuggets or unsuspected strength in the cumulative effect of the quotations.[36]

A number of commentators would add a caution concerning Vom Bauer's suggested liberal use of quotations.[37] Rombauer aptly points out that frequently

> you will make your point more clearly by using your own language. You will probably also avoid falling into the error of placing unintended reliance on dictum or too much emphasis on what the courts say rather than on what they do in relation to the facts of the cases before them. Courts do rely on language from prior opinions, sometimes without consideration of the relationship of the language to the decision, but you should not unintentionally suggest conclusions that can be supported only if a court uses this technique.[38]

In sum, the best approach is to quote language from authorities selectively. Quotations should be used to support conclusions that might be disputed, to identify critical language of a case, statute, contract provision, or other source (especially when paraphrasing may result in a possible change in meaning), and to emphasize critical points in the discussion.[39]

---

[36] Vom Bauer, supra note 15, at 39.

[37] See, e.g., H. Weihofen, supra note 2, at 231 ("Although more use may be made of quotations in a memorandum than in a[n] [appellate] brief, one should still be on guard against falling into the easy habit of having the typist copy lengthy quotations from opinions and statutes").

[38] M. Rombauer, supra note 1, at 301.

[39] See id. at 300-01.

Section 6E. Composing the Brief Answer

The brief answer section follows the question section. The commentators on legal writing suggest that the answer should be written *after* the discussion section has been drafted.[40] The purpose of the answer is to state the researcher's conclusions in a summary form. Along with the questions, the brief answer thus provides the reader with a "ready reference," as Cohen aptly puts it.[41]

1. FORMAT OF THE ANSWER

THE ANSWER SHOULD BE IN PROPER FORM.

Traditionally, the answer is presented in either of two ways, depending on the writer's preference and the nature of the research problem. One way is simply to answer each question with a few sentences or even a "yes" or "no" answer, labeled to correspond with the questions ("1.," "2.," etc.). The other way is to answer the questions in a succinct paragraph in which no more than one or two sentences are devoted to answering each question.

ILLUSTRATION 6.9

Consider the following brief answer to the real estate broker example reproduced in Problem 6.4 above:

> Smith should be able to sue successfully for his commission in a Washington court. Although it would appear that he acted as a "real estate broker" in finding a purchaser of a "business opportunity" within the meaning of the licensing statute, the Washington court has evidenced a willingness to construe the licensing statutes liberally so as to enforce the claims of brokers properly licensed in other states. Montana law will govern the validity of the commission promise because the promise-offer was made and accepted in Montana (acceptance by performance). The oral promise is enforceable because the Montana court has confined the term "real estate" to estates of

---

[40] See, e.g., Vom Bauer, supra note 14, at 40; L. Squires & M. Rombauer, supra note 5, § 6.3, at 154 ("Although the Brief Answer appears before the Discussion section, it is often written after the Discussion section is in final or nearly final form. The clear understanding required for a succinct answer may come only with the discipline of writing a detailed Discussion").

[41] M. Cohen, supra note 14, at 488.

in construing statutes analogous to the statute of frauds. A leasehold interest is not a freehold estate and the statute of frauds therefore should not apply to this commission promise.[42]

2. MANNER OF FORMULATING THE ANSWER

BE SURE TO GIVE A DEFINITE ANSWER, AND, IF APPROPRIATE, A SPECIFIC RECOMMENDATION.

One virtue of the answer reproduced in Illustration 6.7 is that the example gives a definite answer. The failure to give a definite answer is a principal defect of many office memoranda, perhaps because lawyers (and law students) do not like to be "tied down." Making definite predictions about the application of the law is sometimes difficult and increases the risk of embarrassment if the predictions turn out to be wrong. Nevertheless, a memorandum is more useful to the reader if advice and predictions are given. Furthermore, a definite answer is expected in quality legal work.

Even when a categorical answer cannot be given, a researcher should be as definite as possible. For example, it may be necessary to state that the authorities are in conflict or that the state of the law is uncertain. In such a situation, however, a researcher should still express a considered judgment on the probable resolution of the matter.[43]

DO NOT REFER TO MATTERS IN THE BRIEF ANSWER OR THE CONCLUSION IF THEY ARE NOT DISCUSSED FULLY IN THE DISCUSSION SECTION OF THE MEMORANDUM.

To refer to matters in the brief answer or the conclusion that are not discussed fully in the discussion section of the memorandum is improper. In other words, the brief answer (and the conclusion) "should summarize only."[44]

---

[42] M. Rombauer, supra note 1, at 297 (stating the above answer).

[43] See M. Cohen, supra note 14, at 482, 488.

[44] M. Rombauer, supra note 1, at 297, 300.

CITE PRECEDENTS IN THE BRIEF ANSWER ONLY IF THEY ARE THE CRUX OF THE PROBLEM.

Unless "they are the crux of the problem," cases, statutes, or other precedents should not be cited in the brief answer.[45] To refer to them in the discussion section is usually sufficient.

THE "BRIEF ANSWER" SHOULD BE BRIEF. IF THE ANSWER IS COMPLICATED OR LENGTHY, GIVE A SHORT ANSWER WITH A REFERENCE TO THE CONCLUSION SECTION.

Because the purpose of the brief answer is to provide a capsule conclusion in conjunction with the question presented, it should be brief. Sometimes, however, you may not be able to give a brief answer because the answer is extremely complicated or lengthy. In that situation, you should give a short answer with a reference to the conclusion section at the end of the memorandum.[46]

Section 6F. Writing the Conclusion

A conclusion is usually given at the end of a long legal memorandum.

1. PURPOSE OF THE CONCLUSION

USE THE CONCLUSION TO PROVIDE THE READER A FINAL SUMMARY AND TO GIVE PERSPECTIVE TO THE RESEARCH.

The conclusion section provides a final summary of the research. The conclusion also provides the writer a place to put in perspective the issues, substantive law, findings, solutions, recommendations, and areas in which further research or inquiry are needed. Thus, the conclusion is a good place to state specific advice about how a matter should be handled or the prospects for

---

[45] L. Squires & M. Rombauer, supra note 6, § 6.3, at 154.

[46] See id. at 488.

success.[47] Furthermore, it may be used "to relate the specific legal issues discussed to factual or legal issues that you do not believe warrant detailed discussion."[48]

2. CONTENT OF THE CONCLUSION

DO NOT INTRODUCE NEW AUTHORITIES IN THE CONCLUSION.

The conclusion should not introduce authorities that have not been discussed. Remember, the principal purpose of the conclusion section is a final summary for the reader.

DO NOT REPEAT THE BRIEF ANSWER VERBATIM AS THE CONCLUSION.

The conclusion should not repeat the brief answer verbatim. On the other hand, because the conclusion and the brief answer perform similar functions, the conclusion is likely to parallel the brief answer.[49]

Section 6G. Preparing the First Draft of a Memorandum From A Detailed Outline and Research Notes

Before drafting the memorandum, a detailed outline should be prepared, as shown in the following Illustration.

ILLUSTRATION 6.10

I. Sudden Illness Defense

  A. General Background

    1. Unavoidable accidents

---

[47] See M. Rombauer, supra note 1, at 300.

[48] Id.

[49] See J. Dernbach & R. Singleton, supra note 2, at 73-74 (pointing out that the conclusion is usually longer than the brief answer because it should contain a more thorough description of the reasoning supporting the ultimate conclusions).

2. Common applications--heart attacks, epileptic seizures, blackouts, etc.

B. Requirements

1. Restatement rule on sudden physical illness

2. Summary of basic requirements

a. Suddenness

b. Lack of forewarning

c. Burden of proof

II. Application of the Sudden Illness Rule to Sudden Mental Illnesses or Aberrations

A. Support for adoption of a sudden mental illness rule

1. Leading cases recognizing sudden mental illness to be within the sudden illness rule

a. <u>Buckley</u>

b. <u>Breunig</u>

2. Dictum on wide spread acceptance of the rule (<u>Moore</u>)

3. Support for rule among commentators

4. Restatement rule 283C

B. What must be shown and potential problems of application (especially in relation to the facts presented by the research problem)

1. Effect on ability to understand or appreciate the duty of care or the ability to discharge that duty

2. Suddenness and lack of forewarning vs. prior mental illness

C. Authorities Rejecting Sudden Mental Illness as a Defense

1. <u>Kuhn</u>

2. <u>Turner</u>

3. <u>Sforza</u>

4. <u>Williams v. Hays</u> (?)

D. Evaluation of these authorities and application to the facts of the research problem

III. Prior Existing Insanity--The Common-Law Rule

A. The common-law rule holding insane persons to a reasonable person standard

1. Potential problem presented by the facts of the research situation

2. <u>Williams v. Hays</u> (leading case) and judicial support for the rule

3. Restatement rule 283B

4. Reasons in favor of the common-law rule

a. Purpose of tort law

b. Fairness

c. Allocating the loss between innocent parties

d. Ease of feigning insanity

e. Difficulty of distinguishing between degrees of incapacity and bad judgment

f. Introducing unsatisfactory tests from the criminal law

g. Encouraging control of mentally ill persons

h. Liability for necessities

i. Reasonable expectations of the parties

j. Insurance and other policy arguments

B. Arguments against holding insane persons accountable for their negligence as if they were normal, prudent persons

1. Purpose of tort law

2. Injustice of the reasonable person standard

3. Imposing strict liability on one of the "innocent" victims

4. Ability to bear losses

5. Feigning mental illness

6. Difficulty fashioning test

7. Disparity of treatment of the mentally ill

8. Control of the mentally ill

9. Liability for necessities

10. Victim's reasonable expectations

C. Contributory negligence cases

D. Likely resolution or solutions to the issue

When the first draft of the memorandum (shown in Appendix E) was written using this outline, minor changes were made in the titles of the sections and levels of division. Examples of memoranda of law can be found in many sources.[50]

Examine the memorandum drafted from this outline in Appendix E.

---

[50] See, e.g., M. Rombauer, supra note 1, at 369-378; H. Weihofen, supra note 2, at 234-36; J. Dernbach & R. Singleton, supra note 2, at 183-95; M. Cohen, supra note 14, at 490-94; W. Statsky & R. Wernet, supra note 15, at 235-41; H. Shapo, M. Walter, & E. Fajans, supra note 19, at 250-55; V. Charrow & M. Erhardt, supra note 24, at 200-18; D. Pratt, supra note 25, at 326-60; K. Porter, N. Schultz, L. Scott, L. Sirico, & A. Young, Introduction to Legal Writing and Oral Advocacy app. D-1 to D-22 (1989); L. Katz, Winning Words: A Guide to Persuasive Writing for Lawyers 121-36 (1986) (office memoranda); C. Good, Mightier Than the Sword 229-39 (1989); W. Gilmer, Legal Research, Writing & Advocacy 148-55 (2d ed. 1987); K. Woolever, Untangling the Law: Strategies for Legal Writers 138-58 (1987) (sample office memorandum and trial brief compared).

Chapter 7

REVISING, REORGANIZING, AND PROOFREADING LEGAL WRITING

Section

WHAT YOU WILL LEARN IN THIS CHAPTER

* How to revise sentences to make them more effective
* How to avoid excessive wordiness in legal writing
* How to avoid "sexist" language in legal writing
* How to improve the organization of legal writing
* How to use numbers, symbols, and italics correctly in legal writing
* How to proofread legal writing more effectively

Section 7A. Introduction

An important prerequisite to achieving a command of the English language is an awareness of matters of usage and a mastery of basic stylistic techniques. Such a command--along with other basic writing skills--allows good writers to adjust the tone, emphasis, and content of their writing to reflect the purpose of a document and to achieve the desired effect on the audience who will read it.

The Oxford English Dictionary states that "style" relates to "[t]hose features of literary composition which belong to form and expression rather than to the substance of the thought or matter expressed"; in other words, "style" is simply "a writer's mode of expression considered in regard to clearness, effectiveness, beauty, and the like."[1] This chapter examines basic stylistic techniques for writing, revising, organizing, and proofreading legal writing. Many of the points that are discussed and illustrated, however, are ones widely suggested for improving writing generally; they are by no means unique to legal writing. Several problems are included in this chapter to provide you practice in using these techinques.

Section 7B. Effective Sentences

PLACE THE MAIN IDEA OF THE SENTENCE AT THE END (IN A STRESS POSITION).

Strunk and White suggest that "[t]he proper place in the sentence for the word or group of words that the writer desires to make most prominent is usually the end."[2] Legal writing commentators often echo this suggestion.[3]

ILLUSTRATION 7.1

Block illustrates how the emphasis in a sentence can be changed by placement. Consider the following three examples:

> (a) If the defendant can prove that the state statute did not give adequate notice because it was vaguely written, the federal statute would override it. (**Most important point**: the federal statute would override.)
>
> (b) The federal statute would override the state statute if the defendant can prove that the state did not give adequate notice because it was vaguely written. (**Most important point**: the state statute may be vaguely written.)
>
> (c) The federal statute would override the state statute if the defendant can prove that, because the state statute was vaguely written, it did not give

---

[1] 10 The Oxford English Dictionary 1206 (1933).

[2] W. Strunk & E. White, The Elements of Style 32 (3d ed. 1979).

[3] See, e.g., G. Block, Effective Legal Writing 38 (3d ed. 1986); Gopen, Let the Buyer in the Ordinary Course of Business Beware: Suggestions for Revising the Prose of the Uniform Commercial Code, 54 U. Chi. L. Rev. 1178, 1186 (1988) ("In the structure of a sentence, readers tend to expect that the material the writer intends to emphasize will appear at the end of the sentence," which can conveniently be called the "stress position").

adequate notice. (**Most important point**: the state statute might not have given adequate notice.)[4]

PLACE EACH MAIN IDEA IN A STRESS POSITION.

Syntactic closures (such as periods, colons, and semi-colons) create stress positions ("when the reader knows there is nothing but the present material left in the sentence").[5] As discussed and illustrated in Chapter 5 ("Statutory Interpretation and Analysis"), avoid trying to put several points or ideas into a sentence that does not provide structural stress positions for each of the points or ideas.

Thus, one important function of periods and other punctuation marks is to signal readers that it is time to pause to digest the new ideas. If you do not provide readers with appropriate structural signals, they will try to break up the sentence anyway--sometimes with the result that they get lost in the process.

When readers get lost, you have failed as a writer and have missed the opportunity to communicate effectively.

PLACE THE FOCUS OF THE DISCOURSE AT THE BEGINNING OF THE DISCOURSE UNIT.

As discussed and illustrated in Chapter 5, readers tend to expect the focus of the discourse to be announced at the beginning of the discourse unit.[6]

KEEP THE SUBJECT, VERB, AND OBJECT NEAR ONE ANOTHER IN A SENTENCE. AVOID INTERRUPTING PHRASES AND CLAUSES THAT COULD BE TRANSFERRED TO THE BEGINNING OF THE SENTENCE OR TO A SEPARATE SENTENCE.

---

[4] Block, supra note 3, at 38 (providing these examples).

[5] Gopen, supra note 3, at 1187.

[6] See id. at 1191-95 ("topic position").

The subject and principal verb should not be separated with a phrase or clause that could be placed at the beginning of the sentence.[7]

ILLUSTRATION 7.2

The "final judgment" rule, by insisting that the case be entirely completed at the trial level before an appeal is permitted, prevents constant disruption of the trial process.

This sentence could be rewritten as follows:

By insisting that the case be entirely completed at the trial level before an appeal is permitted, the "final judgment" rule prevents constant disruption of the trial process. (Subject (rule), verb (prevents), and object (disruption) now near each other.) Sometimes, the interrupting clause is best placed in a separate sentence.

PLACE QUALIFYING ADVERBS, SUCH AS "ONLY," "MERELY," AND "ALMOST," IMMEDIATELY BEFORE THE WORD OR WORDS THAT THEY MODIFY.

Qualifying adverbs, such as "only," "merely," and "almost," should be placed immediately before the words or words that they modify.

ILLUSTRATION 7.3

Consider the effect of the placement of "rarely" on the meaning of this sentence:

Public indecency rarely is a crime committed by law students.

Is it rarely a crime or is it a crime rarely committed by law students? This ambiguity can be remedied by placing "rarely" just before "a crime" or "committed," depending on the meaning intended.

Wydick aptly points out that the word "only" is particularly troublesome in legal writing. Wydick suggests that if placing "only" immediately before the word that is meant to be modified still creates ambiguity, it should be isolated at the beginning or the end of the sentence.

---

[7] See W. Strunk & E. White, supra note 2, at 29; Gopen, supra note 3, at 1190-91 ("Readers generally expect a grammatical subject to be followed immediately by the verb, which will in turn be followed immediately by the complement of the sentence").

ILLUSTRATION 7.4

Wydick gives the following examples:

Lessee shall use the vessel only for recreation. (ambiguous)
Lessee shall use the vessel for recreation only. (clear)

Shares are sold to the public only by the parent corporation. (ambiguous)
Only the parent corporation sells shares to the public. (clear)[8]

AVOID "SQUINTING" CONSTRUCTIONS IN WHICH MODIFIERS MAY REFER TO EITHER A WORD PRECEDING OR FOLLOWING THE MODIFIER.

"Squinting" constructions should be avoided.

ILLUSTRATION 7.5

Block gives the following illustration of a squinting modifier: "The trial that was postponed twice *apparently* will take place next month." To remove the inherent ambiguity, "apparently" should be placed either before "postponed" or before "take," depending on the meaning intended:

The trial that was apparently postponed twice will take place next month.

The trial that was postponed twice will apparently take place next month.[9]

USE SHORT SENTENCES FOR IMPACT.

In his book *Writing for Lawyers*, Hurd aptly points out that a short sentence is "like a jab in boxing. It doesn't necessarily knock the reader out, but it snaps [the reader's] head back and makes [the reader] take notice."[10]

---

[8] R. Wydick, Plain English for Lawyers 45 (2d ed. 1985).

[9] G. Block, supra note 3, at 9. Accord R. Wydick, supra note 8, at 44-45.

[10] H. Hurd, Writing for Lawyers 39 (1982).

ILLUSTRATION 7.6

Hurd gives the following example of the useful effect of a short sentence (in this instance, "this is false"):

> Defendant's motion to dismiss the complaint is utterly without merit, for so many reasons that it is virtually impossible to mention them all in five pages. Briefly, defendant claims first that the Fund has no standing to sue. This is false: the Fund has standing to sue because ERISA expressly says it does. Defendant claims second that the Fund has alleged no breach of the terms of the plan. This is false: the Fund has clearly alleged that the plan required employer contributions and defendant has failed to contribute.[11]

IN FORMAL LEGAL WRITING, PLACE A PREPOSITION AT THE END OF A SENTENCE WHEN (1) IT SOUNDS MORE COMFORTABLE, (2) IT IS PART OF THE SENTENCE THAT YOU WANT TO EMPHASIZE, AND (3) IT IS NOT LIKELY TO DISTRACT OR ANNOY THE READER. OTHERWISE, FOLLOW THE "TRADITIONAL" RULE THAT PREPOSITIONS SHOULD NOT BE USED TO END A SENTENCE.

The "traditional" rule is that prepositions should not be used to end a sentence.

ILLUSTRATION 7.7

Consider the following example of noncompliance with this rule:

The attorneys identified two issues which a dispute existed *about*.

To comply with the traditional rule and to avoid distracting or annoying the reader, the preposition should be moved to before "which":

The attorneys identified two issues about which a dispute existed. (Better yet, this sentence could be rewritten: "The attorneys identified two disputed issues.")

This traditional rule, however, is honored in its breach. Fowler suggests this approach:

---

[11] Id. at 39-40.

> Follow no arbitrary rule, but remember that there are often two or more possible arrangements between which a choice should be *consciously* made. If the final preposition that naturally presented itself sounds comfortable, keep it; if it does not sound comfortable, still keep it if it has compensating vigor, or when among awkward possibilities it is the least awkward.[12]

ILLUSTRATION 7.8

Consider the following example of an acceptable use of a preposition at the end of a sentence:

The defendant's attorney refused to tell me what he objected to. (This sentences uses the "natural" word order.)

Compare the above sentence with the following:

The defendant's attorney refused to tell me what it is to which he objected.[13]

Remember that when it makes little difference in how smoothly a sentence reads, judges and others who are "traditionalists" may be annoyed unnecessarily by sentences that end with a preposition.

Section 7C. Eliminating Excessive Wordiness

Wydick suggests that one way to identify excessive wordiness is to divide sentences into "working words" and "glue words":

> In every English sentence are two kinds of words: working words and glue words. The working words carry the meaning of the sentence. In the preceding sentence the working words are these: *working*, *words*, *carry*, *meaning*, and *sentence*. The others are glue words: *the*, *the*, *of*, and *the*. The glue words do perform a vital service. They hold the working words together to form a proper, grammatical sentence. Without them, the sentence would read like a telegram. But if the *proportion* of glue words is

---

[12] H. Fowler, A Dictionary of Modern English Usage 475 (2d ed. 1965) (emphasis added). See also Romm, Prepositions to End It All With, 71 A.B.A. J., Apr. 1985, at 119 (advocating that it is appropriate and often better to end sentences with prepositions). Cf. Gopen, supra note 3, at 1187-88 (discussing stress positions).

[13] See Romm, supra note 12, at 119.

> too high, that [excess] is a symptom of a badly constructed sentence.
>
> A well-constructed sentence is like fine cabinetwork. The pieces are cut and shaped to fit together with scarcely any glue. When you find too many glue words in a sentence, take it apart and reshape the pieces to fit together tighter.[14]

Similarly, Strunk and White explain:

> A sentence should contain no unnecessary words, a paragraph no unnecessary sentences, for the same reason that a drawing should have no unnecessary lines and a machine no unnecessary parts.[15]

This section identifies various situations which signal that excessive wordiness may be present.

ELIMINATE EXCESSIVE WORDINESS: PASSIVE VOICE

A sentence written in the passive voice often signals a situation in which excessive "glue" words may be eliminated.[16] The passive voice uses a form of "be" with the passive form of the verb (the past participle).

ILLUSTRATION 7.9

Wigits are made in the United States.
The provision was held unconstitutional.

In the above sentences, the subject does not do the acting. Furthermore, a "by" phrase could be added after the passive verb to identify the actor.

ILLUSTRATION 7.10

Wigits are made *by the Wigit Company of America* in Toledo, Ohio.

The provision was held unconstitutional *by the United States Supreme Court.*

---

[14] R. Wydick, supra note 8, at 7-8.

[15] W. Strunk & E. White, supra note 2, at 17.

[16] See id. at 8, 45-46. See also H. Weihofen, Legal Writing Style 111-12 (2d ed. 1982); W. Strunk & E. White, supra note 2, at 13-14.

By using the active voice, you could make these sentences more forceful. At the same time, you could eliminate some of the "glue" words.

ILLUSTRATION 7.11

The Wigit Company of America *makes* wigits in Toledo, Ohio.

The United States Supreme Court *held* the provision unconstitutional.

In certain circumstances, the passive voice will be preferred even though some "wordiness" will result. For example, the passive voice is a means of de-emphasizing the performer of the action if the "by" phrase is omitted. It is also a means of shifting emphasis within a sentence. The passive voice must be used when the actor is unknown.

Furthermore, Gopen points out that readers ordinarily "expect a unit of discourse to be about whoever shows up first." Thus, the passive voice may be necessary to convey who's story the writer intends to recount.[17]

PROBLEM 7.1

An important part of a command of the English language is the ability to manipulate sentences between the active and the passive voice. Practice changing the following sentences from passive voice to active voice.

(a) The lower court was correct in its decision in this case.

(b) The prison is constitutionally bound to provide inmates with some form of court access.

(c) An inmate's right to access to counsel was first recognized by the Supreme Court in Ex parte Hull, 312 U.S. 546 (1941).

(d) In the court order, the defendants were enjoined from enforcing the regulations.

Stop here, and revise the above sentences before consulting the discussion of this problem in Appendix A.

ELIMINATE EXCESSIVE WORDINESS: "OF"-PHRASES INDICATING POSSESSION.

[17]Gopen, supra note 3, at 1190-91.

A sentence containing an "of"-phrase indicating possession often signals a situation in which excessive wordiness may be eliminated. The sentence can be shorted by the use of an apostrophe or a personal pronoun.

ILLUSTRATION 7.12

the decision of the judge = judge's decision
or his (her) decision

ELIMINATE EXCESSIVE WORDINESS: NOUNS DERIVED FROM VERBS

Another signal indicating the opportunity to reduce excessive wordiness is the use of nouns (e.g., determination, supervision, delegation, violation, etc.) derived from verbs (e.g., determine, supervise, delegate, violate, etc.). Wydick aptly recognizes that "surplus words begin to swarm like gnats" when derivative nouns (nominalizations) are used instead of their "base" verbs.[18]

ILLUSTRATION 7.13

Compare the following two sentences:

The President made an appoint*ment* of a new ambassador.
The President appointed a new ambassador.

ELIMINATE EXCESSIVE WORDINESS: INDEFINITE LANGUAGE STATING A CONCEPT.

Another signal of excessive wordiness is the use of indefinite language stating a concept.

ILLUSTRATION 7.14

Compare the following two sentences:

The plaintiff entered into a doctor-patient relationship with the doctor.

The plaintiff became the doctor's patient. (This sentence uses direct, specific words to express the concept. As Strunk and

---

[18] R. Wydick, supra note 8, at 23 (noting that nominalizations can be spotted by their endings; common ones include "-al," "-ion," "-ence," "-ment," "-ance," "-ancy," "-ency," "-ant," "-ent," and "-ity"). See also Gopen, supra note 3, at 1188 ("Readers expect the action of a sentence to be located in the verb or the verb phrases").

White suggest, "[p]refer the specific to the general, the definite to the vague, the concrete to the abstract.")[19]

PROBLEM 7.2

Shorten the "of-phrases" and eliminate the nominalizations in the following sentences.

(a) The insurance policy contains a provision for a premium refund if the age of the applicant is stated incorrectly.

(b) In such a case, the contracting parties plainly had the intention that the age adjustment clause should override the stated age.

(c) The search is a violation of the constitutional rights of the plaintiff.

(d) Another court held that ten to fourteen hours per week placed an unreasonable impediment upon access to the courts.

Stop here, and revise the above sentences before consulting the discussion of this problem in Appendix A.

ELIMINATE EXCESSIVE WORDINESS: NEEDLESS REPETITION.

Excess wordiness can be avoided by eliminating redundancies.

ILLUSTRATION 7.15

The woman was seeking a divorce *from her husband*.[20]

ELIMINATE EXCESSIVE WORDINESS: USE OF "IT" OR "THERE" WITH A FORM OF THE VERB "BE."

---

[19] W. Strunk & E. White, supra note 2, at 15. Accord R. Wydick, supra note 8, at 49-53 (use concrete and familiar words). Cf. Gopen, supra note 3, at 1188 ("Readers expect the action of a sentence to be located in the verb or the verb phrases").

[20] Slips of the TV Tongue, Omaha World-Herald Magazine of the Midlands, Oct. 30, 1983, at 12, col. 1.

Sentences beginning with "It is," "It was," "There are," "There were," and similar constructions often signal opportunities to shorten sentences.[21]

ILLUSTRATION 7.16

Compare the following pairs of sentences:

There have been several decisions in which the state action immunity doctrine has been properly applied.
The state action immunity doctrine has been properly applied in several decisions.

It was impossible for the defendant to avoid the accident because he was in a position of helpless peril.
The defendant could not avoid the accident because he was in a position of helpless peril.

ELIMINATE EXCESSIVE WORDINESS: EXPRESSIONS THAT CAN BE REDUCED TO SINGLE ADVERBS.

Watch for expressions that can be reduced to single adverbs. They signal opportunities to eliminate words.[22]

ILLUSTRATION 7.17

in a negligent manner = negligently
in many instances (cases, circumstances, or situations) = often

ELIMINATE EXCESSIVE WORDINESS: EXPRESSIONS THAT CAN BE REDUCED TO SINGLE CONJUNCTIONS OR PREPOSITIONS.

Many expressions in common use can be reduced to single conjunctions or prepositions. Again, they signal opportunities to reduce needless words.

ILLUSTRATION 7.18

The following examples are drawn (with a few exceptions) from Weihofen's text:

---

[21]See R. Wydick, supra note 8, at 16-17. Accord H. Weihofen, supra note 16, at 45. Cf. Gopen, supra note 3, at 1188 ("Readers expect the action of a sentence to be located in the verb or the verb phrases").

[22]See R. Wydick, supra note 8, at 12-14.

at the present time = now
at the time at which = when
be of help to = help
by means of = by
during the course of = during
during the time that = while
for the period of = for
for the purpose of = for
for the reason that = because
in accordance with = by
in order to = to
in the same way as = like
notwithstanding the fact that = although
subsequent to = after
with the exception that = except
until such time as = until
with the result that = so that[23]

Watch particularly for "the fact that." Strunk and White suggest that "[i]t should be revised out of every sentence in which it occurs."[24]

PROBLEM 7.3

Eliminate excessive wordiness from the following sentences.

(a) Many statutes at the present time require incontestability clauses in insurance contracts.

(b) Notwithstanding the fact that in some instances other types of insurance policies contain incontestability clauses, life insurance policies always contain such clauses.

(c) The insurer's cancellation of the policy was illegal under the law.

(d) There are several ways that this problem can be resolved.

Stop here, and revise the above sentences before consulting the discussion of this problem in Appendix A.

ELIMINATE EXCESSIVE WORDINESS: "NOT."

---

[23]H. Weihofen, supra note 16, at 46. See also R. Wydick, supra note 8, at 11-14 (avoiding compound constructions and word-wasting idioms).

[24]W. Strunk & E. White, supra note 2, at 18. Accord R. Wydick, supra note 8, at 13 ("almost always surplus"); G. Block, supra note 3, at 46-47 (avoid this common "long wind-up").

Still another signal of excessive wordiness is "not." Many negative phrases may be stated more succinctly (and more forcefully) in a positive form.

ILLUSTRATION 7.19

Consider the following examples drawn from Strunk and White's book:[25]

not honest = dishonest
did not remember = forgot
did not pay any attention to = ignored

ELIMINATE EXCESSIVE WORDINESS: "WHICH" OR "WHO" USED WITH A FORM OF "BE."

Clauses beginning with "which is," "who is," etc. often signal situations in which an appositive can be used to shorten the sentence.[26]

ILLUSTRATION 7.20

Compare the following sentences:

The plaintiffs, *who were* pilots licensed by the state of Texas, sought to enjoin the unlicensed offering of pilotage services in the port of Galveston.

The plaintiffs, pilots licensed by the state of Texas, sought to enjoin the unlicensed offering of pilotage services in the port of Galveston.

ELIMINATE EXCESSIVE WORDINESS: CLAUSES THAT CAN BE REDUCED TO PHRASES, ADJECTIVES, OR ADVERBS.

Watch for clauses that can be reduced to phrases, adjectives, or adverbs.

ILLUSTRATION 7.21

Compare the following two sentences:

---

[25] W. Strunk & E. White, <u>supra</u> note 2, at 14-15 (use "not" for denials and antithesis).

[26] <u>See id</u>. at 18.

Although the defendant's actions were unintentional, the defendant caused serious harm.

The defendant unintentionally caused serious harm.

ELIMINATE EXCESSIVE WORDINESS: WIND-UPS AND THROAT-CLEARING.

Several commentators suggest that long "wind-ups" and "throat-clearing" should be eliminated from legal writing. Block points out that long "wind-ups" add to verbiage and diminish "force and directness by filling the important part of the sentence with language containing little or no content."[27]

ILLUSTRATION 7.22

Block lists the following examples, among others:

It is important to note that . . . .
I cannot fail to point out . . . .
I intend to discuss . . . .
I should like to stress that . . . .
There can be no question but that . . . .
It is a true fact that . . . .[28]

Wydick calls this practice "throat clearing" and recommends deletion of not only such introductory phrases but also deletion of words like "clearly."[29]

PROBLEM 7.4

Eliminate excessive wordiness from the following sentences.

(a) It is important to note that many statutes now require incontestability clauses.

(b) The statements are not relevant.

(c) The seller, who is a cross-claimant in the present action, did not make honest statements.

(d) There can be no doubt whatsoever that the plaintiff is clearly entitled to recover lost profits.

---

[27] G. Block, Effective Legal Writing 40 (2d ed. 1983).

[28] Id.

[29] R. Wydick, supra note 8, at 67.

Stop here, and edit these sentences before consulting the discussion of this problem in Appendix A.

Section 7D. Avoiding "Sexist" Language

Chapter 1 highlighted several fundamental principles of good legal writing, including an awareness of the audience. This awareness includes a sensitivity to possibly offending readers by using "sexist" (although grammatically correct) language. This section addresses how you can avoid this problem.

Many documents that lawyers prepare are directed to persons who may be offended by (1) traditional grammatical use of masculine singular pronouns (he, his, him) to refer generally to previously named titles or positions (pilot, judge, President, advocate, etc.) or (2) use of male gender titles or terms (congressman, remainderman, mankind, etc.). Commentators now present several widely recognized ways of avoiding "sexist" language.[30]

USE THE PLURAL TO AVOID THIRD PERSON SINGULAR PRONOUNS.

Often the context will allow you to change your sentences to the plural to refer to a class of individuals. In this way, you can avoid using third person singular pronouns.

ILLUSTRATION 7.23

Compare the following two sentences:

A *lawyer* must always complete *his* work on time if *he* wants to maintain the respect of *his* colleagues.

Lawyers must always complete their work on time if they want to maintain the respect of their colleagues.

REPLACE MALE AND FEMALE GENDER TITLES OR TERMS WITH SEX-NEUTRAL ONES.

Another approach is to replace male and female gender titles or terms with sex-neutral ones.

---

[30] See, e.g., D. Mellinkoff, Legal Writing: Sense and Nonsense 47-50 (1982) ("Special case: grammar v. sexism"); R. Wydick, supra note 8, at 65-67.

ILLUSTRATION 7.24

Workman's Compensation vs. Worker's Compensation
policeman, police woman vs. police officer
garbage man, trash man vs. garbage collector
steward, stewardess vs. flight attendant

The use of "person" is also rapidly replacing the "-man" ending.

ILLUSTRATION 7.23

Consider the following examples accepted by *Webster's Ninth New Collegiate Dictionary*:[31]

chairperson
congressperson
spokesperson

REPLACE THIRD PERSON SINGULAR POSSESSIVES WITH ARTICLES.

Often, third person singular possessives (his, her) can be replaced with articles (a, the).

ILLUSTRATION 7.26

Compare the following two sentences:

Rule 12(a) of the Federal Rules of Civil Procedure originally provided that "[t]he plaintiff shall serve *his* reply to a counterclaim in the answer within 20 days after service of the answer . . . ."

Rule 12(a) of the Federal Rules of Civil Procedure now provides that "[t]he plaintiff shall serve a reply to a counterclaim in the answer within 20 days after service of the answer . . . ."

ADDRESS YOUR READERS DIRECTLY IN THE SECOND PERSON ("YOU," "YOUR," "YOURS").

Instead of referring to your readers indirectly, address them using the second person.

ILLUSTRATION 7.27

Compare the following two sentences:

---

[31] See Webster's Ninth New Collegiate Dictionary 224, 227, 1139 (1983).

A lawyer should be sensitive to the far-ranging purposes of the legal documents that *he* prepares.

As a lawyer, you should be sensitive to the far-ranging purposes of the legal documents that you prepare.

PROBLEM 7.5

Revise the following Federal Rules of Civil Procedure to make them sex-neutral:

(a) If a party becomes incompetent, the court upon motion service as provided in subdivision (a) of this rule may allow the action to be continued by or against his representative. (Rule 25(b))

(b) The notice shall state the time and place for taking the deposition and the name and address of each person to be examined, if known, and if the name is not known, a general description sufficient to identify him or the particular class or group to which he belongs. (Rule 30(b)(1))

(c) No judgment by default shall be entered against the United States or an officer or agency thereof unless the claimant establishes his claim or right to relief by evidence satisfactory to the court. (Rule 55(e))

(d) The filing of pleadings and other papers with the court as required by these rules shall be made by filing them with the clerk of the court, except that the judge may permit the papers to be filed with him, in which event he shall note thereon the filing date and forthwith transmit them to the office of the clerk. (Rule 5(e))

Stop here, and edit the above sentences before consulting the discussion of this problem in Appendix A.

Section 7E. Improving Organization

This section reviews some of the basic principles of organizing written work. Specific applications and additional suggestions are given in several other chapters.

ORGANIZE WORDS, PHRASES, CLAUSES, SENTENCES, AND PARAGRAPHS IN A PARALLEL STRUCTURE TO IMPROVE CLARITY.

A traditional method of improving sentence clarity is to arrange words, phrases, clauses, and sentences in a parallel structure.[32] Parallel structure is also an excellent way of creating stress positions.[33]

ILLUSTRATION 7.28

Consider initially the following example of improper parallel structure given by Block:

> A valid banker's acceptance contains the following: (1) a time draft; (2) signature of an officer of a bank; (3) when and where the acceptance is payable; (4) statement of the underlying transaction; and (5) "accepted" written across the face of the instrument.[34]

Block suggests the following revision using "time draft" as the introductory words and beginning each listed item with a present participle (-ing form of the verb):

> In order to be valid, a banker's acceptance must be a time draft: (1) containing the signature of an officer of the bank; (2) stating when and where acceptance is payable; (3) referring to the underlying transaction; and (4) bearing the word "acceptance" on its face.[35]

PROBLEM 7.6

Revise the following sentence to reflect a parallel structure:

Such an analysis would include the following four factors: (1) the extent to which ultimate buyers are well-informed, sophisticated purchasers; (2) whether alternative names are

---

[32] See, e.g., H. Weihofen, supra note 16, at 132-33, 150-51, 319-321.

[33] See Gopen, supra note 3, at 1187, 1189, 1202-03.

[34] Block, supra note 3, at 41. Block points out that this excerpt violates the two requirements of parallel structure:

> (1) The word that introduces the list must be appropriate to all items on the list. (Here, the words "contain the following" are inappropriate for item (1), [because] a banker's acceptance "is" (not "contains") a bank draft. The introductory words also connect awkwardly with items (3) and (5).
>
> (2) The grammatical structure of all the items must be similar. If the first item on this list begins with a verb, all items should begin with a verb; if a noun, all items should begin with a noun. But, in the above example, items (1), (2), and (4) begin with nouns; item (3) begins with an adverbial phrase; and item (5) begins with a past participle.

Id.

[35] Id. at 42.

available; (3) if the product is purchased primarily on the basis of experience or test purchases; and (4) the degree to which the trademarked goods have associated with them invisible product-category attributes or characteristics.

Stop here, and revise this sentence before consulting the discussion of this problem in Appendix A.

IN ORGANIZING MATERIAL, LOOK FOR UNIFYING FACTORS SUCH AS COMMON IDEAS, SIMILARITY OF EVENTS, TIME SEQUENCE, LOGICAL SEQUENCE, ORDER OF IMPORTANCE, OR SHARED CHARACTERISTICS.

You will often have several ways in which material can be organized. The key to finding those ways is to look for unifying factors, such as time sequence, order of importance, or other shared characteristics.

Be careful to avoid an illogical development. Block points out that one especially troublesome form of development is "hysteron-proteron" (the Greek term which means "the last before the first").[36]

ILLUSTRATION 7.29

Block provides the following example of hysteron-proteron:

> In [Jones v. Jones], involving a man and woman who had just been divorced, the man had signed a note evidencing a loan from his wife, while they were still married. Then, after the divorce, by mutual consent, the former wife released the former husband from his debt. The woman took a bad debt deduction because she had not been repaid by her former husband.

Block suggests the following revision:

> In [Jones v. Jones], involving a man and woman who had just been divorced, the man had signed a note evidencing a loan from his wife, while they were still married. Then the couple were divorced and, by mutual consent, the man was released from the debt. The woman took a bad debt deduction because she had not been repaid by her former husband.[37]

---

[36]Id. at 81.

[37]Id. at 82.

CHOOSE ONE OVERALL ORGANIZATIONAL SCHEME. USE UNIFYING FACTORS TO ORGANIZE THE PRESENTATION WITHIN A GIVEN PART OR PARAGRAPH, PROVIDED THE OVERALL ORGANIZATIONAL SCHEME REMAINS CLEAR AND IS FOLLOWED.

Section 7F. Numbers, Symbols, and Italics in Legal Writing

This section discusses various technical rules concerning numbers, symbols, and italics.

1. NUMBERS

SPELL OUT ANY NUMBER THAT BEGINS A SENTENCE.

Any number that begins a sentence should be spelled out.[38]

ILLUSTRATION 7.30

Seventy-five out of the ninety persons interviewed thought "Formica" was the common descriptive name of high-pressure, decorative plastic laminate. ("Seventy-five" begins the sentence.)

IN THE TEXT, SPELL OUT NUMBERS THAT REQUIRE ONE OR TWO WORDS; USE FIGURES FOR OTHER NUMBERS; USE NUMERALS WITH (1) AN ENTIRE SERIES, (2) SECTION SIGNS OR OTHER SUBDIVISIONS, (3) DECIMALS, AND (4) REPEATED PERCENTAGES OR DOLLAR AMOUNTS.

Spell out numbers in the *text* that require one or two words; use figures for other numbers. The *USOC* provides that *round* numbers such as "hundred," "thousand," or "million" may be spelled out if they are consistently treated in that manner. Further, it provides that figures should be used for numbers used in a series,

---

[38] The Harvard Law Review Ass'n, Yale Law Journal, Columbia Law Review, and University of Pennyslvania Law Review, A Uniform System of Citation 30 (14th ed. 1986) [hereinafter USOC and USOC Rule] (Rule 6.2(a)).

with section signs or other subdivisions, with decimals, and with repeated references to percentages or dollar amounts.[39]

ILLUSTRATION 7.31

ten
five million
22, 150, and 188 (use figures in a series)
§ 2001(a)
section one
3.5
16%, 22%, and 38%
forty percent
$24,500

Note that there is no space between the percent or dollar symbols and the numerals.[40]

USE COMMAS TO SEPARATE GROUPS OF THREE DIGITS WHEN THE NUMBER CONTAINS FIVE OR MORE DIGITS.

Commas should be used to separate groups of three digits when the number contains *five* or more digits.[41] Be aware that many secretaries, however, will have learned to insert a comma in *four* digit numbers (e.g., 4,682).

ILLUSTRATION 7.32

17,650
4682
10,350,128

IN FOOTNOTES, SPELL OUT ONLY ZERO THROUGH NINE.

In *footnotes*, spell out only zero through nine.[42]

---

[39] Id. at 30 (Rule 6.2(c)).

[40] Id.

[41] Id. (Rule 6.2(a)).

[42] See id.

2. SYMBOLS

IN TEXT, SPELL OUT "SECTION" AND "PARAGRAPH"; IF THEY ARE USED IN A CITATION, SYMBOLS SHOULD BE USED.

In legal writing *text*, the words "section" and "paragraph" should be spelled out.[43]

ILLUSTRATION 7.33

The defendant disregarded *paragraph* seven of the contract. ("Paragraph" spelled out in the text.)

AFTER A STATUTE HAS BEEN MENTIONED AND PROPERLY CITED, SHORT FORMS USING A SECTION SYMBOL MAY BE USED IN THE SAME GENERAL DISCUSSION IN THE TEXT AND RELATED FOOTNOTES, EXCEPT THAT A SECTION SIGN MAY NOT BE USED TO BEGIN A SENTENCE.

In Rule 4.3(b), the *USOC* allows short form references to sections of *statutes* after a statute has been mentioned and properly cited. Permissible short forms use a section symbol (e.g., 15 U.S.C. § 1; § 1 of the Sherman Act; § 1).[44]

ILLUSTRATION 7.33

Surprisingly, only one significant case has arisen under *section* fifteen of the British Trade Marks Act of 1938. 1 & 2 Geo. 6, ch. 22, § 15. ("Section" spelled out in the first reference in the text; a section symbol was used in the citation.)

Section fifteen provides that trademark registrations do not become invalid by reason of the use of the registered mark as the name of an article or substance. ("Section" spelled out because it is the first word of the sentence.) The effect of § 15 is to afford word marks adopted by the public as the name of the goods more favorable treatment. (Symbol was used in a permissible short-form reference to the section previously cited and discussed.)

---

[43] See id. (Rule 6.2).

[44] See id. at 24-25 (Rule 4.3(b)).

DO NOT BEGIN A SENTENCE WITH A DOLLAR OR PERCENTAGE SYMBOL; USE SYMBOLS ("$" OR "%") WHENEVER NUMERALS ARE USED.

A dollar or percentage symbol should not be used to begin a sentence.

ILLUSTRATION 7.34

Five hundred *dollars* (*not* "$500") was bet on the horse, of which $250 was the plaintiff's. ("Five hundred" is spelled out because it begins the sentence.)

ILLUSTRATION 7.35

A dollar or percentage symbol should be used whenever numerals are used.[45]

ILLUSTRATION 7.36

Smith bet $500 on the horse.

PROBLEM 7.7

Edit the following sentences and accompanying footnotes in light of the above numeral and symbol rules. Indicate insertions using a caret. Indicate deletions by crossing out the material or otherwise showing that the material should be omitted. Assume that each entry follows the preceding one in a memorandum.

(a) In 1919, § 6(1) of the British Trade Marks Act of 1905 was amended to give statutory effect to the Linoleum case. 9 & 10 Geo. 5, ch. 79, sec. 6(1) (1919).

(b) Under § 6(1), all exclusive rights ceased if the trademark was the name of an article or substance manufactured under a patent upon its expiration.

(c) Section 15(1)(b), however, provides that the owner of the mark loses those exclusive rights only if it remains the only practicable name of the article or substance after a period of 2 years following cessation of the patent. British Trade Marks Act of 1938, 1 & 2 Geo. 6, ch. 22, § 15(1)(b).

(d) A study of 1,250 British cases found that this "protective" provision caused a 92 % decrease in claims of invalidity.

---

[45] See id. at 31 (Rule 6.2(c)).

Stop here, and mark the necessary corrections before consulting the discussion of this problem in Appendix A.

3. ITALICS

Italics developed as a style of slanted cursive handwriting in the fifteenth and sixteenth centuries. Today, it survives as a type style with characters that slant upward to the right as a means of setting off or emphasizing certain portions of the text. In typewritten legal writing, italics are shown by underscoring (single underlining).

(a) Names of Vehicles and Titles of Works of Art and Motion Pictures

ITALICIZE NAMES OF VEHICLES AND OTHER MEANS OF TRANSPORTATION AND TITLES OF WORKS OF ART AND MOTION PICTURES.

Italicize names of ships, trains, aircraft, and other means of transportation. Likewise, italicize titles of works of art and motion pictures.

ILLUSTRATION 7.37

Monet's *Rouen Cathedral in Full Sunlight*
Sea Princess
the *Enterprise*
Jaws 2

(b) Foreign Words

ITALICIZE FOREIGN WORDS WHEN THEY HAVE NOT BEEN ANGLICIZED.

Although many Latin and French words or phrases are commonly used in legal writing, they should be italicized as foreign words only if they have *not* been Anglicized.

ILLUSTRATION 7.38

habeas corpus (not italicized)
prima facie (not italicized)
voir dire (not italicized)
droit de suite (italicized foreign words)

According to the *USOC*, there is a strong presumption that such phrases have been incorporated into common usage.[46]

(c) Case Names and Publications

ITALICIZE CASE NAMES, TITLES OF BOOKS, ARTICLES, CONGRESSIONAL PUBLICATIONS, AND OTHER MATERIAL IN ACCORD WITH THE USOC OR OTHER ACCEPTED RULES.

In briefs, memoranda, and similar types of material, all case names should be italicized.[47] Different *USOC* typeface rules apply to material appearing in law reviews.[48]

ILLUSTRATION 7.39

State v. Jones, 579 S.W.2d 670 (Mo. Ct. App. 1979).
the *Jones* case

Titles of books and articles in periodicals are also italicized.

ILLUSTRATION 7.40

R. Keeton, *Basic Text on Insurance Law* (1971).
Folsom & Teply, *Trademarked Generic Words*, 89 Yale L.J. 1350 (1980).

Periodicals, newspapers, rules of procedure, and other publications are not italicized except when they are referred to textually.[49]

ILLUSTRATION 7.41

The article was published in the *Yale Law Journal*. (Reference to the name of a periodical in the text is italicized.)

---

[46] See id. at 31 (Rule 7). Cf. University of Chicago, The University of Chicago Manual of Legal Citation 9 (1989) [hereinafter Chicago Manual and Chicago Rule] (italicize "uncommon foreign words").

[47] USOC, supra note 38, at 3 (Rule 1.1(b)). Accord Chicago Manual, supra note 46, at 9.

[48] USOC, supra note 38, at 3 (Rule 1.1(b)).

[49] Id. at 3-4 (Rule 1.1(b)).

According to the *USOC*, titles of congressional hearings and documents should be italicized.[50] According to the *Chicago Manual*, they should not.[51]

ILLUSTRATION 7.42

Hearings on H.R. 82 Before the Subcomm. of the Senate Comm. on Patents, 78th Cong., 2d Sess. (1944). (*USOC* form)

Congressional reports that are cited without a title or author are not italicized.[52]

ILLUSTRATION 7.43

S. Rep. No. 1333, 79th Cong., 2d Sess. 4 (1946).

(d) Citation Signals and Short Forms

Signals such as "*see*," "*cf.*" and others that introduce cited authorities are used to indicate support, contradiction, profitable comparison, or background material in legal writing. According to the *USOC*, such signals should be italicized except when they are used as verbs in a complete English sentence.[53] Likewise, phrases introducing related authority, relevant history, or commentary, such as "reprinted in," "affirmed," "certiorari denied," "construed in," and others, are italicized.[54] According to the *Chicago Manual*, signals and explanatory phrases should not be italicized.[55]

ILLUSTRATION 7.44

See, e.g., *E.W. Wiggens Airways v. Massachusetts Port Auth.*, 362 F.2d 52 (1st Cir.), *cert. denied*, 385 U.S. 947 (1966). (*USOC* form)

According to the *USOC*, "*Id.*" (a short form of citation meaning the "same" and referring to the immediately preceding source), "*supra*" (meaning "above" or "before"), and "*infra*" (meaning

---

[50] Id.

[51] Chicago Manual, supra note 46, at 9, 22 (Rules 1 and 4.7).

[52] USOC, supra note 38, at 4 (Rule 1.1(c)). Accord Chicago Manual, supra note 46, at 9, 22 (Rules 1 and 4.7).

[53] USOC, supra note 38, at 3, 10 (Rules 1.1(a) and 2.2(e)).

[54] Id. (Rule 1.1(a)).

[55] Chicago Manual, supra note 46, at 9, 12 (Rules 1 and 3.1).

"below") also should be italicized.[56] According to the *Chicago Manual*, these words should not be italicized.[57]

(e) The Letter "l" in Subdivisions

It is common practice to italicize the letter "*l*" when it is used as a subdivision to avoid confusion with the number "1."[58]

ILLUSTRATION 7.45

§ 409(*l*)

PROBLEM 7.8

Indicate words that should be italicized in the following sentences from an office memorandum. Show the italics by placing a single underline under the words. When the *USOC* and *Chicago* rules differ, use the rules that you are learning.

(a) In Phelps v. The Camilla, 19 F. Cas. 441 (C.C.D. Md. 1838), agents and consignees of the brig Camilla ordered certain repairs on credit.

(b) The court pointed out that those necessary repairs are prima facie a lien on the vessel.

(c) The court carefully noted in the Phelps case, however, that if the credit had been given to the owner or anyone else, and not the vessel, then no lien would be created.

(d) Id. at 442.

Stop here, and indicate the words that should be italicized (single underlined) before consulting the discussion of this problem in Appendix A.

Section 7G. Spelling and Proofreading

PROOFREAD CAREFULLY FOR FORMAT, TYPING, AND SPELLING ERRORS.

---

[56] USOC, supra note 38, at 4 (Rule 1.1(d)).

[57] Chicago Manual, supra note 46, at 9, 25 (Rules 1 and 5).

[58] See USOC, supra note 38, at 31 (Rule 7).

Proper spelling is a technical skill that has more importance than many may think. Misspellings (or typing errors) interrupt the reader's concentration. In an article about appellate brief writing, one commentator aptly explains:

> Consider what happens when your [appellate] brief ends up on some judge's desk. It's good, nicely readable, but there is a misspelled word in the second sentence. Then another in the fifth sentence; and another in the sixth. The judge will wince at each misspelling, as if he or she were driving down a superhighway hitting a pothole every now and then. No matter how well the brief is written the misspellings will detract from its overall effect. After the third or fourth misspelling the judge feels like chucking the thing in the wastebasket.[59]

USE A DICTIONARY WHENEVER YOU HAVE ANY DOUBT WHATSOEVER ABOUT THE SPELLING OF A WORD.

Proofreading is a surprisingly difficult technical skill. Often lawyers are pressed for time and careful proofreading may get sacrificed. Furthermore, when technical errors occur in the drafting or typing process, they are frequently difficult to correct because in proofreading we are influenced by the natural tendency to "see" what we expect to see. Therefore, it is particularly useful to have someone else (in addition to the author) proofread the material.

Fortunately, some problems of proofreading have been eliminated. With the advent of sophisticated word processing systems, the problem of introducing new errors in successive drafts has been diminished substantially. Furthermore, spell checking software programs are available for many word processors, and those programs aid in proofreading.

What is the best way to proofread? Pinckert suggests the following approach:

> First, check the form. . . .
> Now comes the trick of proofreading, a trick requiring you to do two things at once, like rubbing your belly and patting your head. *You have to coordinate looking and listening*. Novices listen too much and look to little, tired proofreaders look too much and listen too little. Unless you have been proofreading all your life, you must do it out loud. Reading aloud catches

---

[59] Grey, Writing a Good Appellate Brief, 88 Case & Com., Nov.-Dec. 1983, at 44, 44.

> ugly constructions and faulty spelling and punctuation.
>
> . . .
>
> . . . Read the manuscript twice, aloud and with feeling. If you're some place where you can't read aloud, read softly while moving your tongue and lips. If everything sounds OK, move to the next sentence. Stumbling while reading shows where repairs are needed.[60]

If someone else is available to help you proofread, read the document out loud and have the other person check the accuracy of each word on a photocopy of the document.[61]

TAKE EXTRA CARE IN SPELLING (1) LEGAL TERMS AND (2) NAMES AND ADDRESSES.

As most lawyers are well aware, secretaries are not always familiar with a lawyer's vocabulary, particularly specialized legal terminology.

ILLUSTRATION 7.46

Spelling of legal terms such as the following should be carefully checked.

ad valorem	amicus curiae
forum non conveniens	demurrer
quantum meruit	escheat
res ipsa loquitur	per stirpes
certiorari	voir dire
subpoena duces tecum	injura absque damno

INSIST ON THE USE OF THE PREFERRED SPELLING OF LEGAL TERMINOLOGY, SUCH AS "ACKNOWLEDGMENT," "JUDGMENT," AND "WILLFUL."

Especially when you have dictated a document, your typist may misspell words. In proofreading, be particularly careful when the typed word appears, by itself, to be correct. A spell-checking program will not eliminate these errors.

---

[60] R. Pinckert, Pinckert's Practical Grammar 166-67 (1986) (emphasis added).

[61] V. Charrow & M. Erhardt, Clear and Effective Legal Writing 173 (1986). Charrow and Erhardt also suggest other means of forcing a proofreader to concentrate on the words rather than absorbing ideas, such as reading (1) the last sentence to the first, (2) each page from bottom to top, (3) line-by-line, with a ruler placed under the line being read, and (4) each line right to left instead of left to right. Id.

ILLUSTRATION 7.47

A lawyer may say the words on the left, but they are typed as shown on the right:

the lessor of the premises vs. the lesser of the promises
breach of contract vs. breech of contract
equitable doctrine of laches vs. equitable doctrine of latches

WATCH FOR WORDS THAT SOUND ALIKE.

Watch for words that sound alike--like those immediately above.

ILLUSTRATION 7.48

You may dictate "I am going to Bayou La Batre" (a town near Mobile, Alabama); the typed letter could read, "I am going to buy you a battery."

Watch especially for the words (principle/principal, accept/except, affect/effect, there/their/they're, and its/it's) to be sure that the word you use is typed correctly.

WATCH FOR THE INADVERTENT OMISSION OF LETTERS.

ILLUSTRATION 7.49

The following words illustrate the kind of errors you should look for in addition to the more obvious ones:

accident*al*ly (not "accidently")
re*s*cind (not "recind")
enviro*n*ment (not "enviroment")
statu*t*e (not "statue")
gover*n*ment (not "goverment")
undoubt*ed*ly (not "undoubtly")

WATCH FOR THE INADVERTENT OMISSION OF WORDS, PHRASES, OR SENTENCES.

Sometimes when a writer drafts material, a word or phrase may be omitted. More often, however, a typist may miss a word or phrase, particularly when the writer is making extensive revisions in the text. Another problem sometimes occurs when the same words or phrases are used in two adjoining sentences:

typists may skip over the material in between those words or phrases.

Many errors should be spotted by the typist, and, indeed, it is a good idea to insist that the typist *always* proofread each draft before it is returned to you.

CAREFULLY EXAMINE QUOTED MATERIAL FOR ERRORS.

Check quotations carefully against the original source or a photocopy thereof, especially when the document in which the quoted material appears will be filed with a court. Errors in a quotation may diminish the persuasiveness of the quoted material and may cause confusion or cast doubt on the accuracy of other statements.

CAREFULLY CHECK THE TYPING OF CITATIONS, PARTICULARLY THE SPACING OF REPORTER ABBREVIATIONS.

Unless the typist is thoroughly familiar with the citation system that you are using, take care to make clear exactly how you want the citations to be typed. You may want to use a signal, such as a caret or some other symbol, to indicate spacing, particularly to show that a space should be left in a reporter or court designation.

IN SUM, REMEMBER THAT PROOFREADING SHOULD BE TAKEN SERIOUSLY.

Technical errors detract from the overall quality of the final product. In particular, they create an unfavorable first impression of you, your abilities, and the value to be attached to what you write. On occasion, they also may have disastrous effects on substance. Remember, too, that proofreading is closely connected with precision--a valuable trait to develop as a professional.

Chapter 8

FORMULATING ARGUMENTS AND USING PERSUASIVE WRITING TECHNIQUES

WHAT YOU WILL LEARN IN THIS CHAPTER

* To recognize logical, emotional, and ethical arguments in legal writing
* To formulate arguments using the standard logical techniques, the "handcuff" method, purpose-of-the-rule approach, the "paradigm" case, the "extreme consequences" technique, and policy-level approaches
* To recognize and use stylistic language techniques that are useful in persuading the reader

Section 8A. Persuasive Writing in Law Practice

Persuasion is one of the important skills that lawyers use, and it frequently takes place in written form: memoranda in support of motions, trial briefs, settlement proposals, letters, and appellate briefs. This type of persuasive writing is often referred to as "argumentative" legal writing.

Argumentative legal writing relies heavily on several basic methods of formulating contentions. These methods are discussed in section B of this chapter. The particular language chosen to state facts or to express positions also plays a key role in argumentative legal writing. Language may make a sentence weak or forceful, tentative or firm, unimpressive or dramatic. As discussed in section C of this chapter, these effects are achieved by choosing words carefully, arranging sentences and paragraphs to convey desired emphasis, and controlling the tone of the presentation.

PERSUASIVE WRITING IN LAW PRACTICE IS ORDINARILY A BLEND OF THREE TYPES OF ARGUMENTS: (1) LOGICAL; (2) EMOTIONAL; AND (3) ETHICAL.

First and foremost, persuasive legal writing uses *logical arguments*--principally deductive reasoning and analogy. As discussed in prior chapters, these arguments most often rely on the authority of prior decisions or the application of statutes.

Second, persuasive legal writing uses, in part, *emotional arguments*--principally fairness and bias. Courts are sensitive to appeals contending that the application of the "letter of the law" may result in unfairness. Thus, judges usually will be receptive to resolutions that avoid harsh or undesirable results. As it is often said, hard cases make bad law.

Furthermore, lawyers have traditionally argued in subtle ways for positions that aid the poor, the feeble, the oppressed, and the suffering. Arguments based on such biases, however, are to be distinguished from appeals to prejudice.[1]

Third, persuasive writing in law practice uses, in part, *ethical arguments*--principally the honesty, good faith, and straightforwardness of the attorney and his client. This type of argument is achieved by (1) appearing to present arguments in a fair, well-balanced, and reasonable manner and by not inserting too much emotion into the presentation and (2) carefully characterizing the client's actions in a favorable manner.[2]

If appropriate, the dishonesty, unreasonableness, duplicity, or morally reprehensible conduct of opposing counsel or the opposing party can be carefully mentioned. This type of appeal most significantly affects the *tone* of the presentation.

DO NOT UNDERESTIMATE THE PERSUASIVE EFFECTS OF EMOTIONAL AND ETHICAL ARGUMENTS.

Justice Holmes aptly pointed out that there may be "some accident of immediate overwhelming interest which appeals to the feelings and distorts the judgment [so that] [t]hese immediate interests exercise a kind of hydraulic pressure which makes what

---

[1] See R. Aronson & D. Weckstein, Professional Responsibility 300 (1980) (unethical to appeal to a judge's racial, religious, national, or regional prejudices).

[2] See L. Squires & M. Rombauer, Legal Writing § 7.8, at 196-97 (1982).

previously was clear seem doubtful, and before which even well-settled principles of law will bend."[3]

One of the first steps in mastering persuasive writing techniques is to be able to recognize the type of argument being made. In the following series of problems, identify the excerpts from the briefs in *California v. Krivda* (previously discussed in Chapter 1) as primarily (a) logical, (b) emotional, or (c) ethical arguments. Recall that this case involved a police search of the defendant's trash.

PROBLEM 8.1

The attorneys for the petitioner (the State of California) included a statement of facts in their brief. What facts they included and how these facts were stated, in part, presented an opportunity for persuasion. Consider the following excerpt from the petitioner's "Statement of Facts":

> On July 1, 1968, Officer Stephen C. Gates of the Los Angeles Police Department received a telephone call from an anonymous female informant who told him that "Rodger" and "Judy" were engaging in narcotic activities, *i.e.*, smoking marijuana and injecting methedrine. (App. pp. 12-13.) The informant indicated that there were many sex parties at their 1901 Nolden residence in Los Angeles and that a Lesbian named "Frankie" was living there. The informant also indicated that both Rodger and Judy were injecting the two children who resided at that location with methedrine. The informant said that she had heard this from Judy, who said she enjoyed the effects of methedrine and that she also wanted her children to experience the feeling of being under the influence of methedrine. (App. pp. 12-13.)[4]

(Primarily) (a) logical argument, (b) emotional argument, or (c) ethical argument

Stop here, and decide what type of argument is primarily being made in the above excerpt before consulting the discussion of this problem in Appendix A.

PROBLEM 8.2

In the *Krivda* case, the petitioners asked the court to limit the scope of the exclusionary rule. In their reply brief, the

---

[3] Northern Sec. Co. v. United States, 193 U.S. 197, 400-01 (1904) (Homes, J., dissenting).

[4] Petitioner's Opening Brief at 5, California v. Krivda, 409 U.S. 33 (1972).

attorneys for the American Civil Liberties Union as amicus curiae asserted:

> Petitioners direct their attack upon the exclusionary rule to the issue of deterrence, deliberately failing to acknowledge that they are asking this Court to participate in and sanction prosecutorial deprivations of constitutional liberties.[5]

(Primarily) (a) logical argument, (b) emotional argument, or (c) ethical argument

Stop here, and decide what type of argument is primarily being made in the above excerpt before consulting the discussion of this problem in Appendix A.

PROBLEM 8.3

The attorneys for the respondents argued that the respondents were entitled to a reasonable expectation of privacy in their private trash containers while those containers were adjacent to their home. In this regard, the attorneys asserted, in part, the following:

> Both the exigencies of time and a lack of interest in stinking, putrid refuse, containing everything from used Kotex, disposable baby diapers, and overripe fruit, literally covered with maggots, to discarded personal letters, perused, dog-eared old magazines and junk mail, operate to cause these harried and muscled sanitation workers to rapidly propel such vile matter into the gaseous anonymity of the bellies of their huge mechanical scavengers. Few Los Angeles residents have not had the experience of watching neighbors, at the last opportunity to catch the truck, gallantly struggling to pull their garbage cans from the protective environs of the home onto the curb, having forgotten to do so previously. The point is that the even minimally alert and cognizant citizen expects, *knows*, that the usual garbage hauler has neither the time nor interest to conduct a "search" or a "view" of the individual garbage can, and he has a reasonable expectation of privacy in that he therefore expects, *knows*, that refuse there deposited will flow in an uninterrupted manner out to the dump

---

[5] Brief of the American Civil Liberties Union and the American Civil Liberties Union of Southern California, Amici Curiae, at 6, California v. Krivda, 409 U.S. 33 (1972).

> where it will be burned and/or plowed under by a bulldozer.[6]

(Primarily) (a) logical argument, (b) emotional argument, or (c) ethical argument

Stop here, and decide what type of argument is primarily being made in the above excerpt before consulting the discussion of this problem in Appendix A.

PROBLEM 8.4

The attorneys for the petitioner pointed out:

> The California Supreme Court concluded that an abandonment of one's trash to the trash collector was not ". . . necessarily an abandonment of one's trash to the police or general public." *People v. Krivda, supra,* 5 Cal. 3d at 366, 96 Cal. Rptr. at 68, 486 P.2d at 1268. Unfortunately, the California Supreme Court cites no authority for the novel doctrine of partial abandonment. Like pregnancy, abandonment by definition cannot be partial. Either one has voluntarily relinquished all of his property interest in discarded items, or he has not.[7]

(Primarily) (a) logical argument, (b) emotional argument, or (c) ethical argument

Stop here, and decide what type of argument is primarily being made in the above excerpt before consulting the discussion of this problem in Appendix A.

PROBLEM 8.5

At the end of their brief, the attorneys for the petitioner noted the following:

> The State of California has been authorized by the Attorneys General of the following states and territories to list them as joining with us in our brief on the merits.

Honorable William J. Baxley	Alabama
Honorable Ray Thornton	Arkansas
Honorable Gary K. Nelson	Arizona
Honorable Duke W. Dunbar	Colorado

---

[6]Respondent's Brief at 43-44, California v. Krivda, 409 U.S. 33 (1972).

[7]Petitioner's Opening Brief at 28, California v. Krivda, 409 U.S. 33 (1972).

Honorable John D. La Belle, Chairman Council of State's Attorneys	Connecticut
Honorable W. Laird Stabler, Jr.	Delaware
Honorable Robert L. Shevin	Florida
Honorable Arthur K. Bolton	Georgia

[The list continues with the names of attorney generals from twenty-nine more jurisdictions.][8]

(Primarily) (a) logical argument, (b) emotional argument, or (c) ethical argument

Stop here, and decide what type of argument is primarily being made in the above excerpt before consulting the discussion of this problem in Appendix A.

PROBLEM 8.6

The petitioner's attorneys asserted the following:

> Even if one were to assume that an abandonment of trash to the trash collector was not an abandonment to the public at large or to the police, it is clear that there are circumstances when an owner may give another such complete and unrestricted freedom over his property that he will have accepted the risk that the person so entrusted would consent to a search, thus losing his right to privacy. *See United States v. Edwards*, *supra*, 441 F.2d at 752 and cases cited. The case of *Clarke v. Neil*, 427 F.2d 1322 (6th Cir. 1970) is an apt illustration of this point. In *Clarke*, the manager of a dry cleaning establishment let the police conduct a laboratory examination of a suit delivered to him by the defendant for cleaning. The laboratory examination revealed the presence on the suit of certain fibers matching those in the murder victim's clothing. The Court of Appeals for the Sixth Circuit held that the evidence from the laboratory examination was admissible because the court was unable to find any significant invasion of anything which appellant had sought to preserve as private. The court noted that appellant had delivered the suit to the cleaners open to public view, that he knew the suit could be handled and examined by many persons in the course of the cleaning process, but that he in no way tried to conceal the suit or anything contained thereon, nor did he try to restrict the number of persons who handled it. 427 F.2d at 1325.

---

[8] Id. at 53.

The same reasoning should apply with even more force in the instant case. For here the respondents retained no property interests in the trash examined by the police whereas the defendant in *Clarke v. Neil* still retained the rights of a bailor under implied bailment. The rule adopted by the court below could only serve to deprive the police of information and evidence provided by citizens, such as the dry cleaner in *Clarke* and the garbage men in this case, who have come to the aid of law enforcement. It is well recognized that the effective enforcement of our criminal law depends in large part on the voluntary cooperation of public spirited citizens. *See, e.g.*, Report of the President's Commission on law Enforcement and Administration of Justice, *The Challenge of Crime in a Free Society* 99 (1967).

The decisions of this Court support the reasoning of the Sixth Circuit in *Clarke*. In *Hoffa v. United States*, 385 U.S. 293, 302 (1966), this Court held that the Fourth Amendment does not protect ". . . a wrongdoer's misplaced belief that a person to whom he voluntarily confides his wrongdoing will not reveal it." Subsequently in *United States v. White*, 401 U.S. 745, 752 (1971), this Court further observed:

> [I]nescapably, one contemplating illegal activities must realize and risk that his companions may be reporting to the police. If he sufficiently doubts their trustworthiness, the association will very probably end or never materialize. But if he has no doubts, or allays them, or risks what doubts he has, the risk is his. . . .

It is hardly a meaningful distinction that the respondents in this case confided the evidence of their wrongdoing to a garbage collector instead of a police informant or turncoat accomplice. Under the circumstances of this case, the respondents assumed the risk that the garbage collectors might permit the police to examine their trash upon request.[9]

(Primarily) (a) logical argument, (b) emotional argument, or (c) ethical argument

Stop here, and decide what type of argument is primarily being made in the above excerpt before consulting the discussion of this problem in Appendix A.

---

[9] Id. at 28-30.

PROBLEM 8.7

The petitioners asserted that the exclusionary rule failed to achieve its purported reason for existence (deterrence of police misconduct) and cited statistical studies, numerous articles, and other support for this view.

The respondents countered, in part, with the following:

> Respondents suggest that the citizens of this nation do not share the "gestapo" mind of petitioner, and, moreover, the vibrant and freedom-loving United States of America is too great a country to need or to desire to require its citizens to be faced with uncertainty of identity of local garbage haulers. To allow warrantless garbage can searches to be a mandate from this Honorable Court, and one that we are to live with in fear henceforth, bespeaks of a 1939 environment on the European continent which respondents believe to have been laid to rest in 1945.[10]

(Primarily) (a) logical argument, (b) emotional argument, or (c) ethical argument

Stop here, and decide what type of argument is primarily being made in the above excerpt before consulting the discussion of this problem in Appendix A.

Section 8B. Formulating Arguments

Lawyers use several basic methods of formulating arguments, including: (1) standard logical techniques; (2) the "handcuff" technique; (3) emphasizing the purpose of a rule; (4) the "paradigm" case; (5) use of the hypothetical case; (6) the "extreme consequences" technique; and (7) policy arguments. This section focuses on these methods.

1. STANDARD LOGICAL TECHNIQUES

Of the standard logical techniques, inductive reasoning, deductive reasoning, and a fortiori arguments are the most often used approaches.

---

[10] Respondent's Brief, supra note 6, at 97.

(a) Inductive Reasoning

When the ratio decidendi of a judicial decision that a lawyer wants to assert is not specifically or clearly stated in a court's opinion, a lawyer must formulate it. Even when the legal proposition has been stated, the lawyer may want to reformulate it in light of other decisions. This formulation or reformulation process often involves inductive reasoning.

As discussed in earlier chapters, the lawyer sometimes must synthesize several opinions to reach the "new" characterization of the legal principle. Thus, a lawyer might analyze the facts of several cases that, when viewed together, form the basis for a proposition that had not been articulated before. This process of analysis, as we have seen, is aided by the use of analogy.

ILLUSTRATION 8.1

Consider the following excerpt showing how the lawyers representing the State of California in the *Krivda* case used inductive reasoning to establish the legal proposition that the fourth amendment protects only reasonable expectations of privacy:

> Prior to *Katz v. United States*, 389 U.S. 347 (1967), the search and seizure decisions of this Court tended to focus on whether the location searched was a "constitutionally protected area." *See e.g., Berger v. New York*, 388 U.S. 41, 57, 59 (1967); *Lopez v. United States*, 373 U.S. 427, 438-39 (1963); *Silverman v. United States*, 365 U.S. 505, 510, 512 (1961). In *Katz*, the Court eschewed this phrase as a mode of analysis, stating that ". . . the correct solution of Fourth Amendment problems is not necessarily promoted by incantation of the phrase 'constitutionally protected area.'" 389 U.S. at 350. The Court explained that the term was only descriptive of a conclusion and was not meant to serve as a "talismanic solution to every Fourth Amendment problem." *Id.* at 351 n.9. Mr. Justice Stewart's opinion for the Court further states:
>
> > [O]nce it is recognized that the Fourth Amendment protects people--and not simply 'areas'--against unreasonable searches and seizures, it becomes clear that the reach of that Amendment cannot turn upon the presence or absence of a physical intrusion into any given enclosure[.] *Id.* at 353.
>
> Rejecting the traditional formulation of the Fourth Amendment, the Court found that the government's electronic eavesdropping activities had

violated the privacy upon which the petitioner had justifiably relied while using a telephone booth. *Id.* The *Katz* opinion did not elaborate on the concept of "justifiable reliance," except to state that ". . . what [a person] seeks to preserve as private, even in an area accessible to the public, may be constitutionally protected." *Id.* at 351-52.

The concurring opinion of Mr. Justice Harlan has served as a gloss to explain what the Court intended by its reformulation in *Katz* of the approach to search and seizure questions arising under the Fourth Amendment. In Justice Harlan's view, these questions were to be resolved in terms of the individual's "reasonable expectation of privacy." *Id.* at 360. His concurring opinion explains this phrase in these terms:

> . . . My understanding of the rule that has emerged from prior decisions is that there is a twofold requirement, first that a person have exhibited an actual (subjective) expectation of privacy and, second, that the expectation be one that society is prepared to recognize as "reasonable." Thus a man's home is, for most purposes, a place where he expects privacy, but objects, activities, or statements that he exposes to the 'plain view' of outsiders are not 'protected' because no intention to keep them to himself has been exhibited. On the other hand, conversations in the open would not be protected against being overheard, for the expectation of privacy under the circumstances would be unreasonable. (Citation omitted.) *Id.* at 361.

Justice Harlan's test directed towards "reasonable expectations of privacy" has since been adopted by the majority of the Court in several subsequent decisions. *Terry v. Ohio*, 392 U.S. 1, 9 (1968); *Alderman v. United States*, *supra*, 394 U.S. at 179 n.11. Other decisions after *Katz* have contained variations on the same theme. *Mancusi v. De Forte*, *supra*, 392 U.S. at 368 ("reasonable expectation of freedom from governmental intrusion"); *United States v. White*, 401 U.S. 745, 752 (1971) ("what expectations of privacy are constitutionally 'justifiable'--what expectations the

Fourth Amendment will protect in the absence of a warrant").[11]

USE INDUCTIVE REASONING TO FORMULATE OR GENERALIZE A LEGAL PROPOSITION FROM A SERIES OF PARTICULAR HOLDINGS OR APPLICATIONS.

(b) Deductive Reasoning

DEDUCTION STARTS WITH A MAJOR PREMISE, SUCH AS A LEGAL DOCTRINE THAT IS ACCEPTED AS TRUE. THE MINOR PREMISE PLACES THE PARTICULAR SITUATION OR CASE WITHIN THE CLASS OR TERMS DESCRIBED BY THE MAJOR PREMISE (USUALLY A FACTUAL STATEMENT OF THE CASE AT HAND).

Lawyers often assert a ratio decidendi of a judicial decision or a proposition based upon a statute as the major premise of a syllogism.

A PROPOSITION DERIVED THROUGH INDUCTIVE REASONING CAN BE THE MAJOR PREMISE IN A DEDUCTIVE ARGUMENT.

The facts of the case that the lawyers are arguing form the minor premise. The conclusion is then, supposedly, apparent. As previously noted, the debate usually centers on whether the facts of the current case are as the lawyer asserts them to be and whether the lawyer has properly classified those facts.

PROBLEM 8.8

Prior to the *Krivda* case, a series of United States Supreme Court cases had apparently focused on whether the individual seeking constitutional protection under the fourth amendment had a "reasonable expectation of privacy" in the place searched or the items seized.

Formulate the basic structure of the prosecution's argument using the facts of the *Krivda* case and deductive reasoning.

---

[11] Petitioner's Opening Brief, supra note 4, at 21-23.

Major premise:

____

____

____

____

____

Minor premise:

____

____

____

Conclusion:

____

____

____

Stop here, and formulate the above premises and conclusion before consulting the discussion of this problem in Appendix A.

(c) A Fortiori Arguments

Another standard logical technique used in persuasive legal writing is an "a fortiori" argument. Such an argument is "to the effect that because one ascertained fact exists, therefore another, which is included in it, or analogous to it, and which is less improbable, unusual, or surprising, must also exist."[12]

ILLUSTRATION 8.2

In *Motor Vehicle Manufacturers Association v. State Farm Mutual Automobile Insurance Co.*,[13] the United States Supreme Court reviewed the National Highway Traffic Safety Administration's rescission of certain crash protection standards for automobiles sold in the United States. In ruling that the Highway Administration acted arbitrarily and capriciously, the Court stated:

---

[12] Black's Law Dictionary 56 (5th ed. 1981).

[13] 463 U.S. 29 (1983).

> [T]he Motor Vehicle Safety Act was necessary because the industry was not sufficiently responsive to safety concerns. The Act intended that safety standards not depend on current technology and could be "technology-forcing" in the sense of inducing the development of superior safety design. . . . If, under the statute, the agency should not defer to the industry's failure to develop safer cars, which it surely should not do, *a fortiori* it may not revoke a safety standard which can be satisfied by current technology simply because the industry has opted for an ineffective seatbelt design.[14]

USE A FORTIORI REASONING TO DRAW A CONCLUSION THAT IS INFERRED TO BE EVEN MORE CERTAIN THAN ANOTHER.

2. "HANDCUFF" TECHNIQUE

THE "HANDCUFF" TECHNIQUE USES A LOGICAL CHAIN OF PROPOSITIONS EMANATING FROM A SIMPLE GENERAL PROPOSITION THAT THE READER WOULD NOT READILY DISPUTE.

The "handcuff" technique involves stating a simple premise that the reader would not readily dispute. Often, the premise is relatively abstract in nature.

ILLUSTRATION 8.3

Such a premise might be as follows: "Under the Constitution the states retained all of their sovereign powers except those specifically ceded to the federal government." Another might be: "It is a fundamental principle of contract law that men [and women] ought to perform their promises."

Once this basic premise is established--to which the reader is "handcuffed"--the writer then can lead the reader through a deductive chain to specific conclusions.

ILLUSTRATION 8.4

Recall the No-Pay research problem (discussed in earlier chapters) involving the defendant driver's mental illness. A simple starting proposition for the defendant in this situation might be

[14] Id. at 49.

that "the law of negligence is based on fault." From this proposition, the defendant's lawyer could lead the reader to the following conclusion: "Because the defendant's mental illness was sudden and unexpected (and thus not the defendant's fault), the defendant was not negligent."

TO BREAK OUT OF A HANDCUFF ARGUMENT, ATTACK THE INITIAL PREMISE; SUGGEST INSTEAD A DIFFERENT STARTING POINT FOR ANALYSIS.

If one is faced with attacking such an argument, the point of attack should be the innocuous-appearing premise.

3. EMPHASIZING THE PURPOSE OF A RULE

In considering the potential application of a rule, particularly a statutory rule, conclusions are often reached based on the *purpose* of the rule.

ILLUSTRATION 8.5

Assume that a statute provides that "no vehicle may be brought into the park." When someone tries to drive a tank into the park, the statute without doubt applies. A tank is commonly understood to be a "vehicle." But what about a boy riding a tricycle? Is a tricycle a vehicle for purposes of the statute? If the purposes of the statute are to maintain peace and order within the park, certainly a boy riding a tricycle would not violate those purposes.[15]

LEGAL RULES ARE NOT SELF-EXECUTING. A GOOD WAY TO DETERMINE HOW A RULE SHOULD BE APPLIED IS TO EXAMINE THE PURPOSE OR PURPOSES OF THE RULE.

4. THE "PARADIGM" CASE

Another accepted means of formulating legal arguments is to use the "paradigm" case.

[15] Compare Hart, Positivism and The Separation of Law and Morals, 71 Harv. L. Rev. 593, 607 (1958) with Fuller, Positivism and Fidelity to Law--A Reply to Professor Hart, 71 Harv. L. Rev. 630, 662-64 (1958) (debating various applications of this hypothetical statute).

A PARADIGM IS AN OUTSTANDINGLY CLEAR OR TYPICAL EXAMPLE. USE THE PARADIGM (ALONG WITH DECIDED CASES) FOR COMPARISON.

Assume that the application of a statute is in issue. For purposes of developing an argument, a lawyer may present a case which the lawyer asserts *is* covered by a statute--without regard to whatever else may also be covered by the statute. The lawyer then asserts that the instant case is or is not significantly different from the paradigm case.[16]

In some instances, the paradigm may be a hypothetical situation, perhaps derived from the legislative history of the statute or the apparent purpose of the enactment. In other instances, the paradigm may be derived from a prior judicial decision applying the statute. In theory, the court should decide the instant case "different from that of decided cases and from the paradigm cases under statutes only if it can point to a significant difference between the instant case and each of the decided cases and paradigm cases."[17]

ILLUSTRATION 8.6

In discussing whether abstention in a particular situation would be proper, the United States Supreme Court noted that abstention is proper only in narrowly limited "special circumstances." The Court then referred to the paradigm case: "The paradigm of the 'special circumstances' that make abstention appropriate is a case [in which] the challenged state statute is susceptible of a construction by the state judiciary that would avoid or modify the necessity of reaching a federal constitutional question."[18] The Court then used that paradigm for purposes of comparison to decide whether abstention was proper under the circumstances of the case the Court was considering.

Thus, the paradigm case is another useful technique of formulating arguments.

5. HYPOTHETICAL CASES

Closely related to arguments based upon paradigm cases is using hypothetical cases for purposes of comparison.

---

[16] See Christie, Objectivity in the Law, 78 Yale L.J. 1131, 1334 (1969).

[17] Id. at 1336.

[18] Kusper v. Pontikes, 414 U.S. 51, 54 (1973).

A HYPOTHETICAL CASE IS ONE IN WHICH FACTS ARE ASSUMED FOR THE PURPOSE OF EXPLAINING AND DISCUSSING THE APPLICABLE LAW.

Christie explains use of hypothetical cases as follows:

> In deciding the case before it, the court may also refer to hypothetical cases posed by the parties or by the court itself. The consideration of hypothetical cases is an important adjunct to the [use of the paradigm case] for hypothetical cases are of material assistance in establishing the relation of the instant case to the prior cases and to the paradigm cases. To be pertinent, a hypothetical case must be one not significantly different from the instant case. A court which has constructed or which is referred to such a hypothetical case must then determine whether the hypothetical case is itself significantly different from the prior cases and the pertinent paradigm cases. For the court to decide the instant case in a particular way, not only the instant case but also all pertinent hypothetical cases must be significantly different from the prior cases and the paradigm cases pointing to a contrary result. Only then can it be said the instant case is truly significantly different from the these cases and not just apparently significantly different.
>
> The use of hypothetical cases thus broadens the scope of a court's inquiry and helps it to deal with the body of law which it is administering. Hypothetical cases, for example, help a judge to appreciate the reach of his decision by indicating the extent to which, in deciding the instant case, he is committing himself to decide future cases in a particular way. Similarly, hypothetical cases are a bridge between the instant case and previously decided cases whose relevance to the instant case the judge has not initially appreciated. In this way, hypothetical cases broaden his understanding of existing legal materials and help him to comprehend more fully their restraining influence on the choices available to him in the instant case. At the same time, [this approach] required that hypothetical cases themselves pass the significant difference test and thereby prevent their use from degenerating into a ludicrous and improper *reductio ad absurdum*, the so-called "parade of horrors" which law students are quite properly told to avoid.[19]

[19] Christie, supra note 16, at 1336-37.

TO ATTACK AN ANALYSIS BASED ON A HYPOTHETICAL CASE, TRY TO SHOW THAT THE HYPOTHETICAL CASE IS SIGNIFICANTLY DIFFERENT FROM THE INSTANT CASE.

The best approach to attacking a hypothetical case is to show that it is significantly different from the case at hand.

6. "EXTREME CONSEQUENCES" TECHNIQUE

THE "EXTREME CONSEQUENCES" TECHNIQUE DEMONSTRATES THE POTENTIAL ADVERSE EFFECTS OF A RULE.

Hypothetical cases are usually directed to possible *applications* of a rule. The "extreme consequences" technique focuses on the *effects* of a rule--its costs, disruption, and potential harm.

ILLUSTRATION 8.7

In *CPG Products v. Anti-Monopoly, Inc.*,[20] the Ninth Circuit held that the "Monopoly" trademark had become generic. In requesting the United States Supreme Court to grant certiorari, the petitioner used, in part, an extreme consequences argument:

> Unless this Court reviews this decision and clarifies the law, the opinion of the Ninth Circuit will sow chaos in the manufacture and merchandising of brandname products affecting all spheres of life. Actual or potential competitors of many highly successful products that have become publicly identified by their brand names may henceforth pirate such brand names for their own benefit with impunity.[21]

The petitioner's arguments, however, were unsuccessful, and the Supreme Court refused to review the Ninth Circuit's decision.

---

[20] 684 F.2d 1316 (9th Cir. 1982), cert. denied, 459 U.S. 1227 (1983).

[21] Brief of Petitioner For Certiorari at 12, CPG Prods. v. Anti-Monopoly, Inc., 684 F.2d 1316 (9th Cir. 1982), cert. denied, 459 U.S. 1227 (1983).

TO COUNTER AN EXTREME CONSEQUENCES ARGUMENT, CONSIDER CAREFULLY WHETHER THE ASSERTED CONSEQUENCES ARE LIKELY TO OCCUR. WATCH ALSO FOR IMPROPER REDUCTIO AD ABSURDUM IN THE GUISE OF LEGITIMATE USE OF THE EXTREME CONSEQUENCES TECHNIQUE.

7. "POLICY" ARGUMENTS

POLICY ARGUMENTS CAN BE CRITICAL TO THE OUTCOME OF CASES IN WHICH CONFLICTING LEGAL RULES MAY BE APPLICABLE.

Sometimes a court is faced with two or more rules that plausibly could apply to a situation before it. In addition to using precedent, legislative history, hypotheticals, and the like, a lawyer will often attempt to bolster the argument in favor of a particular rule by using "policy" arguments. This subsection considers these types of arguments.

(a) "Lesser of Two Evils"

Sometimes, none of the solutions available in a case offers a particularly satisfactory resolution of the matter. In that situation, an argument can be made that a solution should be chosen because it is the lesser of two evils.

ILLUSTRATION 8.8

In *Devine v. White*,[22] for example, the D.C. Circuit took this approach:

> If government agencies and unions in the federal sector are to bind themselves through collective bargaining agreements to arbitrate disciplinary matters, one would hope that the arbitrators selected--who are given broad authority to construe and enforce labor contracts--have the time, talent and experience to write intelligible opinions. An opinion such as that submitted here forces the court to choose between placing its stamp of approval on utter gibberish or conducting what would amount to de novo review on

[22] 711 F.2d 1082 (D.C. Cir. 1983).

a hopelessly inadequate record. Both options, of course, are undesirable.

Notwithstanding our dismay over the quality of the arbitral opinion in this case, consistency of the *result* reached in the arbitrator's decision with the test established in our original opinion leads us to conclude that approving that result is the lesser of two evils. We therefore affirm the judgment, but not the rationale or opinion, of the arbitrator.[23]

(b) "Floodgates" Arguments: Difficulty of Circumscribing the Area of Liability

In deciding whether a particular rule should be adopted, several variants of a "floodgates" argument are sometimes made.

FLOODGATES ARGUMENTS GENERALLY FOCUS ON THE EXPECTED SUBSEQUENT ADVERSE CONSEQUENCES OF AN INITIAL DECISION (IF MADE IN A CERTAIN WAY).

One form of a floodgate argument is that there is no rational way to confine liability within reasonable limits.

ILLUSTRATION 8.9

Consider the following discussion of this problem in the context of a mother's action for mental pain and suffering from seeing her child injured:

> The final and most difficult factor is any reasonable circumscription, within tolerable limits required by public policy, of a rule creating liability. Every parent who loses a child or whose child of any age suffers an injury is likely to sustain grievous psychological trauma, with the added risk of consequential physical harm. Any rule based solely on eyewitnessing the accident could stand only until the first case comes along in which the parent is in the immediate vicinity but did not see the accident. Moreover, the instant advice that one's child has been killed or injured, by telephone, word of mouth, or by whatever means, even if delayed, will have in most cases the same impact. The sight of gore and exposed bones is not necessary to provide special impact on a parent. Again, the logical difficulty of excluding the grandparent, the relatives, or other *in loco parentis*,

[23] Id. at 1084.

> and even the conscientious and sensitive caretaker, from a right to recover, if in fact the accident had the grave consequences claimed, raises subtle and elusive hazards in devising a sound rule in this field.
>
> This case is particularly illustrative--just because the pretrial examination reveals that if the pleaded cause of action is sustained the trial court will be faced not with an eyewitncss mother, but with one who comes upon the scene immediately following the accident.[24]

(c) *"Floodgates" Arguments: Fraudulent Claims*

Another type of floodgates argument relates to a potentially dramatic increase of fraudulent claims.

ILLUSTRATION 8.10

In *Mitchell v. Rochester Railway*,[25] the New York Court of Appeals stated:

> If the right of recovery in this class of cases [based upon fright] should be once established, it would naturally result in a flood of litigation in cases where the injury complained of may be easily feigned without detection, and where the damages must rest upon mere conjecture or speculation. The difficulty which often exists in cases of alleged physical injury, in determining whether they exist, and, if so, whether they were caused by the negligent act of the defendant, would not only be greatly increased, but a wide field would be opened for fictitious or speculative claims. To establish such a doctrine would be contrary to principles of public policy.[26]

Such arguments will not, however, necessarily survive.

ILLUSTRATION 8.11

For example, the *Mitchell* case (discussed in Illustration 8.10 above) was overruled by the court in *Battalla v. State*:[27]

---

[24] Tobin v. Grossman, 24 N.Y.2d 609, 617, 249 N.E.2d 419, 423, 301 N.Y.S.2d 554, 560 (1969).

[25] 151 N.Y. 107, 45 N.E. 354 (1886).

[26] Id. at 110, 45 N.E. at 354-55.

[27] 10 N.Y.2d 237, 176 N.E.2d 729, 219 N.Y.S.2d 34 (1961).

> We presently feel that even the [fraudulent claim] public policy argument is subject to challenge. Although fraud, extra litigation and a measure of speculation are, of course, possibilities, it is no reason for a court to eschew a measure of its jurisdiction. "The argument from mere expediency cannot commend itself to a Court of Justice, resulting in the denial of a logical legal right and remedy in all cases because in some a fictitious injury may be urged as a real one. . . ."
>
> . . . .
>
> . . . The ultimate result is that the honest claimant is penalized for his reluctance to fashion the facts within the framework of the exceptions.
>
> Not only, therefore, are claimants in this situation encouraged by the *Mitchell* disqualification to perjure themselves, but the constant attempts to either come within an old exception, or establish a new one, lead to excess appellate litigation. . . . In any event, even if a flood of litigation were realized by abolition of the [rule], it is the duty of the courts to willingly accept the opportunity to settle these disputes.[28]

(d) "Floodgates" Arguments: Unlimited Liability

The problem of unlimited liability is another type of floodgates argument.

ILLUSTRATION 8.12

This type of argument was also used in the *Tobin* case, discussed in Illustration 8.9 in subsection (b) above. The court stated:

> The problem of unlimited liability is suggested by the unforeseeable consequence of extending recovery for harm to others than those directly involved in the accident. If foreseeability be the sole test, then once liability is extended the logic of the principle would not and could not remain confined. It would extend to older children, fathers, grandparents, relatives, or others *in loco parentis*, and even to sensitive bystanders. Moreover, in any one accident, there might be more than one person indirectly but seriously affected by the shock of injury or death to the child.

---

[28] Id. at 239, 176 N.E.2d at 731, 219 N.Y.S.2d at 37-38.

The factor of unduly burdensome liability is a kind of dollars-and-cents argument. It does not vanish, however, by reference to wide-spread or compulsory insurance. Constantly advancing insurance costs can become an undue burden as well, and the aggregate recoveries in a single accident of this kind are not likely to stay within ordinary, let alone, compulsory insurance liability limits.[29]

(e) "Floodgates" Arguments: Burden on the Courts

Sometimes the "floodgates" argument is specifically focused on the burden that increased litigation would place on the courts. This type of argument seems to be more frequently accepted in the federal courts.

ILLUSTRATION 8.13

In *Colligan v. Activities Club*,[30] a group of 153 students sued an operator of an interstate ski tour service in federal court. They alleged that they had been deceived and damaged by the operator's use of false descriptions and representations in conjunction with a ski trip. Specifically, they alleged, contrary to the operator's representations, that:

> Only 88 pairs of skis and boots were provided for the 153 children: only one "qualified" ski instructor was provided, who because of the equipment shortage spent all of Saturday morning fitting the children with such skis and boots as were available; the other "instructors" were high school and college students whose agreements with defendants provided for only a few hours of instructions per day; one of the buses broke down on a country road en route to Great Barrington, stranding 40 children and two chaperons in the middle of the night; another bus had faulty brakes and only one headlight and was ticketed by the Massachusetts police; another bus en route back to New York poured exhaust fumes into its interior; one of the bus drivers was intoxicated and therefore unable to drive his bus on the return trip to New York; neither the buses nor the Club were licensed or certified by the Interstate Commerce Commission; and one busload of children was required to pay an unrefunded total of $71.75 for

---

[29] Tobin, 24 N.Y.2d at 616-17, 249 N.E.2d at 423, 301 N.Y.S.2d at 559-60.

[30] 442 F.2d 686 (2d Cir. 1971).

an extra meal in Great Barrington due to unsafe bus transportation.[31]

The students sought to base their suit on Section 43 of the Lanham Act, which provides that "[a]ny person who shall use in connection with any goods or services . . . any false description or representation . . . shall be liable to a civil action . . . by any person who believes that he is or is likely to be damaged by the use of any such description or representation." Section 39 of the Act permits actions based upon violation of the Lanham Act to be brought without regard to diversity of citizenship or amount in controversy. In holding that "any person" does not include consumers, the Second Circuit relied in part on a floodgates argument:

> Moreover, consumers use of § 39 of the Act, which requires the allegation of neither a minimum monetary amount in controversy nor diverse citizenship, in combination with the expansive jurisdictional delineation given the phrase "in commerce," and the procedural advantages of bringing suit in federal court, would lead to a veritable flood of claims brought in already overtaxed federal district courts, while adequate private remedies for consumer protection, which to date have been left almost exclusively to the States, are readily at hand.[32]

(f) Economic and Social Policy Arguments: Distribution of Costs

When the proper rule is in doubt, a variety of economic arguments can often be made. One approach is to consider the distribution of costs.

ILLUSTRATION 8.14

Consider the classic example in the area of products liability. This type of policy argument is well stated by Justice Traynor in *Escola v. Coca Cola Bottling Co.*:[33]

> In these [prior] cases the source of the manufacturer's liability was his negligence in the manufacturing process or in the inspection of component parts supplied by others. Even if there is no negligence, however, public policy demands that responsibility be

---

[31] Id. at 688.

[32] Id. at 693 (footnote omitted).

[33] 24 Cal. 2d 453, 150 P.2d 436 (1944).

> fixed wherever it will most effectively reduce the hazards to life and health inherent in defective products that reach the market. It is evident that the manufacturer can anticipate some hazards and guard against the recurrence of others, as the public cannot. Those who suffer injury from defective products are unprepared to meet its consequences. The cost of an injury and the loss of time or health may be an overwhelming misfortune to the person injured, and a needless one, for the risk of injury can be insured by the manufacturer and distributed among the public as a cost of doing business. It is to the public interest to discourage the marketing of products having defects that are a menace to the public. If such products nevertheless find their way into the market it is to the public interest to place the responsibility for whatever injury they may cause upon the manufacturer, who, even if he is not negligent in the manufacture of the product, is responsible for its reaching the market. However intermittently such injuries may occur and however haphazardly they may strike, the risk of their occurrence is a constant risk and a general one. Against such a risk there should be general and constant protection and the manufacturer is best situated to afford such protection.[34]

(g) Economic and Social Policy Arguments: Who Can Avoid the Costs Most Cheaply

Another type of economic and social policy argument focuses on who can avoid the costs most cheaply.

ILLUSTRATION 8.15

In *Union Oil Co. v. Oppen*,[35] commercial fisherman sued several oil companies for damages they allegedly sustained as a result of an oil spill. In deciding to permit the action, the Ninth Circuit relied, in part, on the following argument:

> The same conclusion is reached when the issue before us is approached from the standpoint of economics. Recently a number of scholars have suggested that liability for losses occasioned by torts should be apportioned in a manner that will best contribute to the achievement of an optimum allocation of resources. *See, e.g.*, Calabresi, *The Cost of*

---

[34]Id. at 462, 150 P.2d at 440-41 (concurring opinion).

[35]501 F.2d 558 (9th Cir. 1974).

Accidents 69-73 (1970) (hereinafter Calabresi); Coase, *The Problem of Social Cost*, 3 J. Law & Econ. 1 (1960). This optimum, in theory, would be that which would be achieved by a perfect market system. In determining whether the cost of an accident should be borne by the injured party or be shifted, in whole or in part, this approach requires the court to fix the identity of the party who can avoid the costs most cheaply. Once fixed, this determination then controls liability.

It turns out, however, that fixing the identity of the best or cheapest cost-avoider is more difficult than might be imagined. In order to facilitate this determination, Calabresi suggests several helpful guidelines. The first of these would require a rough calculation designed to exclude as potential cost-avoiders those groups/activities which could avoid accident costs only at an extremely high expense. Calabresi at 140-43. While not easy to apply in any concrete sense, this guideline does suggest that the imposition of oil spill costs directly upon such groups as the consumers of staple groceries is not a sensible solution. Under this guideline, potential liability becomes resolved into a choice between, on an ultimate level, the consumers of fish and those of products derived from the defendants' total operations.

To refine this choice, Calabresi [provides] additional guidelines which, in this instance, have proven none too helpful. For example, he suggests an evaluation of the administrative costs which each party would be forced to bear in order to avoid the accident costs. Calabresi at 143-44. He also states that an attempt should be made to avoid an allocation which will impose some costs on those groups or activities which neither consume fish nor utilize those products of the defendants derived from their operations in the Santa Barbara Channel. Calabresi at 144-50. On the record before us, we have no way of evaluating the relative administrative costs involved. However, we do recognize that it is probable that by imposing liability on the defendants some portion of the accident costs in this case may be borne by those who neither eat fish nor use the petroleum product derived from the defendants' operations in Santa Barbara.

Calabresi's final guideline, however, unmistakably points to the defendants as the best cost-avoider. Under this guideline, the loss should be allocated to that party who can best correct any error in allocation, if such there be, by acquiring the activity

> to which the party has been made liable. Calabresi at 150-52. The capacity "to buy out" the plaintiffs if the burden is too great is, in essence, the real focus of Calabresi's approach. On this basis there is no contest--the defendants' capacity is superior.[36]

It is unusual for a court to be this directly articulate about cost efficiency. The underlying policy argument, however, is one that can be used effectively.

(h) Economic and Social Policy Arguments: Economic Efficiency

Economic efficiency is another policy argument that may be used in support of (or against) a particular rule. Such arguments may arise in a variety of contexts.

ILLUSTRATION 8.16

In contract law, it is argued that "[r]epudiation of obligations should be encouraged where the promisor is able to profit from his default after placing his promisee in as good a position as he would have occupied had performance been rendered. . . . To penalize such adjustments through over-compensation of the innocent party is to discourage efficient reallocation of community resources."[37]

Another aspect of economic efficiency sometimes considered is transaction costs.[38]

PROBLEM 8.9

When you are conducting legal research, you may find that several reasons are stated in favor of a particular rule or position. For example, the research problem presented in prior chapters focused, in part, on the common-law rule holding mentally disabled persons to an ordinary standard of reasonable conduct. Classify the following "policy" reasons given in support of this rule using the framework outlined in this section:

---

[36] Id. at 569-70.

[37] Birmingham, Breach of Contract, Damage Measures, and Economic Efficiency, 24 Tul. L. Rev. 273, 284 (1970).

[38] See, e.g., Folsom & Teply, Trademarked Generic Words, 89 Yale L.J. 1323, 1350 (1980) (trademark law).

1. Lesser of Two Evils
2. Floodgates--Difficulty of Circumscribing the Area of Liability
3. Floodgates--Fraudulent Claims
4. Floodgates--Unlimited Liability
5. Floodgates--Burden on the Courts
6. Economic and Social Arguments--Distribution of Costs
7. Economic and Social Arguments--Who Can Avoid the Costs Most Cheaply
8. Economic and Social Arguments--Economic Efficiency

Write the relevant identifier (for example, 1) in the space provided.

______ (a) When one of two innocent persons must suffer a loss, it should be borne by the one who occasioned it. W. Prosser & W. Keeton, *supra* § 135, at 1073.

______ (b) One basis for holding the mentally disabled liable is that since insanity is easily feigned, the temptation to pretend it would be too great. W. Prosser & W. Keeton, *supra* § 135, at 1073; *McIntyre v. Sholty*, 121 Ill. 660, ___, 13 N.E. 239, 240 (1887) ("strong temptation to simulate insanity, with a view of masking the malice and revenge of an evil heart").

______ (c) One basis for holding the mentally disabled liable is the difficulty of distinguishing true incapacity from mere bad judgment. W. Prosser & W. Keeton, *supra* § 32, at 177; Restatement (Second) of Torts § 283B, comment b(1) (1965) (pointing out the practical difficulty of drawing any satisfactory line between mental deficiency and other variations of temperament, intellect, and emotional balance).

______ (d) Potential liability will encourage the custodians of mentally ill persons and those interested in their estates to keep them under control. W. Prosser & W. Keeton, *supra* § 135, at 1073; *McIntyre v. Sholty*, 121 Ill. 660, ___, 13 N.E. 239, 240 (1887) (liability tends to secure a more efficient custody and guardianship of insane persons).

______ (e) It is legitimate to identify insurance companies as the real parties in the resolution of the liability issue. In this day of broad coverage for general liability in family insurance policies, the ultimate recourse probably will be to such policies "in a large percentage of cases." Alexander & Szasz, *supra* at 36.

Stop here, and classify these policy reasons before consulting the discussion of this problem in Appendix A.

Section C. Command of the English Language: Argumentative Writing

Prior chapters and Appendix B reviewed various technical writing skills relating to proper spelling, capitalization, punctuation, and grammar. They also reviewed basic stylistic techniques for creating effective sentences and writing clearly and precisely. This section focuses on the use of the English language for persuasive purposes: (1) choosing words carefully; (2) shifting emphasis; and (3) controlling tone.

1. CHOOSING WORDS CAREFULLY

The words chosen by a writer influence the persuasive impact of a written presentation. Consider the following suggestions.

(a) *Unnecessary Qualifiers*

Weihofen cautions that "because the need for exactness so often calls for qualifications, lawyers [and law students] are likely to fall into the habit of qualifying everything they say . . . even [in] the most innocuous sentences."[39] Sentences can be qualified in a variety of ways.

ILLUSTRATION 8.17

The forcefulness of a sentence is often weakened by such phrases as "it seems," "it appears," "it may be," "it is possible," "apparently," "it could be," "possibly," "somewhat," "it would seem to be," and the like.

UNLESS IT IS TO YOUR ADVANTAGE TO DO SO, DO NOT WEAKEN A STATEMENT BY USING UNNECESSARY QUALIFIERS.

To the extent possible, these qualifiers should be deleted when it is to your advantage. Squires and Rombauer recommend that a strong phrase such as "it must follow that" be used or that the writer "simply begin with the point itself and then state [the] necessary qualifications."[40]

---

[39] H. Weihofen, Legal Writing Style 115 (2d ed. 1980).

[40] L. Squires & M. Rombauer, supra note 2, § 7.8, at 186.

Weihofen also criticizes the use of "very" as a frequent qualifier:

> One of the most overused adverbs is "very." In its original meaning of "truly" this was a word of some force, but it has become so worn out from overuse that it no longer packs even a powder-puff punch. When you catch yourself using it, stop to ask whether it ever would be missed if you deleted it. The answer will almost always be no. To say that a point is "very clear,: a speech "very good" or "very convincing" and its defects "very few," does not add anything to the same statements without "very." On the contrary, "clear," "good", "convincing," and "few" without the qualifying adverbs are stronger.[41]

Similarly, Strunk & White criticize the use of "rather," "very," "little," and "pretty." In their words, they "are the leeches that infest the pond of prose, sucking the blood of words."[42] These types of qualifications are one aspect of what Wydick describes as an "adjective-adverb mania." This "mania" consists of using weak verbs and nouns "held afloat by adjectives and adverbs."[43]

ILLUSTRATION 8.18

Consider one of Wydick's examples: "Defendant's sales agents maliciously took advantage of people with little money and limited intelligence." This sentence could easily be rewritten to be more potent, more direct, and more persuasive: "Defendant's sales agents preyed on the poor and ignorant."[44]

Weihofen makes the same type of suggestion in this way:

> When you feel that the noun you are using is not strong enough, instead of trying to intensify it by adding an adjective find a stronger noun. If "accident" doesn't seem strong enough, don't call it a "terrible accident." Look for a stronger synonym for "accident," such as "disaster," "catastrophe," "calamity," or "tragedy."[45]

---

[41] H. Weihofen, supra note 39, at 107-08.

[42] W. Strunk & E. White, The Elements of Style 59 (1959).

[43] R. Wydick, Plain English for Lawyers 62 (1979).

[44] Id.

[45] H. Weihofen, supra note 39, at 107.

PROBLEM 8.10

Delete the unnecessary qualifiers from the following sentences:

(a) It appears that the defendant did not act very carefully under the circumstances.

(b) Apparently, it is a rather unsatisfactory rule.

(c) The proposed settlement is merely a reflection of the relative bargaining power of the parties.

(d) It would seem to be a very significant factor.

Stop here and delete the unnecessary qualifiers from the above sentences before consulting the discussion of this problem in Appendix A.

(b) Using "Not"

Chapter 7 noted that the appearance of "not" in a sentence is often a signal of excessive wordiness. In persuasive writing, its use generally depends on the writer's purpose. Use a positive statement to gain force and persuasive effect. Use "not" (along with other qualifiers) to weaken a statement.

AVOID THE USE OF "NOT" EXCEPT WHEN WEAKNESS IS DESIRED; USE POSITIVE STATEMENTS TO GAIN FORCE AND PERSUASIVE EFFECT.

PROBLEM 8.11

Assume that you want to discuss the defendant's lack of honesty in a persuasive writing (or oral argument) context. Formulate how you would describe the defendant's lack of honesty (a) if you are writing from the plaintiff's perspective or (b) if you are writing from the defendant's perspective.

Stop here, and decide how you would describe the situation from each of these perspectives before consulting the discussion of this problem in Appendix A.

(c) Using Words with Favorable Connotations

One of the frequent criticisms of persuasive legal writers is that they have failed to use words with connotations favorable to their positions. Two words may appear to say the same thing, but their implications may differ substantially. The choice of the better word in a given situation is an important way of making an emotional appeal to the reader.

USE WORDS WITH FAVORABLE CONNOTATIONS.

ILLUSTRATION 8.19

Consider the following noun pairs:

"fabrication" / "reconstruction"
"crime" / "offense"
"informer" / "informant"
"junket" / "travel"
"argument" / "debate"
"explosion" / "rapid disassembly"[46]

Similarly, verbs, adjectives, and adverbs carry positive and negative connotations:

"lied" / "misspoke"
"unemployed" / "idle"
"slowly" / "at a snail's pace"

A thesaurus is a good source for finding better words to describe your position.

PROBLEM 8.12

Consider the following list of words. In the space provided, give one word with a favorable connotation and one with an unfavorable one.

	Favorable	Unfavorable
(a) house	____________	____________
(b) adventurer	____________	____________
(c) wealthy	____________	____________
(d) female prostitute	____________	____________

Stop here, and complete the above problem before consulting the discussion of this problem in Appendix A.

---

[46]H. Weihofen, supra note 39, at 13; L. Squires & M. Rombauer, supra note 2, § 7.8, at 192-93 (using the above examples).

2. SHIFTING EMPHASIS

The ability to shift emphasis is another important persuasive writing skill. Consider the following widely recognized methods of emphasizing or de-emphasizing matter within a sentence or paragraph.

PLACE WORDS THAT SHOULD BE EMPHASIZED AT THE END OF THE SENTENCE (IN A STRESS POSITION); DE-EMPHASIZE WORDS BY PLACING THEM IN THE MIDDLE OF A SENTENCE, PREFERABLY IN A PARENTHETICAL EXPRESSION OR A SUBORDINATE CLAUSE.

As discussed in previous chapters, the positioning of words within a sentence affects what the reader will tend to emphasize. Place words that you want to emphasize at the end of the sentence.[47] Place words that you want to de-emphasize in the middle of the sentence, preferably in a parenthetical expression or a subordinate clause.[48]

USE THE ACTIVE VOICE TO EMPHASIZE; USE THE PASSIVE VOICE TO DE-EMPHASIZE.

The passive voice is a means of de-emphasizing the performer of the action. It is also another means of shifting the position of words within a sentence.[49]

ILLUSTRATION 8.20

In a custody case, a lawyer representing the mother may deliberately choose not to say, "The mother neglected the child." Instead, the lawyer could use the passive voice to displace responsibility for the neglect: "The child was neglected," or better still, "The child was left alone."[50]

---

[47] See H. Weihofen, supra note 39, at 125-29; R. Wydick, supra note 43, at 49-50.

[48] See G. Block, Effective Legal Writing 38 (3d ed. 1986) ("Put your **most important ideas** at the **end** of the sentence, the **next most important** ideas at the **beginning** of the sentence, and all of the qualifiers, the amplifiers, and the 'ho-hum' words in the **middle**").

[49] See R. Wydick, supra note 43, at 46-47; H. Weihofen, supra note 39, at 130; L. Katz, Winning Words: A Guide to Persuasive Writing for Lawyers 21-22 (1986) ("When used deliberately, passive . . . forms can be important persuasive tools. When used out of habit, they only weaken the lawyer's real message").

[50] L. Katz, supra note 49, at 21 (suggesting this example).

USE OTHER BASIC STYLISTIC TECHNIQUES TO GAIN EMPHASIS. PUT IMPORTANT WORDS OUT OF THEIR "NATURAL" ORDER. ARRANGE FACTS OR IDEAS IN ORDER OF CLIMAX TO ADD FORCE; DE-EMPHASIZE THEM BY MIXING THEIR ORDER. ABRUPTLY SHORTEN A SENTENCE IN A PARAGRAPH TO EMPHASIZE THE CONTENTS OF THE SHORTENED SENTENCE.

The unexpected draws attention. For example, putting important words out of their natural order creates emphasis.[51]

The arrangement of facts or ideas can influence whether they will gain force or tend to be de-emphasized.[52] Likewise, abruptly shortening a sentence in a paragraph emphasizes the contents of the shortened sentence. Squires and Rombauer properly caution that this latter technique should be used sparingly.[53]

GAIN EMPHASIS BY USING A PERSUASIVE PARAGRAPH STRUCTURE.

In persuasive legal writing in which adverse arguments must be taken into account, a persuasive paragraph structure should be used. Squires and Rombauer recommend the following:

> In each section of [an appellate] brief or in each paragraph, state your argument or position first--not your opponent's--and state it affirmatively. Then dispense with you opponent's argument. To make paragraphs affirmative: (i) State your argument or position first. (ii) Acknowledge contrary evidence, or state the opposing arguments in the middle of the paragraph. (iii) Refute contrary evidence or opposing argument. (iv) Restate your argument as a conclusion.[54]

The purpose of this structure is two-fold:

---

[51] H. Weihofen, supra note 39, at 129; R. Wydick, supra note 43, at 37, n.15.

[52] H. Weihofen, supra note 39, at 131.

[53] L. Squires & R. Rombauer, supra note 2, § 7.8, at 190-92.

[54] Id. § 7.8, at 189.

> One purpose of this structure is to put favorable arguments and facts in the most conspicuous place (the beginning and the end). The interior of a paragraph should contain less important elements. Both unfavorable facts and arguments must be included, of course, but they will be given less emphasis in the middle of a paragraph.
>
> Another purpose of this structure is to give [the appearance of] a balanced analysis of the issue, that is, to reflect fair consideration of both sides even if only one is fully developed in the paragraph.[55]

3. CONTROLLING TONE

In argumentative legal writing, tone plays an important role. Tone is one of the principal means of making an ethical appeal to the reader. Sometimes, however, improper tone, created by over-assertiveness and certain forms of expression, detracts from the appearance of reasonableness, fairness, and honesty of the writer and alienates the reader. This subsection makes several suggestions on how to set a favorable tone.

AVOID MAKING OVERSTATEMENTS.

Overstatements cast doubt on the writer's veracity. Weihofen points out that exaggeration destroys a reader's confidence and undermines the entire presentation.[56]

AVOID EXPRESSIONS OF SUPPOSED CANDOR OR MODESTY.

Avoid expressions of supposed candor or modesty because they undermine the writer's ethical appeal.

ILLUSTRATION 8.21

Squires and Rombauer suggest that the worst offenders are "frankly," "to be frank," "to be honest," "with all candor," "candidly," "I humbly disagree," and "I do not pretend to be an

---

[55] Id. § 7.8, at 190.

[56] Weihofen, supra note 39, at 106 (if a lawyer "hopes to gain and hold respect, [a lawyer] must be careful to avoid reckless superlatives and unrestrained generalizations"). Accord H. Shapo, M. Walter, & E. Fajans, Writing and Analysis in the Law 207 (1989) (avoid "hysterical overstatement").

expert."[57] Similarly, Weihofen suggests that "to tell the truth" or "to be frank" merely raise the question, "haven't you been, so far?"[58]

DO NOT USE WORDING THAT CREATES AN ARROGANT TONE. AVOID FLATTERY.

Avoid using an arrogant tone. Fontham appropriately points out that "[p]ersonal comments about opposing counsel and the trial judge are almost certain to harm the case. Critical characterizations of the conduct, integrity, or intelligence of these persons are unnecessary. In addition, they are unseemly and degrading to the judicial process."[59]

An arrogant tone can be conveyed in a number of ways. First, it can be created by ridiculing opposing counsel or the judge in the court below. Second, it can be created by implying that the result in the case should be a foregone conclusion. Third, it can be created by suggesting that anyone who disagrees with your position is an unenlightened simpleton.[60]

ILLUSTRATION 8.22

Resist the temptation to assert invectives like the following (even if they are true): "This appeal is absurd, ridiculous, and nonsensical. Had the trial judge and opposing counsel had an ounce of understanding of the law in this jurisdiction, this court could have been saved this waste of its valuable time." Likewise, avoid flattering opposing counsel. Fontham points out that "[s]tatements lauding the integrity and ability of opposing counsel are likely to be perceived as insincere."[61]

DO NOT OVERUSE "CLEAR," "CLEARLY," "OBVIOUS," AND "OBVIOUSLY" IN PERSUASIVE WRITING.

---

[57] L. Squires & M. Rombauer, supra note 2, § 7.8, at 194-95.

[58] H. Weihofen, supra note 39, at 108.

[59] M. Fontham, Written and Oral Advocacy 116 (1985) ("Don't get personal").

[60] See L. Squires & M. Rombauer, supra note 2, § 7.8, at 184. Accord H. Shapo, M. Walter, & E. Fajans, supra note 56, at 207 ("[A]void imperative sentences, since it is inappropriate to issue commands to judges. You should also avoid being belittling or sarcastic, especially in regard to other judges. You may say that the judge below misapplied the law, or found the facts incorrectly, or reached an incorrect decision, but you should say it respectfully").

[61] M. Fontham, supra note 59, at 116.

The problem with the use of "clear," "clearly," "obvious," and "obviously" is often that the point is usually far from clear or less than obvious.[62] When they are used in an appellate brief or in a judicial opinion, they usually identify a *weak point*. Using terms like "clearly" and "obviously" in describing the facts makes you appear argumentative rather than objective.[63]

Section D. Conclusion

This chapter has presented several methods of formulating arguments. These methods are essential to persuasive legal writing--in appellate briefs, memoranda in support of motions, trial briefs, letters, and settlement proposals.

Stylistic techniques likewise play an important role in the persuasive process. These techniques include choosing your words carefully to achieve favorable or unfavorable connotations, arranging your words to emphasize or de-emphasize material, and planning your words to maintain a persuasive tone. Paying special attention to these matters is the key to quality persuasive writing.

---

[62] See L. Squires & M. Rombauer, supra note 2, § 7.8, at 194 (these words "do not persuade" and "may irritate the judicial reader").

[63] H. Weihofen, supra note 39, at 261-62 (in stating facts, avoid such expressions as "[i]t is obvious that the Board's decision was based upon an assumption. . .").

Chapter 9

APPELLATE BRIEF WRITING

WHAT YOU WILL LEARN IN THIS CHAPTER

* The basic steps of appellate procedure
* The factors taken into account in deciding to hear cases with a court's discretionary review powers
* The "mechanical" aspects of appellate practice, including filing the notice of appeal, preparation of a record on appeal, and physical requirements for appellate briefs
* The sections of an appellate brief
* The ways of selecting and formulating the questions presented
* The best approaches to writing the statement of the case, the argument, and conclusion

Section 9A. Appellate Practice and Procedure

An appeal to an appellate court is a relatively rare occurrence and is limited to specific situations.

TO APPEAL IN A CIVIL ACTION IN A FEDERAL DISTRICT COURT, THERE MUST BE EITHER (1) A FINAL DECISION, (2) AN APPEALABLE INTERLOCUTORY ORDER, OR (3) A PROPERLY CERTIFIED QUESTION.

A party may appeal a federal district court civil action when there has been a "final decision" or an appealable interlocutory order (principally an order "granting, continuing, modifying, refusing, or dissolving" an injunction).[1] The district court may also certify that an otherwise nonappealable "order involves a controlling question of law as to which there is a substantial ground for difference of opinion and that an immediate appeal from the order may materially advance the ultimate termination of the litigation." Whether an appeal from such an order will be permitted is within the discretion of the court of appeals.[2]

IN FEDERAL COURT ACTIONS, AN APPEAL IS INITIATED BY FILING A NOTICE OF APPEAL WITH THE CLERK OF THE DISTRICT COURT.

An appeal from a final decision or from an appealable interlocutory order in a federal district court civil action is initiated by filing a notice of appeal with the clerk of the district court.[3] Private parties must file this notice within thirty days after the entry of the judgment or order.[4]

If (1) a motion for judgment notwithstanding the verdict under Rule 50(b), (2) a motion to amend or make additional findings of fact under Rule 52(b), or (3) a motion to alter or amend the judgment or for a new trial under Rule 59(b) is made in a timely manner, however, the thirty-day time limit runs from the entry of the order disposing of the motion. A notice of appeal filed before the disposition of such an order has no effect, and a new notice must be filed if an appeal is desired.[5]

In criminal actions in federal district court, a notice of appeal generally must be filed within ten days after the entry of the judgment from which an appeal is taken.[6]

The notice of an appeal is a simple document. It merely specifies:

(1) the party or parties who are appealing;
(2) the order or judgment from which the appeal is taken; and

---

[1] See 28 U.S.C.A. §§ 1291, 1292(a)(1) (West Supp. 1989).

[2] See id. § 1292(b).

[3] Fed. R. App. P. 3(a).

[4] Id. 4(a)(1).

[5] Id. 4(a)(4).

[6] Id. 4(b).

(3) the name of the court to which the appeal is directed.[7]

ILLUSTRATION 9.1

The following example of the format of a notice of appeal to a federal court of appeals is based on Form 1 accompanying the Federal Rules of Appellate Procedure:

UNITED STATES DISTRICT COURT FOR
THE DISTRICT OF UTOPIA

Civil Action, File Number XXX

SNIDELY W. LASH, Plaintiff, v. NO-PAY CASUALTY CO. and IRMA M. DELIRA, Defendants.	NOTICE OF APPEAL

Notice is hereby given that Snidely Whip Lash, the plaintiff in the above-named action, hereby appeals to the United States Court of Appeals for the Thirteenth Circuit from the final judgment entered in this action on the XX day of January, 19xx.

Dated: February 8, 19xx.

Signed: ______________________________
Attorney for the Plaintiff

Address: ______________________________

A filing fee and a court of appeals docketing fee must be paid at the time of the filing of the notice of appeal.[8]

AFTER THE NOTICE OF APPEAL HAS BEEN FILED IN A FEDERAL COURT ACTION, THE APPELLANT IS REQUIRED TO ORDER A TRANSCRIPT. THE TRANSCRIPT BECOMES PART OF THE ENTIRE RECORD ON APPEAL, WHICH ALSO INCLUDES THE ORIGINAL PAPERS AND EXHIBITS FILED IN THE DISTRICT COURT AND A CERTIFIED COPY OF THE DOCKET ENTRIES.

---

[7] Id. 3(c).

[8] Id. 4(e). See R. Stern, Appellate Practice in the United States § 4.4, at 87 (1981).

Within ten days after filing the notice of appeal, the appellant is required to order a transcript from the court reporter.[9] The appellant may order that only part of the proceedings be transcribed. When the entire transcript is not prepared, however, the appellant must file a statement of the issues that the appellant intends to raise on appeal so that the appellee can order other parts of the proceedings transcribed if they are thought to be necessary.[10]

After the transcript has been received by the clerk of the district court, the record on appeal is sent to the appellate court.[11] Unless otherwise controlled by local rule or by stipulation of the parties, the record on appeal consists of the original papers and exhibits filed in the district court, the transcript, and a certified copy of the docket entries prepared by the clerk of the district court.[12] The documents comprising the record are numbered and listed by the clerk of the court. Physical exhibits and documents of unusual bulk or weight, however, normally are not transmitted by the clerk.[13]

IN A FEDERAL COURT APPEAL, THE PRINCIPAL MEANS OF PRESENTING THE ISSUES AND ARGUMENTS IS THROUGH WRITTEN APPELLATE BRIEFS.

The appellant in the case is required to serve a brief on opposing counsel and to file it with the court of appeals within forty days of the date on which the record on appeal is filed.[14] The brief presents the issues for review, a statement of the nature of the case, the course of the proceedings, the disposition of the case in the court below ("Statement of the Case"), and an argument which supports the appellant's contention that the court below committed reversible error.[15]

The appellee is required to file a brief within thirty days after service of the appellant's brief on the appellee.[16] The

---

[9] Id. 10(b)(1).

[10] Id. 10(b)(3).

[11] Id. 10(b).

[12] Id. 10(a).

[13] Id. 10(b).

[14] Id. 30(a).

[15] Id. 28(a).

[16] Id. 30(a).

format of the appellee's brief is similar to the appellant's brief except that a statement of the issues or of the case need not be made unless the appellee is dissatisfied with the appellant's statements.[17] The appellant then may file a reply brief.[18] In most circumstances, the court will hear an oral argument before it renders a decision.[19] Appellate oral argument is discussed in the next chapter.

IN A FEDERAL COURT APPEAL, THE APPELLANT MUST ALSO PREPARE AND FILE AN APPENDIX TO THE BRIEFS.

In addition to preparing a brief, the appellant is required to prepare and file an appendix to the briefs. Unless otherwise provided by court rule, the appendix must be served on the other parties and filed with the court of appeals at the same time the appellant's brief is filed. Federal Rule of Appellate Procedure 30(a) specifies that the appendix shall contain:

(1) the relevant docket entries;
(2) the relevant portions of the pleadings, charges, findings, or opinion;
(3) the judgment, order, or decision in question; and
(4) any other parts of the record to which the parties want to direct the particular attention of the court.[20]

DISCRETIONARY UNITED STATES SUPREME COURT REVIEW OF A DECISION IS SOUGHT THROUGH A PETITION FOR CERTIORARI. THE CONTENTS OF THE PETITION IS GOVERNED BY SUPREME COURT RULE 21.

Discretionary review of decisions by the United States Supreme Court is sought by means of a petition for certiorari. Rule 21 of the Supreme Court Rules provides that the petition must contain the following elements in the order listed:

(1) the questions presented for review;

---

[17] Id. 28(b).

[18] See id. 28(c), 31.

[19] See id. 34.

[20] Id. 30(a). See also id. 30(d) (specifying the arrangement of the appendix).

(2) a list of all parties to the proceeding, except when the caption contains the names of all the parties;

(3) a table of contents and authorities;

(4) a reference to the opinions below;

(5) a jurisdictional statement;

(6) the constitutional or other provisions involved;

(7) a statement of the case;

(8) an argument amplifying the reasons why the writ should be granted; and

(9) an appendix.[21]

When a dissatisfied party (the "petitioner") seeks discretionary review by a petition for certiorari, the party seeking a denial of the writ (the "respondent") normally attempts to show in a brief why the case should not be heard.[22] The character of the reasons that will be influential on whether review will be granted have already been discussed in an earlier chapter.

Section 9B. Format of Appellate Briefs

ALWAYS CONSULT THE RULES OF THE COURT TO WHICH THE APPEAL IS DIRECTED TO DETERMINE THE REQUIREMENTS FOR THE FORM OF THE APPELLATE BRIEF.

The organization, format, and other "mechanical" aspects of appellate brief writing are prescribed in detail by the court to which the brief is directed.

ILLUSTRATION 9.2

Rule 28 of the Federal Rules of Appellate Procedure provides:

> The brief of the appellant shall contain under appropriate headings and in the order indicated:
>
> (1) A table of contents, with page references, and a table of cases (alphabetically arranged), statutes and other authorities cited, with reference to the pages of the brief where they are cited.
>
> (2) A statement of the issues presented for review.

---

[21] S. Ct. R. 21.1.

[22] See id. 22 (brief in opposition).

> (3) A statement of the case. The statement shall first indicate briefly the nature of the case, the course of proceedings, and its disposition in the court below. There shall follow a statement of facts relevant to the issues presented for review, with appropriate references to the record. . . .
>
> (4) An argument. The argument may be preceded by a summary. The argument shall contain the contentions of the appellant with respect to the issues presented, and the reasons therefor, with citations to the authorities, statutes and parts of the record relied on.
>
> (5) A short conclusion stating the precise relief sought.[23]

The size of paper, the size of type, the color of the front cover, and other matters are set forth in Rule 32:

> Briefs and appendices may be produced by standard typographic printing or by any duplicating or copying process which produces a clear black image on white paper. Carbon copies of briefs and appendices may not be submitted without permission of the court, except in behalf of parties allowed to proceed in forma pauperis. All printed matter must appear in at least 11 point type on opaque, unglazed paper. Briefs and appendices produced by the standard typographic process shall be bound in volumes having pages 7 1/8 by 9 1/4 inches and type matter 4 1/6 by 7 1/6 inches. Those reproduced by any other process shall be bound in volumes having pages not exceeding 8 1/2 by 11 inches and type matter not exceeding 6 1/2 by 9 1/2 inches, with double spacing between each line of text. . . . Copies of the reporter's transcript and other papers reproduced in a matter authorized by this rule may be inserted in the appendix; such pages may be informally renumbered if necessary.
>
> If briefs are produced by commercial printing or duplicating firms, or, if produced otherwise and the covers to be described are available, the cover of the brief of the appellant should be blue, that of the appellee, red, that of an intervenor or amicus curiae, green; that of any reply brief, gray. The cover of the appendix, if separately printed, should be white.[24]

---

[23]Fed. R. App. P. 28(a).

[24]*Id.* 32(a).

An action on appeal to a federal court of appeals is docketed under the title given to it in the district court.[25] This title should be used on the front cover; the parties' status should be appropriately indicated, such as "Plaintiff-Appellant," "Defendant-Appellee," "Petitioner," "Respondent," etc. Other aspects of the cover page are governed by Rule 32(a). This rule provides that the front covers of the briefs and of appendices, if separately printed, shall contain:

> (1) the name of the court and the number of the case; (2) the title of the case . . . ; (3) the nature of the proceeding in the court (e.g., Appeal; Petition for Review) and the name of the court, agency, or board below; (4) the title of the document (e.g., Brief for Appellant, Appendix); and (5) the names and addresses of counsel representing the party on whose behalf the document is filed.[26]

ILLUSTRATION 9.3

Although the exact placement and format varies, a typical cover page for an appeal to a United States Court of Appeals is shown in the following Illustration.

---

[25] Id. 12(a).

[26] Id. 32(a).

IN THE
UNITED STATES COURT OF APPEALS
FOR THE THIRTEENTH CIRCUIT

No. xx-xxx

A.B.,

Plaintiff-Appellant,

v.

C.D.,

Defendant-Appellee.

APPEAL FROM THE UNITED STATES DISTRICT COURT
FOR THE DISTRICT OF UTOPIA
Honorable XXX, Judge

BRIEF OF THE APPELLANT A.B.

[Attorney's Name and Firm]
[Attorney's Address]
Attorney for Appellant A.B.

* * * * *

The cover page is followed by a table of contents; many attorneys label it an "Index." It provides a quick reference to the location of particular matters in the brief. More importantly, because it lists the argument headings from the argument section of the brief, it provides the court with a concise summary of the argument presented in the brief. If the brief involves only a single issue, the argument heading (in contrast to the Illustration below) would omit the initial roman number.

ILLUSTRATION 9.4

The table of contents or index might appear as follows:

[Top of the Page]

TABLE OF CONTENTS

Immediately after the table of contents and continuing on the same page is the table of cases, statutes, and other authorities cited. The cases should be grouped together and should be alphabetized. When the cases are numerous, some writers use subdivisions (e.g., United States Supreme Court Cases, Other Federal Court Cases, etc.).

Again, references are made to the pages of the brief where the authorities are cited. If an authority is cited on numerous pages, you may use "passim" in lieu of page numbers.

ILLUSTRATION 9.5

This section might appear as follows:

[Immediately Following the Table of Contents]

CASES CITED

<u>Altrichter v. Shell Oil Co.</u>, 263 F.2d 377 (8th Cir. 1959). 12

<u>Bierczynski v. Rogers</u>, 239 A.2d 218 (Del. 1968). . 14, 16

* * *

[Continue listing all cases cited in alphabetical order]

CONSTITUTIONAL PROVISIONS AND STATUTES CITED

U.S. Const. amend I. 14, 17, 18

42 U.S.C.A. § 1983 (West 19xx). 9

* * *

[Continue listing the provisions and statutes cited; if none are cited, omit this section.]

OTHER AUTHORITIES CITED

Perry & Teply, <u>Interviewing, Counseling, and In-Court Examination of Children</u>, 18 Creighton L. Rev. 1369 (1984-85). 6

* * *

[Continue listing other authorities cited in alphabetical order.]

* * * * *

It is obvious that the above table can be prepared only after the body of the brief has been written, finalized, and the pages numbered. The pages on which the tables appear are numbered with small roman numerals (i, ii, iii, etc.).

A simple way to compile the cases, statutes, and other authorities cited is to use an index card for each, listing the page(s) on which they are cited. The cards then can be sorted and alphabetically arranged for the typist. Some word processing programs will automatically prepare this table if the items to be listed are marked in the text of the brief.

Typically, the first numbered page (1) of the brief repeats the information given on the front cover in the same way, except that the name and address of the attorney are omitted. Immediately following (on the same page if there is room) is the statement of the questions presented.

Section 9C. Writing Suggestions

This section focuses on writing appellate briefs. A large volume of material has been published on how to write good appellate briefs. This material contains a variety of excellent suggestions, the best of which are summarized in the following paragraphs.

Specifically, this section presents suggestions about formulating and writing the critical elements of the brief: the questions presented, the statement of the case, the summary of the argument, the argument, and the conclusion. For the most part, these suggestions are specific applications of the persuasive writing techniques discussed in the preceding chapter.

1. FORMULATING THE QUESTION(S) PRESENTED

EXPRESS THE QUESTION(S) IN THE TERMS AND CIRCUMSTANCES OF THE CASE.

When you are formulating the questions presented, express those questions in the terms and circumstances of the case. This suggestion is frequently made by commentators[27] and has even been specifically incorporated in the Supreme Court Rules.[28] In this way, the reader is given a meaningful understanding of the law as it applies to the present case.

PROBLEM 9.1

Consider the following questions.[29] Which best expresses the question in the terms and circumstances of the case?

(a) Does section 495 of the Pennsylvania Code violate the Equal Protection clause?

(b) Does section 495 of the Pennsylvania Code, which prohibits automobile dealerships from staying open on Sunday, violate the Equal Protection clauses of the Pennsylvania and United States Constitutions?

---

[27] See, e.g., H. Weihofen, Legal Writing Style 247-49 (2d ed. 1980); E. Re, Brief Writing and Oral Argument 118-23 (4th ed. 1974); F. Weiner, Briefing and Arguing Federal Appeals 72-75 (1967).

[28] See S. Ct. R. 15.1(a), 21.1(a).

[29] See R. Stern, supra note 8, at 264 (presenting the questions on which this problem is based).

(c) Does section 495 of the Pennsylvania Code, which prohibits automobile dealerships but no other retail merchants from staying open on Sunday, violate the Equal Protection clauses of the Pennsylvania and United States Constitutions?

(d) Does section 495 of the Pennsylvania Code, which does not permit the defendant but allows others to stay open for business on Sunday, violate the Equal Protection clauses of the Pennsylvania and United States Constitutions?

Stop here, and consider which best expresses the question in the terms and circumstances of the case before consulting the discussion of this problem in Appendix A.

STATE THE ISSUE FAIRLY BUT IN A WAY THAT SUGGESTS A FAVORABLE ANSWER.

An issue may be fairly stated in several ways. A brief writer should work to formulate the issue in a way that leads the reader to be favorably disposed to the writer's position. As discussed and illustrated in the preceding chapter, words with favorable connotations should be used. Furthermore, the wording of the questions should be adjusted to stress favorable aspects of the case.

WHEN STATING A QUESTION, MOVE FROM THE GENERAL TO THE SPECIFIC, AND STATE THE LAW BEFORE THE FACTS.

This suggestion was made and illustrated in Chapter 6 on writing legal memoranda.[30]

AVOID USING A SERIES OF QUESTIONS THAT ARE REPETITIVE OR THAT ARE SIMPLY SUBPARTS OF A PRINCIPAL QUESTION.

Repetitive questions as well as questions that are merely subaspects of a principal question should be eliminated. Again, examples of this point were given in the earlier chapter on writing legal memoranda, and they apply equally in this context.

---

[30] See also H. Weihofen, supra note 27, at 248.

2. STATEMENT OF THE CASE

One common shortcoming in brief writing is the failure to appreciate the importance of the statement of the case section. It has been suggested that "[h]ow the facts are stated may be more important than the argument of law itself."[31]

AT THE OUTSET, STATE THE TYPE OF PROCEEDING AND THE RELIEF SOUGHT; THEN STATE THE DISPOSITION OF THE ACTION, FOLLOWED BY A STATEMENT OF THE FACTS.

The statement of the case should indicate: (1) the nature of the case; (2) the course of the proceedings; (3) the disposition in the court below; and then (4) a statement of the facts relevant to the issues presented for review.[32]

ILLUSTRATION 9.6

Thus, a statement of the case might begin as follows:

In this action, the homeowner sued the builder for damages for breach of contract. After a jury trial, judgment was entered against the builder for $50,000.

Squires and Rombauer suggest that additional procedural details may the be given, but a lengthy summary should be avoided.[33]

WHEN THE RECORD IS AVAILABLE, MAKE SPECIFIC REFERENCES TO IT IN THE STATEMENT OF THE CASE.

The statement of the facts should make appropriate references to the record by citing the appendix filed with the appellant's brief or by clearly citing parts of the record not reproduced in the appendix.[34]

---

[31] L. Squires & M. Rombauer, Legal Writing § 7.4, at 171 (1982).

[32] See Fed. R. App. P. 28(a)(3).

[33] L. Squires & M. Rombauer, supra note 31, § 7.4, at 170 ("human side of the case" should be introduced at an early point).

[34] Fed. R. App. P. 28(e).

EMPHASIZE FAVORABLE FACTS AND DE-EMPHASIZE UNFAVORABLE ONES.

The techniques suggested in the preceding chapter should be employed to create a favorable view of the facts of the case (shifting emphasis, choosing words carefully, etc.).

DO NOT OMIT UNFAVORABLE FACTS.

Although a writer should seek to de-emphasize them, unfavorable facts should not be omitted. They will surely be pointed out by the opposing party, and the writer's ethical appeal will be undermined. Instead, state unfavorable facts at a high level of generality, place them between favorable facts discussed in greater detail, and use words with favorable connotations.

BE SURE TO DISTINGUISH BETWEEN DISPUTED OR ALLEGED FACTS AND UNDISPUTED OR ESTABLISHED FACTS.

Generally speaking, the procedural context of the case will be critical to determining which facts, if any, are merely alleged, which are disputed, and which are established. Thus, *for purposes of the appeal*, you may have to treat certain facts (although disputed) as established.

ILLUSTRATION 9.7

You must treat as established the facts alleged in a complaint that has been dismissed for failure to state a claim.

GENERALLY, USE A CHRONOLOGICAL ORDER TO PRESENT THE FACTS; OR USE A TOPICAL ORGANIZATION WHEN THE EVENTS CAN MORE EASILY BE UNDERSTOOD IN THAT WAY.

This same approach was suggested in Chapter 6 on writing legal memoranda, and it applies here as well.

MINIMIZE THE USE OF THE DESIGNATION OF THE PARTIES ON APPEAL.

Use of descriptive terms (for example, home owner, bailee, or passenger) to refer to the parties is much more likely to enlighten the court than use of their designation on appeal (for example, appellant, petitioner, respondent, or appellee). Rule 28 of the Federal Rules of Appellate Procedure specifically provides:

> Counsel will be expected in their briefs and oral arguments to keep to a minimum references to parties by such designations as "appellant" and "appellee." It promotes clarity to use the designations used in the lower court or in the agency proceedings, or the actual names of parties, or descriptive terms such as "the employee," "the injured person," "the taxpayer," "the ship," "the stevedore," etc.[35]

3. WRITING THE ARGUMENT SECTION

The argument section of a brief is a textual discussion of the authorities and reasons that support propositions that the writer is asserting. The means of formulating the arguments have already been discussed in the preceding chapter. This subsection principally considers the order of presentation and the effective use of point headings.

FOLLOW THE WIDELY ACCEPTED GUIDELINES FOR EFFECTIVE POINT HEADINGS IN THE ARGUMENT SECTION: (1) USE FULL SENTENCES; (2) MAKE STATEMENTS ABOUT THE CASE RATHER THAN ABSTRACT STATEMENTS; (3) MAKE STATEMENTS THAT HAVE LEGAL RELEVANCE.

Argument headings precede each part of the argument. They generally provide, in capsule form, the gist of the argument contained in that section or subsection. Often, these headings are typed or printed in all capital letters.

There are three widely accepted guidelines that should be followed in preparing these headings. First, you should use full sentences, not topical phrases. Second, you should make statements about your case, not about abstract legal principles. Third, you should make statements that demonstrate legal relevance.[36]

---

[35] Id. 28(d).

[36] See, e.g., L. Squires & M. Rombauer, supra note 31, § 7.2, at 175-76.

PROBLEM 9.2

Which of the following argument headings best complies with the above stated guidelines?[37]

(a) THE ALLEGED CONTRACTUAL RELATIONSHIP.

(b) A THIRD PARTY IS LIABLE FOR INTERFERENCE WITH CONTRACTUAL RELATIONS ONLY IF THERE IS AN INTERFERENCE WITH A VALID CONTRACTUAL RELATIONSHIP OR BUSINESS EXPECTANCY.

(c) PLAINTIFF'S EVIDENCE FAILED TO ESTABLISH A VALID CONTRACTUAL RELATIONSHIP OR BUSINESS EXPECTANCY.

(d) PLAINTIFF HAS NOT PROVED THAT DEFENDANT TORTIOUSLY INTERFERED WITH HIS EXCHANGE CONTRACT BECAUSE PLAINTIFF'S EVIDENCE FAILED TO ESTABLISH THE EXISTENCE OF A VALID CONTRACTUAL RELATIONSHIP OF THE TYPE ENTITLED TO PROTECTION AGAINST INTERFERENCE BY THIRD PARTIES.

Stop here, and consider these headings before consulting the discussion of this problem in Appendix A.

INCORPORATE REASONS IN THE POINT HEADINGS. CONSIDER USING SUBPOINT HEADINGS THAT SUPPORT THE PRINCIPAL HEADING AND CONTAIN A CONCLUSION.

The argument heading in (d) in Problem 9.2 above provides both the conclusion and a reason. If there are several reasons, consider using subpoint headings to support a principal heading.[38]

ORDINARILY, PUT THE STRONGEST POINT FIRST.

The order of presentation most often recommended is to discuss the strongest point first. Weihofen suggests that one practical reason for this approach is that first impressions tend to be lasting ones: "If on reading your first point the judge has the

---

[37]See id. (presenting the example on which this problem is based).

[38]See id. § 7.2, at 176.

impression your case is weak, the chances that your later points will change his [or her] mind are not good."[39]

4. SUMMARY OF THE ARGUMENT

The summary of the argument should be a condensed version of the argument presented in the argument section.

DO NOT MAKE ARGUMENTS IN THE SUMMARY OF THE ARGUMENT SECTION THAT ARE NOT MADE IN THE ARGUMENT SECTION OF THE BRIEF.

The summary of the argument should be just that: a summary. It should not introduce new theories or arguments that will not be discussed in the argument section.

IN THE SUMMARY, MAKE AN EFFORT TO CONDENSE THE ARGUMENT IN A WAY THAT PRESENTS THE CRUX OF THE ARGUMENT AND AVOIDS REPEATING THE ARGUMENT HEADINGS.

Although the summary of the argument is likely to track the argument headings, you should avoid simply repeating the argument headings. Instead, try to condense the argument in different terms.

In this regard, consider the requirements of Supreme Court Rule 34.1. It provides that the summary of the argument should be "a succinct, but accurate and clear, condensation of the argument actually made in the body of the brief. It should not be a mere repetition of the headings under which the argument is arranged."[40]

AUTHORITY SHOULD NOT BE DISCUSSED IN THE SUMMARY OF THE ARGUMENT; A CRUCIAL CASE, HOWEVER, MAY BE CITED, PARTICULARLY IF THE CASE IS WIDELY KNOWN.

Avoid discussing authority (for example, stating the facts or holdings of other cases) in the summary of the argument section.

---

[39] H. Weihofen, supra note 27, at 275.

[40] S. Ct. R. 34.1(h).

A crucial case may be cited, however, particularly if it is widely known.[41]

5. WRITING THE CONCLUSION

Traditionally, the conclusion section of a brief has been limited to a statement of the relief requested, such as a reversal, affirmance, etc. Sometimes, writers will add a short summary. Squires and Rombauer suggest that the basic argument be added as reasons for granting the requested relief. This approach provides an opportunity to interrelate multiple arguments.

ILLUSTRATION 9.8

> The judgment for plaintiff should be reversed. Plaintiff did not have a valid contract or a business expectancy of the type protected against tortious interference. In the alternative, the conduct of defendant, as a competitor, was privileged.[42]

Section 9D. Preparing the Initial Draft

This section discusses how to approach the task of preparing an initial draft of the brief.

1. UNDERSTANDING THE FACTS AND ISSUES

TO PREPARE A BRIEF, IT IS ESSENTIAL THAT YOU UNDERSTAND THE SIGNIFICANT "EVENTS" OF THE CASE.

The significant "events" of the case include the facts alleged by each party; the facts that cannot be reasonably disputed; the nature and strength of the proof tending to establish disputed facts; the substantive theories; the procedural posture of the case; the rulings of the judge; and the findings of the jury or other trier of fact. It is from these "events" that the issue on appeal will be framed and argued.

If you are unfamiliar with the events of a case, there are several ways to familiarize yourself with them. One source of information is the office file. Reading the file (or selected

---

[41] See L. Squires & M. Rombauer, supra note 31, § 7.6, at 179.

[42] Id. § 7.7, at 180.

portions of it) should orient you to the litigation. Furthermore, the office file is likely to contain office memoranda, memoranda in support of or in opposition to motions, trial briefs, and other documents that may save you considerable work in preparing the brief.

ILLUSTRATION 9.9

For instance, the documents in the office file may show what arguments have been made, the research that has been conducted, etc.

Another source of information is the transcript if it is relevant to the point to be appealed and available at the time you are beginning your work.

When you have not been previously involved in the litigation that is the basis for the appeal, however, the best initial approach is to discuss the proceedings, possible points for appeal, and relevant arguments with those persons who have been actively involved in the case. Sometimes, these matters may be outlined for you in an office memorandum.

ILLUSTRATION 9.10

Assume that you work for the firm representing Snidely Lash in his lawsuit against I.M. Delira and her insurer. Assume that you have not been actively involved in this litigation, but now you have been asked to prepare the initial draft of an appellate brief. Assume that you have been given the following instructions:

MEMORANDUM

To: Young R. Associate
From: Senior Partner
Date: January xx, 19xx
Re: *Lash v. Delira*
Our File # xx-xxx

As you know, our client received an unfavorable verdict in *Lash v. Delira*, and we have filed a notice of appeal. I would like you to prepare a draft of our appellate brief in final form. Here is a summary of the significant events in this litigation:

On November xx, 19xx, we filed suit against I.M. Delira and her insurer No-Pay Casualty Co. in federal district court in Utopia. Jurisdiction was based on diversity of citizenship and more than $50,000 in controversy. The complaint alleged that I.M. Delira negligently and carelessly operated her automobile and, as a result, severely injured our client.

Delira apparently had suffered a "mental aberration" that caused her to lose conscious control of her automobile. Delira was taken to Lincoln County General Hospital. She remains institutionalized to date. Consistent with her statements at the scene of the accident, she still maintains that she is a real "Wonder Woman" and that her car was controlled by an alien creature.

The defendants asserted in their answer that, *inter alia*, they were not liable because Delira had suffered a sudden, incapacitating mental illness that occurred without prior warning. We moved to strike this defense on the ground that it was insufficient as a matter of law. This defense is one of first impression in Utopia. The defendants principally cited *Breunig v. American Family Insurance Co.*, 45 Wis. 2d 536, 173 N.W.2d 619 (1970), *Buckley & Toronto Transportation Commission v. Smith*, 1946 Ont. L. Rep. 798, and several commentators for the proposition that a sudden mental illness ought to be treated like a sudden physical illness. We relied on *Kuhn v. Zabotsky*, 9 Ohio St. 2d 129, 224 N.E.2d 137 (1967) and the general common-law rule of liability of insane persons.

The court denied our motion. The judge accepted the common-law rule requiring insane persons to conform to an objective standard of a sane person but held that an exception to it should be recognized. The judge thus decided that if the defendants could show that Delira's mental condition prevented her from operating her vehicle in an ordinary prudent manner, the defendant would not be liable.

The lawsuit then centered on Delira's mental state and evidence of possible forewarning. We discovered through interrogatories that Delira had been under the treatment of Dr. Sigmond Psycho for about two years prior to the accident. After some procedural maneuvering, we were able to take Dr. Psycho's deposition. He stated that Delira had been treated for "severe depression," but that she had never suffered from hallucinations or delusions. In Psycho's "expert" opinion, Delira did not have forewarning that she would become ill in the way that she did.

We did the best we could to discredit Dr. Psycho in the deposition but we neglected for some reason to ask him about his background. His demeanor was very unconvincing, so we subsequently investigated his background. We learned that he had graduated last in his class from Ed's Night School of Psychiatry and Auto Mechanics and had been sued for malpractice twelve times.

At the time of the trial, Dr. Psycho was doing research on psychic surgery among the primitives in some foreign country and thus was unable to testify. The defendants introduced Dr. Psycho's deposition. We moved to exclude the part of his deposition in which he opined on the lack of forewarning on the ground that he was not qualified to give an expert opinion in light of his training and current practice. The trial judge, however, ruled that this objection had been waived because it had not been raised at the time of the deposition (so that the defendants could have attempted to obviate it).

The other evidence at trial conflicted about forewarning. Delira's next-door neighbor testified that Delira had acted "sort of strangely" before the accident but the neighbor did not see any prior signs of delusions. On cross-examination, Delira's neighbor stated that Delira had said "Merciful Minerva" several times during the month preceding the accident. Nonetheless, the neighbor maintained that Delira did not give any other indication of illness in the form of delusions.

A good friend of Delira testified that on the morning of the accident Delira "appeared to be her usual self" and there had not been any indications of hallucinations prior to the accident. We attempted to call Delira herself, but the trial judge accepted defense counsel's argument that she was too ill to testify.

We objected to the court's charge to the jury, which permitted the jury to find in favor of the defendant based on a sudden mental illness defense. The jury made the following findings of fact, *inter alia*, pursuant to specific interrogatories:

(a) The plaintiff was not negligent in any way;

(b) The defendant Delira suddenly and without warning became mentally ill; as a result, she was unable to control her vehicle and injured the plaintiff.

(c) The defendant failed to conduct herself in a manner of an ordinary prudent person but under the circumstances was not at fault.

Based upon these findings, the judge entered judgment for the defendants. We moved for judgment notwithstanding the verdict or, in the alternative, for a new trial. Previously, we had moved for a directed verdict. All of these motions were denied.

2. DECIDING ON THE ISSUES TO PRESENT ON APPEAL

During the course of litigation, a number of possible errors may occur. Some of them ordinarily will be more significant than others. Some may be "harmless," and others may be critical.

PROBLEM 9.3

Experienced attorneys and commentators recommend that you carefully select the issues for appeal. In general, the issues should be limited to those that are truly determinative of the outcome of the litigation. Remember that the errors will usually center on actions taken by the trial judge. In the above memorandum, for example, the following possible errors could be identified:

(a) The trial judge erred by not striking the sudden mental illness defense;

(b) The trial judge erred by not excluding Dr. Psycho's opinions because he was not a qualified expert;

(c) The trial judge erred by not requiring Delira to testify;

(d) The trial judge erred by not directing a verdict in favor of the plaintiff;

(e) The trial judge erred in instructing the jury;

(f) The trial judge abused his discretion by not granting a new trial;

(g) The trial judge erred when he failed to enter judgment in favor of the plaintiff notwithstanding the verdict.

Which of these possible errors should be appealed? Stop here, and reach a conclusion before consulting the discussion of this problem in Appendix A.

3. DRAFTING THE QUESTION OR QUESTIONS

Assume that you have decided to limit the appeal to the sudden mental illness defense. One of the first steps in preparing the initial draft of the brief is to tentatively state the question. On a sheet of paper, try to quickly state the issue in several ways.

PROBLEM 9.4

Consider the following formulations of the question presented. What criticism do you have of these initial formulations?

(a) Should a sudden mental illness be recognized in the State of Utopia as a defense to a negligence action when the driver of an automobile suddenly and without warning suffers a hallucination that causes a loss of conscious control of the car and a collision with the plaintiff's vehicle?

(b) If a driver is suddenly stricken with a mental disability and, as a result, causes an accident, should the driver's mental condition be treated like a sudden physical illness (such as a heart attack or epileptic seizure) and thus relieve the driver of responsibility?

(c) Should an insured driver who suddenly begins hallucinating without warning and, as a result, severely injures another driver who is completely free of negligence at the time of the accident be relieved of all responsibility to compensate the innocent injured driver?

(d) Should a driver who suddenly and without warning begins to believe that she is unable to control her car because it is controlled by an alien being and, as a result, severely injures another driver be excused from her failure to conform to the standard of a reasonable person?

Stop here, and consider these initial formulations before consulting the discussion of this problem in Appendix A.

4. DRAFTING THE STATEMENT OF THE CASE

The next step in preparing the initial draft should be to draft a tentative version of the statement of the case. Following the suggestions given earlier, you would open the statement with the nature of the case, a description of the course of the proceedings, and an indication of the disposition of the action below. You would then state the relevant facts. Because the facts of this case are relatively simple and the parties are few, a chronological approach should be used.

This statement of the case should be drafted with the view that it will be refined later to make it as favorable as possible but still fair under the circumstances. An initial draft of the statement of the case should be placed on a sheet of paper separate from the draft of the questions presented.

ILLUSTRATION 9.11

STATEMENT OF THE CASE

The plaintiff driver Lash brought a tort action against I.M. Delira and her insurer for damages as a result of Delira's vehicle crossing the center line and striking the plaintiff's vehicle traveling in the opposite direction. The principal defense was that the defendant driver suffered without warning a sudden mental illness that prevented her from fulfilling her duty of care owed to other travelers. After a jury trial in the United States District Court for the District of Utopia, judgment was entered for the defendants based solely on this defense.

The accident in question occurred on September 1, 19xx, on Highway 8 in Lincoln County, Utopia. Defendant Delira lost control of her vehicle, crossed the center line of the highway, and struck the plaintiff's vehicle. Delira apparently believed that she was a real Wonder Woman and that her vehicle was under the control of an alien being which prevented her from avoiding the accident.

The plaintiff moved to strike Delira's sudden mental illness defense from the answer on the ground that Utopia has not and should not recognize this defense. This motion was denied. At trial, it was shown that Delira had been under psychiatric care for "severe depression" prior to the accident, but Delira's neighbor and a friend testified that there had been no signs warning Delira that a hallucination of this nature would occur. In his deposition, which was read at trial, Delira's psychiatrist also stated that in his opinion this illness occurred without forewarning.

The plaintiff unsuccessfully challenged the validity of this defense again at the close of the defendants' evidence and at its inclusion in the jury charge. The jury found the plaintiff to be free of any negligence, but that defendant Delira was not liable because of the effects of her hallucination. The plaintiff's motions for judgment notwithstanding the verdict or a new trial were denied.

This tentative draft of the Statement of the Case should be put aside for revision.

5. OUTLINING THE ARGUMENT SECTION

The next step in preparing the initial draft of a brief should be to prepare an outline of the argument section. If the research for the brief was prepared in the manner described in the chapter on research notes, you could arrange the research notes in a logical argument.

If you are working from other materials, such as research in the file and memoranda filed with the trial court, it is suggested that you briefly list the basic arguments *without regard to the order or overlap*.

ILLUSTRATION 9.12

(a) Several well-considered cases have rejected the attempt to create an exception for sudden-occurring insanity to the common-law rule holding insane persons to a reasonable person standard. *Kuhn*, *Sforza*, *Turner*, *Williams*.

(b) Traditional public policy allocating liability between two innocent persons should be applied.

(c) Sudden mental illness should not be treated like a sudden physical illness because (1) the risk of feigning a mental illness is greater than that of feigning a physical illness; (2) it is more difficult to the prove existence and effects of a mental illness than of a physical illness; and (3) the requirement of "forewarning" cannot be effectively applied to a mental illness.

One benefit of this process of arranging or listing arguments is that another line of argument might occur to you.

ILLUSTRATION 9.13

For example, in this instance, it may occur to you that you should attack the *entire* sudden illness rule:

(d) Utopia should not recognize any sudden illness (mental or physical) as a defense to an action based on conduct that falls below that of a reasonable person because of (1) the widespread role of insurance today in an automobile context; (2) the modern acceptance of strict liability in inherently dangerous activities; (3) support of commentators; and (4) dictum in the *Kuhn* case.

After you have listed the arguments or arranged the research notes, you should then draft the tentative argument headings (and subheadings).

ILLUSTRATION 9.14

The prior outline was used to formulate the following tentative argument headings:

AN UNEXPECTED, SUDDEN HALLUCINATION SUFFERED BY A DRIVER SHOULD NOT RELIEVE THAT DRIVER OF THE RESPONSIBILITY OF CONFORMING HIS CONDUCT TO THAT OF A REASONABLE PERSON BECAUSE OF THE RULE THAT WHEN ONE OF TWO INNOCENT PARTIES MUST SUFFER A LOSS, THE ONE WHO OCCASIONED IT SHOULD BEAR IT.

A. WELL-REASONED CASES FROM OTHER JURISDICTIONS HAVE REFUSED TO CREATE A "SUDDEN MENTAL ILLNESS" EXCEPTION TO THE GENERAL RULE HOLDING INSANE PERSONS LIABLE TO INJURED INNOCENT VICTIMS.

B. THE ATTEMPT TO ANALOGIZE A SUDDEN MENTAL ILLNESS TO A SUDDEN PHYSICAL ILLNESS RECOGNIZED AS A DEFENSE IN SOME JURISDICTIONS IS ILL-FOUNDED BECAUSE OF SIGNIFICANT DIFFERENCES BETWEEN PHYSICAL AND MENTAL ILLNESSES, THE GREATER UNRELIABILITY OF PROOF OF MENTAL ILLNESS, AND THE GREATER RISK OF FEIGNING A MENTAL ILLNESS.

C. EVEN IF A SUDDEN MENTAL ILLNESS AND A SUDDEN PHYSICAL ILLNESS ARE SEEN AS ANALOGOUS, THE BEST APPROACH IS TO REJECT ALL SUDDEN ILLNESSES AS DEFENSES TO NEGLIGENCE ACTIONS IN LIGHT OF THE PUBLIC POLICY ALLOCATING LOSSES

AMONG INNOCENT PARTIES, THE WIDESPREAD AVAILABILITY OF LIABILITY INSURANCE, AND MODERN CONCEPTS OF STRICT LIABILITY.

After you have prepared your tentative argument headings, you should prepare a detailed outline using complete sentences. Woolever explains as follows:

> Why should you outline in complete sentences and not jotted categories? Writing in whole sentences demands that you think whole thoughts instead of half-formulated ideas. Legal writers often have a general notion of how to go about answering a question, but they soon discover at the writing stage that they don't have conclusive ideas. As a result, they have to backtrack, restate, and travel off on tangents because the boundaries of their arguments are not set. An outline of complete sentences shows you not only the clear progression of topics, but also the conclusion you have drawn about each one. Sentence outlines force completeness of thought in preliminary stages, saving you time and energy in the long run.[43]

6. DRAFTING THE ARGUMENT SECTION

After preparing an outline, you are then ready to prepare a first draft of the argument section (using your research notes).

ILLUSTRATION 9.15

You might begin the argument section as follows. Note that if there were more than one main heading, the heading below would be identified with the roman numeral "I."

ARGUMENT

AN UNEXPECTED, SUDDEN HALLUCINATION SUFFERED BY A DRIVER SHOULD NOT RELIEVE THAT DRIVER OF THE RESPONSIBILITY OF CONFORMING HIS CONDUCT TO THAT OF A REASONABLE PERSON BECAUSE OF THE RULE THAT WHEN ONE OF TWO INNOCENT PARTIES MUST SUFFER A LOSS, THE ONE WHO OCCASIONED IT SHOULD BEAR IT.

A. WELL-REASONED CASES FROM OTHER JURISDICTIONS HAVE REFUSED TO CREATE A "SUDDEN MENTAL

---

[43] K. Woolever, Untangling the Law: Strategies for Legal Writers 47 (1987). Cf. Vom Bauer, How to Look Up Law and Write Legal Memoranda--Revisited, 11 Prac. Law., May 1965, at 23, 28 (stating each idea or legal principle in a complete sentence when you are taking research notes). See also Woolever, supra, at 40, 42-43 (recommending and illustrating the use of visual aids such as grid charts to organize your notes before outlining).

ILLNESS" EXCEPTION TO THE GENERAL RULE HOLDING INSANE PERSONS LIABLE TO INJURED INNOCENT VICTIMS.

Under the common law, persons who are insane or otherwise mentally deficient are held liable in negligence actions when their conduct fails to conform to the standard of conduct of reasonable persons. W. Prosser & W. Keeton, *The Law of Torts* § 135, at 1074 (5th ed. 1984). . . .

7. ABBREVIATED SAMPLE DRAFT

On the following pages is an abbreviated sample draft of this brief. It is designed primarily to illustrate the general appearance of an appellate brief.

IN THE
UNITED STATES COURT OF APPEALS
FOR THE THIRTEENTH CIRCUIT

No. xx-xxx

SNIDELY WHIP LASH,

Plaintiff-Appellant,

v.

NO-PAY CASUALTY CO. AND I.M. DELIRA,

Defendant-Appellee.

APPEAL FROM THE UNITED STATES DISTRICT COURT
FOR THE DISTRICT OF UTOPIA

Honorable Jack Gleason, Judge

BRIEF OF THE APPELLANT SNIDELY WHIP LASH

[Attorney's Name and Address
or Student's Name or Number]
[Legal Writing § __]

Attorney for Appellant Lash

TABLE OF CONTENTS

CASES CITED

[Continue listing all cases cited in alphabetical order, followed by a listing of other authorities cited in the brief.]

IN THE
UNITED STATES COURT OF APPEALS
FOR THE THIRTEENTH CIRCUIT

No. xx-xxx

SNIDELY WHIP LASH,

Plaintiff-Appellant,

v.

NO-PAY CASUALTY CO. AND I.M. DELIRA,

Defendant-Appellee.

APPEAL FROM THE UNITED STATES DISTRICT COURT
FOR THE DISTRICT OF UTOPIA
Honorable Jack Gleason, Judge

BRIEF OF THE APPELLANT SNIDELY WHIP LASH

QUESTION PRESENTED

Should an insured driver who suddenly begins hallucinating without warning but, as a result, severely injures another driver who is completely free of negligence at the time of the accident be relieved of all responsibility to compensate the innocent injured driver?

STATEMENT OF THE CASE

The plaintiff driver Lash brought a tort action against I.M. Delira and her insurer for damages as a result of Delira's vehicle crossing the center line and striking the plaintiff's vehicle traveling in the opposite direction. The principal defense was that the defendant driver had suffered without warning a sudden mental illness that prevented her from fulfilling her duty of care owed to other travelers. After a jury trial in the United States District Court for the District of Utopia, judgment was entered for the defendants based solely on this defense.

The accident occurred on September 1, 19xx, on Highway 8 in Lincoln County, Utopia. Defendant Delira lost control of her vehicle, crossed the center line of the highway, and struck the plaintiff's vehicle. Delira apparently believed that she was a real Wonder Woman and that her vehicle was under the control of an alien being which prevented her from avoiding the accident.

The plaintiff moved to strike Delira's sudden mental illness defense from the answer on the ground that Utopia has not and should not recognize this defense. This motion was denied. At trial, it was shown that Delira had been under psychiatric care for "severe depression" prior to the accident, but Delira's daughter and husband testified that there had been no signs warning that a hallucination of this nature would occur. In his deposition, which was read at trial, Delira's psychiatrist stated that in his opinion this illness occurred without forewarning.

The plaintiff again unsuccessfully challenged the validity of this defense at the close of the defendants' evidence and objected to its inclusion in the jury charge. The jury found the plaintiff to be free of any negligence, but found that Delira was not liable because of the effects of her hallucination. The plaintiff's motions for judgment notwithstanding the verdict and a new trial were denied.

SUMMARY OF THE ARGUMENT

The question of whether proof of a sudden, unanticipated mental illness is a defense in a negligence action is one of first impression in the State of Utopia.

. . . [Continue the summary of the argument.]

2

ARGUMENT

AN UNEXPECTED, SUDDEN HALLUCINATION SUFFERED BY A DRIVER SHOULD NOT RELIEVE THAT DRIVER OF THE RESPONSIBILITY OF CONFORMING HIS CONDUCT TO THAT OF A REASONABLE PERSON BECAUSE OF THE RULE THAT WHEN ONE OF TWO INNOCENT PARTIES MUST SUFFER A LOSS, THE ONE WHO OCCASIONED IT SHOULD BEAR IT.

A. WELL-REASONED CASES FROM OTHER JURISDICTIONS HAVE REFUSED TO CREATE A "SUDDEN MENTAL ILLNESS" EXCEPTION TO THE GENERAL RULE HOLDING INSANE PERSONS LIABLE TO INJURED INNOCENT VICTIMS.

Under the common law, persons who are insane or otherwise mentally deficient are held liable in negligence actions when their conduct fails to conform to the standard of conduct of reasonable persons. W. Prosser & W. Keeton, The Law of Torts § 135, at 1074 (5th ed. 1984). This rule has been accepted by the Restatement of Torts: "Unless the actor is a child, his insanity or other mental deficiency does not relieve the actor from liability for conduct which does not conform to the standard of a reasonable man under the circumstances." Restatement (Second) of Torts § 283B (1965). . . .

[Continue the argument.]

CONCLUSION

The judgment for the defendant should be reversed and a new trial ordered.

* * * * *

Examples of complete appellate briefs can be found in many sources.[44]

After you have prepared your initial draft of the appellate brief, you are ready to edit your draft in light of the style suggestions in Chapters 1 and 7 and the persuasive writing suggestions in Chapter 8.

---

[44] See, e.g., D. Pratt, Legal Writing: A Systematic Approach 376-414 (1989); M. Fontham, Written and Oral Advocacy 309-37 (1985); H. Shapo, M. Walter, E. Fajans, Writing and Analysis in the Law 256-75 (1989); J. Gaubatz, The Moot Court Book 127-96 (1979) (briefs with commentary); V. Charrow & M. Erhardt, Clear and Effective Legal Writing 229-86 (1986); L. Katz, Winning Words: A Guide to Persuasive Writing for Lawyers 175-99 (1986).

Chapter 10

APPELLATE ORAL ARGUMENT

Section

WHAT YOU WILL LEARN IN THIS CHAPTER

* The goals and benefits of appellate oral argument
* The situations in which it is appropriate to submit the case on the briefs without oral argument
* The necessary steps to prepare adequately for appellate oral argument
* The mechanics of scheduling and delivering an oral argument in an appellate court
* The best ways to prepare the appellant's argument, the appellee's answering argument, and the appellant's rebuttal
* The best approaches to dealing with questions from the court

Section 10A. Purpose of Appellate Oral Argument

After the appellate briefs have been filed, the appellate court ordinarily hears oral argument, during which all sides orally present their arguments to a panel of judges. The decision to have oral argument in a case and its success if it is undertaken depends, in part, on a conscious attention to the purpose of oral argument.

In this regard, this section addresses three basic areas: (1) Why have oral argument? In other words, what does each side and the court hope to accomplish? (2) When should counsel submit the case for decision without oral argument? (3) When can and when should an appellate court dispense with oral argument even if the parties want it?

1. GOALS AND BENEFITS OF ORAL ARGUMENT

Oral argument has a long tradition in England and the United States.

ILLUSTRATION 10.1

In the early days of the United States Supreme Court, for example, the Court heard six days of oral argument in *McCullogh v. Maryland*,[1] and ten days of argument in *Vidal v. Mayor of Philadelphia*.[2] Today, of course, the time permitted for oral argument is limited. In the United States Supreme Court, each side is allowed only one-half hour, unless otherwise directed by the Court.[3] Despite the time limitation, oral argument is still highly valued by most appellate judges.

The Supreme Court rules state that "[o]ral argument should undertake to *emphasize* and *clarify* the written argument" in the briefs.[4] The value of oral argument lies, in part, in its "power to *vivify* what otherwise would be a cold and lifeless printed document."[5]

ORAL ARGUMENT IS A SUPPLEMENT AND AN AID TO THE UNDERSTANDING OF THE CASE. IT IS NOT A SUBSTITUTE FOR THE BRIEF.

As counsel, your basic goal in oral argument is to guide the appellate court "through the maze of facts to the conclusion that the appeal *must* be decided in favor of your client."[6] The persuasive techniques discussed in Chapter 8--logical, emotional, and ethical arguments--should be used to accomplish this goal.

Your goal should not be to "win" the case on oral argument by establishing the absolute legal correctness of a position directly. You will not have enough time to establish such a position. If you attempt to do so within the time allotted, you will be driven to making overstatements that will "catch up" to you.

---

[1] 17 U.S. (4 Wheat.) 316 (1819).

[2] 43 U.S. (2 How.) 127 (1844). See Davis, The Argument of an Appeal, 26 A.B.A. J. 895, 895 (1940).

[3] S. Ct. R. 38.3.

[4] Id. 38.1 (emphasis added).

[5] See C. Walter, Brief-Writing and Advocacy 161 (1931) (emphasis added).

[6] Steinheimer, Winning on Appeal, 29 Mich. St. B.J. 16, 21 (1950).

Instead, **ON THE INTELLECTUAL LEVEL**, the emphasis of the argument should be to interest the court in the controlling phase of the case so that the court sees the record from your point of view. **ON THE EMOTIONAL LEVEL**, the emphasis of the argument should be to convince the court of *your confidence* in the correctness of your client's cause so that the court is left with a sense of urgent importance of deciding the case in a particular way.[7]

Knapp explains as follows:

> If your client happens to have a sympathetic case, then you have an easy job. You have the emotional job of showing the court what a terrible deal your client has gotten, and the relatively simple intellectual job of providing a rational basis for vindicating your client's rights.
>
> If, on the other hand, your client [does not have] a sympathetic case--for example, if your client is pleading the statute of limitations and doesn't even want the judges to find out what your opponent says he has done--then you have an entirely different problem. You must emotionally convince the court that the particular legal point involved is so important that it would be a disservice to the administration of justice to let this particular judgment stand.
>
> But let me repeat: You shouldn't use the oral argument to establish the correctness of your position; you should use it to impress upon the judges your own moral conviction, which communicates itself to them in various ways, and then direct their attention to that phase of the case which will establish your point for you when they start discussing it in conference.[8]

2. SUBMISSION OF THE CASE FOR DECISION WITHOUT ORAL ARGUMENT

It is possible for the attorneys appealing an action to stipulate that the case will be submitted on the briefs for decision without oral argument. As a matter of strategy, when should counsel so stipulate?

---

[7] See Knapp, Why Argue an Appeal? If So, How? 1960 Ins. L.J. 29, 35.

[8] Id. at 35-36.

UNDER MOST CIRCUMSTANCES, THE PREVAILING VIEW IS THAT COUNSEL SHOULD SEEK ORAL ARGUMENT RATHER THAN SUBMITTING THE CASE ON THE BRIEFS.

The prevailing view among commentators is that counsel should seek appellate oral argument and that you should forego oral argument only in limited circumstances.[9]

FOREGO ORAL ARGUMENT (1) WHEN THE RECORD IS UNCOMPLICATED, (2) WHEN YOU WERE SUCCESSFUL IN THE COURT BELOW, (3) WHEN YOUR OPPONENT WANTS TO SUBMIT THE CASE ON THE BRIEFS, AND (4) WHEN YOU ARE SATISFIED WITH THE PRESENTATION IN YOUR BRIEF.

ILLUSTRATION 10.2

Judges suggest that oral argument would not be helpful on appeal from an order requesting that numerous paragraphs in a pleading be stricken, or in the event that is not done, that the alleged causes of action be separately stated and numbered, and in the event that is not justifiably required, that the action should be dismissed on the ground that no cause of action has been stated.[10]

Even though the parties agree to submit a case for decision on the briefs, the appellate court may nevertheless order that the case be argued orally.[11]

3. REFUSAL TO HEAR ORAL ARGUMENT

Even though the parties want to argue the case orally, the court may not let them do so. It has long been asserted that appellate courts have the power to dispense with oral argument

---

[9] See, e.g., Wilkins, The Argument of an Appeal, 33 Cornell L.Q. 40, 48 (1947).

[10] See M. Pittoni, Brief Writing and Argumentation 63 (3d ed. 1967) (quoting suggestion of Hon. William B. Carswell of the New York Supreme Court, Appellate Division).

[11] See, e.g., Fed. R. App. P. 34(f); S. Ct. R. 38.1 (United States Supreme Court is "reluctant to accept the submission of briefs, without oral argument, of any case in which jurisdiction has been noted or postponed to the merits or certiorari has been granted. Notwithstanding any such submission, the Court may require oral argument").

altogether.[12] Many courts have established a screening process to determine whether oral argument should be dispensed with or limited.[13]

ILLUSTRATION 10.3

Rule 34 of the Federal Rules of Appellate Procedure is typical:

> Oral argument shall be allowed in all cases unless pursuant to local rule a panel of three judges, after examination of the briefs and record, shall be unanimously of the opinion that oral argument is not needed. Any such local rule shall provide any party with an opportunity to file a statement setting forth the reasons why, in his opinion, oral argument should be heard. A general statement of the criteria employed in the administration of such local rule shall be published in or with the rule and such criteria shall conform substantially to the following minimum standard:
>
> Oral argument will be allowed unless (1) the appeal is frivolous; or (2) the dispositive issue or set of issues has been recently authoritatively decided; or (3) the facts and legal arguments are adequately presented in the briefs and record and the decisional process would not be significantly aided by oral argument.[14]

In most courts, counsel for parties appearing as amicus curiae are permitted to argue only if permission for them to do so has been previously granted.

ILLUSTRATION 10.4

The rules of the United States Supreme Court provide that a party may consent to have *amicus curiae* argue the case as the one counsel for that side. In absence of such consent, leave of Court must be sought, and permission will be "granted only in the most extraordinary circumstances."[15]

---

[12] See, e.g., Schmidt v. Boyle, 54 Neb. 387, 390, 74 N.W. 964, 956 (1888) (court may dispense with oral argument without violating state constitutional provision requiring court to hear the appeal).

[13] See R. Stern, Appellate Practice in the United States 361 (1981).

[14] Fed. R. App. P. 34.

[15] See S. Ct. R. 38.7.

Section 10B. Scheduling of Oral Argument

The methods of scheduling oral arguments are not uniform and the rules and practice of each court must be consulted.

ILLUSTRATION 10.5

Some courts require that notice of an intention to argue orally be printed on the brief and that counsel register before the court convenes on the day the case is called. Some courts require notice be served a stated number of days in advance of the call of the case. Others have a call of the term calendar at which counsel must request oral argument.[16]

Generally speaking, when an appeal is taken, the case will be docketed, given a number, placed in the clerk's files, and calendared. The cases are usually assigned on a rational basis to the judges who are responsible for reviewing the file and preparing a summary for other members of the court.[17] Some courts begin with the oldest case on file and proceed to the end of the docket.[18] In many courts, other factors are taken into account in setting the argument calendar. Priority may be given to certain types of cases, such as criminal appeals, or to those of particular importance in which an expedited appeal would be beneficial.[19]

Counsel will ordinarily be notified by the clerk's office when a case is to be argued. Often, this information may be determined before that notice is received. Provided it is received before the argument calendar has been formally set, a request to avoid scheduling argument on particular days or weeks will generally be accommodated when the request is reasonable and undue delay will not result. After the argument calendar has been set, a change in the scheduling will be more difficult to obtain.[20]

If there is a long calendar call, Knapp suggests that a young associate should not be sent to answer it because it may provide an opportunity to communicate with the court.

---

[16] See Rall, Effective Oral Argument, 1952 U. Ill. L.F. 114, 116-17 (1952).

[17] See Wigginton, General Aspects of Appellate Practice, 33 Fla. B.J. 421, 431-32 (1959).

[18] See Thompson, Practice in the Supreme Court of Illinois, Chi. B.A. Rec. 97, 102 (1927).

[19] R. Stern, supra note 13, at 373.

[20] Id. at 373-74. See Fed. R. App. P. 34(b).

ILLUSTRATION 10.6

Knapp illustrates this point with the following story:

> I remember a case [in which] George Z. Medalie represented the appellant. The case was on the calendar in the Appellate Division, on the last day of the June term. This was a long time ago when Appellate Division calendars used to be inordinately long and no appellant wanted to appear on the closing day of the June term.
>
> When the case was called, as frequently happened in those days, there were about 25 cases on the calendar. The presiding justice had announced at the outset that the whole calendar was going to be disposed of within the four hours. About the twentieth case down, *People v. Zilch* was called. The presiding justice said: "What kind of case is this?"
>
> The learned district attorney--this was in the days before Thomas E. Dewey, I might hasten to say--was represented by a young man in his office. He got up very brightly and said: "It is a criminal case, your Honor." This obviously was not much news to the court.
>
> Mr. Medalie just sat there and waited until the young man and the presiding justice had gotten themselves completely embroiled, and the young man was offering to telephone his office and find out what the case was really about. Then Mr. Medalie came up, very quietly said, "Your Honor, I represent the defendant" and in a word stated the argument for reversal. He didn't argue; he just stated what the case was about in such a way that all five judges were immediately interested.
>
> The net result was that the judges had a huddle and then agreed to come back at seven-thirty that evening for a special session to hear this particular case. As I subsequently learned from Mr. Medalie, the argument lasted until ten o'clock. There was a unanimous reversal.
>
> Obviously, I don't know what would have happened had this not transpired. But it is clear that by being there at the call of the calendar when his opponent wasn't there, by waiting until the court was irritated with the young representative from the other side, he got the greatest possible receptiveness in the court's mind and was able to get this extraordinary privilege of a special hearing at seven-thirty that

> evening. I wager that most of the day, while they were listening to dull arguments, including mine, they had in the back of their minds: "I wonder what Mr. Medalie is going to be saying tonight." By the time he got there, he had them vitally interested in his problem. Half his battle was won. If you remember Mr. Medalie, you know that if you gave him half the battle, you rarely won the other half.[21]

The appellant (or petitioner) routinely has the right to open the oral argument and to close the argument in rebuttal.[22] The amount of time permitted for oral argument is regulated by court rule or order.

ILLUSTRATION 10.7

In the United States Supreme Court, each side is allowed one-half hour for argument.[23]

Additional time may be granted upon request when it is shown that the case cannot be presented within the time limitation.[24] Time is sometimes, though rarely, extended in advance.[25]

IT IS YOUR OBLIGATION TO KEEP TRACK OF THE TIME AND TO STAY WITHIN THE TIME LIMITS.

One recommended method is to have an assistant keep track of the time.[26] Another method is to use a stop watch that is set at the beginning of the argument to an arbitrary time. Fitzgerald and Hartnett explain:

> The pressure of time on an appellate advocate is so formidable, and so dangerous to [the] case if [counsel] mishandles it, that [counsel] should take special care to assure that time does not get out of hand and that the precautions [counsel] has taken will not be upset unexpectedly.

---

[21] Knapp, supra note 7, at 36-37.

[22] See, e.g., S. Ct. R. 38.2; Fed. R. App. P. 34(c).

[23] S. Ct. R. 38.3.

[24] Id. See also Fed. R. App. P. 34(b).

[25] Jackson, Advocacy Before the Supreme Court: Suggestions for Effective Case Presentations, 37 A.B.A. J. 801, 861 (1951).

[26] Id.

The vital nature of oral argument as an engagement of the minds of the judges and the mind of the appellate advocate in an intellectual contest of a very high order, resembling certain forms of combat, is intensely absorbing to the advocate. [The advocate's] full faculties are involved, his [or her] adrenaline is pumping, and [the advocate] is totally absorbed in his [or her] work for considerable periods of time, if [the advocate] is worth his [or her] salt. This can cause even the best of counsel to forget the time.

But as the heat of an interchange subsides and counsel looks back to his [or her] notes to move on to the next point, [counsel] would be well advised to have built in some simple reminder system to keep . . . posted on the time requirements of [the] argument. Familiarity coming from repeated use, in your rehearsals and in your arguments, will naturally make whatever time notation system you devise become second nature. . . .

It is cumbersome and dangerous to use notations on your lectern notes that do not refer directly to the time on the clock. It is better to have none at all, or else shift to a time notation system that will indicate that you should begin a certain section of the argument when you have a certain number of minutes to go.

The trouble with the clocks that are available in the courtroom (including the face of the timer clock that may be on the lectern) is that they are set to the correct time of day. You have no idea, even if you are the first case, of precisely what minute you will be asked to begin your argument, and you therefore cannot make accurate notations on your lectern notes that correspond to the actual time on the clock.

One method followed by some counsel is to take one's own watch to the lectern--a pocket watch or possibly a stop watch. It is set to begin at an arbitrary time, which is then keyed to the lectern notes.

For example, an ordinary pocket watch could be brought to the lectern and taped to an upper corner with masking tape, out of the way but visible, with the hands set at precisely 12:00 o'clock. As the minute hand moves to 5 minutes past 12:00, 10 minutes past, and so on, it will mark the elapsed time of the argument, which will then relate directly to the time notations in the margin of your lectern notes.[27]

The United States Supreme Court and other courts provide some assistance by use of a warning light system. In the Supreme Court, a white warning light on the lectern goes on five minutes before counsel's time expires, and a red light indicates that counsel's time has expired.[28] Counsel is expected to finish his sentence and "not much more" without obtaining the court's permission.[29]

If the time limit expires before all important points have been covered, a request for a short extension may be made, particularly when questioning from the court has consumed a significant portion of counsel's time.[30]

YOU MAY ASK FOR TIME TO SUMMARIZE IF TIME EXPIRES WHILE YOU ARE ARGUING.

How successful requests for additional time to cover other important points or to summarize will be may depend on a variety of factors: "whether the presiding judge believes that counsel has been unduly harassed or that further argument will be helpful, on how rushed the court is that day to keep up its calendar, and, of course, on the subjective attitude of the judge or judges toward such requests."[31]

YOU SHOULD CONTINUE TO REPLY TO QUESTIONS FROM THE COURT EVEN AFTER TIME HAS EXPIRED.

As Justice Jackson stated, "[s]uccessful advocacy will keep the Justices' minds on the case, and off the clock."[32]

---

[27] Fitzgerald & Hartnett, Effective Oral Argument, 18 Prac. Law. 51 (Apr. 1972).

[28] R. Stern, supra note 13, at 373.

[29] Id. See J. Gaubatz, The Moot Court Book 81 (1979) (similar custom for moot court arguments).

[30] See Hesse, Suggestions for Appellate Practice, 10 Pa. B.A.J. 133, 140 (1939) (suggesting that such leave will be granted almost without exception, but it is "not a license to re-argue points already covered").

[31] R. Stern, supra note 13, at 372.

[32] Jackson, supra note 25, at 861. See also R. Stern, supra note 13, at 372.

Some courts require that the attorneys personally appear in the clerk's office and "sign in" prior to the convening of court. Appleman suggests that in this situation counsel should either arrive in the city where the session is held the preceding evening or relatively early on the morning of the argument so that counsel can eat a leisurely breakfast and skim over his or her notes for last minutes observations.[33]

Stern recommends that all out-of-town attorneys arrive the night before to avoid last minute problems and to obtain a good night's sleep. Stern also recommends an even earlier arrival if the lawyer is unfamiliar with the court so that the lawyer can listen to a few arguments on the day before the case will be argued.[34] Prior to argument counsel should determine the availability of parking, where lunch can be quickly and conveniently obtained, and the location of rest rooms in the courthouse, if counsel is not familiar with these matters.[35]

Other courts require counsel be present at a particular time of the day. For instance, they may require all counsel be present at 10:00 a.m. for cases to be argued that morning. Still other courts require counsel be present a certain number of cases before his case is to be heard.

ILLUSTRATION 10.8

The United States Supreme Court "wants counsel in or close to the courtroom when the second preceding argument on that day begins, and in the courtroom when the preceding argument begins."[36]

THE BEST SOURCE OF INFORMAL ADVICE IS FROM THE CLERK'S OFFICE AND FROM OTHER LAWYERS WHO HAVE APPEARED BEFORE THAT PARTICULAR COURT.

In the federal courts of appeals and other appellate courts, the judges may be sitting in rotation. In some instances, one or more judges may be absent because of illness or other reasons. Attorneys should determine who will be hearing the argument because "an alert appellate attorney always bears in mind the

[33] J. Appleman, Successful Appellate Techniques 1003 (1953).

[34] R. Stern, *supra* note 13, at 375.

[35] *Id.* at 376.

[36] *Id.* at 375.

idiosyncrasies and backgrounds of the justices to whom his [or her] remarks will be addressed."[37]

Some courts will identify the names of the judges who will hear the oral argument a few days in advance; other courts inform the attorneys through the clerk's office on the morning of the oral argument. The names of the judges may also appear in front of the bench or on the rostrum.[38]

Section 10C. Preparation Before Oral Argument

PREPARATION FOR AN ORAL ARGUMENT IS VITAL TO A SUCCESSFUL ARGUMENT.

Preparation principally involves (1) the selection and arrangement of the points to be argued and (2) rehearsal for the argument. Subsumed in this process is the preparation of notes, visual aids, and other matters of detail.

One of the principal concerns will be the content of the argument. In other words, what points will be raised and how will they be arranged? The most frequent advice is that counsel for the appellant should focus on the central point of law on which a reversal is most likely. Most commentators feel that dealing with several miscellaneous points leaves an unfavorable impression on the court. In this regard, consider the following comments, which are illustrative of this widely held view:

> In [counsel's] argument of questions of law, it is suggested that in general the most strategic procedure for counsel to follow is to select the one big central point of law on which he [or she] hopes to obtain a reversal, to concentrate on that and so to arrange the various phases of his argument that this point will be fully and clearly understood in every aspect. Peppering away with a lot of miscellaneous points of more or less importance is apt to leave the court without any very definite impression that the judgment or order should be reversed. If the forces are marshalled so as to deliver one good, solid blow, the appellant's chances are greatly enhanced. Naturally, the selection of this point requires considerable skill and judgment. Furthermore, it is not a rule of universal application, as some cases are of such a character as to make it possible and

---

[37] J. Appleman, supra note 33, at 1003.

[38] R. Stern, supra note 13, at 374-75.

advisable to argue two or more points with almost equal force. In other cases, however, the points are of a more or less contradictory character so that it is absolutely indispensable to decide on one and hammer away at that, leaving the rest to be studied by the members of the court when they read appellant's brief.[39]

THE CRITICAL ASPECT OF SELECTING THE POINTS TO BE ARGUED IS AN EVALUATION OF WHAT POINTS WILL BE DISPOSITIVE OF THE ACTION.

In an oral argument, counsel should "go for the jugular vein."[40] Some points will ordinarily have to be left to be in the brief. They will not be waived if they are not included in the oral argument.[41]

ILLUSTRATION 10.9

Davis illustrates the value of focusing on the dispositive "cardinal point" by telling of a lawyer who customarily addressed "a single point, often speaking for not more than twenty minutes but with compelling force. When [the lawyer] had concluded, it was difficult for his adversary to persuade the court that there was anything else worthy to be considered."[42] Note that only points that have been briefed should be argued and that counsel should stay within the record.[43]

Counsel prepare for oral argument in a variety of ways. Some prepare from the brief. Others dictate the argument or write an outline with headings and subheadings. Some write down a few catch-words or phrases in a sketchy fashion.[44]

It has been suggested that counsel should outline the points of the argument even if the outline is not consulted in the

[39] Medina, The Oral Argument on Appeal, 20 A.B.A. J. 139, 140 (1934).

[40] Davis, supra note 2, at 897.

[41] See Qua, Suggestions About Briefs and Arguments, 32 Mass. L.Q. 16, 22 (1947).

[42] Davis, supra note 2, at 897.

[43] Pope, Argument on Appeal, 14 Prac. Law. 33, 44 (Dec. 1968).

[44] See C. Walter, supra note 5, at 173 (reviewing how counsel prepare for oral argument and suggesting it depends on personal idiosyncrasies). See also R. Stern, supra note 13, at 383-98 (suggestions incorporating responses to a questionnaire sent to approximately one hundred experienced appellate advocates).

argument because observing the points on paper may suggest something that might otherwise remain dormant. Such an outline aids in establishing sequences and serves as a useful way of recording cross-references to the record and the briefs. These cross-references may be needed during argument because, as you will see, one of the most effective rebuttals is a quick reference to the record.[45] In conjunction with preparing an outline for oral argument, it is widely recommended that the record be re-read and mastered.[46]

In addition to knowing the record, another step in preparation is reading or re-reading every case cited by either advocate. Searles suggests that familiarity with the facts and principles embodied in each case not only will aid an advocate in argument, but will also impress the court. By mastering the opponent's cases, counsel will be able to anticipate his arguments and questions from the court and will be ready to meet them.[47] As part of this preparation, the cases should be brought up to date by means of *Shepard's Citations* and, if possible, a computer search on WESTLAW or LEXIS.[48]

After the basic content and emphasis of the oral argument has been determined, some form of oral preparation is widely recommended.[49] Justice Jackson has suggested that counsel argue the case aloud to himself or herself and other persons, such as an associate or a secretary.[50]

ORAL PREPARATION WILL ASSIST YOU IN CLARIFYING YOUR THOUGHTS AND WILL HELP YOU TEST THE EFFECTIVENESS OF DIFFERENT ARRANGEMENTS.

---

[45] See Haight, The Advocate in Courts of Review, 1940 Wis. L. Rev. 327, 331.

[46] See, e.g., id. at 300 ("one must know the case to argue it well"); C. Walter, supra note 5, at 164 (record must be known sufficiently well so counsel will be able to turn readily to each important fact if the occasion arises); D. Karlan & C. Joiner, Trials and Appeals 528 (1971) (preparation for oral argument begins with a thorough understanding of all of the facts, not only the major ones, but all facts having any bearing upon the issues).

[47] J. Searles, Advocacy in the Moot Court Program 13-14 (3d ed. 1971).

[48] See R. Stern, supra note 13, at 383.

[49] See Medina, supra note 39, at 140 (oral statement "helps to whip the case into shape in a way that no amount of silent study will do").

[50] Jackson, supra note 25, at 861.

Medina points out that it is particularly useful practicing stating the facts of the case to someone without legal training: "If one can describe a complicated set of facts in such a clear and simple fashion as to make them intelligible to a layman, they will be even more intelligible and plain [for] an appellate [court]."[51]

Tape recording and videotaping are other possibilities for oral preparation. Rehearing an argument on audio tape helps an attorney "recognize weaknesses, awkward phrases, hesitations, excess wordiness, and other areas needing improvement."[52] Furthermore, videotape allows a lawyer to spot distracting mannerisms.

Thus, although the specific methods may vary according to the individual involved, both written and oral preparation are widely recognized as essential prerequisites for effective appellate oral argument.

DO NOT MEMORIZE YOUR ARGUMENT.

Memorizing your argument makes the final argument stale and appear to be lacking in sincerity. Stern suggests it is "dangerous" because questioning or other interruptions by the court "may throw the memorizer off his [or her] stride" and make it difficult . . . to return or reorganize his [or her] arrangement.[53]

ALTHOUGH MANY LAWYERS WRITE OUT THE PLANNED ORAL ARGUMENT, SUCH AN EFFORT SHOULD NOT BE DONE FOR THE PURPOSE OF READING THE TEXT AT THE ORAL ARGUMENT.

Section 10D. Appellant's Argument

AN ATTORNEY APPEARING IN AN APPELLATE COURT SHOULD BE AWARE OF TRADITIONAL CUSTOMS.

---

[51] Medina, supra note 39, at 140.

[52] Fitzgerald & Hartnett, supra note 27, at 60.

[53] R. Stern, supra note 13, at 388. See also id. at 389 (avoid reading a prepared oral argument).

When the judges enter the courtroom, everyone should rise and wait to be invited to be seated.[54] Traditionally, appellant's counsel sits to counsel's own left side of the counsel table and respondent's counsel sits to the right.[55] Furthermore, when a judge speaks to an attorney who is seated, the attorney should rise to answer the court.

A judge should never be addressed as "you."[56] Instead, refer to the judge as "Your Honor."[57] The traditional method of addressing the court is, "May the court please," not "If the court please."[58]

As noted in section B of this chapter, the appellant (or petitioner), under normal circumstances, has the right to open the oral argument and to close it in rebuttal.

THE APPELLANT OPENS THE ORAL ARGUMENT BY ADDRESSING THE BENCH FORMALLY ("May it please the court"). YOU SHOULD THEN INTRODUCE YOURSELF ("My name is Walter Smith"). YOU SHOULD THEN IDENTIFY THE NATURE OF THE CASE, HOW IT GOT TO THE APPELLATE COURT, WHOM YOU REPRESENT, WHAT YOU WANT, AND, IN A SENTENCE, WHY.

ILLUSTRATION 10.10

> This is a patent case. It is here on appeal from the District Court for the Eastern District of Wisconsin. I represent the Appellant, who was the plaintiff below. The patent relates to a mouse trap. The District Court found it void for lack of invention over the prior art, and entered a decree dismissing the plaintiff's bill of complaint for want of enquiry. We here seek a reversal of that decree because the device is not anticipated and the defendants failed to show lack of invention by proof adequate to overcome the presumption of validity.[59]

---

[54] See Hinshaw, Court Room Decorum, 40 Ill. B.J. 85, 85 (1951).

[55] Lasher, Oral Argument for Fun and Profit, 48 Cal. B.J. 398, 402 (1973).

[56] Hinshaw, supra note 54, at 85.

[57] J. Searles, supra note 47, at 17.

[58] Hinshaw, supra note 54, at 85.

[59] Haight, supra note 45, at 332.

This information should then be followed by a brief statement of the points that will be orally argued and the points that will be left to the brief.

ILLUSTRATION 10.11

Consider the following opening, which effectively states the points to be argued as follows:

> May it please the court. I am John Jones from Pear Valley. This is a boundary case [and I represent the defendant]. It was tried before a jury and the court gave judgment for the plaintiff on the verdict. We are before this court on five points, but we shall discuss only three of them. We shall leave the others to the briefs. Our first point is that the surveyor of the tract in question went to the thread of the stream instead of the cut bank. Our second point is that the verdict is incomplete. Our third point is that one of the jurors received outside information about the boundary line in question. We shall show that the case should be remanded.[60]

Such an opening orients the court and can help to capture the court's interest. It also helps prevent later interruptions caused by a mystery style of development of the argument.[61]

AFTER A BRIEF OPENING, YOU SHOULD REQUEST TIME FOR REBUTTAL IF YOU WANT IT.

Searles suggests that this request be made in the following manner: "[A]t this time counsel wishes to reserve five minutes for rebuttal."[62] Counsel should not proceed with argument until this request to reserve time is acknowledged by the court by a nod of the head or oral permission.[63]

THE TIME RESERVED IS DEDUCTED FROM THE TIME YOU ARE INITIALLY ALLOWED TO SPEAK.

---

[60] Pope, supra note 43, at 39-40.

[61] See id. at 39.

[62] Searles, supra note 47, at 17.

[63] Id.

Failure to reserve rebuttal at the outset is likely to mean that no rebuttal will be permitted.

SUBSTANTIVE POINTS SHOULD NOT BE SAVED FOR REBUTTAL.

As discussed in section G below, you should not use the rebuttal to introduce entirely new points of substance.[64]

THE APPELLANT IS ORDINARILY EXPECTED TO STATE THE FACTS OF THE CASE.

The appellant is ordinarily expected to state the facts of the case at the beginning of the argument. This statement should present the "case fairly and completely."[65] It has been suggested that the facts should be stated in less detail than in the briefs, focusing only on the most prominent.[66] Nevertheless, counsel must not leave gaps that make the judges wonder whether something essential has been omitted.[67] Generally, a chronological presentation avoids this problem.[68]

In deciding which facts to present, counsel should "try to anticipate the thoughts and questions that might occur to the judges as they listen to the recital of facts."[69] Stern points out that straining to mention irrelevant facts in an attempt to arouse the court's sympathy is more likely to produce an adverse reaction.[70]Furthermore, as noted previously, counsel must be careful to stay within the record.[71]

---

[64]See, e.g., S. Ct. R. 38.5.

[65]Id.

[66]Carter, Preparation and Presentation of Cases in Courts of Review, 12 Ill. L. Rev. 147, 156 (1917).

[67]Medina, supra note 39, at 140.

[68]See Carter, supra note 66, at 156. See also R. Stern, supra note 13, at 415 (usually a chronological presentation is more clearly understood, but a topical presentation in some instances may take less time and may be more persuasive).

[69]Id. at 140.

[70]R. Stern, supra note 13, at 416.

[71]Steinheimer, supra note 6, at 21.

Recent factual developments outside the record that could conceivably affect the outcome of the case, however, should be brought to the court's attention early in the presentation.[72]

Adverse facts should be "met squarely" without any evasion or lengthy explanations of excuses.[73]

It is particularly important not to intersperse parenthetical or diversionary arguments between narrative factual accounts.[74]

ILLUSTRATION 10.12

Norvell gives the following example of the confusing nature of a parenthetical argument intermixed with the statement of facts:

> Now, in the trial court, in order to prove that her husband was acting within the scope of his employment, we put Mrs. Jones on the stand. She testified she prepared a meal for her husband at 10:30 p.m. and he immediately left thereafter for the plant. Now let me say here that in the trial court the other side cited a lot of out of state cases which they said showed, as a matter of law, this man couldn't have been within the scope of his employment. They've abandoned that now, they know that isn't any good, but they've gotten hold of a Commission of Appeals case which they found later, and that's what they'll talk about here. Mrs. Jones said she handed her husband his lunch, etc.[75]

With respect to speaking style, commentators have made numerous useful suggestions. It has long been recognized that making an oral argument is different from making a public address.

THE USE OF A CONVERSATIONAL TONE AND A LOW PITCH OF VOICE ARE GENERALLY THOUGHT TO BE BETTER SUITED TO ADVANCING REASONS THAN A LOUDER AND MORE RAPID DELIVERY.

---

[72] R. Stern & E. Gressman, Supreme Court Practice 760 (5th ed. 1978) (late-breaking developments should be discussed early even if it means that the case becomes moot or is otherwise lost).

[73] Medina, supra note 39, at 140-41 ("Nothing can ruin an oral argument so completely as the slightest tendency toward evasion, concealment, straddling or running away from the facts").

[74] Norvell, The Case on Appeal, 1 So. Tex. L.J. 229, 238 (1954).

[75] Id.

Commentators suggest that you use a conversational tone and a low-pitch voice in making your argument.[76] Just as an overly aggressive style should be avoided, so should an obsequious style be avoided.[77] The focus should be on using a clear and distinct voice with a certain amount of rise and fall by way of contrast and emphasis.[78] How does an advocate provide proper contrast and emphasis? Consider the following suggestions:

> [E]mphasis is a kind of artifice; but the spoken word without emphasis would be as ineffective--and often as unintelligible--as the written word without punctuation or capitalization. A lawyer worthy of the name cannot afford to use the same tone for "This case comes here on appeal from a decree of the District Court for the Eastern District" as for "This is a gross and shocking fraud which was perpetrated by these respondents."
>
> The matter of proper emphasis can be broken down into four basic admonitions:
>
> (I) Avoid a monotone. Perhaps the best way to attempt to reproduce a monotone in print is to omit punctuation:
>
> > At this point the shipper called on the railroad to deliver livestock directly to its siding but the railroad refused to do so contending that by reason of its contract with the stockyards it was bound not to deliver such competitive traffic over the track in question without the payment of yardage charges which yardage charges it was no longer willing to absorb and thereupon the shipper instituted its complaint against the railroad before the Commission.
>
> That statement is just as difficult to follow by ear as by eye.
>
> (II) Avoid the ministerial cadence. Here the voice goes up and down but without emphasis on the proper words:

---

[76] See, e.g., W. Stawn, Nebraska Supreme Court Practice and Forms 317-18 (1900); Medina, supra note 39, at 139 (shouting creates an atmosphere of discomfort for the hearers and distracts the judges).

[77] M. Josephson, Handbook of Appellate Advocacy 173 (1967).

[78] Medina, supra note 39, at 139-40.

court,
this that
to if
say these
we practices
so about
And which
we

remain
to in
permitted effect,
are the
complained Act
have has been

dead letter.
a
made
and
nullified

(III) Avoid mumbling.

This-ah-case, turns on the-ah-validity of the-ah-Gadget Restriction Act of-ah-1948. We--that is, the petitioners--ah-contended-ah-that the measure-ah-clearly transcends-ah-the powers vested in the-ah-Congress.

(IV) Use the pause. The only way that an oral statement can be punctuated is by a pause--a short one for commas (which, after all, are simply signals for a breath), a longer one at the end of sentences, and a still longer one when you reach the end of a paragraph. If more emphasis is desired, as to mark the taking up of an entirely new point, underscore the pause and make it longer by taking a sip of water.

The pause is also helpful as a device to regain the court's attention. Sometimes the court's lack of interest is the fault of the case, more often it is the fault of the lawyer, and sometimes for no good reason the justices just aren't paying attention. They are whispering and passing notes, and reading the record. Your main proposition is coming up. How are you going to make certain that it will have their full attention? Very simple, just use the public speaker's oldest trick--pause. The sudden silence makes every one look up; every member of the court eyes the speaker expectantly. It's an ancient dodge, but still one of the most effective.[79]

Closely connected with speaking style are the physical aspects of delivery of an oral argument.

STAY PHYSICALLY CLOSE TO THE ROSTRUM.

In general, counsel should stay physically close to the rostrum. Striding back and forth across the courtroom tends to distract judges and creates the appearance of confusion.[80]

AVOID DISTRACTING MANNERISMS AND AFFECTATIONS.

Counsel should avoid other distracting mannerisms and affectations.[81]

THE BEST IMPRESSIONS ARE MADE WHEN COUNSEL LOOKS THE JUDGES IN THE EYE DURING THE PRESENTATION AND ENGAGES IN AN ORAL DISCUSSION.

Josephson describes this visual interaction as creating a "personal link" with the judges.[82] Reading, of course, similarly prevents counsel from maintaining eye contact with the judges.[83] Maintaining eye contact has the further advantage of allowing counsel to detect quickly when a particular judge is failing to grasp counsel's argument or "when the speed of presentation has

---

[79] F. Wiener, Oral Advocacy, 62 Harv. L. Rev. 56, 61-63 (1948).

[80] See Freedman, On Advocacy, 1 Vill. L. Rev. 290, 303 (1956).

[81] See, e.g., M. Josephson, supra note 77, at 172 (pounding on the lectern, slouching, pacing, and pointing at the judges should be avoided); J. Searles, supra note 47, at 21 (avoid rustling papers, clicking pens, toying with the microphone, and constant "talking" with the hands; however, a few points can be aided and emphasized by sophisticated gesture); Rossman, Appellate Court Advocacy: The Importance of Oral Argument, 45 A.B.A. J. 675, 675 (1959) (avoid leaning heavily on the lectern and thrusting "their hands into their pockets and assum[ing] a posture which is more becoming to a different kind of bar").

[82] M. Josephson, supra note 77, at 172.

[83] Rall, supra note 16, at 121 (also noting that apart from failing to look the court in the eye, the reader is speaking a written language, not a spoken language).

been too great and a pause for relaxation or a dropping of the tone is indicated."[84]

Searles cautions that you should avoid glancing quickly over the courtroom. Never glance over your shoulders. Furthermore, looking at the court should not become a stare. Instead, it is suggested that counsel look at each justice individually, which assists in maintaining the attention of the entire court.[85]

THE WELL-ESTABLISHED "RULES" OF PROFESSIONAL ETIQUETTE SHOULD BE OBSERVED DURING AN ORAL ARGUMENT.

Opposing counsel should be treated with the appearance of respect, even if you dislike the opposing counsel or feel that the opposing counsel has acted unfairly during the trial below. Opposing counsel should not be referred to as "my opponent." Instead, use "counsel for the appellant," counsel's name ("Mr. Smith"), "counsel for the defendant," "opposing counsel," or the like.[86]

It is inappropriate to grimace or smile derisively during opposing counsel's argument.[87] Harsh exchanges and controversies between counsel impose on the appellate court "the wholly unnecessary burden and annoyance of preserving order and maintaining the decorum of its proceedings."[88] In sum, personalities should be avoided because they detract the court from the issues at hand.[89]

Care should be taken to avoid unfair or harsh criticism of a lower court. Such attacks often offend an appellate court.[90] Searles points out that "[r]espect for the judiciary must always be uppermost in the advocate's mind [and that] [a]ny degradation is

---

[84] Carson, Conduct of the Appeal--A Lawyer's View, in American Law Institute, Appeals 94 (1957).

[85] J. Searles, supra note 47, at 19.

[86] See Board of Student Advisors of Harvard Law School, Introduction to Advocacy 142 (4th ed. 1985).

[87] J. Searles, supra note 47, at 20.

[88] Davis, supra note 2, at 898.

[89] Id.

[90] Id.

certainly unbecoming to an officer of the [c]ourt."[91] Justice Jackson suggested that counsel be both respectful of the court as well as self-respectful: neither flatter the justices nor disparage yourself.[92] Attacks on the opposing party may also arouse a sympathy for the person attacked.[93]

It has already been noted that counsel should not read the argument to the court. Nonetheless, counsel should use some *unobtrusive* form of notes. One helpful form is an outline of the major points, highlighted with key words. The notes can be annotated for purposes of responding to questioning. Stern explains the headings and catchwords can be derived from a written draft of the oral argument.[94] Other commentators suggest counsel rely on notes without writing a draft of the argument in order to preserve the spontaneity of the argument.[95]

In any event, the notes should be functional. The notes should be legible so that counsel can easily see them on the rostrum at a glance and they should be flexible. Levy suggests that the outline be typed double-spaced on a series of large index cards, using only one side of each card. If possible, each card should be self-contained, with only one point and its subpoints so that counsel does not have to look for his place on a page.[96] Use of large "orator" type facilitates the use of the notes.

Levy points out that the index cards can be used in a different way:

> [I]f you have no doubts of your ability to think and speak on your feet, the "key-point" method of oral argument is generally the best. The method is extremely simple. It consists of writing on one side of separate index cards the three or four, or possibly five or six, aspects of the matter that you wish to stress before the appellate court. Do not write the crucial points themselves, but some key word or phrase which will inevitably and quickly bring the specific point to mind. Spread these cards on the podium or desk which will be provided for you, explore each key point, turn over its card and put it in a pile. Organize them so that you will have the

---

[91] J. Searles, supra note 47, at 19.

[92] Jackson, supra note 25, at 802.

[93] Davis, supra note 2, at 898.

[94] R. Stern, supra note 13, at 390-91.

[95] See, e.g., F. Wiener, Briefing and Arguing Federal Appeals 283 (1967).

[96] H. Levy, How to Handle an Appeal 206 (2d ed. 1982).

outline of a running legal argument. In this fashion, you will be able to touch upon every key point which you wish to make.

The key-point method also permits flexibility. Nothing distracts a court more than to evade or postpone answers to its questions. If you work from a prepared outline, the inevitable tendency is to say that you will come to that point in a few minutes. But the judge wants the answer, not a promise. The court is not interested in the order or content of what you think would be a good argument, but in those aspects that are troubling it. By not tying yourself down to any preconceived organizational structure of your argument, you will be much freer to answer questions as they are asked, not worrying about the thread of your argument, knowing that you will not omit any major points since you have your index cards to remind you of those points. Thus, using key points is a more comfortable method of argument. It may make you a little apprehensive before you begin, but much more confident once you start to speak.[97]

Commentators emphasize that a critical element in the success of an oral argument is flexibility. Wiener states

> [that] [c]ounsel must . . . be sufficiently flexible to vary his argument on the basis of the reception it receives. If [counsel] has planned to spend ten minutes on Proposition A, and finds that [this] initial statement thereof gets nods of approval from the bench, [counsel] need not--indeed, [counsel] should not--proceed to elaborate that proposition further. If [counsel's] statement of the second principle evokes a similar attitude of assent, [counsel] should once more move on. But if the court does not react favorably, [counsel] should elaborate upon the bare statement. And if [counsel] encounters doubts or active opposition, [counsel] may have to expand and detail his [or her] argument on a particular proposition far beyond what [counsel] had originally planned.
>
> Sometimes these alternatives can be planned far in advance by setting up the notes on each point in three parts: the basic proposition, its elaboration, and its further elaboration. Then, depending on the

---

[97] Id. at 207-08.

reaction from the court, the lawyer can use one, two, or all three portions.[98]

Sometimes counsel's presentation will be assisted by the use of visual aids. But caution is urged by a number of commentators.[99]

Typical visual aids include enlarged maps, charts, and photographs. They should be used when the matter illustrated is essential to the controversy. Otherwise, they are prone to be distracting and ineffective.[100] Fitzgerald and Hartnett suggest four worthwhile rules to follow in using charts:

> [1] Use only one chart and have it blown up large enough that even the judge who has left his [or her] glasses at home that day can easily see and read everything on it.
>
> [2] Don't give each judge a copy of the chart. Since you are going to explain it, they need to be looking at the chart you are explaining, not some small copy handed out.
>
> [3] Use a pointer and stand to the side so that each judge will be able to see what you are pointing out on the chart.
>
> [4] When you finish explaining your point, either cover or somehow remove the chart so that it does not continue to stand beside you as a distraction from the other arguments that you make after you finish with the chart.[101]

In using a visual aid, counsel should find out from the marshal or bailiff where it can be placed during the argument.[102]

---

[98]Wiener, supra note 79, at 75.

[99]See, e.g., Medina, supra note 39, at 141 ("Some lawyers will come into an appellate court with several assistants carrying models and a pile of books and these will be spread out on a counsel table with what the lawyer may regard as great dramatic effect [but] [u]sually the effect is just opposite to the one desired").

[100]See Rall, supra note 16, at 126 (helpful when one or two enlarged exhibits will graphically illustrate the entire argument).

[101]Fitzgerald & Hartnett, supra note 27, at 63.

[102]Rall, supra note 16, at 587.

AVOID READING LONG EXCERPTS FROM CASES IN AN ORAL ARGUMENT.

It has long been recognized that reading long excerpts from cases (like reading the argument itself) should be avoided in an oral argument.[103] Most commentators suggest that it is better to discuss as few cases as possible, describing those discussed without quotations.

FOCUS THE ORAL PRESENTATION ON PROPOSITIONS OF LAW THAT YOU WANT THE COURT TO APPLY.

In general, the oral presentation should focus on propositions of law that you want the court to apply. When it is appropriate, counsel may indicate that the propositions are supported by cases cited in the briefs. In such instances, counsel should be thoroughly familiar with the cases so that counsel could give an explanation of them in response to questioning by the court.[104]

When the meaning or application of precise words of a statute, regulation, contract, specific testimony, or other document are at issue, however, the court will want the language quoted, preferably from the record, and not paraphrased.[105]

Upon reaching the end of the planned argument, counsel customarily closes with a brief conclusion. To the extent that the points of an argument are recapitulated at its close, it should be done with the fewest possible words so that it does not appear that you are re-arguing the points again. It is widely thought that re-arguing the points nearly always weakens the argument already made.[106] You should try to end the argument on a positive note.[107]

---

[103] See, e.g., W. Stawn, supra note 76, at 319.

[104] Hesse, supra note 30, at 140-41.

[105] R. Stern & E. Gressman, supra note 72, at 767-68 (counsel should refer to the page of the brief or record so that the court may read along with counsel).

[106] W. Stawn, supra note 76, at 320.

[107] Rossman, supra note 81, at 675-76. See M. Josephson, supra note 77, at 170-71.

IN GENERAL, A POSITIVE ENDING CAN BE CREATED BY REPEATING THE THESIS STATEMENT OF THE ARGUMENT AND ASKING THE COURT TO GRANT THE RELIEF REQUESTED.

Similarly, counsel should try not to end the argument in an atmosphere of disappointment caused by counsel's failure to budget his or her time.[108] In that situation, counsel should attempt to dispel the possible disappointment by bringing the uncovered issues to the court's attention by summarizing them quickly and inviting the court's attention to their discussion in the brief before closing.[109] The final words in closing customarily are: "Thank you, your honors."[110]

Section 10E. Questions From the Court

It is reasonable to expect that the court will ask questions of counsel during the oral argument. The extent of the questioning, however, varies with the tribunal. The United States Supreme Court, for example, is given to questioning counsel more than most tribunals.[111] Davis maintains that counsel should "[r]ejoice when the [c]ourt asks questions."[112] First, it assures counsel "that the court is not comatose" and that at least a "vestigial interest" has been awakened. Second, it affords counsel the opportunity "to penetrate the mind of the court."[113]

One commentator explains this point as follows:

> Some lawyers are inclined to regard questions from the bench as a necessary evil which interferes with their orderly plan of oral presentation. If counsel has such an attitude, the court's questions are usually ineffectively answered, if at all. I say you should be encouraged by questions. They indicate the court is interested and is following your argument. Questions are a guide to the court's initial reaction to the case

---

[108] Rossman, supra note 81, at 676.

[109] See M. Josephson, supra note 77, at 170.

[110] J. Gaubatz, supra note 29, at 81.

[111] Jackson, supra note 25, at 862.

[112] Davis, supra note 2, at 897.

[113] Id.

and point out the particular problems which seem to be troubling the court. With questions as indicators, the effective appellate lawyer will be able to adjust his [or her] presentation to give greater force and emphasis to matters in which the court seems most interested and about which it seems to be troubled.

The most important admonition with regard to questions from the bench is not to postpone answering the question. The psychological time to answer is now. It is the time when the court's interest in that particular point is keenest and the time when the court will probably be most receptive to an intelligent attempt to satisfy its curiosity. Delay in answering risks loss of the inquiring judge's attention which may be diverted to something far afield or concentrated on another point by the time the answer is belatedly given. Delay in answering risks loss of the interrogating judge's attention in subsequent parts of your argument while he [or she] sits and ponders the problem posed by his [or her] question which you have not answered. Delay in answering risks the possibility that the judges will gain the impression that it is futile to seek your help in informing them on matters which are troubling them and will sit back throughout the balance of your argument without attempting to elicit further information from you by way of questions no matter how puzzled they may be. Delay in answering also risks the possibility that you will forget about the question at a later stage of the argument and will leave it unanswered. The judges are then left to speculate whether the failure to answer was the result of lack of a satisfactory answer or something else.[114]

COUNSEL SHOULD ANSWER THE COURT'S QUESTIONS IN A DIRECT AND UNEQUIVOCAL MANNER.

If counsel's answer is timid and inconclusive, the court may feel that counsel is not convinced of the point himself.[115] If the question admits of a "yes" or "no" answer, counsel should give the answer, followed by the reasons.[116] A categorical answer should

[114]Steinheimer, supra note 6, at 22.

[115]Medina, supra note 39, at 143.

[116]Hesse, supra note 30, at 140.

be accompanied with a respectful form of address: "Yes, your honor" or "No, your honor."[117]

YOU SHOULD NOT BECOME CONCERNED IF THE COURT ASKS QUESTIONS THAT SEEM UNFAVORABLE TO YOUR POSITION.

Rombauer explains that the unfavorable character of the questions does not necessarily signal a judge's view:

> [Q]uestions fall into three general categories--neutral, favorable, and unfavorable. Neutral questions are genuinely directed toward seeking information or clarification. A judge persuaded as to the correctness of your position may ask favorable questions that put your view in the best light. A judge already persuaded to your viewpoint may also ask unfavorable questions, however, in order: (1) to permit you to suggest favorable resolution of points that are bothering him or her, or (2) to permit you to suggest favorable resolution of points that he or she knows are bothering a judge who is neutral or opposed to your position. Finally, a judge already persuaded as to the invalidity of your position may ask unfavorable questions that reveal the weaknesses of your position.[118]

Some members of the judiciary unfortunately abuse their position by constantly asking questions of an insincere, humiliating, offensive, or irrelevant nature. The universal advice from the commentators for the advocate in such circumstances is clear: whatever the nature of the questions or the attitude of the judge, counsel should attempt to retain his poise and composure; an oral argument is no place to lose one's temper or to become disrespectful or impertinent.[119]

If a question is irrelevant, counsel should diplomatically show how it is irrelevant. If the facts assumed in the question are contrary to the record, counsel should explain to the court why they are.[120]

---

[117] E. Re, Brief Writing and Oral Argument 198 (4th ed. 1974).

[118] M. Rombauer, Legal Problem Solving: Analysis, Research and Writing 342 (4th ed. 1983).

[119] See, e.g., Medina, supra note 39, at 143.

[120] Goldberg, The Art of Oral Argument on Appeal, 41 Cal. St. B.J. 109, 124 (1966).

RETAINING ONE'S POISE AND COMPOSURE AND BEING RESPECTFUL DOES NOT MEAN THAT COUNSEL MUST GIVE EXCESSIVE DEFERENCE TO THE COURT.

Counsel should not give excessive deference to the court. In particular, "there is no deference due the court which requires [counsel] to forebear from setting the judges straight."[121] On the other hand, if counsel does not know the answer, counsel should tell the court so without attempts at bluffing or evasion. If counsel makes a mistake in answering a question, the best advice is to admit the mistake and to restate the answer.[122]

If a question is not understood, counsel should ask for clarification.[123] Care should be taken in asking other types of questions of the judges.[124]

WHEN A JUDGE ASKS A QUESTION, YOU SHOULD IMMEDIATELY STOP, EVEN IF THE JUDGE IS INTERRUPTING YOU IN THE MIDDLE OF A SENTENCE.

When you answer a question, it has been suggested that you should not rush to answer. A pause before answering conveys the impression that you are giving serious thought to the question even though the answer immediately comes to mind.[125] A pause is also useful for another reason. It tends to eliminate an over-enthusiastic answering of questions.

Counsel should avoid developing a "sparring context between the court and counsel, in which the main points of the argument are lost in the verbal fireworks."[126] It has also been suggested that counsel should prepare for anticipated questioning by using

---

[121] Id.

[122] M. Rombauer, supra note 118, at 342.

[123] Lasher, supra note 55, at 403.

[124] See, e.g., Proctor, Briefs and Argument on Appeal, 48 Mass. L.Q. 278, 290 (1963) (inappropriate to ask whether you have satisfactorily answered a judge's question).

[125] J. Searles, supra note 47, at 20.

[126] Goldberg, supra note 120, at 134.

brackets or other marks to identify material in the argument that can be discarded if necessary.[127]

Section 10F. Appellee's Answering Argument

If the appellant has clearly and accurately stated the facts, the appellee (respondent) should not repeat all the facts again.[128] On the other hand, some restatement of the facts may be necessary so that they fit into appellee's view of the proceeding. Llewellyn states that such a re-characterization is essential when counsel faces an intelligent opponent.[129] This re-characterization, however, must be done tactfully. Llewellyn, for example, suggests:

> If you start to say, "The facts are different," or "These are the facts," they'll go to sleep on you, or get mad at you. But if on the other hand you say, "There is one point that I don't think [counsel for the appellant] has developed quite as fully as [counsel] might," and pick up some fact or other that you can build on, by the time you get done with that, you can swing into the recital of the whole.[130]

When the appellant's counsel has misstated the facts, the best approach is not to charge opposing counsel with trying to mislead the court. Instead, counsel should state that because of some misunderstanding the facts have become a little confused.[131] Such a misstatement likewise provides an opportunity to re-characterize the facts.

It is often stated that the appellee should not simply attempt to meet the appellant's argument.[132] Counsel for the appellee should make clear why the appellee won in the court below or why the appellant was unsuccessful.[133]

---

[127] R. Stern, supra note 13, at 430.

[128] Medina, supra note 39, at 142 (long, repetitious rehashing of the facts bores the court).

[129] Llewellyn, A Lecture on Appellate Advocacy, 29 Chi. L. Rev. 628, 639 (1962) (appellee needs to state a positive case, including the facts).

[130] Id.

[131] Medina, supra note 39, at 143 (an appropriate reference to the record bolsters counsel's position).

[132] See, e.g., id. at 142 (nothing could be a more serious mistake than to merely respond to the appellant's argument, which may be skillfully designed to lead opposing counsel "off into the woods").

[133] J. Appleman, supra note 33, at 1039.

THE APPELLEE SHOULD SEIZE UPON THE CENTRAL FEATURE OF THE CASE AND SHOULD DISPEL THE IMPRESSION LEFT BY THE ADVERSARY.

It is also often suggested that the counsel for the appellee should open the argument with force to dispel the appellant's contentions before the court's reaction has crystallized in favor of finding error.[134] With respect to the substance of an appellee's argument, counsel must decide what should be emphasized.

Stern points out that in a number of ways counsel for the appellee "has it a lot easier." Stern explains as follows:

> [The appellee] need not spend as much time stating the issues or the facts, but need only correct or improve upon what appellant has said. [The appellee] can also usually concentrate on the legal points covered in the appellant's oral argument, as well as upon the reactions of the judges. If [counsel] can win on any of a number of alternative grounds, [counsel] should, of course, emphasize his [or her] strongest, irrespective of the points which appellant has stressed, for this would be adhering, from his [or her] point of view, to the principle that counsel should argue the issues which "are likely to be dispositive."[135]

As part of appellee's preparation, it has been suggested that counsel for the appellee should take notes indicating exactly what matters of fact or principles of law have been erroneously asserted or omitted.[136] Likewise, counsel may want to answer a question that the court has asked the appellant, but was either not answered or was answered unsatisfactorily.[137]

Section 10G. Appellant's Rebuttal

As noted previously, the appellant must reserve time for rebuttal during the initial presentation if the appellant wants to

---

[134] Id. (open with a sharp and direct disagreement with a major assumption or conclusion of the opposing counsel). See also Wiener, supra note 79, at 63 (seize upon the central feature and dispel the impression left by your adversary).

[135] R. Stern, supra note 13, at 409.

[136] See E. Re, supra note 117, at 201.

[137] Id. at 202.

make a rebuttal. The rebuttal period may give the appellant the opportunity to supply important and definite corrections.[138]

IN THE REBUTTAL, FOCUS ON THE WEAKEST LINK IN THE APPELLEE'S CASE.

The rebuttal also allows counsel to focus on the weakest link in the appellee's case. That link should be in a point that is controlling to the court's determination and it should be "hit" with "dynamic force."[139]

KEEP IN MIND THAT THERE ARE SEVERAL DANGERS IN MAKING A REBUTTAL.

There are several dangers in making a rebuttal. One danger is that counsel will be asked an accumulation of questions.[140] Appleman explains:

> [Rebuttal] may well develop that the entire period, or almost all of it, will be consumed by questions of the court which must be answered tersely and in an incomplete and unsatisfactory manner. The replies to these questions may produce a feeling of dissatisfaction or lack of conviction in judges who--had they only the forceful opening statement and appellee's arguments to weigh--could remain with their initial convictions produced by appellant's prior argument.[141]

Similarly, if it is disorganized, rebuttal may have the effect of an anti-climax.[142] Another danger is that the court may be irritated if counsel attempts to introduce new arguments or to repeat previous ones.

---

[138] Jackson, <u>supra</u> note 25, at 804.

[139] J. Appleman, <u>supra</u> note 33, at 1043 ("Go directly to the point of vulnerability, point it out clearly, tell the court that the other matters have been fully covered and sit down").

[140] Jackson, <u>supra</u> note 25, at 804.

[141] J. Appleman, <u>supra</u> note 33, at 1042.

[142] Rossman, <u>supra</u> note 81, at 85.

Many experienced advocates do not make use of rebuttal time.[143] Because of the dangers, Appleman suggests that unless it is vital to reply, counsel may well want to close as follows:

> "If Your Honors please, I have dealt fully in my argument-in-chief with the contentions which the appellee has raised and have also discussed the cases which he has cited. Since it would serve no purpose to discuss these a second time, and bearing in mind the heavy schedule of this court for today, I will waive rebuttal argument."[144]

This type of closing leaves the court with an impression that you are confident of your position.[145]

---

[143]Jackson, supra note 25, at 804.

[144]J. Appleman, supra note 33, at 1043.

[145]Rall, supra note 16, at 134.

Appendix A

DISCUSSION OF THE PROBLEMS IN THE TEXT

Chapter 1

Written Work in Law Practice

DISCUSSION OF PROBLEM 1.1

In this problem, you were to assume Louis wants you to deny the allegations that Louis provoked the fight and threw the first punch because Louis thinks that a jury will not believe the plaintiffs. You were also to assume Louis is probably right and that a jury is not likely to believe the plaintiffs. You were then asked to decide whether the denial would be proper.

Under the facts given, the proposed denial of the allegations would be improper under both the disciplinary rules and Rule 11 of the Federal Rules of Civil Procedure. In the interview, the client flatly admitted he had started the altercation and had thrown the first punch. You have no other information, and the assumed facts stated that it was "clear to you from the interview with your client that Louis [had] started the argument, [had] provoked the fight and [had] struck the first blows." Furthermore, there were no other witnesses to the altercation.

Answer (d) is correct. The denial would be improper because Rule 11 of the Federal Rules of Civil Procedure requires you to plead in good faith to the best of your knowledge, information, and belief. If you denied the allegations, you would be making a false statement of fact--one directly contrary to information your client gave you in the interview. Therefore, you must admit the allegation. All of the other answers state the denial would be proper and are thus incorrect.

This situation can be distinguished from pleading an apparently "guilty" defendant "not guilty" in a criminal case.[1] This

---

[1] See R. Aronson & D. Weckstein, Professional Responsibility in a Nutshell 281 (1980) ("[T]here [is no] ethical impropriety in pleading [an apparently guilty] client 'not guilty.' This plea does not assert the fact of innocence but simply allocates the burden of proof. It invokes the defendant's [constitutional] right to have the state attempt to prove his [or her] guilt beyond any reasonable doubt of the judge or jury.").

situation can also be distinguished from the situation in which a lawyer is required to remain silent (as opposed to making *affirmative* statements or allegations). Such a situation typically arises when the court makes possibly erroneous findings and the attorney gained knowledge of contrary facts in a confidential interview with a client.[2]

Rule 11 provides that the pleading must be well grounded in fact "to the best of the [attorney's] knowledge, information, and belief formed *after reasonable inquiry* . . . ."[3] This language was intended to stress "the need for some prefiling inquiry into both the facts and the law to satisfy the *affirmative* duty imposed by the rule."[4]

DISCUSSION OF PROBLEM 1.2

In this problem, you were to assume that Louis also wants you to file a counterclaim asserting that the plaintiffs negligently caused the crash. You were reminded that during the interview, Louis stated he should have been more careful and that "he caused the accident." You were then asked to determine (from the choices stated) what is the best argument that it is ethical to file this counterclaim.

The situation in this problem can be distinguished from the proposed action in Problem 1.1. Unlike the fact of the client throwing the first punch, determining causation and concluding someone is negligent may involve a complicated weighing and interpretation of a variety of facts--though the client believes he was negligent and should have been more careful.

Furthermore, under the law of some jurisdictions, the plaintiffs might be liable even though the defendant had been negligent if the plaintiffs had the "last clear chance" to avoid the accident. In these circumstances, the defendant's attorney does not have to rely on the client's statements concerning his possible negligence.

The best argument is thus provided in the second answer: "an attorney does not have to rely on a client's interpretation of complex factors involved in a negligence case, particularly the issue of causation. If the attorney's view of the facts, however remote, would support plaintiff liability, the professionally prudent course of action is to preserve your client's claim."

---

the judge or jury.").

[2] See id. at 299.

[3] Fed. R. Civ. P. 11 (emphasis added).

[4] Fed. R. Civ. P. 11 advisory committee's note (1983 amendment) (emphasis added).

DISCUSSION OF PROBLEM 1.3

In this problem, you were asked to decide what is the best argument supporting the assertion that it would be unethical to file the counterclaim described in Problem 1.2.

On the facts given, the intention to harass or delay is not apparent. Thus, it is doubtful that the claim is *intended* to delay trial, answer (a). Nor is the claim likely to qualify as a nuisance or frivolous claim. In light of the complex factors involved in determining causation and whether someone has acted negligently, answers (b) and (c), the attorney may arguably have a good faith belief in the merits of the claim.

The best argument is provided by answer (d): "[F]iling the counterclaim would be contrary to the facts apparently known by the attorney at the time. An attorney has an obligation to make a reasonable inquiry before filing the counterclaim and cannot simply follow the client's strategy unless the counterclaim 'to the best of his knowledge, information, and belief . . . is well grounded in fact.'" As discussed in Problem 1.2, Rule 11 establishes an affirmative duty to investigate, which may not have been satisfied in this case.

DISCUSSION OF PROBLEM 1.4

In this problem, you were to assume Louis had specifically told you that the only reason he wants you to file the counterclaim is that he believes "the best defense is a good offense" and he is sure the cost of litigating the counterclaim will induce a settlement in the case. You were also to assume (1) you now believe your client has such a weak case that no possibility exists that a jury could plausibly find in Louis' favor and (2) if the jury would find in favor of Louis, the finding would be reversed on appeal under the applicable rules of appellate review. Based on these additional facts, you were asked whether filing the counterclaim would be proper.

Unlike the facts assumed for the previous problems, the added assumptions (the nonexistent chances of success and the client's statements) now are sufficient to establish the client's *sole* intent and purpose: to harass the other side into buying peace through a settlement to avoid the cost of defending the suit.

Disciplinary Rule 7-102(A)(1) prohibits attorneys from filing suits or taking similar action in the form of a counterclaim when they should know or it is obvious that such action would serve merely to harass or maliciously injure another. Thus, under the disciplinary rules, the client's intention is relevant and does restrict lawyers from pursuing otherwise legitimate claims, and answer (c) is correct. Answer (a) (proper because everyone is entitled to a day in court regardless of the merits of the claim) and (b) (proper because an attorney must zealously represent a client; a client's motivation is irrelevant) are incorrect.

Furthermore, no rule treats weak cases like frivolous ones, answer (d).[5]

DISCUSSION OF PROBLEM 1.5

In this problem, you were to assume instead that (1) Louis lies to you and claims the plaintiffs started the altercation; (2) Louis wants you to file a counterclaim against the plaintiffs asserting that they provoked and initiated the altercation; (3) Louis wants you to threaten to seek to have the proper authorities file a criminal complaint asserting that the plaintiffs provoked and initiated the altercation; (4) a jury might award substantial damages on the counterclaim in the civil action; and (5) a jury could plausibly convict the defendants based on Louis' testimony in a criminal proceeding.

You were also to assume that the prospect of the criminal charges would induce a substantial settlement in the case (of which you would receive a third) because a conviction may lead to barring the boxers from participating in future boxing matches. Your preliminary investigation establishes that no one except the parties witnessed the events and either your client or the other parties are lying. You were then asked to consider which of the statements (listed in the problem) is correct.

Under these circumstances, in absence of some direct or indirect indication that your client was lying, most attorneys would agree that it would be proper to file the counterclaim. Indeed, the attorney probably would be required to file the counterclaim to represent the client adequately.

On the other hand, the attorney could not threaten criminal charges to *solely* gain an advantage in the civil action.[6] The facts posed make this conclusion easy because the client's intent is clear. A much more difficult case ethically would be presented if the client had indicated a *mixed* motive.

In relation to the statements that you were asked to consider, the correct answer is thus answer (b): "In absence of some direct or indirect indication that your client is lying, filing the counterclaim would be proper because an attorney is ethically obligated to represent a client zealously. Filing the criminal

---

[5] See American Bar Ass'n, Model Code of Professional Responsibility DR 7-102 (1980) [hereinafter Model Code]. See also American Bar Ass'n, Model Rules of Professional Conduct Rule 3.1 (meritorious claims and contentions), Rule 3.2 (expediting litigation), Rule 4.4 (respect for rights of third persons) (1983); Fed. R. Civ. P. 11.

[6] See Model Code, supra note 5, DR 7-105(A).

complaint, however, would be improper because an attorney may not threaten criminal charges solely to gain advantage in a civil matter."

DISCUSSION OF PROBLEM 1.6

In this problem, you were to assume that Soda Popinski's attorney refuses to discuss settlement or to convey your settlement offer of $50,000 to Popinski. Louis wants you to send the offer directly to Popinski to get the matter settled. Louis is sure Popinski will accept the offer. You were then asked to consider the propriety of this proposed course of action.

Popinski's attorney should have passed on the proposed settlement offer to the client. DR 7-104(A)(1)[7] and Model Code Rule 4.2,[8] however, clearly prohibit direct communication with a party who is known to be represented by counsel and the settlement offer is related to the subject of the representation--the lawsuit.

Thus, the correct answer is (b): "unethical because an attorney is prohibited from communicating directly with a party known to be represented by counsel."

DISCUSSION OF PROBLEM 1.7

In this problem, you were to assume that you had decided not to contact Soda Popinski directly. You were then asked to decide which of the courses of action listed in the problem would be the clearest violation of professional ethics.

The course of action that is the clearest violation of professional ethics is stated in (a): "talking to the judge privately about the merits of the case and the refusal of Popinski's counsel to communicate the offer to Popinski." Disciplinary Rule 7-110(B) prohibits ex parte judicial communications to a judge or other official without prior notice to the opposing counsel.[9]

The information probably can be released to the news media without violating the disciplinary rules, answer (b).[10] To threaten to report the opposing counsel's failure to communicate the offer to the disciplinary committee of the bar, answer (d), is also not improper. Indeed, Disciplinary Rule 1-103 requires lawyers

---

[7]Mode Code, supra note 5, DR 7-104(A)(1).

[8]Model Rules, supra note 5, Rule 4.2.

[9]Model Code, supra note 5, DR 7-110(B). Accord Model Rules, supra note 5, Rule 3.5(b).

[10]See Model Code, supra note 5, DR 7-107(G).

"possessing unprivileged knowledge of a violation [of the disciplinary rules to] report such knowledge to a tribunal or other authority empowered to investigate or act upon such violation."[11]

A closer question of propriety exists about answer (c) ("allowing your client to communicate the offer directly to Popinski"). Disciplinary Rule 7-104 clearly prohibits a lawyer from causing another to communicate the offer. One could argue that a legitimate difference exists between "causing" and "allowing" a client to convey the information.[12]

DISCUSSION OF PROBLEM 1.8

In this problem, you were to assume that a legal issue has arisen in the lawsuit concerning whether professional boxers have a special duty to avoid participating in fist fights outside the professional ring. You were to assume that, in the course of your research, you have found that the courts in the jurisdiction where the litigation is taking place have not considered the issue. Other jurisdictions have considered the issue and are split on the question of whether a special duty exists.

You were to assume further that you have told your client about these decisions. The court has requested each side to prepare a memorandum of law for the court on this issue. Louis wants you to cite only the favorable cases in support of your position. Your client strongly feels you should not be doing the other side's work for them.

On these facts, mandatory disclosure of adverse cases from other jurisdictions is not required by DR 7-106(B)(1) because they are not "directly controlling."[13] These cases are merely "persuasive" authority that the jurisdiction in question is not bound to follow under the rules of stare decisis (the doctrine governing when previously decided cases will be recognized as authority for the disposition of future ones).

Assuming a false statement of law is not being made (for example, "all courts that have considered this issue have uniformly held . . . ."), most lawyers probably would agree that the disciplinary rules would not prohibit the conduct proposed by the client. Thus, answer (c), "[t]he proposed course of action would not violate the disciplinary rules because mandatory disclosure of adverse cases from other jurisdictions is not required," is correct.

---

[11]Model Code, supra note 5, DR 1-103. Accord Model Rules, supra note 5, Rule 8.3(a), (c).

[12]See Model Rules, supra note 5, Rule 4.2.

[13]Model Code, supra note 5, DR 7-106(B)(1). Accord Model Rules, supra note 5, Rule 3.3(a)(3).

Note, however, that a lawyer might decide to inform the court of the split of authority in other jurisdictions and attempt to show why one line of authority is more persuasive than the other. This approach may be a better means of advocacy on behalf of the client.

DISCUSSION OF PROBLEM 1.9

In this problem, you were to assume that in the course of your research you have found a favorable case (*Sandman v. Tiger*) from a neighboring jurisdiction which directly supports your legal position. Upon further research, you have discovered the *Sandman* case has been substantially undermined by another recent decision (*Flamenco v. Machoman*) in that jurisdiction.

You were also to assume that you have told your client about these two cases and that Louis thinks that you should cite only the *Sandman* case. Louis maintains you do not have to make the other side's case for them by explaining how a recent case has affected an earlier one.

The best argument that this proposed course of action would be unethical is contained in the first answer ("the disciplinary rules prohibit citing a case or a statute when an attorney knows that the case has been overruled or the statute has been repealed. Citing a case which an attorney knows has been substantially undermined is different only in degree, not kind, from citing an overruled case and, therefore, should be considered a knowingly false statement of law"). This position is the one taken by Aronson and Weckstein in their work on professional responsibility (although some lawyers might disagree with the view of these two commentators).[14]

The other answers are incorrect. An attorney does not have to disclose every adverse precedent to the court, answer (b). Nor can the failure to disclose the existence and effect of the subsequent case be properly considered a prohibited dilatory tactic designed to needlessly increase the cost of litigation, answer (c). Also, this case is not a controlling precedent, answer (d).

DISCUSSION OF PROBLEM 1.10

The sentences in this problem contain several errors as well as several correct applications of the capitalization rules stated in this section.

In (a), "The eighth circuit affirmed the refusal to grant the injunction," "***Eighth Circuit***" should be capitalized because it is derived from the proper name identifying a specific court (the United States Court of Appeals for the Eighth Circuit).

---

[14] See R. Aronson & D. Weckstein, supra note 1, at 299.

In (b), "The U.S. Department of Justice then sought review in the United States Supreme Court," no changes are necessary. The full names of specific governmental departments (***U.S. Department of Justice***) and specific courts (***United States Supreme Court***) are capitalized in legal writing.

In (c), "The U.S. attorney general argued on behalf of the Federal Government that (1) the federal district courts did have the power to hear the case even though the state of Minnesota was a party to the action and (2) the U.S. District Court for the District of Minnesota could enjoin the Minnesota supreme court from hearing the case," several correct applications of the capitalization rules as well as errors appear.

First, "***Attorney General***" in "***U.S. Attorney General***" should be capitalized because it is the full title of a governmental officer.

Second, "***federal government***" should not be capitalized in legal writing pursuant to the generally accepted rule.

Third, "***federal district courts***" is correctly not capitalized because that phrase refers to a general class of courts.

Fourth, "***state***" in "***the state of Minnesota***" is correctly not capitalized because "state" precedes the proper name (Minnesota). Note that "state" should be capitalized if it is an essential part of a specific name ("Washington State") or if it is used in persuasive writing. (The instructions at the outset of the problem, however, indicated that these sentences appear in an office memorandum.)

Fifth, "***U.S. District Court for the District of Minnesota***" is correctly capitalized because it is the full name of a specific court. For the same reason, "***Minnesota Supreme Court***" should have been capitalized.

In (d), "On the other hand, the Respondents argued that the Eleventh Amendment to the U.S. Constitution and the Anti-Injunction Act, 28 U.S.C. § 2283, applied to this case," "***respondents***" should not have been capitalized because it is a descriptive name of a litigant. Likewise, "***eleventh amendment***" should not be capitalized in an office memorandum. (It may be capitalized in persuasive legal writing when it is to your advantage.) Both "***U.S. Constitution***" and "***Anti-Injunction Act***" are properly capitalized because full names of constitutions and laws are capitalized in legal writing.

In (e), "Under that act, writs of injunction to stay proceedings in any court of a state have been prohibited since 1793. <u>See</u> Durfee & Sloss, <u>Federal Injunctions against Proceedings in State Courts: the Life History of a Statute</u>, 30 Mich. L. Rev. 1145 (1932)," "***Act***" should be capitalized because it refers to a specific law--the Anti-Injunction Act. In this same sentence, "**court**" is properly not capitalized because it does not refer to the

U.S. Supreme Court. Likewise, "***state***" is properly not capitalized because it refers to the state generally.

Both "***Against***" and "***The***" should be capitalized in the article title because the initial word, the word immediately following a colon ("***The***"), and all other words except articles, conjunctions, and prepositions of four or fewer letters ("***Against***") in headings and titles cited are capitalized in legal writing.

In (f), "In an opinion accompanying the court's refusal to hear the case this term, the justices refused to speculate on whether the constitution or that act applied to a state court appeal because the issue was moot," "***Court's,***" "***Term,***" and "***Justices***" should be capitalized because they refer to the U.S. Supreme Court.

"***Constitution***" should be capitalized because it refers to the U.S. Constitution. "***Act***" should also be capitalized because it refers to a specific law, the Anti-Injunction Act. In "***state court,***" "***state***" is properly not capitalized because it refers to the state generally. Likewise, "***court***" in "***state court appeal***" is properly not capitalized because it does not refer to the U.S. Supreme Court.

DISCUSSION OF PROBLEM 1.11

In this problem, you are to assume that you are reviewing a proposed elevator maintenance contract. Your client wants you to be sure that the contract provides protection against the various possible equipment failures that might occur. You are asked what you think of the following provision: "This company will repair or replace worm and gear bearings and housings."

If you were doing your job well, you should state that this provision is unacceptable. Why? When your client sought to have a worn-out worm or gear repaired or replaced, the maintenance company could point out the above provision covered repair or replacement of the worm and gear *bearings* or the worm and gear *housings*, not the worm or gear itself.

Thus, to provide coverage, the above provision needs, at a minimum, a comma after "gear" to make clearer that the worm and gear themselves are covered:

> This company will repair or replace worm and gear, bearings and housings.[15]

---

[15] See Romm, Comma Sense, 70 A.B.A. J., Dec. 1984, at 132, 132 (stating the above example). The failure to notice the missing comma cost the client in this instance $8,000, plus attorney's fees. Id.

Better still, the provision could have been rewritten:

> This company will repair or replace (1) the worm, (2) the gear, and (3) their bearings and housings.

DISCUSSION OF PROBLEM 1.12

In this problem, you were asked to correct the misplaced clauses and phrases in the following sentences:

(a) The French government is preparing television commercials encouraging the use of condoms that are blunt enough to shock even liberal Americans.

(b) Establishments such as the Bright Star in Bessemer, for instance, will have lines of people waiting for seats extending outside their own premises.

(c) On Monday, March 30, at 7:30 p.m., there will be an Interfaith Support Group meeting for parents who have lost a child [through] death at the First Presbyterian Church.

(d) One pharmacist told us of a trying moment recently when he had to explain to a young woman how to administer a douche in front of a small audience of onlookers.

In (a), the misplaced modifier ("that are blunt enough to shock even liberal Americans") is best placed in a separate sentence: "The French government is preparing television commercials encouraging the use of condoms. ***The commercials*** are blunt enough to shock even liberal Americans." (This example appeared in the *Portland Oregonian*.)

In (b), the sentence could be rewritten as follows: "For instance, to obtain seats, *patrons* of establishments such as the Bright Star in Bessemer ***will have to wait in lines*** extending outside the premises." (This example appeared in the *Birmingham (Ala.) News*.)

In (c), "at the First Presbyterian Church" should be moved to the beginning of the sentence: "On Monday, March 30, at 7:30 p.m. ***at the First Presbyterian Church***, there will be an Interfaith Support Group meeting for parents who have lost a child [through] death." (This example appeared in a church notice in North Palm Beach.)

In (d), this sentence could be rewritten in two sentences: "One pharmacist recently told us of a trying moment. ***In front of a small audience of onlookers, he*** had to explain to a young woman how to administer a douche." (This example appeared in the *Augusta (Ga.) Chronicle*.)

DISCUSSION OF PROBLEM 1.13

In this problem, you were asked to correct remote, ambiguous, or improper references in the following related sentences:

(a) Holding social hosts liable for injuries to third parties caused by their drunken driving would cause practical problems.

(b) In this instance, for example, it was impossible for a host to keep his "eye" on each guest and for him to monitor his drinking habits.

(c) When they left, the host and hostess went with the guests to the door, wished them good night, and reminded everyone who was driving to use caution.

(d) Clearly, this indicated that the social hostess exercised the same degree of care that a reasonable person would have exercised toward social guests under these circumstances.

In (a), the sentence should be clarified to indicate whose drunken driving is involved (presumably, that of the guests, not the host). The sentence should read, "Holding social hosts liable for injuries to third parties caused by their ***guests'*** drunken driving would cause practical problems."

In (b), the sentence should be clarified to indicate clearly the references. For example, the sentence could be edited as follows: "In this instance, for example, it was impossible for a host to keep his 'eye' on each guest and for ***a host*** to monitor ***the guests'*** drinking habits."

In (c), "when they left" appears to refer to "the host and hostess," but the writer probably means "when **the guests** left."

In (d), "this" by itself should not be used to refer indefinitely to the preceding material. A specific reference should be added, such as "Clearly, this ***action*** indicated that the social hostess exercised . . . ."

DISCUSSION OF PROBLEM 1.14

In this problem, you were asked to revise the following sentences to reflect a proper legal writing style:

(a) In this memorandum, I'll discuss the law concerning incontestability clauses in insurance contracts.

(b) The court refused to tackle certain kinds of violations, such as the failure to pay parking tickets.

(c) The rule is simple: Never fail to file the complaint on time.

(d) Smith distinguished the Jones case.

In (a), the personalized writing style should be deleted: ***This memorandum discusses*** the law concerning incontestability clauses in insurance contracts. Note also that you should avoid using a contraction ("I'll") in formal legal writing.

In (b), "tackle" may be too colloquial for formal legal writing: "The court refused to ***hear*** certain kinds of violations, such as the failure to pay parking tickets."

In (c), the use of multiple negatives should be avoided: "The rule is simple: ***Always*** file the complaint on time.

In (d), make the court the subject: "The court in Smith distinguished the Jones case."

DISCUSSION OF PROBLEM 1.15

In this problem, you were asked to read the "Statement of Facts" and "Summary of Argument" from the Petitioner's Opening Brief in *California v. Krivda*, 409 U.S. 33 (1972). You were asked to consider the following four questions:

1. How does the petitioner characterize the case?
2. What parts of the presentation are not strictly necessary (and thus perhaps designed to influence and persuade)?
3. Does the argument seem convincing?
4. How would you respond? In other words, what seem to be the weak points on these facts and in the legal arguments?

First, note how the petitioner characterized the case. The petitioner presented the case as one involving police officers who, using ingenuity, discovered discarded evidence of violations of the law. The petitioners implied that the possible violation of the fourth amendment was a minor one (not involving "truly lawless" police conduct) and that the application of the exclusionary rule would serve no useful purpose in this case.

Second, the excerpt included several factual details that were not strictly necessary. For instance, the petitioner pointed out that the officers observed the defendant "wearing only a towel around his waist" when he took the can back to the house. The petitioner also included statements by the informant which were not directly relevant to the drug charges ("there were many sex parties at their residence" and "a Lesbian named 'Frankie' lived there"). Thus, while it may be relevant that someone named "Frankie" resided at the residence to connect the handwritten letter found in the trash with the Frankie's name to the informant's statement, it is irrelevant that Frankie was a lesbian. Note also that the brief writer opted to use the capitalized form of the term (of or relating to Lesbos), which provides further emphasis.

Third, in response to the petitioner's brief, the respondents in this case made the following arguments and observations:

(a) On the facts, the respondents emphasized that "an untested, unreliable, anonymous informant placed a telephone call."

(b) The officers decided to intercept the garbage truck "[a]pparently, as an afterthought," and "[n]o information was in the possession of the police which in any way indicated that [r]espondents' garbage can was utilized by them to dispose of contraband or in any way played a role in the lives of respondents save to dispose of routine refuse."

(c) The petitioner could not have obtained a search warrant based on the anonymous "tip" because the informant was prima facie unreliable and nothing was proffered to indicate the informant spoke with personal knowledge of the events alleged to have occurred at the residence.

(d) Respondents had a reasonable expectation of privacy in their trash container.

(e) Respondents did not reasonably accept the risk that trash collectors would cooperate with the police in search of the respondents' trash cans.[16]

Fourth, the United States Supreme Court disposed of the *Krivda* case without reaching the merits of the arguments presented by the litigants. In a per curiam opinion, the United States Supreme Court vacated the judgment of the California Supreme Court and remanded the case to that court for further proceedings.

The United States Supreme Court found, after briefing and argument of the case, that the Court was unable to determine whether the California Supreme Court based its holding on the fourth and fourteenth amendments of the U.S. Constitution or upon equivalent provisions in the California Constitution, or both. (The United States Supreme Court did not have jurisdiction to hear the *Krivda* case if the California Supreme Court had based its holding only on the California constitutional provisions.)

---

[16]Respondent's Brief, passim, California v. Krivda, 409 U.S. 33 (1972).

Chapter 2

Analyzing The Facts, Identifying Legal Problems, Defining The Writing Project, Developing a Research Plan, and Taking Research Notes

DISCUSSION OF PROBLEM 2.1

In this problem, you were to assume that you work for a law firm representing No-Pay Casualty Company and that you had been given the documents reproduced in Illustration 2.1 in Chapter 2 to review. You were asked to prepare a preliminary analysis of this information.

The following is an example of an acceptable preliminary problem analysis:

Preliminary Problem Analysis (Lash v. No-Pay Casualty Co.)

(a) Legal Subject(s)

Tort law, negligence, and insurance law;

(b) Legal Description of the Parties, Places, and Things

Insurer, insured, driver, insane person, highway, automobile, motor vehicle, loss of conscious control, delusion, mental illness, and mental aberration;

(c) Legal Issues (Theories, Defenses, Relief, and Other Problems)

Negligence, direct action, damages, sudden mental illness, mental capacity, insanity, and failure to notify insurer of accident;

(d) Research Leads

(1) The jurisdiction involved (place of accident and suit) is the State of Utopia, U.S.A.;

(2) The action was brought in federal district court based on diversity of citizenship and an amount in controversy that exceeds $50,000;

(3) The law likely to be applied is that of Utopia (state tort law).

Based upon the above problem analysis and the information provided in the text, the following factual summary and tentative issue formulation could be prepared:

MEMORANDUM

To: File
From: Legal Researcher
Re: Lash v. No-Pay Casualty Co.
No-Pay Policy No. 89-199
Date: January 12, 19xx

No-Pay is a co-defendant in a direct action in the newly admitted State of Utopia. The plaintiff is suing for $750,000 in damages arising out of No-Pay's obligation to pay any liability incurred by its insured Irma Marie Delira that has resulted from her negligent operation of a motor vehicle. Delira apparently suffered a mental delusion that caused her to lose conscious control of the automobile she was driving. Delira currently is institutionalized in Freud Memorial Mental Hospital.

The police report stated that Delira had told the officer at the scene that she was a real "Wonder Woman." She claimed that she was from Paradise Island, which was "hidden deep within the Bermuda Triangle." The report also quoted the "Wonder Woman" as stating, "I was totally powerless to do anything."

Delira claims that the accident was not her fault because she was attacked by an alien creature. She apparently had seen a beer commercial on television and was taking three cases of beer to the local cemetery at the time of the accident because a television commercial had told her to do so.

The principal legal issue is whether Delira's insanity is likely to be recognized under the law of Utopia as a defense to a negligence action. A secondary legal issue is whether Delira violated her obligation as the insured by failing to notify her insurance carrier.

DISCUSSION OF PROBLEM 2.2

In this problem, you were to determine from the entries in Burton's *Legal Thesaurus* a synonym for "insanely deluded." The index identifies "non compos mentis" as a synonym for "insanely deluded." The main entry for insanity lists many more synonyms.

DISCUSSION OF PROBLEM 2.3

In this problem, you were asked which index entry or entries you would try to consult *first*. Some indexes, such as those accompanying West's digests, have entries that tend to include broad descriptions of the parties, places, and things involved. In contrast, indexes in most treatises and legal encyclopedias tend to emphasize legal subjects, theories, defenses, relief, or specific legal issues.

In this instance, the principal legal subjects or issues identified in the preliminary problem analysis (negligence, sudden mental illness, and insanity) would probably be the best ones to consult first.

DISCUSSION OF PROBLEM 2.4

In this problem, you were to assume that you have decided initially to consult the entries for "Negligence" and "Insanity." You were asked to underline the entries that you feel might direct you to a relevant discussion of law relating to the No-Pay research problem.

In this instance, several entries may be relevant. Under "Negligence," you might have marked "Insane persons, 1074" and "Mental capacity, 176." Under "Insanity," you might have marked "Immunity of insane persons, 1072," "Immunity of mentally disabled, 1072," "Negligence, 1074," and "State compensation for acts of mentally disabled, 1075."

DISCUSSION OF PROBLEM 2.5

In this problem, you were to assume that in your research using Prosser and Keeton on Torts that you decided to start with the references to pages 1072 through 1075 because they appear to be the most relevant. You were asked to read these pages and to mark in the margin the portions of the discussion that appear to relate to the research question.

Upon reading this section, you should have recognized several general legal principles that appear to be relevant. Here are two examples of important principles that you should have noted:

(1) When it occurs suddenly and without warning, insanity should be treated like a heart attack; in such circumstances, insane defendants are not held to the standard of conduct of the reasonable person which is ordinarily used in negligence actions; and

(2) Under the common law in negligence actions, insane persons are liable for their failure to conform to the standard of conduct of reasonable persons.

DISCUSSION OF PROBLEM 2.6

In this problem, you were asked to read Prosser and Keeton's discussion of "Mental Capacity" and to mark in the margin the portions of the discussion that appear to relate to the research question.

This section cites some additional support for the common-law insanity rule (footnote 32). The new cases should be added to those already listed on the relevant sheet. A reference to this section of Prosser & Keeton should be added to that sheet also.

The text (see the discussion accompanying footnote 33) articulates another slightly different argument against the common-law rule: the apparent injustice of holding insane defendants accountable on the basis of a standard they cannot meet. This argument should be recorded on a new sheet of paper.

The authors also repeat one of the justifications for the common-law rule (see the text following footnote 34 concerning encouraging control of incompetents by their custodians). Two other reasons in support of the common-law rule (also discussed in the text following footnote 34) are stated in a sufficiently different way, and they probably should be listed on new sheets.

Prosser and Keeton state again (see the text accompanying footnote 37) that there is "some sentiment for treating a sudden delirium or loss of mental faculties as a 'circumstance' depriving the actor of control over his conduct, thus shielding him from liability, provided the lapse was foreseeable." A reference to this section of Prosser and Keeton should be added to the earlier sheet containing this point. This time, however, the authors cite a case (*Kuhn v. Zabotsky*) in footnote 37 as *contrary* authority for the proposition (indicated by the "But see" signal).

Thus, there appears to be a split of authority on whether sudden mental illness should be treated like other sudden illnesses or losses of consciousness. A new sheet should be made for the contrary proposition:

> Even if a mental illness is sudden and without warning, such a mentally ill person should not be shielded from liability.
>
> ✓ W. Prosser & W. Keeton, § 32, at 178, n.37 (citing authority for the above proposition).
>
> * <u>Kuhn v. Zabotsky</u>, 9 Ohio St. 2d 129, 224 N.E.2d 137 (1967).

A star should be placed in front of the *Kuhn* case to indicate its possible critical significance as authority for the contrary position.

Finally, Prosser and Keeton indicate again (see text accompanying footnote 36) the similarity in treatment between sudden mental illness and other sudden illnesses and the standard applied in a contributory negligence context (see text accompanying footnotes 38 and 39).

DISCUSSION OF PROBLEM 2.7

In this problem, you were asked to examine the beginning page of section 29 from Prosser and Keeton's hornbook and to determine how that section is relevant to the research problem, if at all.

Section 29 deals with unavoidable accidents. Because this doctrine sets the framework for the sudden mental illness rule, you should record a basic statement of that doctrine (along with the supporting citations) before leaving this text. Section 29 defines unavoidable accidents as occurrences that were not intended and which, under all the circumstances, could not have been foreseen or prevented by the exercise of reasonable precautions (see the text accompanying footnotes 1 and 2).

In the context of a driver operating an automobile, this rule is applied in this way (see text accompanying footnote 4): A driver "who suddenly loses control of the car because the driver is seized with a heart attack, a stroke, a fainting spell, or an epileptic fit is not liable, unless the driver knew that he might become ill, in which case he may have been negligent in driving the car at all." W. Prosser & W. Keeton, § 29, at 162. Again, this rule should be recorded along with the cited support for the rule.

DISCUSSION OF PROBLEM 2.8

In this problem, you were to assume that you are specifically interested in determining whether a "sudden mental illness" is a defense to a negligence action in West Virginia (instead of the State of Utopia as previously assumed). You were asked how you could determine the relevant topic and key number under which you should look in a relevant digest to find West Virginia cases on point (if any exist).

Your research so far has identified several cases, but none of them apply West Virginia law. Recall, however, that a star was placed by three cases in your notes--the *Breunig* case from Wisconsin, the *Buckley* case from Ontario, and the *Kuhn* case from Ohio. These sources are likely to be the most promising ones from which you can directly identify the relevant topic(s) and key number(s). In this instance, it probably would be best to start with the *Breunig* case, which appears to be a leading United States case directly on point in favor of recognizing the defense.

DISCUSSION OF PROBLEM 2.9

In this problem, you were to assume that you had decided to consult the *Breunig* opinion to determine the relevant topic(s) and key number(s). The page containing the relevant headnotes from the *Breunig* opinion is reproduced in Figure 2-O in Chapter 2. You were asked to examine these headnotes and to place a check by the headnotes that appear to contain relevant points of law.

The most relevant headnotes appear to be the first three: Headnote 1--Negligence 105; Headnote 2--Automobiles 157; and Headnote 3--Automobiles 157. You have now identified the topics and key numbers under which you could look in West's Digests to determine if any West Virginia cases have dealt with this point of law.

Under the system of note taking described earlier in this chapter, however, complete notes should be taken on the *Breunig* case before you leave it. The notes on the *Breunig* case should either (1) be added directly to the sheet(s) that contain(s) the *Breunig* citation or (2) be written on a separate sheet and then paper-clipped to the principal sheet containing the *Breunig* citation. Your notes should also include the relevant topics and key numbers and the headnote number for each point. The format for taking these notes is presented in the next chapter.

New principles and ideas appearing in the case should be recorded on separate sheets. Likewise, new authorities cited in support of previously recorded principles and ideas should be added to the sheets containing them. After you have personally read this case, a check mark should be placed on the sheet next to the citation.

After completing your notes on the *Breunig* case, you would then consult one of West's digests covering West Virginia.

DISCUSSION OF PROBLEM 2.10

In this problem, you were to assume that you had found the relevant page from West's *South Eastern Digest* showing Automobiles 157. That page is reproduced in Figure 2-P in Chapter 2. You were asked to examine that entry and to determine whether a West Virginia case has dealt with this point of law.

The relevant entry indicates that the case of *Keller v. Wonn*, 140 W. Va. 860, 87 S.E.2d 435 (1955), appears to support the proposition that a sudden mental illness will be recognized as a defense in West Virginia. You should add that case to the page prepared earlier containing this principle:

> When it occurs suddenly and without warning, insanity should be treated like a heart attack; in such circumstances, insane defendants are not held to the standard of conduct of the reasonable person ordinarily used in negligence actions.

✓ W. Prosser & W. Keeton, The Law of Torts § 135, at 1074-75 (5th ed. 1984) (pointing out this line of authority).

✓ * Breunig v. American Family Insurance Co., 45 Wis. 2d 536, 173 N.W.2d 619 (1970) (annotated at 49 A.L.R.3d 179) (see attached case brief).

* Buckley & Toronto Transportation Commission v. Smith Transport, Ltd., [1946] Ont. L. Rep. 798, [1946] 4 Dom. L. Rep. 721.

Picher, The Tortious Liability of the Insane in Canada, 13 Osgoode Hall L.J. 193 (1975).

W. Prosser & W. Keeton, § 32, at 178.

Cf. Restatement (Second) of Torts § 283C, comment b (______).

Keller v. Wonn, 140 W. Va. 860, 87 S.E.2d 453 (1955).

DISCUSSION OF PROBLEM 2.11

In this problem, you were asked to examine the annotation scheme and index of 49 A.L.R.3d 189 shown in Figures 2-Q and 2-R in Chapter 2 and then to determine which section discusses sudden insanity. Both the annotation scheme and the index indicate that section 5(b) is the most relevant section.

DISCUSSION OF PROBLEM 2.12

In this problem, you were asked to examine the "Table of Jurisdictions Represented" shown in Figure 2-R in Chapter 2 and then to determine in which sections of the annotation New York cases could be found. The Table indicates that New York cases are cited and discussed in sections 4, 5[a], and 6 of the annotation.

DISCUSSION OF PROBLEM 2.13

In this problem, you were asked to examine section 1[a] dealing with the scope of the annotation and to determine where a discussion of contributory negligence of the mentally ill could be found. Section 1[a] indicates that a treatment of contributory negligence of mentally ill persons can be found in 91 A.L.R.2d 392.

DISCUSSION OF PROBLEM 2.14

In this problem, you were asked to examine the first page of section 5(b) in Figure 2-S in Chapter 2. Based on this page, you were asked to determine the following: (a) whether the annotation concludes that it is foreseeable that sudden and unforeseeable mental illness might be recognized as a defense to a negligence claim; and (b) what argument the annotation makes (in footnote 13) about *Restatement (Second) of Torts* § 283C.

In § 5(b) "Sudden insanity," the annotation concludes that it is foreseeable that sudden and unforeseeable mental illness might be recognized as a defense to a negligence claim. In support of that conclusion, it indicates in footnote 13 that comment b to § 283C of the *Restatement (Second) of Torts* treats a sudden transitory delirium under the rule governing heart attacks and temporary dizziness rather than under the less favorable rule governing mental deficiency and insanity.

Chapter 3

Reading, Analyzing, and Briefing Cases for Legal Research and Writing Purposes

The following problems are based on the *Theisen* case reproduced in Chapter 3.

DISCUSSION OF PROBLEM 3.1

It is apparent from the heading of the case that Sharon Theisen was the plaintiff in the trial court and that the insurance company was the defendant.

At the time the action was commenced Sharon Theisen was a seventeen-year-old "infant." This term has a special legal meaning: she had not yet reached the legal age of majority in Wisconsin. Traditionally, this age has been twenty-one, but many states have changed the age of majority to eighteen. Her father, as her natural guardian, represents her interest.

When someone is appointed by the court to prosecute or defend a suit on behalf of an infant or incompetent person, the person appointed is called a guardian ad litem. In some jurisdictions, a person who appears in the action to look after the interests of a minor is called his or her next friend. Thus, Sharon Theisen, answer (a), and her father Fred Theisen, answer (c), are correct answers.

The style of the case and the syllabus prepared by the court both indicate that the *only* defendant is an insurance company. Thus, the other correct answer to Problem 3.1 is the Milwaukee Automobile Mutual Insurance Company, answer (d). You may be wondering, if Shepard was the negligent party, why his estate, answer (b), was not named as a defendant. The answer is that Wisconsin permits a "direct action" against the tortfeasor's liability insurer. In contrast, most states hold that a liability insurer can be sued only after a judgment has been obtained against the insured or only after the execution of that judgment against the insured has been returned unsatisfied.

DISCUSSION OF PROBLEM 3.2

West's synopsis and the court's syllabus both describe the action as a "guest-host action." The plaintiff Sharon Theisen was a guest riding in the insured's automobile. This phrase summarizes their legal relationship: Sharon Theisen was a non-paying passenger. Thus, one possible description of the case could include this term. This guest-host relationship is to be contrasted with one in which passengers are transported for hire (through a contract created by purchasing a ticket or through an oral or written agreement to pay for the transportation). Answer (b) is defective because it describes the action as one based on contract.

West's synopsis and the court's syllabus mention instances that the action involved an alleged claim of negligence (falling asleep at the wheel of the automobile). In the second paragraph of the syllabus, details of the jury's findings in the case are given. The reference to the apportionment of damages indicates that the plaintiff was seeking damages and that Wisconsin uses "comparative negligence" in making this determination. The action is thus accurately and aptly described as follows: "comparative negligence action," answer (a).

Answer (c), "Negligent homicide action for damages," improperly describes the action with a criminal-law term (homicide). Answer (d), "The case of the sleeping driver," might be a good title for an article about the case. It does not, however, describe the basic *legal* nature of the action.

DISCUSSION OF PROBLEM 3.3

In this problem, you were give the following descriptions of the basic facts involved in the action:

(a) Louis Shepard brought a fifth of liquor to a cast party after the senior class play. He consumed part of it, and beer was also served at the party. Apparently influenced by the consumption of this alcohol, Shepard fell asleep at the wheel of the car he was driving on the way home from the party. Sharon Theisen, a minor who was a guest passenger sleeping in the rear seat of the car, was injured when the car struck a large tree stump. Shepard, who was insured by the defendant Milwaukee Automobile Mutual Insurance Company, was killed.

(b) Louis Shepherd, a participant in the senior class play, attended a party at the home of one of the members of the cast. Some liquor was served at the party, but there was no evidence that anyone became intoxicated. About 3:00 a.m. the party broke up and five girls, including the plaintiff Sharon Theisen, got into Shepherd's car for the ride home. About four miles from the party, Shepherd fell asleep at the wheel. The car left the road and hit a tree. Sharon Theisen, who at the time of the accident was sleeping in the rear seat of the car, was injured. Shepard, who was insured by the defendant Milwaukee Automobile Mutual Insurance Company, was killed.

Each of the above statements is an expansion on the most basic facts: The plaintiff, a passenger in a car, was injured in an accident late at night when the driver, insured by the defendant, fell asleep and the car hit a tree. The principal difference between (a) and (b) is the emphasis in (a) on the consumption of alcohol.

The opinion states that "[a]t the party, beer or sloe gin, or both, were consumed, but there was no evidence anyone became intoxicated." Contrary to the statement in answer (a), "[Shepard]" consumed part of [the fifth of liquor]," the opinion states that "[t]he only evidence concerning Shepard's drinking is by one of the girls who said she saw him with a drink in his hand." Thus, answer (a) is inaccurate. It places too much emphasis on the drinking of alcohol and fails to state that the accident occurred at 3:00 a.m. Answer (a) also fails to identify the specific relationship of the parties as plaintiff or defendant.

DISCUSSION OF PROBLEM 3.4

The first sentence of the court's syllabus states that the plaintiffs sought "to recover damages for personal injuries." Answer (b) is thus correct. Note that the plaintiff did not seek punitive damages, answer (c). Nor was sequestration, answer (a), involved. Answer (d) is obviously incorrect.

DISCUSSION OF PROBLEM 3.5

The information identifying the lower court in which the proceedings took place is contained in West's synopsis. The action was tried in the Circuit Court for Buffalo County, Wisconsin. Thus, answer (a), "Wisconsin Circuit Court," is correct.

DISCUSSION OF PROBLEM 3.6

The heading at the outset of the opinion identifies the court rendering the opinion as the Supreme Court of Wisconsin. Thus, answer (b), "Supreme Court of Wisconsin," is correct.

DISCUSSION OF PROBLEM 3.7

The plaintiffs were successful in the trial court because the insurance company is the appellant (the party who appeals from the decision below). Correspondingly, Sharon Theisen and her father Fred Theisen (as her guardian) are designated as the respondent. In many jurisdictions, they would be called the appellee (the party who will be arguing against setting aside the judgment below). At common law, the insurance company would have been designated as the plaintiff-in-error and Sharon Theisen and her father would have been the defendants-in-error. Thus, answer (a), "Sharon Theisen/Fred Theisen," is correct.

The facts recited in the syllabus and the opinion give some indication of how the jury reached its verdict in favor of the plaintiff. Shepard was viewed as negligent in falling asleep. This negligence was found to be the principal cause of the accident.

If it had been the sole cause, Shepard would have been one hundred percent responsible. The jury apparently found that Sharon Theisen's conduct (riding with Shepard under the circumstances) fell below that of a person of ordinary prudence but that her conduct was not a *proximate* cause of the accident (not the primary or moving cause that produced the accident).

The jury, however, apparently found that the passengers, including the plaintiff, were a contributing cause of the accident by falling asleep because they failed to keep a proper lookout to aid the driver. When one of the passengers did awaken, it was too late. Because Sharon Theisen thus was apportioned five percent of the total negligence, her recovery was reduced by that amount.

DISCUSSION OF PROBLEM 3.8

Both West's synopsis and the court's syllabus describe the basic procedural context of the case. A Wisconsin circuit court tried the case, and the "defendant appealed." This language indicates that this case involved an appeal. Thus, answer (b) ("Appeal") is correct.

DISCUSSION OF PROBLEM 3.9

West's synopsis states that the circuit court's judgment was reversed and that the case was remanded for a new trial on questions of negligence only. Thus, answer (c) is correct. In the opinion, the court explained that neither the plaintiff nor the defendant raised any question concerning the amount of damages. Therefore, there was no need to determine again the amount of damages suffered by the plaintiff.

DISCUSSION OF PROBLEM 3.10

In this problem, you were asked to consider the following statements:

(a) Acts done while a person is asleep cannot constitute negligence. Because Shepard hit the tree while he was asleep, he could not have been negligent (and thus was not liable).

(b) Negligence is based on fault, and a person who suffers from a physical impairment, such as a heart attack, epileptic seizure, or other loss of consciousness, is always an innocent victim of that impairment. Such a person cannot be said to be "at fault."

(c) The direct cause of the accident was the car hitting the tree, not Shepard's falling asleep. Thus, Shepard was not at fault and cannot be liable.

(d) This case should be governed by the general rule that a driver is not liable for an accident caused by a sudden and unforeseen disability (such as a heart attack). Shepard unknowingly fell asleep from physical exhaustion without warning. Under such circumstances, it would be unfair to hold him responsible because the subsequent acts were involuntary.

The defendant's approach was to argue that this case falls outside of the general rules governing negligence. Instead, the defendant contended that a different general rule should have controlled. The defendant argued that persons who unexpectedly and unknowingly are victims of heart attacks, epileptic seizures, and other losses of consciousness (including sleep resulting from physical exhaustion) should not be liable.

Presumably, it would be unfair to hold individuals liable under such circumstances (no control over their actions), and the court points out, *arguendo*, that acts done after loss of consciousness are involuntary and do not in and of themselves constitute negligence. This argument is best summarized in answer (d) above. The defendant's argument was not based on causation, answer (c). Nor is it correct to say that a victim of a physical impairment is "always" innocent because such a person may have been able to foresee the likelihood of a subsequent attack occurring. Answer (a) is less complete than answer (d) and thus is not the best explanation of the defendant's argument.

The last sentence of the paragraph of this portion of the opinion sets the stage for the court's response to the defendant's argument: "The basis, however, for liability of the sleeping driver is his negligence in falling asleep." The events leading up to the loss of consciousness play an important role in the rule asserted by the defendant. If a person knows that the event is likely to occur, imposing the duty to avoid the dangerous situation is reasonable. The court thus states that negligence, and hence liability, may arise from falling asleep while driving.

DISCUSSION OF PROBLEM 3.11

In this problem, you were asked which of the following statements *best* identifies the court's basic approach in this case:

(a) Greater skill and attention are needed in driving an automobile now than were needed forty years ago. This change justifies liability without fault if one falls asleep while driving.

(b) To recover in a negligence action, the defendant must have breached a duty of care owed to others. Because of the risks involved, drivers have a duty to stay awake while they are driving, and it is within their control either to stay awake, to cease driving, or not to drive at all when they are sleepy.

(c) Modern, high-powered automobiles have become inherently dangerous. Because of this increased danger, a special duty arises to cease driving if one becomes sleepy.

(d) Physical impairments are no longer a valid excuse because of the increase in the frequency and in the seriousness of the consequences of accidents involving modern automobiles.

To recover in a negligence action (i.e., "state a cause of action"), there must be (1) a recognized legal duty on a person to exercise due care; (2) a failure by that person to conform to the duty; (3) a direct causal connection between the person's conduct and the injury inflicted upon another person; and (4) some actual damage to the injured party. A plaintiff thus must present evidence of facts showing that a duty of care existed (driving the automobile on the public highway) and a breach of that duty (falling asleep) that caused actual injury to the plaintiff.

In the above excerpt, the court identified the duty: "[T]he driver has the duty to stay awake while he drives and it is within his control either to stay awake, to cease driving, or not to drive at all when sleepy." It also stated that it is within the driver's *control* to stay awake or to avoid driving. This approach is summarized in answer (b) above. Answer (a) is not an accurate summary because it makes the driver liable without regard to fault (strict liability), rather than based on the driver's negligence. Nor does the court condemn automobiles as being "inherently dangerous" (like a gun), answer (b). The court also does not attack the general rule (sudden illness or impairment) proposed by the defendant, answer (d).

DISCUSSION OF PROBLEM 3.12

In this problem, you were asked (1) why proof of falling asleep is enough to establish an inference of negligence for purposes of a prima facie case and (2) under prior cases, what was the effect of that proof. You were given the following choices:

(a) Sleep does not ordinarily occur without some notice and to fall asleep while driving is the usual result of negligence in failing to heed the warnings. The case goes to the jury and a verdict for the plaintiff will be upheld if no circumstances tending to excuse or justify such conduct are proven.

(b) No circumstances can be proven that would justify any conclusion other than that the driver had been negligent by falling asleep while driving. The plaintiff wins and is entitled to a directed verdict.

(c) The inference of negligence is based on the well-established medical principle that sleep is always accompanied by premonitory warnings. A jury verdict may be based on falling asleep after receiving those warnings and will be upheld on appeal because no circumstances can be proven to excuse or justify that conduct.

(d) Sleeping is inherently negligent. Thus, proof of sleep at the wheel allows the case to go to the jury and will support a jury verdict in favor of the plaintiff if the court is satisfied that it was the proximate cause of the accident.

In the prior cases, proof of falling asleep had been sufficient to support an inference of negligence for purposes of establishing the breach-of-the-duty-of-care element of a prima facie case. When the plaintiff has presented at least the minimum necessary to prove each of the elements of a negligence claim, the plaintiff has presented a prima facie case and ordinarily is entitled to have the case go to the jury.

The prior decisions recognized that "sleep ordinarily does not occur without some notice and to fall asleep while driving is the usual result of negligence in failing to heed the warning." On review, the effect of such a prima facie showing would be to support a verdict for recovery, provided "no circumstances tending to excuse or justify [falling asleep were] proven." Answer (a) is thus correct.

The court did not state that falling asleep was inherently dangerous, answer (d). Contrary to answers (b) and (c), the prior cases allowed defendants to justify or excuse their falling asleep or failure to heed the warnings. The prior cases do not state that sleep is *always* accompanied by warnings, answer (b).

DISCUSSION OF PROBLEM 3.13

In this problem, you were to consider the effect of the court's declaration that a person's falling asleep while driving an automobile is negligence as a matter of law. You were given the following choices:

(a) the court will determine whether any excuse is sufficient to be submitted to the jury.

(b) negligence will no longer be a question of fact to be submitted to the jury when the plaintiff alleges that the defendant driver fell asleep at the wheel.

(c) defendants will be held strictly liable because no facts can exist which will justify, excuse, or exculpate falling asleep at the wheel.

(d) all the plaintiff needs to prove is the fact of falling asleep. If the plaintiff proves this fact, the plaintiff is entitled to recover, assuming the other elements of his cause of action are sufficiently shown.

"Negligence as a matter of law" was used in the synopsis, in headnote one, and in the text of the opinion. Negligence is an act or omission that falls below the standard established by law for the protection of others against unreasonable risk of harm.

Ordinarily, the trier of fact determines what care a reasonably prudent and careful person should have used under similar circumstances. Sometimes, however, the standard of care may be derived from a statute setting a specific legal standard by which the defendant's conduct will be measured. The defendant's violation of the statute is considered negligence as a matter of law. The standard of care also may be established by the court when it finds that certain conduct is so opposed to the dictates of common prudence that no careful person would have committed the act or omission (falling asleep while driving).

In these latter two situations, the trier of fact will be concerned only with whether the conduct in fact occurred or the statute in fact was violated. Thus, answer (d) is correct. This limited question is still submitted to the jury, and thus answer (b) is incorrect. Furthermore, in future cases, the court will refuse to hear or pass on any excuses, and thus answer (a) is incorrect. Note that negligence as a matter of law is sometimes referred to as "negligence per se," particularly when the violation of a statute forms the legal standard of care.

DISCUSSION OF PROBLEM 3.14

In this problem, you were asked the meaning of the following statement: "If while driving a car one is in such a state of exhaustion that he falls asleep without any premonitory warning, [the defendant] is *chargeable* with the knowledge of any ordinary prudent man that such exhaustion is reasonably likely to cause sleep while driving" (emphasis added). You were given the following choices:

(a) even if credible evidence could be offered that, because of inexperience, the driver *in fact* did not know that a result of exhaustion is falling asleep, the defendant would not be allowed to offer that evidence under the rule established by the court.

(b) on retrial, the plaintiff must show that Shepard was an ordinary prudent person.

(c) on retrial, the plaintiff must show that Shepard was in a state of exhaustion; otherwise, the burden shifts to the defendant to show that ordinary prudent persons, faced with the same circumstances as those facing the defendant, would have attempted to drive.

(d) on retrial, the defendant will have to show through medical and scientific proof that in some instances sleep resulting from exhaustion can *in fact* occur without premonitory warning in order to win.

Words like "chargeable" or "deemed" often indicate that the court is adopting a legal fiction (an assumption of law or fact that the legal system permits to be established). Thus, even if credible evidence could be offered that, because of inexperience, the defendant *in fact* did not know that a result of exhaustion is falling asleep, the defendant would not be allowed to offer that evidence under the rule established by the court. Thus, answer (a) is correct.

To the extent that a contrary rule has been recognized in earlier decisions, the court expressly overrules them. Answer (d) is thus incorrect. The negligence-as-a-matter-of-law rule thus has this important effect. The driver may no longer attempt to prove facts to justify, excuse, or exculpate falling asleep at the wheel. The plaintiff must only prove circumstances tending to show that the driver fell asleep, contrary to the assertions in answers (b) and (c).

DISCUSSION OF PROBLEM 3.15

In this problem, you were to assume that on retrial the defendant could offer *credible* medical evidence from Shepard's autopsy that Shepard's falling asleep was caused by his first (and last) attack of narcolepsy (a condition characterized by brief attacks of deep sleep). You were asked, based on the court's opinion, which of the following provides the best argument in favor of allowing the defendant to introduce this evidence:

(a) The plaintiff assumed the risk as a matter of law that the defendant might be struck with an attack of narcolepsy.

(b) Narcolepsy is different from ordinary sleep because it involves deep sleep. Thus, this case does not fall within the court's rule excluding justifications or excuses for ordinary sleep.

(c) Narcolepsy is an illness which occurred without warning and resulted in a sudden incapacitation of the driver.

(d) Narcolepsy does not involve "permitting oneself to fall asleep," and driving under such circumstances should not be *deemed* to be negligence as a matter of law.

Does the defendant in this narcolepsy hypothetical have a way of avoiding the court's rule concerning negligence as a matter of law? The court left the door open when it "exclude[d] from this holding those exceptional cases of loss of consciousness resulting from [an] illness which [without foreseeable warning] suddenly incapacitates the driver." The best argument is thus to characterize narcolepsy as an illness that occurred without warning, answer (c). If the court accepted this classification, the principal issue would be whether the first attack of narcolepsy could occur suddenly and without warning and not be reasonably foreseen.

The other answers are incorrect. Assumption of risk is not relevant, answer (a). Answer (b) fails to state the argument clearly, and answer (d) is not responsive to the question. Note that the court's exclusion of "exceptional cases" is dictum (a nonessential comment that is unnecessary to resolving the specific issues before the court).

DISCUSSION OF PROBLEM 3.16

Based on the paragraph of the opinion discussing the subject, you were asked which of the following statements about the "burden of proof" in cases involving allegedly sleeping drivers is correct:

(a) The party claiming that the driver fell asleep has the initial burden of going forward with the evidence tending to show that the driver fell asleep.

(b) If the party claiming that the driver fell asleep presents evidence tending to establish that fact, the burden of going forward with the evidence shifts to the other side to show that the driver did not fall asleep, for example, that the driver suffered a heart attack.

(c) If the burden shifts as described in answer (b), the driver will be held negligent as a matter of law unless the driver can show that a greater probability exists that the loss of consciousness is excusable on some nonactionable basis, such as a heart attack.

(d) The court does not appear to be addressing the ultimate burden of proof (persuasion), which remains on the plaintiff throughout the proceeding.

The phrase "burden of proof" has two distinct meanings. First, it can refer to the ultimate burden of persuasion, which under the traditional view never shifts from one party to another party during the course of the proceeding. Second, it can refer to the burden of going forward with the evidence, which may shift back and forth between the parties during the course of the trial. The court in the text of the opinion is using this term in the latter sense.

Here, the plaintiff must present evidence that "tends to establish the fact" that the driver fell asleep (a prima facie case). If the plaintiff does, then the burden of going forward with the evidence shifts to the defendant to show that the driver did not fall asleep--for example, that the driver had a heart attack.

After the burden has shifted, the defendant will be held negligent as a matter of law unless the defendant can show that there is a "greater probability that the loss of consciousness is excusable on some nonactionable basis." The ultimate burden of persuasion, however, apparently remains on the plaintiff. Thus, all the above statements are correct.

DISCUSSION OF PROBLEM 3.17

In this problem, you were asked the reason why the trial court's exclusion of the defendant's offer of proof concerning Shepard's physical exhaustion was not error. You were given the following choices:

(a) [The evidence] was offered for the purpose of proving a proposition which was not properly at issue.

(b) [The evidence] lacked any tendency to make the existence of any fact more probable or less probable than it would have been without the evidence.

(c) [The evidence] was based on a preconceived view of the facts which would have confused the determination of liability.

(d) [The evidence] tended to prove a proposition favorable to the plaintiff, not the defendant (who offered the evidence); only evidence favorable to one's side may be offered by that side.

At this point in the opinion, the court began to examine errors that the defendant claimed the trial court had committed. The court first addressed the contention that it was an error to have excluded the defendant's offer of proof that Shepard was physically exhausted from the considerable loss of sleep, practice for the play, and continuing his usual chores. The reason that this exclusion was proper was *because this evidence was offered as a justification for falling asleep.*

The court previously had stated that no justifications would be permitted. If the driver fell asleep (as opposed, for example, to having a heart attack), then the driver was negligent as a matter of law. The reasons why he fell asleep are "immaterial." In other words, the trial court's exclusion of the defendant's offer of proof concerning Shepard's physical exhaustion was not error because that evidence "was offered for the purpose of proving a proposition which was not properly at issue," answer (a).

Answers (c) and (d) are erroneous propositions, and answer (b) is an inaccurate statement of the reason for the exclusion.

DISCUSSION OF PROBLEM 3.18

In this problem, you were told that the defendant contended that an instruction should have been given on the presumption of due care accorded a deceased party. You were asked why the defendant wanted this instruction given. You were given the following choices:

(a) Had the instruction been given, the driver would have been conclusively presumed to have operated the vehicle with due care.

(b) Had the instruction been given, the verdict would have been improper because it rested on speculation.

(c) Because there was no direct evidence of the cause of the driver's loss of consciousness, the defendant wanted the jury to be told that the driver should be presumed to have acted with due care. This instruction would have been favorable to the defendant, who could have tried to convince the jury that the plaintiff was only speculating as to the cause of the loss of consciousness and thus had not met the required burden of rebutting the presumption.

(d) Because no direct evidence of the cause of the driver's loss of consciousness was offered by the plaintiff, the defendant would have been entitled to a directed verdict had the instruction been given.

As previously noted, the plaintiff must prove that the driver fell asleep. What happens if there is no direct evidence of the cause of the driver's loss of consciousness? It was in this context that the court considered another of the defendant's contentions: the trial court erred in not instructing the jury that a deceased party (the driver) is entitled to a *presumption* that the deceased party had exercised due care.

A presumption (in this instance, a "rebuttable" presumption) is one that results from the proof of certain facts (that the driver was deceased). This presumption establishes prima facie (not requiring further support) the existence of a certain conclusion (that the driver was exercising due care). The party against whom it operates (here the plaintiff because she must prove the driver's lack of due care) must introduce facts to rebut the presumption or it becomes "conclusive." Answer (c) best explains the reasons why the defendant wanted this instruction given.

The presumption was not a conclusive presumption, answer (a), because it could be rebutted by the plaintiff. Even if the instruction had been given, a directed verdict would not have resulted because there was sufficient evidence to take the issue to the jury. For the same reason, a jury verdict in favor of the plaintiff would not be overridden by the court on the ground of speculation had the instruction been given, answer (d).

Although the court recognized that no direct evidence of the cause of the driver's loss of consciousness existed, the court found that the circumstantial evidence (car on the wrong side of the road, no sudden turning, distance and length of time until impact, time of night, others in the car fell asleep) was sufficient to raise an inference that the driver had fallen asleep.

Note that the court was faced with a problem here. The trial judge had *excluded* an offer of proof that Shepard was physically exhausted from the loss of considerable sleep, practice for the play, and continuing his usual chores. The exclusion of this offer of proof was upheld (as previously noted) because the defendant could not offer evidence to prove a justification for falling asleep. Had this evidence been *admitted*, it could have been used to prove physical exhaustion--not as a justification for falling asleep but rather to infer that Shepard fell asleep from exhaustion.

The court sidestepped this problem by relying on the fact that the car was on the wrong side of the road, coupled with the other circumstances mentioned above (time of night, etc.). In Wisconsin (but not in all states), once these circumstances have been introduced, the "presumption is eliminated and drops out of the case." Therefore, it was proper for the trial court not to give the instruction dealing with the presumption of due care of a deceased party.

Chapter 4

Authority of Judicial Decisions, Basic Legal Reasoning, and Case Synthesis

DISCUSSION OF PROBLEM 4.1

In *Fuentes v. Shevin*, the United States Supreme Court was divided four-to-three, with two Justices not participating. In this problem, you were asked whether you thought the binding nature of the decision is affected because a majority (five Justices) did not concur in the result.

As noted in the preceding section of this chapter, ordinarily United States Supreme Court decisions on questions of federal law bind all federal courts. Such decisions also bind all state courts pursuant to the supremacy clause of the Constitution. The issue is whether decisions of less than a majority of the Court have the same binding effect.

Commentators generally take the view that decisions by less than a majority of the Court should not affect the binding nature of the Court's decision,[17] but the Arizona Supreme Court held otherwise in *Roofing Wholesale Co. v. Palmer*.[18] In *Palmer*, the Arizona Supreme Court conceded that the four Justices in *Fuentes* fully intended in their opinion to apply the due process clause to situations such as the one (prejudgment attachment) before the Arizona court. Nevertheless, the court concluded it was not bound:

> The petitioner, however, asserts that because two [J]ustices did not participate in this opinion the four [person] opinion is clearly not a majority opinion, is advisory only, and therefore not binding upon this court. Admittedly, were we convinced that the four man majority of the United States Supreme Court in [*Fuentes*], *supra*, would become at least a five man majority when the two [Justices] who did not participate in the particular case are called up to participate in a similar question, we would then be inclined to follow the decision as set down in *Fuentes*, *supra*. When, however, we have doubts that once the full court hears the case that the opinion will stand, we are reluctant to declare unconstitutional Arizona

---

[17] See Annotation, Binding Effect Upon State Courts of Opinion of United States Supreme Court Supported by Less Than A Majority of All Its Members, 65 A.L.R.3d 504, 516-17 (1975).

[18] 108 Ariz. 508, 502 P.2d 1327 (1973).

> statutes based upon a decision by less than a clear majority.[19]

Dissenting in *Palmer*, Justice Struckmeyer countered:

> I cannot believe the important aspects of the United States Constitution and federal statutes so construed are not binding on all other courts of this country simply because all nine members of the Court did not enter into the decision. Cases such as these must be held to be binding precedent; otherwise, important areas of constitutional law and congressional enactments remain in limbo, until finally the court in a subsequent action has an opportunity, years later perhaps, to re-examine the questions presented. The resulting mischief is intolerable.[20]

One would suspect that should it specifically review the question, the United States Supreme Court would hold that the opinion of a majority of the Court sitting, even if it is a minority of the whole court, is binding.[21]

DISCUSSION OF PROBLEM 4.2

In this problem, you were asked to assume that you had found the following case during the course of your research: *Plata v. Gohman*, 359 S.W.2d 163 (Tex. Civ. App. 1962). By examining (1) the page reproduced from *Shepard's South Western Reporter Citations* covering the entry for this case in Figure 4-A and (2) *Shepard's* table of abbreviations for Texas writ history in Figure 4-B, you were to determine the writ history of *Plata v. Gohman*.

Shepard's South Western Reporter Citations uses an asterisk to alert the researcher to the existence of writ history for cases appearing in volumes prior to volume 306 of *South Western Reporter Second*; thereafter, *Shepard's* uses abbreviations (e.g., "R" = application for writ of error refused, "RNRE" = application for writ of error refused, no reversible error, etc.) to show the specific disposition of the writ.

In this instance, the Texas Supreme Court refused the application, indicating that no reversible error existed ("RNRE").

---

[19] Id. at 1329-30.

[20] Id. at 1332.

[21] But cf. Sculthorp v. American Motors Corp., 4 Mich. App. 65, 67, 143 N.W.2d 767, 768 (1966) (3-2 decision of the seven-member Michigan Supreme Court was "not precedent as to future cases").

This information is indicated immediately below the listed page number ("163") on which the report begins.

DISCUSSION OF PROBLEM 4.3

In this problem, you were asked what the refusal of the application for the writ of error in the *Plata* case means. You were given the following choices:

(a) the authority of the decision below is strengthened.

(b) the principles declared in the opinion of the Texas Court of Civil Appeals were decided correctly.

(c) the authority of the decision below must be analyzed carefully because the Texas Supreme Court was not convinced that the opinion of the Texas Court of Civil Appeals correctly stated the law in all respects.

(d) the Texas Supreme Court lacked jurisdiction to hear the case, and thus it refused the application for the writ of error. A refusal of the writ indicates that "no reversible error" existed.

Generally speaking, when a writ of error is simply "refused" by the Texas Supreme Court, the authority of the decision below is strengthened because this notation indicates the judgment below was correct, and the principles or questions of law declared in the opinion were decided correctly. Because the writ was not simply refused, answers (a) and (b) are incorrect.

On the other hand, when such a writ is "refused, no reversible error," the authority of the decision below must be analyzed carefully. This indication means that the Texas Supreme Court was not convinced that the opinion below correctly stated the law in all respects but that the application presented no error that required a reversal. Thus, answer (c) is correct. The disposition of this case did not involve a lack of jurisdiction, and answer (d) is therefore incorrect.

DISCUSSION OF PROBLEM 4.4

In this problem, you were to assume that Grandmother Hood's attorneys sought to take the oral deposition (pretrial testimony taken under oath) of Peter Hood, Ms. Hood's younger brother. Wolf objected that Peter was too young to testify. After the parties took the appropriate procedural steps to present the issue to the trial court for decision, the trial judge ruled that Peter was competent and allowed his deposition to be taken. At trial, Wolf again objected that Peter was incompetent to testify. You were asked which of the following doctrines would be the proper basis for denying Wolf's objection:

(a) stare decisis

(b) res judicata

(c) full faith and credit

(d) law of the case

The proper basis for denying Wolf's objection is stated in answer (d), "law of the case." Under this doctrine, once a question of law has been determined in a case, that determination will be treated as correct in subsequent stages of the same case (until the question is reviewed by a higher court).

DISCUSSION OF PROBLEM 4.5

In this problem, you were to assume that Grandmother Hood won her action against Wolf and that Ms. Hood's action was then brought to trial. Ms. Hood called her little brother (Peter) to testify, and Wolf objected on the ground that Peter was too young to testify reliably. You were asked which of the following doctrines would support the trial judge's denial of Wolf's motion:

(a) stare decisis

(b) collateral estoppel

(c) full faith and credit

(d) law of the case

Full faith and credit, answer (c), does not apply to this kind of situation. Had Grandmother Hood, for example, sought to enforce the judgment that she had won, other courts would ordinarily be required to honor that judgment pursuant to the full faith and credit clause. Stare decisis, answer (a), also does not apply because the ruling in the *Grandmother Hood v. Wolf* action was that of a *trial* court. Recall that trial courts do not make binding precedents.

Nor is law of the case, answer (d), involved in any way in this problem because that doctrine does not apply to proceedings in different actions. On the other hand, answer (b), collateral estoppel, is correct. Under the modern law of collateral estoppel (issue preclusion), Wolf may be bound by the prior determination, provided the necessary requirements are met, such as a full and fair opportunity to litigate the issue.

DISCUSSION OF PROBLEM 4.6

In this problem, you were to assume that at trial, Wolf claimed that "he didn't touch Ms. Hood" and that she had attacked him without provocation. Assume that the jury believed Wolf's testimony and that the trial court entered a judgment in favor of Wolf based on the jury's verdict. Dissatisfied with that result,

Hood sued again on the same claim in a different California Superior Court. You were asked on what basis the second action would be barred. You were given the following choices:

(a) the doctrine of stare decisis

(b) the doctrine of res judicata

(c) the doctrine of full faith and credit

(d) the doctrine of law of the case

The res judicata doctrine precludes the second action. In this instance, Ms. Hood is bound by the results in the first action, and thus answer (b), "res judicata," is correct. Ms. Hood's proper course of action was to appeal the case rather than to file a new action. Stare decisis, answer (a), and full faith and credit, answer (c), do not apply for the reasons stated in the preceding problem. Law of the case, answer (d), does not apply to proceedings in different actions.

DISCUSSION OF PROBLEM 4.7

In this problem, you were to assume that instead of filing a new action, Hood appealed the judgment entered on the jury's verdict to a California Court of Appeal. On appeal, Ms. Hood asserted that the trial court erred when it allowed certain testimony that Hood considered to be inadmissible hearsay evidence. You were also to assume that the California Supreme Court had decided a prior case involving the same point of evidence law and similar facts. You were asked on what basis the California Court of Appeal would be bound by that earlier decision. You were given the following choices:

(a) the doctrine of stare decisis

(b) the doctrine of res judicata

(c) the doctrine of full faith and credit

(d) the doctrine of law of the case

This problem presents a classic example of a binding or mandatory precedent. All inferior courts have a duty to adhere to decisions of their higher courts until they have been overruled or altered by legislation. Thus, answer (a) is correct.

Had the decision been from a different California Court of Appeal or from another jurisdiction, the decision would have been merely persuasive (not binding).

DISCUSSION OF PROBLEM 4.8

In this problem, you were to find the entry for *Plata v. Gohman*, 359 S.W.2d 163 (Tex. Civ. App. 1962) on the page of Shepard's Citations in Figure 4-A. You were to assume that you were particularly interested in the subsequent treatment of the point of law summarized in headnote 4 of the opinion shown in Figure 4-C. You were asked what the subsequent treatment of headnote 4 has been.

The page reproduced from *Shepard's* in Figure 4-A indicates, *inter alia*, that the point of law summarized in headnote 4 was distinguished in

d390SW2d^{4}383

This entry means that a *subsequent* case reported in volume 390 of the *South Western Reporter Second* at page 383 discussed and distinguished headnote 4 of the *Plata* case. If you consulted that case in the reporter, you would find that the subsequent case was another decision of the Texas Court of Civil Appeals--*Gonzales v. Perry*, 390 S.W.2d 382 (Tex. Civ. App. 1965).

To help you understand the significance of this entry in *Shepard's*, examine the relevant portions of pages 383-84 of the *Gonzales* case shown below.

> [1, 2] It has been definitely decided in this State that a pedestrian under certain circumstances and surroundings must keep a lookout to his rear for approaching automobiles. Plata v. Gohman, Tex.Civ.App., 359 S.W.2d 163. In that case this Court in a divided opinion held that Plata, who was walking along the extreme left edge of the road, was required to keep a lookout to his rear for approaching vehicles, where he had some warning that one was approaching. The writer of this opinion dissented in that case, but the Supreme Court refused an application for a writ, n. r. e. There were more circumstances requiring Gonzalez to keep a lookout to his rear for the approaching vehicle than in the Plata case. Here the two boys were running down the middle of the street. When the horn was sounded, Lopez, who was the front runner, turned to his right and occupied the right-hand lane of the street, and Gonzalez, who was running behind him, is presumed to

have seen Lopez turn into the right-hand lane. Thus Gonzalez knew that a vehicle was approaching from his rear and that Lopez was in the right-hand lane of the street. This should have been sufficient to cause Gonzalez concern as to the side on which the vehicle would attempt to pass. He did not look to the rear, but continued on down the center of the street. When the vehicle was about even with him, he turned into the left-hand lane and collided with the side of the vehicle. The evidence was sufficient to support the jury's answer to Special Issue No. 7, to the effect that Gonzalez failed to keep a proper lookout for his own safety, and its answer to Issue No. 8, that such failure was a proximate cause of the collision. 4 Tex. Jur.2d 390–395, § 837; 7 Am.Jur.2d, § 401,

FIGURE 4-D
SOUTH WESTERN REPORTER SECOND

The entry for the *Plata* case in *Shepard's* also indicates two other instances in which that case has been *cited* with reference to the point of law summarized in headnote 4:

404SW2d[4]926 and 408SW2d[4]952

In both instances, the citing court quoted the *Plata* case (as shown in Figure 4-E):

VOL. 404 AT PAGE 926

[10, 11] In a case involving a vehicle and a pedestrian and the failure of the pedestrian to keep a proper lookout, judgment for the driver of the vehicle was affirmed. Plata v. Gohman, 359 S.W.2d 163, Tex.Civ.App., 1962, ref. n. r. e. The Court said:

> "* * * Intersection cases are not precisely in point, but they suggest similar rules and results with respect to the facts and circumstances which must be considered. The principle is the same. Even one who has the right of way is not excused from exercising ordinary care for his own safety. Even though one is not required to anticipate negligent conduct, he is not entitled to close his eyes to that which is plainly visible and which would have been observed by a person of ordinary prudence similarly situated. Lynch v. Ricketts, 158 Tex. 487, 314 S.W.

VOL. 408 AT PAGE 952

[11] In an opinion written by Justice Pope while on the San Antonio Court of Civil Appeals in the case of Plata v. Gohman, supra, it was said:

> "* * * Even though one is not required to anticipate negligent conduct, he is not entitled to close his eyes to that which is plainly visible and which would have been observed by a person of ordinary prudence similarly situated. (cases cited)"

See also De Winne v. Allen, 154 Tex. 316, 277 S.W.2d 95, (S.Ct.) 1955; Lynch v. Ricketts, 158 Tex. 487, 314 S.W.2d 273, (S.Ct.) 1958. It has also been held that the abstract statement that one may assume that others will act in a lawful and non-

FIGURE 4-E
SOUTHWESTERN REPORTER SECOND

DISCUSSION OF PROBLEM 4.9

In this problem, you were to assume that a trial judge in Wisconsin is asked to decide whether a defendant should be permitted to offer evidence to prove certain unusual circumstances in an attempt to excuse the defendant's apparent negligence in the operation of his automobile. Assume further that the request to rule on the admissibility of the evidence occurred after the decision of *Theisen v. Milwaukee Automobile Mutual Insurance Co.*, 18 Wis. 2d 91, 118 N.W.2d 140 (1962), discussed in Chapter 3. You were asked how would you, as the plaintiff's attorney, attempt to convince the court that the evidence should be excluded.

Ordinarily, a plaintiff's attorney would attempt to convince the court through deductive reasoning. You would first refer to the decision in the *Theisen* case: "The Supreme Court of Wisconsin has decided that if a driver falls asleep at the wheel of an automobile, the driver is negligent as a matter of law and no facts may be introduced into evidence to excuse that negligence." This statement would be the *major premise* of the syllogism that a plaintiff's attorney would plan to construct.

The defendant's attorney may disagree with this interpretation of the *Theisen* case and assert that the *ratio decidendi* (the principle of law that links the essential facts with the ultimate decision in the case) is not the one asserted by opposing counsel. Presumably, however, in this instance the judge would agree with the proposition stated by the plaintiff's attorney.

The plaintiff's attorney then would attempt to establish that the facts of the present case show that the defendant fell asleep at the wheel of the automobile. This proposition would be the attorney's *minor premise*. The defendant's attorney may dispute this characterization of the evidence by arguing, for example, that the defendant did not fall asleep at the wheel of the automobile. This type of factual dispute is often the central focus of many lawsuits. If the judge agrees with the asserted major and minor premises, the judge will then *conclude* that the evidence offered to excuse the driver's negligence (falling asleep) should be excluded.

DISCUSSION OF PROBLEM 4.10

In this problem, you were to assume again the basic facts presented in Chapter 2 involving Irma Marie Delira. You were also to assume that (1) you have found three Wisconsin opinions during your research that appear to be related to this problem and (2) you are going to analyze and apply the principles in those cases to the facts of the Delira problem.

The first case is *Karow v. Continental Insurance Co.*, 57 Wis. 56, 15 N.W. 27 (1883). You were asked to note the basic facts of the *Karow* case and decide what its holding is. You were also asked to mark in the margin the parts of the opinion that are relevant to the research problem. [The text of the *Karow* case is reproduced in Chapter 4 in Figure 4-F.]

As indicated in Chapters 2 and 3, you should prepare research notes on the cases you read during the course of your research. For example, for the *Karow* case, your principal case brief might be as follows:

> An insurer is liable under a fire insurance policy if the burning was not caused by the voluntary act, assent, procurement, or design of the insured. If the insured was insane at the time of the burning, his actions could not be considered, from a legal point of view, to be voluntary ones because an insane person has no control over his mental faculties.
>
> ✓ Karow v. Continental Insurance Co., 57 Wis. 56, 15 N.W. 27 (1883).
>
> The plaintiffs sued a fire insurance company in a Wisconsin circuit court to recover under two fire insurance policies. The plaintiffs were heirs at law and legal representatives of the owner of the policies that covered the buildings on his homestead. In a special verdict (one in which the jury only finds the facts in response to specific questions submitted to it), the jury found, inter alia, (1) that the insured had set fire to the buildings and (2) that he was not insane when he had done so. Based on the jury's findings, the circuit court entered judgment for the defendant, apparently because the insured had burned his own buildings while he was sane. The plaintiffs asserted that the insurer had waived this defense, but both the trial and appellate courts found that it had not.
>
> On the question of insanity, the trial judge charged the jury that it must look outside the commission of the act of burning the buildings and the immediately preceding crime (the murder of his wife and attempted murder of the members of his family) in judging the insured's sanity. In effect, it could find the owner insane only from other independent testimony. The Supreme Court of Wisconsin found "manifest error" in this charge because the owner's acts themselves should be considered in determining what his mental condition was at the time of the commission of the act. On appeal, the insurance company argued that the insured's insanity was immaterial, and thus the error in the charge could be disregarded.

The Wisconsin Supreme Court held that the insurance company was liable if the burning had not been caused by the voluntary act, assent, procurement, or design of the insured. The insured's insanity was relevant because an insane person has no control over his mental faculties and thus no control, from a legal viewpoint, over his physical action. The court emphasized the absence of a specific provision in the policy relieving the insurer of liability in these circumstances. Thus, the error was material and the court reversed the judgment below and remanded the case for a new trial.

This problem asked you, in part, to mark the portions of the opinion that possibly could be related to the research issue. The court discussed in several places the legal responsibility of an insane person for his acts, including those that could be considered to be negligent. Much of this discussion was in response to the following argument made by the defendant insurer (found near the middle of page 28 of the opinion):

> [The] learned counsel contends that, while an insane person cannot be guilty of a crime, nor liable for a tort wherein the *intent* is a necessary ingredient, yet that a lunatic has always been held liable for other torts resulting in damage. In support of this, counsel cite [sic] several cases, and argues from them that if a lunatic burns the buildings of [A], he is liable to [A] for the amount of the actual damages sustained; and that, since this is so, it must follow that a lunatic cannot burn his own buildings upon which he has previously obtained an insurance, and then turn around and recover [from] the insurer the damages he has sustained by reason of his own act.[22]

The court noted several decisions from other states that supported the above proposition. Because this idea or principle is different from the one that was stated in the research notes above, you should not include it in your principal case brief.

Recall the discussion of note taking in Chapter 2 that each idea, concept, principle, or legal rule should be stated on a *separate* sheet of paper (under the system of note taking suggested). This approach allows you to compile authorities and notes thereon without interference or confusion with other ideas. It also allows you to arrange and rearrange those ideas or principles conveniently without rewriting. Thus, using this system, you could state the above idea at the top of a new sheet, along with the authorities cited in support of it:

---

[22] 57 Wis. at 60, 15 N.W. at 28.

Except when intent is an essential element in the action, insane persons are liable for their torts (including negligence).

✓ Karow v. Continental Insurance Co., 57 Wis. 56, 15 N.W. 27 (1883) (respondent insurer's argument was rejected as not applicable in that case because the instant case did not involve an innocent third party; instead, it involved an insurer that assumed the risk by contract from which the insurer could be relieved only if the burning was caused by the voluntary act, assent, procurement, or design of the insured).

Krom v. Schoonmaker, 3 Barb. 657 (_____) (civil action for personal injury may be maintained against a lunatic because the intent with which the act is done is not material).

Morse v. Crawford, 17 Vt. 499 (_____) (lunatic who killed plaintiff's ox liable for unintentional trespass).

Behrens v. McKenzie, 23 Iowa 333 (_____).

In the discussion of the cases listed on the above sheet, the *Karow* court identified (near the bottom of page 28 of the opinion) a reason for the above rule. Again, that reason should be recorded on a separate sheet of paper in your notes:

An insane person is civilly liable for his torts because of the principle that where a loss must be borne by one of two innocent persons, it should be borne by the one who occasioned it.

✓ Karow v. Continental Insurance Co., 57 Wis. 56, ____, 15 N.W. 27, ____ (1883) (apparently recognizing the above rule but holding it did not apply to insurance contract cases).

Beals v. See, 10 Pa. St. 61 (Chief Justice Gibson stated that "[a]s an insane man is civilly liable for his torts, he is liable to bear the consequences of his infirmity, as he is liable to bear his misfortunes, on the principle that where a loss must be borne by one of two innocent persons, it shall be borne by him who occasioned it").

Lancaster v. Moore, 78 Pa. St. 433 (_____) (quoting the reason stated in Beals approvingly).

_. Cooley, Torts 99, 103 (_____).

In your reading of the opinion, you may also have marked the following passage (which appears near the top of page 30):

> Of course, negligence involves a want of care in one who ought to bestow care. It is an omission of duty. But the law imposes no duty--no obligation of care--upon one who has no control over his mental faculties, and hence no control over his physical action. Being under no obligation of care, and under no restraint of duty, and incapable of exercising either, it would be inapt, if not inaccurate, to say that, by his omission, an insane person was guilty of negligence.[23]

This statement supports the conclusion that an insane person is incapable of being guilty of negligence. This conclusion is undercut, however, by the court's prior recognition that liability rests on the principle of allocating losses between two innocent parties. Furthermore, immediately after the above statement, the court continued:

> So, while the burning of his own property by an assured under no restraint of duty and incapable of care, and without any intent or design, does not relieve the company from liability, yet the same act of burning another's property might subject such person to damages therefor, not on the ground of negligence, as that word is usually understood, but in the language of Chief Justice Gibson, *supra* "on the principle that where a loss must be borne by one of two *innocent* persons, it should be borne by him who occasioned it."[24]

Therefore, although the language in isolation appears to support a possible defense based on insanity, recording this language as an authoritative statement from the *Karow* opinion would be improper.

In sum, the initial reading of *Karow* supports the following conclusions. First, certain language in *Karow* suggests that an insane person cannot be guilty of negligence because he has no control over his mental faculties and hence no control over his physical action. Second, the court indicated that an insane person "might" be subject to liability, however, on the ground that when "a loss must be borne by one of two *innocent* persons, it should be borne by him who occasioned it." Note, however, that these conclusions are based on dicta because the court emphasized the contractual obligation of the insurer; the court was not concerned with liability to third parties in the case before it.

---

[23] Id. at 63, 15 N.W. at 30.

[24] Id. at 64, 15 N.W. at 30.

DISCUSSION OF PROBLEM 4.11

In this problem, you were asked to read the second Wisconsin case, *In re Meyer's Guardianship*, 218 Wis. 381, 261 N.W. 211 (1935), reproduced in Chapter 4. You were also asked to mark in the margin the parts of the case that are relevant to the research issue and to consider how it could be related to the research problem and the *Karow* case.

The court in the *Meyer's Guardianship* case recognizes the basic rule (identified in the *Karow* case) holding insane persons liable for their unintentional torts. Thus, you could add this case to the list of authorities on the sheet prepared previously. Furthermore, you could add any *new* cases supporting this proposition discussed in the *Meyer's Guardianship* opinion as follows:

> Except when intent is an essential element in the action, insane persons are liable for their torts (including negligence).
>
> ✓ Karow v. Continental Insurance Co., 57 Wis. 56, 15 N.W. 27 (1883) (respondent insurer's argument was rejected as not applicable in that case because the instant case did not involve an innocent third party; instead, it involved an insurer that assumed the risk by contract from which the insurer could be relieved only if the burning was caused by the voluntary act, assent, procurement, or design of the insured).
>
> Krom v. Schoonmaker, 3 Barb. 657 (_____) (civil action for personal injury may be maintained against a lunatic because the intent with which the act is done is not material).
>
> Morse v. Crawford, 17 Vt. 499 (_____) (lunatic who killed plaintiff's ox liable for unintentional trespass).
>
> Behrens v. McKenzie, 23 Iowa 333 (_____).
>
> ✓ In re Meyer's Guardianship, 218 Wis. 381, 261 N.W. 211 (1935).
>
> Pursuant to an assignment of a right of action by persons who had been paid for a fire loss, the plaintiff in Meyer's, an insurance company, attempted to recover the amounts paid. The insurer sued the estate of the insane person (hereinafter referred to as the defendant), who had started a fire. The jury found, inter alia, that the defendant did not "intentionally" set the fire and was insane, but the trial court refused to enter judgment for the plaintiff;

instead, it did grant a new trial on the ground that justice had not been done.

On appeal, the Supreme Court of Wisconsin found that the evidence proved beyond doubt that the defendant set the fire. The court then held that insanity was not a defense in this case and entered judgment in favor of the plaintiff insurance company.

14 Ruling Case Law § 51, at 596 (______) (stating the above rule).

Hutchting v. Engel, 17 Wis. 230, 231 (______) ("lunatic is as liable to compensate in damages as a man in his right mind").

Williams v. Hays, 143 N.Y. 442, 446, 38 N.E. 449, 450 (______) (stating the above rule).

Cross v. Kent, 32 Md. 581 (______) (recognizing rule but stating an insane person is civilly liable "for any tort he may commit").

McIntyre v. Sholty, 121 Ill. 660, 13 N.E. 239 (______) (insane persons liable for their torts).

Seals v. Snow, 123 Kan. 88, 254 P. 348 (______) ("great weight of authority is that an insane person is liable for his torts").

Annotation, Liability of Insane Person for Tort, 51 A.L.R. 833 (______).

Note that the *Meyer's Guardianship* opinion relied on three reasons for the above rule. These reasons were summarized in *Ruling Case Law* (quoted by the court) as follows:

> This rule is usually considered to be based on [1] the principle that where a loss must be borne by one of two innocent persons, it shall be borne by him who occasioned it, and [2] it has also been held that public policy requires the enforcement of the liability in order that those interested in the estate of the insane person, as relatives or otherwise, may be under inducement to restrain him and [3] that tortfeasors may not simulate or pretend insanity to defend their wrongful acts causing damage to others.[25]

---

[25] 218 Wis. at 385, 261 N.W. at 213.

Because two *new* reasons ([2] and [3] above) are relied on, you should again state those reasons on separate sheets of paper, along with all supporting authorities for them.

Combining the analysis of the *Karow* case with this case, it appears that insanity is not a general defense to liability for an insane person's act except when evil intent or express malice are an essential element in the tort. Neither an evil intent nor express malice are elements of a cause of action for negligence. Thus, insane persons may be held liable for their negligent acts.

DISCUSSION OF PROBLEM 4.12

In this problem, you were to assume that the third Wisconsin case that you have found is *Theisen v. Milwaukee Automobile Mutual Insurance Co.*, 18 Wis. 2d 91, 118 N.W.2d 140 (1962), reproduced in Chapter 3. You were asked to examine that case again and to decide how that case might support a possible defense. You were also asked to consider how the *Theisen* case relates to the *Karow* case and *Meyer's Guardianship* case.

In the *Theisen* case, the plaintiff, a passenger in a car, commenced a negligence action for damages to recover for injuries resulting from the driver's falling asleep at the wheel. The Wisconsin Supreme Court held, *inter alia*, that the driver, insured by the defendant insurance company, was negligent per se. The court refused to accept the defendant's argument that the driver

> went to sleep unknowingly from physical exhaustion and the case should be governed by the principles applicable to sudden unforeseen *physical disability* over which a driver has no control, such as being the victim of a heart attack, epileptic seizure, or other loss of consciousness which is sudden and unforeseen. Arguendo, it may be stated acts done while one is asleep are not voluntary and in and of themselves do not constitute negligence. . . . The basis, however, for liability of the sleeping driver is his negligence in falling asleep.[26]

This initial reference to the asserted rule was stated in terms of a sudden unforeseen physical disability over which the driver has no control. The court stated this rule in a slightly different manner later in its opinion:

> We exclude from this holding those exceptional cases of loss of consciousness resulting from injury inflicted by an outside force or fainting or heart attack, epileptic seizure, or *other illness* which suddenly incapacitates the driver of an automobile and when

[26]Id. at 98, 118 N.W.2d at 142-43 (emphasis added).

> the occurrence of such disability is not attended *with sufficient warning or should not have been reasonably foreseen.* When, however, such occurrence should have been reasonably foreseen, we have held the driver of a motor vehicle negligent as a matter of law, as in the sleep cases.[27]

You would again prepare notes in the manner previously described, recording this new idea.

In the above statement, the court does not limit the rule to *physical* disabilities. The court refers to an "illness" that (1) suddenly incapacitates the driver, provided that (2) the occurrence was without sufficient warning, and (or?) (3) the illness was not reasonably foreseeable. Thus, this decision could be interpreted to support the view that if a *mental illness* suddenly incapacitates a driver, the driver will not be held liable if the illness occurred without warning and was not reasonably foreseeable.

Based upon *Karow* and *In re Meyer's Guardianship*, *prior* insanity of the defendant as a general defense cannot be relied on to relieve the defendant of liability. In fact, evidence of prior insanity may undercut the "sudden illness" rule recognized (but not applied) in *Theisen*. Furthermore, you should note that nothing in *Karow* and *In re Meyer's Guardianship* expressly limits the "insanity rule" to *pre-existing* insanity.

To meet the sudden illness rule, then, a "mental aberration" would have to be considered a physical or mental disability. Furthermore, it must have been "sudden" and "without warning." Thus, the defendant's prior "mental" history should be carefully investigated.

One matter of concern is how the court's requirement in *Theisen* (that the defendant could not have reasonably foreseen the events) should be applied when the illness is a mental one. Would the court judge the defendant by an objective standard or by a subjective one? What if there were indications of mental illness, but the very nature of the illness caused the person to deny the existence of the illness? In *Theisen*, the court charged the driver with knowledge of an ordinary prudent person even though the defendant, *in fact*, may not have realized that exhaustion might cause sleep.

Thus, one might suspect that a driver would be charged with objective knowledge of his prior mental illness if there had been sufficient warnings. This conclusion is supported by a general policy consideration recognized in *Meyer's*: those interested in the estate of the insane person would be under an inducement to restrain the driver if there were sufficient warnings.

---

[27] Id. at 99, 118 N.W.2d at 144 (emphasis added).

Another more critical concern is whether a mental illness (resulting in a loss of conscious control of an automobile) should be classified within the sudden illness rule. One might argue that this rule should be limited to *physical* disabilities and illnesses. One basis of the rule in *Meyer's* was to discourage tortfeasors from simulating or pretending insanity to defend their wrongful acts. Physical disabilities arguably could be proven by more objective evidence than mental illnesses.

Another concern is how to harmonize the principal basis for the rule in *Meyer's* (as between two innocent persons, the person causing the damage should be liable) with the rule recognized in *Theisen* (that sudden disabilities do not give rise to liability for negligence). Is not a person struck by a sudden heart attack or a sudden mental illness an innocent person who caused injury to another innocent person? One difficulty in resolving this apparent conflict lies in the lack of explanation of the reasons for the sudden illness rule in *Theisen*. Other cases supporting the sudden illness rule might establish the reasons. Is the suddenness the key to distinguishing the two rules? Or is the inability to control or anticipate the events the reason?

At this point in the synthesis, what conclusions can be drawn? First, it is clear that prior insanity of the driver is not a defense. Second, a sudden mental illness may provide a defense if (a) the illness occurred without warning or (b) the illness could not have been reasonably anticipated. Third, it seems likely that the driver would be charged with objective knowledge of the warnings even if the driver did not realize that loss of conscious control of an automobile was a possible result of the illness. Fourth, some risk exists that the line of cases refusing to recognize insanity as a defense may be applied to any case of mental illness, limiting the sudden illness rule to physical disabilities.

In *Karow*, there was apparently very little evidence of insanity except at the time the events (burning) occurred. In *Meyer's*, there is no discussion of whether there had been indications of insanity prior to the burning. However, in *Meyer's*, one of the reasons that supports the insanity liability rule is lacking: unlike the case of persons with a history of insanity, there is no opportunity for others to control the person who, without warning, becomes mentally ill.

Chapter 5

Statutory Interpretation and Analysis

DISCUSSION OF PROBLEM 5.1

In this problem, you were asked to identify and list what you regarded to be the key elements of the following Wisconsin statute:

> No cardholder shall use a credit card issued to him or allow another person to use a credit card issued to him with intent to defraud the issuer, a person or organization providing money, goods, services or anything else of value or any other person.[28]

Several key elements could be listed. Here are some possibilities: (1) cardholder; (2) use; (3) credit card; (4) issued to him; (5) allow another person to use; (6) intent to defraud; (6) issuer; (7) person or organization providing money, goods, services or anything of value; and (8) any other person.

Statsky points out that "[t]here are no absolute guidelines on how many thoughts, concepts or words should be [included] in any one element . . . . *You* must make the decision on how many elements exist and the test you use is: does the element say enough so that it can be analyzed and discussed separately?"[29]

DISCUSSION PROBLEM 5.2

In this problem, you were asked to decide "whose story" the following provision is primarily attempting to tell:

> § 1-102(3) . . . *Variation by Agreement* (original)
>
> The effect of provisions of this Act may be varied by agreement, except as otherwise provided in this Act and except that the obligations of good faith, diligence, and reasonableness and care prescribed by this Act may not be disclaimed by agreement but the parties may by agreement determine the standards by which the performance of such obligations is to be measured if such standards are not manifestly unreasonable.

---

[28] Wis. Stat. Ann. § 943.41(5)(b) (West 1982).

[29] W. Statsky, Legislative Analysis: How to Use Statutes and Regulations 50-51 (1975).

The primary agents in this section are the parties. They have the power to vary the effects of the Act, except in limited circumstances. Thus, based on reader expectation theory, the provision could be clarified by beginning it with the "parties" in the topic position.[30]

DISCUSSION OF PROBLEM 5.3

In this problem, you were asked to decide "whose story" is being told by the two exceptions in the provision ("except as otherwise provided in this Act and except that the obligations of good faith, diligence, and reasonableness and care prescribed by this Act").

The Act is the principal agent in the exceptions. The Act prohibits the parties from varying the effects of the provisions. Thus, based on reader expectation theory, the exceptions could be clarified by beginning them with the "Act" in the topic position.[31]

DISCUSSION OF PROBLEM 5.4

In this problem, you were asked to focus on the beginning of the provision: "The effect of provisions of this Act may be varied by agreement, except as otherwise provided . . . ." You were asked to assume that the provision is going to begin with the word "Parties." You were asked what verb or verb phrase you could use to locate the action of the sentence (what the parties are allowed to do) in that verb or verb phrase.

Several different verbs or verb phrases could be used. For example, the provision might begin as follows: "Parties are free to agree to vary the effects of the provisions of this Act except . . . ." or "Parties may agree to vary the effects of the provisions of this Act except . . . ."[32]

DISCUSSION OF PROBLEM 5.5

In this problem, you were asked how many stress positions may be found in the original version. The original provision is a single sentence containing only one stress position, which is identified by the punctuation mark at the end of the sentence.

---

[30]Gopen, Let the Buyer in the Ordinary Course of Business Beware: Suggestions for Revising the Prose of the Uniform Commercial Code, 54 U. Chi. L. Rev. 1178, 1186, 1189 (1987).

[31]*Id.* at 1189.

[32]*See id.* at 1188-89.

DISCUSSION OF PROBLEM 5.6

In this problem, you were asked how many stress provisions are there in Gopen's revision of this subsection:

> § 1-102(3) . . . *Variation by Agreement* (revision)
>
> Parties are free to agree to vary the effects of the provisions of this Act except
>
> (a) when this Act explicitly provides otherwise, and
>
> (b) when this Act prescribes obligations of good faith, diligence, reasonableness and care.
>
> When the obligations listed in Section 1-102(3)(b) are involved, parties may agree to determine the standards by which the performance of the obligations is to be measured, as long as those standards are not manifestly unreasonable.

The revised version contains three stress positions, created by (1) the comma at the end of exception (a), (2) the period at the end of exception (b), and (3) the period at the end of the final sentence (embodying the prohibition arising from the general concept of "reasonableness"). These stress positions allow the three separate ideas of the original to be presented more clearly.[33]

Consider the following version of the provision. The stress positions are shown in the braces. The story focuses are underlined. The verb phrases are capitalized.

> <u>Parties</u> ARE FREE TO AGREE TO VARY the effects of provisions of this Act except
>
> (a) when <u>this Act</u> EXPLICITLY PROVIDES {otherwise}, and
>
> (b) when <u>this Act</u> PRESCRIBES obligations of {good faith, diligence, reasonableness and care}.
>
> When <u>the obligations listed in Section 1-102(3)(b)</u> ARE INVOLVED, <u>parties</u> MAY AGREE TO DETERMINE the standards by which the performance of the obligations IS TO BE MEASURED, as long as those standards ARE {not manifestly unreasonable}.[34]

---

[33] *Id.* at 1189.

[34] *Id.*

DISCUSSION OF PROBLEM 5.7

In this problem, you were asked to identify the principal subject-verb separation in the following U.C.C. provision:

> § 2-202 *Final Written Expression: Parol or Extrinsic Evidence* (original)
>
> Terms with respect to which the confirmatory memoranda of the parties agree or which are otherwise set forth in a writing intended by the parties as a final expression of their agreement with respect to such terms as are included therein may not be contradicted by evidence of any prior agreement or of a contemporaneous oral agreement but may be explained or supplemented
>
> (a) by course of dealing or usage of trade (Section 1-205) or by course of performance (Section 2-208); and
> (b) by evidence of consistent additional terms unless the court finds the writing to have been intended also as a complete and exclusive statement of the terms of the agreement.

The grammatical subject of the provision is "Terms." The subject is separated from the verb ("may not be contradicted") by 40 words. By putting the subject and verb together, a different focus becomes evident. This provision tells the story of "evidence of prior agreement," not of "terms with respect to which . . . ." Thus, the wrong phrase occupies the topic position. Gopen explains further steps in the revision process:

> In further rearranging the prose to make sure that the stress positions were filled with the proper occupants, we discover that there were *two* stories being told here. The first is of parol evidence; it now occupies the primary topic position. The second turns out to be a sub-story about "terms;" they can therefore occupy topic positions in the subunits. Beyond that, there is a story of an exception concerning those terms. The need for stress positions for that story requires us to build a completely separate unit of discourse, in which "terms" is justly deserving the topic position. The result:
>
> § 2-202 *Final Written Expression: Parol or Extrinsic Evidence* (revision)
>
> (1) No evidence of any prior agreement or contemporaneous oral agreement may be used to contradict

(a) terms which the parties have agreed to in their confirmatory memoranda; or

(b) terms in a writing which the parties have intended as a final expression of their agreement.

(2) However, the terms referred to in (1)(a) and (1)(b) may be explained or supplemented

(a) by course of dealing or usage of trade (Section 1-205);

(b) by course of performance (Section 2-208); or

(c) by evidence of consistent additional terms, unless

> (i) the court finds the writing to have been intended as a complete and exclusive statement of the terms of the agreement.

Note in the second subsection how simple it was to arrange the three indented methods neatly in parallel fashion, each with its own topic and stress positions. In this revision, the mind does not have to deal with a sub-unit of discourse longer than 15 words until the final sub-sub-section, (2)(c)(i). We can afford to expend the extra energy at that point because we can see that the whole section is quickly coming to an end.[35]

DISCUSSION OF PROBLEM 5.8

In this problem, you were to assume that you are trying to decide whether minimum wages must be paid to the following persons performing various services necessary to production at a factory producing goods for commerce:

(a) janitors who clean the floors of the factory

(b) persons who wash the windows of the factory

(c) persons who sell sandwiches to the factory workers

(d) employees who exterminate cockroaches in the factory buildings

It is impossible in the abstract to know whether these persons are covered by the Act. You could *logically* conclude that each of the above types of employees are ultimately necessary to production. For example, how many people would continue to work in a factory that had thousands of roaches crawling on the

[35] Id. at 1192-93.

floors, in the machines, and on the controls? Is not the person who sells sandwiches to the factory workers supplying nourishment essential to production?

Justice Frankfurter stated, "The process of construction [of statutory language] is not [a mere] exercise in logic or dialectic: The aids of formal reasoning are not irrelevant; they may simply be inadequate."[36]

DISCUSSION PROBLEM 5.9

In this problem, you were asked what information would be helpful to you in evaluating the decisions of the courts and the administrative agency about the application of the provision cited in the preceding problem.

To decide the proper application of the provision, useful information would include, *inter alia*, (1) what problem or evil Congress was trying to solve, (2) what the normal meaning of "necessary" would be in this context (necessary = closely related? indispensable? directly essential?), and (3) what examples of the application of this provision did the legislative committees give to illustrate its intended application.

DISCUSSION OF PROBLEM 5.10

In this problem, you were asked, based on the principle of ejusdem generis, which of the following should *not* be included within "other vegetation" in the phrase, "oaks, elms, and other vegetation":

(a) grass

(b) clover

(c) honey locust trees

(d) palm trees

Under the ejusdem generis principle, grass, answer (a), would not be included. Likewise, clover, answer (b), would not be included. On the other hand, the various types of trees listed above, honey locust and palm trees, answers (c) and (d), are similar to the enumerated items. They are all trees.

DISCUSSION OF PROBLEM 5.11

In this problem, you were asked to (a) apply Statsky's first and second steps to the phrase, "oaks, elms, and other vegetation"

---

[36] Frankfurter, Some Reflections on the Reading of Statutes, 47 Colum. L. Rev. 527, 529 (1947).

and (b) list the possible common characteristics of the specific language.

The first step in Statsky's analysis is simply mechanical. The specific language is "oaks" and "elms." The general language is "vegetation." The second step requires more creative skills. In analyzing the characteristics of any listing, several common ones are likely to exist. Finding common characteristics is your job.

As Dickerson points out, the existence of multiple characteristics may create an ambiguity. For instance, one could just as plausiblely limit the class to deciduous trees (oaks and elms are both deciduous trees) rather than trees generally.[37] Another common characteristic is that oaks and elms are broadleaf trees. Still another approach might be to include in the class only vegetation within the same plant family as oaks and elms.

---

[37] See R. Dickerson, The Interpretation of Statutes 234 (1975).

Chapter 6

REPORTING LEGAL RESEARCH

DISCUSSION OF PROBLEM 6.1

In this problem, you were asked to consider how the following research questions (involving the viability of sudden mental illness as a defense to a negligence action) could be criticized:

(a) Does the defendant have a valid defense to the plaintiff's cause of action?

(b) Whether a sudden mental illness, which a motorist asserts after a negligence claim by another motorist, is a defense to such an action?

(c) Is a sudden and unforeseeable mental illness equivalent in effect to a sudden and unforeseeable physical illness, and therefore, should sudden and unforeseeable mental illness be recognized as a defense?

Question (a) is vague and incomplete. This question would be meaningless to the reader. Question (b) is poorly worded and incomplete. Question (c) is misdescriptive of the issue.

A better statement of the question involved in the preceding examples would be:

Should a sudden mental illness be recognized as a defense to a negligence action when the driver of an automobile suddenly and without warning suffered a mental aberration that caused the driver to lose conscious control of the automobile and to collide with another vehicle?

DISCUSSION OF PROBLEM 6.2

In this problem, you were asked how each of the following questions could be specifically criticized:

(a) Is the franchisor liable for treble damages for violating the Sherman Act?

(b) Is it necessary to evaluate the necessity and proportionality of the foreign sovereign's action to determine the illegality of the foreign sovereign's acts?

Without the aid of other questions providing factual detail, question (a), standing alone, would not be meaningful to a reader.

This question would be improved by integrating the relevant facts into the question.

Question (b) suggests that some issue of international law is involved, but without other questions or unless the reader reviews the statement of facts, the question would not be meaningful to a reader.

DISCUSSION OF PROBLEM 6.3

In this problem, you were asked to consider how the following series of questions could be revised to avoid the specific problem of having too many questions:

1. Is mental illness a general defense to negligence?

2. Is sudden physical illness a defense to negligence?

3. Is sudden mental illness a defense to negligence?

4. Is sudden mental illness likely to be recognized as a defense to negligence in Utopia?

These questions could be combined by incorporating the ideas and tying them to the basic facts of the research problem. For example, consider the following revisions:

1. If an insane driver negligently causes an accident, is the driver's preexisting insanity likely to be recognized as a defense?

2. If a driver is suddenly stricken with insanity and thereby negligently causes an accident, should the driver's mental condition be treated like a sudden physical illness (such as a heart attack or epileptic seizure) and thus relieve the driver of responsibility?

DISCUSSION OF PROBLEM 6.4

In this problem, you were asked to consider (1) whether the question below states the legal issue clearly and (2) whether the use of subquestions would present the significant facts or the precise legal issue or issues more fully:

> Can a broker, licensed in Montana but not in Washington, recover a promised commission for procuring a purchaser for hotel furnishings and a lease on the hotel property, located in Washington, whe[n]:
>
> 1. the oral promise to pay a commission was made in Montana,
>
> 2. the broker found the purchaser in Montana, and

3. the seller accepted the purchaser's offer, sent from Montana, by telegram sent from Seattle?

Rombauer points out the above questions illustrate the tendency of some students "to present only the ultimate question to be resolved, dressing it up with the significant facts"[38] Rombauer states that such questions "may be helpful as a tentative formulation to aid in identifying significant facts, but it does not identify precise legal questions."[39] Compare the above questions with the following, much improved revision:

1. Does the lack of a Washington real estate broker's license prevent a Montana-licensed broker from recovering a promised commission for finding a purchaser for Washington property?

a. Does a person act as a "real estate broker," within the meaning of the Washington licensing act, in finding a purchaser for a real property leasehold interest and personal property used in the conduct of a hotel business?

b. Does [Washington Revised Code section] 18.85.100, providing that no action shall be brought by a real estate broker for collection of compensation without proof that he was a "duly licensed real estate broker" at the time the cause of action arose, close Washington courts to all but Washington-licensed brokers?

2. Is an oral promise to pay a commission for finding a purchaser of a real property leasehold interest enforceable?

a. Will Montana or Washington law govern the validity of the commission promise where the promise was made in Montana and the broker [was also] located in Montana, but the property was located in Washington and the promisor-seller accepted the purchaser's offer, sent from Montana, by telegram sent from Seattle?

b. Assuming that Montana law will govern, does the requirement of the Montana statute of frauds that brokerage contracts for the "sale or purchase of

---

[38] M. Rombauer, Legal Problem Solving: Analysis, Research, and Writing 296 (4th ed. 1983).

[39] *Id.*

real estate" be in writing prevent recovery under the oral promise?[40]

DISCUSSION OF PROBLEM 6.5

In this problem, you were asked to revise the following question:

1. Should a driver be excused from liability for negligence when he is suddenly overcome, without warning, by a mental disability that prevents him from conforming his conduct to the standard of a reasonable person under like circumstances?

a. Should the question of liability in every case depend on the nature and extent of the driver's insanity?

Short of a complete rewriting, the above subquestion, at a minimum, should be stated as a second question (2). In other situations, a single subquestion may be a more detailed statement of the principal question or a second subquestion may have been omitted. In those situations, Squires and Rombauer suggest that you should either "substitute the more specific formulation for the primary question or identify and state the other parts of the whole."[41]

DISCUSSION OF PROBLEM 6.6

In this problem, you were asked how could state the following facts more clearly and concisely:

> [1] The defendant, ABC, an Ohio Corporation for profit, is engaged in the subsidized housing business and incident thereto is the owner of six dwelling units containing 46 apartment units housing 100 people. To provide for the culinary and sanitary needs of the occupants the defendant purchases from LeAx approximately 5300 gallons (22 tons) of water per day, and since opening for business in July 1975 has purchased 11,308,000 gallons of water which is all collected following use, placed in a sewage plant, treated, and discharged into a drainage ditch, which in turn discharges onto the plaintiff's property.
>
> [2] This case involves an incident which occurred on November 16, 1978. The plaintiff, Oilcorp, was the owner of a drilling rig which was located in a rural section of Athens County for the purpose of drilling for petroleum. Prior to November

---

[40] Id.

[41] L. Squires & M. Rombauer, Legal Writing § 6.3, at 154 (1982).

> 16, 1978, it had been determined that the drilling was completed and it was necessary to move the rig to another location. The defendant was notified of this need and was requested to bring equipment to the drill site for the purpose of moving the drilling rig and associated apparatus from that location to a new location.[42]

Consider Grey's rewritten versions of these statements of facts. Although Grey was discussing appellate brief writing in his article, his revisions are equally applicable to stating facts in memoranda:

> [1] The defendant, ABC Corp., owns and operates a 46-unit apartment complex containing 100 residents. Water for the apartments is supplied by LeAx at the rate of 5300 gallons, 22 tons, per day. All waste water from the apartments is treated in defendant's sewage plant and discharged into a drainage ditch which runs across plaintiff's property.
>
> [2] The plaintiff, Oilcorp, owned an oil drilling rig located in rural Athens Country. It was necessary to move the rig to another location. Oilcorp requested [the] defendant to bring his equipment to the drill site to move the drilling rig.[43]

As the above revisions demonstrate, a simple, direct, and concise statement of facts can be written. This kind of statement will greatly benefit the reader.

---

[42] Grey, Writing a Good Appellate Brief, 88 Case & Comm., Nov.-Dec. 1983, at 44, 49.

[43] Id. at 49.

Chapter 7

Revising, Reorganizing, and Proofreading Legal Writing

DISCUSSION OF PROBLEM 7.1

In this problem, you were asked to change the sentences from passive voice to active voice.

In (a), the sentence should be revised as follows: "The lower court correctly decided this case."

In (b), one way to change the sentence to the active voice is to make "Constitution" the subject: "The **Constitution requires** the prison to provide inmates with some form of court access."

In (c), make the "Supreme Court" the subject: "The **Supreme Court first recognized** an inmate's right to access to counsel in Ex parte Hull, 312 U.S. 546 (1941)."

In (d), the sentence could be revised as follows: "In the order, **the court enjoined** the defendants from enforcing the regulations."

DISCUSSION OF PROBLEM 7.2

In this problem, you were asked to shorten the "of-phrases" and eliminate the nominalizations from the sentences.

In (a), the following changes could be made: "The insurance policy **provides** for a premium refund if the **applicant's** age is stated incorrectly."

In (b), "had the intention" could be reduced to "intended" "In such a case, the contracting parties plainly **intended**" that the age adjustment clause should override the stated age."

In (c), "is a violation of" and "constitutional rights of the plaintiff" could be shortened to "violates" and "plaintiff's constitutional rights" respectively: "The search **violates** the **plaintiff's** constitutional rights."

In (d), "impediment" could be changed to "impeded": "Another court held that ten to fourteen hours per week unreasonably **impeded** access to the courts."

DISCUSSION OF PROBLEM 7.3

In this problem, you were asked to eliminate excessive wordiness from the sentences.

In (a), "at the present time" can be reduced to "now": "Many statutes **now** require incontestability clauses in insurance contracts."

In (b), "Notwithstanding the fact that" can be reduced to "although" and "in some instances" can be reduced to "sometimes": "**Although sometimes** other types of insurance policies contain incontestability clauses, life insurance policies always contain such clauses."

In (c), the redundancy "under the law" should be eliminated.[44] "The insurer's cancellation of the policy was **illegal**."

In (d), "There are" can be eliminated and the sentence revised as follows: "This problem can be resolved in several ways."

DISCUSSION OF PROBLEM 7.4

In this problem, you were asked to eliminate excessive wordiness from the sentences.

In (a), the wind-up "It is important to note that" can be eliminated: "Many statutes now require incontestability clauses."

In (b), the sentence could be revised as follows: "The statements are **irrelevant**."

In (c), the following changes could be made: "The seller, **a cross-claimant in the present action, lied.**

In (d), the wind-up "There can be no doubt whatsoever that" and the word "clearly" can be eliminated: "The plaintiff is entitled to recover lost profits."

DISCUSSION OF PROBLEM 7.5

Compare your editing with that of the Advisory Committee (adopted in 1987):

(a) If a party becomes incompetent, the court upon motion service as provided in subdivision (a) of this rule may allow the action to be continued by or against **the party's** representative.

(b) The notice shall state the time and place for taking the deposition and the name and address of each person to be examined, if known, and if the name is not known, a general description sufficient to identify **the person** or the particular class or group to which **the person** belongs.

---

[44] See Slips of the TV Tongue, Omaha World-Herald Magazine of the Midlands, Oct. 30. 1983, at 12, col. 1.

(c) No judgment by default shall be entered against the United States or an officer or agency thereof unless the claimant establishes **a** claim or right to relief by evidence satisfactory to the court.

(d) The filing of pleadings and other papers with the court as required by these rules shall be made by filing them with the clerk of the court, except that the judge may permit the papers to be filed with **the judge**, in which event **the judge** shall note thereon the filing date and forthwith transmit them to the office of the clerk.

DISCUSSION OF PROBLEM 7.6

In this problem, you were asked to revise the following sentence to reflect a parallel structure:

Such an analysis would include the following four factors: (1) the extent to which ultimate buyers are well-informed, sophisticated purchasers; (2) whether alternative names are available; (3) if the product is purchased primarily on the basis of experience or test purchases; and (4) the degree to which the trademarked goods have associated with them invisible product-category attributes or characteristics.

This sentence could be improved by using a parallel structure in listing the four factors:

Such an analysis would include the following four factors:
(1) **whether ultimate buyers** are well-informed, sophisticated purchasers;
(2) **whether effective alternative names** are available;
(3) **whether the product** is purchased primarily on the basis of experience or test purchases; and
(4) **whether invisible product-category attributes or characteristics** are associated with the trademarked goods.

DISCUSSION OF PROBLEM 7.7

In this problem, you were asked to edit the following sentences and accompanying footnotes in light of the numeral and symbol rules discussed in the text. For purposes of this problem, you were to assume that each entry follows the preceding one in a memorandum.

(a) In 1919, § 6(1) of the British Trade Marks Act of 1905 was amended to give statutory effect to the Linoleum case. 9 & 10 Geo. 5, ch. 79, sec. 6(1) (1919).

(b) Under § 6(1), all exclusive rights ceased if the trademark was the name of an article or substance manufactured under a patent upon its expiration.

(c) Section 15(1)(b), however, provides that the owner of the mark loses those exclusive rights only if it remains the only practicable name of the article or substance after a period of 2 years following cessation of the patent. British Trade Marks Act of 1938, 1 & 2 Geo. 6, ch. 22, § 15(1)(b).

(d) A study of 1,250 British cases found that this "protective" provision caused a 92 % decrease in claims of invalidity.

In (a), section in the text should be spelled out in "§ 6(1)." On the other hand, a symbol should be used in the citation. Thus, the sentence and citation should read as follows: "In 1919, **section** 6(1) of the British Trade Marks Act of 1905 was amended to give statutory effect to the Linoleum case. 9 & 10 Geo. 5, ch. 79, § 6(1) (1919)."

In (b), no changes are needed. According to the *USOC*, after the statute was initially mentioned and properly cited in (a), a short form reference using a section sign (§ **6(1)**) is proper.

In (c), "section" is properly spelled out because it is the first word of the sentence. The section sign is also properly used in the citation. However, numbers requiring only one or two words should be spelled out in the text. Thus, "2" should be written as "two" in "after a period of **two** years following cessation of the patent."

In (d), according to the *USOC*, no comma should be used in "1,250," and "92" should be written out because it requires only one or two words. Because a numeral is no longer used, percent should then be spelled out. Thus, the sentence should read as follows: "A study of **1250** British cases found that this "protective" provision caused a **ninety-two percent** decrease in claims of invalidity." Note that had the numeral and a section sign been used in the sentence, no space should be left (**92%**, not 92 %).

DISCUSSION OF PROBLEM 7.8

In this problem, you were asked to indicate words that should be italicized in the following sentences from an office memorandum. When the *USOC* and *Chicago* rules differ, you were asked to use the rules that you are learning.

(a) In Phelps v. The Camilla, 19 F. Cas. 441 (C.C.D. Md. 1838), agents and consignees of the brig Camilla ordered certain repairs on credit.

(b) The court pointed out that those necessary repairs are prima facie a lien on the vessel.

(c) The court carefully noted in the Phelps case, however, that if the credit had been given to the owner or anyone else, and not the vessel, then no lien would be created.

(d) Id. at 442.

In (a), "***Phelps v. The Camilla***" should be italicized because all case names should be italicized (single underlined) in briefs, memoranda, and similar types of material. Also, "**Camilla**" in "the brig ***Camilla***" should be italicized because it is the name of a ship--a "brig" is a two-masted, square-rigged ship.

In (b), no words should be italicized. Latin words like "prima facie" have long been Anglicized and should not be italicized in legal writing.

In (c), "***Phelps***" should be italicized (single underlined) because it is part of a case name.

In (d), "***Id.***" should be italicized (single underlined) if you are using *USOC* rules. "Id" should not be capitalized (and no period is necessary after "Id") if you are learning *Chicago* rules.

Chapter 8

Formulating Arguments and Using Persuasive Writing Techniques

DISCUSSION OF PROBLEM 8.1

This excerpt stating the "facts" of the case is primarily an ethical argument because it points out the morally reprehensible and illegal conduct of the respondents.

DISCUSSION OF PROBLEM 8.2

This excerpt suggests that the petitioner *deliberately* failed to acknowledge what the petitioner was really asking for, and thus it is primarily an ethical argument.

DISCUSSION OF PROBLEM 8.3

This excerpt, which describes the pick-up of garbage using vivid descriptions and examples, primarily constitutes an emotional argument (made in the course of a logical argument).

DISCUSSION OF PROBLEM 8.4

This excerpt, which argues that, by definition, no partial abandonment is possible, is primarily a logical argument.

DISCUSSION OF PROBLEM 8.5

This except, which simply lists a large number of state attorney generals, constitutes primarily an ethical argument.

DISCUSSION OF PROBLEM 8.6

This excerpt, which reasons by analogy from other cases that the respondent assumed the risk that the trash collector might consent to a search, constitutes primarily a logical argument.

DISCUSSION OF PROBLEM 8.7

This excerpt, which labels the petitioner as having a "gestapo" mentality, could be reasonably classified as either primarily an ethical argument or an emotional argument.

Based on these problems, you can see that all of these methods of arguing--logical, emotional, and ethical--are useful in a writing meant to persuade a decision maker.

DISCUSSION OF PROBLEM 8.8

In this problem, you were asked to formulate the basic structure of the prosecution's argument using the facts of the *Krivda* case and deductive reasoning. In the *Krivda* case, the petitioner asserted that the constitutional bounds of the fourth amendment were limited to those areas or items in which an individual had a reasonable expectation of privacy. That concept would be the major premise. The petitioner stated it in this way: "Only when the purported victim of an illegal search or seizure has a 'reasonable expectation of privacy' in the place searched or the items seized can he be said to have 'justifiably relied' on the privacy interests protected by the Fourth Amendment."[45]

The minor premise would be that a person does not have a reasonable expectation of privacy in "abandoned" property placed in the trash for public disposal.

The conclusion would be that a person who placed trash out for public disposal is not protected by the fourth amendment. This problem thus demonstrates how basic deductive legal arguments can be formulated.

DISCUSSION OF PROBLEM 8.9

In this problem, you were asked to classify the following "policy" reasons given in support of this rule using the following framework:

1. Lesser of Two Evils
2. Floodgates--Difficulty of Circumscribing the Area of Liability
3. Floodgates--Fraudulent Claims
4. Floodgates--Unlimited Liability
5. Floodgates--Burden on the Courts
6. Economic and Social Arguments--Distribution of Costs
7. Economic and Social Arguments--Who Can Avoid the Costs Most Cheaply
8. Economic and Social Arguments--Economic Efficiency

Compare your answers with the following:

1 or 7 (a) When one of two innocent persons must suffer a loss, it should be borne by the one who occasioned it. W. Prosser & W. Keeton, *supra* § 135, at 1073.

3 (b) One basis for holding the mentally disabled liable is that since insanity is easily feigned, the temptation to pretend it would be too great. W. Prosser & W. Keeton, *supra* § 135, at 1073; *McIntyre v. Sholty*, 121 Ill. 660, ___, 13 N.E. 239, 240

[45] Petitioner's Opening Brief at 24, California v. Krivda, 409 U.S. 33 (1972).

(1887) ("strong temptation to simulate insanity, with a view of masking the malice and revenge of an evil heart").

___5___ (c) One basis for holding the mentally disabled liable is the difficulty of distinguishing true incapacity from mere bad judgment. W. Prosser & W. Keeton, *supra* § 32, at 177; Restatement (Second) of Torts § 283B, comment b(1) (1965) (pointing out the practical difficulty of drawing any satisfactory line between mental deficiency and other variations of temperament, intellect, and emotional balance).

___7___ (d) Potential liability will encourage the custodians of mentally ill persons and those interested in their estates to keep them under control. W. Prosser & W. Keeton, *supra* § 135, at 1073; *McIntyre v. Sholty*, 121 Ill. 660, ___, 13 N.E. 239, 240 (1887) (liability tends to secure a more efficient custody and guardianship of insane persons).

___7___ (e) It is legitimate to identify insurance companies as the real parties in the resolution of the liability issue. In this day of broad coverage for general liability in family insurance policies, the ultimate recourse probably will be to such policies "in a large percentage of cases." Alexander & Szasz, *supra* at 36.

DISCUSSION OF PROBLEM 8.10

In this problem, you were asked to delete the unnecessary qualifiers from the following sentences:

(a) It appears that the defendant did not act very carefully under the circumstances.

(b) Apparently, it is a rather unsatisfactory rule.

(c) The proposed settlement is merely a reflection of the relative bargaining power of the parties.

(d) It would seem to be a very significant factor.

The above sentences contain several unnecessary qualifiers:

In (a), "It appears that" and "very" should be deleted ("The defendant did not act carefully under the circumstances").

In (b), "Apparently" and "rather" should be deleted ("It is an unsatisfactory rule" or "The rule is unsatisfactory").

In (c), "merely" should be deleted ("The proposed settlement is a reflection of the relative bargaining power of the parties" or "The proposed settlement reflects the relative bargaining power of the parties").

In (d), "It would seem to be" and "very" should be deleted ("It is a significant factor").

DISCUSSION OF PROBLEM 8.11

In this problem, you were asked to formulate how you would describe the defendant's lack of honesty (a) if you are writing from the plaintiff's perspective or (b) if you are writing from the defendant's perspective.

If your purpose is to emphasize the defendant's lack of honesty, it is stronger and more persuasive to assert that "the defendant was dishonest." Other words with stronger connotations could be used (for example, "cheated" or "lied"). On the other hand, if your purpose is to down play the defendant's lack of honesty, you might state that "the defendant was not honest." Even better, you might state that "the defendant was not as forthright as he could have been in hindsight."[46]

DISCUSSION OF PROBLEM 8.12

In this problem, you were asked to give (for the words listed) one word with a favorable connotation and one word with an unfavorable connotation. Several possibilities exist, including the following:

For (a), "house," "home" would be a favorable word; depending on the circumstances, "mansion," "hut," "shack," "residence," or "dwelling" might have less favorable connotations.

For (b), "adventurer," "traveler," "voyager," and "free-lancer" would be favorable words; "fortune-hunter" and "soldier of fortune" would be less favorable.

For (c), "wealthy," "well-off" and "well-to-do" would be favorable words; "rich," "filthy rich," "opulent," and "high roller" would be less favorable.

For (d), "female prostitute," "lady-of-the night" or "self-employed streetwalker," or "victim of adverse circumstances forced to engage in sex for money" would be favorable choices; "whore" or "hooker" would be less favorable.

---

[46] See W. Strunk & E. White, The Elements of Style 14-15 (1959); G. Block, Effective Legal Writing 54-55 (2d ed. 1983).

Chapter 9

Appellate Brief Writing

DISCUSSION OF PROBLEM 9.1

In this problem, you were asked to consider which of the following questions best expresses the question in the terms and circumstances of the case:

(a) Does section 495 of the Pennsylvania Code violate the Equal Protection clause?

(b) Does section 495 of the Pennsylvania Code, which prohibits automobile dealerships from staying open on Sunday, violate the Equal Protection clauses of the Pennsylvania and United States Constitutions?

(c) Does section 495 of the Pennsylvania Code, which prohibits automobile dealerships but no other retail merchants from staying open on Sunday, violate the Equal Protection clauses of the Pennsylvania and United States Constitutions?

(d) Does section 495 of the Pennsylvania Code, which does not permit the defendant but allows others to stay open for business on Sunday, violate the Equal Protection clauses of the Pennsylvania and United States Constitutions?

The best expression of the facts and circumstances of the case is best presented in answer (c). Obviously, answer (a) is not helpful to the reader. The difference between answers (b) and (c) is the insertion of "but no other retail merchants" after "automobile dealerships" which identifies the real point of the litigation. Answer (d) lessens the clarity of the problem by referring to the dealership as the "defendant."[47]

DISCUSSION OF PROBLEM 9.2

In this problem, you were asked which of the following argument headings best complies with the guidelines stated in the text:

(a) THE ALLEGED CONTRACTUAL RELATIONSHIP.

(b) A THIRD PARTY IS LIABLE FOR INTERFERENCE WITH CONTRACTUAL RELATIONS ONLY IF THERE IS AN

---

[47] See R. Stern, Appellate Practice in the United States 264 (1981) (presenting this example from which the above problem was adapted).

INTERFERENCE WITH A VALID CONTRACTUAL RELATIONSHIP OR BUSINESS EXPECTANCY.

(c) PLAINTIFF'S EVIDENCE FAILED TO ESTABLISH A VALID CONTRACTUAL RELATIONSHIP OR BUSINESS EXPECTANCY.

(d) PLAINTIFF HAS NOT PROVED THAT DEFENDANT TORTIOUSLY INTERFERED WITH HIS EXCHANGE CONTRACT BECAUSE PLAINTIFF'S EVIDENCE FAILED TO ESTABLISH THE EXISTENCE OF A VALID CONTRACTUAL RELATIONSHIP OF THE TYPE ENTITLED TO PROTECTION AGAINST INTERFERENCE BY THIRD PARTIES.

The heading in (d) best complies with the guidelines stated in the text. The heading in (a) uses a topical phrase rather than a sentence. The heading in (b) is better than (a), but it concentrates on an abstract legal proposition. The heading in (c), standing alone, fails to demonstrate the legal relevance of the proposition asserted in the heading.[48]

DISCUSSION OF PROBLEM 9.3

In this instance, several of the trial judge's rulings have a common basis: acceptance of the sudden mental illness as a defense to a negligence action. The unrecognized existence of this defense thus would be the most obvious ground for appeal and is critical. In contrast, there is probably little hope for a reversal based on an alleged abuse of discretion in not granting a new trial.

The other errors fall between these two extremes. It is hard to assess Delira's ability to testify from the information given. The question of Dr. Psycho's qualifications seems to be a more plausible ground for appeal, but there are at least three major problems.

First, a major part of the problem is that the attorneys representing the plaintiff did a poor job because of their failure to examine Dr. Psycho concerning his background or to object to the defendant's apparent lack of foundation at the deposition establishing Dr. Psycho's qualifications.

Second, there appears to be very little evidence that indicates that Delira had any forewarning. Thus, even if Dr. Psycho's testimony should have been stricken, there is probably sufficient *other* evidence to support the verdict.

---

[48] See L. Squires & M. Rombauer, supra note 41, § 7.2, at 175-76 (presenting the example on which this problem is based).

Third, research would have to be conducted to see whether qualifications come within the relevant rule governing waiver of defects that could have been obviated at the deposition. Initially, it seems that the judge's interpretation might be the proper one.

In this instance, a reasonable approach would be to attack the recognition of the sudden illness mental defense as the sole issue on appeal. It is a question of first impression in Utopia and critical to the outcome of the case.

DISCUSSION OF PROBLEM 9.4

In this problem, you were asked to criticize the following initial formulations of the question presented:

(a) Should a sudden mental illness be recognized in the State of Utopia as a defense to a negligence action when the driver of an automobile suddenly and without warning suffers a hallucination that causes a loss of conscious control of the car and a collision with the plaintiff's vehicle?

(b) If a driver is suddenly stricken with a mental disability and, as a result, causes an accident, should the driver's mental condition be treated like a sudden physical illness (such as a heart attack or epileptic seizure) and thus relieve the driver of responsibility?

(c) Should an insured driver who suddenly begins hallucinating without warning and, as a result, severely injures another driver who is completely free of negligence at the time of the accident be relieved of all responsibility to compensate the innocent injured driver?

(d) Should a driver who suddenly and without warning begins to believe that she is unable to control her car because it is controlled by an alien being and, as a result, severely injures another driver be excused from her failure to conform to the standard of a reasonable person?

None of the above tentative formulations is entirely satisfactory. The first two formulations are too "objective." The others seem more persuasive but are awkwardly worded. At this point in the preparation of the first draft, however, it is better to put these tentative questions aside and to return to them after you have written the argument section.

Appendix B

REVIEW OF TECHNICAL ENGLIGH LANGUAGE SKILLS

One of the seven fundamental principles of legal writing discussed in Chapter 1 was that good legal writing requires a command of the English language. Such a command results from a mastery of those technical writing skills and basic stylistic techniques that allow good writers to consciously adapt them to achieve their basic goal: to adjust the tone, emphasis, and content to reflect the purpose of a document and to achieve the desired effect on the audience who will read it. Thus, knowing those skills and techniques is an essential prerequisite to achieving that goal.

This appendix is designed to provide a quick check on those skills and techniques. Several problems have been included to allow you to assess your level of expertise. For many of you, use of technical writing skills in a legal context will be simply an extension of your prior learning. For you, this appendix will involve a simple review and perhaps some fine tuning.

For others, however, writing in a legal context will require a constant effort to avoid prior bad habits. Your situation will be somewhat akin to that of the farmer who washes up a pig for a fair: the farmer may have the pig smelling nice and looking clean, but it is a constant struggle to keep the pig from going back and wallowing in the mud.

1. GRAMMAR

This section reviews basic points of grammar.

(a) Complete Sentences and Verb Agreement

MAKE SURE THAT EACH SENTENCE HAS A VERB AND A SUBJECT.

This type of grammatical error--failure to have a subject and a verb in a sentence--frequently occurs when writers inadvertently combine appositives and subordinate clauses.

ILLUSTRATION B.1

An early draft may contain the following:

Kuhn v. Zabotsky, 9 Ohio St. 129, 224 N.E.2d 137 (1967), a case which did not allow sudden mental illness as a defense because it was prejudicial.

This sentence should be rewritten when the error is spotted in proofreading:

In Kuhn v. Zabotsky, 9 Ohio St. 129, 224 N.E.2d 137 (1967), the Ohio Supreme Court did not allow sudden mental illness as a defense because it was prejudicial.

MAKE SURE THAT THE VERB AGREES IN NUMBER WITH ITS SUBJECT.

This type of grammatical error--lack of agreement between the subject and the verb--often occurs in the revision process. For example, the subject may have been changed from singular to plural or vice versa in editing, but the verb was inadvertently left unchanged--especially when the subject and the verb are separated by a phrase or clause.

ILLUSTRATION B.2

Assume that the initial draft states the following:

The *defendants* who remained in control of the lawsuits *were* required to post security.

Assume that in the next draft this sentence is changed as follows:

Each of the defendants who remained in control of the lawsuits were required to post security. ("Were" was inadvertently left unchanged; the sentence should read, "Each . . . *was* . . . .")

Remember that plural nouns derived from Latin ("data," "dicta," "criteria," and "addenda") use plural verb forms.

(b) Pronoun Agreement

MAKE SURE A PRONOUN AGREES IN NUMBER WITH ITS ANTECEDENT.

The lack of agreement between pronouns and their antecedents often results from careless editing. Remember that collective nouns such as "jury," "court," "board," and "committee" use singular pronouns.

ILLUSTRATION B.3

In *Thompson v. Commercial Union Insurance Co.*, 250 So. 2d 259 (Fla. 1971), the Florida Supreme Court did not offer an explanation of *its* [not "their"] damage measure in excess liability cases.

The board of directors exercises control over the officers and affairs of a company. *It* has [not "They have] a duty to the corporation and the stockholders to manage the affairs of the corporation in a manner that is consistent with the shareholders' interests.

(c) Verb Tense

USE THE PROPER TENSE TO INDICATE THE TIME OF THE ACTION, PARTICULARLY WHEN FACTS ARE STATED. DO NOT NEEDLESSLY SHIFT THE TENSE, MOOD, OR VOICE IN A SENTENCE, PARAGRAPH, OR OTHER UNIT.

In general, use the past tense to state the *prior* events giving rise to an action.

ILLUSTRATION B.4

In *Theisen v. Milwaukee Automobile Mutual Insurance Co.*, 18 Wis. 2d 91, 118 N.W.2d 140 (1962), the plaintiff *was injured* when the car in which she *was riding* hit a large tree stump. The plaintiff *sued* the driver's insurance company in a comparative negligence action to recover damages for personal injuries. (Past tense is used to state the facts of the case.)

Be careful, however, that the verbs in the same sentence or paragraph reflect the proper time relationship, particularly when you are using the past tense.

ILLUSTRATION B.5

The following sentence is *incorrect*:

Respondent also *alleged* that petitioners *conspired* with an electric power company to engage in vexatious litigation to forestall respondent from building a nuclear power generation facility. (The conspiracy took place *before* the allegations.)

The above sentence should be rewritten as follows:

Respondent also *alleged* [past tense] that petitioners *had conspired* [past perfect tense] with an electric power company to engage in vexatious litigation to forestall respondent from building a nuclear power generating facility. (Past perfect tense should be used to show that the action occurred before an indicated time in the past.)

Avoid needless shifts in the tense, mood, or voice in a sentence, paragraph, or other unit.

ILLUSTRATION B.6

The driver's loss of control over his mental and physical conduct *renders* him incapable of guarding against any dangers his conduct *might* (should be "may") cause. (The tense needlessly shifts in the sentence.)

If he *were* a woman and she *was* (should be "were") a man, they still would not be entitled to different recoveries under the statute. (The mood needlessly shifts from the subjunctive to the indicative in the sentence.)

It *is* unjust to hold insane persons liable for their negligence because *the ordinary-person standard of care can never be met by them* (should be "they can never meet the ordinary-person standard of care").

The subjunctive was traditionally used in situations involving uncertainty and suppositions. Today, the use of the subjunctive is in transition and it has now generally been displaced by the indicative. The use of the subjunctive is now considered to be optional in most situations.

USE THE SUBJUNCTIVE IN FORMAL LEGAL WRITING TO EXPRESS IMPOSSIBILITY, A HIGH DEGREE OF IMPROBABILITY, OR A WISH.

ILLUSTRATION B.7

Consider the following classic example: (1) (subjunctive) "Suppose he *were* to die" versus (2) (indicative) "Suppose he *dies*." Note that the past singular subjunctive form of "to be" is "were."

The subjunctive, however, is still used when conditions "contrary to fact" are expressed in formal legal writing. Thus, in situations that are impossible or highly improbable, use the subjunctive.

ILLUSTRATION B.8

Were he a woman, he would be entitled to dower. (*Not: Was* he a woman, he would be entitled to dower; note the extreme improbability of the condition.)

In "if"-clauses that involve impossibility or a high degree of improbability, the subjective should also be used.

ILLUSTRATION B.9

If he *were* a woman, he would be entitled to dower.

In "if"-clauses that do not involve impossibility or a high degree of improbability, the indicative is acceptable, particularly when such clauses read smoothly.

ILLUSTRATION B.10

If the defendant *was* a citizen of another state, the plaintiff would not be able to sue the defendant in the state where the accident occurred. (Assume that this sentence expresses a hypothetical situation that may or may not be true and that you do not want to imply that there is a high probability that the defendant is, in fact, a citizen of another state.)

USE THE SUBJUNCTIVE IN "THAT"-CLAUSES EXPRESSING A RECOMMENDATION, COMMAND, REQUEST, WISH, MOTION, ORDER, DEMAND, OR RESOLUTION.

The subjunctive is used in "that"-clauses expressing a desire in varying forms.

ILLUSTRATION B.11

The judge ordered *that* the memorandum *be* filed immediately.

I move *that* the charges *be* dismissed.

The defendant demanded *that* he *receive* fair and impartial treatment.

Note that the present singular subjunctive form of "to be" is "be" and that the third person singular subjunctive form of other verbs such as "receive" is "receive," not "receives."

(d) Dangling Modifiers

AVOID DANGLING MODIFIERS.

A dangling modifier is a verbal phrase or elliptical clause (one in which one or more words are omitted but are understood) that causes a confusing or illogical association in a sentence.

ILLUSTRATION B.12

Having heard all of the plaintiff's witnesses, the case was dismissed. (Dangling participial phrase--the case did not hear the witnesses.)

After hearing all of the plaintiff's witnesses, the case was dismissed. (Dangling gerund phrase--again the case did not hear the witnesses.)

Both of these errors could be corrected by rephrasing the sentence as follows:

Having heard [*or* After hearing] all of the plaintiff's witnesses, the judge dismissed the case.

A similar type of error occurs when an infinitive phrase refers to the wrong word.

ILLUSTRATION B.13

To bring a diversity action in federal district court, a claim of more than fifty thousand dollars must be alleged. (Dangling elliptical clause--a claim does not bring a diversity action.)

This sentence should be rephrased as follows:

To bring a diversity action in federal district court, the plaintiff must allege a claim of more than fifty thousand dollars.

Another error arises when a dangling elliptical clause improperly refers to the subject of the main clause. Dangling elliptical clauses often begin with "when" or "while."

ILLUSTRATION B.14

A *claim* of more than fifty thousand dollars must be alleged *when* seeking monetary relief in a diversity action. (Dangling elliptical clause--a claim is not the one who is seeking monetary relief.)

This sentence should be rephrased as follows:

When seeking monetary relief in a diversity action, the plaintiff must allege a claim of more than fifty thousand dollars.

One other error involves dangling phrases of result.

ILLUSTRATION B.15

The *case* was dismissed, *thereby* [or thus] saving considerable expense. (Dangling phrase of result--the phrase using a present participle ("saving") technically modifies case and the case did not save the expense.)

This sentence could be rephrased in several ways to avoid this problem:

The case was dismissed, which saved the defendants considerable expense.

The dismissal of the case saved the defendants considerable expense.

The defendants saved considerable expense because the case was dismissed.

(e) Split Infinitives

BE AWARE OF SPLIT INFINITIVES; SPLIT THEM ONLY WHEN IT IMPROVES THE CLARITY AND SMOOTHNESS OF A SENTENCE.

A split infinitive occurs when an adverb is placed between the word, "to," and the verb. In considering whether to split an infinitive, follow the advice of William Safire:

> No stigma attaches to the splitting, nor did it ever in the minds of many of the most prestigious usagarians. Let us put the modifier in place--before the *to*, just after it, or after the verb--where it works best for our purpose of stress or grace.[1]

ILLUSTRATION B.16

You may split the infinitive in a sentence such as this one:

Child witnesses may not be able *to effectively accept* the finality of death for months or even years.

---

[1]Safire, N.Y. Times, Oct. 9, 1983, § 6 (Magazine), at 14, col. 1.

In contrast, compare the awkward splitting of the infinitive in the following sentence:

I shall have no other alternative but *to immediately criminally prosecute* you for assault against my client.

PROBLEM B.1

Edit the following sentences for grammatical errors. Write in changes using a caret symbol to indicate insertions. Cross out or circle words or phrases in a manner showing where they should be moved or indicating that they should be deleted.

(a) Having been severely injured in the automobile accident and seeking compensation, the plaintiffs' complaint alleged that the defendant had operated his vehicle in an unsportsmanlike manner.

(b) The defendant's motion to dismiss for failure to state a claim was denied and the case was submitted to the jury, thus creating a question whether the law in this jurisdiction had been followed.

(c) To the credit of the jury, they returned a special verdict in favor of the plaintiffs.

(d) The jury specifically found that the defendant was intoxicated at the time of the accident.

Stop here, and edit the above sentences for grammatical errors before consulting the discussion of this problem at the end of this Appendix.

PROBLEM B.2

Edit the following sentences for grammatical errors. Write in changes using a caret symbol to indicate insertions. Cross out or circle words or phrases in a manner showing to where they should be moved or indicating that they should be deleted.

(a) On appeal, raising the question for the first time, dismissal of the action was requested by the defendant on the ground that the trial court lacked subject-matter jurisdiction over the action.

(b) In order to file the appeal, however, each of the defendants were required to post a supersedeas bond.

(c) To effectively and quickly resolve the matter, an expedited appeal was granted by the appellate court.

(d) After hearing oral argument on the issue, a dismissal was granted.

Stop here, and edit the above sentences for grammatical errors before consulting the discussion of this problem at the end of this Appendix.

2. PUNCTUATION

Punctuation (1) separates groups of words for meaning and emphasis, (2) conveys an idea of varying pitches, volumes, pauses, and intonations, and (3) helps avoid contextual ambiguities. This section examines the more frequent errors in punctuation in legal writing.

(a) Joining Independent Clauses

USE A COMMA TO SEPARATE INDEPENDENT CLAUSES JOINED BY A COORDINATING CONJUNCTION ("AND," "OR," "NOR," "FOR," "YET," "SO," AND "BUT"). WHEN ONE OR BOTH OF THE INDEPENDENT CLAUSES CONTAINS COMMAS OR WHEN THE SECOND CLAUSE REVEALS A STRIKING CONTRAST, CONSIDER USING A SEMICOLON.

ILLUSTRATION B.17

The Dade County Commissioners are the Port Authority, but a professional staff oversees the daily management of their work. (A comma is used to separate two independent clauses joined by a coordinating conjunction; an independent clause is one that can stand alone.)

The Port Authority regulates the port of Miami and operates Miami International Airport. (No comma is used because "and" does not join two independent clauses.)

When the independent clauses are *short*, many legal writers omit the comma, particularly before "and" or "or."

A semicolon is preferable when one of the independent clauses contains commas or when the second clause strikes a contrast with the first.

ILLUSTRATION B.18

Often the courts couched the standards in language that reflected elements of the common-law notice requirements, such as "personal service within the state"; but territorial power, not convenience, was their ultimate concern. (Second clause contrasts with the first and both clauses contain commas.)

USE A SEMICOLON TO SEPARATE TWO INDEPENDENT CLAUSES NOT JOINED BY A COORDINATING CONJUNCTION ("AND," "OR," "NOR," "FOR," "YET," AND "BUT"). THUS, USE A SEMICOLON WHEN TWO INDEPENDENT CLAUSES ARE JOINED BY A CONJUNCTIVE ADVERB OR A TRANSITIONAL PHRASE.

Conjunctive adverbs and transitional phrases frequently are used in legal writing to introduce conclusions, to enhance continuity, and to provide transitions. When they are used to join two independent clauses, they should be punctuated with a semicolon.

ILLUSTRATION B.19

From the outset of the opinion, the assumption was made that "Shredded Wheat" was the name of the product; *nonetheless*, it was apparent that the Privy Council thought that if the Canadian Shredded Wheat Co. could have adequately shown distinctiveness, exclusive rights would have been enforced. (conjunctive adverb)

Separate sentences may be used.

ILLUSTRATION B.20

If the alleged infringing use is outside the product category, use of the term ought to be enjoined. *On the other hand*, competition on the merits ought to prevail when the products are substantially identical. (transitional phrase)

The following words and phrases are useful conjunctive adverbs and transitional phrases:

CONJUNCTIVE ADVERBS	**TRANSITIONAL PHRASES**
also	after all
anyway	as a result
besides	at any rate
consequently	at the same time
finally	by the way
furthermore	even so
hence	for example
however	in addition
incidentally	in fact
indeed	in other words
instead	in the second place
likewise	on the contrary
meanwhile	on the other hand
moreover	nevertheless

next
otherwise
then
thus
nonetheless
still
therefore

(b) Subordinate Clauses and Long Phrases

USE A COMMA TO SEPARATE A SUBORDINATE CLAUSE, OR A LONG PHRASE THAT PRECEDES OR INTERRUPTS AN INDEPENDENT CLAUSE, OR TO PREVENT MISREADING OF SHORT INTRODUCTORY PHRASES.

When a subordinate clause (usually introduced by a subordinating conjunction such as "although," "because," "when," "if," "while," "until," etc.) or a long phrase *precedes* or *interrupts* an independent clause, use a comma or comas to separate it from the main clause.

ILLUSTRATION B.21

Although the amount of time varies, a twenty-four hour total cessation in urban areas should suffice. (Comma is used after the subordinate clause.)

To prevent a subsequent action that would closely duplicate the present suit, Smith's joinder should be compelled. (Comma is used after a long phrase.)

The appellate court opinion, written by Justice Holmes, was a masterpiece of legal reasoning. (Commas are used to separate interrupting phrase, "written by Justice Holmes," from the main clause.)

A comma also is sometimes necessary to prevent misreading of short introductory phrases.

ILLUSTRATION B.22

Compare the following two sentences:

In Florida courts have lots of spectators.
In Florida, courts have lots of spectators.

DO NOT USE A COMMA TO SEPARATE A SUBORDINATE CLAUSE THAT FOLLOWS AN INDEPENDENT CLAUSE UNLESS THE SUBORDINATE CLAUSE IS PARENTHETICAL OR LOOSELY CONNECTED WITH THE REST OF THE SENTENCE.

Set off subordinate clauses that *follow* an independent clause with a comma only when the subordinate clause is parenthetically or loosely connected with the main clause. To identify when a subordinate clause is parenthetical or loosely connected with the independent clause, read the sentence aloud; if you do not pause between the two, do not use a comma.

ILLUSTRATION B.23

The court refused to grant the injunction because irreparable harm had not been shown. (No comma is needed because the subordinate clause is not loosely connected with the main clause or parenthetical.)

The complaint stated four causes of action, although only one of them is now relevant. (A comma is used to separate the parenthetical subordinate clause from the main clause.)

(c) Restrictive and Nonrestrictive Clauses and Phrases

USE COMMAS TO SET OFF NONRESTRICTIVE ("EXTRA") CLAUSES OR PHRASES; DO NOT SET OFF RESTRICTIVE ("ESSENTIAL") CLAUSES OR PHRASES.

ILLUSTRATION B.24

There is a true story of an English teacher who was once helping a young student to understand the difference between restrictive and nonrestrictive clauses. She explained that adjective clauses (introduced by "who," "which," or "that") are *restrictive when they are needed for identification of the word they modify*; they limit (restrict) the meaning of the sentence and cannot be omitted.

In an effort to check the student's understanding, the teacher asked the student whether the following sentence had a restrictive or nonrestrictive clause: "Get the painting *that is on the wall*."

Sensing that the student was uncertain, she asked: "If I asked you to get the painting [there was a painting on the desk, one on the table, and one on the wall], what would be the first thing you would say?" The teacher expected the student to respond by asking, "Which one?" and thus identifying the clause ("that is on the wall") as restrictive (no commas). Instead, the student responded that the first thing he would say would be: "Yes, ma'am."

Another author specializing in language suggests the following way to remember to insert commas in nonrestrictive clauses or phrases:

> I like the term "essential clauses" for those you must keep glued (without commas) to the rest of the sentence or else the meaning changes. I use "extra clauses" for those you can separate out (with commas) without changing the meaning. "Extra" reminds me that the extra clause requires the extra commas.[2]

ILLUSTRATION B.25

Any person who exercises control over any place which offers seclusion or shelter for the practice of prostitution commits the offense of keeping a place of prostitution. (restrictive or "essential"--which person?) (no commas)

Public indecency, which is defined by statute as an exposure of the genitals of the body done with an intent to affront or alarm any person, is a crime rarely committed by medical students. (nonrestrictive) (commas needed) ("extra clause, extra commas")

(d) Appositives, Contrasted Elements, Conjunctive Adverbs, and Transitional Expressions

SET OFF NONRESTRICTIVE APPOSITIVES, CONTRASTED ELEMENTS, CONJUNCTIVE ADVERBS, AND TRANSITIONAL EXPRESSIONS WITH COMMAS.

Commas should be used to set off appositives, conjunctive adverbs, contrasted elements, and transitional expressions.

ILLUSTRATION B.26

Mrs. Wilson, the insured, offered no excuse for failure to make the payment before the grace period expired. (The appositive is set off by commas--assuming that the information in the appositive merely supplies additional information and is not needed for identification.)

---

[2]Romm, Comma Sense, 70 A.B.A. J., Dec. 1984, at 132-33.

Early pleading in the United States, unlike discovery, was derived principally from procedures developed in English common-law courts. (The contrasted element is set off with commas.)

The rules should not frustrate legitimate state and local efforts to meet local problems; however, the rules should not cut too deeply into national interests. (A comma is used after the conjunctive adverb.)

Specific evidentiary survey questions, for example, should be directed to each relevant universe to identify the three categories of consuming persons likely to be present in any generic litigation. (Commas set off the transitional phrase.)

(e) Lists, Series, and Coordinate Adjectives

USE A COLON TO INTRODUCE A LIST, A SERIES, A LONG QUOTATION, OR AN EXPLANATION.

A colon should be used to introduce a list, a series, a long quotation, or an explanation.

ILLUSTRATION B.27

The court should identify three categories of consumers: those for whom the mark is solely source-significant and not the generic name of the product; those for whom the mark lacks any source significance and is the generic name of the product; and those for whom it performs both functions.

The crime of rape consists of three elements: (1) unlawful (2) carnal knowledge of a woman (3) against her will.

WHEN A SERIES OR LIST IS INTRODUCED BY A COLON AND THE SERIES OR LIST IS COMPLICATED OR LENGTHY, USE SEMICOLONS TO SEPARATE THE ITEMS IN THE SERIES. LIKEWISE, USE SEMICOLONS TO SEPARATE ITEMS WHEN THE SERIES CONTAINS COMMAS. IN OTHER SERIES, USE COMMAS TO SEPARATE THE ITEMS.

In the first example given in Illustration B.27, semicolons were used to separate the items in the series because the items were complicated and lengthy. Otherwise, commas should be used to separate items in a series.

Semicolons should be used to separate items in a series that contains commas so that the reader can easily distinguish the principal divisions of the series.

ILLUSTRATION B.28

The law of procedure establishes, among other things, the method by which the injured party may begin a lawsuit against the tortfeasor; the degree of detail with which the injured party must describe his "claim" for the court and the opposing party; the rules governing how the injured party must prove the facts constituting the breach of duty, the injury, and the other elements of the tort; and the ways in which the injured party may enforce any award of damages against the tortfeasor.

USE COMMAS TO SEPARATE WORDS, PHRASES, AND CLAUSES IN A SERIES.

Follow the traditional rule of placing a comma before the conjunction as well as between the other items of a series (three or more items).

ILLUSTRATION B.29

The sellers may be able to reduce their promotional expenditures, maintain a price premium, or hold a larger market share.

Avoid the usual practice of journalists and other writers of omitting the final comma in a series.

ILLUSTRATION B.30

The company will replace the worm, gear, bearings, and housings.

USE A COMMA BETWEEN COORDINATE ADJECTIVES MODIFYING THE SAME NOUN BUT NOT BETWEEN CUMULATIVE ADJECTIVES THAT MODIFY THE WHOLE CLUSTER OF SUBSEQUENT ADJECTIVES AND THE NOUN.

Coordinate adjectives are adjectives that modify the same word or word group and should be separated by a comma.

ILLUSTRATION B.31

A bona fide, nonrevocable offer was made. ("Bona fide" and "nonrevocable" both modify "offer.")

The assailant was wearing a dark blue tweed suit. ("A," "dark," and "blue," cumulatively modify "tweed suit.")

(f) Citations Within a Sentence

USE COMMAS TO SET OFF CITATIONS WITHIN A SENTENCE.

Citations within a sentence should be set off with commas.[3]

ILLUSTRATION B.32

To prove a defendant's prior conviction, a permanent record book of a circuit court is admissible without compliance with the Business Records Acts, *see, e.g.*, *State v. Jones*, 579 S.W.2d 670, 670 (Mo. Ct. App. 1979), but other courts have required compliance with the Act. (The citation is set off with commas.)

(g) Possessives

USE AN APOSTROPHE TO INDICATE THE POSSESSIVE CASE OF NOUNS AND INDEFINITE PRONOUNS ("THE JUDGE'S DOCKET" OR "NO ONE'S PROPERTY") BUT NOT WITH PERSONAL PRONOUNS (HERS, YOURS, THEIRS, OR ITS). WATCH CAREFULLY THE USE OF "ITS" AND "IT'S."

Particularly in proofreading, take care to see that the contraction of "it is" ("it's") has not been used in place of the possessive "its" or vice versa.

IN FORMAL LEGAL WRITING, USE A PREPOSITIONAL PHRASE RATHER THAN AN APOSTROPHE TO INDICATE POSSESSION FOR INANIMATE NOUNS.

Possession of inanimate nouns in formal writing (such as an appellate brief) should *not* be indicated by an apostrophe; instead *use a prepositional phrase*.

---

[3]The Harvard Law Review Ass'n, Yale Law Journal, Columbia Law Review, and University of Pennsylvania Law Review, A Uniform System of Citation 7 (14th ed. 1986) [hereinafter USOC and USOC Rule] (Rule 2.1).

ILLUSTRATION B.33

the headlights of the automobile
(*not* the automobile's headlights)

Most legal writers, however, use a possessive with inanimate nouns referring to groups that are composed of human beings.

ILLUSTRATION B.34

the association*'s* recommendation
the jury*'s* verdict

(h) Hyphenation

The primary function of a hyphen is to indicate to the reader that two or more words should be read together as a single word with its own meaning.[4]

WHEN TWO OR MORE WORDS JOINTLY SERVE AS AN ADJECTIVE BEFORE A NOUN OR WHEN PREFIXES ["EX-," "SELF-," "ALL-," AND "QUASI-"] OR THE SUFFIX, "-ELECT," ARE ADDED TO A WORD, USE A HYPHEN. A HYPHEN IS ALSO USED WHEN A PREFIX IS ADDED TO A CAPITALIZED WORD.

ILLUSTRATION B.35

self-incrimination
quasi-contract
ex-offender
pro-American
self-defense
common-law rules
self-dealing

(i) And / Or

AVOID JOINING "AND" AND "OR" WITH A VIRGULE ("/").

---

[4] H. Fowler, A Dictionary of Modern English Usage 255 (2d ed. 1965).

Avoid the use of "and/or" in legal writing.[5] In this regard, consider the following discussion:

> The difference between "and" and "or" is usually explained by saying that "and" stands for the conjunctive, connective, or additive and "or" stands for the disjunctive or alternative. The former connotes "togetherness" and the latter tells you to "take your pick." So much is clear. Beyond this point, difficulties arise.
>
> One difficulty is that each of these two words is on some occasions ambiguous. Thus, it is not always clear whether the writer intends the *inclusive* "or" (A or B, or both) or the *exclusive* "or" (A or B, but not both). This long recognized uncertainty has given rise to the abortive attempt to develop "and/or" as an acceptable English equivalent to the Latin "vel" (the inclusive "or").
>
> . . . .
>
> Observation of legal usage suggests that in most cases "or" is used in the inclusive rather than exclusive sense . . . . If true, this is significant for legal draft[ers] and other writers because it means that in absence of special circumstances they can rely on simple "or's" . . . to carry [this inclusive meaning]. This, incidentally, greatly reduces the number of occasions for using the undesirable expression "and/or" or one of its more respectable equivalents, such as "A or B, or both," or "either or both of the following."[6]

(j) Dashes

USE DASHES FOR EMPHASIS OR CLARITY; OTHERWISE, AVOID USING THEM AS SUBSTITUTES FOR COMMAS OR OTHER PUNCTUATION MARKS.

---

[5] See H. Weihofen, Legal Writing Style 24-25 (2d ed. 1980).

[6] Dickerson, The Choice Between "And" and "Or," 46 A.B.A. J. 310, 310-11 (1960) (footnotes omitted). See also Gopen, Let the Buyer in the Ordinary Course of Business Beware: Suggestions for Revising the Prose of the Uniform Commercial Code, 54 U. Chi. L. Rev. 1178, 1197 (1987) ("It is often difficult to perceive whether the words "and" and "or" are being used (a) for joining phrases/clauses or (b) for joining parallel individual words within phrases/clauses. . . . My suggestion: We should use "and" and "or" only to join phrases/clauses, using in their place a slash (/) to join individual words whenever necessary. The new compound slash-word will be read as the single unit it represents").

Dashes set off parenthetical material and should be used if, for some reason, the parenthetical material should be emphasized.

ILLUSTRATION B.36

Consistent application of the rules--achieved through detailed analysis of the nature of the state action involved in a particular case--would adequately protect the public interest. (Assuming that it is useful to emphasize the parenthetical material, dashes should be used.)

Dashes emphasize material at the end of a sentence.

ILLUSTRATION B.37

The adversary system is based on a number of assumptions about the best path to justice and efficiency--assumptions that often are untrue. (Dashes emphasize the phrase at the end of the sentence.)

Dashes also can provide clarity. For example, when appositives or contrasted elements contain several items separated by commas, dashes can be used to set them apart from the rest of the sentence.

ILLUSTRATION B.38

The attorney should be concerned about what kind of death the child client witnessed--shooting, stabbing, violent beating, or drug overdose--and what kind of effects it has had on the client's life. (Dashes are used for clarity here.)

Dashes in typewritten material are indicated by two hyphens without spacing, as shown above.

PROBLEM B.3

Based on the rules discussed in this section, punctuate the following sentences. Indicate insertions using a caret. Cross out or circle punctuation marks in a manner that indicates deletions.

(a) When it is rendered a judgment will ordinarily award costs to the prevailing party.

(b) Examples of taxable costs are fees of the clerk, marshall, court reporters and/or witnesses but attorney fees are not taxable costs.

(c) Furthermore a judgment will embody a remedy.

(d) Four general kinds of final remedies are available, (1) damages, (2) restitution, (3) coercive remedies, and (4) declaratory remedies.

(e) Note however that common law remedies did not include a declaratory judgment.

Stop here, and properly punctuate the above sentences before consulting the discussion of this problem at the end of this Appendix.

PROBLEM B.4

Based on the rules discussed in this section, punctuate the following sentences. Indicate insertions using a caret. Cross out or circle punctuation marks in a manner that indicates deletions.

(a) An injunction is a court order that commands a party to do or cease doing certain things.

(b) A party who violates the injunction can be punished by contempt of court which may involve monetary fines or imprisonment.

(c) Two types of contempt exist--civil and criminal.

(d) Several cases, see, e.g., In re Lazarus, 276 F. Supp. 450 (C.D. Cal. 1967) illustrate the difference between civil and criminal contempt.

(e) The distinction primarily depends ". . . upon the objective to be served by the contempt citation". J. Friedenthal, M. Kane, & A. Miller, Civil Procedure § 15.8, at 715 (1985).

Stop here, and properly punctuate the above sentences before consulting the discussion of this problem at the end of this Appendix.

PROBLEM B.5

Based on the rules discussed in this section, punctuate the following sentences. Indicate insertions using a caret. Cross out or circle punctuation marks in a manner that indicates deletions.

(a) Certain remedies which are known as "provisional remedies" are granted at or near the outset of the lawsuit.

(b) Provisional remedies as their name suggests are available for only a limited period of time.

(c) These remedies are designed for three purposes: to preserve the status quo, to safeguard against the dissipation of assets that might later be needed to satisfy a final judgment in the action, and to prevent other serious harm from accruing to one of the parties during the period of the litigation.

(d) Some of the most useful provisional remedies--the ones you need to remember--are attachment, garnishment, preliminary injunctions, and replevin.

Stop here, and properly punctuate the above sentences before consulting the discussion of this problem at the end of this Appendix.

3. USAGE

BE CAREFUL NOT TO CONFUSE WORDS WITH SIMILAR BUT DISTINCT MEANINGS.

In legal writing, be careful not to confuse words with similar but distinct meanings.

The following are some of the words that cause problems in legal writing:

"Assume" should be used to express "taken for granted" or to express "suppose." Because "presume" is closely associated with several legal terms with technical meanings, such as "rebuttable presumption," the word "presume" should be limited to formal, traditional uses, such as "presumed innocent until proved guilty."[7]

ILLUSTRATION B.39

Assuming (*not* "presuming") that it was properly enacted, the bailiff complied with the statute.

"Express" refers to matter that is set forth in sufficient detail and is worded with intention. On the other hand, "explicit" refers to clearly developed and plainly stated matters that do not have a disguised meaning.

ILLUSTRATION B.40

The explicit holding of the court (the clearly stated holding) left no doubt about its view on the subject.

The express (*not* "explicit") language of the testator's will granted a life estate to his wife.

"Infer" means to derive a conclusion from premises or facts. In contrast, "imply" means to express indirectly.

---

[7] See H. Weihofen, supra note 5, at 34.

ILLUSTRATION B.41

Although the defendant did not specifically state that the plaintiff would be fired, the defendant implied (*not* "inferred") that event would occur if the plaintiff reported the violation.

From the evidence presented, the court inferred (*not* "implied") that a binding offer had been made.

AVOID IMPROPER USE OF "DUE TO."

"Due to" is an adjective and means "attributable to." It ordinarily introduces an adjectival phrase that immediately follows a form of the verb "to be" and modifies the noun that is the subject of the sentence.

ILLUSTRATION B.42

The dismissal was due to factors unrelated to the merits of the lawsuit. (The adjectival phrase ("due to factors unrelated to the merits of the lawsuit") immediately follows a form of the verb "to be" ("was") and modifies the noun that is the subject of the sentence ("dismissal"); "*attributable to*" could readily be substituted for "due to," and thus it is correctly used in this illustration.)

In other circumstances, "due to" and "due to the fact that" should be replaced with "because" or "because of." In particular, "due to" should not be used to introduce an adverb clause modifying the verb.

ILLUSTRATION B.43

The suit was dismissed because of (*not* "due to") factors unrelated to the merits of the lawsuit. ("Because of factors unrelated to the merits of the lawsuit" is an adverb phrase modifying the verb--"was dismissed"); "attributable to" could *not* be readily substituted for "because of.")

DO NOT MISUSE "WHERE."

Traditionally, "where" should be used to designate place and not as a substitute for "when" or "in which."[8]

---

[8] See id. at 40 ("states where the rule is followed" is correct, but not "cases where the rule is followed").

ILLUSTRATION B.44

Summary judgment is not appropriate when (*not* "where") a genuine issue of fact exists.

Situations in which (*not* "where") a dispute exists about the law, as opposed to the facts, are rare.

AVOID AMBIGUOUS USES OF "WHILE" AND "SINCE."

Unlike "where," which denotes only place, "while" and "since" are no longer limited to their original meanings denoting time: "during the time that" (while) and "subsequent to the time that" (since). "While" also means "although," and "since" also means "because."

Because of these differing meanings, care should be taken to assure that the intended meaning is clear to the reader.

ILLUSTRATION B.45

Because (*not* "since") the case has not been overruled, the district court should apply it.

Consider also the meaning of "while" in the following example given by Weihofen:

While such combinations were expressly prohibited by statute, this venture flourished.

Did the venture flourish during the time that it was prohibited or did the writer mean to say that although it was prohibited, it flourished?[9]

AVOID USING "SO" TO JOIN CLAUSES IN FORMAL LEGAL WRITING.

One of the meanings of "so" is "therefore" or "as a result." In formal legal writing, however, "so" should not be used to join clauses.

ILLUSTRATION B.46

Juries no longer need be concerned with technical differences between the several types of theft, *so* they may return

[9] See id. at 36, 40.

a general verdict of guilty if they find that any type of unlawful taking has been proved. (improper)

Instead, consider subordinating one of the clauses:

Because juries no longer need to be concerned with technical differences between the several types of theft, they may return a general verdict of guilty if they find that any type of unlawful taking has been proved.

AVOID IMPROPER OR AMBIGUOUS USES OF "AS."

"As" has developed several meanings--including "while," "when," "though," "because," "since," and "like." In some contexts, use of "as" is improper, and in others, it may cause confusion.

If a comparison is meant, do not use "as" in place of the preposition "like."

ILLUSTRATION B.47

Compare the difference in meaning of these two sentences:

The directors of the corporation, *as* its officers, owe a duty of loyalty to the shareholders.

The directors of the corporation, *like* its officers, owe a duty of loyalty to the shareholders.

Legal writing frequently involves causal or explanatory discussions. To avoid possible ambiguities, use "since," "because," or "while" instead of "as." Consider the possible meanings of the following sentence:

ILLUSTRATION B.48

As the plaintiff approached the door, the defendant fired several warning shots. (Did the defendant fire *because* the plaintiff approached the door? Did the defendant fire *while* the plaintiff was approaching?)

PROBLEM B.6

Assume that the following sentences are the conclusion of a memorandum. Edit them for usage errors. Indicate appropriate insertions using a caret symbol. Cross out or circle words or phrases in a manner showing to where they should be moved or indicating that they should be deleted.

(a) Some courts have held that even innocent accident victims should be prevented from recovering rewards for their injuries where tortfeasors can successfully demonstrate that they were mentally incapacitated at the time of the accident.

(b) On the other hand, due to the difficulty of proving mental illness by objective criteria and the high probability of fraudulent assertions of mental illness, other courts have refused to recognize this defense.

(c) In other words, an insane person, just as a sane person, is liable.

(d) The latter approach is the better one. The defendant relies completely on the insanity defense, so the plaintiff is likely to win.

Stop here, and edit the above sentences for usage errors before consulting the discussion of this problem at the end of this Appendix.

BE CAREFUL TO USE "SHALL," "WILL," "MAY," AND "MUST" CORRECTLY. AVOID USING "MAY NOT."

Significant differences in meaning exist when you use "shall," "will," "may," or "must" in creating or describing legal rights, legal authority, duties, or conditions precedent. In particular, problems may arise when "shall" is used to refer to obligatory or mandatory (imperative) action and later it is used to refer to nonobligatory future action.

The safest approach to using these terms correctly is as follows:

(1) To create or refer to a right, use "is entitled to";
(2) To create or refer to discretionary authority, use "may";
(3) To create or refer to a duty, use "shall";
(4) To create or refer to a mere condition precedent, use "must";
(5) To negate a right, use "is not entitled to";
(6) To negate a duty or a mere condition precedent, use "is not required to";
(7) To create a duty not to act (a prohibition), use "shall not."[10]
(8) To refer to future (nonobligatory) action, always use "will" (*not* "shall").
(9) To express discretion in acting or not acting, use "need not," "does not have to," or "has the option to" instead of

---

[10] See R. Dickerson, Materials on Legal Drafting 182 (1981).

"may not"; to express a complete prohibition, use "shall not" (or "must not") instead of "may not" (see (7) above).

PROBLEM B.7

Based on the above suggestions, circle the correct word to indicate the proper meaning:

(a) To be eligible to take the state bar examination, a person (shall) (must) be a graduate of an accredited law school. (Assume that you are creating or referring to a condition precedent to taking the bar examination.)

(b) Persons charged with crimes (are entitled to) (shall) have counsel present during a line-up. (Assume that you are referring to a legal right.)

(c) Doctors (may not, shall not) perform operations on nonconsenting patients. (Assume that you want to impose a legal duty not to act in the manner specified).

(d) The director (will) (may) (shall) (must) allow interested parties to file comments on the proposed regulations. (Assume that you want to indicate that the director has discretionary authority under these circumstances.)

(e) Cars (may not) (shall not) (will not) be left unattended on the highway for more than three hours. (Assume that you want to create a duty in unnamed persons not to act in the manner mentioned.)

Stop here, and select your answers before consulting the discussion of this problem at the end of this Appendix. (The discussion of the problems in this Appendix begins on the following page.)

DISCUSSION OF PROBLEM B.1

In this problem, you were asked to edit several sentences for grammatical errors.

In (a), a dangling participial phrase ("Having been severely injured in the automobile accident and seeking compensation") needs to be corrected (the plaintiff was injured, not the complaint). This sentence should be rewritten to make the plaintiff the subject: "Having been severely injured in the automobile accident and seeking compensation, the plaintiffs **alleged** in their complaint that the defendant **had operated** his vehicle in an unsportsmanlike manner." Note that the verb tenses (highlighted above) correctly reflect the proper time relationship.

In (b), a dangling phrase of result ("thus creating a question whether the law in this jurisdiction had been followed") needs to be corrected (the judge's actions, not the defendant's motion or the case, created the question).

This sentence could be rewritten in several ways. One way would be to use a dependent clause ("which created a question whether the law . . . "). Another way would be to rewrite the sentence: "The judge's denial of defendant's motion to dismiss for failure to state a claim and the submission of the case created a question whether the law in this jurisdiction had been followed."

In (c), "they" should be changed to "it" because collective nouns like "jury" use singular pronouns ("To the credit of the jury, **it** returned a special verdict in favor of the plaintiffs").

In (d), "was" should be changed to "**had been**" to reflect the proper time relationship (the intoxication preceded the jury's finding).

DISCUSSION OF PROBLEM B.2

In this problem, you were asked to edit several sentences for grammatical errors.

In (a), a dangling participial phrase ("raising the question for the first time") needs to be corrected (the dismissal of the action did not raise the question). The sentence could be rewritten as follows: "On appeal, raising the question for the first time, **the defendant requested that** the action **be dismissed** on the ground that the trial court lacked subject-matter jurisdiction." Note that the subjective ("be dismissed") is used in the "that"-clause expressing a request.

In (b), the verb (were required) does not agree with the subject ("each"). The sentence should read "each of the defendants **was** required to post a supersedeas bond."

In (c), you should have noted the split infinitive ("**To** effectively and quickly **resolve**"). Although it involves a matter of personal judgment, not splitting the infinitive would probably improve the way the sentence reads. More important, the infinitive clause itself modifies the wrong word ("appeal"). To correct this error, the sentence should be rewritten to make the "court" the subject: "**To resolve** the matter **effectively and quickly, the appellate court granted** an expedited appeal."

In (d), a dangling gerund phrase ("After hearing oral argument on the issue") needs to be corrected (the court, not the dismissal, heard the argument). This error should be corrected by making "the court" the subject of the sentence: "After hearing oral argument on the issue, **the court** granted a dismissal."

DISCUSSION OF PROBLEM B.3

In this problem, you were asked to punctuate several sentences based on the rules discussed in this Appendix.

In (a), a comma should be inserted after "rendered" to separate the subordinate clause ("When it is rendered,") from the independent clause that follows ("a judgment will . . . ").

In (b), "and/or" should be changed to just "and" in this sentence. Furthermore, a comma should be added after "reporters" in the same series because in legal writing the final comma is generally not omitted. Thus, the series in the sentence should preferably read "fees of the clerk, marshall, court reporters, and witnesses." It is also appropriate to add a comma after "witnesses" to separate the two independent clauses ("witnesses, but attorney fees are not taxable costs").

In (c), a comma should be added after "furthermore" to set off the conjunctive adverb ("Furthermore, a judgment . . . ").

In (d), a colon should replace the comma after "available" to introduce a list ("Four kinds of final remedies are available: (1) damages, (2) restitution, (3) coercive remedies, and (4) declaratory remedies.") Note that commas (rather than semicolons) are correctly used in the list. Semicolons would have been appropriate had the series been complicated and lengthy.

In (e), the conjunctive adverb "however" should be set off by commas, and "common-law" should be hyphenated because "common-law" serves as an adjective before a noun ("remedies"). The sentence should read as follows: "Note, however, that common-law remedies did not include a declaratory judgment."

DISCUSSION OF PROBLEM B.4

In this problem, you were asked to punctuate several sentences based on the rules discussed in this Appendix.

In (a), no changes are necessary. Note that a comma is not used between "order that" because restrictive ("essential") clauses are not set off.

In (b), a comma should be inserted between "court, which" because the clause ("which may involve monetary fines or imprisonment" is nonrestrictive ("extra"). Note also that no comma is needed between "party who" for the reason stated in (a) above.

In (c), the dash should be changed to a colon ("Two types of contempt exist: civil and criminal.") Dashes should be used for emphasis or clarity. You should avoid using them as substitutes for commas or other punctuation marks.

In (d), a comma should be inserted after the closing parenthesis at the end of the citation as follows: "(C.D. Cal. 1967), illustrate . . . ." Commas should be used to set off citations within a sentence.

In (e), two changes should be made. First, the ellipsis should not have been used at the beginning of the quotation. The rule is that when the material quoted appears as a clause or phrase in one of *your* sentences, ellipses are not used to indicate language omitted before or after the quoted material.

Second, the period at the end of the quotation should be inside of the ending quotation mark. Semicolons and colons, not commas, are placed outside of quotation marks. The sentence should read as follows: The distinction primarily depends "**upon** the objective to be served by the contempt citation." The citation in (e) is correct.

DISCUSSION OF PROBLEM B.5

In this problem, you were asked to punctuate several sentences based on the rules discussed in this Appendix.

In (a), the quotation marks surrounding "provisional remedies" should be omitted. Quotation marks are used to enclose items introduced by "entitled," "endorsed," "marked," "the term," and "the word." They are not ordinarily used with the terms "known as," "called," or "so-called." Furthermore, the clause itself should be set off by commas for the reason stated in the discussion of Problem B.4(b) above.

In (b), the subordinate clause ("as their name suggests") should be set off by commas because it interrupts an independent clause ("Provisional remedies, as their names suggests, are available . . . ").

In (c), the colon has been used properly, but semicolons should be used rather than the commas because the series is complicated and lengthy. Note that a comma is not used to set off the restrictive ("essential") clause "that might later be needed to satisfy a final judgment in the action" for the reason stated in the discussion of Problem B.4(a) above.

In (d), the sentence is properly punctuated. Dashes properly can be used to emphasize the interrupting material.

DISCUSSION OF PROBLEM B.6

In this problem, you were asked to edit several sentences for usage errors.

In (a), two usage errors exist. First, accident victims do not recover "rewards" for their injuries. The correct legal term of art is "compensation." Second, "where" should be used to designate place, not as a substitute for "when" or "in which." Thus, the sentence should read as follows: "Some courts have held that even innocent accident victims should be prevented from recovering **compensation** for their injuries **when** tortfeasors can successfully demonstrate that they were mentally incapacitated at the time of the accident."

In (b), "due to" is used incorrectly. It should be replaced with "because of." Note that "due to" is an adjective meaning "attributable to" and ordinarily introduces an adjectival phrase that immediately follows a form of the verb "to be" and modifies a noun that is the subject of the sentence. This sentence should read as follows: "On the other hand, **because of** the difficulty of proving mental illness by objective criteria and the high probability of fraudulent assertions of mental illness, other courts have refused to recognize this defense."

In (c), "as" is used incorrectly. Because a comparison is most likely intended in this sentence, "as" should be replaced with the preposition "like." The sentence should read: "In other words, an insane person, **like** a sane person, is liable."

In (d), "so" is used to join two clauses. In formal legal writing, this use of "so" should be avoided. The easiest solution is to subordinate one of the clauses: "**Because** the defendant relies completely on the insanity defense, the plaintiff is likely to win."

DISCUSSION OF PROBLEM B.7

In this problem, you were asked to circle the word that indicates the proper meaning.

In (a), you should use "must" to create or refer to the condition precedent; you are not creating or referring to a duty ("shall"): "To be eligible to take the state bar examination, a person **must** be a graduate of an accredited law school."

In (b), the proper method to refer to a legal right is with "entitled to": "Persons charged with crimes **are entitled to** have counsel present during a line-up."

In (c), you should use "shall not" to impose a duty not to act: "Doctors **shall not** perform operations on nonconsenting patients." If you wanted instead to express discretion in acting or not acting, you should use "need not," "does not have to," or "has the option to." In any event, do not use "may not" because it is ambiguous.

In (d), "may" is the proper term to indicate discretionary authority: "The director **may** allow interested parties to file comments on the proposed regulations."

In (e), you should use "shall not" to create a duty not to act in the manner mentioned: "Cars **shall not** be left unattended on the highway for more than three hours." If you wanted to refer to future (nonobligatory) action, you would use "will." Again, avoid using "may not."

Appendix C

"CLASSROOM" CASE BRIEF

A traditional aspect of law study has been the briefing of cases (technically, the briefing of "opinions"), which is largely a result of the case method of teaching. Briefing cases for classroom study has three principal benefits. First, it provides a systematic method of analyzing judicial opinions. Second, it encourages an understanding of many aspects of trial and appellate procedures. Third, it assists in learning to distill the facts of a case and the court's reasoning into workable statements.

Briefing judicial opinions for research and writing purposes differs in several ways. The suggested approaches for preparing classroom briefs place a central emphasis on *structure*. Use of a rigid structure encourages careful reading and analysis. The particular structure recommended varies, but the following items ordinarily are covered in one order or another:

(1) an identification of the case;
(2) a brief statement of the relevant facts;
(3) a statement of the procedural context;
(4) a statement of the issues or questions before the court;
(5) a statement of the court's decision on each of the issues or questions; and
(6) a summary of the court's reasoning.

A seventh item is sometimes added:

(7) a critical evaluation of the decision or other comments.

Opinions reprinted in casebooks have been edited to eliminate discussion of issues not relevant to the point that the author of the casebook is making through the case. When multiple issues appear in an opinion in a casebook, however, students are expected to include each issue in their briefs. The following case brief is based on the unedited *Theisen* opinion in Chapter 3. Under normal circumstances, many of the issues briefed in the example below would have been eliminated by the author of the casebook.

Note that in the brief below, "P" stands for "plaintiff"; "D" stands for "defendant"; and "J" stands for "judgment."

Theisen v. Milwaukee Automobile Mutual Insurance Co., 18 Wis. 2d 91, 118 N.W.2d 140 (1962).

Facts:

P, a passenger in a car, was injured in an accident late at night when the driver, insured by D, fell asleep and the car hit a tree.

Procedure:

Comparative negligence action for damages. Judge (1) excluded D's offer of proof of the driver's physical exhaustion to excuse the driver's falling asleep, (2) refused to instruct the jury that a deceased party is presumed to have exercised due care, (3) refused to submit the case to the jury under the assumption of risk doctrine, but (4) used assumption of risk language in the negligence questions submitted to the jury, and (5) asked the jury whether P's negligence was the cause of the accident and resulting injuries to P. Verdict: Driver 95% negligent; P 5% negligent for failing to keep a proper lookout; P also negligent by riding with driver under the circumstances, but P's negligence in riding with the driver was not causal. J/P

Issues:

(1) Is falling asleep at the wheel of an automobile negligence as a matter of law, thus making it proper to exclude evidence attempting to justify falling asleep?

(2) When evidence is introduced which would support a jury finding contrary to the presumption that a decedent exercised due care, is it proper to refuse to instruct the jury on the presumption?

(3) Is it proper in a comparative negligence action to refuse to recognize assumption of risk as a defense based upon plaintiff's implied consent?

(4) In determining P's negligence, is it proper to ask the jury whether P voluntarily exposed himself to the risk of injury (assumption of risk language) rather than whether P acted unreasonably under the circumstances?

(5) In determining whether the negligent acts caused the injury, is it improper to ask whether the lack of due care by the parties found negligent caused the accident and P's injuries?

Decision:

(1)-(3) Yes (4)-(5) No J/P/reversed; new trial granted on negligence questions only (no dispute as to P's damages).

Reasoning:

(1) Because it is within the driver's control to stay awake, to cease driving, or not to drive at all when sleepy and because falling asleep does not occur without warning, falling asleep at the wheel of an automobile is so opposed to the dictates of common prudence that no careful person would permit it to occur. Therefore, such conduct will be deemed to be negligence as a matter of law. When conduct is so deemed, proof of facts attempting to justify or excuse that conduct will not be permitted.

Rule: Falling asleep at the wheel of an automobile is negligence as a matter of law, and no facts can exist that will excuse that negligence.

(2) Because P proved that the car was driven on the wrong side of the road, that the other occupants who had participated in the events of the night had fallen asleep, and all the other circumstantial evidence indicated that the driver had fallen asleep, the presumption that the decedent exercised due care was eliminated, and it was, therefore, proper not to instruct the jury on the subject.

Rule: The presumption of due care accorded deceased persons only places upon the other parties the risk incidental to a failure to come forward with such testimony as may be within their control. When evidence is introduced that would support a jury finding contrary to the presumption that the decedent exercised due care, the presumption is eliminated, and no instruction on the subject should be given.

(3) After the court's decision in McConville v. State Farm Mutual Automobile Insurance Co. (Wis. 1962), assumption of risk based upon implied consent has been abolished as a defense in a comparative negligence action; therefore, it was proper for the court to submit P's decision to ride with the driver to the jury in terms of negligence (whether P acted unreasonably under the circumstances).

Rule: Implied assumption of risk is not a defense in a comparative negligence action.

(4) Assumption of risk involves a voluntary exposure to the risk of injury. Because the court's question to the jury should have been phrased in terms of negligence, but the question used by the court emphasized exposure to risk instead, the court erred in its instruction.

Rule: In determining whether guests failed to exercise ordinary care for their own safety, the jury should be asked whether the guests acted unreasonably in proceeding under the circumstances.

(5) If the jury intended to find P negligent in riding with the driver under the circumstances, the jury might have answered

that such negligence was not causal because it was not a cause of the collision. However, when the guest's negligence in riding with the driver consists of an exposure to a hazard that is found to be causal negligence on the part of the driver, the guest's negligence necessarily would be a cause of the guest's injuries, which is the legally relevant matter. On the other hand, the jury might not have found P negligent in riding with the driver at all had the negligence question been stated only in terms of negligence rather than exposure to risk. Because of this confusion and the court's failure to limit the questions of cause to P's injuries, the court erred.

Rule: All questions of cause in comparative negligence actions should be framed in terms of whether the various parties caused the plaintiff's injuries.

Evaluation and Comment:

(1) The prior rule in Wisconsin, which followed the leading case of Bushnell v. Bushnell (Conn. 1925), was that proof of falling asleep at the wheel establishes an inference of negligence sufficient to establish a prima facie case unless that evidence is rebutted by exculpatory evidence. By adopting the "negligence as a matter of law" rule, the court precluded the possibility of showing that the driver's falling asleep was somehow justified or excusable or that it was otherwise unanticipated. The underlying social policy for the court's rule seems sound because of the inherent danger of operating motor vehicles and the serious consequences of falling asleep at the wheel. The court's rule reinforces the duty of a driver to heed the forewarning of sleep and imposes liability (without excuses) on the driver who fails to do so.

(2) The court stated in dictum that this rule does not cover loss of consciousness (as distinguished from going to sleep) resulting from an injury inflicted by an outside force, fainting, heart attack, or some other illness that incapacitates the driver. To be successful as a defense, the court indicated that this loss of consciousness (a) must be sudden, (b) must be without sufficient warning, and (c) should not have been reasonably foreseen.

Appendix D

OPINION SYNTHESIS

For purposes of illustration, the synthesis shown below is limited to the Wisconsin cases analyzed in the text. Note especially that the research notes shown in the discussion of Problems 4.10, 4.11, and 4.12 in Appendix A form the direct basis for presentation.

MEMORANDUM

TO: Senior Partner
FROM: John Q. Clerk
DATE: October 1, 19xx
RE: Synthesis of Karow, Meyer's, and Theisen Cases

ASSUMED FACTS:

Defendant I.M. Delira suffered a mental aberration that caused her to lose control of the automobile that she was driving. She negligently caused an accident. The details of the accident and her mental condition are unknown at this time because the defendant currently is institutionalized.

OPINION SYNTHESIS:

In Karow v. Continental Insurance Co., 57 Wis. 56, 15 N.W. 27 (1883), the plaintiffs sued a fire insurance company to recover for a loss under two fire insurance policies. The plaintiffs were heirs at law and legal representatives of the owner of the policies that covered the buildings on his homestead. The plaintiffs asserted that the owner had burned his buildings while he was insane, and thus the burning was not caused by his voluntary act. They also asserted that the insurer had waived the defense that the insured had burned his own buildings while sane by calling for proofs of loss. Id. at ____, 15 N.W. at 27.

The Wisconsin circuit court rejected the argument that the insurer had waived this defense. On the question of insanity, the trial judge charged the jury that it must look outside the commission of the act of burning the buildings and the immediately preceding events--the murder of his wife and the attempted murder of other members of his family. Under this charge, the jury, in effect, could find the owner insane only from other independent testimony. In a special verdict, the jury found, inter alia, that (1) the owner had set fire to the buildings and (2) he was not insane when he had done so. Based on these findings, the court entered judgment for the defendant. Id.

On appeal, the plaintiffs argued that the trial court erred in two ways. First, the trial court should have entered judgment for the plaintiffs because the defense that the insured had burned his own buildings while sane had been waived. Second, the trial court should have allowed the jury to consider the owner's acts and the immediately preceding events in deciding whether the insured was insane. On the other hand, the insurer argued that the defense had not been waived and that the insured's insanity was immaterial. Thus, any error in the charge could be disregarded. Id.

The Wisconsin Supreme Court upheld the trial court's ruling that the defense had not been waived, but it found "manifest error" in the charge because the owner's acts themselves should have been considered in determining what his mental condition had been at the time of the burning. The court held that the insurer is liable if the burning was not caused by the voluntary act, assent, procurement, or design of the insured. If the insured was insane at the time of the burning, his actions could not be considered, from a legal point of view, to be voluntary ones because an insane person has no control over his mental faculties. The court emphasized the absence of a specific policy provision relieving the insurer of liability in these circumstances. Id. at _____, 15 N.W. at 27, 32.

In Karow, the Wisconsin Supreme Court focused on whether the risk had been assumed by contract. The court was not concerned with the insured's liability to third parties for negligence. In dictum, however, the court indicated that an insane person "might" be liable on a different basis:

> [T]he . . . act of burning another's property might subject [an insane] person to damages therefor, not on the ground of negligence, . . . but . . . "on the principle that where a loss must be borne by one of two innocent persons, it should be borne by [the one] who occasioned it."

Id. at 30 (quoting Beals v. See, 10 Pa. St. 61, ___ (_____) (Gibson, C.J.).

In In re Meyer's Guardianship, 218 Wis. 381, 261 N.W. 211 (1935), persons who had been paid for a fire loss by their insurer assigned their right of action to the insurer. The insurer sued the defendant's estate (hereinafter referred to as the defendant) to recover the amounts paid. In prior proceedings, the defendant had been charged with the crime of arson but had been found insane and committed to a mental hospital. The evidence offered by the insurer proved beyond doubt that the defendant had set the fire. The jury found, inter alia, that the defendant had not "intentionally" set the fire and that he was insane at the time the fire occurred. Both the plaintiff and defendant moved for judgment, but the trial court refused all motions except the one granting the plaintiff a new trial on the ground that justice had not been done. The defendant appealed from the entry of this order. Id. at ____, 261 N.W. at 212.

The Wisconsin Supreme Court held that insanity was not a defense in this case and entered judgment in favor of the plaintiff insurer. In reaching its decision, the court relied on the following "well-settled" rule: "A person non compos mentis is liable in damages to one injured by reason of a tort committed by him unless evil intent or express malice constitutes an essential element in the plaintiff's recovery." Id. at ____, 261 N.W. at 213. The court also cited and discussed several cases in which this rule had been applied. Id. at ____, 261 N.W. at 213-15.

The court set forth three reasons in support of this rule. First, the loss should be borne by the person who caused it when one of two innocent persons must bear it. This reason is the one announced by the court in Karow. Second, imposing liability on insane persons will encourage relatives and others interested in their estate to restrain them. Third, recognizing insanity as a defense to a negligence action would permit tortfeasors to simulate or pretend insanity to avoid liability. Id. at ____, 261 N.W. at 213 (quoting a summary of the reasons in Ruling Case Law derived from prior decisions).

Based on the Karow and Meyer's cases, it can be concluded that insanity is not recognized as a general defense to liability to third parties for an insane person's acts except when evil intent or express malice is an essential element in the tort. Neither are elements in a cause of action for negligence. Thus, insane persons may be held liable for their negligent acts.

In Theisen v. Milwaukee Automobile Mutual Insurance Co., the plaintiff, a passenger in a car, commenced a comparative negligence action for damages to recover for injuries resulting from the driver's falling asleep at the wheel. The Wisconsin Supreme Court held, inter alia, that the driver, insured by the defendant insurer, was negligent per se. The court refused to accept the defendant's argument that the driver

> went to sleep unknowingly from physical exhaustion and [that] the case should be governed by the principles applicable to sudden unforeseen physical disability over which a driver has no control, such as being the victim of a heart attack, epileptic seizure, or other loss of consciousness which is sudden and unforeseen. Arguendo, it may be stated acts done while one is asleep are not voluntary and in and of themselves do not constitute negligence.

> . . . The basis, however, for liability of the sleeping driver is his negligence in falling asleep.

Id. at ____, 118 N.W.2d at 142-43 (emphasis added).

The court stated this rule in a slightly different manner later in its opinion:

> We exclude from this holding those exceptional cases of loss of consciousness resulting from injury inflicted by an outside force or fainting or heart attack, epileptic seizure, or other illness which suddenly incapacitates the driver of an automobile and when the occurrence of such disability is not attended with sufficient warning or should not have been reasonably foreseen. When, however, such occurrence should have been reasonably foreseen, we have held the driver of a motor vehicle negligent as a matter of law, as in the sleep cases.

Id. at ____, 118 N.W.2d at 144 (emphasis added).

In this latter statement, the court did not limit the rule to physical disabilities; instead, it referred to an "illness" that (1) suddenly incapacitates the driver, provided that (2) the occurrence was without sufficient warning, and (3) it was not reasonably foreseeable. This decision could be interpreted to support the view that if a mental illness suddenly incapacitates a driver, the driver will not be held liable if the illness occurred without warning and was not reasonably foreseeable.

Based upon Karow and In re Meyer's Guardianship, prior insanity of the defendant as a general defense cannot be relied on to relieve the defendant of liability. In fact, evidence of prior insanity may undercut the "sudden illness" rule recognized (but not applied) in Theisen. Furthermore, it should be noted that nothing in Karow and In re Meyer's Guardianship expressly limits the "insanity rule" to pre-existing insanity.

To meet the sudden illness rule, a "mental aberration" would have to be considered a physical or mental disability. Furthermore, it would have to occur suddenly and without warning. Thus, I.M. Delira's prior "mental" history should be investigated carefully.

One matter of concern is how the court's requirement in Theisen that the defendant should not have reasonably foreseen the events should be applied when the illness is a mental one. Would the court judge the defendant by an objective standard or by a subjective one? What if there were indications of mental illness, but the very nature of the illness caused the person to deny the existence of the illness? In Theisen, the court deemed (charged) the driver with knowledge of an ordinary prudent person even though the defendant, in fact, may not have realized that exhaustion might cause sleep. Id. at ____, 118 N.W.2d at 143-44. Thus, one might suspect that a driver would be charged with objective knowledge of his prior mental illness if there had been sufficient warnings. This conclusion is supported by a general policy consideration recognized in Meyer's: those interested in the estate of the insane person would be under an inducement to restrain the driver if there were sufficient warnings.

Another more critical concern is whether a mental illness (resulting in a loss of conscious control of an automobile) should be classified within the sudden illness rule. One might argue that this rule should be limited to physical disabilities and illnesses. One basis of the rule in Meyer's was to discourage tortfeasors from simulating or pretending insanity to defend their wrongful acts. Physical disabilities arguably could be proven by more objective evidence than mental illnesses.

Still another concern is how to harmonize the principal basis for the rule in Meyer's (as between two innocent persons, the person causing the damage should be liable) with the rule recognized in Theisen (that sudden disabilities do not give rise to liability for negligence). Is not a person struck by a sudden heart attack or a sudden mental illness an innocent person who caused injury to another innocent person? One difficulty in resolving this apparent conflict lies in the lack of explanation of the reasons for the sudden illness rule in Theisen. Other cases supporting the sudden illness rule might establish the reasons. Is the suddenness the key to distinguishing the two rules? Or is the key the inability to control or anticipate the events?

CONCLUSION:

Based on this synthesis of the Karow, Meyer's, and Theisen cases, four conclusions can be drawn:

First, prior insanity of the driver is not a defense.

Second, a sudden mental illness may provide a defense if (l) it occurred without warning and (2) it could not have been reasonably anticipated.

Third, the driver would more than likely be charged with objective knowledge of the warnings even if the driver did not realize that loss of conscious control of an automobile was possible as a result of the illness.

Fourth, some risk exists that the line of cases refusing to recognize insanity as a defense may be applied to any case of mental illness, limiting the sudden illness rule to physical disabilities. In Karow, there was apparently very little evidence of insanity except at the time the events (burning) occurred. In Meyer's, there is no discussion of whether there had been past indications of insanity prior to the burning. However, one of the reasons that supports the insanity liability rule is lacking: unlike the case of persons with a history of insanity, there is no opportunity for others to control the person who, without warning, suddenly and unexpectedly becomes mentally ill.

Appendix E

DRAFT OF A MEMORANDUM OF LAW

MEMORANDUM

TO: Senior Partner
FROM: John Q. Clerk
DATE: February 29, 19xx
RE: Sudden Mental Illness and Preexisting Mental Illness as Defenses to Negligence Actions

QUESTIONS PRESENTED:

1. In the State of Utopia, should a sudden mental illness be recognized as a defense to a negligence action when the driver of an automobile suddenly and without warning suffered a mental aberration that caused the driver to lose conscious control of the automobile and to collide with the plaintiff's vehicle?

2. In the State of Utopia, should a driver who has a prior and continuing history of mental illness be required to conform to a reasonable person standard when a mental aberration prevents the driver from either recognizing a duty of care or being able to discharge that duty?

BRIEF ANSWER:

1. Although some authority to the contrary exists, it is likely that the State of Utopia will recognize sudden mental illness as a defense to a negligence action.

2. The traditional arguments in favor of requiring mentally ill persons to meet a reasonable person standard are not persuasive, but so far the courts have not permitted the use of a subjective standard (one tailored to their ability to personally meet it). The common-law rule imposes, in effect, strict liability on insane defendants and is inconsistent with the standard imposed on young children. Based upon the almost unanimous agreement among modern commentators who have considered the issue and the erosion of the common-law rule in contributory negligence cases, a good chance exists that the Utopia courts will reject the common-law rule.

STATEMENT OF FACTS:

Our firm represents No-Pay Casualty Company (No-Pay). S.W. Lash has commenced a $750,000 direct action against No-Pay and Irma Marie Delira. Lash alleges that No-Pay and Delira are liable for his injuries resulting from Delira's negligent operation of her motor vehicle on a highway in the State of Utopia. Delira maintains that her car was controlled by an alien creature and that she "was totally powerless to do anything." Delira also claims that she was a real "Wonder Woman" from Paradise Island, which was "hidden deep within the Bermuda Triangle." Delira currently is institutionalized in the Freud Memorial Hospital of the Insane. The question whether Delira's mental illness should be a defense is one of first impression in Utopia.

DISCUSSION:

I. Sudden Illness Defense

A. Sudden Illnesses as Unavoidable Accidents

The law of negligence is based on fault. When a person engages in a potentially dangerous activity such as operating a motor vehicle, the law imposes a duty of care on that person. If that person fails to operate the motor vehicle in a reasonably prudent manner and thus breaches that duty, liability is imposed when property damage or personal injuries result. On the other hand, it is well established that a driver is not liable when an accident is "unavoidable." Thus, no liability is imposed when the events were not intended and, under all the circumstances, the accident could not have been foreseen or prevented by the exercise of reasonable precautions. W. Prosser & W. Keeton, The Law of Torts § 29, at 162 (5th ed. 1984).

Within this broad category of unavoidable accidents are sudden emergencies. Id. § 29, at 162, n.1. Drivers who suddenly lose control of their automobiles when they are seized with a heart attack, stroke, fainting spell, or epileptic fit are not held liable. See, e.g., Moore v. Presnell, 38 Md. App. 243, 379 A.2d 1246 (1977) (blackout) ("overwhelming weight of authority" supports this rule); Restatement (Second) of Torts § 283C (1965) ("If the actor is ill or otherwise physically disabled, the standard of conduct to which he must conform to avoid being negligent is that of a reasonable [person] under like disability"); 7A Am. Jur. 2d Automobiles & Highway Traffic § 773 (1980). But see Leary v. Oates, 84 S.W.2d 486, 490 (Tex. Civ. App. 1935) (writ dissm'd w.o.j.) (apparently rejecting the sudden illness defense).

B. Elements of the Sudden Illness Defense

To establish a sudden illness defense in a negligence action, the illness must have been sudden and without warning. Thus, if the illness was foreseeable, liability may be imposed because the driver may have been negligent in driving the car at all. W. Prosser & W. Keeton, supra § 29, at 162. See, e.g., Reliance Ins. Co. v. Dickens, 279 So. 2d 234 (La. App. 1973) (epileptic attack foreseeable to driver with an 8-year history of seizures).

Whether an illness is foreseeable depends on the facts of each case. For example, in Keller v. Wonn, 140 W. Va. 860, 87 S.E.2d 453 (1955), a driver ran up onto the sidewalk and injured the plaintiff. Just before the accident, the driver suffered a massive cerebral hemorrhage. In a suit to recover damages, the primary issue was whether the driver had been negligent by driving at all in light of his physical condition and background. The circuit court entered judgment in favor of the plaintiff and the defendant appealed.

The West Virginia Supreme Court of Appeals reversed. The court recognized that when "the driver of a motor vehicle suddenly becomes physically or mentally incapacitated without warning, he cannot be held liable for any injury resulting from the operation of his vehicle while he is so incapacitated." Nonetheless, when "a prima facie case of negligence has been established by the plaintiff, the burden is upon the defendant to show the sudden illness or attack, and to further show that the illness or attack was unanticipatable and unforeseen." Id. at ____, 87 S.E.2d at 459.

The court's careful analysis of the record showed that the driver had sought medical treatment for hypertension but had not been informed by the doctors that if he operated an automobile he might have a sudden attack of some kind which could result in serious injury to himself or others. Furthermore, there was no evidence in the record that prior to the day of his death the defendant had suffered from a stroke, fainting spell, or other type of attack that rendered him dizzy or unconscious. Id. at ____, 87 S.E.2d at 461. Finding that the defense had clearly met its burden and with no contrary evidence before the trial court, the West Virginia Supreme Court of Appeals held that the trial judge erred in not directing a verdict in the defendant's favor and remanded the case.

II. Application of the Sudden Illness Rule to Sudden Mental Illnesses or Aberrations

A. Support for Adoption of a Sudden Mental Illness Rule

The first case to allow a defense based on a sudden mental illness was Buckley & Toronto Transporation Commissionn v. Smith Transport Ltd., [1946] Ont. L. Rep. 798, [1946] 4 Dom. L. Rep. 721. In that case, a street-car was damaged and its operator was injured when the driver of a tractor-trailer transport jack-knifed and collided with the street-car (the Commission). They sued the owner of the transport for damages based on the driver's alleged negligence. The owner of the transport presented an "unavoidable accident" defense. The owner asserted that its driver "suddenly and without warning, had become insane and was labouring under an insane delusion that the transport unit was under some sort of remote electrical control manipulated from the head office of his employer in the city of Toronto, as a result of which he was unable to control the speed of the vehicle or stop it." [1946] Ont. L. Rep. at 800.

The trial judge found that the driver turned the steering wheel of the transport quickly (causing it to jack-knife) to avoid hitting a fence ahead of him. That action, the trial judge found, indicated that the driver was not under any delusion concerning his control at the time of the accident. Id. at 802. On this basis, the defense was rejected, and judgment was entered for the plaintiffs.

On appeal, the Ontario Court of Appeal found that the evidence indicated that the driver was affected by the delusion a short time before the collision. About an hour before the accident about three miles from the point of the collision, he had telephoned his employer and reported that his transport was stalled on the highway. Another driver was directed to render assistance and get the transport started. That driver arrived and found nothing wrong with the transport. As they were separating, the affected driver said, "It must be under electric control and the beam must be on."

The court of appeal likewise found that there was ample proof of the existence of the delusion after the accident. Id. at 800-03. Based on this proof, the court recognized a legal presumption that "he was also labouring under it at the time of the collision." Id. at 803. The court of appeal rejected the argument that his last-second turning of the steering wheel rebutted the presumption. The nature of the insane delusion was important to the court of appeals. Id. at 805-06. The delusion had to be related to the accident in such a way that (1) it affected the insane person's ability to understand the duty which rested on him to take care or (2) if it could be said that he did understand and appreciate that duty, the particular delusion prevented him from discharging it. Id. at 807.

There was apparently no forewarning of this delusion. The insane driver had been employed only a few days with the defendant company and had no indication of abnormal conduct or conversation, apart from the comment that he made to the other driver on the night of the accident. Id. The driver had syphilis of the brain. He died from the effects of that disease approximately one month after the accident. Id. at 799-800. Thus, the court of appeal allowed the sudden mental illness defense.

Citing the Buckley case favorably, the Wisconsin Supreme Court reasoned in the leading American case, Breunig v. American Family Insurance Co., 45 Wis. 2d 536, 173 N.W.2d 619 (1970), that a sudden mental illness was "equivalent in its effect" to sudden physical illnesses and thus should be treated under the rules governing sudden illnesses rather than under the general rule developed under the common law refusing to recognize insanity as a defense. Id. at ____, 173 N.W.2d at 624. In Breunig, the plaintiff had been injured when his truck collided with an automobile driven by the defendant's insured. While driving home after taking her husband to work, the insured saw a white light on the back of the car ahead of her. According to her psychiatrist, she became under the impression that God was taking hold of the steering wheel and was directing her car.

When she saw the plaintiff's truck approaching her, she stepped on the gas to become airborne. She told the psychiatrist that she knew she could fly because Batman does; to her surprise, she was not flying before striking the truck but after the impact she was. When a traffic officer came to her car to investigate, he found her sitting behind the wheel looking off into space and could not get a statement of any kind from her. She was taken to the hospital and later transferred to a psychiatric ward. Id. at ____, 173 N.W.2d at 622.

The defendant asserted that its insured was not negligent under these circumstances. The circuit court tried the case on the theory that some forms of insanity preclude liability. The jury, however, found for the plaintiff, and, after the plaintiff accepted a reduction in damages, the court entered judgment in favor of the plaintiff.

The defendant asserted on appeal, inter alia, that its insured was not negligent as a matter of law because no evidence existed upon which the jury could have found that she had knowledge or warning or should have reasonably foreseen that she might be subject to a mental delusion that would cause her suddenly to lose control of the car. On the other hand, the plaintiff argued that such evidence of forewarning did exist and that insanity should not be a defense in negligence cases. Id. at ____, 173 N.W.2d at 622-23.

The court distinguished the various common-law cases holding insane persons liable for their torts because they generally have dealt with preexisting insanity of a permanent nature. The court concluded that

> the statement that insanity is no defense is too broad when it is applied to a negligence case where the driver is suddenly overcome without forewarning by a mental disability or disorder which incapacitates him from conforming his conduct to the standards of a reasonable man under like circumstances. These are rare cases indeed, but their rarity is no reason for overlooking their existence and the justification which is the basis of the whole doctrine of liability for negligence, i.e., that it is unjust to hold a man responsible for his conduct which he is incapable of avoiding and which incapability was unknown to him prior to the accident.

Id. at ____, 173 N.W.2d at 624.

The Wisconsin Supreme Court nonetheless upheld the jury's verdict. Even though the psychiatrist testified that the insured was suffering from a "schizophrenic reaction, paranoid type, acute" and that she had no knowledge or forewarning that such an illness would be likely to occur, the psychiatrist's opinion was not conclusive. It was for the jury to decide whether the factual underpinning of an expert opinion was true. Prior to the accident, the insured had told her daughter of certain visions. Id. at ____, 173 N.W.2d at 622-63, 624. On this basis, the court held that the

> jury could find that a woman, who believed she had a special relationship to God and was the chosen one to survive the end of the world, could believe that God would take over the direction of her life to the extent of driving her car. Since these mental aberrations were not constant, the jury could infer she had knowledge of her condition and the likelihood of a hallucination just as one who has knowledge of a heart condition knows the possibility of an attack.

Id. at ____, 173 N.W.2d at 625 (emphasis added).

Other American courts apparently have recognized that sudden mental incapacities should be treated like sudden physical illnesses. See, e.g., Keller v. Wonn, 140 W. Va. 860, ____, 87 S.E.2d 453, 459 (1955) (cerebral hemorrhage) (including "mental incapacity" in its statement of the sudden illness rule); Lutzkovitz v. Murray, 339 A.2d 64, 67 (Del. Super. 1975) (apparent black-out) (similar statement of the rule). Accord Moore v. Presnell, 38 Md. App. 243, _____, 379 A.2d 1246, 1248 (1977) (loss of consciousness) (including mental incapacity in the rule and recognizing that it represents "the overwhelming weight of authority).

Comment c to section 283C of the Restatement (Second) of Torts (dealing with physical disabilities) provides further support for treating a sudden mental illness or aberration like a physical disability: "Thus a heart attack, or a temporary dizziness due to fever or nausea, as well as a transitory delirium, are regarded as circumstances to be taken into account in determining what the reasonable [person] would do." Restatement (Second) of Torts § 283C comment b (1965) (emphasis added). Recognizing sudden mental illness as a defense also is well accepted among the commentators who have considered the subject. See, e.g., Curran, Tort Liability of the Mentally Ill and Mentally Deficient, 21 Ohio St. L.J. 52, 62 (1960) (supporting adoption of the rule).

B. Application of the Rule

1. Nature of the Mental Illness

As discussed at the outset of this memorandum, the fundamental basis for not imposing liability for otherwise negligent conduct is the unavoidability of the accident. In other words, when the defendant's mental illness does not affect the ability to avoid the accident, the defendant will be held liable. Thus, to establish this defense, the nature of the mental illness must be examined. In Breunig, for example, the Wisconsin Supreme Court stated:

> Not all types of insanity vitiate responsibility for a negligent tort. The question of liability in every case must depend upon the kind and nature of the insanity. The effect of the mental illness or mental hallucinations or disorder must be such as to affect the person's ability to understand and appreciate the duty which rests upon him to drive his car with ordinary care, or if the insanity does not affect such understanding and appreciation, it must affect his ability to control his car in an ordinarily prudent manner.

Breunig, 45 Wis. 2d at _____, 173 N.W.2d at 623. Accord Buckley, 1946 Ont. L. Rep. at 806-07.

In the instant case, like in Breunig and Buckley, the defendant was suffering from a delusion at the time of the accident. Delira apparently believed that she was a Wonder Woman and that an alien creature controlled her vehicle. Based on Breunig, the existence and effect of Delira's mental aberration will be questions for the jury.

The burden of proof rests on the defendants. Buckley, 1946 Ont. L. Rep. at 806. Unlike in Buckley, however, there appears to be no evidence that Delira was laboring under the delusion other than her own testimony. Thus, the defendant cannot take advantage of a presumption that the defendant was laboring under the delusion at the time of the accident based upon evidence of the existence of the delusion shortly before the accident and shortly after it. Cf. id. at 803 (evidence of delusion shortly before and after the occurrence gave rise to a legal presumption). On the other hand, the defendant's case is stronger on the facts than Buckley because there appears to be no last-second turning of the wheel in an apparent attempt to avoid the accident.

2. Suddenness and Lack of Forewarning

Both the Ontario Court of Appeals in Buckley and the Wisconsin Supreme Court in Breunig specifically required the illness to be sudden and without forewarning. In Buckley, the court emphasized that the defendant employer had no indication of the illness of the driver and that the driver had acted normally during the few weeks that he had worked for the company. Id. at 799-800. In Breunig, however, the jury apparently believed that the prior visions of the driver were sufficient to establish prior knowledge of the possibility of another hallucination. Breunig, 45 Wis. 2d at _____, 173 N.W.2d at 625.

The facts of the instant case are silent on whether Delira had experienced any prior delusions. If she had, the illness might not be viewed as "sudden." Furthermore, if the delusions were intermittent, the jury might decide that Delira had sufficient forewarning that the delusion might occur again. Cf. Johnson v. Lambotte, 147 Colo. 203, 363 P.2d 165 (1961) (defendant driver apparently knew that he was in a mental hospital for treatment of mental disorder) (auto accident caused by an escaping insane defendant). Thus, it is important to inquire into Delira's past mental history to determine if she has received treatment or otherwise manifested symptoms of mental illness.

Two additional factors concerning forewarning based on prior illness should be considered. First, it has been argued that in order to hold mentally ill persons who suffer from intermittent visions to the standard of a reasonable person, evidence of lucidity (equivalent to that of a reasonable person) at the time they decided to drive should be required. Otherwise, a capacity may be imputed to them that they, in fact, may have lacked because, to them, their prior visions may have seemed entirely rational and not indicative of an impaired ability to operate a car. Seidelson, Reasonable Expectations and Subjective Standards in Negligence Law: The Minor, the Mentally Impaired, and the Mentally Incompetent, 50 Geo. Wash. L. Rev. 17, 36-37 (1981). Second, it has been asserted that "if a person suffering from intermittent periods of insanity were told by his doctor that he was no longer ill, then he should not be required to guard against his insanity, at least not in the near future." Comment, The Tort Liability of Insane Persons for Negligence, 39 Tenn. L. Rev. 705, 721 (1972).

C. Authorities Rejecting the Sudden Mental Illness Defense

A few jurisdictions refuse to treat sudden mental illnesses occurring without warning like sudden physical illnesses and hold a mentally ill person to the standard of conduct of a reasonable person. In Kuhn v. Zabotsky, 9 Ohio St. 2d 129, 224 N.E.2d 137 (1967), the plaintiff was travelling about 25 miles per hour when his car was struck in the rear by the defendant's car. It appeared from the evidence that it was struck at least once more before the plaintiff brought his car to a stop. The plaintiff commenced a negligence action in an Ohio Common Pleas court for damages. The defendant at trial asserted that he "had been suddenly stricken by a mental illness which he had no reason to anticipate and which rendered it impossible for him to control the car which he was driving." Id. at _____, 224 N.E.2d at 138.

The defendant testified that he had no recollection of what happened after he drank a cup of coffee at work until he was in the psychiatric ward. The undisputed evidence showed, however, (1) that the defendant followed the plaintiff to a phone booth and tore the page out of the telephone book that the plaintiff was attempting to use; (2) that he threw a glass of water in the investigating officer's face; (3) that he tried to leave the scene of the accident by running along the road so that the police had to chase and apprehend him; and (4) that, upon being asked for his name, he said he was St. Michael the Archangel. The psychiatrist testified that the defendant was suffering from a psychotic depression reaction. Id. at _____, 224 N.E.2d at 139-40.

The trial judge charged the jury on this basis and the jury found for the defendant. Id. at _____, 224 N.E.2d at 138-39. On appeal, the Ohio Court of Appeals affirmed the judgment of the trial court in favor of the defendant, but the Ohio Supreme Court reversed. It held that this jury charge did not correctly state the law of Ohio. Id. at _____, 224 N.E.2d at 139. The court stated that there were not many negligence cases in any jurisdiction in this country dealing with the defense of sudden mental illness or temporary insanity but it thought that "the rule seems well established." The court quoted section 283B of the Restatement (Second) of Torts ("Under the common law, insane persons are liable for their failure to conform to the standard of conduct of reasonable persons in negligence actions") and from the third edition of Prosser at pages 156 and 1030 and cited 1 Cooley on Torts §§ 64-65, at 186-87 (4th ed. 1932). Id. at ____, 224 N.E.2d at 140. The court emphasized "the public policy that as between two parties to an accident, where one party is mentally sound, blameless and injured and the other is at fault and mentally ill or insane, the loss which must be done by someone should be suffered by the person at fault." Id. at ____, 224 N.E.2d at 141.

The Ohio Supreme Court rejected the defendant's attempt to characterize the events as a "blackout" to bring it within the rule of Lehman v. Haynam, 164 Ohio St. 595, 133 N.E.2d 97 (1956), which involved a sudden disability caused by unconsciousness. The evidence clearly indicated that the defendant had not blacked out prior to the accident. Id. at ____, 224 N.E.2d at 139. In any event, the court indicated in dictum that if the defendant had blacked out, it would have to reexamine Lehman in light of subsequent decisions. Id. at ____, 224 N.E.2d at 141.

A more recent case rejecting the sudden mental illness defense is Turner v. Caldwell, 36 Conn. Supp. 350, 421 A.2d 876 (Super. Ct. 1980). In Turner, the plaintiff commenced a negligence action in a Connecticut superior court. In a special defense, the defendant alleged that "she was suddenly stricken by mental illness which she had no cause to anticipate, thereby rendering it impossible for her to control her vehicle." The plaintiff moved to strike that defense "on the ground that temporary insanity is not a defense to an action grounded in negligence." 36 Conn. Supp. at ____, 421 A.2d at 876.

The court granted the motion. The court cited Kuhn v. Zabotsky, 9 Ohio St. 2d 129, 224 N.E.2d 137 (1967), and relied on (1) the policy ground of allocating liability among two innocent persons to the one at fault and mentally ill and (2) the stated view that "mental illness, particularly that which is temporary, is difficult of proof and susceptible of being feigned." Id. at ____, 421 A.2d at 877. This latter view seems to imply that if the illness remains, then there may be less of a concern with proof and feigning. The court distinguished an earlier Connecticut decision, Fitzgerald v. Lawhorn, 29 Conn. Supp. 511, 294 A.2d 338 (Conn. Super. 1972) on the ground that Fitzgerald involved (1) an intentional tort, not negligence and (2) a prior adjudication of not guilty in criminal proceedings by reason of insanity, not a "momentary attack of mental illness." Id. at ____, 421 A.2d at 876.

Two other cases that factually may support a rejection of a sudden illness defense are Williams v. Hays, 143 N.Y. 442, 38 N.E. 449 (1894), qualified in 157 N.Y. 541, 52 N.E. 589 (1899) and Sforza v. Green Bus Lines, 150 Misc. 180, 268 N.Y.S. 446 (N.Y.C. Mun. Ct. 1934). In Williams, the captain of a ship became temporarily insane and was subsequently sued by the insurer for his negligence in managing the vessel. The Williams opinions (discussed in detail in the next section) did not focus on the suddenness of the defendant's insanity but instead adopted the common-law rule refusing to recognize insanity as a defense in tort actions.

In Sforza, the plaintiff was chopping ice on his parked ice truck when a bus owned by the corporate defendant and driven by the individual defendant hit the ice truck. The plaintiff brought a negligence action to recover for property damage and personal injuries. The bus driver was committed for observation and later was confined in an insane asylum. The court indicated that there was evidence of unusual and irrational acts by the driver at the time of and immediately following the accident. Id. at ____, 268 N.Y.S. at 446-47. Relying on the opinion in the second appeal in Williams v. Hays, 157 N.Y. 541, 52 N.E. 589 (1899), the defendant argued that a distinction should be made between torts of misfeasance and nonfeasance when they are committed by an insane person.

The court pointed out that if the defendant were sane, his acts in driving the bus into the standing truck would constitute a tort of misfeasance or his failure to swerve the course of the bus to prevent a collision would constitute a tort of misfeasance. Thus, the court concluded that the adoption of one theory or the other as a practical matter would not conflict with the result. Id. The court stated that if such a distinction was adopted, it "would be unreal and unsubstantial, and, if given judicial sanction, would readily induce an influx of simulated or pretended insanity." Further, the court stated that the question whether a lunatic is responsible in all cases of negligence was not before the court because "there was no evidence in the case at bar as to how the insanity was occasioned." The defendants had suggested that the insanity may have been produced by a state of mind induced by his wife's expected motherhood that morning. Id. at ____, 268 N.Y.S. at 447-48.

D. Evaluation of the Authorities

The Sforza opinion was distinguished by the Wisconsin Supreme Court in Breunig on the ground that it was a trial court decision that did not discuss directly the issue of sudden insanity and was "unconvincing." 45 Wis. 2d at ____, 173 N.W.2d at 624. Although the facts of Sforza do appear to present sudden insanity, the court's view in Breunig does seem to be correct because the Sforza opinion is devoted primarily to the misfeasance/nonfeasance distinction.

The Breunig court did not cite or discuss Kuhn v. Zabotsky, supra, decided by Ohio Supreme Court three years before Breunig. These cases must be viewed as taking diametrically opposed positions. In my opinion, it is more likely that the courts in the State of Utopia would adopt the view expressed by Breunig and thus would allow the defense. Sudden mental illness fits within the general sudden illness rule, which has been accepted by all but a few jurisdictions. As long as the focus stays on fault--the central basis of the law of negligence--and the law of unavoidable accidents is accepted, a strong likelihood exists that the sudden mental illness defense will be permitted in Utopia.

III. Prior Existing Insanity--The Common-Law Rule

A. Common-Law Rule Holding Insane Persons to a Reasonable Person Standard

Although the sudden mental illness rule is essentially an application of the sudden emergency (unavoidable accident) doctrine, it should be recognized that the sudden mental illness rule also can be viewed as an exception to the common-law rule generally holding insane persons liable for their torts, including negligence (noted in the preceding section). The stated facts indicate that Delira's mental illness was sudden but are silent on whether she had been ill previously or whether any prior signs of her mental problems existed. Assuming that a trier of fact might find sufficient warning, Delira would have to argue that the common-law rule should not be adopted and applied. The common-law rule holding mentally disabled persons liable for their torts appears to have originated from dictum in Weaver v. Ward, 80 Eng. Rep. 284 (K.B. 1616). In Weaver, two soldiers were skirmishing in a military exercise. The plaintiff was involuntarily wounded when the defendant fired his musket. Judgment was rendered for the plaintiff on the ground that the accident was not inevitable. Insanity was not a defense.

In dictum, the court stated that "if a lunatic hurt a man, he shall be answerable in trespass: and therefore no man shall be excused of a trespass . . . except it may be judged utterly without his fault." Id. at 284. It should be noted that at the time of Weaver, a strict liability theory of trespass was used and the concept of negligence based on an individual's fault had not developed yet. When the modern law of negligence did develop, however, the dictum nevertheless was repeated and adopted.

The leading American case holding mentally deranged or insane defendants accountable for their negligence as if they were normal, prudent persons is Williams v. Hays, 143 N.Y. 442, 38 N.E. 449 (1894), qualified in 157 N.Y. 541, 52 N.E. 589 (1899). In Williams, the defendant commanded a vessel. After remaining on constant duty for two days during a severe storm, the defendant retired to his cabin in a state of exhaustion. The defendant took a large dose of quinine and laid down. The mate in charge found that the rudder was broken and that the vessel could not be steered. The defendant came back on deck but refused to believe that the vessel was in any trouble. The defendant refused the help of two tugs and allowed the vessel to drift upon the shore and be wrecked. The assignee of the insurer sued the defendant for his negligence in managing the vessel. The defendant claimed that he had become temporarily insane and knew nothing of what had occurred from when he retired until he found himself in the life-saving station. 143 N.Y. at ____, 38 N.E. at 449-50.

The case was submitted to the jury on the theory that the defendant, if insane, was not responsible for the loss through any conduct on his part which, in a sane person, would have constituted actionable negligence. The jury found for the defendant and the plaintiff appealed. Id. The New York Court of Appeals reversed and ordered a new trial in a four to three decision. The court held that insanity was not a defense. The court, however, stated that if the defendant had become insane solely in consequence of his efforts to save the vessel, a different case would be presented. The court relied heavily on Cooley's discussion and an analogy to the liability of children for their torts at that time. 143 N.Y. at ____, 38 N.E. at 450-53.

On remand, the trial court directed a verdict for the plaintiff and the appellate division affirmed. 157 N.Y. at ____, 52 N.E. at 591. The Court of Appeals again reversed because the trial court failed to submit to the jury the questions (1) whether the defendant's condition was the result of exhaustion caused by his efforts to save the ship from the perils of the storm and (2) whether the mate was guilty of negligence in not assuming command. The court questioned: "What careful and prudent man could do more than to care for his vessel until overcome by physical and mental exhaustion? To do more was impossible . . . . [T]here is no obligation to perform impossible things." Id. at ____, 52 N.E. at 592.

The rule imposing liability appears to be "remarkably well settled in this country." Ellis, Tort Responsibility of Mentally Disabled Persons, 1981 A.B. Found. Research J. 1081, 1083. Statutory law in five jurisdictions makes insane persons fully liable for their torts but shields them from punitive damages. Curran, supra, at 52. The first Restatement of Torts, however, took no position on the issue, apparently in the hope that a rule of nonliability would be espoused in subsequent cases. In 1948, the Restatement changed its position and added section 283B. Id. at 53. See Restatement (Second) of Torts § 283B app., reporter's note (1965).

Section 283B now provides that "[u]nless the actor is a child, his insanity or other mental deficiency does not relieve the actor from liability for conduct which does not conform to the standard of a reasonable man under the circumstances." Id. § 283B. This change was based on the idea that since courts had made insane persons liable for their intentional torts, they would also hold them liable for their negligent torts. Restatement of the Law 654-58 (Supp. 1948).

This basis for adopting the Restatement rule has been severely criticized. Curran, for example, points out that the underlying theory appears to be that negligence is a lesser tort and liability more easily established. Curran points out that a court can examine the rudiments of the insane's conduct, uncontrolled though it may be; to impose liability for negligence, however, the court must blindly apply the objective reasonable person standard. Thus, Curran suggests that imposition of liability for negligence is a clear extension of responsibility which does not readily follow from the imposition of liability for intentional torts. Curran, supra, at 65.

A typical case applying the traditional common-law rule is Johnson v. Lambotte, 147 Colo. 203, 363 P.2d 165 (1961). In Johnson, the defendant was under observation and being treated for a chronic schizophrenic state of a paranoid type. The defendant escaped, found a car with its motor running, and drove off. Having little or no apparent control of the car, she collided with the plaintiff's car. The plaintiff brought a negligence action against the mentally ill driver in Colorado District Court to recover for damage to the plaintiff's car and personal injuries. The plaintiff recovered $5,257 in a nonjury trial.

On appeal, the defendant argued that the trial court erred as a matter of law in finding the defendant negligent because she was physically and mentally incapable of performing any volitional act and did not realize the risk involved to herself and others. Id. at ____, 363 P.2d at 166. The Colorado Supreme Court affirmed. The court assumed, without deciding, that the evidence showed that the defendant was insane. Quoting the "general rule" set out in 44 C.J.S. Insane Persons § 122, at 281 (1945) ("an insane person is liable for injuries caused by his tortious negligence" and "is held to the same degree of care and diligence as a person of sound mind"), the court found the general rule to be "clearly applicable." Id.

The Johnson opinion has been criticized as "a poor precedent because it is not a well reasoned opinion," failed to discuss policy factors or cases, and "blindly" relied on C.J.S. See Note, The Tort Liability of Insane Persons for Negligence, 39 Tenn. L. Rev. 705, 719 (1972). Other courts and commentators, however, have asserted several reasons for imposing liability.

1. Purpose of Tort Law

It has simply been stated that liability should be imposed on the insane because the purpose of tort law is compensation. See, e.g., Williams v. Hays, 143 N.Y. 442, 447, 38 N.E. 449, 450

(1894) ("The law looks to the person damaged by another and seeks to make him whole, without reference to the purpose or the condition, mental or physical, of the person causing the damage").

2. Fairness

It has been asserted that there is a "perceived sense of fairness, even in the absence of moral blame, of a rule requiring mental defectives who live among the rest of society to conform to the general standards of conduct or pay their innocent victims for the damage they cause." See, e.g., Jolley v. Powell, 299 So. 2d 647, 648 (Fla. Dist. Ct. App. 1974), cert. denied, 309 So. 2d 7 (Fla. 1975) ("one price men pay for membership in society"); Restatement (Second) of Torts § 283B, comment b (3) (1965).

3. Allocating the Loss Between Innocent Parties

Another frequently stated basis for holding the mentally disabled liable is the view that "where one of two innocent persons must suffer a loss, it should be borne by the one who occasioned it." See W. Prosser & W. Keeton, supra § 135, at 1073. Thus, Prosser and Keeton point out that to the extent that it is "anything more than an historical survival," the rule placing liability on the innocent person who inflicted a loss on another innocent person represents the conclusion that it is better that for the estate of the insane person to use its resources to provide compensation than to let those assets remain to be administered by the guardians for the incompetent's benefit. Id.

Thus, some courts have feared that if liability were not imposed, it might create "the anomaly of an insane person having abundant wealth depriving another of his rights without compensation." See, e.g., McGuire v. Almy, 297 Mass. 323, ____, 8 N.E.2d 760, 762 (1937) ("an insane person with abundant wealth ought not to continue in unimpaired enjoyment of the comfort which it brings while his victim bears the burden unaided").

4. Ease of Feigning Insanity

It is often asserted that since insanity is easily feigned, the temptation to pretend it would be too great if the defense was allowed. See, e.g., McIntyre v. Sholtz, 121 Ill. 660, ____, 13 N.E. 239, 240 (1887) ("strong temptation to simulate insanity, with a view of masking the malice and revenge of an evil heart"); G. Smoot, The Law of Insanity 363 (1929) ("So deep is the cunning of the evil that it is extremely difficult to detect the use, when he is feigning insanity as a cloak under which he may safely work his nefarious ends. The rule is therefore necessary, in order that the evil doer may not be led to simulate madness as a means of escaping the consequence of his tortious acts"). Smoot notes, however, that this reason has little weight by itself, but adds considerable force to the other reasons for liability.

5. Difficulty of Distinguishing Between Degrees of Incapacity and Bad Judgment

Another basis for holding the mentally disabled liable is the difficulty of distinguishing true incapacity from mere bad judgment. Restatement (Second) of Torts § 283B, comment b (1) (1965) (pointing out the practical difficulty of drawing any satisfactory line been mental deficiency and those variations of temperament, intellect, and emotional balance). Furthermore, it has been suggested that relaxation of the objective standard for the mentally ill would introduce a new inequity in the law between the mentally disabled defendants, who would escape liability, and defendants whose disability (e.g., congenital awkwardness accompanied by typical or superior intelligence) would still be held to an objective standard.

Since the law certainly is unwilling to forego liability because of poor education, absentmindedness, pathological lack of consideration for others, and other varieties of human nature, any claim for a subjective standard must stand on a perception of extraordinary injustice to such defendants and on assurances of a workable standard. Ellis, supra, at 1088 (suggesting this possible argument). Cf. O. Holmes, The Common Law 108 (1881) (the law takes no account of the infinite varieties of temperament, intellect, and education of defendants; but on the following page Holmes states that an incapacitating insanity should be regarded as a proper exception).

6. Introducing Unsatisfactory Tests from the Criminal Law

Some fear that failure to impose liability would lead to the introduction into the law of torts the confusing and unsatisfactory tests of insanity developed in criminal cases. See, e.g., Jolley v. Powell, 299 So. 2d 647, 649 (Fla. Dist. Ct. App. 1974), cert. denied, 309 So. 2d 7 (Fla. 1975) (accepting this consideration as a practical consideration in the administration of justice); Restatement (Second) of Torts § 283B comment b (2) (1965).

7. Encouraging Control of Mentally Ill Persons

Still another basis for holding the mentally disabled liable is the view that potential liability will encourage the custodians of mentally ill persons and those interested in their estates to keep them under control. See, e.g., McIntyre v. Sholty, 121 Ill. 660, ____, 13 N.E. 239, 240 (1887) (liability tends to secure a more efficient custody and guardianship of insane persons); Restatement (Second) of Torts § 283B, comment b (4) (1965); T. Cooley, The

Law of Torts 116 (2d ed. 1888) ("Would it not be an important stimulus to [those who have a personal, family, or financial interest] if the estate is to be held responsible for all injuries committed by [the insane person] to others; and would it not tend to indifference on their part if the law were to leave any injured party to bear the loss without redress?").

8. Liability for Necessities

Another argument in favor of imposing liability is that since insane persons are liable for their necessities, they should be liable for their torts. Seidelson, supra at 39 (1981) (stating this argument, but criticizing it).

9. Reasonable Expectations of the Parties

One commentator has pointed out that the reason courts may persist in imposing liability is a tacit judicial sensitivity to the reasonable expectations of the victim of the insane person's conduct. Id. at 41-43 (suggesting that existing law does reflect this reluctance and that it is more likely to be overcome when there are other potentially viable defendants than when the incompetent or his estate is the only defendant).

10. Insurance and Other Policy Arguments

Finally, two commentators, Alexander & Szasz, have raised several unique policy arguments not directly addressed by the courts. They argue that it is legitimate to identify insurance companies as very much parties in the resolution of the liability issue. They argue in this day of broad coverage for general liability in family insurance policies that the ultimate recourse probably will be to such policies "in a large percentage of cases." Alexander & Szasz, Mental Illness as an Excuse for Civil Wrongs, 43 Notre Dame Law. 24, 36 (1967).

Alexander and Szasz also argue that it would be contrary to the interest of the insane to deny them liability. Id. at 35-38 (arguing that "the price paid for legal irresponsibility"--the stigma, loss of freedom, and other privileges of the mentally healthy adult world--is too great; it is better to treat them as responsible so that persons (the family who stands to benefit and the insurer) would not be induced to assert the defendant's mental irresponsibility). See also Picher, The Tortious Liability of the Insane in Canada, 13 Osgoode Hall L.J. 193, 226, n.155 (1975) (suggesting this argument is "interesting but not of widespread currency").

B. Arguments Against Holding Insane Persons Accountable for Their Negligence as if They Were Normal, Prudent Persons

Virtually all modern commentators have been sharply critical of the common-law rule. See, e.g., Hornblower, Insanity and the Law of Negligence, 5 Colum. L. Rev. 278, 297 (1905) ("The true rule and the only rule consistent with justice and reason . . . is that a person who is non compos mentis cannot be held liable for negligence"); Sadoff, Tortious Liability of the Insane, 39 Pa. Bar. Q. 73, 82 (1967) (all-or-nothing approach of the common law too inflexible). Indeed, none of the explanations that have been given in support of the mentally disabled have gone unchallenged. W. Prosser & W. Keeton, supra § 135, at 1073 (citing law review discussion).

1. Purpose of Tort Law

The policy argument that the insane should be liable because the purpose of tort law is compensation has been criticized as misleading and failing to address the real issues. If that was the only aim of tort law, then the law of negligence should be stricken so that all, not only the insane, would be subject to the same hardship. Picher, supra at 228; Comment, The Tort Liability of Insane Persons for Negligence, 39 Tenn. L. Rev. 705, 716 (1972) ("If the law is primarily interested in compensating innocent victims, then the concept of negligence should be eliminated and all torts should be placed on a strict liability basis"). Instead, a different purpose is emphasized: the law exists to control the conduct of individuals in society and since the insane cannot be controlled by an understanding of the law, the law should not be imposed on them. See, e.g., Picher, supra at 224. Cf. Ellis, supra at 1108 (imposing higher standard no deterrence to accident-causing behavior).

2. Injustice of the Reasonable Person Standard

The commentators also argue that there is an apparent injustice in making persons responsible according to a standard they cannot meet. See, e.g., Ague, The Liability of Insane Persons in Tort Actions, 60 Dick. L. Rev. 211, 221, 225 (1956); C. Morris & C. Morris, Morris on Torts 50 (2d ed. 1980) ("a reasonably-prudent-insane-person" is a contradiction in terms; insanity disabling a defendant from using care should be recognized as a proper excuse for conduct that otherwise would be negligent). See also Fitzgerald v. Lawhorn, 29 Conn. Supp. 511, _____, 294 A.2d 338 (C.P. 1972) ("it is unjust to hold one responsible for a wrong he is incapable of avoiding") (dictum). Contra Jolley v. Powell, 299 So. 2d 647, 648 (Fla. Dist. Ct. App. 1974) ("It is surely not unusual or unfair that persons may be held responsible for failing to live up to a standard which, as a matter of fact, they cannot meet").

Similarly, it also is pointed out that it is unjust to impose responsibility without fault upon the mentally disabled when fault is the standard of liability for others. See, e.g., Hornblower, supra at 28 ("if a man be non compos mentis, . . . he should be no more liable for negligence than if he were blind or paralyzed and thereby physically incapacitated from doing or refraining from doing what an ordinarily prudent man should do or refrain from doing").

3. Imposing Strict Liability on One of the "Innocent" Victims

It is pointed out that the policy argument "of protecting the innocent victim is simply a modernized method of stating the obsolete rule of absolute liability." Picher, supra at 228. See also Ague, supra at 222 (this reason "is nothing more than strict (or absolute) liability dressed up in Sunday-go-to-meetin' garb"); Bohlen, supra at 17 ("so obviously a mere restatement of the old concept of liability without fault dressed up in a new form so as to appear modern and just") (also noting that this formulation was adopted from dicta in a Pennsylvania case and "given vogue and currency" by Cooley in his early treatise on torts).

Furthermore, this policy argument has been criticized as an inaccurate statement of law and represents a legal conclusion. For example, if a person had a sudden, unexpected fainting spell, the loss would not be shifted from the original victim to the nonculpable actor. "That 'special treatment' seems to be reserved for the mentally incompetent actor." Seidelson, supra at 38.

It has been asserted that the modern view of strict liability does not support the use of that approach for the mentally ill for two reasons: (1) Unlike someone who voluntarily engages in a dangerous enterprise for his own purposes and profit, insane persons have not voluntarily created their insanity. (2) Nor is there a better allocation of costs because (a) insane persons are not likely to be wealthier than the persons they injure and (b) they have no way of distributing their loss evenly on the public (unlike manufacturers, for example, who can better administer and distribute losses than consumers). Comment, The Tort Liability of Insane Persons for Negligence, 39 Tenn. L. Rev. 705, 716-17 (1972).

With regard to unfairness, while it may be unfair to the victim not to be compensated when the insane persons can pay, it is equally unfair to the insane to compensate the victim if the victim can pay. On this basis, it is said that the "two possibilities cancel each other out so that a consideration of their competing merits will lead nowhere." Picher, supra at 229.

4. Ability to Bear Losses

Implicit in the imposition of liability on the insane is the conclusion that it is better to provide compensation than to let those assets remain to be administered for the insane's benefit. But it has been suggested that "[f]ar from being able to bear losses, the insane usually need to preserve their funds in order to pay expensive bills for psychiatric care and treatment." Id. at 228. See also Comment, The Tort Liability of Insane Persons for Negligence, 39 Tenn. L. Rev. 705, 716-17 (1972) (insane may have a greater need because of the expense of psychiatric care and treatment).

5. Feigning Mental Illness

Commentators have disagreed with the view that feigning insanity is a likely result if an insanity defense is allowed. Id. at 715 (impossible to determine to what extent a sham might be successfully attempted--perhaps "a handful of cheats"); Bohlen, supra at 36, n.38 ("This consideration has no force where the insane person is guilty at most of negligence, for it is inconceivable that a man would feign insanity in order to act inadvertent"; at trial, it "seems improbable" that a defendant would do so to escape payment of money damages).

It has also been pointed out that the concern about feigning mental illness overlooks the stigma that still attaches to insanity and the threat of involuntary commitment. See, e.g., Comment, The Tort Liability of Insane Persons for Negligence, 39 Tenn. L. Rev. 705, 715 (1972) (enormous stigma counterbalances to any great extent any tendencies to feign insanity); Seidelson, supra at 39 ("Only a rare defendant would be eager to embrace this stigma in exchange for the possibility of avoiding liability in a negligence action") (also noting the risk of appointment of a guardian).

The concern about feigning mental illness, in part, appears to be based on the experience of the allowance of that defense in criminal law cases. It has been pointed out that some criminal defendants may be willing to assume that substantial stigmatizing effect to escape the death penalty or lengthy imprisonment, it does not necessarily follow that tort defendants would be willing to do so when simply money damages are at issue. Further, many tort defendants have liability insurance. It has been suggested that the better analogy is to the experience of contract law. In that area, the existence of a mental incompetency defense has not led to a large number of false claims of mental incapacity. Ellis, supra at 1087.

Furthermore, the concern about feigning mental illness to avoid liability for negligence underestimates the ability of psychiatrists to identify those who are fakers. See, e.g., Seidelson, supra at 39 (no basis for a unique concern either that the defendant will be able to deceive the expert or that the expert will cooperate with the defendant's desire to present perjurious testimony; also noting that the defendant's uncorroborated testimony is unlikely to be persuasive); Sadoff, supra at 250 (comparing the recognized ability of psychiatrists to detect false claims of mental disturbance in intentional infliction of emotional distress cases). But cf. Ellis, supra at 1086-87 (question still open to debate; diagnosis still an imprecise science despite the elaborate new classification scheme developed by the American Psychiatric Association; "[p]erhaps the best conclusion is that many individuals can be identified with some certainty as mentally ill").

Thus, it is argued that imposing liability in all cases to prevent feigning by a few persons "is another unfortunate example of legislating to the lowest common denominator." Picher, supra at 229; Comment, The Tort Liability of Insane Persons for Negligence, 39 Tenn. L. Rev. 705, 715 (1972) ("not proper to penalize a large number of insane persons in hopes of preventing a handful of cheats"). Contra T. Cooley, supra at 117 ("it seems better to exclude [the fakers] by an invariable rule that mental disease or infirmity shall be no defense to an action for tort").

6. Difficulty in Fashioning Test

It is asserted that the difficulty of fashioning an appropriate judicial definition as seen in criminal cases "seems hardly more than an abdication of judicial responsibility. It implies a shoulder-shrugging attitude of preferring ease of resolution over propriety of result." See, e.g., Seidelson, supra at 40; Ague, supra at 222 ("Mental disease is a nebulous thing at best, and no rule governing it will be infallible, but certainly an imperfect rule is better than no rule at all in such a case"); Bohlen, supra at 36, n.38 ("It seems unworthy of the law, whose purpose should be to do justice and to perfect its machinery so that justice may be done, to deny immunity to persons so insane as to be incapable of culpability because of the difficulty of evolving a test" that defines the precise degree of mental deficiency).

Specifically, in response to the problem of delineating a cut-off point, one possible answer is to set up criteria that would relieve insane persons of the reasonable person standard when they are "totally disoriented." Comment, Tort Liability of the Insane for Negligence, 39 Tenn. L. Rev. 705, 714 (1972) (some types of insanity should relieve the defendant of the reasonable person standard). See also Slattery v. Haley, [1923] 3 D.L.R. 156, 160 (1922) (dictum to the effect that the lunacy may be so extreme as to preclude any genuine voluntary act at all) (quoting the 5th ed. of Salmond on Torts 74-75); O. Holmes, The Common Law 109 (1881) (in many cases an insane person may be perfectly capable of taking precautions, but when insanity of a pronounced type manifestly incapacities the sufferer from complying with the rule of law, "good sense would require it to be admitted as an excuse").

7. Disparity of Treatment of the Mentally Ill

The commentators are concerned about the difference in treatment between children and the insane. It is argued that if a child who is too young cannot be held liable for negligence, then an insane person should not be held liable. See, e.g., Fitzgerald v. Lawhorn, 29 Conn. Supp. 511, ____, 294 A.2d 338, 339 (C.P. 1972) (recognizing and accepting this argument, among others); Ellis, supra at 1102-08 ("Is it less fair to ask accident victims (or their insurers) to bear the costs of injury when caused by mentally disabled persons than it is in cases involving children or the physically handicapped?").

Indeed, it is flatly asserted that the reason that insane persons are treated differently from infants, the handicapped, and the suddenly overcome is prejudice. "Few people relate to the plight of the insane and assume insanity won't befall them; it is therefore easy to put the insane in a separate category and [to] apply different principles." Picher, supra at 227.

8. Control of the Mentally Ill

The policy argument that those who have charge of insane persons or their estates will be stimulated to look after them and see that they do no harm is attacked as "nothing more than a legal fiction." For the most part, guardians and those interested in their estates are layman. In all probability they believe insanity is a defense to a negligence action since it is a defense to a criminal charge. Furthermore, even if they were aware of the law, it is doubtful that possible tort liability to the estate will make them discharge their duties more carefully. Comment, Tort Liability of Insane Persons for Negligence, 39 Tenn. L. Rev. 705, 717 (1972). See Ellis, supra at 1085 (alternative incentives such as concern for the disabled individual, embarrassment of the relatives, fear, revulsion, and concern for society are probably sufficient to induce most, if not all, to restrain the mentally disabled--without even considering the possibility of tort liability); Bohlen, supra at 35, n.38 (arguing it is "neither effective nor just to impose upon the family the indirect incentive of self-interest at the price of making the insane persons answerable for the faults of those who should be his guardians").

Commentators also maintain that imposing liability on the insane is unlikely to vary the conduct of the custodians and those interested in the estate because the torts often occur within the hospital setting or upon a sudden attack of insanity--in both instances the guardian and the heirs who are not the custodian could not prevent the tort. See, e.g., Picher, supra at 228; Ellis, supra at 1084 (this policy argument "is limited because it presupposes a greater control over the acts of mentally disabled people than is exercised by any but the most draconian of caretakers").

In addition, stimulating interested persons to attempt to control a person's conduct, based on their belief that person is insane, may very well generate a painfully abrasive familial relationship, which as a matter of policy, is undesirable. Seidelson, supra at 38 (suggesting that this reason is "hardly more than a cynical fabrication to support a rule of law almost facially unfathomable"). Instead, the better way to make custodians be more attentive is to impose liability on them when they have been negligent. Id. at Seidelson, supra at 38 (If a court is really serious about having the imposition of liability influence those interested in the insane's estate to restrain the insane's conduct, it should impose liability on the interested persons for failing to take reasonable steps to prevent the insane from driving once they were aware of the insane's condition); Ellis, supra at 1084, n.27 ("If an incentive for caretakers were thought desirable, an action for negligent supervision would probably be more effective").

9. Liability for Necessities

According to Seidelson, the attempted analogy between an insane's liability for necessities and torts is unpersuasive because the two liabilities are different. The obligation to pay for the insane's acquired necessities is wholly unrelated to fault, on which negligence is based. Further, this argument presupposes that the insane's conduct was tortious, which subsumes the basic question of the standard by which the insane's conduct should be judged. Seidelson, supra at 39.

10. Victim's Reasonable Expectations

It is asserted that it is proper to frustrate legally a victim's reasonable expectations by giving the benefit of a subjective standard to the incompetent who is the only potentially viable defendant. Seidelson, supra at 44-46. Seidelson explains:

> In cases concerning actors who are mentally incompetent, the courts should reject the objective standard and afford the incompetent the benefit of a standard that acknowledges his mental condition. The resulting frustration of the other actor's reasonable expectations is justified in such cases by the analogous result in cases in which the actor's conduct is the faultless product of physical infirmity, by the incompetent's lack of capacity to attain the reasonable person standard, and by the

> incompetent's vulnerability to formal adjudication [of incompetency, appointment of a guardian,] and deprivation of freedom of action.

Id. at 46.

In sum, the common-law rule holding the mentally disabled liable is the "product of an era when confinement of the mentally limited was the accepted social goal"--one which is no longer accepted. W. Prosser & W. Keeton, supra § 135, at 1073; Ellis, supra at 1107 ("We no longer expect (or wish) the majority of mentally disabled to live in institutions far removed from the rest of us"). The early argument that if mental defectives live among the rest of society, then they should be required to conform to general standards of conduct was based on the conventional wisdom of the time. This argument was buttressed by what appeared to be a substantial body of scientific opinion that mentally ill and mentally retarded people constituted a grave threat to society.

This argument (and a supposed sense of fairness) thus developed when it was thought that they would swamp society through their wicked actions and through their incompetence if they were allowed to reproduce. Ellis points out that it is not surprising that such an atmosphere fostered retention of a strict liability rule. Attitudes and scientific opinion have changed so that they bear little resemblance to the historical attitudes that shaped the policies of current tort law. Ellis, supra at 1080, 1085-86.

C. Erosion of the Standard in Contributory Negligence Cases

Judicial doubts about the common-law rule requiring insane persons to conform to the standard of conduct of reasonable persons have been expressed in contributory negligence cases. In those cases, they usually are held only to the standards that they personally can meet. W. Prosser & W. Keeton, supra § 135, at 1075; Annotation, Comment Note--Contributory Negligence of Mentally Incompetent or Mentally or Emotionally Disturbed Persons, 91 A.L.R.2d 392 (1963). The Restatement (Second) of Torts expressly refused to take a position on the appropriate standard in contributory negligence situations. Restatement (Second) of Torts § 464 (1965).

For example, in Mochen v. State, 43 A.D.2d 484, 352 N.Y.S.2d 290 (1974), a 17-year-old mental patient brought suit against the State of New York to recover for injuries sustained in an escape attempt from a second-story window of a state hospital. The New York Court of Claims dismissed the claim. On appeal, the Appellate Division reversed. The court held that a plaintiff who suffers from a mental disability which is the product of impulse or irrational behavior beyond his control should not be held to any greater degree of care for his own safety than that which he was capable of exercising. The court explained:

> We find no reason to adhere to the inelastic view that the disabled plaintiff is either "totally" insane or legally accountable for his own contributory negligence. Considering the present state of medical knowledge, it is possible and practical to evaluate the degrees of mental acuity and correlate them with legal responsibility.

Id. at ____, 352 N.Y.S.2d at 293.

D. Likely Resolution of the Question

In light of the sudden illness and the contributory negligence cases, Prosser and Keeton have concluded that "the permanent direction of the law may be in doubt even now." W. Prosser & W. Keeton, supra § 135, at 1075. Cf. Annotation, Liability of Insane Person for His Own Negligence, 49 A.L.R.3d 189, 192 (1973) (it remains to be seen whether Breunig will be the turning point for the alteration of the rule or graft upon it the exception of sudden and unforeseeable insanity). In terms of administering a legal rule providing a subjective standard for the mentally ill, the key issue is whether expert testimony can provide sufficient assistance to jurors to allow them to implement such a standard. Ellis, supra at 1103.

One commentator has suggested that "perhaps the ideal solution would be to allow the trial court to exercise discretion in ordering the lunatic to pay such compensation as seems equitable under the circumstances of the case, having regard especially to the relative pecuniary situations of the parties." Ague, supra at 227, citing 22 Minn. L. Rev. 853, 862 (1938). Cf. Ames, Law and Morals, 22 Harv. L. Rev. 97, 100 (1908) (citing provision of German Code taking this approach). It seems unlikely, however, that this discretionary approach would be adopted.

Other possible approaches involve legislation. For example, proposals have been made to compensate the injured through payment from a state fund. This approach "would avoid the harshness of liability for the insane and at the same time protect the injured." Crime Victim's Compensation Acts operate on a similar principle. See W. Prosser & W. Keeton, supra § 135, at 1075 and n.40. Cf. Sadoff, supra at 82 (state should be liable for the torts of those declared incompetent or insane and sent to a state mental institution).

It should be remembered that the arguments made by commentators have had little effect on the courts so far. The courts in Illinois have frankly stated: however justly imposing liability on the insane may have originally been subject to criticism on the grounds of reason and principal, "it is now too firmly supported by the weight of authority to be disturbed." McIntyre v. Sholty, 121 Ill. 660, 664, 13 N.E. 239, 240 (1887); Vosnos v. Perry, 43 Ill. App. 3d 834, _____, 357 N.E.2d 614, 615 (1976) (favorably quoting McIntyre). Obviously, the State of Utopia does not suffer from the hindrance of a long-accepted rule because this question is one of first impression. Thus, there is a better chance that the arguments favoring a sudden mental illness defense will be successful.

CONCLUSION:

Delira's best defense is to argue that she was incapacitated by a sudden mental illness without warning. This defense is supported by the leading case of Breunig v. American Family Insurance Co., 45 Wis. 2d 536, 173 N.W.2d 619 (1970). This defense is consistent with the central basis of negligence law--fault--and is a specific application of the law of unavoidable accidents. Although some authority to the contrary exists, it is more likely that the courts in the State of Utopia will adopt the view expressed by Breunig and thus will allow this defense. Delira would have the burden of proof, and the issue of the nature, extent, and effect of Delira's illness will be one for the jury.

The principal difficulty that Delira is likely to face is the question of forewarning. In Breunig, the defendant's delusions were intermittent, and the jury apparently found that she had knowledge of the condition and the likelihood of hallucination. The facts given do not indicate whether Delira had any prior occurrences or delusions or other signs of mental illness prior to the accident. Thus, further factual inquiry should be undertaken to determine the existence and extent of such illness. Even if Delira had previous illnesses, however, it should be argued that evidence of lucidity at the time she decided to drive should be required. Furthermore, if Delira's doctor told her she was no longer ill, then it should be argued that she should not be required to guard against her future insanity.

Assuming that the facts show that Delira had a preexisting mental illness, Delira would have to argue that the generally accepted common-law rule should not be adopted and applied. That rule requires mentally ill persons to conform to a reasonable person standard. In other words, for purposes of assessing their conduct, they are judged as if they were normal, prudent persons. In effect, they become strictly liable.

This approach is inconsistent with the standard imposed on young children. The traditional arguments supporting the common-law approach are not persuasive and have been roundly criticized by virtually all modern commentators. On the other hand, the courts so far have been reluctant to reject the common-law rule and to measure a defendant's conduct by a subjective standard. This rule, however, has been eroded in judging a plaintiff's contributory negligence. Because the matter is one of first impression, Utopia courts will be considering the matter anew, and a good chance exists that they will reject the common-law rule.

INDEX

Notes

Notes

Notes

Notes

Notes

Notes

Notes

Notes

Notes

Notes

Notes

Notes

Notes

Notes